Talcott Parsons
1902–1979
Dean of American sociology during the mid-1900s promoted a conception of society as a social system with subsystems of human action, in which individuals fulfill the systems needs of the societies of which they are members.

Samuel Delbert Clark
1910–2003
Canadian historical sociologist and educator founded the University of Toronto's Department of Sociology (1963).

Robert K. Merton
1910–2003
American sociologist and educator developed middle-range theory, which sought to bridge the gap between high-level theories and low-level observations.

Guy Rocher
b. 1924
Canadian educator and pioneer in the sociology of education, law, and medical ethics has sat on several commissions and boards of inquiry at the provincial and federal levels and wrote a lucid and highly regarded introduction to the discipline, *Introduction à la sociologie* (1968).

Erving Goffman
1922–1982
Canadian-born sociologist advanced microsociology and studied social roles, deviance, stigma, and "total institutions."

Michel Foucault
1926–1984
French thinker, famous for historical studies of madness and civilization, imprisonment, and sexuality, portrayed science as an arbitrary instrument for control and power, and constructed a theory of power as actions and relations.

Herbert Blumer
1900–1987
American student of Mead, who coined the term "symbolic interactionism."

Theodor Adorno
1903–1969
German Frankfurt School philosopher argued that philosophical authoritarianism is inevitably oppressive.

John Porter
1921–1979
Canadian sociologist examined connections between ethnicity and barriers of opportunity in Canadian society, which he characterized as a "vertical mosaic."

Dorothy Smith
b. 1926
English-born Canadian sociologist developed standpoint theory, which sought to frame and understand everyday life from a feminist point of view.

Everett C. Hughes
1897–1983
American sociologist studied economic organization, work and occupations, and ethnic relations, including a key study of the "ethnic division of labour" in Quebec.

Oswald Hall
1908–2007
Canadian educator researched the sociology of work and medicine and served on the Royal Commission on Health Services and the Royal Commission on Bilingualism and Biculturalism.

C. Wright Mills
1916–1962
American critical sociologist studied power structure in the US and coined the term "sociological imagination."

Jean Baudrillard
1929–2007
French cultural theorist influenced postmodernism and showed how capitalist consumer society erases distinctions between reality and reference, leading to a loss of meaning.

Margrit Eichler
b. 1942
Canadian sociologist has studied family sociology, feminist research methods, and gender inequality.

1900   1940   2000

1969
Doctors and Doctrines: The Ideology of Medical Care in Canada, an examination of Canada's healthcare system in terms of role strain, conflict in values, and relations to the public, by Bernard Blishen (b. 1919)

1978
The Double Ghetto: Canadian Women and their Segregated Work, a study of gender inequality in the labour force and the home, by Pat Armstrong (b. 1945) and Hugh Armstrong (b.1943)

1983
Green Gold: The Forest Industry in British Columbia, an early study in the social, political, and economic aspects of a particular staples industry, the BC forest industry, by Patricia Marchak (1936–2010)

2002
"The Impact of Feminism on Canadian Sociology," a study of the rise of sociology as a feminist discipline, by Margrit Eichler

1996
The Barbershop Singer: Inside the Social World of a Musical Hobby, a study of leisure and hobbies in society, by Robert Stebbins (b. 1938)

1986
"The 'Wets' and the 'Drys': Binary Images of Women and Alcohol in Popular Culture," a study of gender inequalities and mass media, by Thelma McCormack (b. 1921)

1968
Introduction to the Mathematics of Population, a landmark contribution to the field of population studies, by Canadian demographer Nathan Keyfitz (1913–2010)

1987
The Everyday World as Problematic: A Feminist Sociology, an argument that sociology has developed without proper insight into women's experiences, by Dorothy Smith

2004
Perspectives de recherche en santé des populations au moyen de données complexes, an analysis of the Quebec healthcare system, by Paul Bernard (1945–2011)

1975
The Rise of a Third Party: A Study in Crisis Politics, a sociological analysis of the growth of nationalist politics in Quebec, by Maurice Pinard (b. 1929)

The Canadian Corporate Elite: An Analysis of Economic Power, a response to *The Vertical Mosaic* examining corporate elites and their impact on class and social stratification, by Wallace Clement

1988
Quebec Society: Tradition, Modernity, and Nationhood, a study of Quebec's rising middle class and the separatist movement, by Hubert Guindon (1929–2002)

Families in Canada Today: Recent Changes and Their Policy Implications, a study of how the way we think and talk about gender roles pre-empts useful changes in family policy, by Margrit Eichler

1965
Lament for a Nation: The Defeat of Canadian Nationalism, an examination of the dangers of Canadian cultural absorption by the US, by Canadian social philosopher George Grant (1918–1988)

The Vertical Mosaic: An Analysis of Social Class and Power in Canada, a ground-breaking and influential study of Canada's class structure, depicting a complex system of groups organized in hierarchy across lines of ethnicity and class, by John Porter

2006
Do Men Mother? Fathering, Care, and Domestic Responsibility, an examination of the changing role of fathers, by Andrea Doucet

1989
The Social Significance of Sport, a study of how individuals take control of and participate in society through voluntary association, by James Curtis (1943–2005)

2008
Canada's Rights Revolution: Social Movements and Social Change, 1937–82, a study of post-war Canadian social movements, by Dominique Clément

Milestones in Canadian Sociology

Principles of Sociology
Canadian Perspectives
Third Edition

EDITED BY Tepperman ◎ Albanese ◎ Curtis

OXFORD
UNIVERSITY PRESS

Oxford University Press is a department of the University of Oxford.
It furthers the University's objective of excellence in research, scholarship, and education by publishing worldwide.
Oxford is a registered trade mark of Oxford University Press in the UK and in certain other countries.

Published in Canada by
Oxford University Press
8 Sampson Mews, Suite 204,
Don Mills, Ontario M3C 0H5 Canada

www.oupcanada.com

Library and Archives Canada Cataloguing in Publication
Sociology : a Canadian perspective / editors, Lorne Tepperman, Patrizia Albanese & Jim Curtis. — 3rd ed.

Includes bibliographical references and index.
ISBN 978-0-19-544666-1

1. Sociology—Textbooks. 2. Canada—Social conditions—
1991– —Textbooks. I. Tepperman, Lorne, 1943– II. Albanese, Patrizia III. Curtis, James E., 1943–

HM586.P75 2013   301   C2013-901113-7

Introduction opener: zaragyemo/BigStock.com; Part 1 opener: Norman Hollands/The Bridgeman Art Lilbrary/Getty
Images; Chapter 1 opener: © Deco/Alamy; Part 2 opener: Reuters/China Daily; Chapter 2 opener: © imagebroker/
Alamy; Chapter 3 opener: © Whisson/Jordan/Corbis; Chapter 4 opener: Reuters/Damir Sagolj; Chapter 5 opener:
© Jim Cornfield/Corbis; Part 3 opener: ©CP Images/Shehzad Noorani; Chapter 6 opener: © Kamyar Adl/Alamy;
Chapter 7 opener: © Hugh Smith/Demotix/Demotix/Corbis; Chapter 8 opener: ©iStockphoto.com/Bartosz
Hadyniak; Part 4 opener: © Agnieszka Pastuszak-Maksin/istock; Chapter 9 opener: Sophia Fortier; Chapter 10
opener: © Marmaduke St. John/Alamy; Chapter 11 opener: © Gu Feng/epa/Corbis; Chapter 12 opener: © Gunter
Marx/Alamy; Chapter 13 opener: © Images & Stories/Alamy; Chapter 14 opener: AFP/Getty Images; Part 5 opener:
© Baci/Corbis; Cgaoter 15 opener: © iStockphoto.com/Bartosz Hadyniak; Chapter 16 opener: © Megapress/Alamy;
Chapter 17 opener: © Robert Harding World Imagery/Alamy.

Figure 3.3, p. 65: "Generation M2: Media in the Lives of 8- to 18-Year-Olds", (#8010), The Henry J. Kaiser Family
Foundation, January 2010. This information was reprinted with permission from the Henry J. Kaiser Family
Foundation. The Kaiser Family Foundation, a leader in health policy analysis, health journalism and communication,
is dedicated to filling the need for trusted, independent information on the major health issues facing our nation and
its people. The Foundation is a non-profit private operating foundation, based in Menlo Park, California.

Cover image: Chris Schmidt/Getty

Oxford University Press is committed to our environment.
Wherever possible, our books are printed on paper
which comes from responsible sources.

Printed and bound in the United States of America

1 2 3 4 — 17 16 15 14

brief contents

detailed contents

CHAPTER 5: Deviance   93
Vincent F. Sacco and Alicia D. Horton

Part III Types of Social Inequality   111

**CHAPTER 6: Class, Status,
and Social Inequality   113**
Ann D. Duffy and Sara J. Cumming

CHAPTER 7: Gender and Sexuality   133
Janet Siltanen, Andrea Doucet, and Patrizia
Albanese

CHAPTER 8: Ethnic and Race Relations   151
Nikolaos I. Liodakis

Part IV Social Institutions   171

CHAPTER 9: Families and Personal Life   173
Maureen Baker

CHAPTER 10: Education   191
Terry Wotherspoon

CHAPTER 11: Work and the Economy   213
Pamela Sugiman

CHAPTER 12: Health Issues   233
Juanne Clarke

CHAPTER 13: Religion in Canada   253
Lori G. Beaman

CHAPTER 14: Politics and Social Movements 273

Randle Hart, Howard Ramos, Karen Stanbridge, and John Veugelers

Part V Canadian Society and the Global Context   297

CHAPTER 15: Globalization and Social Change   299

Liam Swiss

CHAPTER 16: Population, Urbanization, and the Environment   319

Cheryl Teelucksingh

CHAPTER 17: Mass Media and Communication   343

David Young

tables

figures

boxed features

SOCIOLOGY in ACTION

Research That Helps Us Understand Our World

HUMAN DIVERSITY

World Views and Ways of Life of Different Cultures and Social Groups

OPEN for DISCUSSION

Contemporary Social Issues and Debates

GLOBAL ISSUES

A Sociological Perspective on Cases from around the World

UNDER the WIRE

Exploration of the Ways in Which Media and Technologies Intersect with Social Behaviours

preface

From the Publisher

While preparing this third edition of *Principles of Sociology: Canadian Perspectives*, the general editors, contributing authors, and publisher kept in mind one paramount goal: to produce the most authoritative, accessible, and interesting introduction to sociology available for Canadian students.

The revision builds on the strengths of the well-received first and second editions and incorporates many new features designed to enhance the book's usefulness for students and instructors alike.

Highlights of the Third Edition

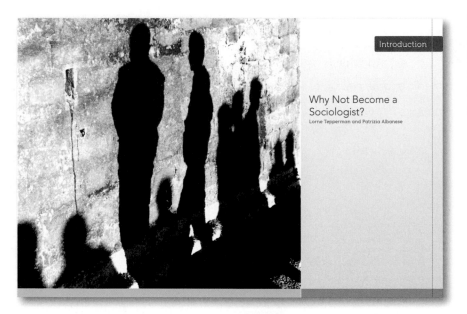

NEW INTRODUCTION

An introduction has been added to better acquaint students with the discipline of sociology and its origins, development, and significance.

NEW CHAPTER ON THEORY AND RESEARCH METHODS

Tony Thomson joins Bruce Arai to craft a new chapter. Revamped for the third edition to provide better linkages between classical theory and contemporary ideas, this chapter uses clear and accessible language to break down complex theory and ensure that students are engaged and prepared for the chapters that follow.

NEW CONTRIBUTING AUTHORS

For the third edition, we welcome several new contributing authors: Tony Thomson (sociological theory and research methods), Barbara Mitchell (being social), Dorothy Pawluch and William Shaffir (status, roles, and identities), Alicia D. Horton (deviance), Sara J. Cumming and Ann D. Duffy (class status and inequality), Janet Siltanen and Andrea Doucet (gender relations), Howard Ramos and Karen Stanbridge (politics and social movements), Liam Swiss (globalization and social change), and Cheryl Teelucksingh (population, urbanization, and the environment). These prominent sociologists join our seasoned team of contributors to produce a new edition of the highest quality.

NEW "UNDER THE WIRE" THEME BOX

New "Under the Wire" boxes analyze the ways in which current media and new technologies influence social patterns and behaviours.

Teamed with four additional theme boxes, these features are spread throughout the text to keep students motivated and encourage them to think analytically about key concepts.

- "**Sociology in Action**" boxes show how sociological research can help us to better understand the everyday world.

- **"Open for Discussion"** boxes use contemporary social issues and debates to focus understanding of core sociological concepts.

---

20 PART I: Theory and Methodology

OPEN for DISCUSSION

Max Weber and *Verstehen*

In many of the chapters in this text, you will come across the ideas of Max Weber. One of his most enduring contributions to research methods in sociology is his elaboration of a concept he called *verstehen* (German for "to understand"). His idea is that in order to properly study the cultures of other peoples, a researcher needs to develop more than knowledge but an "empathetic understanding" of their lives as well in order to see the world as that group sees it.

Verstehen became a cornerstone of qualitative sociology as researchers tried to understand the lives of others "from the inside." In Weber's view, developing verstehen was a bit of an art, but in theory anyone who was good at it could understand the world view of any other group. In other words, the views of any group could be understood regardless of the personal characteristics of the researcher.

But this view has been criticized as too simplistic. That is, some researchers have argued that there are limits to verstehen, because the personal characteristics of the researcher will affect how the group reacts to her or him. And this will limit the depth of verste-

hen or understanding that a researcher can achieve. For instance, Margaret Mead's classic anthropological study in Samoa has been criticized because the Samoans later claimed that they were not completely honest with her. Similarly, men are able to reach only a certain limited level of understanding with women. And because of this, it may not even be appropriate for men to study women, or vice versa. If we relate this to Killingsworth's (2006) study of mom and tot groups discussed later in this chapter, it might be the case that as a male, he might not have had the same access to the ongoing discussions around motherhood and child care. So, are there factors that would limit the level of verstehen that a researcher can achieve? And if so, what are those factors, and how do we identify them? At one extreme, this would mean that a researcher would have to match up with her or his participants on everything from gender, to education level, to hair colour, to fashion sense. So neither extreme position is particularly convincing, but exactly where we draw this line remains "open for discussion."

then the experiment is allowed to run, while in quasi-experiments observations of "naturally occurring" phenomena are made and an attempt is made to remove the effects of confounding variables during the analysis stage.

SURVEYS

Surveys are the most widely used technique in social scientific research. Sociologists, economists, political scientists, psychologists, and others use them regularly (Gray and Guppy 2008). They are an excellent way to gather data on large populations that cannot be studied effectively in a face-to-face manner. The goals of almost all social scientific surveys are to produce detailed data that will allow researchers to describe the characteristics of the group under study, to test theories about that group, and to generalize results beyond the people who responded to the survey.

At first glance, it might seem that designing good questions for a survey would be easy. The reality is that it is quite difficult—sociologists can spend months trying to figure out what

questions they will ask, how they will word them, and the order in which they will ask them. One of the reasons it is so difficult is that each question must be unambiguous for both the respondent and the researcher. A question with several different interpretations is not useful, because respondents may answer it from a perspective different from that intended by the researcher. Similarly, questions that are too complicated for respondents to answer, or that presume a level of knowledge that respondents do not have, will not produce useful data. There are many, many issues to consider in designing good questions and the order they appear on the questionnaire, and unless sufficient attention is paid to these issues before the survey is administered, the results will affect the legitimacy of the whole research project.

Random Sampling, Sample Size, and Response Rates
In virtually all social science research, it is impossible to include each member of the whole population in a study. For instance,

---

CHAPTER 15: Globalization and Social Change **307**

GLOBAL ISSUES

Glocalization and the Maharaja Mac

What is glocalization, and how does it function? We might think that seeing the effects of the mixing of global and local might be a difficult thing to do, but we do not have to look much further than the McDonald's restaurants that have so often been a major referent of the **Americanization** of the world associated with globalization.

In India, for instance, the Big Mac has been replaced on the McDonald's menu by the "Maharaja Mac." Originally based on goat or lamb meat, all McDonald's "burgers" in India are now chicken-based. Why would we see a change to such an American staple? Not surprisingly, the double beef patties of the original Big Mac would not go over too well in a country where the majority of the population follows the Hindu faith, revere the cow as sacred, and do not eat

beef. Moreover, some customers might mistake mutton for beef. Thus, the Maharaja Mac was born out of a process of glocalization that still enables Indian customers to partake of the McDonald's experience but in a way that caters to local tastes. Other glocalized items on the McDonald's menu in India include items such as the "McSpicy Paneer" (a battered, deep-fried patty composed of the Indian curdled milk cheese, paneer) or the "McAloo Tikki" (a potato- and pea-based patty in a burger bun with typical burger trimmings, representing a McDonald's version of the traditional "Aloo Tikki" snack common throughout north India). These examples demonstrate the concept of glocalization but provide clear evidence of the mixing of cultures at work in the globalization of fast food.

the way that relationship is conventionally interpreted as fixed and static (Pieterse 1994). This notion of globalization as at once converging and diverging is an important counterpoint to views of globalization that would argue for uniformity as a chief outcome of globalization.

Though less cohesive than either the world system or world society perspectives, the space/time perspective grapples with an equally important aspect of how society is changing in the era of globalization. Through examination of how time and space are reshaped by technological advances and increasing global awareness, this perspective offers a number of convincing models of why we see altogether different forms of social relations emerging in the realms of economics, politics, and culture. This move away from conventional relationships to time and space can be seen in the increased flows of ideas, communication, capital, and people throughout the increasingly compressed global community. At once connecting peoples and societies, removing national boundaries and barriers, and at the same time encouraging hybrid forms of glocal cultural interpretation to emerge, this perspective can simultaneously support arguments for both convergence and divergence—a contradiction we will examine in the following sections.

Ronald McDonald welcomes visitors with a traditional greeting at a McDonald's restaurant in Bangkok, Thailand. The success of McDonald's in foreign markets like Thailand relies on the food chain's adaptability to local customs and environment.

- **"Global Issues"** boxes draw on examples from around the world to illustrate the effects of globalization and show what sociologists have to say about key international topics.

- **"Human Diversity"** boxes recognize the overwhelming and unavoidable fact of human diversity and seek to introduce students to the ways of life and world views of different cultures and social groups.

THEORETICAL BALANCE

The very mention of the term "theory" seems to make first-year undergraduates uneasy, but the overriding goal in *Principles of Sociology: Canadian Perspectives* has been not just to make the theories that underpin the discipline comprehensible but to show how they inform an understanding of the data that sociologists gather—and how the choice of which theoretical perspective to employ can yield new and surprising insights. Throughout the text, emerging paradigms are also discussed when they shed new light on long-standing questions.

CHAPTER 8: Ethnic and Race Relations　159

HUMAN DIVERSITY

The "Veil Issue"

Many Muslim women choose to cover parts of their face with veils. It is part of their religious tradition, just as many southern European Christian women in mourning choose to wear long black dresses and cover their heads. In the post 9/11 world, xenophobia and Islamophobia are on the rise worldwide. The "veil issue" has sparked heated debates in the UK, Belgium, France, and elsewhere. Canada is no exception. In September 2007, three federal by-elections took place in Quebec. Marc Mayrand, Canada's chief electoral officer, was under pressure from politicians, the media, and "concerned citizens" to take a stand against allowing veiled Muslim women to vote unless they first showed their faces. Should women wearing veils be allowed to vote? How could their identity be verified? Mayrand argued that veiled Muslim women have the same rights as everyone else. There is nothing in the current electoral law to prevent veiled people from voting. The law allows citizens—for religious reasons—to vote with their face covered provided they show two pieces of valid ID and swear an oath. After all, in the previous federal election, 80,000 people cast votes by mail.

How would you feel if you were a Canadian Muslim woman and were not allowed to vote because you wear a veil? Do you think that veiled women want to hide their identities? Canada is considered a tolerant society and has an official policy of multiculturalism. Freedom of religion is protected by the Charter of Rights and Freedoms. Should we allow veiled citizens to cast ballots? Before you grapple with this last question, you should know that both the Canadian Islamic Congress and the Canadian Council of Muslim Women agreed that veiled women should show their faces before voting.

and Aboriginals. In Quebec, multiculturalism was seen as an attempt by the federal government to undermine the legitimate Quebec aspirations for "nationhood." By severing culture from language, multiculturalism rejected the "two founding nations" metaphor of Canada's historical development and reduced the status of French Canadians from that of "founding people" to just another ethnic group (Abu-Laban and Stasiulis 1992, 367). Multiculturalism also became a mechanism to "buy" allophone votes. Assimilationist language policies in Quebec, directed toward allophones, can be understood in this context. Successive Quebec governments have pursued a policy of **interculturalism** instead of multiculturalism. According to Kymlicka (1998), interculturalism is based on three important principles: (1) it recognizes French as the language of public life; (2) it respects liberal-democratic values (political rights, equality of opportunity); and (3) it respects pluralism (openness to and tolerance of differences). These principles constitute a "moral contract" between the province of Quebec and immigrant groups. Interculturalism may sound a lot like the federal policy of multiculturalism, but there are some nuanced differences. For example, it promotes linguistic assimilation. The "centre of convergence" for different cultural groups in Quebec is the "collective good" of the French language, which is seen as an indispensable condition for the creation of the *culture publique commune* (common public culture) and the cohesion of Quebec society.

Some researchers have argued that interculturalism is the most advanced form of pluralism today (Karmis 2004, 70), since it combines multiculturalism and multinationalism and is more inclusive than either. It does not apply only to ethnic groups or nations but also to "lifestyle" cultures and world views associated with new social movements, including cultural, gay, punk, environmental, feminist, and other non-ethnic-based identities. In principle, no cultural community is excluded from québécois identity.

TIME to REFLECT
Would you prefer to live in a country without official multiculturalism and/or interculturalism? Would you rather live in the US, France, or Germany? Why?

14　PART I: Theory and Methodology

TIME to REFLECT
How would Durkheim respond to the figure depicting the capitalist system?

The working class in global capitalism was not only oppressed, Marx reasoned, but also "alienated." In simple terms, alienation means to be separated from something. Generally, for Marx, the original alienation (separation) of humanity from nature in the earliest stage of social evolution was a good thing, and it was necessary for all the progress that followed—potentially, for a world of shared wealth and high living standards for all. But power over nature has now proved to be a double-edged sword. In our current environmental crisis, which is one of the consequences of constant-growth capitalism, it is clear that our power over and alienation from nature have had some disastrous consequences.

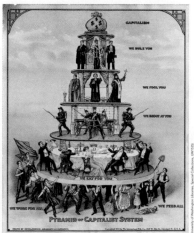

Social stratification has been a central concern since the founding of sociology. Even non-sociologists have long understood that their lives are shaped by class structure.

18　PART I: Theory and Methodology

UNDER the WIRE

What Difference Do the Differences Make?

In contemporary times—at least in the Western world—new technology, international travel, and the Internet have modified the way we experience our world. The implications our new and different lifestyle will have for us and future generations are issues of vital public interest.

Sociologists are not just interested in what the differences are—they want to know *what difference* the differences make. Does modern communication technology enable us to be better informed about socially significant events or only about everyday trivia? Do the new media provide platforms for greater realization of democratic decision-making, or are they tools of Big Brother? Do they create more communities of interest and sharing, or do they more thoroughly individualize us? Do they deepen our actual engagement with the world or merely make even the most horrendous event seem like a spectacle, to be gazed at but not acted upon?

Every new communication technology creates new possibilities for control, but also for resistance.

Protesters in Egypt and Tunisia in 2011, who (perhaps temporarily) drove their dictatorial leaders from power, frequently communicated via social networking. Blurred Vision, a Toronto-based rock group fronted by two Iranian brothers, covered Pink Floyd's transgressive anthem "Another Brick in the Wall." Posted on YouTube in 2010, the song created an underground sensation among disaffected Iranian youth.

One of the most controversial theorists in contemporary times, Jean Baudrillard, challenged our view of "the real." For Baudrillard (1998), we perceive society through the veil of mass media so that "reality" has been overtaken by simulations, such as Disney World, that impose upon us images of what we take to be real. No wonder the Hollywood "culture industry" is full of questions about what is "real" versus virtual (*The Matrix*, *Tron*) or sanity versus madness (*Shutter Island*, *Black Swan*) and what is only a dream (*Dark City*, *Inception*).

Theory and Research

For most sociologists, it is important that their research be closely connected with a theory or set of theories. Briefly, *theories* are abstract ideas about the world. Most sociological research is designed to evaluate a theory, either by testing it or by exploring the applicability of a theory to different situations. As can be seen throughout the many chapters in this text, sociologists investigate substantive problems and try to use their theories to help them understand these problems better. For instance, sociologists may be interested in understanding crime, the family, the environment, or education, and they will almost always use their theories to provide a deeper appreciation of these issues.

Sociologists use theories as models or conceptual maps of how the world works, and they use research methods to gather data that are relevant to these theories. Thus, theories and methods are always intertwined in the research process. There are hundreds of different theories in sociology, but most of them can be grouped into the four main theoretical perspectives that can be found throughout this text: structural functionalism, conflict theory, symbolic interactionism, and feminism. Theories cannot be tested directly, because they are only abstract ideas. Theories must be translated into observable ideas before they can be tested. This process of translation is called **operationalization**.

OPERATIONALIZATION

Operationalization is the process of translating theories and concepts into hypotheses and variables. Theories are abstract ideas, composed of concepts. **Concepts** are single ideas. Usually, theories explain how two or more concepts are related to each other. For instance, Karl Marx used concepts such as "alienation," "exploitation," and "class" to construct an abstract explanation (theory) of capitalism.

Once we have a theory, we need some way to test it. We need an observable equivalent of a theory or at least a set of observable statements that are consistent with our theory. These are called hypotheses. In the same way that theories express relationships between concepts,

GLOBAL PERSPECTIVE

Although this book was written by and for Canadians, the editors and authors never forget that Canada is but one small part of a vast, diverse, and endlessly fascinating social world. Along with Canadian data, examples, and illustrations, a wealth of information about how humans live and interact around the world is presented in every chapter.

Polygyny is legal in Pakistan and permitted Azhar Haidri to marry both the woman he loves and the woman his family arranged for him to marry when he was a child.

AIDS TO STUDENT LEARNING

Numerous features designed to enhance usefulness and interest for students and instructors alike are incorporated throughout the book and encourage a mastery of sociological concepts. They include:

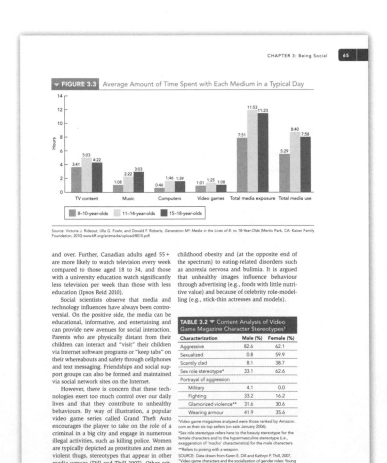

- **Learning Objectives** at the start of each chapter provide a concise overview of the key concepts that will be covered.

- **Graphs and Tables.** Colourful and informative graphs and charts are featured throughout the text and allow students to accurately analyze quantitative data.

- **New Cross-Chapter References** highlight the interconnectedness of content across chapters to ensure a comprehensive study of the material.

- **Time to Reflect** questions placed throughout the text prompt students to analyze the material both in and out of the classroom.

---

with other kids in "real time." Consequently, it is deemed that children are increasingly being socialized to become self-indulgent life-long consumers as well as to form imaginary "para-social" (one-sided) relationships (Chung, Debuys, and Nam 2007).

Finally, socialization also takes place in other institutionalized settings, such as in religious contexts and in the workplace, the latter of which will be discussed in the next section. With respect to religious institutions, Statistics Canada documents that attendance at formal religious services has fallen dramatically over the past several decades, particularly among younger age groups (Lindsay 2008a), a trend that has many implications. Religious norms influence many facets of family life, such as gender roles, parent–child relations, attitudes toward moral issues (e.g., abortion), and how families celebrate rituals and holidays. At the same time, the number of adherents to religions such as Islam, Hinduism, Sikhism, and Buddhism has increased substantially in Canada as the result of changing sources of immigration (Statistics Canada 2001).

> The religious landscape in Canada is constantly evolving. See Chapter 13, "Religion in Profile," p.???, to better understand what religion looks like in Canada.

TIME to REFLECT

How have your family and religious/spiritual background influenced your current opinions or attitudes with respect to some controversial social issues (e.g., abortion, same-sex marriage, assisted suicide, the death penalty)?

The Life Course, Aging, and Socialization

Throughout this chapter, it has been emphasized that socialization occurs throughout the life course, although the basic, formative instruction occurs fairly early in life. Some of the socialization that takes place during this

time is called **anticipatory socialization**, a term used to refer to how individuals acquire the values and orientations they will likely take up in the future. In childhood, this might include doing household chores, a childhood job, sports, dance lessons, and dating, experiences that give youngsters an opportunity to rehearse for the kinds of roles that await them in adulthood (Newman 2006).

As we age, many other kinds of experiences also give us the opportunity to rehearse for the kinds of adult roles that we might eventually adopt. In particular, many educational or training settings prepare us for our future work roles. A recent ethnographic study by Chappell and Lanza-Kaduce (2010) on police academy socialization explores the socialization that takes place during training to serve on the police force. The researchers found that despite the philosophical emphasis on "community policing" and its powerful themes of decentralization and flexibility, the most important lessons learned in police training are those that reinforce the paramilitary structure and culture.

Socialization to many new roles continues as we age and face new transitions and responsibilities. Older adults, for example, may have to "reverse" and learn new family roles as they care for frail and dependent **aging** parents. Moreover, adjustment to grandparenthood, retirement, and the death of friends and family members, as well as acceptance of the inevitability of one's own death, are part of socialization for aging adults.

TIME to REFLECT

Think back to your first paid work experience. What kinds of skills and "lessons" did you learn? How did your interactions with others on the job (e.g., bosses, co-workers, customers) influence your experience and what you learned?

Socialization Processes: Pawns, Puppets, or Free Agents?

In summary, we have learned that socialization is lifelong and shapes the individual and

---

questions for critical thought

1. What criteria would you use to differentiate human populations, and why? What makes you a member (or not) of an ethnic and/or racial group? Should Ontarians be considered an ethnic group? Quebecers? Why? Apply the criteria listed in the first part of this chapter to answer these questions.

2. Can the policy of multiculturalism alone provide solutions to the problems of racism and the attendant issues of immigrant and minority group integration into Canadian political, social, and economic institutions? What should policy-makers do to address the issues of racism and immigrant integration into Canadian society? Explain.

3. What is reasonable accommodation? Who decides what is reasonable? Explain the rise of post-9/11 xenophobia and Islamophobia in the US, Canada, and elsewhere. Choose a particular issue (e.g., the veil), and survey the opinions of your friends and family. What do you conclude?

4. What account better for the economic inequalities among different ethnic/racial groups—cultural or structural differences? Assume that all members of ethnic/racial groups share the same cultural and behavioural characteristics. If culturalist explanations account for the economic inequalities among ethnic/racial groups, what would explain the significant economic inequalities within ethnic/racial groups?

recommended readings

Grace-Edward Galabuzi. 2006. *Canada's Economic Apartheid: The Social Exclusion of Racialized Groups in the New Century*. Toronto: Canadian Scholars Press.
In this controversial argument that supports the view of Canada as characterized by a new colour-coded vertical mosaic, Galabuzi presents evidence of persistent income inequalities between racialized and non-racialized Canadians.

Frances Henry and Carol Tator. 2005. *The Colour of Democracy: Racism in Canadian Society*. 3rd edn. Toronto: Thomson Nelson.
This thorough and caustic critique of racism in Canadian policies and institutions points to the contradictions of multiculturalism and democratic racism in Canadian society.

Peter Li. 2003. *Destination Canada: Immigration Debates and Issues*. Toronto: Oxford University Press.
This is an excellent and up-to-date review of the major debates about the social and economic consequences of immigration to Canada.

Vic Satzewich and Nikolaos Liodakis. 2010. *"Race" and Ethnicity in Canada: A Critical Introduction*. 2nd edn. Toronto: Oxford University Press.
This work summarizes theoretical approaches to the study of race and ethnicity, Canadian immigration policies, Aboriginal–non-Aboriginal relations, economic inequalities among and within ethnic groups, multiculturalism, racism, and transnationalism.

recommended websites

Assembly of First Nations
www.afn.ca
This excellent website of the national organization for status Indians, established in 1982 out of the earlier National Indian Brotherhood, includes press releases, publications, news, policy areas, information on past and future annual assemblies, and links to provincial and territorial organizations. You might also want to check out the fine websites of the other two major Aboriginal organizations in Canada: Inuit Tapiriit

Kanatami, at www.itk.ca, and the Métis National Council, at www.metisnation.ca.

Canadian Heritage: Multiculturalism
www.canadianheritage.gc.ca/progs/multi/index_e.cfm
This federal department site includes information on multicultural programs, definitions of multiculturalism and diversity, news releases, publications, and links to numerous Canadian and international organizations.

- **Questions for Critical Thought, Recommended Readings, Recommended Websites** at the end of each chapter encourage readers to think deeply and point students toward useful sources for further research.

Supplements

Principles of Sociology: Canadian Perspectives is supported by an outstanding array of ancillary materials for both students and instructors.

FOR INSTRUCTORS

- **Online Instructor's Manual** This fully revised online resource includes comprehensive outlines of the text's various parts and chapters, additional questions for encouraging class discussion, suggestions on how to use videos to enhance class learning, and extra resource material for use in lectures.

- **Online Test Generator** A comprehensive test generator allows instructors to sort, edit, import, and distribute hundreds of questions in multiple-choice, short-answer, and true/false formats.

- **PowerPoint® Slides** Hundreds of slides for classroom presentation—rewritten for this edition—incorporate graphics and tables from the text, summarize key points from each chapter, and can be edited to suit individual instructors' needs.

- **Online Video Library** Carefully chosen video clips, matched to relevant chapters and streamed from our companion website, provide case studies, documentary footage, and conversations that enhance students' experiences of critical concepts and issues discussed in the textbook.

Details on instructor's supplements are available from your Oxford University Press sales representative or at our website: www.oupcanada.com/principles3e.

FOR STUDENTS

- **Companion Website** A comprehensive online study guide site provides automatically graded study questions, chapter summaries, annotated links to other useful Web resources, additional review questions, and applied exercises. To access the companion website, visit www.oupcanada.com/Principles3e.

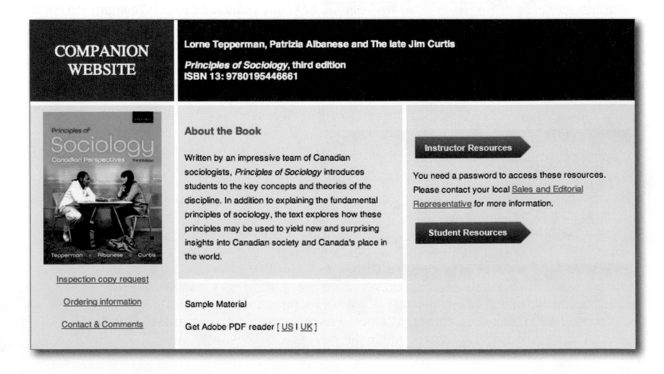

From the General Editors

So much has changed since the first edition of this book. Canada has been jolted (again) by events originating in our neighbour-state, the USA. The economy has melted down, leading to global fears of an economic depression nearly equalling that of the 1930s when so many Canadians were thrown out of work and lost their homes and savings. As well, the Americans have elected a new president—their first African-American president ever—leading to hopes that global power will be exercised in a new, more peaceful and collegial way than in the recent past.

But the mere change of personnel, even of presidents, is not likely to change the institutional structure and fundamental interests of the world's power-brokers, as you will see through various chapters in this book and in a new chapter by Cheryl Teelucksingh. A separate but related enduring reality, represented by another chapter in this edition, is that religion will continue to exercise a dominant ideological force in the world. For reasons made clear in Lori G. Beaman's chapter in this book, religion continues to shape the thoughts, hopes, and actions of people around the world—especially in the war-torn Middle East. Religion still inspires people to noble deeds, as well as to violent, foolhardy ones.

Some things haven't changed much in recent years. Here in Canada, we are still governed by a Conservative government; the country is still fractured by regional differences; and we are still a minor player in the world's political and military dramas. Our everyday lives are still mainly focused on friends and family, school and work, cyberspace and popular culture. As Canadians, we still live in a society widely—and correctly—viewed as moderate, civilized, tolerant, and healthy. Therefore, many people around the world want to immigrate here, and many do, giving us one of the highest rates of immigration in the world. With this comes continuing concern about immigrant assimilation—economically, culturally, and socially.

For all that, Canadian society is still relatively safe and peaceful, although many continue to express fears and concerns about crime, especially violent crime. Even though sociologists have shown repeatedly that violent crime is not increasing, the media continue to fan the fears of older people, small-town people, and people who stay indoors and watch a lot of television. Some of this fear, particularly about handguns and gang violence, has been imported from the United States. Some is an indirect result of anxiety about immigration and the problems of assimilating new immigrants. Some is justifiable, given the high rates of school dropout, especially by young men, who are the prime candidates for committing violent crime. Regrettably, the federal government has encouraged this unwarranted anxiety about crime with plans to fill new mega-prisons with (yet to be identified) violent criminals.

Canada, then, continues to be a complicated society: peaceful and violent, calm and fearful, cooperative and conflictual, stable and tempestuous. This new version of *Principles* tries to capture, describe, and explain Canadian society today, and we think you will like it. We think you will find it even more interesting, provocative, and readable than the last edition. And our mission is no less important than it was the last time: namely, to educate Canadians about the society in which they live. We have a duty to study and understand this country and to make it serve our collective needs.

The publisher, Oxford University Press Canada, has continued to help our contributors provide the clearest possible portrait of Canadian society. Developmental editor Meagan Carlsson has done a masterful job of keeping us on track, smoothing chapters and otherwise taking care of the backstage, practical matters at Oxford—making sure that all the pieces come together when and where they should. We also want to thank Dorothy Turnbull for performing a very thorough read-through of the manuscript. And thanks go to those talented people who selected the photos that appear in this great-looking book.

We would also like to acknowledge the following reviewers, along with the reviewers who chose to remain anonymous, whose insightful comments have helped to shape the new edition of *Principles of Sociology: Canadian Perspectives*:

Alexandre Enkerli, Concordia University
Susan Miller, University of Manitoba
Diane Naugler, Kwantlen Polytechnic University
Isher-Paul Sahni, University of New Brunswick
Tamy Superle, Carleton University
Linda Quirke, Wilfrid Laurier University

We extend our most profound thanks to the authors of the chapters in the most recent version of *Sociology: A Canadian Perspective*, whose work formed the main basis of this streamlined version. Without their contribution, this book would not exist. They put up with our (seemingly endless) demands, and somehow everything was done on time and as needed. It has been a great privilege working with this distinguished group of Canadian scholars from all over the country. Thank you, authors.

In closing, we dedicate this book to our students, who face many challenging decisions. Never in recent times has the world economy been so troubled or the future so murky. It will take great courage, dedication, and maturity to forge ahead, to make plans, and to keep them alive. We wish you well; you are the next generation of our country and our best chance. We hope sociological analysis will prove a useful guide in your lives.

Lorne Tepperman, University of Toronto
Patrizia Albanese, Ryerson University

contributors

Patrizia Albanese is associate professor in the Department of Sociology at Ryerson University and the co-director of the Centre for Children, Youth, and Families at Ryerson.

Bruce Arai teaches courses in research methods, statistics, and the sociology of work at Wilfrid Laurier University.

Maureen Baker is professor of sociology at the University of Auckland.

Shyon Baumann is associate professor of sociology at the University of Toronto.

Lori G. Beaman is professor of classics and religious studies at the University of Ottawa.

Juanne Clarke is professor of sociology at Wilfrid Laurier University.

Sara J. Cumming is a PhD candidate in the Department of Sociology and Legal Studies at the University of Waterloo.

Andrea Doucet is professor of sociology at Brock University and the Canada Research Chair in Gender Work and Care.

Ann D. Duffy is professor of sociology and associate chair of the Department of Sociology at Brock University.

Randle Hart is assistant professor in the Department of History and Sociology at Southern Utah University.

Alicia D. Horton is a PhD candidate in the Department of Sociology at Queen's University.

Nikolaos I. Liodakis is associate professor of sociology at Wilfrid Laurier University.

Barbara A. Mitchell is professor of sociology at Simon Fraser University.

Dorothy Pawluch is associate professor of sociology at McMaster University.

Howard Ramos is a political sociologist in the Department of Sociology and Social Anthropology at Dalhousie University.

Vincent F. Sacco is professor of sociology and teaches courses relating to crime, deviance, and social control at Queen's University.

William Shaffir is professor and associate chair in the Department of Sociology at McMaster University.

Janet Siltanen is professor of sociology at Carleton University and director of the Institute of Political Economy.

Karen Stanbridge is associate professor of sociology at Memorial University of Newfoundland.

Pamela Sugiman is professor of sociology at Ryerson University.

Liam Swiss is assistant professor of sociology at Memorial University of Newfoundland.

Cheryl Teelucksingh is associate professor of sociology at Ryerson University.

Lorne Tepperman is professor of sociology at the University of Toronto and past president of the Canadian Sociological Association.

Anthony Thomson is professor of sociology at Acadia University.

John Veugelers is associate professor of sociology at the University of Toronto.

Terry Wotherspoon is professor and head of sociology at the University of Saskatchewan.

David Young is assistant professor of sociology at McMaster University.

Why Not Become a Sociologist?

Lorne Tepperman and Patrizia Albanese

Introduction

Why do people become sociologists? There are many answers to this question, and it is likely that everyone at one point or other has been on the brink of becoming a sociologist. This is because at some point or other, all people experience odd facts of social life that affect their opportunities, and they try to understand them. This is where sociology begins for most people. When people continue from here, there is even more motivation to actually study sociology. What can be more fascinating, more empowering, and more personal than to begin to understand the society that shapes our lives? For these reasons, sociology is an inherently attractive area of study, and many people do study it.

Maybe as a child you noticed the following:

- Parents sometimes treat their sons differently from their daughters.
- Teachers often treat pretty little girls better than plain-looking ones.
- Salespeople treat well-dressed youth better than poorly dressed youth.
- Movies typically portray people with "accents" as strange or ridiculous.

If you noticed these things, you may have wondered why they happen. They may even have affected you, as a daughter or son, a plain-looking or attractive person, a poorly dressed or well-dressed person, or a person with or without an "accent." You may have felt ashamed, angry, or pleased, depending on whether you identified with the favourably treated or the unfavourably treated category of people.

If you noticed or experienced these things, you may have wanted to understand them better. These are the kinds of circumstances in which sociological curiosity begins. All sociologists got hooked on trying to better understand their own lives and the lives of people around them. They came to understand that common sense gave them incomplete or inaccurate explanations about people's behaviour and the society in which they live. They were not satisfied with the explanations they received and wanted to know more.

For much of what we do, common-sense understanding is just fine. But for anyone who wants to understand how society works, it is not good enough. You may already realize there are many questions common sense cannot answer adequately, such as the following:

- Why do seemingly similar people lead such different lives?
- Why do we often treat "different" people much worse than others?
- What do people do to escape from being treated badly?
- What can citizens do to make Canadian society a more equitable place?
- Can we bring about social change by changing the laws of the country?

Sociologists want to understand how societies change and how people's lives change with them. Social changes, inequalities, and conflicts captivate sociologists because such issues—war and peace, wealth and poverty, environmental destruction and technological innovation, for example—are important for people's lives. Sociologists know that "personal problems" are similar across many individuals. They also know that many of our personal problems are the private side of public issues. American sociologist C. Wright Mills called this knowledge or ability "the sociological imagination." With this ability or approach, we know we need to deal with personal problems collectively and, often, politically—with full awareness that we share these problems and their solution with others.

However, solving problems entails clear thinking and careful research. So social theorists and social science researchers have developed concepts, theories, and research methods that help them to study the social world more effectively. Our goal as sociologists is to be able to explain social life, critique social inequities, and work toward effecting social change. In this book, you will learn how sociologists go about these tasks and some of what sociologists have found out about the social world.

Our starting point is a formal definition of *sociology*, comparisons of sociology with other related fields of study, and a discussion of sociology's most basic subject matter.

A Definition of *Sociology*

Scholars have defined sociology in many ways, but most practising sociologists think of their discipline as the systematic study of

(©iStockphoto.com/benadek)

Sociologists are particularly interested in social change. What do you think a sociologist would say about the LGBT movement in Canada?

social behaviour in human societies. Humans are intensely social beings and spend most of their time interacting with others. That is why sociologists study the social units people create when they join with others. As we will see in the following chapters, these units range from small groups—comprising as few as two people—to large corporations and even whole societies (see, for example, Chapter 4, on social organization). Sociologists are interested in learning about how group membership affects individual behaviour. They are also interested in learning how individuals change the groups of which they are members.

However, it is impossible for any sociologist to study all social issues or to become an expert in all the sub-disciplines of sociology. As a result, most sociologists specialize in either macrosociology or microsociology—two related but distinct approaches to studying the social world—and choose problems for study from within these realms.

Macrosociology is the study of large social **organizations** (for example, the Roman Catholic church, universities, corporations, or government bureaucracies) and large social categories (for example, ethnic minorities, seniors, or university students). Sociologists who specialize in the macrosociological approach to the social world focus on the complex social patterns that people form over long periods.

On the other hand, **microsociology** focuses on the typical processes and patterns of face-to-face interaction in small groups. A microsociologist might study a marriage, a clique, a business meeting, an argument between friends, or a first date. A macrosociologist would study the common, everyday interactions and negotiations that together produce lasting, secure patterns. You can see many examples of this in Chapter 3 on being social.

Combining macro and micro approaches improves our understanding of the social world. Consider a common social phenomenon: the domestic division of labour—who does what chores around the home. From the micro perspective, who does what is constantly open to negotiation. It is influenced by personal characteristics, the history of the couple, and many other unique factors. Yet viewed from a macro perspective, different households have similar divisions of labour despite different personal histories. This suggests the answer lies in a society's history, culture, and economy. It is far from accidental that across millions of households, men enjoy the advantage of a better salary and more social power both in a great many workplaces and at home.

While these approaches are different, they are also connected. They have to be: after all, both macro- and microsociologists are studying the same people in the same society. All of us are leading unique lives within a common social context, faced by common problems. The question is, how can sociologists bring these elements together? As noted above, C. Wright Mills (1959) gave the answer when he introduced the notion of the sociological imagination as something that enables us to relate personal biographies—the lives of millions of ordinary people like ourselves—to the broad sweep of human history. The sociological imagination is what we need to use to understand how societies control and change their members and, at the same time, are constantly changed by the actions of their members.

(©iStockphoto.com/Igor Skrbic)

Even though they are utilized by sociologists simultaneously, micro- and macrosociology are two distinct approaches. For example, a macrosociology approach would examine rates of homelessness in Canada, whereas a microsociology approach would investigate how the homeless in downtown Vancouver choose to construct their identity.

How Sociology Differs from Other Academic Fields

Sociology is just one of several fields of study designed to help describe and explain human behaviour; others include journalism, history, philosophy, and psychology. How does sociology differ from these other endeavours? Canadian sociologist Kenneth Westhues (1982) has compared sociology's approach with those of the other fields. He stresses that journalism and history describe real events, as does sociology. However, journalism and history only sometimes base their descriptions on a theory or interpretation, and then it is often an implicit or hidden theory.

Sociology strives to make its theories clear, to be able to test them. Telling a story is important for sociologists but less so than the explanation on which the story is based. Besides, stories often make the news because they are unusual; sociologists instead are drawn to issues because they are common events or are recurring patterns.

Sociology also differs from philosophy. Both are *analytical*—that is, concerned with testing and refining theory. However, sociology is firmly *empirical*, or concerned with gathering evidence and doing studies, while philosophy is not. Philosophy has greater concern with the internal logic of its arguments. Sociological theories must stand up logically, but they must also stand up to evidence in a way philosophical theories need not. Sociologists, no matter how logical the theory may be, will not accept a sociological theory whose predictions are not supported by evidence gathered in a sound way.

Finally, sociology differs from psychology, which is also analytical, empirical, and interpretive. The difference here lies in the subject matter. Psychologists study the behaviour of individual humans or, sometimes, animals. Generally, they do so under experimental conditions. Sociology's subject matter is **social relationships** or groups viewed in society. As you will see, sociologists study the family, schools, workplaces, the media—even the total society. Sociology and psychology come close together in a field called *social psychology*, but this field is defined differently by sociologists and by psychologists. Studies by sociologists are more likely to focus on the effects of group living on people's views and behaviours. By contrast, psychologists are more likely to focus on particular individuals and how they respond under certain experimental conditions.

Another way of characterizing sociology and what makes it unique has been put forward by Earl Babbie (1988). He states that sociologists hold some basic or fundamental ideas that set them apart from those in other fields:

1. Society has an existence of its own.
2. Society can be studied scientifically.
3. Society creates itself.
4. Cultures vary over time and place.
5. Individual identity is a product of society.
6. Social structure must satisfy survival requirements.
7. Institutions are inherently conservative.
8. Societies constrain and transform.
9. Multiple paradigms or fundamental models of reality are needed.

As we will see in the chapters that follow, these are many of the most basic ideas or assumptions of sociology. Chapter 1 introduces the theoretical underpinnings and methodologies of sociology. This is followed by chapters on culture (Chapter 2), being social (Chapter 3), social organization (Chapter 4), and deviance (Chapter 5). The next three chapters present different forms of inequality people experience: class and status (Chapter 6), sexuality and gender relations (Chapter 7), and ethnic and race relations (Chapter 8). Reading the next part of the book, you will learn about different

(©iStockphoto.com/Nikada)

Sociology is one of the fields of study designed to help describe and explain human behaviour. Unlike psychologists, who focus on the individual, sociologists prefer to study social relationships and groups.

social institutions that shape and constrain our lives, including families (Chapter 9), education (Chapter 10), work and the economy (Chapter 11), health (Chapter 12), religion (Chapter 13), and politics and social movements (Chapter 14). Increasingly, understanding Canadian society means also understanding global issues (Chapter 15), population, urbanization, and the environment (Chapter 16), and the mass media and communication (Chapter 17).

People who major or specialize in sociology gain valuable skills in critical thinking and research methods. This prepares them for a variety of second-entry college and university programs, including law, social work, teaching, industrial relations, human resources, opinion polling, public health, and public administration as well as other fields. People who go on to get an MA or PhD in sociology often end up teaching in colleges or universities or holding positions as researchers, consultants, or policy planners.

Conclusion

Sociology is a broad field of study. This is obvious in the broad theoretical perspectives used to guide most sociological research. Sociology highlights both micro- and macro-level analyses and the complex relationships between the two, as noted in Mills's idea of the sociological imagination. Sociology also covers a broad subject matter—consider the subject matter of the following chapters, ranging across deviance, family, education, religion, politics, the economy, health, and beyond.

Sociology allows people to move beyond a purely common-sense approach to a better understanding of social life. It gives people more powerful tools to explore the connections between social institutions and processes. As they do so, they recognize that much common-sense knowledge is faulty. Sociology will help you to see that things are not always what they seem.

Sociology stresses the relationships among individuals, social structure, and culture. As you will see, social structure and culture constrain the behaviour of individuals. However, they are both essential for social life. As well, social structure and culture are both created by humans in social interaction. Therefore, they are both subject to future changes in the same way. In short, sociology "demystifies" social life, showing that social arrangements are in our own hands. That said, powerful interest groups play a disproportionate role in controlling the kinds of social and cultural change that take place.

Sociology has obvious personal relevance, since it addresses everyday life issues. And, finally, sociology has an important goal overall: to contribute positively to the future of humanity. Our sincere hope is that this text will set you on your way to developing your own sociological imagination.

PART I

Theory and Methodology

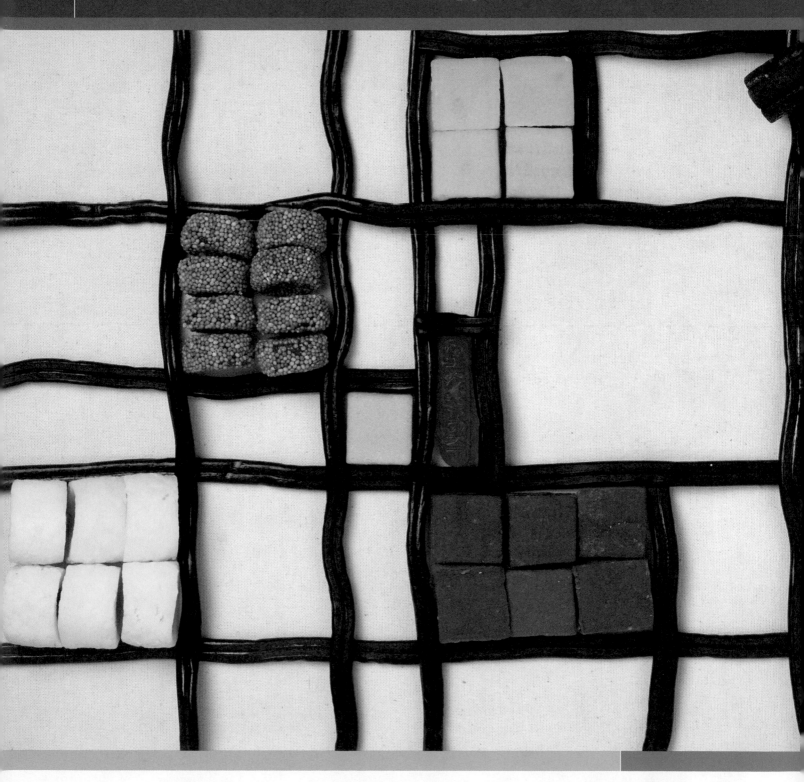

chapter 1

Sociological Theory and Research Methods

Bruce Arai and Anthony Thomson

In this chapter you will:

▶ Distinguish between objectivity and subjectivity in social theory.

▶ Identify the key ideas of the major classical theorists: Durkheim, Marx, and Weber.

▶ Relate classical social theory to modern perspectives in sociology—functionalist, conflict, interactionist, and feminist—and to contemporary sociology.

▶ Gain a better grasp of social survey design.

▶ Learn about field research, interviewing, and ethnographic research.

▶ Study the different types of existing data and how they are analyzed.

Introduction: Why Theory and Methods?

In one sense, we are all sociologists. We all use our mind and our actions to make sense of the world in which we live. At the same time, even though we may fry an egg for breakfast, we are not all kitchen wizards. Professional sociologists are like chefs who concoct ideas and conduct systematic research to explain the world that people construct and inhabit.

In this chapter, we focus on the theories sociologists have devised to understand social life and the methods they use to collect the data that have informed these theories and produced the many findings you will read about throughout this text.

Understanding the world and our places within it is almost as important as eating. The majority of Canadians (though certainly far from all) can take eating pretty much for granted. This is a great privilege. In our increasingly connected but greatly unequal globe, a full stomach cannot be assumed. Our privilege is also our responsibility. Not only are we able to use our intellect to understand the world, it is a crucial ingredient for guiding the actions we take. From a sociological perspective, what we do—our day-to-day actions—are part of the making and remaking of the actual world we live in.

Like eating, much of our understanding of the world, of what we do and think, is simply taken for granted, as if it were natural. But the rules of nature—for example, if you are deprived of food long enough, you will die—are not the same as the rules of society—you will not have enough to eat if you don't have the money to pay for it.

Many sociologists want specifically to understand the taken-for-granted nature of social life. People live, day to day, with simple formulas that help them to understand the way things work: we tend to think that the world is the way it is and couldn't be much different. We even begin to study sociology with the blasé attitude that sociologist Georg Simmel talks about—the rock band Pink Floyd would call it "comfortably numb."

We don't, however, just act blindly or randomly or make up these ways of understanding as we go along. To borrow from the film industry, we follow scripts that are given to us and play the roles assigned. We are born into an existing society of things and people and into a world of ideas of what we should and shouldn't think or do. We are told who we are by other people; our identity is not something we make by ourselves willy-nilly.

Our ideas about the world and our place within it reflect theories of society that have been built into our intellect. The process goes on so automatically that, like digestion, it seems to just happen. We begin ingesting ideas about the world along with our mother's milk, as Chapter 3 on socialization demonstrates. But the ideas that we swallow may be open to question. They may be popular fictions or myths. They may be part of the problems in the world, not the solutions.

Most of the sociologists you will read about in this book have been motivated by a desire not only to understand society but to change it for the better. Sociology challenges existing ways of thinking and researching. This book is as much about helping you to see the world through different lenses as it is about providing information.

The Birth of Sociology in the Age of Revolution

How do theorists go about building a theory for understanding social life? Quite a lot depends on how they approach some basic questions about individuals and society. Are people's actions the result of a choice they have made? Or are people really just the puppets of objective social forces that work the strings behind their backs, determining what they do or think? Should you look only at the existing facts, such as how food is unevenly distributed, or should you also ask questions about values, such as how food *should* be distributed?

On the one hand, we are born into pre-existing social arrangements or structures, including physical objects such as buildings as well as social codes of behaviour and morality. Social theory focuses much of its attention on the working of the pre-existing structures and institutions that set the limits and boundaries of our lives.

On the other hand, we choose one course of action over others. For example, you chose to enter university, but you may toss the whole thing aside tomorrow and travel to Bali. People are thinking and acting individuals; in short, they exercise **agency**. Sociology considers both the existing **objective** facts and our **subjective** understanding of them.

Social thinkers have examined society—the ways that people organize their lives together—for thousands of years. Sociology was developed by scholars who were aware that their world was changing rapidly and fundamentally (Thomson 2010). What was new when sociology was invented about two centuries ago was the idea that society could be studied scientifically. People who are part of the generation now reaching adulthood are used to rapid change, at least in many of the ways they go about their lives—how they communicate, travel, work, and experience diversions and pleasures. There is a sense that the gap between generations is widening, that the old generation can't understand the new

one or appreciate the microchip revolution. "I *used to be* with it," Grandpa Simpson says, but now what's "it" seems pretty weird and scary to him. Sociology thrives in these periods of large-scale social change. It is harder to take things for granted when the ground that had seemed so familiar is shifting under your feet.

When European social theorists in the 1800s surveyed their "new" society, they believed that a more modern view of the world had replaced the older, traditional view. Traditional society had been a world of magic, mystery, and arbitrary authority. In contrast, modern society had entered a new world of **Enlightenment**. Through the use of reason or rationality, the human mind could shine light into the darkest caves and discover "true" knowledge. More than 200 years later, we seem no closer to this elusive and improbable "universal" understanding.

The French social theorist who invented the term *sociology*, Auguste Comte (1798–1857), intended to create a "science" of society that would allow us to understand social life the

© Mike Baldwin / Cornered

BALDWIN

(© Mike Baldwin, www.CartoonStock.com)

"iPad, huh? When I was your age, I remember getting hold of a piece of carbon paper once. Amused myself for days – after I figured out how it worked."

way that biology understood physical life. But the "natural" sciences—astronomy, physics, chemistry—were more advanced in their knowledge at that time than any purported science of social life. There was a lot of catching up to do.

The way forward for sociology, then, was to discover the "natural" laws that determined social life, just as Sir Isaac Newton had discovered the law of gravity. Once these laws of society were discovered scientifically, they could be applied to make social life orderly, peaceful, and secure. As Comte (1974, 19–27) saw it, the knowledge developed by the new social science of "sociology" would give humans power over social change. Throughout most of the nineteenth century, sociological thinking involved the search for law-like certainties that could explain social life. But as sociologists proliferated, the search for social "laws" led to quite different—indeed opposite—conclusions.

TIME to REFLECT

What does it mean to live in a revolutionary age? How is the word *revolution* used today?

Studying sociological theory entails grasping the perspectives of the early developers of sociology who strove to carve out the new discipline, the new science of understanding social life. We refer to members of the founding generation of sociologists as classical theorists. Three of the most important are Émile Durkheim, Karl Marx, and Max Weber. They are cited frequently throughout this text, so at this point it is useful to outline their thinking.

Émile Durkheim

Émile Durkheim (1858–1917) would become the most famous French sociologist of the late nineteenth and early twentieth century, but he was originally destined to become a rabbi. He was born in eastern France to a close-knit, strictly moral, and orthodox Jewish family, part of a small and cohesive community. Educated in Paris among the intellectual elite of his generation, Durkheim broke with the Jewish faith and with religious belief generally, but he

understood the powerful hold that religion has on people in society (Lukes 1972, 39–46).

In contemporary society, Durkheim's theory is seen as **structural functionalism**. His theories explain the ways that different institutions function to maintain social order and reproduce society over time. A strong sense of social togetherness, Durkheim said, originated in the simplest societies through regular feasts and celebrations. In joyous, often delirious festivals, people experienced a "collective effervescence" that bound them together and generated a feeling of spirituality. They sensed a sacred or spiritual power greater than themselves that, Durkheim argued, actually originated from the shared social experience itself.

Modern society, however, seemed to have lost that solid and shared code of morality that had acted as the glue holding traditional society together—in Durkheim's terms, people no longer shared a collective conscience (Durkheim 1965 [1912], 5–6). People were no longer united by a single code of right and wrong, an uncertainty that he termed **anomie**. Over time, the sacred part of life had become overshadowed by the secular.

For Jean Baudrillard (1929–2007), it may paradoxically be the definition of the sacred that is changing. Through the ostentatious display of goods-for-sale in shop windows and big-box malls, "things" take on an almost sacred aura, even when they are merely worshipped through gazing (window-shopping). At every moment in consumer society, "in the streets . . . on advertising hoardings and neon signs," individuals are trained into a modern collective consciousness of mass consumption (Baudrillard 1998, 166).

Durkheim believed that other traditional institutions, such as marriage and the family, also seemed to be breaking down in modern society. He believed that men had an inborn sexual passion that had to be curbed and regulated by marriage. Otherwise, he thought, men's sexual desires would lead them into the pursuit of novelty and excess. A typical Victorian man, Durkheim also opposed sex education, which, he said, was like treating a mysterious and private act as if it were no more than digestion (Lukes 1972, 530–4). Women sociologists, on the other hand, soon recognized that the writings of classical male sociologists reflected their culturally induced gender biases.

For Durkheim, modern society had evolved away from the spirit of community. Feeling closely connected to others, as in a close-knit community, was good for society, but it was also essential for the well-being of an individual. Durkheim's best-known application of sociological methods to understand a social problem was his examination of suicide, perhaps the loneliest act. The key to the sociological explanation for suicide was the strength or weakness of the individual's ties to his or her community and society (Durkheim 1951 [1897], 208–23). Durkheim saw self-destruction as a social fact that could be understood scientifically through his research methods.

Durkheim's social theory examined society as a totality of interconnected parts, an approach that is fundamental to theory. Through his publications, his teaching, and the work of his followers, he stamped his functionalist approach to understanding society on the new discipline he helped to create.

Karl Marx

While he did not describe his work as "sociological," the theories of Karl Marx (1818–83) have inspired movements of revolution and reform that have had deep and lasting consequences for sociological theory. Marx was born into a respectable middle-class family in Germany and married into the minor aristocracy. The match was a romance, however, not a route into the upper class. The groom was not conventionally ambitious but instead was steeped in youthful radicalism (Berlin 1963, 27–32).

For Marx, the way to begin the analysis of any society was to examine the way it produced and distributed the basic necessities of life—its economic system. Over time, land and goods, which had originally been the common property of all, became the private property of a few. Class divisions and conflict became basic features of most societies and the keys to understanding social change. The majority of people produced more goods than they required for their own use. The excess or **surplus** went to support the elite few who were free from the burden of daily labour. Over time, the few grew into a rich and powerful dominant class, and society became increasingly unequal.

Economically, what distinguished traditional from modern society, Marx said, was the rise of **capitalism**. Under the control of the capitalists, the economic system was revolutionized. People were driven from the countryside into the poorest sections of the booming new cities and into the factory system, which became the dominant economic form—migration from rural to urban is now a worldwide phenomenon (Marx and Engels 1985 [1848]; Marx's perspective is illustrated in the image on the following page, "Pyramid of Capitalist System": the labour of the working class toiling at the bottom provides surplus in the form of profit for the livelihood of the opulent capitalist class [shown at dinner], for priests [second from the top], and for the government, which orders the soldiers to shoot the workers when they rebel).

SOCIOLOGY in ACTION

Michel Foucault

Born in France, Michel Foucault (1936–84) established an early and highly successful career in intellectual history, and he remains influential in many disciplines, including sociology. Educated at an elite school in France, the solitary Foucault found life unbearable. He became fascinated with authors who dealt with "transgression," "limit experiences" (such as death), and "excess." His book *Discipline and Punish* uses the rise of the penitentiary, with its constant surveillance of prisoners and strict discipline, as a metaphor for the same processes as they spread throughout modern society (schools, hospitals, the army).

As an "engaged philosopher," Foucault became politically active in the 1970s. He supported prisoners' rights and exposed the intolerable realities of incarceration. By then, he had come to terms with a homosexual identity and followed his new lifestyle with abandon. Foucault died at 47 from complications linked to AIDS (Eribon 1991).

TIME to REFLECT

How would Durkheim respond to the figure depicting the capitalist system?

The working class in global capitalism was not only oppressed, Marx reasoned, but also "alienated." In simple terms, *alienation* means to be separated from something. Generally, for Marx, the original alienation (separation) of humanity from nature in the earliest stage of social evolution was a good thing, and it was necessary for all the progress that followed—potentially, for a world of shared wealth and high living standards for all. But power over nature has now proved to be a double-edged sword. In our current environmental crisis, which is one of the consequences of constant-growth capitalism, it is clear that our power over and alienation from nature have had some disastrous consequences.

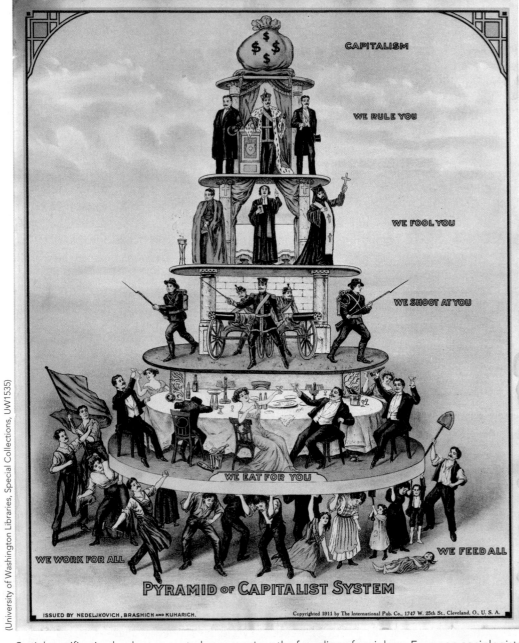

(University of Washington Libraries, Special Collections, UW1535)

Social stratification has been a central concern since the founding of sociology. Even non-sociologists have long understood that their lives are shaped by class structure.

Max Weber

The way people interpret and respond to social rules was important to the theories of German sociologist Max Weber (1864–1920). In his view, neither individualism nor capitalism captured the fundamental way that modern society differed from traditional society. For Weber, the growing importance of rationality was the basic underlying difference.

Weber was born near Weimar, Germany, and grew up under the iron-fisted power of Kaiser Wilhelm (Käsler 1988, 1–3). In Germany, Marxism was an influential political force by the time Weber had begun to address sociological issues. As with Marx, Weber's sociology is historical and comparative, two essential elements of sound social theory. But Weber sought to uncover the social, cultural, and political factors that shaped modern society independently of economic processes.

For Weber, modern society differed from traditional society in that it was highly rational, and the most direct example was modern science. Arising in a traditional society dominated by religion, science tended to erode mystical and supernatural beliefs. Weber referred to this process as the disenchantment of the world (Weber 1946 [1915], 350–1). He saw the modern world as characterized by "formal rationality," which involves calculating the most efficient means to achieve a goal, just as politicians plot how to manipulate public opinion and win votes.

Society had not always been fundamentally rational. In traditional monarchies, for example, the first-born son of the sovereign automatically becomes the next king, but this form of "traditional authority" does not mean he is actually fit to rule. In *The King's Speech*, the shy, speech-impaired second son of the deceased king learns to play the role of king in place of his older but decadent, pro-Nazi brother. The ability to exercise power over others can also be based on personal, "charismatic authority"—an irrational power that compels people to follow a leader, such as Jesus or Hitler.

In the modern world, Weber said, tradition and charisma had been replaced by "legal–rational authority." All of the institutions of modern life, including government, were regulated by a rational set of rules that defined a hierarchy of positions and power. When you get a job as an assistant bank manager, your work will be judged according to objective standards of performance. Traditional types of evaluation and judgment—such as to whom you are related—become less important than your qualifications, experience, and work habits.

TIME to REFLECT

Weber said that traditional authority and charismatic authority had been largely superseded by legal–rational authority. Thinking about Canadian elections, would you say this is largely true?

In contemporary sociology, French social theorist Pierre Bourdieu (1930–2002) has redefined Weber's analysis of modern society to examine the various ways in which people can acquire resources of power and control. For Bourdieu (1984), if you are well educated and have acquired the necessary knowledge and "taste" to be able to fit seamlessly into higher classes, you have **cultural capital**. If you are well-connected and have an "in" with important people, you can benefit by using these connections and have **social capital**, says Bourdieu.

Calculating the most efficient means to attain an end such as private profit is central to contemporary globalization. George Ritzer terms the spread of rationality in the global economy McDonaldization, since the fast-food chain's calculated techniques of production and marketing have become the model for others. McDonaldization is evident in "education, work, health care, travel, leisure, dieting, politics, the family, and virtually every other aspect of society" (Ritzer 2000a, 1–2).

As life becomes increasingly dominated by rational calculation, however, people often try to escape from rationality into other, competing, and non-rational realms. Workaday life has no deep or ultimate meaning, so people strive for other life-affirming, personal goals. The value we sometimes put on erotic love, for example, can provide meaning to our existence. Erotic love, Weber said, is not only a joyous triumph over the all-too-rational but appears to be the gateway into the irrational, "real kernel of life" (1946 [1915], 341–7). Weber's focus on the meaning of things, on people's understandings and interpretations, is at the root of some contemporary sociological theories, such as symbolic interactionism.

Symbolic Interactionism

As the challenge of the irrational side of humanity suggests, there are two sides to sociology. It isn't possible to study people the way you study rocks or plants. If you push a rock, the results are quite predictable. You can calculate how far and in what direction it will move. But what happens if you push a human being? Rocks don't push back; they don't run away or turn and fight. Human beings are not simply objects that are analyzed and acted upon; they have intentions they want to carry out; they have interpretations of their own actions and those of others; they have desires and needs they seek to fulfill; and they make choices.

These subjective processes became the research focus of a group of sociologists and social psychologists called the Chicago School. Over time, the Chicago approach led to **symbolic interactionism**, a theory that is a form of microsociology because it focuses attention on the smallest units of society—individual people and their interactions.

In symbolic interactionism, society emerges from social interaction—the way people orient their actions to take other people into account. In his modern novel *Ulysses*, James Joyce (1968, 602) asks this question about Leopold Bloom and Stephen Dedalus, two of his characters: "What . . . were Bloom's thoughts about Stephen's thoughts about Bloom, and Bloom's thoughts about Stephen's thoughts about Bloom's thoughts about Stephen?" In sociology, this complex calculation involves **intersubjectivity**—people orient their action according to what they think (subjectively) others think. In addition, as W.I. Thomas (Thomas and Znaniecki 1958, 68–9) said, everyone enters a social occasion with a specific "definition of the situation," and this definition affects how they act and what they hope to get out of the interaction.

Similarly, G.H. Mead (1863–1931) argued that we learn to put ourselves in the position of the other person and see what he or she sees, feel what he or she feels. The better socialized we are, the better we are able to stand in others' shoes and see the world from their point of view—in Mead's terms, we "take the role of the other" and learn to think reflexively (1934, 73, 133–4).

For a more complete discussion of symbolic interactionism and Mead's perspective, see "Symbolic Interactionist Frame of Reference" in Chapter 3, p. 55.

The more closely or significantly we are attached to these others, the more their opinion toward us affects how we feel about our self. It doesn't matter to the Mark Zuckerberg character in *The Social Network* if a neighbour down the hall thinks he's an "asshole," but it does matter when, in the opening scene, his girlfriend comes to the same conclusion.

Interactionism and microsociology generally see society from the bottom up, as an ensemble of relationships maintained through communication and interpretation. Social institutions exist only because people continually, minute by minute, act in ways that reproduce them. Some people, however, particularly those in positions of power, have more opportunity to construct society according to their interests. This insight is crucial to **conflict theory** in sociology.

Conflict Theory

The concept of **power** in society—including top-down domination and resistance from the bottom—is an important element in the modern conflict perspective in sociology that derives from Marx and Weber. The imposition of discipline on bodily movements may become so ingrained that people respond unthinkingly, like Pavlov's dog, a poor creature who drooled every time he heard a bell ring because an experimenter had conditioned him to associate bell-ringing with getting his dinner. It may be useful, however, to think of a person's body as both the target of rules imposed on the person by authority and as an object that is manipulated and modified by the person. After all, we do pay a great deal of attention to a person's body, and we sculpt our body through various means, including exercise and diet. We adorn the body with ornaments, tattoos, hairstyles, and clothing styled for various occasions.

Kindergarten is referred to in sociology as "boot camp" for children, because teachers impose rules on the way students direct their bodily movements. Besides learning to control such bodily needs as elimination, eating, and drinking, children are taught to observe rules about covering parts of the body, lining up at the bell, sitting straight in specified places (traditionally in rows), and obeying the rule of silence. In Michel Foucault's terms, people are taught to regulate themselves.

Nevertheless, no one is powerless. Ask any teacher or parent. When people such as teachers, judges, or parole officers exercise power, they simultaneously provoke "resistance"— the ways people find to subvert power and achieve their aims against external authority (actions that transgress rules). Students have invented many strategies to resist school rules. They copy homework, skip classes, feign sickness, carve their desks, cheat on tests, plagiarize—in short, they learn the informal anti-rules of schooling (Raby 2009, 127). Children as a group may be the most oppressed of all—Charles Dickens thought so—but **feminism**, which focuses on the inequality between men and women, is one of the most important contemporary perspectives to emerge from conflict theory.

Feminist Sociology

As more and more women entered sociology and undertook professional studies in the middle of the last century, it became increasingly clear that women were absent from classical, male theory or were apparently subsumed under a male point of view. In response, feminists such as Marianne Weber (1870–1954) have integrated a distinctly female standpoint into sociological theorizing and research. The earliest feminist writings, such as Mary Wollstonecraft's *Vindication of the Rights of Women*, asserted the equal

rationality of women and men, from which she inferred the right for women to be equal in all aspects of society. Similarly, liberals in the women's movement seek to equalize conditions for women within the existing economic structures (Friedan 1963). Over time, women in modern society have made great advances, but they have been more successful in acquiring the *rights* to equality than in achieving *actual* equality in many spheres of modern life.

In contrast to liberal feminists, radical feminists demand more than an equal chance to gain access to the formal structures of power in modern society (Firestone 1970). They demand changes in the everyday relationships between men and women, such as stopping patriarchal violence, and the equal recognition of alternative forms of families and different sexualities.

Feminist theorists in contemporary sociology have understood that the experiences of poor, or minority, or sexually differentiated women are likely to be misunderstood when seen through the eyes of middle-class, professional, heterosexual women. While there are many kinds of feminisms, one of the most pervasive strains within feminist sociology is the need to understand society from women's standpoint and to focus on women's subjectivity. In Canada, sociologist Dorothy Smith (b. 1926) developed a perspective that is critical of the top-down model of sociology that dominates the discipline. Smith argues that feminist research should begin with the everyday experiences of women and with their understanding of these "lived experiences."

Radical feminism is engaged, explicit in its goals, and not value-free. Smith's activist research method is consciously interested, not disinterested. She integrates her "subjects" into all aspects of the research process and produces results that are shared with the participants and are aimed at addressing the issues that sparked the research.

Dorothy Smith was a pioneer of Canadian feminist sociology. To learn more about her perspective, see "Gender and Sexuality as Critical Vantage Points" in Chapter 7, p. 134.

UNDER the WIRE

What Difference Do the Differences Make?

In contemporary times—at least in the Western world—new technology, international travel, and the Internet have modified the way we experience our world. The implications our new and different lifestyle will have for us and future generations are issues of vital public interest.

Sociologists are not just interested in what the differences are—they want to know *what difference the differences make.* Does modern communication technology enable us to be better informed about socially significant events or only about everyday trivia? Do the new media provide platforms for the greater realization of democratic decision-making, or are they tools of Big Brother? Do they create more communities of interest and sharing, or do they more thoroughly individualize us? Do they deepen our actual engagement with the world or merely make even the most horrendous event seem like a spectacle, to be gazed at but not acted upon?

Every new communication technology creates new possibilities for control, but also for resistance.

Protesters in Egypt and Tunisia in 2011, who (perhaps temporarily) drove their dictatorial leaders from power, frequently communicated via social networking. Blurred Vision, a Toronto-based rock group fronted by two Iranian brothers, covered Pink Floyd's transgressive anthem "Another Brick in the Wall." Posted on YouTube in 2010, the song created an underground sensation among disaffected Iranian youth.

One of the most controversial theorists in contemporary times, Jean Baudrillard, challenged our view of "the real." For Baudrillard (1998), we perceive society through the veil of mass media so that "reality" has been overtaken by simulations, such as Disney World, that impose upon us images of what we take to be real. No wonder the Hollywood "culture industry" is full of questions about what is "real" versus virtual (*The Matrix, Tron*), or sanity versus madness (*Shutter Island, Black Swan*), and what is only a dream (*Dark City, Inception*).

Theory and Research

For most sociologists, it is important that their research be closely connected with a theory or set of theories. Briefly, *theories* are abstract ideas about the world. Most sociological research is designed to evaluate a theory, either by testing it or by exploring the applicability of a theory to different situations. As can be seen throughout the many chapters in this text, sociologists investigate substantive problems and try to use their theories to help them understand these problems better. For instance, sociologists may be interested in understanding crime, the family, the environment, or education, and they will almost always use their theories to provide a deeper appreciation of these issues.

Sociologists use theories as models or conceptual maps of how the world works, and they use research methods to gather data that are relevant to these theories. Thus, theories and methods are always intertwined in the research process. There are hundreds of different theories in sociology, but most of them can be grouped into the four main theoretical perspectives that can be found throughout this text: structural functionalism, conflict theory, symbolic interactionism, and feminism. Theories cannot be tested directly, because they are only abstract ideas. Theories must be translated into observable ideas before they can be tested. This process of translation is called **operationalization**.

OPERATIONALIZATION

Operationalization is the process of translating theories and concepts into hypotheses and variables. Theories are abstract ideas, composed of concepts. **Concepts** are single ideas. Usually, theories explain how two or more concepts are related to each other. For instance, Karl Marx used concepts such as "alienation," "exploitation," and "class" to construct an abstract explanation (theory) of capitalism.

Once we have a theory, we need some way to test it. We need an observable equivalent of a theory or at least a set of observable statements that are consistent with our theory. These are called hypotheses. In the same way that theories express relationships between concepts,

hypotheses express relationships between variables. Unlike the typical definition of a hypothesis as simply an "educated guess," it is important to point out that hypotheses must be observable or testable. This means they must express relationships between variables.

A **variable** is the empirical or observable equivalent of a concept. The two key points about a variable are that it must be observable and that it must have a range of different values it can take on. For instance, ethnicity, age, years of schooling, and annual income are variables. We can collect information on all of these items (that is, they are observable), and people can have different ages, ethnicities, and so on. "French," "45 years old," "12 years of schooling," and "$50,000 per year" are not variables because although they are observable, they do not vary. They are *values* of variables, not variables in themselves, and it is important not to confuse the two.

In most cases, our hypotheses contain a minimum of two types of variables: independent variables and dependent variables. Independent variables are roughly equivalent to causes, and dependent variables are roughly equivalent to effects. Another way to keep them straight is to remember that the value of a dependent variable depends on the value of an independent variable. For instance, if you wanted to investigate differences between the average earnings of men and women, then sex or gender would be the independent variable, and earnings would be the dependent variable. This is because people's earnings may depend on their gender. Indeed, it is easy to keep the independent and dependent variables straight in this example, because it makes no sense to say that a person's gender can depend on his or her earnings.

Research Techniques

A popular image is that the experiment is the primary method scientists use to conduct research. However, even in the natural sciences, experiments often are the exception rather than the rule. A great deal of biology, astronomy, geology, and other science is not done—and in many cases cannot be done—experimentally. Nevertheless, the image persists, and it has traditionally been the standard against which science of all types, natural or social, has been measured.

The main advantages of experiments are that (1) they provide a controlled environment in which it is possible to (2) manipulate specific factors in an attempt to determine their effect on an outcome. Experiments can show the effects of one variable on another variable quite convincingly because of these two features.

Despite the fact that sociologists do not use experiments very often, the logic of the experiment still dominates at least one of the major techniques of sociological research. Surveys almost always collect a great deal of extra information from respondents in an attempt to recreate the controlled environment of the experiment after the fact. Surveys are often referred to as *quasi-experimental* designs, because they are only able to construct a controlled environment after the data have been collected. In other words, in true experiments the controlled conditions are set in place, and

(© Marlene Ford / Alamy)

It is important to understand the difference between dependent and independent variables. For example, your hypotheses may be that finding a well-paid job is *dependent* on obtaining a higher level of education. Thus, higher education is an independent variable, while a well-paid job is a dependent variable.

OPEN for DISCUSSION

Max Weber and *Verstehen*

In many of the chapters in this text, you will come across the ideas of Max Weber. One of his most enduring contributions to research methods in sociology is his elaboration of a concept he called *verstehen* (German for "to understand"). His idea is that in order to properly study the cultures of other peoples, a researcher needs to develop not just knowledge but an "empathetic understanding" of their lives as well in order to see the world as that group sees it.

Verstehen became a cornerstone of qualitative sociology as researchers tried to understand the lives of others "from the inside." In Weber's view, developing *verstehen* was a bit of an art, but in theory anyone who was good at it could understand the world view of any other group. In other words, the views of any group could be understood regardless of the personal characteristics of the researcher.

But this view has been criticized as too simplistic. That is, some researchers have argued that there are limits to *verstehen*, because the personal characteristics of the researcher will affect how the group reacts to her or him. And this will limit the depth of *verste-hen* or understanding that a researcher can achieve. For instance, Margaret Mead's classic anthropological study in Samoa has been criticized because the Samoans later claimed that they were not completely honest with her. Similarly, men are able to reach only a certain limited level of understanding with women. And because of this, it may not even be appropriate for men to study women, or vice versa. If we relate this to Killingsworth's (2006) study of mom and tot groups discussed later in this chapter, it might be the case that as a male, he might not have had the same access to the ongoing discussions around motherhood and child care. So, are there factors that would limit the level of *verstehen* that a researcher can achieve? And if so, what are those factors, and how do we identify them? At one extreme, this would mean that a researcher would have to match up with her or his participants on everything from gender, to education level, to hair colour, to fashion sense. So neither extreme position is particularly convincing, but exactly where we draw this line remains "open for discussion."

then the experiment is allowed to run, while in quasi-experiments observations of "naturally occurring" phenomena are made and an attempt is made to remove the effects of confounding variables during the analysis stage.

SURVEYS

Surveys are the most widely used technique in social scientific research. Sociologists, economists, political scientists, psychologists, and others use them regularly (Gray and Guppy 2008). They are an excellent way to gather data on large populations that cannot be studied effectively in a face-to-face manner. The goals of almost all social scientific surveys are to produce detailed data that will allow researchers to describe the characteristics of the group under study, to test theories about that group, and to generalize results beyond the people who responded to the survey.

At first glance, it might seem that designing good questions for a survey would be easy. The reality is that it is quite difficult—sociologists can spend months trying to figure out what questions they will ask, how they will word them, and the order in which they will ask them. One of the reasons it is so difficult is that each question must be unambiguous for both the respondent and the researcher. A question with several different interpretations is not useful, because respondents may answer it from a perspective different from that intended by the researcher. Similarly, questions that are too complicated for respondents to answer, or that presume a level of knowledge that respondents do not have, will not produce useful data. There are many, many issues to consider in designing good questions and the order they appear on the questionnaire, and unless sufficient attention is paid to these issues before the survey is administered, the results will affect the legitimacy of the whole research project.

Random Sampling, Sample Size, and Response Rates

In virtually all social science research, it is impossible to include each member of the whole population in a study. For instance, sending a

TABLE 1.1 ▼ Guidelines for Designing Good Survey Questions

Focus	Each question should have one specific topic. Questions with more than one topic are difficult to answer, and the answers are often ambiguous.
Brevity	Generally, shorter questions are preferable to longer questions. They are easier for respondents to understand. An important exception to this guideline is when asking about threatening topics, when longer questions are often preferable.
Clarity	Use clear, understandable words, and avoid jargon. This is especially important for general audiences, but if you are surveying a distinct group or population (such as lawyers), then specialized language is often preferable.
Bias	Avoid biased words, phrases, statements, and questions. If one answer to a question is more likely or is more socially acceptable than others, then the question is probably biased and should be reworded. For instance, if you are asking people about their religious preferences, do not use words like *ungodly*, *heathen*, or *fanatic* in your questions or you will bias your answers.
Relevance	Ensure that the questions you ask of your respondents are relevant to them and to your research. Also, in most surveys, some questions will not be relevant to all respondents; filter questions allow people to skip questions that are not pertinent to them. For instance, if you want to know why some people did not complete high school, you should first filter out high school graduates and ask them not to answer the questions about not completing high school.

SOURCE: Adapted from George Gray and Neil Guppy, *Successful Surveys: Research Methods and Practices*, 4th edn (Toronto: Nelson Thomson, 2008).

survey to everyone in Canada each time a sociologist wants to conduct some research is not practical for obvious reasons. Luckily, we can use a small **sample** of a population in any study, as long as we choose that sample randomly. Random sampling is so important because it is the only way that we can be confident that our sample is representative of (that is, it looks like) the population we are interested in. If our sample is representative, then we can be fairly confident that the patterns we find among our sample also will be present in the larger population. If it is not representative, then we have no idea whether what we found in our sample also is present in our population. Using a proper randomization procedure ensures that we do not deliberately bias our sample and guards against any unintentional biases that may creep into our selection process. And although randomization does not guarantee that our sample will be representative, by minimizing both intentional and unintentional biases we maximize our chances that the sample will be representative. However, randomization does not solve all problems in sociological research and is not always appropriate or necessary in field research.

There are many procedures for choosing a truly random sample, but all are based on the principle that each person (or element) in a population has an equal (and non-zero)

chance of being selected into the sample. The simplest random-sampling procedure is known as *simple random sampling*: each person in a population is put on a list, and then a proportion of them are chosen from this list completely at random. The usual way of ensuring that people are chosen at random is to use a table of random numbers either to select all of the people or to select the starting point in the list from which the sample will be chosen.

Generating truly random samples is not as easy as the word *simple* suggests. The problem lies not in choosing the actual people or

Many organizations create pools of respondents who are willing to answer polls and surveys online. In many cases, respondents are rewarded for their participation with gifts or cash. Does this make you wonder about bias in polling more generally? Why?

elements but in constructing a complete list of every person or element in the population. For this reason, other sampling techniques, such as **stratified** sampling and cluster sampling, are frequently used to choose samples. So how big a sample do you need in order to be able to generalize your results? Actually, this is the wrong question to ask—it is not the size of the sample but rather how it is chosen that determines how confident you can be that your results are applicable to the population. That is, even a very large sample, if it is not chosen randomly, offers no guarantee about the generalizability of the results. On the other hand, a small sample, properly chosen, can produce very good results. So never assume that because a sample is large it must be representative. Always make sure you find out about how the sample was chosen before making any judgments about its generalizability.

Another crucial factor in determining the generalizability of survey results is how many people from the original sample actually complete the survey. This percentage is called the *response rate*, and it is an important, although not the only, issue to consider in determining the generalizability of the results of a survey. The reason it is important is that unless a large proportion of the people in the original sample actually complete the survey, it is quite possible that the people who do not respond to it are different from those who do respond.

FIELD RESEARCH

In surveys, the primary aim is to collect quantitative or numerical data that can be generalized to a larger population. In contrast, field researchers are concerned about collecting qualitative or non-numerical data that may or may not be generalized. In field research, the aim is to collect rich, nuanced data by going into the "field" to observe and talk to people directly. Researchers spend time getting to know their subjects in order to be able to capture their world view.

Several separate techniques fall under the rubric of field research. They include participant observation or ethnography, in-depth interviewing, and documentary analysis. In many studies, more than one of these techniques is used.

Ethnographic or Participant Observation Research

In *ethnographic* or *participant observation* research, the researcher participates in the daily activities of his or her research subjects, usually for an extended period of time. This may include accompanying them on their daily activities (such as following police officers on patrol), interviews and discussions about their lives, and occasionally even living with them. During these activities, researchers take field notes (or make recordings) during and after an episode in the field.

A good example of participant observation research is Killingsworth's study (2006) of how mothers interact with each other in a "moms and tots" playgroup to construct ideas about what a good mother is and how mothers can reconcile that with the consumption of alcohol. Killingsworth participated in a playgroup of mothers and toddlers in Australia over a period of several months. As is typical of participant observation research, he did not have a rigid research design that he followed strictly over the time he was in the field. Rather, his main interest was in the women's conversations about alcohol and their own personal consumption of it and how they used these conversations to define, alter, and reconstruct ideas about "good mothers." He did not direct the women's conversations or ask them to focus their talk on particular issues. Instead, he simply participated in the playgroup and allowed the conversations to occur naturally. He found that the women were able to reconcile their understandings of good motherhood with the consumption of alcohol by recapturing the importance of alcohol to their previous identities as childless women and using that to build ideals of themselves as women first and good mothers second.

Killingworth's research is interesting for several reasons, but one is particularly relevant to his use of participant observation. By focusing on naturally occurring conversations, he was able to show how cultural ideals about things like motherhood and womanhood are embedded in and recreated by seemingly mundane discussions among mothers. In other words, ideals about good mothers do not just appear out of nowhere and exert pressure on people through "norms" or "society." Instead, ideals about good mothers are defined, interpreted, and reconstructed by actual people in actual interactions.

TIME to REFLECT

What role did Killingsworth's gender play in his research? Would he have reached different conclusions if he were a woman?

In-Depth Interviews

The in-depth interview is another popular field research technique and may be used in conjunction with participant observation. *In-depth interviews* are extensive interviews that are often tape-recorded and later transcribed into text. In some cases, these interviews are highly structured, and neither the researchers nor the respondents are permitted to deviate from a specific set of questions. At the other extreme, unstructured interviews may seem like ordinary conversations in which researchers and respondents simply explore topics as they arise. In many cases, researchers use semi-structured in-depth interviews that ask all respondents a basic set of questions but that also allow participants to explore other topics and issues. Striking the right balance between structured and unstructured questions can pose problems for sociologists, as can asking the right questions.

Documentation

In some field studies, researchers have access not only to people but also to documents. This is more common in the study of formal organizations like police forces or law firms, but it can also be the case with churches, political groups, and even families. These documents (case records, files, posters, diaries, even photos) can be analyzed to provide a more complete picture of the group under study.

Conducting Field Research

The elaborate procedures needed to choose a sample for a survey are not necessary for selecting the research site and the sample in field research. Strictly following a randomization protocol is necessary only if statistical analysis and generalization are the goal of the research. Field research is done to gain greater understanding through the collection of detailed data, not through generalization. Nevertheless, it is important to choose both the research site and the subjects or informants carefully (Bryman, Teevan, and Bell 2009).

The first consideration in choosing a site for field research is the topic of study. A field study of lawyers or police officers likely will take place at the offices or squad rooms of the respective groups. Choosing which offices and squad rooms to study involves many factors, including which ones will be most useful for the purposes of the research. But a practical element impinges on much field research—the actual choice of research site can come down to which law offices or squad rooms will grant access. This is not a criticism of field research but recognition of the realities facing scholars doing this kind of research.

Once the site has been chosen, the issues of whom to talk to, what types of data to record, and how long to stay in the field become important. Some things can be planned in advance, but many things are decided during the course of the field research. The selection of key informants—the people who will be most valuable in the course of the study—cannot always be made beforehand. Similarly, figuring out what to write down in field notes, whom to quote, and which observations to record cannot always be determined until after the research has begun.

When to leave the field is almost always determined during the course of the research. Most researchers stay in the field until they get a sense that they are not gaining much new information. In many cases, researchers decide to leave the field when they find that the data coming from new informants merely repeat what they have learned from previous informants. This is often taken as a sign that the researcher has reached a deep enough level of understanding to be confident that he or she will not learn much from additional time in the field (Bryman, Teevan, and Bell 2009).

This flexibility during the course of the study is one of the great advantages of field research over survey research. Mistakes in research design and the pursuit of new and unexpected opportunities are possible in field research but not usually possible in quantitative survey research. Once a survey has been designed, pre-tested, and administered to a sample, it is impractical to recall the survey to make changes. This is one of the reasons that pre-testing is so important in surveys.

EXISTING DATA

Both in surveys and in field research, sociologists are involved in collecting new, original data. However, a great deal of sociological research is done with data already collected. Of the several different types of existing data, most are amenable to different modes of analysis. Some of the major types of existing data are official statistics and surveys done by other researchers; books, magazines, newspapers, and other media; case files and records; and historical documents.

Secondary Data Analysis

The analysis of official statistics and existing surveys—also known as *secondary data analysis*—has grown immensely with the development of computers and statistical software packages. It has become one of the most common forms of research reported in major sociological journals such as the *American Journal of Sociology*.

Quantitative data can be presented in tables like Table 1.2. However, tables can be designed in many different ways, and the type of information being presented will determine the types of comparisons that can be made. In Table 1.2, on marital status in Canada, comparisons can be made within or across the values of marital status (for example, how many people are married versus single), by sex, and across five different years.

We can see that the number of divorced males increased by more than 90,000 between 2003 and 2007 (712,531 − 620,679 = 91,852) and the number of divorced females rose by more than 119,000 (972,183 − 852,277 = 119,906), while the numbers of married men and women increased by 209,161 and 267,727, respectively. However, the table does not tell us anything about why these numbers may have changed, nor can we make any comparisons with the number of married and divorced people in other countries. Also, notice that the numbers are very precise, but the fact is that these are estimates of the true numbers. So while it is possible to discern trends in tables like this, be careful about reading too much into the precision of the numbers.

TABLE 1.2 ▼ Population by Marital Status and Sex, Canada, 2003–7

	2003	2004	2005	2006	2007
Total					
Both sexes	31,676,077	31,995,199	32,312,077	32,649,482	32,976,026
Male	15,688,977	15,846,832	16,003,804	16,170,723	16,332,277
Female	15,987,100	16,148,367	16,308,273	16,478,759	16,643,749
Single					
Both sexes	13,231,209	13,368,674	13,507,149	13,653,059	13,800,997
Male	7,078,089	7,155,622	7,233,428	7,314,611	7,396,835
Female	6,153,120	6,213,052	6,273,721	6,338,448	6,404,162
Married[1]					
Both sexes	15,438,972	15,558,054	15,675,089	15,802,300	15,916,860
Male	7,701,393	7,752,882	7,803,419	7,860,087	7,910,554
Female	7,737,579	7,805,172	7,871,670	7,942,213	8,006,306
Divorced					
Both sexes	1,472,956	1,524,245	1,576,351	1,630,267	1,684,714
Male	620,679	642,882	665,553	688,975	712,531
Female	852,277	881,363	910,798	941,292	972,183

[1]Includes persons legally married, persons legally married and separated, and persons living in common-law unions.
SOURCE: Statistics Canada. CANSIM, Table 051-0010. Last modified: 16 Dec. 2009

Personal computers, statistical software packages, and the ready availability of many national and international datasets have made secondary data analysis possible for almost every social scientist. The advantages of secondary analysis are that the coverage of the data is broad and that the hard work involved in constructing and administering a survey has already been done, usually by an agency with far more expertise and resources than most individual researchers. The disadvantages are that the data collected are often not precise enough to test the specific ideas that interest researchers and that mastering the techniques to analyze the data properly can be challenging.

Historical Research and Content Analysis

The analysis of historical documents, print and other media, and records and case materials can be done by several methods. The two most common forms of analysis are historical research and content analysis. Historical sociology relies on *historical research* into all kinds of historical documents, from organizational records, old newspapers, and magazines to speeches and sermons, letters and diaries, and even interviews with people who participated in the events of interest. In *content analysis*, documents such as newspapers, magazines, TV shows, and case records are subjected to careful sampling and analysis procedures to reveal patterns. (See Warren and Karner 2009 for a good discussion of historical research and content analysis.)

One of the major issues facing historical sociologists is that someone or some organization has created the records used in their analyses but the potential biases and reasons for recording the information in the documents are not always clear. Further, some documents are lost or destroyed with the passing of time, so the historical sociologist must be aware that the extant documents may not give a complete picture of the events or time period under study. Why have certain documents survived while others have not? Is there any significance to the ordering or cataloguing of the documents? These and other issues must be dealt with continually in historical research.

Content analysis can be done in a number of ways, but it usually involves taking a sample of relevant documents and then subjecting these documents to a rigorous procedure of identify-

ing and classifying particular features, words, or images in these documents. For instance, in studying political posters, content analysis could be used to determine whether the posters from particular parties put more emphasis on the positive aspects of their own party or on the negative aspects of other parties. These results could then be used to better understand styles of political campaigning in a particular country or time period.

SELECTING A RESEARCH METHOD

To summarize, all of the methods described here are used by sociologists to collect data on particular research problems, and they use theories to help them understand or solve these problems. Any of these methods can be used to investigate problems from any of the theoretical perspectives encountered in this text, although some methods are almost never used in some perspectives. For instance, symbolic interactionists rarely if ever use quantitative surveys, while most conflict theorists prefer surveys to participant observation.

How do you know which method to use with which theory or theoretical perspective? A complete answer to this question is beyond the scope of this chapter, but the rule of thumb in sociology has been that you let the problem determine the method. For example, if you want to find out something about the national divorce rate and how divorced people differ from those who remain married, then you need a method that will give you data from people all over the country, such as a survey. But if you want to find out how nurses manage the many pressures of their jobs, then participant observation is a more appropriate method.

Conclusion

Sociologists use a wide range of methods to gather data about the people and groups they study. Each method produces a different type of data, which requires a specific form of analysis and can only be used to answer some questions, but not others, about the topic of study. All of this means that it is very important to specify what you want to know about a particular issue and then choose the data collection and analysis methods based on that. But since no single method guarantees that we will get the "truth" about our topic of study, it is usually a good idea to use multiple methods in sociological research.

Dorothy Smith's action research is only one way to approach the practical and ethical questions of obtaining information from people. Numerous other methods have been developed in sociology to address the social and personal problems that beset modern society. Rather than discovering the "laws" of society, sociologists make generalizations about social phenomena that are tentative in given circumstances. Scientific predictions are actually probabilities, not certainties. As with any science, these answers are open to modification or refutation by new evidence. But the questions asked in sociology and the methods used to answer them are of vital importance to our world and our life, as demonstrated by the reasoned, critical analyses that follow in this book.

questions for critical thought

1. Are modern communication devices increasing our sense of social collectivity, or do they tend to individualize us more?

2. As the world becomes increasingly rational, new forms of irrationality continually arise and compete. What forms of irrationality are important in the contemporary world?

3. What difference would it make in your life, whether you are a man or a woman, if you decided that you were a "feminist"?

4. When you read about a social scientific finding in the newspaper, what kinds of evidence persuade you of its veracity? In other words, do you need quantitative, statistical results, are you persuaded by the detailed accounts of individuals, or are both equally convincing?

5. If you were going to investigate across Canada the effects of a person's ethnicity on his or her educational attainment, what method would be most appropriate? Why?

6. When you read a "human interest" story in a magazine, what persuades you that the story is true? Does the author need to demonstrate that he or she has a deep understanding of the group? If the story contains numbers or statistics, do you find it more believable? If so, should you rethink this idea, given how hard it is to conduct good quantitative research?

recommended readings

Earl Babbie. 2009. *The Practice of Social Research.* 12th edn. Belmont, CA: Wadsworth.
Babbie's books are used in more research methods courses across North America than those of any other author. This one is a comprehensive, undergraduate treatment of research methods.

Bruce Berg. 2011. *Qualitative Research Methods for the Social Sciences.* 8th edn. Boston: Allyn and Bacon.
Berg's book is the current standard for qualitative research methods courses.

George Gray and Neil Guppy. 2008. *Successful Surveys: Research Methods and Practices.* 4th edn. Toronto: Nelson Thomson.
Gray and Guppy have written an accessible and comprehensive introduction to survey research methods. This book can be used as a step-by-step guide to conducting a basic survey.

Robert D. Putnam. 2000. *Bowling Alone: The Collapse and Revival of American Community.* New York: Simon and Schuster.

Based on extensive research, Putnam argues that community, community feeling, and collective behaviour have declined in American society, to the detriment of grassroots democracy.

Eric Schlosser. 2001. *Fast Food Nation: The Dark Side of the All-American Meal.* New York: Houghton Mifflin.
Schlosser describes the history of the fast-food industry in the United States, covering familiar terrain such as marketing to children and the "obesity" panic. His most searing indictment is aimed at the meat industry.

Naomi Wolf. 1991. *The Beauty Myth: How Images of Beauty Are Used against Women.* New York: W. Morrow.
Wolf exposes the social pressures behind the manipulation of women's self-image. The "perfect body" is virtually unattainable for most, underscoring many physical and health problems facing girls and women today.

recommended websites

Dead Sociologists Index
http://media.pfeiffer.edu/lridener/DSS
The Dead Sociologists Index provides detailed information on 16 classical theorists, including biographies, commentary, and links to original works.

Free Resources for Program Evaluation and Social Research Methods
http://gsociology.icaap.org/methods
This is a free resource page on social science research methods, with an emphasis on quantitative rather than qualitative methods.

Organisation for Economic Co-operation and Development (OECD)
www.oecd.org
The OECD is a major data-generating organization, but the focus is international rather than national and is more directly tied to economic and social development policies around the world. Much of the data held by the OECD is quantitative.

Sociology Online
www.sociologyonline.co.uk
This site, produced in Britain, provides a "Classics" link to classical theory. The "Sociology News" link has many items of interest.

Statistics Canada
www.statcan.gc.ca
Statistics Canada is one of the world's most respected national statistical organizations. This is a huge site full of quantitative data, survey materials, statistical analyses, and much more on Canada.

www Virtual Library: Sociology
www.mcmaster.ca/socscidocs/w3virtsoclib/socnet.htm
Hosted by McMaster University, this site covers a number of classical and contemporary sociologists and includes a link to the Durkheim Pages at the University of Illinois.

PART II

Major Social Processes

chapter 2

Culture and Culture Change

Shyon Baumann

In this chapter, you will:

▶ See that culture has many meanings and dimensions.

▶ Learn that culture is powerful: it integrates members of society but can also cause great conflict.

▶ Learn that culture quintessentially carries meaning and facilitates communication.

▶ See that change in culture is inevitable: it is within the nature of culture to evolve.

▶ Learn that important social institutions—like the government, the family, the media—are shaped by culture and, in turn, influence culture.

Introduction: Why Study Culture?

Why do sociologists care about culture? Briefly, **culture** is a powerful social force that influences events as diverse as whom we marry and whether we go to war. Marriage and war are interesting examples—while they seem unrelated, they are similar insofar as both involve the bonds between people, in one case bringing people closer together and in the other pushing them further apart.

Let us consider how culture is implicated in each of these events. How we choose whom to marry is incredibly complicated, but what is clear is that in general people marry other people with whom they share interests and experiences. Such shared ideas and preferences create feelings of comfort and familiarity. If we like the same music and the same kind of movies, if we share a belief in the importance of family and the role of religion in our lives, if we share a notion of the different roles and responsibilities of men and women, if we support the same political ideals, then we feel more connected to each other. Culture includes all these preferences and ideas, and these are the things that allow us in our daily lives to feel connections to other people. Cultural similarities influence our decisions not only about getting married but about all kinds of connections—with whom we become friends, even with whom we work.

Just as we often are brought closer to other people, so too we often experience social divisions, some relatively minor and others quite significant. Like marriage, war is an enormously complicated phenomenon; it can result from a wide array of social, economic, and geopolitical factors. But it is also clear that culture can play a role in creating or worsening the divisions between groups or societies that can lead to war. While a conflict of material interests usually sets the stage for war, culture can play a large role in determining whether war is waged. If we differ in fundamental beliefs about such things as democracy and human rights, if we speak different languages and cannot easily communicate, if we cannot understand others' religious concepts and practices, if we do not share preferences for what we consider to be the normal and good ways to live our lives, then we feel less connected to each other. In all these ways, culture plays a role in dividing us, and it is only when we feel essentially different and disconnected from others that we are able to pursue as drastic a course of action as war. In addition, culture plays a role in many more minor social divisions that are not as significant as war, such as the various social cleavages between many social groups within the same society.

Culture, then, is important because it is the key to understanding how we relate to each other; specifically, it is behind both what unites us and what divides us. Our cultural differences and similarities continually come into play in our daily face-to-face interactions and on a global scale. To truly understand the dynamics of war and peace, love and hate, and more, we need to look at the ways that culture facilitates or inhibits the bonds and the rifts between us.

The goals of this chapter are to review the many nuances to the meaning of culture and to explain how culture is implicated in many important social processes. First, we will specify what culture is through a clear conceptualizing of culture's many dimensions. Second, we will summarize how culture is used in sociological theorizing about society. We will also examine those realms of social life that are primarily cultural—the loci of culture. The nature of culture change is a third focus of this chapter, and we will examine the reciprocal relationship between culture change and social change. Finally, we will discuss the insights of this chapter as they pertain to Canadian culture.

What Is Culture?

Think of the many ways that you might use the word *culture* in conversation, from the way that an entire society lives (e.g., "Thai culture"), to refined aesthetic productions (e.g., symphony concerts), to a phrase such as "consumer culture," which focuses on a major pattern of people's behaviour and a set of economic institutions in contemporary society. Perhaps the best way to tie together these divergent meanings is to recognize that culture is those elements of social life that have meanings that social actors interpret and can also convey.

TIME to REFLECT

Before beginning this chapter, how would you have defined *culture*? As you read, think about how your own understanding of culture is changing or expanding.

The Canadian flag is a symbol and would be considered a *cultural* aspect of society. The Lester B. Pearson government that officially introduced the flag in 1965 is a *structural* aspect of society.

To clarify how cultural elements of social life embody meanings, we can create a list of specific things that are usually classified as "culture" in sociology. Languages, symbols, discourses, texts, knowledge, values, attitudes, beliefs, norms, world views, folkways, art, music, ideas, and ideologies all are "culture," as are the practices through which these things are often performed or put into concrete form. To clarify why these things are culture, it is helpful to consider the distinction between *culture* and *structure*, two terms that have specific meanings within sociology. Structural aspects of society are the enduring patterns of social relations and **social institutions** through which society is organized. For example, our political system with its elections, taxation, and rule of law is a structural element of society. Our economic system with the role of financial institutions and a free market orientation is another structural element. The patterns of relationships that constitute families, schools of all levels, and health care are further examples of structures in our society.

Recall that cultural elements are those that carry meaning and can be interpreted, so it is true that the structures named above contain or interact with culture. With regard to the labour market, the fact that there exists a high degree of occupational segregation by gender—with some jobs (for example, elementary school teachers) primarily done by women and others (for example, elementary school principals) primarily done by men— is not cultural. Rather, this segregation is "structural." It is an enduring pattern of social behaviour, existing primarily at the level of lived experience. The *idea* that it is normal or proper for men to be principals and women to be elementary school teachers is a cultural value. The fact that this pattern exists (although it is changing) is a structural property of our society, but the gender beliefs that underlie this pattern are cultural.

We can find another example of the distinction between culture and structure in the realm of politics. In Canada, the widely held preference for representative democracy represents a deep-rooted aspect of Canadian culture. This political orientation is related to many other beliefs about authority, individual rationality, and justice, and so it is an element of culture that is enmeshed in a web of other cultural elements. In contrast, representative democracy is not merely an idea, it is a practice that involves immense material resources and engenders long-standing patterns of social behaviour. Known in the sociological literature as the **state**, our democratic government is a structural dimension of social life. It influences our work lives, our consumption patterns, our health outcomes, and our educational outcomes, so it is a material element of social life that is enmeshed in a web of other important structural elements. It does not qualify as culture, because it is not in itself a symbol; it does not exist to be received and understood as having a meaning. However, there is no shortage of politically oriented culture. Political ideologies of the left, centre, and right, expressed in political discourses, conversations, newspaper articles, and books, both fiction and non-fiction, are squarely in the realm of culture. The national anthem and the Canadian flag are both explicit political symbols. While these and other political symbols are culture, the state itself is a key structure in Canadian society.

Why is it sociologically useful to focus on culture? To answer this question, we will first learn about how culture varies over time and between places. We will then proceed to highlight culture's role in shaping the actions of groups and individuals, as well as culture's role in shaping their lived experiences and identities.

CULTURE IN PLACE AND TIME

In some popular uses, *culture* can refer to the entire social reality of particular social and geographical groups—Western culture, for example. However, we often think of culture in more specific geographic terms than just Western or Eastern. We frequently think in national terms, with fairly strong ideas of what we mean by, for example, Japanese culture, Italian culture, or Mexican culture. The pervasive use of such terms points to the reality that culture can vary systematically between nations. Nation-states have often (although not always) coalesced around a common cultural foundation, or if one was not clearly defined from early on, they have tended to promote such a cultural foundation for the sake of national unity and cohesion.

Although references to national cultures are ubiquitous, on closer inspection we can see that national cultures also entail a great deal of regional and local variation. Obvious examples are the cultural differences between Quebec and Ontario or between Alberta and British Columbia. We can continue to spatially limit our concept of culture by pointing to the social differences between various cities and even between parts of cities. The culture of downtown Toronto, for example, brings up notions of a lifestyle that is business-oriented, cosmopolitan, and culturally rich. Toronto's **urbanism** is often cited for its impersonality and inward-looking character and contrasts with the habits and interaction styles of, for example, St John's, Newfoundland. It is worth noting that such local cultural variations exist in a broader cultural environment of greater similarities than differences (i.e., they all share a Canadian culture).

Just as we can differentiate cultures with respect to physical space, we can observe that cultures vary according to social space or social groupings. For example, we can think of the culture of adolescent males as distinct from that of adolescent females and adult males, whether their geographic location is Vancouver or Halifax. Acknowledging culture's social, not just physical, boundedness provides us with a second dimension for understanding the meaning of culture.

Age and **gender** are just two of many social boundaries that can differentiate between cultures. Other social lines along which cultural elements may fall include **race** and **ethnicity**, **sexual orientation**, religion, and many other ways that people distinguish themselves. Another social space with important cultural implications is that of social class. Stereotypes of working- and upper-class cultures are at least as pervasive as national stereotypes. We have firm ideas about the typical speech, mannerisms, dress, culinary preferences, occupations, and leisure activities of the working class and the upper class.

TIME to REFLECT
Can you think of television shows that depict working-class and upper-class cultures? How are these class cultures portrayed differently?

It is important to note that just as the cultures of urban Ontario and rural Alberta share more similarities than differences, the culture of different social groups within a society likewise share more similarities than differences. By enumerating the ways in which, for example, social classes in Canada differ, we neglect myriad ways in which they are similar: difference in accent is trivial to the overall nature of a language; a similar reliance on automobiles overshadows any consideration of whether those automobiles are foreign or domestic; and a propensity to vote for different political parties cannot diminish the tremendous importance of a shared faith in parliamentary democracy.

In addition, it is necessary to point out that the dimensions of physical and social space are not entirely independent of each other. For example, if we were to study the culture of retirement communities, we would see that these are physical spaces populated mostly by a specific social group defined by age. The social boundedness of culture by age (the culture of an older generation) overlays a physical boundedness of culture by residential location (the culture of a retirement community). Likewise, there is a great deal of overlap between, for example, the physical space of Anglican churches and the social space of Anglicans.

Cases in which the physical and social spatial dimensions of culture intersect to the exclusion of other social groups are fairly narrowly circumscribed. For the most part, our social lives are messier, and different **subcultures** interact with each other all the time. Quite frequently, individuals of various social classes occupy the same classrooms, malls, and workspaces (although with different functions within those workspaces); segregation on the basis of race sometimes occurs residentially, although for the most part the common venues of daily life are racially integrated.

Adding to the fuzziness of cultural boundaries, borrowing across cultures happens all the time. Often such borrowing occurs without anyone noticing, but sometimes it can happen in ways that are thought to be illegitimate, leading to charges of cultural appropriation. In those cases, the borrowing of

culture across social boundaries can offend a group's sense of identity and cultural heritage.

Other times, culture crosses social and geographic borders through global commerce and communication channels, with the involvement of multinational corporations. The case of skin-bleaching is one highly controversial example (see Global Issues box). Many observers interpret the practice as an example of cultural imperialism whereby cosmetics companies flog Western cultural ideals to global audiences in order to create anxiety-driven sales. This view also implicates the fashion industry as a whole for promulgating Eurocentric images of fair skin as a beauty ideal. Other observers point to long-standing discrimination on the basis of skin tone, particularly in India, where it is argued as deriving from the caste system's relationship between skin tone and social standing. Regardless of the origin, it is clear that corporations are playing a role at least in promoting cultural similarity, of however dubious merit, between disparate global regions.

(© J Marshall - Tribaleye Images / Alamy)

Not all cultural borrowing is considered offensive. In addition to Hiragana and Katakana, the Japanese also use a set of characters called Kanji that were borrowed from the Chinese thousands of years ago. Kanji is now an integral component of the Japanese language.

GLOBAL ISSUES

Global Voices: Skin-Lightening, Commerce, and Culture

Estimated by some marketing analysts to be a $10-billion global industry by 2015, the market for skin-lightening products is enormous and widespread. Various creams that reduce melanin production or bleach skin are used in countries in Asia, Africa, and Latin America and also in Europe and in North America. How are we to understand this market and the consumers of these products?

In many countries, there are long-standing preferences for lighter skin tones, especially for women, and these preferences have both aesthetic and moral overtones. There is debate over the origins of these cultural values around the appearance of skin, as well as differences between global regions. However, the origins of these values notwithstanding, what is clear is that global cosmetics and personal products companies are facilitating the maintenance and even the growth of this market.

The range of companies involved in marketing and selling skin-lightening products globally includes Shiseido, Chanel, and Unilever, the parent company of Dove, among many others. In some cases, the marketing for these products focuses on the benefi-

cial effects of evening out "dark spots," skin discoloration, and acne marks. Shiseido is one example, and its website explains that the company "began focusing on skin-brightening approximately 100 years ago when Japanese women still wore kimonos" ("Skin-brightening," 2013). The equation of fair skin and attractiveness is left implicit (and the notion that uneven skin could be improved by making it uniformly darker is never suggested). However, Unilever's Fair and Lovely skin-lightening product uses advertising campaigns in India that make explicit reference to lighter skin being simply more beautiful than darker skin.

The industry and its marketing campaigns have been criticized on multiple grounds. The promotion of light skin for aesthetic reasons reinforces hegemonic Western beauty ideals and ties into a larger system of global hierarchy with Western nations at the top. The skin-lightening market also includes many products with potentially harmful ingredients such as mercury or bleach, and consumers who cannot afford the more expensive products sometimes resort to the cheaper and riskier products or to equally risky homemade versions.

Finally, we can recognize that culture varies over time. The temporal dimension is an important qualifier because of the magnitude of differences that accumulate to produce cultures that are vastly different from what came before. In other words, culture evolves.

Leaving aside the precise mechanisms of cultural evolution for now, we can recognize that culture is always developing new features and characteristics. Therefore, Western culture of today is remarkably different from that of 500 years ago and is in many ways quite different even from Western culture 10 years ago. The temporal dimension of culture is independent of its physical and social locations—culture changes over time in all countries and regions and for all social groupings. Norwegian culture today is different from what it was in 1900; French-Canadian culture, irrespective of actual geographic roots, has evolved over the century as well; and the culture of Canadians in their sixties has changed dramatically over time— the leisure, work options, and values of older

Canadians bear little resemblance to what they were in earlier time periods. Many observers of culture argue that cultural changes are occurring more frequently in recent times. When we turn to the specifics of cultural dynamics, we will learn more about the reasons behind this increase in the rate of change.

TIME to REFLECT

Provide examples of things that can serve both cultural and structural roles simultaneously, and explain how these roles can coexist.

The Role of Culture in Social Theory

Now that we have a clear idea of what culture is, we can gain an understanding of how it has figured in the works of some of the major sociological theorists. In this section, we will outline how these thinkers have employed culture in their writings about the fundamental driving forces of society. In doing so, we answer our earlier question of why sociologists study culture.

ORTHODOX MARXIST AND NEO-MARXIST THEORIES

One of the most influential theoretical perspectives in sociology is Marxism. In developing his theory of society, Karl Marx was responding to previous philosophical arguments about the central role of ideas (squarely cultural) in determining the path of history and the nature of social reality. In such arguments, the general cultural environment worked at the level of ideas to shape people's thoughts and actions and so was in principle the root cause behind events and social change.

In contrast, Marxism argued that the nature of society was determined primarily by the prevailing *mode of economic production,* evolving through history from agrarian societies to slave ownership to feudalism and then to industrial capitalism. This perspective is squarely structural, because it argues that all social change is a result of the economic organization of society. In Marxist terminology, the economic mode of production forms the "base" of society on which the **superstructure** rests, including all cultural elements of society.

Neo-Marxist perspectives do not adhere so strictly to the view that culture is entirely dependent on society's mode of production. These perspectives share with Marxism a focus on the role of culture in maintaining and supporting capitalism and inequality, but they differ from Marxism insofar as they view culture as more than simply the reflection of the underlying economic base.

One particularly important neo-Marxist perspective on culture is the argument that our current economic mode of production is accompanied by a **dominant ideology**. This ideology is a system of thoughts, knowledge, and beliefs that serves to legitimate and perpetuate capitalism. Where does this dominant ideology come from? Neo-Marxists recognize that culture can be shaped by specific groups and individuals who seek to achieve certain social outcomes. For example, members of the Frankfurt School, who began writing in the 1920s, identified pro-capitalist functions in much of popular culture, which promotes capitalist ideals and stifles critical, independent thinking. The groups responsible for the creation and promotion of popular culture are themselves members of the ruling class, known as the **bourgeoisie**. In the view of the Frankfurt School, the entertainment industry is of great use to the capitalist order through the cultural products it creates.

Growing out of a neo-Marxist perspective, cultural studies is a field with roots in British literary scholarship and in sociology. The specific insight that cultural studies borrows from neo-Marxists is that culture can be shaped and manipulated by dominant groups and employed to maintain **hegemony**, which is a common-sense understanding that inequality and domination by elites is natural and inevitable. Cultural studies has thus provided a more sophisticated understanding of the ways in which culture can work to reproduce inequality; the meanings that are embedded in cultural works can be hegemonic and can therefore legitimize inequality.

Cultural studies practitioners agree with neo-Marxists that culture can function to maintain social divisions, keeping some groups dominant over others. Where they break from Marxists and early neo-Marxists is in the recognition that class conflict is only one of many sites of ideological dominance. As Philip Smith writes of cultural studies, "a move has gradually taken place away from Marxism toward an understanding of society as textured with multiple sources of inequality and fragmented local struggles" (2001, 152). Dominant groups can be defined not only by class but also by race, gender, geography, and sexual orientation. One of the main figures in this tradition from the Birmingham School is Stuart Hall, who has produced some of the seminal concepts of cultural studies. One significant insight of Hall's is that meaning does not simply exist within cultural creations but instead is constructed by individuals through the process of interpreting culture. Meaning is created by people while they make sense of the culture they consume.

A significant continuity between Marxist and neo-Marxist views of culture is that culture is implicated in the essentially conflictual nature of society. Culture, in a sense, supports dominant groups in their efforts to maintain their dominance.

CULTURAL FUNCTIONALISM

A different approach to understanding culture can be found in work that is based on the theoretical insights of Émile Durkheim. In contrast to the conflictual emphasis of the Marxists and neo-Marxists, Durkheimian approaches focus on culture's integrative ability. Durkheim (1964 [1912]) identified the ways in which culture can create social stability and solidarity, focusing on how culture unites us rather than on how culture divides us.

Culture, in terms of norms, values, attitudes, and beliefs, is not reflective of the economic mode of production. Instead, these cultural elements rise out of a particular society's **social structure** to produce a general consensus about the goals and nature of society. For example, our values about the importance of education evolve in response to the changing needs of a modernizing society in which higher general levels of education allow for a more smoothly functioning society. Thus, culture serves a necessary function: through common values and beliefs, society is able to remain coherent, and all the different parts of society can effectively carry out their specific purpose.

Durkheim paid special attention to the role of religion as a motivating force in society, one that made possible the affirmation of collective sentiments and ideas and therefore could play an important role in strengthening social bonds that then reinforced the fabric of society.

For a more complete discussion of Durkheim's perspective on religion, see "Definitions of Religion" in Chapter 13, p. 259.

SYMBOLIC INTERACTIONIST AND DRAMATURGICAL PERSPECTIVES

A third important perspective treats culture as a product of individuals' interactions. In symbolic interactionist thought, culture is a vehicle for meaning (hence "symbolic") that is generated by individuals in face-to-face encounters (hence "interactionist"). Culture is the enacted signals and attitudes that people use to communicate effectively in order to go about their daily lives. Body language and the signals we send through it, however subconsciously, are a clear element of culture in this perspective.

The symbolic interactionist approach contrasts with Marxist and functionalist approaches to culture insofar as it attributes more responsibility to individuals as the active creators and implementers of culture. Rather than originating from an economic order or indirectly from the general social structure, culture is a product of creative individuals who use it to manage their everyday tasks and routines.

One of the most influential theorists to write about the interactions of individuals was Erving Goffman. Goffman developed a framework that analogizes social interaction to what goes on in a theatre. For that reason, it is known as a dramaturgical perspective. In a theatre, there are actors with roles to play for an audience. Likewise, when we interact with people, we assume a role for the situation and perform that role according to a well-known script that defines the boundaries of what is expected and acceptable. We learn these rules of social behaviour through socialization and use them to create meaningful and effective interaction with others. When we are interacting with others, we are managing impressions and performing in a front-stage area. When we let down our guard and behave informally, we are in the back-stage area.

Much like actors in a play, Goffman argues, we act out different social roles every day. What different roles do you play in your everyday life? How do the scripts differ for these various roles? See "Identity" in Chapter 4, p. 76, for a detailed exploration of Goffman's perspective.

Culture plays a central part in the dramaturgical perspective: social order is constituted by the creation and use of meanings embodied in interaction. The sending and receiving of signals is the key to understanding why society functions at all when there is so much potential for chaos. When you think about it, we are remarkably efficient at maintaining social order most of the time, and this achievement is made possible through the shared meanings in face-to-face interactions.

This view of culture, however, is perhaps less rich than that offered by the cultural functionalist perspective. Rather than culture

Sometimes art is employed to achieve ideological ends. This painting by Franklin Carmichael, a member of the Group of Seven, depicts the landscape of the Canadian North. The Group sought to express their nationalistic sentiments through paintings of scenes that were uniquely Canadian. (Franklin Carmichael [1890–1945] *Northern Tundra*, 1931. Oil on canvas. 77.4 92.5 cm. Gift of Col. R.S. McLaughlin. McMichael Canadian Collection. 1968.7.14)

playing a fundamental role in shaping individuals' consciousness, as the functionalist perspective would argue, the dramaturgical perspective sees culture as a tool for creative individuals to manipulate strategically. Rather than persons being fully subject to the influence of culture, culture is subject more to the influence of individuals.

THE PRODUCTION OF CULTURE PERSPECTIVE

The "production of culture" perspective takes as an object of study those aspects of culture that are created through explicit, intentional, and co-ordinated processes. This approach focuses on material culture, including **mass media**, technology, art, and other material symbol-producing realms such as science and law. The guiding insight of this perspective is that culture is a product of social action in much the same way that non-cultural products are. The implication of this view is that culture is studied best according to the same methods and analysis that are standard in other fields of sociology.

A key figure in the production of culture perspective, Richard A. Peterson (1994), notes that the perspective developed to account for perceived shortcomings in the prevailing "mirror" or "reflection" view, which posits that culture is a manifestation of underlying social-structural needs or realities. This view, held by orthodox Marxists and by functionalists, is vague about the specific mechanisms through which culture is created. The metaphor of a mirror describes the content of culture—it represents the true character of society—but is mute about culture's production.

Such a view would find, for instance, that the contours of Canadian national identity are visible in the literary output of Canadian authors. Likewise, baroque art forms are seen as expressions of society in the baroque period, and modernist art is explained as an expression of societal values in the early decades of the twentieth century.

By contrast, the production of culture perspective insists on specifying all of the factors involved in cultural production, as well as how culture is "distributed, evaluated, taught, and preserved" (Peterson 1994, 165). By analyzing these processes, we can better account for the specific content of culture. We need to examine the resources and constraints that specific actors were working with and that influenced the kind of art or other symbols that they created. In this way, the production of culture perspective provides a means of explaining the shape of culture.

TIME to REFLECT

Which of the above theoretical traditions do you find most useful for understanding culture's role in social inequality?

CONFLICT, INTEGRATION, AND CULTURE'S ORIGIN

It is useful to compare these various perspectives according to their views on key features of culture. Marxists and neo-Marxists argue that culture is a tool of conflict in society. By contrast, functionalists emphasize the integrative function of culture. Functionalists are interested in explaining social order, and they see culture as a key factor in creating social stability.

For symbolic interactionists, culture is the means by which individuals create order out of potentially chaotic and unpredictable social situations, so they support an integrative view of culture. The production of culture perspective has little to say about characterizing culture as integrative or as implicated in conflict. Instead, it focuses on explaining the origin of culture. While Marxism and functionalism rely on a "reflection" metaphor to explain where culture comes from, the production perspective locates cultural origin in "purposive productive activity" (Peterson 1994, 164). Cultural studies sees culture as originating in the work of hegemonic leaders who create the texts, symbols, and discourses that embody particular ideologies. Symbolic interactionists also pro-

vide an explanation for the origin of culture: it is produced in the meanings that people create through social interaction at the micro level.

In the Open for Discussion box, renowned sociologist William Julius Wilson (2010) integrates both a cultural and a structural perspective to understand the enduring poverty of many urban African Americans. He skilfully frames cultural traits as integral to processes of both conflict and integration, precisely through their role in guiding and shaping modes of social interaction. Inner-city poverty in Canada differs from that in the United States, given the dramatic overlay of race and inequality that characterizes many American cities. However, Wilson's view of cultural traits as potentially simultaneously conflictual, integrative, and interactionist could be usefully applied to understanding group differences in Canada, perhaps in the case of underemployment among First Nations people or underemployment among young adults in Canada.

Cultural Realms

The stage is now set for a discussion of those realms of social life most commonly located at the core of the sociology of culture. Although we could discuss the cultural dimension of almost any area of society, we will limit our discussion to language and discourse, the mass media, and art. Within each realm, we will highlight the insights that the sociology of culture can bring to bear.

LANGUAGE AND DISCOURSE

Language, a system of words both written and spoken, is but one means of communication. Communication is the sharing of meaning, by which the thoughts of one person are made understandable to another. Communication can occur through a variety of signs and symbols, but we reserve a special place for the study of language because it is the primary means by which our communication takes place.

Languages are complicated systems of many symbols deployed according to a set of rules, and their use gives rise to a number of interesting social phenomena. It is argued, for instance, that the presence of language structures our very thoughts and consciousness such that without a vocabulary with which to label events, we cannot remember them. The character of social reality is tied to language

OPEN for DISCUSSION

Why Both Social Structure and Culture Matter in a Holistic Analysis of Inner-City Poverty

Considerable research has been devoted to the effects of racism in American society. However, there is little research on and far less awareness of the impact of emerging cultural traits in the inner city on the social and economic outcomes of poor blacks. . . .

[F]rom a historical perspective it is hard to overstate the cumulative impact of structural impediments on black inner-city neighborhoods. We have to consider, of course, the racialist structural factors such as the enduring effects of slavery, Jim Crow segregation, public school segregation, legalized discrimination, residential segregation, the Federal Housing Administration's redlining of black neighborhoods in the 1940s and 1950s, the construction of public housing projects in poor black urban neighborhoods, employer discrimination, and other racial acts and processes. . . .

Nonetheless, despite the obvious fact that structural changes have adversely affected inner-city neighborhoods . . . for many Americans . . . cultural traits are at the root of problems experienced by the ghetto poor, because most Americans tend to focus on the outlooks and modes of behavior shared by many inner-city residents.

Culture provides tools (habits, skills, and styles) and creates constraints (restrictions or limits on outlooks and behavior) in patterns of social interaction. These constraints include cultural frames (shared group constructions of reality) developed over time through the processes of meaning-making (shared views of how the world works) and decision-making (choices that reflect shared definitions of how the world works). For example, in the inner-city ghetto, cultural frames define issues of trust—street smarts and "acting black" and "acting white"—that lead to observable group characteristics.

One of the effects of living in a racially segregated, poor neighborhood is the exposure to cultural traits that may not be conducive to facilitating social mobility. For example, some social scientists have discussed the negative effects of a "cool-pose culture" that has emerged among young black men in the inner city, which includes sexual conquests, hanging out on the street after school, party drugs, and hip-hop music. These patterns of behavior are seen as a hindrance to social mobility in the larger society. . . .

SOURCE: Abridged from Wilson 2010.

---

insofar as we make sense of all our experiences in terms of the logic made available through the language we speak.

Discourse refers to a set of ideas, concepts, and vocabulary that are regularly used together. We use specific discourses to habitually speak about and understand a topic or issue. Take, for example, the issue of crime. In talking about crime, we might employ an *individualist discourse* that understands crime as the actions of an individual who makes certain choices. This discourse of crime encourages an understanding of the psychological factors involved in criminal behaviour and leads to solutions that work at the level of the individual. An individualist solution might suggest that if we alter the attractiveness of the option of committing crime by making penalties harsher for those who are caught, the individual will, we hope, no longer choose to commit crime.

In contrast, a *collectivist discourse* views crime as a social problem. The focus is on crime rates and on the social conditions that influence the likelihood that crime will be committed in society. This discourse encourages a more sociological view of the factors contributing to crime, focusing on the social level rather than on the individual level. Just as the problem is conceived at the group level, so the ideas and terminology of a collectivist discourse promote a conception of solutions at the group level. For example, an effort to reduce crime might be based on a comparison of low- and high-crime societies to determine how certain social differences influence crime rates.

Discourses have the potential for great influence. The promotion of certain discourses, by those with the power to do so, can have the effect of setting the public agenda for certain issues. Discourses play a role in the **social construction** of the categories and definitions we use to understand social life. We constantly refer to these categories and definitions in order to make judgments about good and bad, right and wrong, how to distinguish between "us" and the "other," as well as to understand the very nature of things—Is abortion murder? Are movies an art form, an educational medium, a propaganda tool, or entertainment? Is "race" about biological differences? For all these questions, our answers will be influenced by the way predominant discourses shape our notions of the issues central to them.

MASS MEDIA

The mass media are potent social forces that constitute a key realm of cultural production and distribution. They comprise the technologically based methods and institutions that allow a single source to transmit messages to a mass audience. In Canada, the mass media include print (newspapers, magazines, books, and journals), film, radio, television (broadcast, cable, and satellite), and the Internet. The Internet is a special case, because although it can function as a mass medium, it is also much more—a network medium by virtue of its ability to allow multiple message sources. Potentially, every person on the Internet can be a source of mass media content. The Internet is also more than traditional mass media in the sense that it provides functions that extend to commerce, education, and politics, among other realms (see Table 2.1 on the ways in which Canadians are using the Internet).

The mass media are a central cultural concern because of the nature of the content that they bring to the vast majority of people. That content can be categorized both as *information* and as *entertainment*. In addition to information that is delivered as news on news programs and in newspapers, the mass media provide us with a wealth of other information about the world that we might never have access to through firsthand experience. Through the mass media, we can read about the modernization of industries in China, we can hear about the best way to invest money in a sluggish economy, we can find information about our diagnosed disease and likely find a support group willing to share their experiences with the ailment.

As the providers of so much information, the mass media have an enormous amount of influence on people's attitudes and behaviours, which are dependent on the state of our knowledge. For example, some people will alter their eating habits based on information they learn from magazine articles about the dangers and benefits of certain foods, and some people will form an opinion about strengthening environmental protection regulations based on stories they watch on television news programs. Because the mass media select a limited amount of information to present to audiences from a virtually infinite supply, they serve as informational gatekeepers (White 1950). In addition, just as important as *what* they present is the question of *how* they present media content. It is through the mass media that most discourses are disseminated to the general public.

The mass media are also the primary source for popular culture. While high culture (discussed below) is rarely made available through the mass media, popular culture is everywhere. It has been argued that the popular culture productions brought to us by the mass media can be linked to deep-seated social problems. For example, the mass media are blamed for a culture of violence: it is argued that they contribute to high levels of violence in society to the extent that portrayals of violence incite violent acts and desensitize people to the presence of violence. At the same time, it is argued that the mass media contribute to an unrealistic and shallow understanding of and response to this violence. The list of social problems linked to the ways in which the mass media may negatively influence our culture is long, including such serious issues as body consciousness and eating disorders, racism, and sexism, exacerbated through stereotypical and misleading depictions.

The section "Representation in Mainstream Media" in Chapter 17, p. 351, discusses how the mass media represent the working class, women, and racial and ethnic minorities.

ART AND AESTHETICS

The realm of art is, above all, an expressive area of social life. Whereas much of our behaviour is oriented toward the practical achievement of a useful goal, art stands out as an activity that is done to communicate through aesthetic means. The *New Shorter Oxford English Dictionary*

TABLE 2.1 ▼ Internet Use by Individuals at Home,[1] by Type of Activity

	2005	2007	2009
	% of individuals		
Email	91.3	92.0	93.0
Participating in chat groups or using a messenger	37.9	..	..
Using an instant messenger	..	49.9	44.8
Searching for information on Canadian municipal, provincial, or federal governments	52.0	51.4	56.5
Communicating with Canadian municipal, provincial, or federal governments	22.6	25.5	26.9
Searching for medical or health-related information	57.9	58.6	69.9
Education, training, or school work	42.9	49.5	50.3
Obtaining travel information or making travel arrangements	63.1	66.1	66.2
Paying bills	55.0	..	..
Electronic banking	57.8	..	..
Searching for employment	..	32.3	34.9
Researching investments	26.2	25.5	27.1
Playing games	38.7	38.7	42.1
Obtaining or saving music	36.6	44.5	46.5
Obtaining or saving software	31.8	32.5	35.0
Viewing the news or sports	61.7	63.7	67.7
Obtaining information on weather or road conditions	66.6	69.8	74.6
Listening to the radio over the Internet	26.1	28.1	31.8
Downloading or watching television	8.5	15.7	24.7
Downloading or watching a movie	8.3	12.5	19.8
Researching community events	42.3	44.3	50.0
General browsing (surfing)	84.0	76.0	77.7
Researching other matters (family history, parenting)	..	69.5	72.7
Contributing content (blogs, photos, discussion groups)	..	20.3	26.7
Making telephone calls	..	8.7	13.8
Selling goods or services (through auction sites)	..	8.9	13.4
Other Internet activity	10.9	1.5	7.8

.. : Data not available in that year.

NOTE: The target population for the Canadian Internet Use Survey changed from individuals 18 years of age and older in 2005 to individuals 16 years of age and older in 2007.

[1]Internet users at home are individuals who answered that they used the Internet from home during the past 12 months.

SOURCE: Statistics Canada, CANSIM, table (for fee) 358-0130. www40.statcan.gc.ca/l01/cst01/comm29a-eng.htm

(1993) defines **aesthetics** as "a system of principles for the appreciation of the beautiful," which begs the definition of beauty! Today, many artists would eschew the word *beauty* for *important* (and some might narrow that idea to "what is important to me"). Art, then, employs a set of rules or principles embodied in many different forms and pertaining to the artist's notions of what is beautiful or important. This makes art—whether visual, musical, or literary—a special form of communication: it is an expression of thoughts and emotions not communicated through the ordinary means of language. Instead, it relies on the much more implicit and intuitive rules that people use to assess beauty or truth or, for that matter, societal strengths, values, and shortcomings.

As discussed above, we often distinguish between "popular culture" and "high culture." This distinction points to the existence of a

Is this wall of graffiti in Montreal art or vandalism? What social factors affect your decision?

cultural hierarchy in which certain forms of culture are granted greater legitimacy and prestige. Oil painting is higher on the hierarchy than filmmaking, which in turn is higher than television. It is important to recognize that our categories of "high" and "popular" or "low" are socially constructed. These categorizations reflect differences in the social contexts in which artifacts of culture are produced, distributed, and received. For example, the formality and opulence of the settings in which opera is produced and appreciated, and the fact that audiences who typically attend the opera are wealthy and highly educated, encourage an understanding of opera as high culture.

This approach highlights several of art's sociologically significant features. First, as explained by the production of culture perspective, art does not just spring out of a collective consciousness or even out of an individual's consciousness. Instead, art is a collective activity that requires collaboration between many actors in an art world (Becker 1982). It is this collective activity that helps to determine how artistic genres may be legitimated or become prestigious and how they may be viewed in the wider society.

Second, the socially constructed nature of distinctions between high and low in art also points to the significance of art in helping to determine the contours of social stratification. This link is rooted in the notion of **cultural capital**: the knowledge, preferences, and tastes that people have concerning art and aesthetics. Having abundant cultural capital usually means sharing the knowledge, preferences, and tastes that are common among those of high status in society. Sharing similar artistic tastes and consumption patterns with those in economically privileged positions provides access to networks and opportunities not open to those who do not have the necessary aesthetic preferences and expertise. In sociological terms, our cultural capital can increase our economic capital.

Third, and perhaps most significant, is the role that artistic consumption plays in creating social groupings. The enjoyment of aesthetic products is deeply related to our conceptions of our own identities, of who we really are, and of the kind of people with whom we wish to be associated. In this way, our tastes are profoundly implicated in how our lives are structured. We've already seen how artistic tastes can interact with our class position, but tastes can also be a way of expressing racial, gender, regional, and age-based identities. This last example can be illustrated through reference to "youth culture," which includes the artistic, leisure, and style preferences and habits of young people, who thereby distinguish themselves from prior generations.

Cultural Dynamics

We have already seen that culture changes over time, but we have yet to fully consider any specific mechanisms of cultural change. There are various perspectives we can take to understand why and how culture changes over time. First, we can view changes in culture as responses to social-structural changes; we will focus on the cultural ramifications of economic changes and of technological changes. Second, we can also view changes in culture as responses to other cultural developments, a view that emphasizes the web-like, interconnected nature of culture.

ECONOMIC, TECHNOLOGICAL, AND CULTURAL CHANGE

The discussion of Marxism earlier in this chapter reviewed the case for the economic foundation of culture. But it is not necessary to adopt Marxists' assumptions of culture merely as a reflection of economics to see that important economic changes are capable of provoking specific changes in culture. An example of such a change is the liberalization of attitudes toward women and work. In the mid to late nineteenth century and in the first half of the

SOCIOLOGY in ACTION

Neo-Liberalism and the Realities of Reality Television

Neo-liberalism represents a strategy of economic growth whose principles are associated with global free trade and the deregulation of industry, the weakening of union labour, a decline in welfare assistance and social service provision, and the privatization of publicly owned resources.

At first glance, neo-liberal dogma and reality television seem worlds apart—that is, until one considers exactly why the entertainment industry developed the genre in the first place.

. . . [I]t bears remembering that TV studios and networks introduced the first generation of reality television shows—notably the law enforcement shows "COPS" and "America's Most Wanted"—in response to the 1988 Writers Guild of America strike. Their goal was to create a form of programming that would be largely immune from union tactics from sit-downs to picket lines. Since reality television shows do not rely on traditional scripts, producers avoid the risks and expensive costs associated with hiring unionized writers. By casting amateur participants willing to work for free, rather than professional actors, producers also avoid paying industry-standard union wages to members of the Screen Actors Guild.

. . . While the production of reality television employs neo-liberalism's economic principles, the genre's narrative conventions reflect its morals. Competitive programs celebrate the radical right-wing values championed especially by free-market Republicans. Both "Survivor" and "The Apprentice" require 16 or more participants to fiercely compete against one another in winner-take-all contests guaranteed to produce extreme levels of social inequality. Although team members are initially expected to work cooperatively on "Survivor," they eventually vote their collaborators out of the game in naked displays of individualism and self-interest. . . .

Although the very design of competitive reality programs like "The Apprentice" or "Hell's Kitchen" guarantees that nearly all players must lose, such shows inevitably emphasize the moral failings of each contestant just before they are deposed . . . on programs like "The Biggest Loser" in which fitness trainers personally criticize the show's overweight (and typically working-class) contestants for their poor health. In such instances, the contributions of neo-liberal federal policy to increased health disparities in the US—notably the continued lack of affordable and universal health care and cutbacks in welfare payments to indigent mothers and their children—are ignored in favor of arguments that blame the victims of poverty for their own misfortune.

SOURCE: Abridged from Grazian 2010.

twentieth century, there was a strong belief in Western societies that it was most appropriate for women, especially married women, not to work outside the home but rather to find fulfillment in their roles as mothers and housewives. While the reasons for the change in this attitude are many, it can be argued that an important cause was economic. Maintenance of a middle-class standard of living increasingly required a second income. Changing attitudes about women and work, in this view, were an adaptive response to a changing economic reality.

Over the same period of time, rising levels of affluence made it possible for teenagers to possess a certain amount of disposable income. The development of youth culture, while deriving from various causes, was facilitated by the economic changes that created consumers out of young people and thereby encouraged cultural producers to target youth. The continued growth in spending power of teenagers has also allowed them to become the primary demographic target of Hollywood film studios. Because young people see films in theatres more often than do older groups, a great deal of film production is tailored to their tastes and expectations. This dynamic is representative of the more general dependence of the content of cultural industries on economic conditions.

Technological change can also be viewed as the source of a great deal of the change in our culture. Perhaps the most significant technological influence on culture has been the development of the mass media. The printing press, invented by Johannes Gutenberg in 1452, has been credited with transforming European culture in diverse ways. For example, because the printing press brought down the cost of books, many people could own Bibles and interpret them apart from what priests instructed them to believe: a precondition for the Protestant Reformation.

It would be impossible to enumerate all the ways in which technology has created cultural change. To take an example of a broad cultural pattern, the very idea of "nightlife" and all its attendant activities is predicated on the existence of electricity and the light bulb. Much more narrowly, the technological innovation of the electrification of musical instruments has influenced tastes in musical styles. Suffice it to say that technological change frequently has the potential to create cultural reverberations, sometimes of limited significance and other times life-transforming.

CHANGE FOR THE SAKE OF CHANGE

Despite the strength of the relationship between culture and social structure, culture also has internal dynamics that can account for cultural change. In this view, cultural change is inevitable, because culture is inherently progressive, volatile, and unstable: it is the nature of culture to evolve.

This view is perhaps best exemplified by the phenomenon of fashion. Ongoing change is built into the very idea of fashion. Moreover, fashion is not just the styles of clothes that are popular, although that is one of its most visible manifestations. Rather, elements of fashion can be found in many areas of social life. Consider, for instance, how vocabulary choices acknowledge that some words are "in" while others are "out." To express approval, in the past one might have used adjectives such as *swell*, *groovy*, or *mod*, words that sound dated now despite the fact that the need to express approval has not gone away. New, more fashionable words do the job today. Consider also how changes in interior design occur gradually but consistently enough to evoke associations with particular decades. Few of these changes are linked to changes in function or technological innovations.

Although aesthetic changes do not serve any practical purpose, they may still be related to a social purpose: they satisfy needs for self-expression. In this sense, the aesthetic dimension of life is symbolic—we communicate to others and articulate for ourselves certain thoughts, values, identities, and senses of group affiliation.

Canadian Culture

The concepts and arguments reviewed in this chapter can help us to understand the current state of Canadian culture, along with some of the more contentious issues facing Canadian society. Because of its unique history, Canadian culture is unlike any other national culture, with a unique set of challenges and opportunities.

The challenge for Canada continues to be the forging of a unified Canadian culture that respects the unique characteristics of both traditions. To this end, we employ a policy of official bilingualism, and we foster cultural events that embrace both French and English cultural elements.

MULTICULTURALISM

The conception of two founding peoples can be seen as primarily a legal construct rather than as an accurate historical depiction. In reality, there have always been more than two cultural traditions in Canada. The Aboriginal cultures of **First Nations** and Inuit peoples were, of course, present before the idea of a Canadian society or culture was ever proposed.

More recently, increased immigration from a large number of countries and the formation of an equally large number of ethnic communities in Canada have added to the number of cultural traditions. As a society, we have adopted a stance of official **multiculturalism**, although the merits of this position engender debate. We should distinguish between multiculturalism as a fact of contemporary Canadian society— there are ethnic subcultures that are thriving— and multiculturalism as a policy—the tolerance and encouragement of the maintenance of the national cultures that immigrants bring from their countries of origin.

Proponents of multiculturalism point to its helpfulness in easing the transition of new immigrants into Canadian society. This happens through the fostering of ethnic communities that can provide social support. In addition, proponents argue that multiculturalism is properly respectful to all Canadians and enriches the wider Canadian culture. Detractors, on the other hand, argue that multiculturalism only makes it more difficult to create a unifying Canadian culture. Moreover, they question the wisdom of a policy that encourages, to however small a degree, self-segregation rather than facilitating the full cultural integration of immigrants into Canadian life. Again, just as with the question of two founding peoples, the challenge here is to balance culture's potential for unifying us with our desire to maintain certain cultural partitions.

Food is another cultural aspect that changes rapidly. The humble cupcake was elevated to cult status thanks to an appearance on the popular television show "Sex and the City." An abundance of bakeries, cookbooks, and blogs dedicated to the dessert soon appeared. Although the popularity of cupcakes is still high, many consider that they have lost their dominance to macaroons. What will the next food fad be?

DISTINCT SOCIETIES

One of the defining features of Canadian culture is its basis in "two founding peoples," French and English. The term *peoples* refers not only to the actual members of the French and English colonies but also to their respective ways of life—their cultures. How different or similar are the cultures of French and English Canada? On a global scale, they are quite similar to one another in comparison with, for example, Pakistani or Indonesian culture. However, they do differ in important ways. Most obvious is the linguistic distinction. As discussed earlier, the ability to communicate through verbal and written language is a key element in social bonding—without this form of communication, opportunities for social interaction are limited. Differences in other cultural traditions exist as well, ranging from cuisine and leisure activities to political values and views on marriage and family.

Multiculturalism is a topic of great debate in Canada. For a broader discussion of this debate, see "Multiculturalism and Its Critics" in Chapter 8, p. 158.

GLOBALIZATION AND AMERICAN CULTURAL IMPERIALISM

Globalization typically refers to the fact that goods, services, information, and people, now more than ever, can easily flow between distant countries. One effect of globalization is the internationalization of national cultures as they increasingly are exposed to one another. The mass media, then, are the key channels of the cultural diffusion occurring through the mutual influence of many national cultures.

Globalization, however, can bring with it many cultural challenges. Chief among them is the need to manage the global export of American popular culture. The sheer volume of American cultural export has led to the term "cultural imperialism," describing the scope of the global dominance of American culture. The reaction to this state of affairs in Canada has been one of alarm, and a concerted effort has been mounted to maintain the integrity of Canadian culture. In order to promote Canadian cultural production, the federal government has enacted policies that require Canadian broadcasters to make a sizable proportion of their content of Canadian origin. In addition, a variety of programs exist to subsidize Canadian film, television, music, and book production.

This policy of Canadian cultural protectionism has clearly achieved some measured success. Scores of Canadian artists have achieved a level of success that would have been unlikely if they had been left to compete on the unequal playing field with American artists, who are promoted by vast media conglomerates.

TIME to REFLECT

What are the arguments for and against multiculturalism in Canada? Which do you find more persuasive?

Conclusion

Many different social phenomena can be called "cultural," but we have learned that making and conveying meaning is what they have in common. Culture influences people, but people also use culture to shape their actions. Through a sociological analysis of the nature and significance of cultural meanings, we can better understand a wide range of social phenomena. Culture is always evolving and is intimately tied to other social changes and to other cultural changes. Culture is implicated in the social dynamics both of conflict and of people coming together, and for that reason as well as others it is an essential subject for sociological analysis.

questions for critical thought

1. What is Canadian culture, and what are its most important or distinctive facets?

2. How much do you know about other cultures, and how did you learn about them? How do you know whether your impressions are accurate?

3. How would you go about measuring cultural change?

4. Is cultural change beneficial to society? Is it conceivable to have no changes in our culture?

recommended readings

Victoria D. Alexander. 2003. *Sociology of the Arts: Exploring Fine and Popular Forms.* **Oxford: Blackwell.**
This book is a clear, engaging, thorough, and sophisticated overview of this area of study.

Peter Berger and Thomas Luckmann. 1966. *The Social Construction of Reality: A Treatise in the Sociology of Knowledge.* **Garden City, NY: Doubleday-Anchor.**
This is a seminal work in the sociology of culture, laying the groundwork for social constructionist thought.

David Grazian. 2010. *Mix It Up: Popular Culture, Mass Media, and Society.* **New York: Norton.**
Grazian's book is a highly entertaining and accessible introduction to the sociological significance of the media and cultural production.

Eric Klinenberg. 2005. *Cultural Production in a Digital Age: The Annals of the American Academy of Political and Social Science.* **Thousand Oaks, CA: Sage.**
Taking a broad view of what counts as culture, this edited volume investigates how the technological advances of the digital age have influenced the methods and outcomes of cultural production.

recommended websites

Canadian Broadcasting Corporation (CBC)
www.cbc.ca
In addition to finding the news, you will also find links to the corporate history of the CBC, the broadcasting entity charged with strengthening Canadian culture and identity.

Cultural Sociology
http://cus.sagepub.com
This journal was launched in 2007 to provide an outlet for academic work that specializes in taking a cultural approach toward sociological questions.

National Film Board of Canada (NFB)
www.nfb.ca
There are countless interesting links on the website of the NFB, which is especially renowned for its documentary and animated productions.

United Nations Educational, Scientific and Cultural Organization (UNESCO)
www.unesco.org
UNESCO deals with, among others, issues of cultural diversity and preservation.

chapter 3

Being Social

Barbara A. Mitchell

In this chapter you will:

▶ Situate the social experience within the nature/nurture debate.

▶ Understand basic patterns of socialization and key concepts and consider how they are applied in research and everyday situations.

▶ Learn how different theorists explain processes of socialization.

▶ Examine different agents of socialization, such as the family, the school, the peer group, and the mass media.

▶ Critically evaluate how socialization experiences are socially structured and vary by social class, gender/sexual orientation, ethnicity, generation, and geographical location.

▶ Explore how socialization is a reciprocal, never-ending process that shapes changing family, work, and health-related experiences over the life course.

Introduction: What Is Socialization?

In the recent Discovery television documentary, "Into the Universe with Stephen Hawking," the famous British scientist asserts that "aliens are out there, but it could be too dangerous for humans to interact with extraterrestrial life." Hawking further speculates that most extra-terrestrials would be similar to microbes, or small animals, but that communicating with them could be "too risky." But imagine, for a moment, a slightly different scenario. Imagine that you arrive home one day to a neighbour-hood that has been newly inhabited by crea-tures that are biologically identical to adult humans. Intelligent, co-operative, and peace-ful (although occasionally combative), they do not recognize our language or comprehend our customs, norms, or ways of interacting. Instead, they exchange thoughts sonically using suction-like pods, and they make intense eye contact with strangers. After setting up camp in the local park, they quickly begin to learn our language and engage in local community affairs. Over time, they internalize and copy many of our behaviours, beliefs, and technolo-gies, and most become accepted and produc-tive citizens of our society.

Although this hypothetical situation reads like a scene out of a science fiction movie, it illustrates the process of **socialization**, which can be defined as the acquisition of knowl-edge, skills, and motivation to participate in social life. In other words, it is the process whereby individuals learn, through interaction with others, what they must know in order to survive, function, and become members of our society. Moreover, socialization is not confined to babies and children but constitutes a com-plex, lifelong learning process that enables us to develop our selves, roles, and identities.

Yet socialization is not a uniform phenom-enon whereby we are all churned out by some kind of giant socialization factory. Although humans share many values and norms, differ-ences are found by geographic region, ethnic/immigration background, gender, religion, and social class. Additionally, each generation ex-periences socializing effects particular to their birthplace and historical location. Growing up during the Great Depression (1929–39) in Canada, for instance, would have been differ-ent from what it is today, given the vastly different social, economic, and technological environ-ments. Further, criminologists point out that socialization does not necessarily mean that what is learned is acceptable to the "main-stream" or is positive for us. Take, for example, youth gang behaviour whereby a young adult self-identifies with a certain group (e.g., the Crips, the Blood). Through interaction with other gang members, youths learn and display "anti-social" norms and behaviours, such as participating in delinquent acts, crime sprees, drug trafficking, and slayings.

TIME to REFLECT

How have your opportunities in life been affected by your historical location (e.g., the generational time and place in which you were born)?

Human Behaviour—Nature or Nurture?

For more than a century, social scientists have argued over the relative contributions of biol-ogy and the environment to human develop-ment, popularly called "the nature–nurture debate." By way of example, consider your own musical abilities. Are you an awesome singer, or can you play a musical instrument such as a guitar or piano with ease and finesse? Do you think that your musical talent (or lack thereof) is the result of your biology (nature) or environ-mental influences (nurture)? If you lean toward a biological explanation, you might attribute your musical talent to the unfolding of "hardwired" genetic factors. You might believe, for example, that you inherited strong music genes from your parents or from your Uncle Albert, who might be a professional musician. However, if you lean more toward an environmental explana-tion, you might focus more on the role of social forces (e.g., lots of opportunities to take music lessons) in producing your musical talents.

Alternatively, you might argue that both sides of the debate have some merit. Indeed, recent advances in biology and genetics support the idea that biology and environment interact in

("Group of Children", © Corbis)

The socialization of each generation is very different due to the social, economic, and technological environment. For instance, growing up during the Great Depression would present challenges unknown to most youths now.

dynamic ways to transform us into functioning members of society, each with our own unique sets of skills and abilities. From this lens, there is a continually unfolding interaction between how our genes are expressed (our heredity) and our social world (Paul 2010). In short, we may be predisposed toward certain abilities, but our environment will determine the extent to which these abilities can be realized.

In summary, one useful way to conceptualize socialization is that it provides the link between biology and culture. We are born with the capacity to learn (e.g., music), to use language, and to forge social and emotional bonds, all of which are necessary for normal childhood development. However, our environment may limit (or facilitate) the extent to which innate gifts or propensities are realized. But what happens when our biological potential is not actualized? In order to examine this question more closely, let's consider the effects of social deprivation on human development.

TIME to REFLECT

Many children throughout the world do not have the opportunity to grow up in a safe, secure, and loving environment. For example, they may be living in a war-ravaged country, or they may be forced into child-labour camps. How will these early experiences shape their later adult life?

THE EFFECTS OF SOCIAL ISOLATION

Throughout history, reports have surfaced of young children who have been isolated from society and who, in one way or another, have lived in a "wild" state. One study compiled a list of 53 cases of isolated children, beginning with the Hesse Wolf-Child (purportedly raised by wolves) discovered in Germany in 1344 (Newton 2002). Other examples include the cases of Isabelle, Anna, and Genie. Genie, for instance, was discovered at the age of 13 in her home in Los Angeles, California, on 4 November 1970 (Rymer 1993; Curtiss 1977). Tied to a potty chair during the day, she had been locked in a room alone for more than a decade. After she was found, she was placed into Children's Hospital in Los Angeles, and her mental and physical development started to improve immediately. Yet despite these gains, many concluded that she probably would never completely regain her normal learning capacity.

Although case studies such as this one are obviously extreme, research documents that even milder forms of social isolation can have profound effects for children later in life. Recent studies report that repeated social isolation (measured as a lack of social support and controlling for other factors) leads to poor psychological and physical health, such as an increased risk of cardiovascular disease (e.g., Grant, Hamer, and Steptoe 2009). These health problems are attributed to the cumulative "wear and tear" caused by weak adaptation to stress. Fortunately, social connections (or social "capital") are found to have a buffering effect on our ability to handle life's ups and downs, and this can positively influence how we age.

In conclusion, socialization is the essential bridge between the individual and society, and it is the process through which we become human. All of the evidence points to the crucial role of social experience in personality and healthy human development. Children need to be surrounded by people they trust, who care for them, interact with them, and can meet their basic needs. And although humans are resilient creatures, there is a point at which abuse, neglect, or social isolation (especially in infancy) results in irreparable developmental damage.

Theorizing Socialization

In this section, major theoretical approaches to socialization are reviewed. These approaches include: learning/behaviourist theory, Freud's psychoanalytic theory, developmental approaches (Erikson, Piaget, and Kohlberg), the symbolic interactionist view on the development of the self, functionalist and conflict approaches, and feminist theory (especially in relation to **gender-role socialization**). Although there is sometimes overlap in basic assumptions or ideas, these theories mainly differ in emphasis

and conception of what socialization comprises and how learning occurs.

THEORIES ON CHILDHOOD SOCIALIZATION

Learning/Behaviourist Frame of Reference
Learning theory, which has its roots in behaviourism, assumes that the same concepts and principles that apply to animals apply to humans. Although there are many variations of this theory, socialization as applied to the newborn infant involves changes that result from maturations that include classical or instrumental conditioning. Classical conditioning links a response to a known stimulus. A popular example is Pavlov's dog experiment in which a hungry dog is placed in a soundproof room and hears a tuning fork (a conditioned stimulus) before receiving some meat. After this situation is repeated several times, the dog begins to salivate upon hearing the tuning fork. The same principles are assumed to hold true with an infant upon hearing his or her mother's voice or approaching footsteps.

Operant or instrumental conditioning focuses attention on the response, which is not related to any known stimulus. Instead, it functions in an instrumental manner in that one learns to make a certain response on the basis of the outcome that the response produces. According to Skinner (1953), it is the response that correlates with positive reinforcement or a reward. For example, imagine that a baby is picked up after saying "da-da-da," because the father is convinced that the baby is saying "Daddy." Consequently, the baby begins to say "da-da-da" all day long, because there may be lots of rewards. As children grow older, different reinforcements (e.g., praise, candy, allowances) are used as deliberate techniques to teach children approved forms of behaviour.

While there is some usefulness to this theory, there may be limited applicability of generalizing animal behaviour to socialized humans. Humans, unlike animals, have the capacity to share symbolic meanings and symbols in ways that animals cannot.

Psychoanalytic Frame of Reference
Developed by Sigmund Freud (1856–1939) and his followers, psychoanalytic theory stresses the importance of childhood experiences, biological

drives and unconscious processes, and cultural influences. Beneath the surface of each individual's consciousness are impulsive, pleasure-seeking, and selfish energies that Freud termed "the id." Individuals also have "egos" and engage in cognitive, conscious thought processes that make each one of us a unique individual. Both the id and the ego are controlled by the individual's gradual internalization of societal restraints (the "superego"). Parents play a key role in "impulse taming" by transmitting cultural values and rules that guide the ego and repress the id.

Accordingly, socialization consists of a number of stages of development called the *oral, anal, and phallic stages*, followed later by a period of *latency* and then a *genital phase*. When individuals pass through all of these stages, it culminates in a healthy, mature personality with a well-developed superego, which channels libidinal forces in appropriate directions (Freud 1938). Overall, Freudian ideas have been highly controversial (especially because of his emphasis on childhood sexuality) and have received mixed empirical support. For instance, practices such as breastfeeding and bowel and bladder training (which have been so strongly emphasized in the psychoanalytic literature) are found to be negligible in terms of how they affect personality development.

Child Development Frames of Reference

Similar to Freud, both Erikson (1963; 1982) and Piaget (1932; 1950) emphasized the early stages of childhood development. Unlike Freud, both extended their stages beyond the early years and focused more attention on social structure and reasoning. Erikson, who was one of Freud's students, viewed socialization as a lifelong process. He developed the "eight stages of human development," which range from *trust versus mistrust* (first year of infancy) to *integrity versus despair* (old age). As individuals create solutions to developmental concerns, those solutions become institutionalized in our culture. Swiss social psychologist Jean Piaget, who wrote during the 1920s, was also interested in maturational stages. However, his interest was more in cognitive development, characterizing this as the ability to reason abstractly, to think about hypothetical situations logically, and to organize rules into higher-order, complex operations or structures.

Piaget developed four major cumulative stages of intellectual development, which include the sensorimotor period (birth to two years), pre-operational period (two to seven years), concrete operational period (seven to eleven years), and formal operational period (age eleven through adulthood). In Piaget's view, children develop their cognitive abilities through interaction with the world and adaptation to their environment. They adapt by assimilating, which means making new information compatible with their understanding of the world. Children also learn to accommodate by adjusting their cognitive framework to incorporate new experiences as they become socialized into adults.

Kohlberg (1975; 1969) expanded on Piaget's ideas with his stages of moral development. In the earliest stages, children say "it's wrong to steal" and "it's against the law," but they are unable to elaborate any further. Later on (by Stage 4, the most prevalent stage, usually reached as children mature), moral decisions are made from the perspective of larger society, since we think as a full-fledged member of society.

In summary, so far we have reviewed frames of reference that emphasize overt behaviour (i.e., behaviourism, learning theory), the unconscious role of motives and emotions (i.e., the Freudians), and motor skills, thought, and moral reasoning processes (i.e., child developmentalists). Next we will review perspectives that shine the spotlight on societal influences on socialization.

Symbolic Interactionist Frame of Reference

In sociology, the symbolic interactionist (SI) perspective has had one of the greatest influences on theories of socialization. Central importance is placed on interactions with others and the internalized definitions, meanings, and interpretations of our interactions (Charon 1979). Basic assumptions include the following:

1. *Humans must be studied on their own level.* Social life involves sharing meanings and communicating symbolically via language, which enables humans alone to deal with events in terms of past, present, or future.

2. *An analysis of society is the most valuable method in understanding society.* Individual behaviour needs to be contextualized within the structure of society. When one is born into a given society, one learns the language, customs, and expectations of that culture.

3. *At birth, the human infant is asocial.* Newborns are born with impulses and needs and with the potential to become a social being. Behaviours and expectations do not begin to take on meaning until babies begin to learn to channel their behaviours in specific directions via parental training and socialization.

4. *A socialized being is an actor as well as a reactor.* Humans do not simply react to one another in robotic fashion. Rather, humans are minded beings, actively responding to a symbolic environment that involves responses to interpreted and anticipated stimuli.

Another key concept is the idea of the development of a social self, which takes place in interaction with others. For example, a young adult may occupy the status of child, student, sister, athlete, and many others. These statuses have expectations (roles) assigned to them and are organized and integrated into the social self. In this way, the social self is never fixed, static, or in a final state.

Of central importance are the roles of **significant others** and reference groups. Although parents are usually the most significant socializers, others can also play a part. These individuals can be other family members or even role models presented in the media, such as pop star sensations like Justin Bieber or Lady Gaga. Reference groups, on the other hand, constitute a source of comparison and a standard of conduct that operate in a similar fashion. Examples might include a religious group, a hobby club, peer groups, or an organization (e.g., Boy Scouts, Apple).

TIME to REFLECT

Who are your most significant role models? How do they influence what you say and do? How do they contribute to your feelings of self-worth and your self-identity?

Popular SI theorists include George Herbert Mead (1934) and Charles Horton Cooley (1902; 1962). To Mead, social, not biological, forces are the primary source of human behaviour. He maintained that a newborn baby is *tabula rasa*, or a "blank slate," without predisposition to develop any particular type of personality. Mead referred to this spontaneous and unsocialized self as the "I." Through interaction, our personalities develop, and the socialized ("Me") self emerges. Mead also asserted that although the "Me" becomes predominant with socialization, the "I" continues to exist and that it can be the source of unpredictable or "untamed" social behaviour.

Another central concept is Mead's notion of **generalized other**. Children usually pass through three stages in developing a full sense of selfhood: the play stage (whereby the child models significant others), the game stage (whereby children pretend to be other people), and, finally, the generalized other stage (learning generalized values and cultural rules). This final stage signifies how individuals become consistent and predictable in their behaviour and how people learn to view themselves from the perspective of others. Thus, behaviour results less from drives and needs, unconscious processes, and biological forces and more from social interaction processes and internalized meanings of self and others.

FUNCTIONALIST AND CONFLICT PERSPECTIVES

While many theories of socialization describe and analyze the *process* of socialization, functionalist and conflict theories place emphasis on understanding the *role* and the *importance* of socialization. A functionalist approach addresses the ways in which conformity helps to preserve and meet the needs of society. It does so by providing knowledge that is passed from generation to generation, which helps society to survive and meet the demands of its environment. Through cultural transmission, values and norms that are widely shared in society (e.g., trust) are critical to solidarity and co-operation, although it is also recognized that society needs to adapt to new conditions and situations. Thus, the fundamental task of any society is to reproduce itself such that the needs of society become the needs of the individual.

According to George Herbert Mead, the game stage is one of three stages that children pass through in order to develop a sense of selfhood. The game stage is when children pretend to be other people.

Conflict perspectives (which often have roots in Marxist theories) focus more on issues of power and control and how socialization helps the powerful and wealthy pass on their advantages to the next generation. Socialization does so by supporting ideologies and practices that work to the advantage of dominant groups and by social channelling. It teaches people to accept, rather than to challenge or question, the status quo or ways of society. This creates a "false consciousness," or a lack of awareness and a distorted perception of class realities (Pines 1993). In this way, children are prepared for future societal roles, and gender, class, and racial inequities are reproduced. Notably, poor children are channelled toward a life of poverty through the educational and employment system.

FEMINIST THEORIES AND GENDER-ROLE SOCIALIZATION

Although one unified, feminist theory does not exist, feminists often critique functionalist views and build upon conflict theorizing by empha-

sizing how gender is a fundamental organizing feature of social life. Focus is often placed on how social interaction, including discourse (i.e., the usage of language and symbols), is socially constructed and on how gender-role socialization mirrors and perpetuates inequities found throughout society.

> If the term *discourse* refers to a set of ideas, concepts, and vocabulary that are regularly used together, would you agree that it is socially constructed? A fuller discussion of this can be found under "Language and Discourse," Chapter 2, p. 40.

Gender roles refer to the expectations associated with being masculine or feminine, which may or may not correspond with one's sex, whereas sex roles can be defined as the expectations related to being biologically of one sex or another.

There is little denying that gendered divisions are found in virtually all societies. For many centuries, it was assumed that "anatomy is destiny" and that these differences were largely innate or inborn. However, many feminists assert that this belief provides a major (functionalistic) ideological justification for a system of stratification that subordinates women and privileges men. Instead, we must also consider socialization processes and the organization and practices of society. Fundamental differences in gender-role socialization and stereotyping continue to exist, and this begins at birth and continues throughout one's life. It is seen in the sexual objectification of girls in society and the media (e.g., see Stankiewicz and Rosselli 2008) and the kinds of gender-specific toys and games that continue to be manufactured, marketed, and bought for children.

Another example of how social institutions are highly gendered is our educational system, which also plays an important role in the formation of gender identities through curriculum and its local culture. Connell (1996) maintains that each school has its own "gender regime," which contributes to the ongoing negotiation and renegotiation of femininity or masculinity. For instance, at some schools "the look for boys" is to appear somehow connected to sports, athleticism, strength, and power, and this becomes the hegemonic norm (Swain 2004).

Fox (2009) reveals other structural sources of gender differences and how they can resurface beyond childhood (i.e., in young families). Her research uncovered how the transition to parenthood can produce a more conventional division of labour in the home. Gender inequity arises out of the gendered division of paid and unpaid work, and these conditions further shape and constrain options and behaviours. In today's society, a shortage of outside community supports and the privatization of parenthood also mean that women continue to have the ultimate responsibility for their babies' welfare. This creates women's dependence on men or other family members (e.g., on their own mothers), and this further strengthens gendered divisions.

In short, gender socialization does not end in childhood. It continues (and can even deepen) through certain institutional practices and discourses that produce gendered adults and identities. As a result, despite feminist efforts to challenge gender-role socialization and conventional gender divisions, many inequities persist. And while many couples negotiate the changes in their lives, women in a materially strong position (whose bargaining power tends to be relatively good before motherhood) may be better able to resist dynamics that place them in an unequal position within the family.

TIME to REFLECT

In her bestselling book, *The Beauty Myth* (first published in 1990), Naomi Wolf argues that media images place a great deal of pressure on women to conform to an impossible standard of physical perfection. Do you agree or disagree? Have times changed at all since she wrote the book?

From the preceding discussion, it is clear that families are a primary agent of socialization but that other (secondary) agents also contribute to socialization processes. To further illustrate this point, parents may be significant role models for children and can influence whether children will have drug abuse problems. Yet other **agents of socialization** at the peer group, school, and community/societal level can simultaneously

exert risk and protective factors in the process, as depicted in Figure 3.1. Thus, various agents, in conjunction with individual-level factors (e.g., peer resistance skills) can both complement and compete with one another to produce certain behavioural outcomes such as problem drug use.

In the next section, we will examine more closely the role of families in **primary socialization**, followed by the **secondary socialization** that takes place in the wider society. We will consider how these secondary agents—school, peer group, and mass media/technology—differentially influence our social experiences by considering social class, ethnicity/cultural background, gender/sexual orientation, and age.

The Family

There is little denial that during infancy and childhood, our family constitutes the most significant agent of socialization. Families provide the primary source of our early emotional attachments and learning, although others agents (e.g., daycare, the mass media) also shape children's basic beliefs and values. Families also play a critical role in transmitting culture from one generation to the next. Through countless family rituals (e.g., birthday celebrations, graduation ceremonies) and activities, children are taught to reproduce social patterns and behaviours familiar to adults. Families are also sites of power and control relations prevalent in wider society, in addition to having their own hierarchies based on aspects such as age and gender.

Experiences within contemporary families are very different from what they were in the past. Although family life has never been homogenous, changes in family structure (e.g., the rise in step and single-father families), transformations in work and greater gender role equality (e.g., dual-career households), and continuing high rates of immigration contribute to the diversification and experience of "family." Despite these changes, much continuity in family life exists. As shown in Figure 3.2, most Canadian children still grow up in two-parent households. Bibby (2009, with Russell and Rolheiser) also finds that most young people aspire to marry (for life and formalized with some type of religious ceremony) and want to have children.

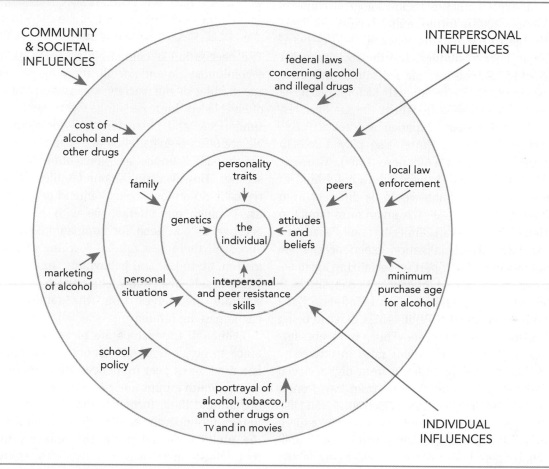

▼ **FIGURE 3.1** Socializing Agents and Risk/Protective Factors for Substance Abuse

COMMUNITY & SOCIETAL INFLUENCES

INTERPERSONAL INFLUENCES

federal laws concerning alcohol and illegal drugs

cost of alcohol and other drugs

personality traits

family

peers

local law enforcement

genetics

the individual

attitudes and beliefs

marketing of alcohol

personal situations

interpersonal and peer resistance skills

minimum purchase age for alcohol

school policy

portrayal of alcohol, tobacco, and other drugs on TV and in movies

INDIVIDUAL INFLUENCES

SOURCE: Image taken from "Educating students about drug use and mental health—Risk and protective factors," retrieved 23 July 2010 from www.camh.net.education/Resources-teachers_school

▼ **FIGURE 3.2** Families with Children, by Family Structure, 1981 and 2006 (%)

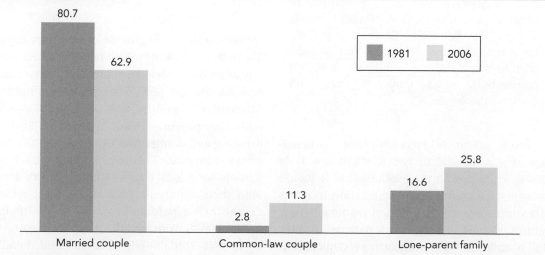

	1981	2006
Married couple	80.7	62.9
Common-law couple	2.8	11.3
Lone-parent family	16.6	25.8

SOURCE: Statistics Canada. 1981, 2006 Census. Retrieved from Human Resources and Skills Development Canada 15 July 2010 at www.statcan.gc.ca/tables-tableaux/sum-som/l01/cst01/famil121a-eng.htm

Regardless of the continuation of many family practices, our experiences are variable and occur within unique socio-ecological contexts (Wilson 2008). Intra-familial factors, such as the age of the parents when a child is born, the number of siblings, and the social support received from others, can profoundly influence socialization. Extra-familial factors, such as the neighbourhood in which the family lives, work/employment experiences, social class background, and culture, also play a role in these experiences (Albanese 2009). Growing up in a one-child Jewish family household in Toronto, for example, would be different from growing up in a large Ukrainian farm family in rural Saskatchewan. Indeed, family size can also influence socialization experiences, since siblings can play a part as socializing agents—for example, as role models or as babysitters.

Further, social class can influence the kinds of life chances and values that are being transmitted to children. Thus, it is not surprising that the enrolment rates in university are higher among children from higher social classes than among children from lower ones. Ethnic and immigration background can also shape opportunities and socialization experiences and produce norms, values, and obligations pertaining to values and many family roles—for example, with respect to how we treat and care for our senior family members.

> The importance of the family in Canadian society is clear, but that doesn't mean it can avoid a number of controversial issues. See "Recent Issues in Canadian Families," Chapter 9, p. 180, for a discussion of the gendered division of household labour, medically assisted conception, child care, divorce, and domestic violence.

Social scientists typically view socialization as a reciprocal or two-way process. Daly (2004, 5), for example, explains that it would be a mistake to think of socialization in terms of a simple linear transmission model whereby culture shapes parents and parents in turn shape children. A more accurate depiction is that of **reciprocal socialization**, or the simultaneity (whereby parents and children are the "players" in this case) of parenting and child behaviours and outcomes.

The Peer Group

The peer group is commonly regarded as the second-most potent socialization agent. The age-grading of our society means that we are often placed into situations with people of similar age and characteristics—for example, we are often segregated by age group in neighbourhoods, schools, and recreational/leisure settings. However, unlike our families, friends typically do not consciously intend to socialize us. Through our interactions with peers and because of our need for companionship and approval, there is a mutual learning of information, attitudes, and behaviours. Interactions with friends also allow children to begin to separate themselves from the family's all-encompassing influence.

Although friendships are of central importance throughout the life course, adolescence is a time when peer influences are particularly strong. Youth groups and the culture that develops around them form a foundation for creating unique subcultures or cliques. In contrast to the adult-dominated world, this allows youths to establish their own identity, with its own norms, rules, and regulations.

> Were you part of a clique in high school? See Chapter 4, "Cliques," p. 84, for a definition and discussion of cliques.

Peer groups also provide a setting for engaging in and trying new behaviours (often without adult supervision), which can have many positive aspects (e.g., learning a new hobby). Alternatively, youths may engage in behaviours that parents do not approve of, such as drinking and doing drugs or engaging in certain sexual activities. This is no doubt why many parents have long expressed great worry about who their children's friends are! Peer groups can also rival parents in influence, as implied by the familiar phrase "the generation gap."

Recent studies (e.g., Tirone and Pendlar 2005; Karakayali 2005) on immigrant youths also reveal multiple or "hybrid" identities of youths and how identities are flexible and subject to multiple influences. In a Canadian study of the narratives among second-generation youths in their early twenties (whose families originated in India, Pakistan, and Bangladesh), most youths had a profound appreciation of their family heritage even as they participated in "dominant" Canadian youth culture. These findings challenge the prevailing discourse that children of immigrants are a "problem group" living in "two worlds"—caught between their "old" culture and the mainstream (Tyyskä 2009).

In addition to age and ethnic background, peer networks are socially structured by other sociological variables such as gender and social class. Research on girls' friendships uncovers a set of social rules, including "reliability, reciprocity, commitment, confidentiality, trust, and sharing" (Hey 1997). Tensions are also observed as girls balance the ethics of friendship with both vying for social position and responding to the male gaze. It is further noted that the ethical rules and foci of girls' cliques vary according to their social class. "Niceness" or getting along with everyone is associated with middle-class femininity, whereas working-class girls tend to present a tougher image and manage their conflicts more openly (Aapola, Gonick, and Harris 2005; Tyyskä 2009).

Schools

As a key socializing agent, schools provide a social environment that is separate from the family, and teachers and schoolmates widen our early learning and experiences. Consequently, a major socializing dimension of schools encompasses its many informal and social elements,

SOCIOLOGY in ACTION

Project Teen Canada and the Emerging Millennials

Project Teen Canada has surveyed more than 5000 Canadian teenagers every eight years since 1984. These surveys examine a wide range of topics of relevance to the everyday lives of teens, such as their values, attitudes, and behaviour. Study findings are made available to all participating schools and to the general public, as well as to a wide range of government departments, educators, and youth workers.

In a recent book entitled *The Emerging Millennials: How Canada's Newest Generation Is Responding to Change and Choice* (2009), sociologist and author Reginald Bibby (University of Lethbridge) summarizes Project Teen Canada 2008. These data came from a sample of 5564 teenagers (aged 15 to 19) who were in secondary schools. A special supplemental over-sample of more than 800 students in Aboriginal schools was also included.

A unique feature of the book is that educator Ron Rolheiser offers responses to each chapter, along with Sarah Russell, an RCMP community relations officer and a former Project Teen Canada research associate. The book also examines the impact of the baby-boomer legacy and compares this generation with those born since the 1980s.

Notable social trends include:

- Top-rated interpersonal values: (1) trust (84 per cent); (2) honesty (81 per cent); (3) humour (75 per cent).
- Sources of influence: Virtually all (92 per cent) of teens perceive that "the way that they were brought up" has influenced their lives "a great deal" or "quite a bit," followed by parents (especially moms), friends, characteristics born with, other adults, music, reading, teachers, television, god/some supernatural force, luck, the Internet, what people in power decide, and advertising.
- Friendship is everything: 72 per cent of teenagers report having four or more close friends; only 1 per cent report having "no close friends."
- Keeping in touch (daily): cellphone (54 per cent); text message (44 per cent); Facebook (43 per cent); email (42 per cent); YouTube (27 per cent).
- Let's talk about sex: 56 per cent state that they have never had sex; the highest rates of sexual activity were found in the North and in Quebec.
- Losing their religion: Quebec teens (22 per cent) were the least likely to "definitely" believe in god, compared to 41 per cent in the rest of Canada, although 54 per cent of Canadian teens acknowledge that they have spiritual needs. Some 85 per cent also say they expect to have a religious wedding ceremony.

SOURCE: Selected material extracted from Project Teen Canada website (www.ptc08.com) and Bibby, Reginald, with Sarah Russell and Ron Rolheiser 2009.

including interactions among students and between teachers and students. On a micro level, the school also plays an important role in political socialization, since it inculcates children with the basic beliefs and values of their society. On a macro level, the educational system provides an allocation function as it channels students through programs of occupational preparation into various positions in the socio-economic and labour structure of society.

In modern society, the role of the school in the socialization process has become even more pronounced. It is relatively common for children under the age of five to attend some type of daycare or pre-school program. According to the Canadian Council on Learning, these experiences provide cognitive, language, socio-emotional, and motor learning that can significantly affect future development. Further, the amount of specialized technical and scientific knowledge required to participate in society has expanded well beyond what parents can teach in the home. Post-secondary education is now an expected part of many young people's lives. And while critics note that this trend has delayed the transition to adulthood and created greater dependency on parents for economic and housing support, benefits are also documented. Living at home with parents, for instance, can help young adults while they attend school and create more peer-like intergenerational socialization experiences (Mitchell 2006).

Yet, as previously mentioned, not all Canadian children have the opportunity to achieve higher levels of education. A recent report on Toronto high school students showed alarmingly high dropout rates among black and Aboriginal youths as well as those with Portuguese, Hispanic, and Middle Eastern backgrounds (Brown 2010). There is also concern over the sizable inequalities in educational pathways of First Nations youth, which can be traced to a legacy of colonization, marginalization, and discrimination. Overall, as presented

(© iStockphoto.com/CEFutcher)

The classroom provides a unique opportunity for socialization separate from the family. Here, interactions between students and teachers widen our early learning and experiences.

TABLE 3.1 ▼ Educational Pathways of Population Groups (%)

	No Post-Secondary	Community College	University	N*
Canadian-born				
European	28	35	37	16,342
First Nations	50	29	21	573
African/Latin American	36	41	23	209
East Asian	11	11	78	185
Other Asian	17	26	58	347
Immigrant				
European	28	29	43	406
African/Latin American	31	41	28	121
East Asian	18	14	68	198
Other Asian	34	32	34	331
Total	28	34	38	18,712

*N = unweighted sample size; further methodological details can be found in Statistics Canada, 2006, "Youth in transition survey (YITS) Cohort B—20–22-year-olds cycle user guide" (Ottawa: Statistics Canada).

SOURCE: Adapted from Victor Thiessen, 2009, "The pursuit of postsecondary education: A comparison of First Nations, African, Asian, and European Canadian youth," *Canadian Review of Sociology* 46 (1): 5–40 (Table 1, p.11).

in Table 3.1, racialized youths, visible minorities, and immigrants (with the exception of Asian students) are less likely to attend college and university (Thiessen 2009).

It is argued that the continuation of unequal educational patterns and experiences lies in the institutionalization of classism, racism, and sexism. Tyyskä (2009) asserts that this is manifested in a pro-middle-class and Eurocentric male mentality that dominates the educational system. One aspect of this is the "hidden curriculum," which refers to implicit messages in education that may not be consciously taught or planned. These messages emphasize "dominant" societal values (such as competition and that our society's way of life is morally good) and social hierarchies based on social class, gender, race, and sexual orientation. The hidden curriculum also perpetuates certain attitudes and practices that create a cultural and social ethos that prevents the full and equal participation of subdominant groups, such as course streaming (e.g., gender tracking), lack of teachers' positive attention, biased testing procedures, and discriminatory practices on the part of guidance counsellors.

In contemporary schools, other pressing issues of concern with respect to student social interactions and how they affect learning and identity include sexual and gender harassment, bullying, and school violence. Bullying, harassment, and social isolation are more commonly experienced by children who differ from the social norm or are perceived as different. "Gay bashing" and the use of homophobic language, for example, is highly prevalent in many schools.

TIME to REFLECT

Why do children bully other children? Consider how various socializing agents play a role in this behaviour. What do you think might prevent children from bullying or from being bullied? For example, should we specifically target "at risk" children, their families, or the school system?

Mass Media

Television, computers, newspapers, radio, magazines, and entertainment such as movies are readily available and constitute another powerful source of socialization. The media environment experienced by children today is vastly different from the one their parents or grandparents faced. As noted by Strasburger, Wilson, and Jordan (2009), terms such as *digital television*, *gangsta rap*, and *Google* did not even exist several decades ago. Children can now participate

UNDER the WIRE

Digital Communications and Social Identities

The concept of social identity is central to understanding the influence that digital information technologies have on social relations. . . . As they are increasingly integrated into everyday life, digital communication technologies have become a significant medium through which children and young people learn about themselves and their relationships to others and the world. Young people's relationships with friends, family, and institutions are conducted in part through the use of cell phones and the Internet. These technologies have become a medium through which meaning and social identities are constructed.

There are two key ways in which information technologies do this. First, digital technologies open up the available positions that individuals can take because they create new social spaces (which are often referred to as 'virtual'). Second, because identity is formed (and performed) through and within the shifting patterns of connections with others, digital technologies offer a wider and different range of possibilities for connecting and communicating with others compared with face-to-face relationships, and hence they increase the possibilities for performing identities.

. . . Digital information technologies provide powerful media through which stories of identity can be narrated: mobile phones, email, chat rooms, and websites such as YouTube and MySpace. Although these spaces are virtual, they nonetheless become part of the everyday practices that are used by significant numbers of young people to construct identities.

Some researchers (Burbules 2004, for example) have challenged the term 'virtual' with regard to digital communications. For many young people the distinction between virtual and real is helpful, it should also be applied to older communication technologies. Pen and paper have traditionally been used for the construction of narratives of identity through letters and diaries. The virtual dimension of these older communication technologies and their role in providing ambiguous spaces for identity construction and performance are illustrated through the contemporary use of surviving letters to construct new interpretations and narratives about people's lives. The point is that the performance of identities always occurs through communication with others, regardless of the medium available; identities do not exist totally apart from everyday life (reality).

. . . Digital communication has also become a tool for furthering what Harris (2004) calls 'the culture of celebrity' (promoted by many television shows). Some young women (and young men, although considerably fewer) have used the available and relatively inexpensive technology of the Internet and web cameras to promote themselves as celebrities, using filmed segments of their everyday lives and turning a private space (such as a bedroom or kitchen) into a very public space that is accessible to viewers on a world scale. Harris (2004) comments that this use of the webcam has turned the electronic surveillance now used in schools, streets, malls, and shops into a tool for their own use and gratification.

SOURCE: Abridged from White, R., J. Wyn and P. Albanese (2011).

(© iStockphoto.com/adipelcz)

There is considerable debate surrounding the idea of the Net Generation and whether or not the education system should be altered to suit their changing abilities and needs.

in a much wider range of media-related activities than ever before, including online social networking, texting, and viewing digitally recorded photographs and home movies. Overall, the sheer proliferation of media outlets and technologies and the amount of time people spend exposed to these outlets has risen dramatically.

Although the adoption of social media has been rapid and widespread, rates and types of usage can vary among socio-demographic groups. As shown in Figure 3.3, children aged 8 to 10 are exposed to the media an average of 7.5 hours a day compared to 11.5 hours for those aged 11 to 14. Other research shows that Internet usage is especially prevalent among younger age groups compared to those aged 65

▼ FIGURE 3.3 Average Amount of Time Spent with Each Medium in a Typical Day

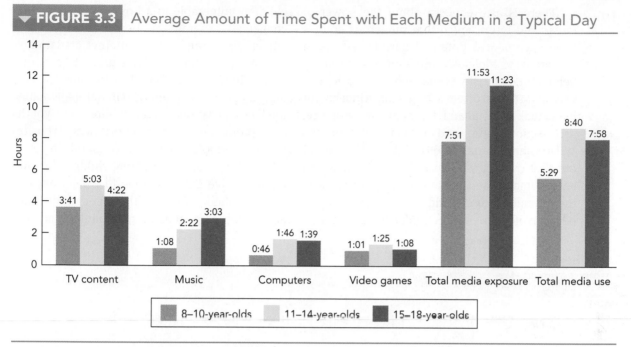

SOURCE: Victoria J. Rideout, Ulla G. Foehr, and Donald F. Roberts, *Generation M²: Media in the Lives of 8- to 18-Year-Olds* (Menlo Park, CA: Kaiser Family Foundation, 2010, p. 5), www.kff.org/entmedia/upload/8010.pdf

and over. Further, Canadian adults aged 55+ are more likely to watch television every week compared to those aged 18 to 34, and those with a university education watch significantly less television per week than those with less education (Ipsos Reid 2010).

Social scientists observe that media and technology influences have always been controversial. On the positive side, the media can be educational, informative, and entertaining and can provide new avenues for social interaction. Parents who are physically distant from their children can interact and "visit" their children via Internet software programs or "keep tabs" on their whereabouts and safety through cellphones and text messaging. Friendships and social support groups can also be formed and maintained via social network sites on the Internet.

However, there is concern that these technologies exert too much control over our daily lives and that they contribute to unhealthy behaviours. By way of illustration, a popular video game series called Grand Theft Auto encourages the player to take on the role of a criminal in a big city and engage in numerous illegal activities, such as killing police. Women are typically depicted as prostitutes and men as violent thugs, stereotypes that appear in other media venues (Dill and Thill 2007). (See Table 3.2.) Other critics link media exposure to the significant rise in

childhood obesity and (at the opposite end of the spectrum) to eating-related disorders such as anorexia nervosa and bulimia. It is argued that unhealthy images influence behaviour through advertising (e.g., foods with little nutritive value) and because of celebrity role-modelling (e.g., stick-thin actresses and models).

TABLE 3.2 ▼ Content Analysis of Video Game Magazine Character Stereotypes[1]

Characterization	Male (%)	Female (%)
Aggressive	82.6	62.1
Sexualized	0.8	59.9
Scantily clad	8.1	38.7
Sex role stereotype*	33.1	62.6
Portrayal of aggression		
Military	4.1	0.0
Fighting	33.2	16.2
Glamorized violence**	31.6	30.6
Wearing armour	41.9	35.6

[1]Video game magazines analyzed were those ranked by Amazon.com as their six top sellers (on sale January 2006).

*Sex role stereotype refers here to the beauty stereotype for the female characters and to the hypermasculine stereotype (i.e., exaggeration of "macho" characteristics) for the male characters.

**Refers to posing with a weapon.

SOURCE: Data drawn from Karen E. Dill and Kathryn P. Thill, 2007, "Video game characters and the socialization of gender roles: Young people's perceptions mirror sexist media depictions," *Sex Roles* 57: 851–64 (Table 1, p. 858).

There is also concern about the power of music and lyrics, given that numerous studies have documented potential harmful effects in the areas of violence, smoking and drinking behaviour, and risky sexual activity. Music television (MTV) is often a target of criticism for its sexual content and for depicting violence, promiscuous sex, and sexism (Strasburger, Wilson, and Jordan 2009). Other critics point out that overall, we live in a society in which sexual images and content (e.g., pornography, the sexualization of children) are predominant because of these new technologies. This makes children vulnerable to a host of new risks and challenges, ranging from health problems (e.g., addictions, depression) to Internet predators.

And as media industries grow, Strasburger et al. (2009) assert that they become increasingly global and commercial in nature. Notably, media corporations target children and youths as a profitable group of consumers. Websites like Nicktropolis (which also contain a lot of advertising) encourage young children to enter an immersive 3-D virtual world where they can create avatars, interact with other cartoon characters (e.g., Spongebob Squarepants), and chat

GLOBAL ISSUES

Globalization, Children, and Media in Times of War and Conflict

In an increasingly global world, even crises and catastrophes that take place in countries thousands of miles away become part of children's daily lives when there is exposure to the news media. News reports from the conflicts in Afghanistan, Chechnya, Iraq, Palestine, Sudan, the former Yugoslavia, to name but a few, as well as events such as the 11 September 2001 attacks on the United States, the bombings of Madrid and London transportation systems, and suicide bombers in Israel, have all been at the centre of world media attention. The sad truth is that war and conflict are an everyday reality for many children all over the globe, either directly or in mediated forms. That violent conflicts have always had detrimental effects on all humans, children included, is self-evident. The physical effects (death, injury, famine, infectious disease, relocation, sexual abuse, and so on), the psychological effect (such as fear, stress, bereavement, post-traumatic reactions, desensitization to suffering, and maladjustment), or even the distant threat of such have proved to have deep and lasting effects on children, even following incidental encounters (Leavitt and Fox 1993).

In her compassionate reflections on the pain of others, Sontag (2003) discusses the meanings of visual portrayals of the suffering of other people in faraway zones of conflicts viewed by privileged and often safe audiences. In her critique, she offers the following observations:

> Being a spectator of calamities taking place in another country is a quintessential modern experience, the cumulative offering by more than a century and a half's worth of those professional, specialized tourists known as journalists. Wars are now also living room sights and sounds. Information about what is happening elsewhere, called "news," features conflict and violence—"If it bleeds, it leads" runs the venerable guideline of tabloids and twenty-four-hour headline news shows—to which the response is compassion, or indignation, or titillation, or approval, as each misery heaves into view (2003, 18).

What is the meaning of this technological and social development? Children hear about, see, and must cope with these troubling, often frightening events that were once only the preserve of adults. They have to endeavour to assimilate the fragments of information they receive from the media and try to make sense of them. They have to deal emotionally with the suffering of others and with gruesome portrayals of atrocities. Children at various ages, developmental levels, media competencies, and personal life experiences have varying skills and cognitive schemes, as well as interests in and experiences with which to make sense of news reports. Clearly, they develop a picture of the events as functions of their personal life history and the media offerings available to them. However, the social-political-cultural environments as well as adult mediation at home and in the educational system also influence them.

SOURCE: Lemish and Götz 2007, 1–2.

with other kids in "real time." Consequently, it is deemed that children are increasingly being socialized to become self-indulgent life-long consumers as well as to form imaginary "para-social" (one-sided) relationships (Chung, Debuys, and Nam 2007).

Finally, socialization also takes place in other institutionalized settings, such as in religious contexts and in the workplace, the latter of which will be discussed in the next section. With respect to religious institutions, Statistics Canada documents that attendance at formal religious services has fallen dramatically over the past several decades, particularly among younger age groups (Lindsay 2008a), a trend that has many implications. Religious norms influence many facets of family life, such as gender roles, parent–child relations, attitudes toward moral issues (e.g., abortion), and how families celebrate rituals and holidays. At the same time, the number of adherents to religions such as Islam, Hinduism, Sikhism, and Buddhism has increased substantially in Canada as the result of changing sources of immigration (Statistics Canada 2001).

> The religious landscape in Canada is constantly evolving. See Chapter 13, "Religion in Profile," p. 255, to better understand what religion looks like in Canada.

TIME to REFLECT

How have your family and religious/spiritual background influenced your current opinions or attitudes with respect to some controversial social issues (e.g., abortion, same-sex marriage, assisted suicide, the death penalty)?

The Life Course, Aging, and Socialization

Throughout this chapter, it has been emphasized that socialization occurs throughout the life course, although the basic, formative instruction occurs fairly early in life. Some of the socialization that takes place during this time is called **anticipatory socialization**, a

term used to refer to how individuals acquire the values and orientations they will likely take up in the future. In childhood, this might include doing household chores, a childhood job, sports, dance lessons, and dating, experiences that give youngsters an opportunity to rehearse for the kinds of roles that await them in adulthood (Newman 2006).

As we age, many other kinds of experiences also give us the opportunity to rehearse for the kinds of adult roles that we might eventually adopt. In particular, many educational or training settings prepare us for our future work roles. A recent ethnographic study by Chappell and Lanza-Kaduce (2010) on police academy socialization explores the socialization that takes place during training to serve on the police force. The researchers found that despite the philosophical emphasis on "community policing" and its powerful themes of decentralization and flexibility, the most important lessons learned in police training are those that reinforce the paramilitary structure and culture.

Socialization to many new roles continues as we age and face new transitions and responsibilities. Older adults, for example, may have to "reverse" and learn new family roles as they care for frail and dependent **aging** parents. Moreover, adjustment to grandparenthood, retirement, and the death of friends and family members, as well as acceptance of the inevitability of one's own death, are part of socialization for aging adults.

TIME to REFLECT

Think back to your first paid work experience. What kinds of skills and "lessons" did you learn? How did your interactions with others on the job (e.g., bosses, co-workers, customers) influence your experience and what you learned?

Socialization Processes: Pawns, Puppets, or Free Agents?

In summary, we have learned that socialization is lifelong and shapes the individual and society. Societal order and continuity rely on

Much like the Canadian Forces basic training, the Cadet Training Program for the Royal Canadian Mounted Police prioritizes fitness, grooming, and discipline.

(© Rolf Hicker / All Canada Photos)

members learning to share norms, values, and language. On an individual level, socialization allows us to realize our potential as human beings. However, because it is such a powerful process, you might ask yourself: To what extent are we free, active agents? Or are we just pawns subject to the invisible hands of larger social forces? This latter view has been called the "oversocialized conception of man," a term coined by American sociologist Wrong in 1961. It reflects a critique of Parsons's functionalist theory of socialization that assumes we passively accept what is taught to us in order to conform to societal norms.

Fortunately, it is well established that while socialization processes have a significant impact on our lives, we are not necessarily prisoners of this process or non-thinking clones. As Peter Berger points out, "unlike puppets, we have the possibility of stopping in our movements, looking up and perceiving the machinery by which we have been moved" (1963, 176). Studies also document that some of us are in a better position (e.g., educationally) than others to decide whether we want to accept what we learn.

Moreover, although we are not completely passive in the socialization process, **resocialization** by **total institutions** can occur. Developed by Goffman (1961), this term refers to any group or organization that has almost total, continuous control over the individual and that attempts to erase the effects of previous socialization. It often denotes a setting in which people are isolated in some way from the rest of society and manipulated by others (e.g., by administrative staff). This might entail brainwashing, religious conversion, military propaganda, physical brutality, and "rehabilitation" programs in prisons and mental hospitals designed to change one's personality.

We are surrounded by total institutions that are designed to modify a person's identity. Do you agree with this approach? For a more complete discussion of Goffman's perspectives on total institutions, see Chapter 4, "Total Institutions," p. 89.

Conclusion

This chapter explored the social experience and what it means to be human. Although there are biological or genetic limits to how socialization shapes us, socialization is an extremely powerful process that makes us functioning, "civilized" members of society. It is a major link between the individual and society, and social relationships are of fundamental importance to our experiences, health, and well-being. Sociologists theorize and study socialization processes at various levels, ranging from day-to-day interactions between individuals to the organization of society as a whole. On an individual level, socialization moulds our tastes and preferences, attitudes and values, and tendencies to act in particular ways in particular situations. Think back to your last family meal or business meeting, for example, and visualize what could have transpired if there were no customs, rules, or rituals governing everyone's behaviour. Similarly, imagine what our society would be like in the absence of such cultural norms and behavioural guidelines.

Another major theme was that beliefs, values, and norms of society are not transmitted through various agents in a uniform, passive, and unidirectional fashion. Diversity is found not only across cultures but also within cultures according to such aspects as family and ethnic background, gender, and age. Further, in line with popular sociological theory, although socialization performs key functions for the individual and society and can perpetuate inequities in society, individuals are not like the fabled lemmings (small rodents) who blindly or unquestioningly follow others. Instead, individuals have some capacity to reflect upon or even resist certain socializing forces, depending on factors such as social and economic position.

Finally, it was emphasized that socialization is a dynamic, lifelong process and that our social experiences change as we age along with other societal transformations. Globalization, rapid population aging, and continuing high rates of immigration in Canadian society may provide the potential to learn and experience an even wider array of roles, identities, and behaviours. Technological advancements in communication and medical fields also mean that our social worlds are constantly shifting, although basic beliefs, norms, and values remain relatively stable with the passage of time.

questions for critical thought

1. Identify some unique socialization experiences of various generations within your family. For example, how did the socialization experience of your grandparents differ from that of your parents and from what you have experienced? Also note any gender differences.

2. The representation of social groups (e.g., by age, gender, race/ethnicity, sexual orientation) in the mass media can be an important socializing experience. Consider how certain groups are portrayed in various media settings (e.g., television, the Internet) and how these portrayals shape our social behaviour (e.g., stereotypes and power relations).

3. What kinds of challenges and opportunities do immigrant children face in trying to become socialized into Canadian society? Consider the role of family and ethnic background, cultural traditions, and values.

4. Recall the last time that you were in a toy store or saw an ad for a child's toy or game. What kinds of toys and games appear to specifically target little boys and little girls? How might this shape gender-role socialization and subsequent behaviours?

5. How might social class shape specific tastes and preferences in food, entertainment, and other activities?

6. Make a list of contradictory lessons that different agents of socialization taught you as a child. How have you resolved these contradictions?

recommended readings

Roberta Berns. 2012. *Child, Family, School, Community: Socialization and Support.* **9th edn. Florence, KY: Wadsworth.**
Examining how the school, family, and community shape children's socialization, this text focuses on issues of diversity. Topics related to culture, ethnicity, gender, sexual orientation, and special needs are addressed, drawing from a social ecological approach.

Norman K. Denzin. 2010. *Childhood Socialization.* **2nd edn. New Brunswick, NJ: Transaction.**
Denzin presents a social psychological exploration of how the lives of children are shaped by social interaction. Emphasis is placed on children's language and the emergence of their self-conception as well as on the role of parents and other caretakers and settings such as daycare centres, playgrounds, and schools.

Gerald Handel, Spencer Cahill, and Frederick Elkin. 2007. *Children and Society: The Sociology of Children and Childhood Socialization.* **Toronto: Oxford University Press.**
A central theme of this book, written from a symbolic interactionist perspective, is the tension between children's active agency and the socializing forces of family, peer groups, school, and mass media and how socialization is shaped by social class, race and ethnicity, and gender.

Mizuko Ito, Sonja Baumer, Matteo Bittanti, et al. 2009. *Hanging out, Messing around, and Geeking out: Kids Living and Learning with New Media.* **Cambridge, MA: MIT Press.**
Grounded in a rich, three-year ethnographic study, this book investigates how young people are learning with new media in settings such the home, after-school programs, and online spaces. Integrating 23 different case studies, such as *Harry Potter* podcasting, video-game playing, music sharing, and online romances, this book offers insight into what it means to grow up in a digital era.

Michael Kimmel and Jacqueline Holler. 2011. *The Gendered Society.* **Canadian edn. Toronto: Oxford University Press.**
This book investigates contemporary gender relations and shows how gender differences are often exaggerated in society. Gender is not viewed as just an element of individual identity but as a socially constructed phenomenon. Students will find the chapter on media and image-driven industries and the portrayal of gender interesting.

recommended websites

MediaSmarts: Canada's Centre for Digital and Media Literacy
www.mediasmarts.ca
The network provides information and resources for anyone interested in media and information literacy. It focuses on such topics as media violence, online hate, media stereotyping, and beauty and body image.

Ontario Federation of Teaching Parents
http://ontariohomeschool.org/socialization.shtml
The Ontario Federation of Teaching Parents provides articles and research on the socialization of home-schooled children in addition to Web links related to various socialization issues in schools.

Sociological Images
www.thesocietypages.org.socimages
Also see www.facebook.com/socimages, www.twitter.com/socimages, www.youtube.com/socimages

Students are encouraged to develop their sociological imaginations through discussions of intriguing visuals that span many topics, including the many postings under the tag "socialization."

Lion's Quest Canada: The Centre for Positive Youth Development
www.lionsquest.ca
Thrive! The Canadian Centre for Positive Youth Development was established in 1988 and is dedicated to fostering positive youth development. Tools to empower and unite caring adults are provided, including programs, products, and training and services for youths, parents, educators, and community leaders.

chapter 4

Social Organization

Dorothy Pawluch, William Shaffir, and Lorne Tepperman

In this chapter, you will:

▶ Be introduced to how sociologists define the terms *status*, *role*, *self*, and *identity*.

▶ Learn how these concepts are interrelated.

▶ Explore themes related to how we define ourselves and others.

▶ Learn about the different sociological "sets" of people.

▶ Understand how groups and cliques function inside larger organizations.

▶ Learn the history of the bureaucratic form of organization.

Introduction

This chapter on social organization is really about two interrelated sociological concerns: how people figure out their personal identity and how people build organizations that give them roles to play and, through those roles, develop identities.

Consider first the question of personal identity. Who am I? Take a moment to think about it. How would you respond? Would you say that you are a woman, man, daughter, son, brother, sister, student, Canadian, atheist, gay? Would you say you are working-class, Aboriginal, or immigrant? Would you say that you are honest, outgoing, shy, athletic, messed up? What difference does it make how you define yourself? How do these definitions affect your experience of life—what you do, the people who are likely to end up around you, how you interact with these people, and how they interact with you?

The study of "social organization" touches on two main questions: (1) How do people typically act in social groupings of different size and purpose? (2) How could we organize social groupings to increase the chances that people will achieve their collective goals? We can address these questions to a wide variety of social groupings ranging in size from (two-person) dyads to cliques, small groups, large groups, social networks, communities, and formal organizations. We will start small and build up to bureaucracies, because large and small organizations are more similar than you might think.

A Functionalist View of Statuses and Roles

A good place to start is by reiterating how structural functionalists understand society. As a macro theoretical perspective, functionalism focuses on entire societies. Functionalists are impressed with how societies organize themselves and persist over time. They are drawn to the part that large-scale structures or institutions, such as the family, religion, and education, play in ensuring that societies endure. The analogy is often made to society as a living organism in which each part contributes to the survival of the whole by serving its own unique function but also by working with other parts.

Just as the heart fulfils the function of pumping blood so that organs receive the oxygen they need to function, so do the "organs" of society play their part to keep societies healthy.

Functionalists underscore the patterned ways in which social institutions are integrated. In response to the question of why people behave in ways that contribute to the integration of society, the functionalist's answer focuses on norms—that is, on sets of socially derived expectations about appropriate behaviour in particular settings. The most important norms are learned in childhood. Later in life, people continue to act in ways that are socially approved. As they enter new social institutions, such as universities, corporations, or organizations, they learn new norms.

Norms in turn are organized around statuses and roles. **Status** refers to the particular social position that an individual holds. All positions occupied by individuals are statuses—hockey player, restaurant server, social worker, or sex trade worker. Attached to every status are one or more roles. **Roles** consist of the responsibilities, behaviours, and privileges connected with the position. In other words, roles are the action elements of status. A status is something we occupy, while a role is something we play. A status describes what one is, while a role describes what one does. "Student" is a status, while studying and attending class are part of the role.

STATUSES

Statuses can be ascribed or achieved. One can be born into a status or have it imposed by nature or by chance; this is an ascribed status. We have little control over whether we are young or old, male or female, black or white. By contrast, other statuses are a matter of choice. We can achieve them through hard work and effort. In our society, most individuals can decide whether to be an entertainer, parent, or vegetarian.

All of us hold many statuses simultaneously. One can be a construction worker, jogger, chess player, and much more at the same time, though not necessarily in the same situation. The cluster of statuses held by any individual at one time is called a status set. People continuously enter into, and exit from, statuses over their lives. As such, status sets are far from fixed—they are regularly reconfigured.

ROLES

The roles connected with any particular status involve both rights and responsibilities. In fact, roles are often organized in such a way that the rights attached to one are linked with the responsibilities of another. Sociologists refer to this as the reciprocity of roles. Members of a sports team have the right to expect training opportunities, expertise, and support from their coach, and a coach has the responsibility to provide these things; on the other hand, coaches have the right to expect commitment and effort from their players, and players are obliged to display the required level of dedication to the team. Parents/children, professors/students, and salespersons/customers are all similarly linked.

Holding different statuses, each with different roles attached, has the potential to create conflict. What happens when the behavioural expectations attached to one role interfere with those of another role? Sociologists refer to this as **role conflict**. Many women today juggle motherhood with a career. Mothering demands devotion to one's children—caring for them, guiding them, and attending to their needs. If they work outside the home, their worker role comes with its own set of demands, including staying late or working on days off if required. To play one role well is to feel that one is letting down those with expectations connected with one's other role.

By contrast, the concept of **role strain** involves competing demands built into a single role, causing tension and stress. For example, multiple expectations are built into most worker roles. For example, lawyers are expected to represent their clients but also to mentor junior colleagues, generate clients, and keep up their billing hours. As in most areas of work, lawyers often feel as though there are not enough hours in the day for them to properly fulfill their duties. Unless they can find some balance, role strain will result.

A functionalist view of roles emphasizes constraints. Although people have some control over the statuses they hold and whether or not to act out institutional roles, they have little choice in *how* to play their roles. Each role comes with pre-existing scripts, demands, and expectations. The scripts are more or less agreed upon by society and do not allow for much flexibility.

Symbolic Interactionism: Roles, Self, Identity

An interactionist view of roles is closely tied to symbolic interactionism, a perspective concerned with how social actors make sense of their worlds. The perspective is captured in three often-cited premises.

From a symbolic interactionist perspective, individuals are constantly involved in assessing and defining things around them and working out how they are going to act. In contrast to the functionalist approach, which sees individuals as buffeted by outside social forces, symbolic interactionism emphasizes how individuals interact to create, sustain, and transform social relationships.

According to symbolic interactionists, human behaviour does not occur in a vacuum but arises out of how social actors define situations. The phrase "definition of the situation" was coined by W.I. and D.S. Thomas (1928, 572), who maintained that "If men define situations as real, they are real in their consequences." The process of defining is ongoing and allows interaction to flow smoothly. Indeed, when a definition of the situation is lacking or unclear, we focus on establishing one that is satisfactory and can help guide ongoing interaction (Shibutani 1961).

The symbolic interactionist approach focuses less on social structure and more on the interactive process. For symbolic interactionists, the conventional approach to roles offers a misleading portrayal of how people actually behave. Statuses and roles, for the interactionist, do not determine social interaction. Rather, they merely provide a context. While human beings make use of norms to guide their interactions, they don't blindly conform to norms. Instead, they engage in ongoing appraisals of what is going on and then act. Individuals carry around a repertoire of roles, determining which of them to use. While they may act within roles, they do so with considerable latitude and flexibility. Far from being locked into particular role configurations or structures, they have the capacity to use and play around with roles.

TIME to REFLECT

How do structural functionalists and symbolic interactionists view roles differently?

TIME to REFLECT

How are role-taking and role-making different? How are they related?

ROLE-TAKING

Two concepts that further emphasize the symbolic interactionist view are **role-taking** and **role-making**. Role-taking is the process by which we co-ordinate or align our actions with those of others. When we engage in role-taking, we put ourselves in the shoes of others and try to determine how they are defining the situation. What roles are they projecting, what meanings are they attaching to the situation, what course of action are they likely to follow? Role-taking also entails looking at ourselves from the point of view of others and trying to anticipate the consequences of our own plan of action. This process continues as we initiate a response. We are constantly monitoring how others are reacting and performing their roles and adjusting or fine-tuning our role performance accordingly. Or we might abandon a particular performance altogether if it isn't working. These ongoing adjustments are what make joint action possible.

ROLE-MAKING

In playing our roles, we do not follow rigid, predetermined, or prewritten scripts. The expectations attached to any given role provide us with a rough guideline at best. There is room for innovation and creativity. Not everyone who performs the role of student does so in precisely the same way as everyone else. Indeed, there is remarkable variability in how the role is played. In this sense, the concept of role-making comes closer than role-playing to describing how we enact our roles.

Role-taking and role-making are linked. There can be no role-making in the absence of role-taking. The construction of a role is impossible without being able to view oneself from the vantage point of another. Behaviour is not simply a matter of repeating pre-set lines of a script, and roles are not merely packages of mandatory behaviour. Roles are perspectives from which people organize lines of behaviour that fit the situation.

THE SELF

We have stressed that symbolic interactionists see human beings as agents, actively defining the things to which they respond. Among the things we define are our selves. Our capacity to role-take means that we can treat ourselves as an object. As with all objects, the meaning we attach to our selves is not fixed but constantly changing. We acquire our sense of **self** by imagining how others see us. This is what symbolic interactionists mean when they say that individuals and society are in a dialectical relationship. Society cannot exist without individuals, but self-aware individuals cannot exist without others (society). Charles Horton Cooley (1902) captures the interdependence between individuals and society in his concept of "the looking glass self." Others (society) are the mirror that reflects back an image of who we are.

According to George Herbert Mead, the capacity to take the role of others is not present at birth but acquired as we develop a self. The self is made up of an "I" and a "Me." The "I" is spontaneous, impulsive, and unsocialized while the "Me" is the socialized part of the self, conscious of social norms, values, and expectations.

The concept of the self is further explained in Chapter 3 under the section "Symbolic Interactionist Frame of Reference," p. 55.

IDENTITY

If the self is an object to which we assign meaning, **identity** refers to the names we give ourselves. Gregory Stone (1962, 93) argues that *identity* is not a substitute word for *self* but instead refers to how an individual casts his or her self as a social object; how an individual tells the self *who* he or she is; and how an individual "announces" to others *what* he or she is. In "announcing" ourselves to others, we enact or suppress certain aspects of our self depending on how we want to come across.

Sociologist Erving Goffman has written extensively about identity. He (1959) analyzes everyday interaction using a dramaturgical approach. Borrowing in a literal sense from the imagery and language of theatre, Goffman argues that every encounter is an occasion for social actors to present one or more of their social roles, much as in a stage performance. Through a process called **impression management**, actors try to shape how others will define them. University of Manitoba sociologists Daniel and Cheryl Albas offer the example of university students receiving their grades on exams. Those who have done well—the *aces*—engage in behaviours like "sitting tall" at their desks, grinning broadly, and walking jauntily. Those who have done poorly or failed—the *bombers*—use these behaviours to figure out who to avoid, since they do not want to come out of the encounter looking (and feeling) lazy, irresponsible, or "dumb" (Albas and Albas 2003).

Goffman distinguishes between role and role performance. For Goffman, role refers to expected behaviours for those in particular positions. By contrast, role performance reflects the actual behaviour of individuals acting out their roles. Goffman also divides the social world into two regions: front-stage and back-stage. In the front-stage, social actors carefully manage the presentations of themselves that they project to others in the hope of creating a positive impression. A student who wishes to impress attends class regularly, participates in class discussions, and may seek out the professor during office hours. In the back-stage region, the same student is likely to be more relaxed, venting perhaps about the course content or the professor's teaching style. Back-stage behaviour is generally displayed among those with whom we share close social bonds and trust with often unflattering information about ourselves.

IDENTITY WORK

Sociologists have focused considerable attention on how individuals present themselves and construct others. These processes are referred to as *identity work*. We project our identities using appearance, behaviours, talk, and props of various kinds. An interesting example appears in a recent study of the "punk" scene. William Force (2009) points out that there is a gendered quality to identity work among punks. Men wear band shirts or pins and baseball caps, while women wear mainstream clothes with a subversive twist, like re-stitched seams. The messy look that most punks work hard to achieve is described as a "scene cut" on men and "JBF" ("just been fucked") hair on women. Another way to communicate membership in the local punk scene is to own and display punk goods, such as certain music.

TIME to REFLECT

Thinking of a role that is central to how you define yourself, what identity work do you engage in to communicate to others who you are?

Over the past several decades, the body and identity have attracted increasing attention. Sociologists have looked at how we experience our bodies and use them to communicate who we are to others. Leanne Joanisse (2005) studied women who had undergone weight loss surgery for obesity. She found that when the surgery was successful, women reported that they were "new" people. Removing the layers of fat, they explained, brought out their "real" selves (2005, 257).

Michael Atkinson (2006; 2008) looked at men who undergo plastic surgery as a way of dealing with what they consider to be deficient (aged, overweight, unattractive) bodies. It is generally assumed that cosmetic surgery is performed almost exclusively on women. However, Atkinson presents data to show that the rate of elective cosmetic surgery among men is rising. Atkinson links the increase to the "crisis of masculinity" or uncertainly about what it means to be a man in the face of gender equity movements, ideologies of political correctness, and attitudes of misandry (male-bashing). In an effort to create what Atkinson calls "a mask of masculinity," men are willing to subject themselves to both invasive (e.g., eyelid surgery, liposuction, hair transplantation) and non-invasive (e.g., chemical peels, hair removal, Botox collagen injections) procedures.

SOCIAL VERSUS PERSONAL IDENTITIES

There can be a gap between the roles we play (social identity) and who we understand ourselves to be (personal identity). Where this gap exists, we may try to distance ourselves from our roles. This role-distancing work can be contrasted with role embracement—situations in which there is such congruence between roles and self-definition that we feel that we *are* our roles.

Another key concept is the authentic self. We typically become aware of our authentic self when we view ourselves as being at odds with normative guidelines concerning appropriate behaviours attached to our roles. In the airline industry, for example, trainers instruct flight attendants in more than serving meals and giving safety instructions. They also train them to control their feelings and expressions in order to shape passengers' emotions, keeping them calm and satisfied. Over time, the forced smiles become divorced from their true feelings. The same must happen to any worker in the service sector—car salespersons, teachers, or entertainers. All require emotional labour both to present themselves and to control the responses of the people they serve.

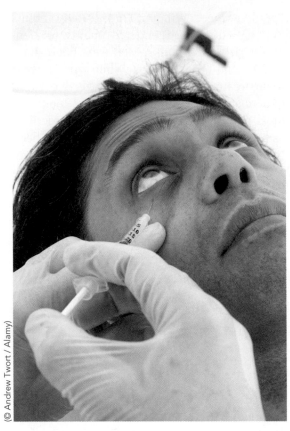

(© Andrew Twort / Alamy)

It is a common misconception that only women choose to have plastic surgery. New research suggests that the way men experience their appearance is pivotal to their self-identity.

UNDER the WIRE

Cellphone Ringtones as Identity Work

You might think that the sole purpose of the ringtone on a cellphone is to signal an incoming call. Not so. Christopher Schneider (2009), a sociologist at the University of British Columbia at Okanagan, describes ringtones as "identity management devices." The ringtone you choose—a clip of your favourite music (classical, hip hop, popular), a line from *The Sopranos*, or the call of an endangered bird—is a way of telling others who you are and what you care about.

Schneider is particularly interested in the use of ringtones by young people. Youths, he insists, are uniquely limited in expressing their identities, especially while they are in school. Drawing on data he collected as a high school substitute teacher, Schneider observed that students downloaded multiple ringtones and switched from one to another much as we choose different outfits depending on the setting and the impression we want to create. Schneider calls this practice *tone shifting*. In certain situations, students would set their cellphones to "silent" or "vibrate" to avoid negative reactions. In spite of these efforts, the students sometimes experienced performance blunders—as when ringtones with crude or sexually explicit lyrics were inadvertently heard by teachers or fellow students who took offence. Schneider calls these situations *identity blitzkriegs*, because they involve the threat that the audience will interpret the information as contradicting the previously formed positive impression. Social interaction can be seriously disrupted, and the effort to create or maintain a favourable impression can be undermined.

PROTECTIVE IDENTITY WORK

How do we shape the view that others have of us in situations in which our identity or actions may invite negative interpretations? In these situations, we often offer disclaimers, accounts, excuses, and justifications. These verbal devices all fall under the category of vocabularies of motive, a concept first used by C. Wright Mills (1940) to describe the standardized forms employed by people to explain and excuse their behaviour. According to Mills, certain stated motives for our actions are more acceptable than others, and how we explain our actions will vary depending on whom we are talking to.

Erving Goffman (1963) too considered the consequences of others' negative views. He pointed out that negative evaluations can be based on physical abnormalities or deformities, membership in a discredited group, or behaviour that deviates from a moral standard. The related concept of courtesy stigma describes a situation in which individuals find themselves dealing with a spoiled identity not by virtue of who they are but because of their connection to someone else whose identity is tainted. Children of "alcoholics," as much as their alcoholic parent(s), often find themselves dealing with the stigmatizing reactions of others.

Deviant labels are consequential, because they generally become a **master status**. Master status, as defined by Everett Hughes (1945), is a status that overshadows all other statuses in terms of how others see us. Someone who suffers from mental illness is more than his/her condition. That person may be a father, mother, business owner, marathon runner. However, in most situations the person will be judged primarily on the basis of the mental illness. Hughes suggested that statuses such as gender, race, class, and age are master statuses. For better or for worse, we generally begin our interactions with assumptions about who people are on the basis of these characteristics. Deviant statuses work in the same way in that they have the power to shape how others see and interact with us.

See Chapter 5, "The Process of Labelling," p. 105, for more information on deviant labels and the master status.

TABLE 4.1 ▼	Sykes and Matza's Techniques of Neutralization
Denial of responsibility	"I'm not to blame."
Denial of injury	"No one got hurt."
Denial of victim	"They deserved it."
Condemning the condemners	"Who are you to judge me?"
Appealing to a higher loyalty	"I didn't do it for me."

According to Sykes and Matza (1957), techniques of neutralization are ways of thinking that allow social actors to maintain a non-deviant image in the face of social disapproval. Based on their research on youth offenders, Sykes and Matza identified five such techniques (see Table 4.1).

TIME to REFLECT

Think of a transgression you have committed—buying an essay, lying to a friend, and so on. What technique(s) of neutralization did you use?

IDENTITY CHANGE

Sociologists are also interested in how individuals move through statuses, roles, and identities. Anselm Strauss (1959) referred to these movements as *status passages* and to the key junctures along the way as *turning points*. According to Strauss (1959, 93), turning points are critical incidents that signal to individuals "I am not the same as I was, as I used to be." How these turning points are experienced depends on whether the changes are voluntary or involuntary, desirable or undesirable, important or insignificant, sudden or gradual, planned or unexpected, reversible or irreversible, and individual or collective (Sandstrom, Martin, and Fine 2006, 77).

An example is offered in a study by William Shaffir (1991) comparing the experiences of secular Jews who decide to become Orthodox Jews (*baalei teshuva* in Hebrew) with those of Jews born into ultra-Orthodox communities who choose to pursue a more secular way of life (*haredim*). There were significant parallels.

SOCIOLOGY in ACTION

Protecting the Self: Stigma Management Strategies

Sociologists who have studied how human beings manage stigmatized identities have shown how endlessly creative we are in developing self-protective strategies:

- Ex-politicians deal with the stigma of defeat by attributing their loss to their political party, the party leader, the party's unpopular decisions, unfair media coverage, or even the timing of the election itself (Shaffir and Kleinknecht 2005).
- Male cheerleaders try to counter the stigma of being men in a "women's" sport by emphasizing the physical stamina required, displaying aggression, and sexually objectifying their female teammates in comments about the great opportunity the sport affords to meet "hot" girls and "grab butts" (Bemiller 2005).

- Pit bull owners deal with courtesy stigma by trying to pass their dogs off as another breed, emphasizing their dogs' personality (cuddly, sweet, docile) over their muscular appearance, and avoiding accessories like studded leather collars and muzzles (Twining, Arluke, and Patronek 2000).
- Students who work as strippers use their socially acceptable identity as "student" to avoid seeing themselves as they know most others see them—that is, as "sleazy." They frame their dancing as a temporary occupation, something they do so that they can afford to stay in school. They are particularly eager to make this clear to customers and co-managers. With others, they carefully manage information about their stripping (Trautner and Collett 2010).

Both processes involved a radical transformation in lifestyle, relationships with others, and self-definition. But there were also significant differences. The *baalei teshuva* changed their behaviours before completely redefining themselves. Outwardly, they adopted the appropriate behavioural trappings of Orthodox Judaism, including dress, language, study, and prayer, while inwardly they were still realigning their understanding of themselves. This sequence was reversed for the *haredim*, who took on a more secular lifestyle only after going through a process of questioning their authenticity as part of the *haredi* community.

At the other end of the continuum is how individuals experience leaving roles and identities behind. The process of exiting from a social role and shedding an identity has been studied by Helen Rose Ebaugh (1988). Ebaugh studied various sorts of "ex's": those who had exited occupational roles (ex-nuns, ex-doctors, alumni, retirees), family roles (divorcees, mothers without custody of their children), and deviant roles (ex-convicts, ex-alcoholics, and transsexuals). She developed a model that divides the exiting process into four stages. In the first stage, *first doubts*, individuals question the roles and identities that they have taken for granted. These doubts can be precipitated

by disappointments, burnout, organizational changes, or changing relationships with others. The second stage, *seeking and weighing alternatives*, involves considering options, weighing the pros and cons, seeking out new reference groups, and in some cases rehearsing new roles. In the third stage, *turning point*, individuals decide that there is no turning back and are ready to "announce to the world" that they have left an old role behind. In the final stage, *creating an ex-role*, individuals adjust to the new self-definitions, working out how to manage such issues as dealing with one's own and others' expectations attached to the hangover identity.

TIME to REFLECT

Think of a role that you have exited. Do Ebaugh's four steps describe your experience?

Now we turn to the discussion of social forms, through which people express their personal identities in social settings.

A founder of sociology, Georg Simmel, defined social interactions and social forms—the essential features of groups and organizations—

as the basic subject matter of sociology. Simmel noted that these two elements are only distinguishable analytically. One element is the purpose or motive of interaction. The other is the *form* through which the interaction communicates its meaning. This is important, because groups and organizations work similarly despite differences in size and purpose.

Fashion is a good example, because it speaks to both interactions and form at the same time. Fashionable dress allows people to display themselves in a way that (they feel) displays their individuality, yet fashion, by nature, is social. The group as a whole decides what is in or out of fashion. Individuals themselves cannot make fashion—they can only select from it and try to personalize it.

Sets of People, Differently Organized

Imagine five sets of 20 people. Call them *categories*, *networks*, *communities*, *groups*, and *organizations*. Sociologists study these five sets differently, because they are organized differently and have different effects on their members.

CATEGORIES

First, imagine that these 20 people are a mere collection of people unconnected with one another—say, a random sample of Canadian 19-year-olds—but fall into the same category: in this case, they are the same age.

This sample of teenagers is of interest to sociologists if they represent the attitudes and behaviours of 19-year-olds across the country. Knowing these attitudes and behaviours may help to predict the future behaviour or explain the current behaviour of 19-year-olds. Categories only become sociologically interesting when people dramatize (or socially construct) meanings for the differences between one category and another. No such meaningful boundaries exist for 19-year-olds compared with 18- and 20-year-olds. However, important cultural boundaries exist between the categories named "male" and "female," "young" and "old," and, in some societies, "white" and "black." As a result, these categories assume social importance.

NETWORKS

Generally, sociologists are more interested in what they call **social networks**. Imagine the same 20 people all connected to one another, whether directly or indirectly. By *direct connections*, we mean links of kinship, friendship, and acquaintance. *Indirect connections* are also of interest to sociologists. In fact, some sociologists, such as Mark Granovetter (1974), argue that *weakly tied networks*, based largely on indirect links, may be even more useful than *strongly tied* or *completely connected networks*. Information, social support, and other valuable resources flow through incompletely connected, or weakly tied, networks.

In recent years, Internet-based social networking services such as LinkedIn, Friendster, and Facebook have rapidly increased in popularity. These services collect information from an individual's profile and their list of social contacts to create a display of their personal social network. Such networking services claim that by allowing members to "get to know one's friends of friends [they can] expand their own social circle" (Adamic and Adar 2005, 188). Increasingly, people are setting up virtual networks of relationships in cyberspace as well as real ones.

Social networks are important and interesting. However, much of social life is not well understood in terms of networks. That is because networks lack several key characteristics. First, people in networks lack a sense of collective identity, such as a community would have. Second, people in networks lack an awareness of their membership and its characteristics, such as a group would have. Third, people in networks lack a collective goal, such as an organization would have.

COMMUNITIES

Sets of people with a common sense of identity are typically called **communities**. Imagine a community of only 20 people—say, a community of like-minded people living together on the land (perhaps a hippie commune in 1960s British Columbia or a utopian farming community in nineteenth-century upstate New York) or in the city (perhaps a community of anarchist or bohemian youths living in a broken-down squat in twenty-first-century Amsterdam).

American popular artists Currier and Ives captured nineteenth-century North American conceptions of "community," in this case the pleasure of sharing one another's company in a simple holiday pastime—skating on the frozen river.

They are likely to be people drawn together by common sentiments, or they may be people who have grown up together and share strong values uncommon in the rest of society. The nineteenth-century German sociologist Ferdinand Tönnies (1957 [1887]) distinguished community life, which he called *Gemeinschaft*, from non-community life, which he called *Gesellschaft*.

Gemeinschaft refers to the typical features of rural and small-town life. They include a stable, homogeneous group of residents with a strong attachment to one particular place. The *Gemeinschaft* is marked by dense or highly connected networks, centralized and controlling elites, and multiple social ties.

By contrast, city life is characterized by *Gesellschaft*. This kind of organization brings together a fluid, diverse group of residents with different personal histories and impersonal, brief relationships. They interact around similar interests, not similar characteristics or histories. They share few moral values and few moral guardians to enforce a common moral code. In short, people who live in a *Gesellschaft* are less cohesive and, largely for this reason, less controlled.

Sociologists since Tönnies have debated whether *Gesellschaft*—especially city life—represents a loss of community or a new kind of community. Most sociologists today believe that people are not as isolated and atomized in large cities as once thought. Rather, most city-dwellers form small communities based on friendship, whether they are residentially close or scattered.

GROUPS

What all groups share is an awareness of membership. Members are connected with one another (directly or indirectly) and, to varying degrees, communicate, interact, and conduct exchanges with one another.

Sociologists have long distinguished between primary groups and secondary groups (Cooley (1962 [1909]). *Primary groups* are small and marked by regular face-to-face interaction; an example is a family household. *Secondary groups* are larger, and many members may not interact with one another regularly.

All small or primary groups have similar characteristics and patterns, whatever their purpose or goal. For example, they are all based on intense, face-to-face interaction, and the members tend to identify with one another. People identify closely with the group and with one another and find it hard to leave or betray the group.

Teams, bands, and gangs (let's use the abbreviation TBG) are three types of larger groups. Unlike families, they do not always command our primary social loyalty. However, many people consider the teams, bands, and gangs they belong to almost like surrogate families. TBGs are very similar, despite the different goals of their members. Each TBG has a clear set of goals and main activities as well as a leadership structure. One or more leaders have the job of setting goals, mobilizing resources to achieve these goals, and motivating members to take part, according to group rules. TBGs also have a simple political

structure (with leaders and followers), legal system (with procedures to resolve conflicts), economy (with a treasury and assets), and culture (with a shared memory of great events, heroes, and villains).

Nowhere is the influence of group membership more evident than in the realm of deviant behaviour—for example, binge drinking. People—especially young people—tend to drink as much as they think is normal in their group, and if they think it is cool to binge drink, because they believe cool people are binge drinking, that is what they will do, even if it hurts them physically or undermines their studies. So efforts to get students to drink more sensibly and moderately will fail unless they address the group dynamic that makes excessive drinking seem not just normal but ideal.

Secondary groups, though less strongly integrated, are no less important. We spend most of our waking hours as members of secondary groups, interacting, communicating, and exchanging resources with other people. Like primary groups, they bind people in fairly stable patterns of social interaction. Formal organizations are subtypes of secondary groups. In turn,

OPEN for DISCUSSION

Binge Drinking Is Especially Awesome for Wealthy, White College Guys

According to a survey of about 1600 undergraduate students attending and revelling at "a selective Northeastern residential liberal arts college" in 2009, binge drinking had a strong correlation to students' social satisfaction, and those students who were best able to maximize their social satisfaction were wealthy, white males . . . According to [sociologist] Carolyn L. Hsu, "Binge drinking is a symbolic proxy for high status in college." . . . It's [binge drinking is] what the most powerful, wealthy, and happy students on campus do. . . . When lower status students binge drink, they may be trying to tap into the benefits and the social satisfaction that those kids from high **status groups** enjoy.

The big binge drinking winners were white, wealthy, Greek-affiliated, heterosexual, and male students, though those who didn't binge drink weren't nearly as happy or affable. . . . As for the other social groups on campus, researchers asked them to assess their social satisfaction through a survey that asked them to gauge their overall social experience on campus. LGBTQ students, for instance, generally found campus to be an . . . unwelcoming environment, [and] women, though more academically successful than their Hellenic male classmates, were more likely to experience **prejudice** and sexual harassment once they ventured beyond the classroom . . . Most surprising to researchers, however, was that not many students were self-medicating with alcohol—those students with the most stress or anxiety were the least likely to drink. Binge drinking at college is a form of social currency, a way for the privileged to flaunt their status and offer the downtrodden a shining example of glamorous dissolution.

SOURCE: Abridged from Barry 2012.

bureaucracies are subtypes of formal organizations. So in the end, almost everything in this chapter—except the discussion of cliques—is about secondary groups.

ORGANIZATIONS

Organizations are secondary groups with a collective goal or purpose. An organization can be a giant multinational corporation, like General Motors, or a small corner variety store; a political party or a government; a church, a school, or a sports club. Given the endless variety of organizational forms and the millions of specific examples, what do all organizations have in common?

Every organization comprises a group of people working together, co-ordinated by communication and leadership to achieve a common goal or goals. At the same time, organizations vary a lot. For example, organizations may come together spontaneously or deliberately. The division of labour within organizations may be crude or complex. The communication and leadership may be *informal* or *formal*. Organizations may have a specific goal or various loosely related goals.

TIME to REFLECT

How is a primary group, like a clique or family, different from a secondary group, like an organization? How they are similar?

One important distinction to make about organizations is between spontaneous and formal organizations. A **spontaneous organization** arises quickly to meet a single goal and then disbands when the goal is achieved. Perhaps the most commonly cited examples of spontaneous organizations are bucket brigades and search parties. They each have a single goal—such as keeping a barn from burning down or finding a lost child. Each arises spontaneously, and its leaders emerge informally, without planning. Each has a crude division of labour—for example, filling buckets, passing them along, emptying them on the fire. Each disappears when the job is completed. Mobs, such as those formed to riot in Vancouver after the final Stanley Cup game in 2011, also fall into the category of spontaneous organization.

Cliques

DEFINING THE CLIQUE

Organizations with unstated goals and/or little division of labour are considered **informal organizations**. One familiar example is the clique. Dictionaries define *clique* as "a small exclusive set," a "faction," a "gang," or a "noisy set." In current sociological thinking, a "clique" is a group of tightly interconnected people—a friendship circle whose members are connected to one another, and to the outside world, in similar ways. Clique members spend more time with one another than with non-clique members, share their knowledge, and think and behave similarly. In short, cliques are built on friendship and the exclusion of "outsiders." They survive largely through what psychologist Irving Janis (1982) called "groupthink."

Though seemingly without goals, cliques have an unstated "mission" or purpose: to raise the status of clique members at the expense of non-members. Though lacking an organizational chart or stated division of labour, school cliques (for example) have a clear hierarchy of influence and popularity, with the leader on top surrounded by his or her favourites. In this sense, then, a clique is a group of people working together and co-ordinated by communication and leadership to achieve a common goal or goals.

CLIQUES IN SCHOOL SETTINGS

Cliques are not only organizations: they are communities and miniature societies. In cliques, children first learn the rules and expectations of society outside their family home. Through games and play with clique members, children internalize the beliefs, values, and attitudes of their group. By these means, children also form judgments of themselves. For example, they learn what it means to be "good-looking," "sexy," and "popular," to be chosen or passed over (Crockett, Losoff, and Petersen 1984).

Cliques, though often supportive, can also offer excellent examples of structured cruelty. It was perhaps unavoidable that the reach of cliques would extend into cyberspace. Online bullying by clique members is a new phenomenon and potentially just as damaging as the

Stop a Bully is a not-for-profit organization that delivers an anti-bullying program nationwide. The program allows students to safely report bullying, helping schools to be more effective at preventing serious bullying.

bullying that occurs face-to-face. With online or e-bullying, youths can constantly harass their victims using text messaging on cellphones and postings on bulletin boards and blogs.

The cohesion of a clique is based both on loyalty to the leader and on loyalty to the group. This loyalty, in turn, is based as much on exclusion as it is on inclusion. Clique members use gossip to reinforce their ignorance of outsiders and keep social distance from them.

Bureaucracies

FORMAL ORGANIZATIONS

Organizations are *formal* if they are deliberately planned and organized. Within formal organizations, roles and statuses provide the skeleton for all communication and leadership. Often, formal organizations have multiple goals, and they usually have a long lifespan. The Roman Catholic Church is a formal organization that has lasted nearly 2000 years.

We can define a **formal organization** as a deliberately planned social group that co-ordinates people, capital, and tools through formalized roles, statuses, and relationships to achieve a specific set of goals.

The most successful form of organization in the past century or so has been the **bureaucracy**. The word calls to mind images of red tape, books of rules and regulations, inefficient and unwieldy groups moving at a tortoise-like pace. To sociologists, however, bureaucracies are merely formal organizations that thrive everywhere in modern societies because they are *relatively* efficient and effective.

THE EMERGENCE OF THE BUREAUCRATIC FORM OF ORGANIZATION

It was obvious to Max Weber—the first sociologist to study bureaucracies—that this form of organization held enormous advantages over earlier organizational forms. Because of its formal characteristics, the bureaucratic organization holds the potential for rational planning. Bureaucracies can state clear goals, plan team strategies, train the most able people, mobilize the needed resources, evaluate effectiveness, and carry out organizational improvements. How different this makes IBM or the University of British Columbia—both bureaucracies—from the Italian mafia or the court of Louis XIV, which are patron–client organizations!

THE CHARACTERISTICS OF BUREAUCRACY

Weber (1958 [1922]) identified seven essential characteristics of bureaucracy in his classic work on the topic:

- Division of labour
- Hierarchy of positions
- Formal system of rules
- Reliance on written documents
- Separation of the person from the office
- Hiring and promotion based on technical merit
- Protection of careers

▼ FIGURE 4.1   Bureacracy

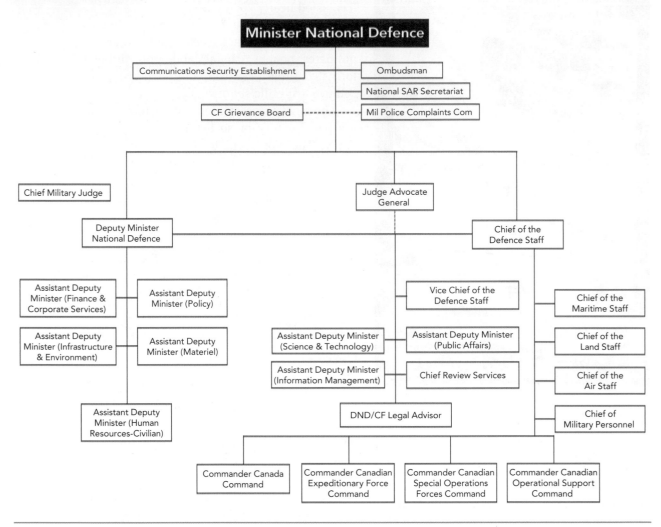

SOURCE: DND Organization Chart, Department of National Defense, 2012. Reproduced with the permission of the Minister of Public Works and Government Services Canada, 2013.
NOTE: CMS, CLS and CMP are also Commanders of Maritime, Land Force, Air and Military Personnel Commands respectively.

Division of Labour

In earlier eras, workers handcrafted specific articles from start to finish to produce society's goods. Gradually, this production process gave way to specialization and a detailed division of labour. A specialized division of labour became the foundation of modern industry and bureaucratization. An automotive assembly line is perhaps the typical modern example of such a division of labour.

As on an assembly line, every member of a bureaucracy performs named and identified duties. The bureaucracy itself provides the facilities and resources for carrying out these duties. Workers work with equipment they do not own; in other words, they are separated from the **means of production**, as Marx had already noted.

Hierarchy of Positions

We can imagine the structure of an organization as a pyramid, with authority centralized at the top (see, for example, the organizational chart in Figure 4.1). Authority filters down toward the base through a well-defined hierarchy of command. Within this hierarchy, each person is responsible *to* a specific person one level up the pyramid and *for* a specific group of people one level down.

The organizational chart of any large corporation is shaped roughly like a Christmas tree. The number of workers increases as you move down toward the bottom of the hierarchy. With the other characteristics of bureaucracy, this feature serves to increase efficiency: all communications flow upward to "control central" from large numbers of workers "at ground level."

TIME to REFLECT

What are the advantages and disadvantages of a bureaucracy? Can you imagine a system that employees would prefer?

Rules

Bureaucracies also work according to written rules. The rules allow a bureaucracy to formalize and classify the countless circumstances it routinely confronts. For each situation, decision-makers can find or develop a rule that provides for an objective and impersonal response. The rules, therefore, guarantee impersonal, predictable responses to specific situations, helping organizations to achieve their objectives.

Separation of the Person from the Office

In a bureaucracy, each person is an officeholder in a hierarchy. The duties, roles, and authority of this office all are clearly defined. For example, the organization spells out the duties of a Level 3 manager in relation to a Level 4 manager (her superior) or Level 2 manager (her subordinate). Thus, the relations between positions in a bureaucracy are impersonal relations between roles, not personal relations between people. This separation of person and office means that people are replaceable functionaries. People come and go, but the organization remains intact. It also means that personal feelings toward officeholders must be subordinated to the impersonal demands of the office.

Hiring and Promotion Based on Technical Merit

An ideal bureaucracy hires employees impartially. Decisions are made based on candidates' technical competence, not on inborn features like gender, race, or ethnicity. Promotion is based on technical competence, or sometimes seniority. People are neither discriminated against nor favoured because of their personalities or connections to the boss.

Protection of Careers

The final characteristic of bureaucracies is that people's careers are protected within them. People can look forward to long careers in a bureaucracy, because they are not subject to arbitrary dismissal for personal reasons. As long as they follow the rules attached to their office or position, they are secure in their job.

MERTON'S BUREAUCRATIC PERSONALITY

Sociologists have found that often bureaucracies do not behave rationally in terms of their long-term interests and survival. This occurs for several reasons.

First, there is the issue of "bureaucratic personalities." As sociologist Robert Merton (1957) pointed out, bureaucracies force their members to conform to rigid bureaucratic rules. This pressure, combined with intensive training, overemphasizes members' knowledge of and adherence to the bureaucracy's rules, which, in turn, makes it easy for bureaucrats to act habitually in routine ways. Inevitably, the routines become similar to blinkers on a horse. Thus, Merton argued, bureaucrats develop a "trained incapacity" for dealing with new situations.

Also, applying the rules means classifying all situations by objective criteria so that they can fit into the correct pigeonhole. The result is that bureaucrats often fail to see clients as people with unique wants and needs, seeing them only as impersonal categories. This viewpoint causes bureaucrats to fail to meet the unique needs of individual clients.

INFORMAL ORGANIZATIONS IN BUREAUCRACIES

Bureaucracy is intended to be an impersonal form of organization; however, bureaucratic roles are filled by actual people. As human beings, workers resist becoming faceless cogs in the bureaucratic machine (replaceable cogs at that). So they develop complex personal and informal networks within the formal organization, creating informal organizations and even cliques within formal organizations.

Informal networks among people who interact on the job serve many purposes. First, they humanize the organization. They also provide support and protection to workers at the lower levels of the hierarchy. They serve as active channels of information flow (the grapevine) and mechanisms for exchanging favours. Paradoxically, informal networks can serve to free people from the limits of formal organization and, occasionally, allow them to protest and subvert their working conditions.

How Bureaucracies Actually Work

Weber's idea of bureaucracy is a useful model for studying this complex form of organization. However, it is an idealization.

Ideally, every member understands his or her role in a bureaucratic network of reporting relationships. In graphic form, as mentioned, a bureaucracy is a Christmas tree–shaped structure that repeatedly branches out as you go down the hierarchy. Thus, at the bottom of the hierarchy there are many people whose job it is to carry out orders from above and report work-related information up the tree to their superiors. At the top of the hierarchy, a few people are responsible for issuing orders, processing information received from below, and preserving links with other organizations.

In practice, organizations do not work this way. There is the ideal or formal structure, which prescribes how a bureaucracy ought to work, and there is an actual, informal structure, which is how it *really* works.

ACTUAL FLOWS OF INFORMATION

In theory, a failure to report information up the hierarchy would never occur. In practice, it occurs all the time, and controlling the flow of information from below is a means of changing the balance of power between superiors and subordinates. And as the French sociologist Michel Crozier (1964) showed, bureaucracies work differently in different societies. This is because people raised in different cultures have different ideas about inequality, deference, openness, and secrecy.

Bureaucracies also appear to work differently for men and women. When playing a managerial role, women often adopt a collaborative approach that draws on qualities learned in family relations. Women's managerial styles stress good employer–employee relations and sharing information and power. By contrast, men are more likely to stress purely economic considerations (Occhionero 1996).

In practice, workers everywhere make friends and acquaintances. As a result, they casually share work information. Often, workers use information purposely to help one another. Sometimes they may even leak information for personal gain or to subvert their boss or the organization as a whole.

TIME to REFLECT

Specifically, how might a bureacracy made up of only women function differently from one of only men?

As in cliques, trust in bureaucracies is built gradually, maintained continuously, and easily destroyed (Lewicki and Bunker 1996). When trust is violated, the result is often revenge, confrontation, withdrawal, or feuding (Bies and Tripp 1996). Within organizations, managers can oversee and enforce rules of reciprocity. Across organizations, rules are harder to enforce. The result is that organizational boundaries tend to limit trust, and this limits the sharing of ideas (Zucker et al. 1996). Within organizations, the flow of information is harder to contain.

TIME to REFLECT

How might an increase in "teleworking" affect the development of trust among workers? How could technology be used to increase trust among workers?

ORGANIZATIONAL CULTURES AND FLEXIBILITY

Organizations need ever-greater flexibility and co-operation from workers. To keep the most able workers, an organization must give them autonomy and rewards for corporate loyalty. Only in this way can they be induced to join, stay, and carry out their duties in conformity with organizational goals.

Some organizations attempt to correct the flaws of bureaucracy by trying to empower their workers. For example, they preach open management, teamwork, continuous improvement, and a partnership between customers and suppliers. Often, however, these tactics aim at obscuring the exercise of power while justifying increased corporate control and a heavier workload.

THE PROBLEM OF RATIONALITY

Over the long term, by making impersonal decisions and rewarding excellence, bureaucracies are able to pursue long-term organizational goals with huge amounts of wealth and power.

However, the sheer size of large bureaucracies and their long-term outlook introduces certain types of irrationality that may also undermine the organization. A concern with the long-term survival of the organization may undermine shorter-term concerns with the quality of decisions, products, and services the organization is providing to its customers. And by creating boundaries between the institution and its environment, the institution may lose touch with its customers—the objects of its efforts (Imershein and Estes 1996).

Another result is the creation of a *bureaucratic personality*— someone willing to ignore ethical concerns in order to follow corporate rules (Ten Bos 1997). This, and anonymity, make moral indifference almost inevitable. As a bureacracy grows and more rules are added, the system becomes increasingly complex. This can lead to a situation in which no one person knows all of the rules. Different offices act independently of each other, creating rules that conflict with one another. The system seems out-of-control.

TOTAL INSTITUTIONS

Total institutions are the ultimate bureaucratic organizations, controlling large numbers of people, 24/7. Including mental hospitals, prisons, residential schools, and military installations, these organizations have a lot in common (Goffman 1961). True, they have different institutional goals and provide different services to society; they also employ different kinds of experts and oversee different kinds of "customers." However, what they have in common organizationally far outweighs these differences. Through the extreme and expert control of human inmates, they are able to bring about identity change through degradation.

What Goffman tells us about mental institutions and prisons reminds us of what we have heard about life in **totalitarian** societies like Nazi Germany and Soviet Russia. Under both Nazism and communism, people are dominated by uncontrollable rulers through government and party bureaucracies (Maslovski 1996). It turns out that totalitarian societies are like Goffman's "total institutions," only larger. It is not surprising they make liberal use of total institutions to punish, brainwash, and resocialize unco-operative citizens.

As Weber warned, modern bureaucratic society is an "iron cage" in which we are all

(© Thinkstock/iStockphoto collection)

In April 2012, the government announced it would close Canada's oldest prison, Kingston Penitentiary. Home to Canada's most notorious criminals, it was designed to simultaneously protect the public and punish the inmates.

trapped by our ambitions for success, efficiency, and progress (1958 [1904], 181). Bureaucracy has enormous potential for enslavement, exploitation, and cruelty. It also has enormous potential for promoting human progress. For example, it can promote economic development and scientific discovery, high-quality mass education, or the delivery of humane social services to the needy. It is to fulfill the second potential that we have risked the first. The jury remains out on whether, in the twenty-first century, the gain has justified the cost.

Conclusion

If sociology is the study of the relationship between the individual and society, there is no question more central than how our statuses, roles, identities, and sense of self connect us to others. Our goal has been to discuss how sociologists have defined and thought about these concepts. We also sought to introduce readers to the types of sociological studies that these concepts have generated.

We started with structural functionalists, explaining the emphasis on statuses, roles, and the more or less predetermined role scripts attached to them. Symbolic interactionists, we went on to explain, reject a view of social actors as mere role players, stressing instead the agency that individuals exercise in deciding what roles to take on and how to play them.

This chapter has also reviewed various "sets" of people, including categories, networks, communities, groups, cliques, and organizations. Sets of people with a common sense of identity are typically called communities. Communities, whether urban or rural, real or virtual, are important, because people are conscious of their membership and make personal investments in remaining members. Formal organizations combine many of the features of networks, groups, cliques, and communities.

The main form of the large, powerful, and long-lived formal organization of the twentieth century is the bureaucracy. The goals of bureaucracy are maximum efficiency and productivity. Largely, bureaucracies achieve their desired goals in the expected ways, but they do so with unwanted side effects.

Finally, this chapter considered total institutions. All of them are organizations that have total control over their "customers"—whether mental patients, nuns, convicts, or soldiers-in-training. Total institutions offer an extreme example of the bureaucratic organization and the bureaucratized society.

questions for critical thought

1. Thinking about the connection between gender and role performance, can you describe how this relationship is shaped by cultural, political, and social contexts both in our society and elsewhere?

2. Can you recall a role you played—son, daughter, boyfriend, girlfriend—that has shifted in how you have played it over time? What prompted the change(s)?

3. Can you think of an instance in which you and/or others felt you had defined a situation inappropriately? What happened? How did you figure out that you had made a mistake? Was the error obvious, or were you able to hide it from others?

4. How might Internet communities, such as comment boards or chat rooms, resemble and affect *Gemeinschaft* and *Gesellschaft*?

5. Robert Bales discovered that in discussion groups, three roles regularly emerged: task leader, emotional leader, and joker. Was he right to infer that the groups "need" these roles to survive?

6. In what ways are bureaucracies rationally and irrationally designed? What kind of organizational system do you think would work more effectively than a bureaucracy?

recommended readings

Michel Crozier. 1964. *The Bureaucratic Phenomenon*. Chicago: University of Chicago Press.
Crozier, a French sociologist, shows that bureaucracies can work differently in different societies and cultures despite their similar organization. Because societies vary—historically, socially, and politically—bureaucracies vary too.

Paul Du Gay. 2005. *The Values of Bureaucracy*. Oxford: Oxford University Press.
This book explores why bureaucracies are such successful, and therefore persistent, organizational structures. The book outlines the characteristics that make bureaucracies efficient in various settings.

Linton C. Freeman. 2004. *The Development of Social Network Analysis: A Study in the Sociology of Science*. Vancouver: Empirical Press.
This book discusses social networks as vast webs of connections between nodes, with huge impacts on the lives of network members.

Anthony Giddens. 1991. *Modernity and Self-Identity: Self and Society in the Late Modern Age*. Stanford, CA: Stanford University Press.
In a clearly argued statement about changes in the experience of self and identity, Giddens emphasizes the challenges of finding an authentic self in a society where trust and intimacy have become problematic.

Erving Goffman. 1959. *The Presentation of Self in Everyday Life*. Garden City, NY: Doubleday.
This is Goffman's classic statement on the dramaturgical approach. "Must" reading for anyone interested in identity work.

John P. Hewitt. 2006. *Self and Society: A Symbolic Interactionist Social Psychology*. 10th edn. Boston: Allyn and Bacon.
This is a good introduction to the central concepts of symbolic interactionism, filled with useful examples that make the perspective accessible to anyone reading about it for the first time.

recommended websites

Cliques in Organizations
http://www.eric.ed.gov/ERICWebPortal/search/detailmini.jsp?_nfpb=true&_&ERICExtSearch_SearchValue_0=EJ078727&ERICExtSearch_SearchType_0=no&accno=EJ078727
This site develops a number of propositions that relate the variables of compliance, mobility, and size to motivation for clique formation.

Community-Based Research
http://communityresearchcanada.ca
This website contains resources for people who support and have an interest in community-based research.

Global Sociology
http://globalsociology.com/tag/identity
This website is maintained by sociologists for those interested in sociological perspectives on globalization, including globalization's effects on identity.

The Mead Project
www.brocku.ca/MeadProject
A useful inventory of documents by or about the founder of symbolic interactionism, George Herbert Mead, and other symbolic interactionists is available on this website.

MIT's Initiative on Technology and Self
http://web.mit.edu/sts/people/turkle.html
This is the website of Sherry Turkle, director of MIT's Initiative on Technology and Self, a centre of research on the relationship between artifacts and identity.

Rumour and Gossip
www.apa.org/science/about/psa/2005/04/gossip.aspx
This website provides useful information about two important means by which people uphold informal social control.

Self-Labelling and Identity
www.youtube.com/watch?v=pxbw7dDMX60
This clip is about how people who have had encounters with the mental health system describe themselves, demonstrating many of the concepts discussed in this chapter.

Shame and Psychotherapy
www.columbiapsych.com/shame_miller.html
This study argues that although shame plays a central role in people's lives, it has been little studied or understood.

Society for the Study of Symbolic Interaction
www.symbolicinteraction.org
This website includes news about a range of conferences related to symbolic interactionism, as well as a link to the journal *Symbolic Interaction*, which regularly publishes papers on self and identity.

Temple Grandin Website
www.templegrandin.com
This is the official website of Temple Grandin, an autistic woman whose life was depicted in an HBO movie of the same name. The movie offers a good example of identity work.

chapter 5

Deviance

Vincent F. Sacco and Alicia D. Horton

Learning Objectives

In this chapter, you will:

▶ Learn to define deviance and social control as sociological concepts.

▶ Identify the major questions that sociological theories of deviance and control are intended to answer.

▶ Examine some of the social and demographic factors that are related to particular forms of deviant conduct.

▶ Learn how behaviours and people come to be labelled as deviant.

Introduction

This chapter has two broad objectives. First, it explains the meaning and use of the terms **deviance** and **social control** in sociological discourse. Second, it focuses on the major theoretical questions that occupy the time and attention of sociologists who study deviance.

What Is Deviance?

Any discussion of the sociology of deviance and social control must begin with some consideration of what these terms mean. Formal sociological conceptualizations of deviance can be contrasted with more popular views that define *deviance* by illustration, statistics, and harm.

BY ILLUSTRATION

When asked to define *deviance*, a first response typically is to list types of people or types of behaviours we think deserve the label. These lists could include criminals, child molesters, drug addicts, alcoholics, cult leaders, chronic liars, and more. The major problem with these stand-alone lists is that they are incomplete and tell us nothing about why some types of people and behaviour are (and why other types are not) included. In short, we are left in the dark regarding the definitional criteria being employed.

IN STATISTICAL TERMS

Statistical rarity suggests a more explicit way of thinking about the meaning of *deviance*. At face value, it makes a certain amount of sense to identify deviance by rarity, since many of the kinds of people we think of as deviant are, in a statistical sense, relatively unusual. A major problem with statistical definitions of deviance is illustrated by Figure 5.1. The area between points X_1 and X_2 represents typical performance levels across some characteristic. The shaded area on the far left represents the minority of statistically rare cases that fall well below the average. On an examination, for instance, people who fail very badly would be represented here. We might tend to think of such people as "deviants" in the conventional sense of "inferior."

However, the shaded portion on the far right-hand side also suggests a statistically rare performance—but in the positive direc-

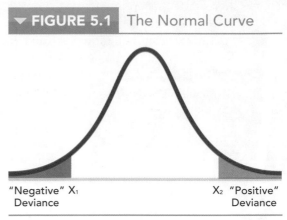

▼ **FIGURE 5.1** The Normal Curve

"Negative" X_1 Deviance X_2 "Positive" Deviance

Statistical definitions of deviance make it difficult to distinguish "negative" deviance from "positive" deviance.

tion (Pascale, Sternin, and Sternin 2010). It could represent people who show superior knowledge on an examination. Statistical definitions obscure distinctions between people who exceed and people who fall short of certain expectations.

AS HARMFUL

Another familiar way of defining *deviance* is by equating deviant action with action that produces destructive outcomes. Again, many of those who would appear on shortlists of deviants seem to be encompassed by this definitional criterion. Murderers, thieves, liars, sexual abusers, and wife-assaulters can all be said to be authors of real and tangible harm. However, while many people considered deviants do cause harm, many do not. The mentally ill, for example, may be treated as deviant, although it is difficult to ascribe harm to their differentness. In contrast, corporate executives and unethical politicians may be able to manage a socially benign image even though their actions might result in considerable damage to life and property. We tend to reserve the label of "deviant" in our society for other categories of people (Simon 2007).

Deviance as a Sociological Concept

As sociologists, we are interested in deviance as a product of **social interaction** and group structure; that is, we understand the study of deviance as the study of people, behaviours, and conditions subject to "social control"—the myriad ways in which members of **social**

groups express their disapproval of people and behaviour. These include name-calling, ridicule, ostracism, incarceration, and even killing. The study of deviance is about ways of acting and ways of being that, within particular social contexts and in particular historical periods, elicit moral condemnation.

To clarify, when the sociologist says, for instance, that LGBT (lesbian, gay, bisexual, transgender) people are an appropriate subject for the scholarly study of deviance, the implication is not that the sociologist thinks of these people as deviant; rather, it is suggested that members of LGBT groups are the targets of various forms of social control in our society. As sociologists, we are interested in why those with the power to exert social control regard LGBT individuals in this way and the consequences of such actions for these targeted groups (Alden and Parker 2005; Nylund 2004).

It is important to distinguish between the *objective* and the *subjective* character of deviance (Loseke 2003). The former refers to particular ways of thinking, acting, and being; the latter, to the moral status accorded such thoughts, actions, and characteristics. From a sociological perspective, the "deviant" character of certain behaviours, world views, or physical features is not implicit in those behaviours, world views, or physical features but conferred on them by society. To be deemed "deviant" by a sociologist, a particular behaviour must not only hold the potential for being called deviant (e.g., unusual or rare behaviour) but also must be labelled as "deviant" by powerful others.

As sociologists, we recognize the need to focus our attention on both sides of the deviance issue. Not everything that could be labelled "deviant" is necessarily labelled "deviant" by society. The ability of some in society to use available resources to resist the efforts of others to consider them deviant also is of sociological interest. For example, although corporations engage in activities that undermine health or safety or weaken the economic

(© iStockphoto.com / ArtisticCaptures)

To be deemed "deviant" by a sociologist, a particular behaviour or attribute must not only hold the potential for being called deviant (e.g., be unusual or rare) but also must be labelled as "deviant" by powerful others. Red hair is the least common hair colour in the world, and as a result redheads often face ridicule and personality stereotypes.

well-being of many in society, they are able to define themselves as morally respectable by making donations to universities and hospitals or by launching public relations campaigns to promote a positive image.

TIME to REFLECT

Why do movies, television, and most other forms of popular culture seem so focused on deviant activities and deviant people?

Researching Deviance

Sociologists who empirically study deviance use the same methodological tools employed in other areas of the discipline. These tools include experiments, surveys, content analyses, and field research. However, attempting to study the degree to which people might be engaging in behaviours that excite widespread disapproval can create rather formidable problems. The problems discussed in this section represent challenges to all forms of social research, but special difficulties arise when the subject is deviance.

When embarking on a study of deviant behavior, it is crucial that sociologists choose the appropriate research method. See "Research Techniques," Chapter 1, p. 19, for more information on the methodological tools used when studying deviance and other sociological topics.

SECRECY

Often, people wish to keep their deviant behaviour secret to protect themselves from social reactions. How do sociologists undertake valid research in a way that does not intrude excessively into the lives of those under study (Humphreys 1970)?

As an example, one of the authors of this chapter undertook an ethnography of participants in a radical body modification ritual referred to as "flesh hook pulling" (Horton 2013). This practice involves partial nudity, cheek skewering, sewing limes to one's back and piercing the flesh of one's chest with hooks attached to ropes. While highly deviant to out-

siders, members of this group claim that the practice meets their need for spiritual fulfillment and personal validation. The event is organized and carried out in secret at an isolated geographic location where the group's activities are shielded from public view. The researcher was able to win the confidence of participants and strengthen the **validity** of the research by gaining the participants' informed consent and respecting the group's need for secrecy by maintaining confidentiality.

DISCOVERY OF REPORTABLE BEHAVIOUR

If research subjects confide in the researcher and reveal information about illegal or harmful circumstances, does the researcher have an obligation to report that wrongdoing to authorities? The problem is brought about by the cross-pressures that the researcher experiences (Bostock 2002). On the one hand, the researcher has a professional obligation to respect the confidentiality of information that research subjects divulge. On the other, one has a social and moral obligation to protect the safety of the public and research subjects.

The complexities involved in the discovery of reportable behaviour are exemplified in sociologist Sudhir Venkatesh's book *Gang Leader for a Day* (2008). The book concerns the author's research activities while he was a graduate student at the University of Chicago. He describes how he began a rather standard piece of survey research in a high-crime, low-income neighbourhood where he became acquainted with the members of a large and powerful local gang. Venkatesh developed close personal friendships with many of the gang's members and their families and in so doing became aware of many of the illegal and often violent activities in which the gang engaged.

SAFETY

Researchers should take no action that could result in harm to those who participate in the research. While we tend to think only of physical harm in this respect, the injunction is much broader and includes emotional, mental, and economic harm.

In the case of one major survey of female victims of male violence, there was a real concern on the part of researchers that calling women and asking questions about violence in their lives could put them in danger if, for instance, a woman's abuser was sitting next to her when she received the phone call and started answering questions (Johnson 1996). It was necessary to take several special precautions, such as training interviewers to be sensitive to cues that the respondent might be under some immediate stress.

The Sociology of Deviant Behaviour

We have defined *deviance* as ways of thinking, acting, and being that are subject to social control—in other words, as kinds of conditions and kinds of people that are viewed by most of the members of a society as wrong, immoral, disreputable, bizarre, or unusual. We recognize that deviance has two distinct yet related dimensions: objective and subjective. *Objective* refers to the behaviour or condition itself; *subjective* refers to the placement of that condition by the members of society in their system of moral stratification. Sociologists do not confuse the physical act of someone smoking marijuana with the designation of marijuana-smoking as a deviant act. Each suggests a distinct realm of experience, and each is an appropriate object of sociological attention, but why some people smoke marijuana and others consider it deviant are indeed separate questions.

Several theoretical problem areas can be identified. They include questions about (1) causes and forms of deviant behaviour, (2) content and character of moral definitions, and (3) issues that arise over deviant labels.

Questions about why deviants do what they do have attracted most of the attention. However, the "why do they do it?" question contains a number of important assumptions. It implies that most of us share a conformist view of the world in which the important thing to understand is why some deviant minority refuses to act the way "we" act and the moral status of deviant behaviour is never called into question. Most of the theoretical thought in this respect reflects the influence of functionalist perspectives. Three dominant ways of thinking about "why they do it" can be identified—strain theory, cultural support theory, and control theory (Cullen, Wright, and Blevins 2007).

STRAIN THEORY

Strain theory derives from the writings of the famous American sociologist Robert Merton (1938). Merton sought to understand why, according to official statistics, so many types of non-conformity such as crime, delinquency, and drug addiction are much more pervasive within the lower social classes. As a sociologist, Merton was interested in understanding the structure of society, rather than individual personalities, as the central explanatory mechanism.

The answer, he argued, resided in the mal-integration of the cultural and social structures of societies. Stated otherwise, the lack of fit between the *cultural goals* people are encouraged to seek and the *means* available to pursue these goals creates a social strain to which deviant behaviour is an adjustment. In a society like the United States, there is little recognition of the role that **class** barriers play in social life. As a result, everyone is encouraged to pursue the goal of material success—and everyone is judged a success or a failure based on the ability to become materially successful.

When people steal money or material goods, it can be said that they are attempting to use "illegitimate means" to achieve the trappings of success. When they take drugs (or become "societal dropouts"), they can be interpreted as having withdrawn from the competition for stratification outcomes. For Merton, these problems are most acute in the lower social classes where people are most likely to experience the disjuncture between the things to which they aspire and the things actually available (see Table 5.1).

Critics note certain problems with Merton's arguments (Downes and Rock 2003; Bernard, Snipes, and Gerould 2009), such as his assumption of the accuracy of official statistics and his failure to account for much middle- and upper-class crime and deviance.

Despite these limitations, Merton's argument has greatly influenced the way sociologists think about the causes of deviant behaviour (Laufer and Adler 1994). More recently, Robert Agnew (1985; 2006) has theorized that in addition to the inability to achieve the things we want in life, a second source of strain involves an inability to avoid or escape some negative condition. For example, youths who cannot avoid abusive parents might use drugs, run away, or become aggressive as a way of coping with this strain.

TABLE 5.1 ▼ Robert Merton's Paradigm of Deviant Behaviour

Robert Merton argued that there are five ways of adjusting to a social structure that encourages large numbers of people to seek objectives that are not actually available to them.

	Attitude to Goals	Attitude to Means	Explanation/Example
Conformity	Accept	Accept	Most people accept as legitimate the culturally approved ways of achieving those goals. In Merton's example, most strive for material success by working hard, trying to get a good education, etc.
Innovation	Accept	Reject	The bank robber, drug dealer, or white-collar thief seeks success too but rejects the conventional means for achieving that success.
Ritualism	Reject	Accept	Some people seem to simply be going through the motions of achieving desired social goals. In large organizations, we use the term *bureaucrat* to describe people who are fixated on procedures at the expense of outcomes.
Retreatism	Reject	Reject	Some people adjust to strain by "dropping out" of the system. Such dropping out could include losing oneself in a world of alcohol or illegal drugs or adopting some unconventional lifestyle.
Rebellion	Reject/ Accept	Reject/ Accept	Rebellion includes acts intended to replace the current cultural goals (and means) with new ones. In this category we might include the radical political activist or even the domestic terrorist.

Strain can also result when individuals lose something they value. A child who is forced to move and thus leave important friendships might experience this type of loss strain.

These arguments share an explanatory logic that focuses on how the organization of our social relations creates problems that require solutions. In this paradigm, the causes of deviant behaviour are located in patterns of social life that are external to but affect individuals.

CULTURAL SUPPORT THEORY

According to **cultural support theory**, people behave in ways that reflect the cultural values to which they have been exposed and then internalize. Writing in the 1930s, Edwin Sutherland proposed that people become deviant because of learning experiences that make deviance more likely. In short, people end up deviant in the same way that they end up as stamp collectors, saxophone players, or French film fans—that is, as a result of exposure to influential learning experiences. According to Sutherland, we must learn to think about deviant conduct as acceptable to ourselves. For instance, we most commonly refrain from committing murder not because we don't know how but because we have come to define such action as morally repugnant. For Sutherland, learning to accept or to value criminal or deviant action in a very real sense makes such action possible.

Sutherland's cultural insights help us to understand how people come to value actions the rest of the society might despise. However, we live in a society that simultaneously condemns and supports deviant behaviour. Is it possible, then, both to believe in and to break important social rules? Most of us think that stealing is wrong but have also stolen something at some point. This is possible because we have learned to define certain deviant situations as ones to which the rules do not apply. When we steal a pen from work, we tell ourselves (and others) that we are underpaid and deserve whatever fringe benefits we can get or that employers expect people to steal and build this cost into their budgets. From this perspective, the broader culture both condemns deviance and makes available cognitive techniques for neutralizing the laws that prohibit deviant action (Fritsche 2005; Maratea 2011; Sykes and Matza 1957).

Cultural arguments have been very influential in the sociological study of deviant behaviour (Akers and Jensen 2003) and have proved more useful than strain arguments in making sense of so-called "respectable crimes" such as **corporate crimes** and "digital piracy" (Ingram and Hinduja 2008; Morris and Higgins 2009). One might argue that corporate crime, at least to some extent, is rooted in a "culture of competition" that legitimates organizational wrongdoing (Calavita and Pontell 1991).

(© Chuck Savage/Corbis)

"Deviant" behaviours such as excessive drinking are not always deviant from a statistical standpoint. Among young men, many risky behaviours (such as binge drinking) are celebrated as signs of masculinity and group conformity.

CONTROL THEORY

Advocates of **control theory** argue that people "lie, cheat, steal" when and if they are free to do so and if these activities can be the most expeditious ways of getting what they want. The important question, then, is not "why do some people break rules?" but "why don't more of us do so?" For control theorists, deviant behaviour occurs whenever it is allowed to occur, so we can expect to find deviance when social controls are weak or broken.

In sociology, this is a venerable idea. In his classic study of suicide, Émile Durkheim (1951 [1897]) sought to explain social variation in suicide rates. Catholics, he found, have lower suicide rates than Protestants, and married people have lower rates than single people. Suicide rates increase both in times of economic boom and during depressions. What is varying in all of these cases? Durkheim suggested that the crucial variable might be social regulation (or *social control*) that forces people to take others into account and discourages behaviours that are excessively individualistic. In short, suicide is more likely when people are disconnected from social regulation and left to their own resources.

In more recent times, sociologist Travis Hirschi (1969) attempted to use social control logic to explain the conduct of youthful offenders. For Hirschi, the problem of juvenile crime could be understood in reference to the concept of the bond to conventional others. For youth, the world of conventional others is represented by parents, teachers, and members of the legitimate adult community. Hirschi reasoned that if youthful bonds to conventional others are strong, youths need to take these others into account when they act; if the bonds are weak, they are free to act in ways that reflect much narrower self-interest. While theories of the bond have been eclipsed by later theoretical developments (Gottfredson and Hirschi 1990), the idea that deviance is a product of weak links to conventional society continues to attract attention (Church, Wharton, and Taylor 2009; Ford 2009.)

THE TRANSACTIONAL CHARACTER OF DEVIANCE

Despite their sociological character, strain, cultural support, and social control arguments tend to focus attention on the individual. However, others encourage us to understand deviant behaviour as an interactional, joint, or collective product rather than as an individual outcome.

Familiar explanations of murder focus on the murderous acts of the individual (see

Figure 5.2 for homicide rates in Canada). As sociologists, we might try to understand how people who commit murder do so in response to social strain (Levin and Madfis 2009; Pratt and Godsey 2003) or as a result of an affiliation with a culture of violence (Chilton 2004; Wolfgang and Ferracuti 1967). Alternatively, we might try to understand how murder results from particular kinds of interactions.

David Luckenbill (1977) has demonstrated that murder can in many cases be understood as a **situated transaction**. Some murder may be seen not as an individual act but an inter-action sequence of participants in a common physical territory. Based on a study of 70 homi-cides in California, Luckenbill identified six common stages of murder:

- *Stage 1.* The transaction starts when the even-tual victim does something that the eventual offender could define as an insult or as an offence to "face." The victim might call the offender a liar or make a sexually suggestive comment about the offender's partner.

- *Stage 2.* The offender defines the victim's actions as threatening or offensive.

- *Stage 3.* The offender makes a countermove intended to respond and save face. This could involve a verbal response or a physical gesture.

- *Stage 4.* The victim responds in an aggressive manner. The problems may be aggravated by onlookers who jeer the participants, hold their jackets, or block convenient exits.

▼ **FIGURE 5.2** Provincial Variations in Rates of Homicide (Number of Homicides per 100,000 Population), 2010

For reasons that are not entirely clear, the rate at which the situated transaction we refer to as homicide occurs varies from province to province.

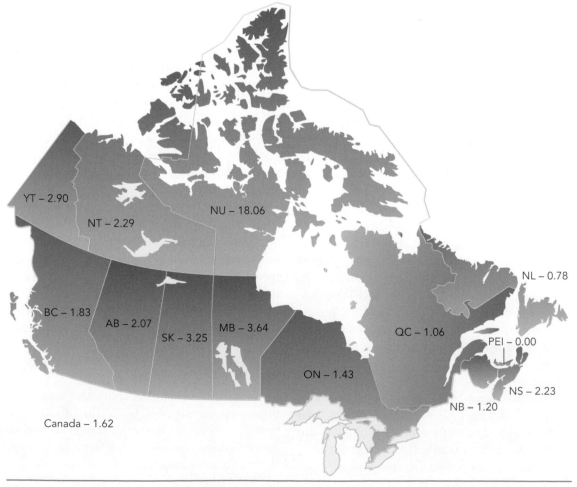

YT – 2.90
NT – 2.29
NU – 18.06
NL – 0.78
BC – 1.83
AB – 2.07
SK – 3.25
MB – 3.64
QC – 1.06
PEI – 0.00
ON – 1.43
NS – 2.23
NB – 1.20
Canada – 1.62

SOURCE: Sara Beattie, "Homicide in Canada, 2008," *Juristat*, Catalogue no. 85-002, vol. 29 no. 02, available at www.statcan.gc.ca/pub/ 85-002-x/2009004/article/10929-eng.pdf

- *Stage 5.* A brief violent exchange occurs. It may involve a fatal blow, stab, or gunshot.

- *Stage 6.* The battle is over; the offender flees or remains at the scene.

Luckenbill's work demonstrates how murder can be understood as a social product. This does not imply an absence of guilt or excuse for killing; rather, it shows that acts of deviance can involve complex and significant interactional dimensions. Sociologist Randall Collins (2008) has proposed an alternative theoretical approach to the role played by situational factors in the development of troublesome behaviour. He argues that in violent situations, people are tense and afraid of being hurt and hurting others. For example, researchers consistently find that many soldiers in battle do not fire their weapons but do exhibit signs of extreme trauma (Crossman 2009). Because the driving force is much more emotional than rational, the eruption of violence depends on a variety of conditions that determine how people negotiate emotional tension.

According to Collins, one of the main pathways around confrontational tension and fear involves identifying and attacking a weak victim. This strategy applies across a wide range of situations including military raids, violence during arrests, domestic violence, and bullying. Another strategy is making third parties the focus of emotional attention. In these situations, observers play a key role in affecting the course of the violent exchange. For violence to be successful, it must turn emotional tension into emotional energy.

TIME to REFLECT

Are theories of situated transaction guilty of victim-blaming?

Making Sense of the "Facts" of Deviant Behaviour

Sociologists have repeatedly demonstrated that deviant acts are not randomly distributed in the population. Instead, people with certain social and demographic characteristics are much more likely to be involved in deviant behaviour than others. The task of sociologists of deviance is to explain these levels of differential involvement.

GENDER

Gender correlates closely with a wide range of behaviours. With respect to deviance, males and females differ in terms of the amounts and types of disapproved behaviours in which they engage. Males are more likely to be involved in behaviours that most members of Canadian society would say they disapprove of. Males are much more likely to be involved in criminal behaviour (crimes related to prostitution are an important exception in this regard). The differential is greatest in cases of violence but is also significant for other kinds of crime (Gannon et al. 2005). While there has been some narrowing of the gender gap in recent years, crime remains a male-dominated activity (Sacco and Kennedy 2012). This pattern is clearly illustrated in Table 5.2.

Males are also more likely to consume both legal and illegal drugs (Health Canada 2009) and to commit suicide by using guns or explosives to do it (Langlois and Morrison 2002). While overall rates of mental illness do not differ markedly between men and women, women are more likely to be diagnosed with depression and anxiety, while men are more likely to experience problems related to addiction and psychosis (Health Canada 2002).

TABLE 5.2 ▼ Accused by the Police by Gender, Rates per 100,000 Population, 2009

	Males	Females
Violations against the person	1560.9	429.3
Violations against property	1806.6	661.7
Other Criminal Code violations	1491.0	387.9
Total Criminal Code violations	5403.1	1580.3

SOURCE: Vincent Ferrao and Cara Williams. 2012. *Women in Canada: A Gender-Based Statistical Report.* Ottawa: Statistics Canada, www.statcan.gc.ca/bsolc/olc-cel/olc-cel?catno=89-503-XWE&lang=eng

Historically, sociologists tended to not be terribly interested in acts of crime or deviance without a significant male dimension. Only through the work of feminist social critics did researchers come to focus on problems that affect women more directly. These include forms of deviance that tend to uniquely victimize women, such as intimate violence and sexual harassment (Alhabib, Nur, and Jones 2010; Chasteen 2001; Comack 2008).

AGE

Age is strongly associated with many kinds of deviant behaviour (Tanner 2009). Crime rates are greatest during the late teens and early adulthood and decline very sharply after that (Sacco and Kennedy 2012).

However, this pattern does not apply to all kinds of crime. Suicide rates actually tend to be lower among younger Canadians (Langlois and Morrison 2002). While older people are traditionally assumed to be those most likely to experience a variety of forms of mental illness, the onset of most mental illness occurs dur-

ing adolescence and young adulthood (Health Canada 2002; Kessler et al. 2005).

CLASS AND ETHNICITY

A great deal of sociological theorizing about the "causes" of deviant behaviour has taken as its central issue the need to explain why social and economic precariousness is related to deviant outcomes. While many studies indicate that poorer people and people from minority groups are more likely to be involved in deviant activity, a consensus does not exist among researchers regarding how concepts such as poverty, inequality, or minority-group status should be measured (Braithewaite 1979; Wortley 1999). As a result, the research regarding the relationships between class and minority status on the one hand and involvement in deviant activity on the other lacks consistency (Brzozowski, Taylor-Butts, and Johnson 2006; Perreault 2009; Tittle, Villemez, and Smith 1978).

Some interpretations of the relationship between social disadvantage and deviant behaviour point to a more general problem in the sociology of deviance. Are poorer or minority people more likely to be deviant, or are they just more likely to get caught and be labelled as "deviant"? Do our definitions of what constitutes crime and deviance themselves reflect class biases?

These observations suggest a need to ask about the subjective character of deviance. Why are some ways of thinking, acting, and being more likely than others to incite indignation and disapproval, and why are some people more likely than others to become the objects of social control?

The Sociology of Deviant Categories

To call something or someone "deviant" is to judge the thing or person to be disreputable. An important set of issues in the sociology of deviance relates to the creation of deviant and non-deviant categories into which people and actions are sorted (Loseke 2003; Best 2013).

We tend to treat categorical distinctions as common sense. The deviant qualities of people and acts, we convince ourselves, reside within the people and acts themselves. However, judged from another standpoint, known as social constructionism (Miller and Holstein

TABLE 5.3 ▼ Suicide Rates by Sex and Age, Rates per 100,000 Population, 2009

	Both Sexes	Males	Females
All ages	11.5	17.9	5.3
10–14	1.3	1.3	1.2
15–19	9.0	12.6	5.2
20–24	11.9	17.1	6.5
25–29	11.0	17.1	4.7
30–34	13.2	20.7	5.7
35–39	14.4	21.7	7.1
40–44	17.4	27.0	7.6
45–49	17.6	26.8	8.3
50–54	18.5	28.4	8.7
55–59	16.7	26.0	7.7
60–64	12.8	19.4	6.3
65–69	9.8	16.4	3.6
70–74	11.3	20.5	3.1
75–79	9.0	16.9	2.6
80–84	10.8	19.6	4.7
85–89	13.1	30.6	3.7
90 and older	9.3	27.5	2.7

SOURCE: Statistics Canada, www.statcan.gc.ca/tables-tableaux/sum-som/l01/cst01/hlth66d-eng.htm; www.statcan.gc.ca/tables-tableaux/sum-som/l01/cst01/hlth66e-eng.htm; www.statcan.gc.ca/tables-tableaux/sum-som/l01/cst01/hlth66f-eng.htm

HUMAN DIVERSITY

What's in a Name?

Does it matter how we label behaviour? In your view, do the labels in each pair below refer to the same or different kinds of behaviour and people? If they are different, then how are they different?

Terrorist	Freedom fighter
Prostitute	Sex worker
Sex assault victim	Sex assault survivor
Cult leader	Religious leader
Disabled	Differently abled
Pro-life	Anti-choice
Pro-choice	Pro-abortion
Addiction	Bad habit
Alcoholic	Drunk
Modification	Mutilation
Stripper	Exotic dancer

1993; Spector and Kitsuse 1977), this logic is flawed. Acts and people are not inherently deviant but are defined as such by those with the power to do so. This perspective maintains that there is nothing commonsensical about the deviant quality of people and their behaviour. Instead, this quality is itself problematic and requires investigation.

Further, we need to recognize that "deviant constructions" change over time (Curra 2011). For example, a relatively short time ago being gay might have been considered grounds for social exclusion, but in the contemporary context it is seen as much less deviant.

Similarly, many ways of acting or being that were once widely tolerated now seem to draw considerable disapproval. One clear example is cigarette-smoking (Stubera, Galea, and Link 2008). Only a few decades ago, people smoked in elevators, restaurants, around children—even in sociology classes. Today, smokers are the object of scorn, and their habit is the sub-

(Nathan Denette/The Canadian Press/ASSOCIATED PRESS)

Thousands gather in a cloud of marijuana smoke in Dundas Square, Toronto, for the annual 420 smoke-off in support of cannabis. While some consider marijuana use a deviant behaviour, others believe that it should be decriminalized, since non-enforcement of the law brings all lawmaking into disrepute.

ject of a variety of forms of legal and extra-legal control. Other examples of behaviour for which social tolerance has decreased include drinking and driving (Asbridge, Mann, and Flam-Zalcman 2004), wife assault (Johnson 1996), and sexual harassment (Lopez, Hodson, and Roscigno 2009).

DEVIANCE AS A CLAIMS-MAKING PROCESS

Social constructionist writers understand the distinctions that people make between deviant and non-deviant behaviour as part of a **claims-making** process (Best 2013; Spector and Kitsuse 1977). This is a process by which groups assert grievances regarding the troublesome character of "other" people or behaviours. Claims-making includes many different activities, such as debating exotic sexual practices on a daytime talk show, marching in protest, or providing expert testimony before a parliamentary committee. In short, it is anything anybody does to propagate a view of who or what is deviant and what needs to be done about it (Loseke 2003).

Claims-making is directed toward three broad types of objectives:

1. *Publicizing the problematic character of the people with the behaviour in question.* People generally need to be convinced that there is good reason to regard others as troublesome. Claims-makers may endeavour to convince us that deviants are dangerous or irresponsible or that their behaviour is contagious (Best 2013).
2. *Shaping a particular view of the problem.* Generally, claims-makers want to convince us that certain people are a problem and a problem of a particular type. "Problem drinking," for instance, can be constructed in many different ways (Holmes and Antell 2001), such as a sin, a crime, or a sickness. The behaviour in question remains the same, but the kind of deviant the problem drinker is varies. Different constructions have very different implications for what it is we think needs to be done.
3. *Building consensus around new moral categories.* Claims-makers endeavour to build widespread agreement about the correctness of a particular moral vision (Macek

2006). This is accomplished by winning the support of the media, officialdom, and the general public (Hilgartner and Bosk 1988). As consensus is built, deviant categories take on a common-sense character.

Who Are Claims-Makers?

Howard Becker (1963) coined the term *moral entrepreneur* to describe those who "discover" and attempt to publicize deviant conditions. These are crusading reformers who are disturbed by some perceived evil and who will not rest until something is done about it.

In the early stages, definitions of deviance are often promoted by those with some direct connection to the problem, such as those who define themselves as the victims of others' actions (Reinarman 1996). Still, many involved in deviance construction have no vested interest in the problem. Lawmakers, journalists, or television talk-show hosts frequently play a significant role in the promotion of deviant designations (Sacco 2005), but their social distance from the issue is often greater than that of victims' groups.

What Are Claims?

When social constructionists speak of *claims*, they are talking about the actual message content that conveys a moral vision of deviance and non-deviance. The study of claims is the study of how communications persuade audiences. Successful claims demonstrate the gravity of a problem in several ways:

- *Using compelling statistics.* Statistics impress upon media consumers the size of a problem and its escalating severity (Best 2004). Statistical estimates of this nature can provide compelling evidence of a problem's urgency.

- *Linking an emergent concern to problems already on the public agenda.* Familiar moral language can be used to provide reference points for emergent problems. For instance, because addiction is widely recognized as a problem in North America, we now hear people speak of "pornography addicts," "gambling addicts," and "Internet sex addiction" (Butters and Erickson 1999; Griffiths 2001).

- *Using emotionally compelling examples to typify the seriousness and character of the threat posed by the behaviour* (see Bromley and Shupe 1981). For example, the Columbine High School killings are often used to exemplify the problem of school violence, even though such an incident is very unusual and most school crime in no way resembles this incident (Fox and Levin 2001).

Deviance and Social Conflict

Disagreement over moral meaning represents forms of social conflict. Such conflicts are evident in the battle over abortion, the movement to legalize marijuana, and efforts to control cigarette-smoking.

Two broad types of conflict theory can be distinguished: conservative and radical (Williams and McShane 2009). These theories suggest different ways of understanding the wider context of the claims-making process. From the perspective of conservative conflict theory, social conflicts regarding the moral meaning of conduct emerge from diverse sources (Turk 1976). As members of various ethnic, religious, professional, lifestyle, or cultural groups pursue their social interests, they may come into conflict with other groups over scarce resources. From this perspective, the study of moral differentiation is the study of how various status groups influence systems of social control as a means of achieving group goals.

In contrast, radical conflict theory draws on the Marxian understanding of society (Spitzer 1975). It views the economic organization of society as the key to understanding moral stratification. The social construction of deviance must be understood as reflecting the economic realities of capitalism and the class exploitation it engenders. From this perspective, the internal logic of capitalism gives deviance both its objective and its subjective character. Capitalism requires a large pool of labour that can be exploited by keeping wages low. This means that there will always be more workers than jobs and some people will inevitably be marginalized. These populations have little stake in the system and are at greater risk of criminal labels and involvement.

TIME to REFLECT

Do you think that the concern over "Internet predators" is another example of exaggerated deviance construction?

THE SOCIOLOGY OF DEVIANT STIGMA

A third key area of study in the sociology of deviance is stigma application and management (see, for example, Table 5.4). This body of research and theory focuses attention on the social interaction between those who exercise social control and those who are thought of as disreputable. In this respect, questions about the application and consequences of deviant stigma tend to be more micro- than macrosociological.

The Process of Labelling

Deviant labels are charged with a great deal of emotion. They sort through the thousands of acts in which a person has engaged and indicate that the person's identity is best understood in terms of the act according to which the label is affixed (Erikson 1966).

The assignment of stigma suggests what sociologists refer to as a master status that overrides all other status considerations (Becker 1963). Being known as a murderer trumps any other status characteristics the person might have (bright, interesting, poor, blonde, left-handed). Sociologists use the term

TABLE 5.4 ▼ Types of Deviant Behaviour

Howard Becker (1963) suggested that once we recognize that deviant stigma is separable from deviant acts, it is possible to recognize at least four types of deviants. These types are created by the contrast between what people actually do (breaking rules or keeping them) and how they are perceived (deviant or not deviant).

		Behaviour	
		Obedient	Rule-Breaking
Perception	Perceived as deviant	Falsely accused	Pure deviant
	Not perceived as deviant	Conforming	Secret deviant

status degradation ceremony to refer to the rituals during which the status of "deviant" is conferred (Garfinkel 1956). Status degradation ceremonies, such as incompetency hearings, psychiatric examinations, and courtroom trials, mark the movement from one social position to another by publicly and officially acknowledging a shift in social roles and the emergence of a new, deviant identity.

Resistance to Labelling

The ability of some in society to confer the status of "deviant" on others reflects differentials in social power. However, people might use a range of strategies to avoid or negotiate a label of deviance. One obvious method involves efforts to undermine social control through *evasion*. "Successful" deviants learn to engage in prohibited conduct in ways that decrease the likelihood of getting caught (Becker 1963).

Individuals try to avoid or negotiate stigma through what Goffman calls *performance* (Goffman 1959). The dramatic roles we might perform when stopped by a police officer for speeding are part of a performance intended to neutralize the efforts of police to impose a deviant designation (Piliavin and Briar 1964). Similarly, *disclaimer mannerisms* are actions intended to signal to agents of social control that one is not the appropriate target of deviant attribution.

Deviant Careers and Deviant Identities

One potential consequence of the labelling process is *deviancy amplification*: the situation wherein the very attempt to control deviance makes deviance more likely (Lemert 1951). Efforts to describe this usually distinguish between primary and secondary deviance (Bernburg, Krohn, and Rivera 2006; Lemert 1951). *Primary deviance* is that in which we all engage that has no real consequence for how we see ourselves or for how other people see us. From time to time all of us might lie, cheat, or engage in some other prohibited behaviour. *Secondary deviance*, in contrast, suggests a deviant identity. While any of us might tell an occasional lie, most of us do not think of ourselves or are thought of by others as liars.

It is societal reaction that turns primary deviance into secondary deviance. The ways

SOCIOLOGY in ACTION

Disclaimer Mannerisms in University Examinations

Sociologists Daniel Albas and Cheryl Albas (1993) have examined how students attempt to distance themselves from charges of academic dishonesty while writing examinations. People writing examinations are at high risk of stigmatization. Invigilators patrol the rooms, and often neither the professor nor graduate assistants have any direct knowledge of the individuals writing the exam. For these reasons, students take steps to ensure that they will not be falsely accused of cheating.

The authors define two major strategies: actions that students take and those they avoid.

Actions taken include:

- *Picayune over-conformity with regulations*. This involves the demonstration of conformity with even the most minor examination rules. A student who needs to blow his or her nose will be sure to wave the tissue around first so it is clear that it is nothing other than a tissue.
- *The expression of repression of creature releases*. Creature releases are those aspects of the self that steal through the facade of social control, including sneezes and yawns.
- *Shows of innocence*. Because students know that a lack of activity might be read as indicative of a lack of preparation, when they are not writing they might be underlining or circling words on the exam sheet.

Actions avoided include:

- *Control of eyes*. Students know that they are not supposed to have roving eyes, so they are careful where they look.
- *Control of notes*. Students might frisk themselves before they enter the exam room to ensure that they are not carrying anything that could cause trouble.
- *Morality of place*. Students worry that where they sit can send a message about their trustworthiness. Care is taken not to sit next to someone they believe is perceived as a potential cheater.

in which agents of social control respond to initial acts of deviance—through stereotyping, rejection, and the degradation of status—can actually make future deviance more rather than less likely (Markin 2005). One of the key intervening mechanisms in this process is the transformation of the **self**. Consistent with social psychological theories, such as the one advanced by Charles Horton Cooley (1902), labelling theorists argue that individuals who are consistently stigmatized may come to accept others' definition of their deviant identity. To the extent that individuals increasingly come to see themselves as others see them, they may become much more likely to behave in ways that are consistent with the label of "deviant." Individuals become committed to a life of deviance largely because others expect them to—deviance becomes a self-fulfilling prophecy (Tannenbaum 1938).

Managing Stigma

Various strategies may be employed to control information about a deviant identity or to alter the meaning of stigma so as to reduce the significance of the deviance in a person's life (Durkin 2009; Hathaway 2004; Park 2002).

For some examples of strategies we employ to manage stigmas, see the Sociology in Action box "Protecting the Self: Stigma Management Strategies" in Chapter 4, p. 80.

A useful distinction is made between the *discreditable* and the *discredited* (Goffman 1963). The former refers to people who might become discredited if their stigma were to become public. Conversely, discredited stigma is either evident or assumed to be known.

For the discreditable, stigma management involves a pressing need to control information others have about them. People with a hidden stigma face the constant worry that others they care about may reject them if information about this stigma becomes public (James and Craft 2002). For instance, those suffering from stigmatized diseases might keep this aspect of their life secret because they fear rejection.

(© john angerson / Alamy)

Some sufferers of anorexia nervosa are known to wear baggy clothes and avoid situations where people are eating as a way of hiding their stigmatized disease.

The discredited person's stigma tends to be apparent, so there is no need to keep it secret. Rather, the discredited attempt to restrict stigma relevance to the ways others treat them. They may attempt purification by trying to convince others that they have left a deviant identity behind (Pfuhl and Henry 1993). One of our contemporary definitions of a hero is someone who has left a deviant stigma behind. Helen Keller and Christopher Reeve, for instance, were thought of as heroic largely because they rose above the stigmatizing character of particular physical conditions.

The discredited may also invoke collective stigma management. Bearers of stigma may join together to form an association intent on changing public perceptions of their disvalued character. Organizations intended to "undeviantize" behaviour include the National Organization for the Reform of Marijuana Laws (NORML); COYOTE (Call Off Your Old Tired Ethics), which promotes the rights of sex workers; and the National Association to Advance Fat Acceptance (NAAFE), which advocates for the rights of the "hugely obese" (Gimlin 2008).

TIME to REFLECT

If deviance is a source of stigma, why are so many kinds of deviants in our society (e.g., gangsta rappers, misbehaving actors and athletes) treated like celebrities?

Deviance and Post-modernism

Post-modernism suggests a more recent theoretical trend that builds upon many earlier insights. Post-modernist theorists of crime and deviance study the way in which language works to marginalize and stigmatize people who come into contact with the criminal justice system or are otherwise labelled deviant. Language is a part of what post-modernists, and other theorists, call "discourse"—large, specialized units of knowledge (such as the scientific, legal, and medical languages) made up of any number of modes of communication. For post-modern criminologists, that which is "criminal" or "deviant" can be understood as resulting from the capacity of powerful groups—such as lawmakers—to "discursively" control the behaviour of less powerful groups.

For post-modernist criminologists, dominant discourses such as law create categories, or binaries, that are organized in a hierarchal fashion. By "deconstructing" or breaking down binaries created by language (such as male/female, rational/irrational, deviant/conforming), post-modernists illuminate the way

UNDER the WIRE

Burglary and New Technologies

How do burglars make decisions about which houses to break into? Are these decisions influenced by social media technologies? Residential occupancy is a primary concern for burglars. Paul Cromwell and colleagues (1991) interviewed 30 burglars about their working patterns and reported that 90 per cent claimed that they "would never enter a residence that they knew was occupied" (Cromwell, Olson, and Avery 1991, 24). To avoid burglarizing occupied homes, burglars typically work during periods when homes are unguarded (Rengert and Wasilchick 1985). For example, burglaries are more likely to occur during the week when people are at work as opposed to on the weekend when residents are at home spending time with family or during the day when people are more likely to be out shopping and running errands rather than at night when families are at home making dinner or sleeping (Cromwell, Olson, and Avery 1991). Cromwell and colleagues found that to avoid burglarizing a house when someone is present, burglars make use of a number of "occupancy probes"; they included:

- Circling a neighbourhood until residents could be seen leaving the home.
- Knocking on the door of a potential target. If someone answered, the prospective burglar would pretend to be lost and needing directions or ask for a non-existent person. A burglar might also pretend that their car had broken down and ask to use the telephone. If the person agreed, the burglar had an extra opportunity to learn about the contents of the home and potential security risks.

- Dressing in jogging attire, taking a piece of mail from a target's mailbox, and then knocking on the door. If someone answered, the burglar would pretend that they found the lost piece of mail and was returning it.
- Probing neighbours adjacent to a target. A house next door to a home with a "For Sale" sign is particularly attractive, because a burglar can pretend to be an interested buyer, snoop around the backyard, and hop the fence into the yard of the target house.

In many ways, burglars are "much more aware of our use of time than we are" (Cromwell, Olson, and Avery 1991, 24), and with the advent of contemporary technologies it would seem that determining residential occupancy has been made easier for potential burglars. With social media sites such as Facebook and Twitter that allow users to post near-constant updates of their whereabouts and services such as Google Earth that provide virtual access to residential properties, it is not surprising that burglars could be using these technologies to their advantage. A recent CBC news story reported that a New Albany home was burglarized shortly after the residents left a Facebook update indicating that they would be out from 8 p.m. onward to attend a concert. According to surveillance footage, two burglars entered their home at 8:42 p.m. and made off with more than $10,000-worth of items. One of the homeowners later recognized one of the burglars as a childhood neighbour who had "friended" her on Facebook six months previously.

SOURCE: Cromwell, Olson, and Avery 1991; www.cbsnews.com/stories/2010/03/25/earlyshow/main6331796.shtml

in which categories privilege the truth claims of some groups over those of others by defining the behaviour of powerless groups as abnormal or criminal (Arrigo 1999). Recently, postmodern theorists of deviance and crime have applied their insights to analyses of housing homeless people (Arrigo 2004), the resistance strategies of female offenders (Geiger 2006), and reality-based television and mental illness (Shon and Arrigo 2006).

Conclusion

Our experience with deviance reflects the influence of the cultural context and the historical period in which we live. As times change, so do the categories of people and behaviour society finds troublesome. By way of example, we need only think about the large number of newly constructed forms of deviance that we already associate with computer use, such as cyberporn, cyberstalking, and Internet addiction.

Deviance can be thought of as having two dimensions: the objective and the subjective. The objective aspect is the behaviour, condition, or cognitive style itself. The subjective aspect is the collective understanding of the behaviour, condition, or cognitive style as disreputable. A comprehensive sociology of deviance needs to consider both dimensions.

There are several major questions around which the study of the sociology of deviance is organized. First, how do we understand the social and cultural factors that make prohibited behaviour possible? Strain theory argues that people engage in deviant behaviour because it is a form of problem-solving; cultural support theories focus on how learned definitions of deviant can be supportive of such behaviour; and control theories maintain that deviance results when the factors that would check or constrain it are ineffective.

Second, there is a need to explain the prevailing system of moral stratification. Definitions of deviance emerge from a process of claims-making. The establishment of consensus around such definitions gives categories of deviance a taken-for-granted quality.

We also need to ask questions about the application and management of deviant stigma. Being labelled "deviant" is a complex process that creates numerous problems for those stigmatized. It is important, therefore, to understand who gets labelled and how people cope with social control. In particular, we need to be alert to the manner in which the imposition of labels can worsen the very problems that the application of social control is meant to correct.

Finally, we need to consider the role of language itself in the creation of categories of deviance and how these categories create power structures that privilege some ways of understanding crime and deviance over others.

questions for critical thought

1. What images of crime and deviance dominate coverage in the local media in your community? What images do they create of troubled and troublesome people?

2. In your view, why are young males so much more likely than other groups to engage in a range of behaviours that many in society find troublesome?

3. Aside from the examples given in the text, can you suggest behaviours or conditions that have undergone a shift in moral status in the past few years? How would you account for these changes?

4. In your opinion, does it make sense to speak of something called "positive deviance"? Why or why not?

recommended readings

Patricia A. Adler and Peter Adler. 2011. *The Tender Cut: Inside the Hidden World of Self-Injury*. New York: New York University Press.
This study employs a range of data sources in order to examine the role that branding, cutting, and other forms of self-injury play in the lives of those affected. The authors discuss the meaning of this behaviour as well as its consequences and likely future.

Joel Best. 2013. *Social Problems*. 2nd edn. New York: W.W. Norton.
This is a thorough and accessible introduction to the social constructionist approach to deviance and social problems. The author makes excellent use of practical examples in order to unravel the complex process by which people and behaviour come to be seen as troublesome.

Julian Tanner. 2009. *Teenage Troubles*. 3rd edn. Toronto: Oxford University Press.
This volume directly addresses the empirical reality of high levels of deviance among young people.

The author examines a number of substantive problems and critically discusses the major theoretical approaches to youth deviance.

Lorne Tepperman. 2010. *Deviance, Crime, and Control: Beyond the Straight and Narrow*. 2nd edn. Toronto: Oxford University Press.
Tepperman provides a detailed discussion of the contemporary field of the sociology of deviance. The book focuses both on theories that structure the field and on their substantive application.

Sudhir A. Venkatesh. 2008. *Gang Leader for a Day: A Rogue Sociologist Takes to the Streets*. New York: Penguin Books.
This is a fascinating first-person narrative in which the author tells of his experiences studying a high-crime neighbourhood on the South Side of Chicago. The book raises a large number of ethical and methodololgical questions.

recommended websites

Sex Professionals of Canada
www.csa-scs.ca/code-of-ethics
This site contains resources for professional sex workers and provides some interesting insights into how those involved in professional pursuits that others regard as deviant think about their own lives.

Society for the Study of Social Problems
www.sssp1.org
This is the main page for the Society for the Study of Social Problems. The journal of the society, *Social Problems*, has been very influential in the development of the sociology of deviance.

Statistical Literacy
www.statlit.org
This is the website of an organization devoted to the promotion of statistical literacy. It is an invaluable resource for researching the various means by which statistics may be manipulated for political and social purposes.

Statistics Canada
www.statcan.gc.ca
This is the main page for Canada's national statistical agency, Statistics Canada. Many different sorts of reports, tables, and graphs relating to a variety of forms of deviance can be found at this site.

SALE

70%

final
clearance

SIZE 8 - 18
NOW AVAILABLE

www.phase-eight.co.uk

chapter 6

Class, Status, and Social Inequality

Ann D. Duffy and Sara J. Cumming

In this chapter, you will:

▶ Come to understand the pivotal role that social and class inequality plays in Canadian society.

▶ Recognize the centrality of class and status inequality in the development of sociology.

▶ Learn some of the key historical as well as contemporary realities of economic and social inequalities in Canadian society.

▶ Recognize the contentious future that Canadians face in terms of economic and social inequalities.

Introduction

One of the foundational insights in sociology is that our lived realities are constructed socially. We become human through a social process, and our understanding of the world is forever framed by these social experiences. For example, a new friend offers to give us a ride home. When we approach her car in the parking lot, we do not simply register the fact that here is a vehicle with four wheels and an engine. Rather, we immediately and unconsciously run through a whole gamut of socially constructed meanings—meanings embedded in patterns of social inequality. The age, make, and upkeep of the car all are noted. That our new friend drives a brand-new, sparkling BMW evokes a whole range of social reactions and connections that are quite different from those we would experience if confronted by a rusty, dented Toyota.

Of course, this example is directly related to the centrality of **class and status** inequalities in our day-to-day experiences. When we look at this car, we generally are making assumptions about the relative class and standing of the individual who drives it. The BMW evokes, rightly or wrongly, an impression of wealth and economic well-being, while the rusty Toyota conjures up images of poverty and social marginalization. Clearly, among the most important sorting devices incorporated in our social construction of daily reality are these divisions between those who have and those who do not.

Within the complex diversity of responses to class inequalities, there is a typical relationship between high economic class and power. Historically, individuals capable of wresting control over a community's assets—land, animals, property—in the process acquire "power." Understood in the simplest terms, the wealthy are in an excellent position to dictate what others do and in this way exercise control over the lives of those who are less well-off. Historically, this power could be demonstrated in the rawest terms as the elite held the power of life and death over those below them.

Over time, the relationships between economic advantage and power have become increasingly nuanced and complex. Today, the power associated with social class is likely to be much more indirect and subtle (Lukes 1974). Bill Gates, founder of Microsoft and one of the wealthiest individuals on the planet, is not only an economic force to be reckoned with on the stock market but has also created a powerful public persona as a revered philanthropist and global activist. Instead of displaying coercive power or brute force, Gates may be said to have successfully mobilized his power in a subtler, though equally effective, manner.

The public nature of Gates's persona is unusual in contemporary global realities. The **economic elite** in Canada and internationally are typically obscured by their corporate connections (Carroll 2010). The power wielded by a globalized manufacturing conglomerate like General Motors may be widely recognized, but the individuals sitting on its corporate boards are not likely to be well known. When they decide to close a factory and lay off thousands of workers, their exercise of power over the lives of others is obscured as the mass media talk about "GM closings" rather than the actions of individual corporate executives.

Not only are economic power relations often indirect, they are likely to be muddied by interconnections with other patterns of inequality. Various social factors—gender, ethnicity, race, age, disability, sexual orientation, and immigrant status—play an important mediating role. Certainly, broad categories of individuals—women, ethnic and racial minorities, the disabled, recent immigrants, the elderly—are generally at much greater risk of being both relatively poor and powerless. Even individuals who combine great advantage and disadvantage often find themselves hobbled. For example, a woman who is a member of the upper class may find that her gender limits the opportunities otherwise provided by her class position (Duffy 1986). In short, as sociologists have suggested, there are complex intersections between economic and other forms of inequalities. When examining economic and status inequalities, it is important to keep these **intersectionalities** in mind (Thomas 2012).

TIME to REFLECT

In what ways do you think age (children, youth, adult, and senior) affects economic inequalities in Canada, and what are the social class implications of the fact that Canada's population is rapidly aging?

Finally, class and status inequalities are further complicated by their ebb and flow through history. Class position may shift dramatically through the course of an individual's life, and certain historical periods have certainly been rife with dramatic change. The recession of 2008 shook up both the RRSP portfolios and the economic future of many Canadians, and the long-term implications remain to be seen. Elites also change throughout history. With corporations going global, along with the expansion of global governance bodies (for example, the **World Trade Organization [WTO]**), the Canadian corporate elite may transform into members of a transnational capitalist class (Carroll 2010; Rothkopf 2008).

In this chapter, we will explore social and economic inequalities in greater detail. Certainly, social class is a pivotal term in sociological thought—indeed, many of the "classics" centre on this concept. Given this centrality, it is not surprising that understanding Canadian society requires an appreciation of the patterns of class structure. As discussed below, these class divisions are sustained not only by various institutions, ranging from elite private schools to political parties, but also by popular ideologies that legitimize and perpetuate specific social class arrangements.

Class and Status Inequalities in Sociological Thought

A number of the key concepts in sociology emanate from concern with patterns of social inequality. Indeed, the term **social stratification** captures one of the foundational ideas in sociological inquiry. It refers to the hierarchical arrangement of individuals based upon wealth, power, and prestige. Social stratification affects almost every aspect of our lives—from where we live, our material possessions, and our level of education to our health and well-being. Rather than focusing on individual circumstances, it stresses the layering of groups of people according to their relative privilege into social classes. Individuals' position within these social class patterns is referred to as their social status. An individual's social status can be achieved or ascribed.

An ascribed status is typically assigned to a person at birth and is connected to many characteristics other than the income of parents—race, gender, disability/ability, age, and other factors that are not chosen or earned. In almost all instances, the factors that determine your ascribed status cannot be changed, although a few people do change their gender, and disabilities may appear or disappear. In contrast, an achieved status is based primarily on earned accomplishments/achievements. If a person goes to university and successfully completes his or her PhD, that person has earned the title of "doctor." If an athlete performs well, he or she can potentially achieve the status of "professional athlete" and the income that accompanies that status.

Although most people would argue that a **meritocracy**, a system based upon achievement rather than ascribed status, is preferable, understanding individual social status and social class is far more complex than equating success or failures to individual strengths and/or weaknesses. Not all positions within the hierarchy are based solely on merit. For instance, under a meritocracy, entrance into university should be based solely on a student's achieving the grades necessary for acceptance. However, the best predictors of university entrance are family income as well as the post-secondary education of one or both parents. If social status were based primarily on earned achievement, we might expect to see a high degree of social mobility—the movement between classes; however, throughout their lifetime most people remain in the social class into which they were born (Western and Wright 1994).

When we look beyond the borders of Canada, however, we find that we appear to have an open stratification system. It is possible in Canada for a person from a poor family to move up in class. A young person from a poor family can win a scholarship or can apply for a student loan to attend college or university. Through hard work and determination, the student may obtain a medical degree and become a practising physician, improving his or her socio-economic status dramatically.

From a global perspective, we see that Canada offers opportunities for upward mobility; however, we also need to recognize the degree to which ascribed status tends to restrict personal advances. For example, Aboriginal peoples, visible minorities, recent immigrants, those with disabilities, and lone mothers all continue to experience disproportionate poverty rates. Additionally, it is important to note that social class is not simply a reflection of income but includes other factors such as wealth and prestige. Resource extraction workers employed in the Alberta oil sands might, with overtime, earn well over $100,000 annually. Although they are earning more money than many teachers and nurses, they are generally not perceived as holding the same social position, because their jobs lack professional prestige. Thus, income and economic assets alone are not clear indicators of social class. Not only are the nature and determinants of social class membership not clear-cut, but sociologists themselves are divided on the overall societal significance of social stratification.

TIME to REFLECT
Is Canada truly a meritocracy?

SOCIOLOGY AND SOCIAL STRATIFICATION

Conflict Approaches to Social Stratification: Karl Marx

The history of all hitherto existing society is the history of class struggles. . . . society is more and more splitting up into two great hostile camps, into two great classes directly facing each other—bourgeoisie and proletariat (Marx and Engels 1985 [1848], 203–4).

In this famous quotation from the *Communist Manifesto*, Karl Marx (1818–83) outlined the two issues that are central to his work on class: he argued that society is characterized by conflict (class struggles) and a distinguishing feature of capitalism is the division of society into two central classes, the **bourgeoisie** and the **proletariat**. Marx maintained that society is divided into these classes on the basis of their relationship to the means of production—their access to the tools, factories,

land, and investment capital used to produce wealth (Marx and Engels 1985 [1848]). As the bourgeoisie, who own the means of production, pursue their self-interest in the form of profit, they necessarily exploit the proletariat, who have little choice other than to sell their labour.

According to Marx, this capitalist mode of organization has several characteristics that distort the structure and meaning of the economic process: private property, expropriation of surplus wealth, division of labour, and alienated labour (Grabb 2007). Marx contended that the drive for private property is primarily responsible for creating the two-class system. Under capitalism, everyone needs to have an income in order to obtain property and ensure survival. Those who exist outside this system—for example, the unemployed who lack an income—serve as a reserve army of labour ready to be called upon if the demand for labour increases or if current workers complain about their exploitation. By paying workers low wages, capitalists are able to expropriate surplus wealth from the labour process. Given the absence of employment opportunities outside the industrial economy, workers have no choice but to exchange their labour for wages that are far below the value of the products they produce for the owners. While working people are responsible for creating a surplus of wealth, they do not reap the benefits.

Marx maintained that the inequality this system produced is neither desirable nor inevitable (Lindsey and Beach 2003). In fact, he held that class conflict between wage-labourers and the owners of the means of production would be historically inevitable as the inequality between these classes became ever more pronounced. As the proletariat class developed **class consciousness**—an awareness of workers' shared interests and their ability to act in those interests—Marx predicted a socialist revolution, the eradication of capitalist economies, and a new mode of production.

Structural Functionalist Approaches to Social Stratification: Durkheim

In contrast to Marx, other sociologists have emphasized the social functions played by social stratification. Émile Durkheim (1858–1917) looked at how social structures, which power and struggle operate within, are even possible in the first place (Grabb 2007). He argued that early societies were held together by mechanical solidarity—union based on minimal division of labour, similarity of people who had roughly the same life experience and shared common beliefs. When a society is comprised of similar individuals, the group feels a sense of solidarity based on these common experiences, values, and beliefs. Durkheim suggested that the division of labour was a crucial force in the historical evolution of social structures. Once the division of labour became more extensive, no one could survive without the co-operation of others. This division of labour weakened the old mechanical solidarity and was the key means by which the new form of solidarity emerged: organic solidarity. Under organic solidarity, Durkheim argued, there was a moral stability as people recognized each other's obligations to and dependence upon one another. However, when people do not recognize this obligation, anomie may occur. An anomic division of labour—conflict between labour and capital—leads to class polarization. Because this division of labour is forced, it encourages class polarization.

TIME to REFLECT

Do you think class inequality is a functional and necessary part of society? Are higher rewards necessary in order to motivate people to fill certain positions?

Symbolic Interactionist Perspectives on Social Stratification: Thorstein Veblen

Symbolic interactionists take a different approach to social stratification. Rather than attempting to explain why stratification exists or how conflict is created because of class inequality, they are interested in how people interpret and represent inequality. As their name suggests, symbolic interactionists consider how meanings and symbols enable people to carry out uniquely human actions and interactions (Ritzer 2000b, 357). In reference to social stratification, they pay particular attention to the use of status symbols.

In *The Theory of the Leisure Class* (1899), Thorstein Veblen (1857–1929) focused on

the role of the leisure class and the role of business in society. From his perspective, business existed only to earn profits for a leisure class. The leisure class was primarily engaged in **conspicuous consumption**—the purchasing of expensive goods and services primarily for the purpose of putting wealth on display. These purchases were status symbols—various signs that identified a particular social and economic status or position. Diamond tiaras, massive country estates, and large retinues of servants would all be status symbols in Veblen's era.

Today, status symbols remain apparent everywhere, although they may manifest themselves differently depending on culture and location. Expensive houses, luxury cars and clothing, along with exotic vacations and elite sports, still communicate wealth and social position. Symbolic statements about wealth are also apparent throughout the university, with name brands such as Lululemon, PINK, and UGG dotting the hallways even though inexpensive yet similar apparel is widely available.

Veblen's main contributions, then, were in highlighting the symbolic embodiment of social inequality through the practice of conspicuous consumption and in his contention that most people want to appear as though they live above their actual social location. Today, conspicuous consumption, even at the risk of indebtedness, has become epidemic, as suggested by the multi-billion-dollar industries dedicated to helping the millions of North Americans live beyond their means—industries ranging from payday loan companies to the credit card divisions of banks and credit unions.

Feminist Explanations for Social Stratification

Predictably, few theorists in the past included women in class analysis. Perhaps the breadwinner ideology (the assumption that a woman's role in the household was to provide unpaid work for her family while her husband provided the economic resources through his paid labour) excluded women as participants in the social class structures (Nakhaie 2002). Certainly, stratification research has repeatedly been critiqued for being "malestream"—excluding women from research samples on the basis of their secondary relationship to the labour market, focusing exclusively on class rather than incorporating gender inequality, and assuming that women's economic and social positions are derived from those of their husbands or fathers (Abbott and Sapsford 1987).

Today, feminist scholars continue to press analysts to recognize that gender intersects with social class in important and complex ways. For example, because of the continued gender segregation of the labour force and women's traditional role in providing unpaid labour in the household, women are at greater risk of poverty than their male counterparts. This **feminization of poverty** is important to an understanding of social class inequalities in Canada and globally. While there have been dramatic changes in women's status over the past 50 years, evidence suggests that women remain disadvantaged both in the world of paid work and in the home. As repeatedly documented in the Canadian census, many continue to undertake the lion's share of domestic labour in the

home and must make the necessary adjustments (including less sleep) when they hold paid employment (Milan, Keown, and Urquijo 2011). Within the labour force, despite employment equity legislation, women continue to be ghettoized, not only into specific employment areas but also at the lower rungs of their work milieu and their professions—they tend to be school teachers rather than principals and so on (Ferrao 2010; Armstrong and Armstrong 1994; Hochschild 1997). In short, feminist analysts continue to underscore the complexities and contradictions embedded in class and status inequalities.

CLASS AND STATUS INEQUALITY IN CANADA

The Wealthy, Elites, and Super Rich

The poor, homeless, and low-income workers seem the natural targets of any analysis of social inequality. However, the opposite end

(© Atlantide Phototravel/Corbis)

Despite gains in education and job opportunities, women in traditional female-dominated occupations such as care workers or housekeepers continue to be marginalized members of society.

of the continuum—those who hold disproportionate financial and other assets—are at least as significant in an understanding of our society. Not surprisingly, the elites have long been of interest to sociologists.

One of the most prominent US sociologists of the twentieth century—C. Wright Mills (1916–62)—played a key role in establishing elites as a central sociological topic. Most notably, his popular book *The Power Elite* (1956) challenged the then-dominant structural-functional approach to social stratification—a viewpoint that minimized class differences among Americans. Indeed, Mills proposed that the elites in US society were so powerful and so co-ordinated that they jeopardized democracy. This book triggered a wide variety of further studies examining US power discrepancies. Most notably in the US, G. William Domhoff (1936–) has produced a steady stream of books profiling the power elite and exploring "who rules America" (2009). His most recent work profiles the growing diversification (by gender and ethnicity) of American business leaders (Zweigenhaft and Domhoff 2011).

Canadian sociologists and social analysts have also studied the powerful. English Canada's pre-eminent sociologist of the twentieth century—John Porter (1921–79)—authored *The Vertical Mosaic* (1965), which provided an eye-opening analysis of the concentration of corporate power in the hands of a few—mostly anglophone Canadian males. Wallace Clement (1951–) advanced Porter's work with his book *The Canadian Corporate Elite* (1975). Clement reveals that in several respects those holding economic power in Canada have become a more diverse (ethnically) group but many of the traditional structures that bound the elite together—private schools, family relations, cultural and charitable organizations—persist.

More recently, popular commentators have joined with academic researchers in revealing the ways in which wealth and power are socially constructed and perpetuated in Canada. Journalists Peter C. Newman and Diane Francis played particularly important roles in drawing Canadians' attention to the key power-holders in our economy. Francis, for example, wrote *Controlling Interest: Who Owns Canada?* (1986) and *Who Owns Canada Now?* (2008). Although she reported in 1986 that 32 families and 5

conglomerates were in control of 40 per cent of Canadian banking, business, and politics, her more recent work suggests that the elite is not becoming an increasingly closed circle, and she identifies new players who have entered these rarefied spheres. By 2007, "[O]nly 21% of the biggest 500 [companies] were family-controlled, by . . . 75 [families, rather than 32]; 30% of the country's biggest 500 [companies] were foreign owned, 8.5% [were] government owned [down from 22% in 1986]" (2008, 16). Family control, while still centralized, has spread out, foreign ownership has increased, and government control has dropped precipitously in the era of privatization. The economic elite described by Francis is a dynamic and shifting reality—but one that still plays a major role in society.

Canadian social scientists have not, however, left the field to the mass media. Jamie Brownlee's *Ruling Canada: Corporate Cohesion and Democracy* (2005) pulls together much of the more recent information on the "ruling class"; he explores the various contemporary mechanisms—including conservative think-tanks such as the Fraser Institute and overlapping memberships on various corporate boards—that serve to draw the Canadian corporate elite together into a self-conscious and integrated social force. Most notable among contemporary researchers is sociologist William K. Carroll. His *Corporate Power in a Globalizing World* (2010) uses network analysis to document the social ties (from shared membership in elite clubs to corporate interlocks with universities) that integrate the elite into every facet of Canadian society while also creating elite solidarity.

In short, elite research has clarified the considerable gap that exists between the top and bottom of our economic hierarchy. Some of this is also communicated through Statistics Canada's income survey (2011b). This analysis divides all Canadian families into quintiles (one-fifths) and determines the average income for those occupying the wealthiest one-fifth all the way down to those in the bottom one-fifth. The latest data indicate that, in 2009, the "average after tax total" of Canadian families in the richest quintile was $83,500, while those in the lowest quintile averaged $15,400 (Statistics Canada 2011b, 2). By 2009, 9.6 per cent, or almost 3.2

Considered one of Canada's most prestigious preparatory schools, Upper Canada College is attended by the sons of some of Canada's wealthiest families—such as the Thomsons. Known as the "Old Boys," the college's alumni occupy positions of wealth and power in Canada.

million Canadians, were living at or below the **Low Income Cut-off (LICO)**, and the income ratio between the wealthy and the poor remained unchanged from 2000 to 2009 (2011b, 2). In short, about one in ten Canadians live in poor circumstances, and the gap between rich and poor has changed little in the past decade.

Within this social stratification pattern, there is a very small number of Canadians who are enormously wealthy and powerful. *Forbes* magazine's yearly list of the world's billionaires reported in 2011 that 24 Canadians had made the list and shared a combined net worth of $85.2 billion. As with many of the global elite, the 2008 recession barely registered on their portfolios, and from 2010 to 2011 their fortunes increased by 14 per cent as the Canadian dollar strengthened (Dolan and Blankfeld 2011). To put these levels of wealth into perspective, consider the strategy proposed by Linda McQuaig and Neil Brooks (2010). If members of one of Canada's wealthiest families—the Thomson family—started counting their wealth ($21.34 billion in 2011) at $1 per second and counted non-stop day and night, they would have it all counted up in approximately 700 years. This is wealth beyond the wildest imaginings of most Canadians. This is wealth that can and is translated into endowments to universities, the creation of cultural institutions, and support for particular political parties. While some might see this pattern as benign, social critics question the desirability of small groups

of individuals holding so much sway over the direction of Canadian society.

Further, the very wealthy, as Mills, Domhoff, Porter, Clement, Carroll, and others have pointed out, tend to be bound together by important shared experiences. Many were themselves born into wealthy families. These families tend to live in exclusive neighbourhoods, vacation at elite resorts, belong to the "best" clubs, send their children to exclusive private schools, and join other wealthy families in participating in specific philanthropic and cultural events. In addition, in the more public domain they sit with one another on corporate boards, university governing councils, and political organizations. These shared experiences inevitably lead to friendships, family intermarriage, and shared perspectives on social issues. The elite are by no means a homogenous, in-grown mass, but—to invoke the famous phrase from F. Scott Fitzgerald— "They are different from you and me."

The bottom line is that there is considerable evidence that a quite small number of Canadians and non-Canadians occupy positions of extreme wealth and privilege, that their power often extends beyond national boundaries, and that there is no sign that their economic dominance is waning, though their wealth ebbs and flows with the state of the world economy (Canadian Press 2011). These social realities necessarily raise two concerns: What are the implications of this narrow consolidation of wealth and power for our democratic structures, and how much of a gap between haves and have-nots is desirable or acceptable in any society that wants to maintain opportunities for social mobility and access?

TIME to REFLECT

What are the implications of the fact that the president of the United States earns $400,000 a year (presiding over a $14-trillion economy) while the CEO of the Potash Corporation of Saskatchewan earns $18 million a year (Olive 2009, B4)?

The Poor and Economically Marginalized

Who are the poor? Do you have to be homeless to qualify? Jobless? Receiving social assistance? Are there status symbols that visibly mark the poor, such as worn-out clothing that lacks a brand name, a neglect of hygiene, criminal behaviour? Why are people poor? Is it because they are lazy? Drunks and/or drug users? Or is it because they cannot find employment or they have too many children? This section will illuminate how poverty rates are determined in Canada and consider the implications of current poverty patterns.

The word *poverty* is often used as an all-encompassing term to describe situations in which people lack many of the opportunities available to the average citizen (Levitas 1998). There is no shortage of poverty measures. The Canadian federal government has developed five measures, while social planning councils, individual researchers, non-profit organizations, and others have developed their own measures (deGroot-Maggetti 2002). The most common distinctions made between these definitions of poverty are the terms "absolute" and "relative." The former definitions refer to a lack of basic necessities, while the latter emphasize inadequacy compared to average living standards (Mitchell and Shillington 2002; Sarlo 1996). Teasing out the differences between absolute and relative definitions of poverty, Ross and Shillington (1994, 3–4) suggest that the first approach assumes that we can ascertain an absolute measure of poverty by calculating the cost of goods and services essential for physical survival. The relative approach is grounded in the belief that any definition of poverty should take social and physical well-being into account. This approach argues that someone who has noticeably less than his or her surrounding community will feel disadvantaged (Ross and Schillington 1994, 4).

Statistics Canada, which collects income data annually from sample surveys of Canadians, relies on two low-income indices—incidence and gap ratio—and three measures to determine which Canadians are poor, living at or below low-income levels: the Low Income Cut-offs (LICO), the Market Basket Measure (MBM), and the low-income measure (LIM). Incidence refers to the numbers of individuals who live below a poverty line. Rather than referring to the incidence of low income in social groupings—for example, lone-parent families—the data refer to the incidence of low income among individuals who live in lone-parent families. The gap ratio refers to the difference between a family's actual income and the low-income level established by the poverty line (Statistics Canada 2011b; Hay 2009; Curwood 2009, 3).

Applying all these statistical measures of poverty gives us a fuller picture of low income than can be ascertained from just one measure. The LICO is a relative measure of poverty

TABLE 6.1 ▼ Percentage of Canadians Living on a Low Income, 2000–9

	2000	2001	2002	2003	2004	2005	2006	2007	2008	2009
					%					
All persons	12.5	11.2	11.6	11.6	11.4	10.8	10.5	9.2	9.4	9.6
Persons under 18 years old in economic families	13.8	12.1	12.3	12.5	12.9	11.6	11.3	9.4	9.0	9.5
In two-parent families	9.5	8.3	7.4	7.9	8.4	7.8	7.7	6.6	6.5	7.3
In female lone-parent families	40.1	37.4	43.0	41.4	40.4	32.9	31.7	26.6	23.4	21.5
Persons 18 to 64 years old	12.9	11.7	12.0	12.2	11.9	11.4	11.2	9.9	10.2	10.5
Persons 65 and over	7.6	6.7	7.6	6.8	5.6	6.2	5.4	4.9	5.8	5.2

SOURCE: Statistics Canada, "*Table 3 Percentage of persons in low income* (1992 base after-tax income low income cut-offs)," *The Daily* 15 June 2011, www.statcan.gc.ca/daily-quotidien/110615/t110615b3-eng.htm

that defines as low-income those Canadians who spend 20 per cent or more of their gross (before tax) income on food, shelter, and clothing than does the average Canadian (Curwood 2009, 3). In 2009, the percentage of Canadians with incomes under the LICO was 9.6 per cent. The MBM estimates the cost of a specific basket of goods and services (food, shelter, and so on) representing a modest, basic standard of living for a reference family made up of one male and one female adult and two children. The MBM is developed for 49 geographical areas within the 10 provinces and in this way reveals the regional variations in the cost of living. In Ontario the incidence of individuals living below the MBM was 11 per cent in 2009, unchanged from 2000. According to this measure, most of the provinces had slightly improved since 2000, and the gap ratio (the difference between actual incomes and the MBM income lines) has decreased (Statistics Canada 2011b).

The LIM is defined as 50 per cent of the median income of all Canadians (but also includes calculations relative to different metropolitan areas and family size). This measure is useful, because it allows for international comparisons. Canada's LIM incidence was 16 per cent in 2009, down from 21 per cent in 2000 (Statistics Canada 2011b).

Although various organizations have developed these systems for drawing a dividing line between the haves and the have-nots, it is clear that the actual choice of a poverty line is ultimately rather arbitrary. Further, many analysts argue that poverty is an issue that extends far beyond income. Amartya Sen (2000) has made a significant intellectual contribution to poverty discourse with his assertion that an impoverished life is more than just the lack of money: "Income may be the most prominent means for a good life without deprivation, but it is not the only influence on the lives we can lead." Arguing for a relational understanding of poverty and deprivation, he suggests, "We must look at impoverished lives, and not just at depleted wallets" (2000, 3). For Sen, poverty is the lack of the capability to live a minimally decent life that, in turn, limits the ability to take part in the life of the community (2000, 4).

Income inequality has a detrimental effect on one of the most important facets of life—health. See "The Social Determinants of Health" in Chapter 12, p. 242, to learn more.

It is a staggering comment on the lack of political and societal will that poverty and

GLOBAL ISSUES

The Occupy Movement

Prompted by a wry suggestion from *Adbusters* magazine (based in Vancouver), social activists came together to "occupy" Wall Street in the summer of 2011. With a somewhat scattered agenda, they targeted the world's financial hub as the key to achieving necessary social change. Some in the groups held signs challenging the unrepentant greed of financiers who despite a very public government bailout in 2008 were now happily awarding themselves enormous salaries and prodigious stock options. Others demanded an end to poverty and increased assistance for those who are marginalized. Still others coined the popular phrase "we are the 99 per cent"—drawing attention to the 1 per cent of the population who owned so much of US wealth. The action, while not a movement, soon generated copycat events throughout North America, including gatherings across Canada. Occupy Bay Street took over a downtown public park in Toronto for several weeks and generated heated public debate about social inequality as well as the rights of protesters. Finally, as the winter of 2011–12 settled in and police pressure intensified, the occupations ended. However, following so closely in the wake of the "Arab Spring," in which so many citizens of Arab countries took to the street to oppose despotism, demand democracy, and assert their rights to a decent standard of living, these actions sent a perceptible ripple through North American politics (Elliott-Buckley 2011; Shallhorn 2011/12).

One in ten Canadian children lives in poverty and may have to go to school without breakfast. Organizations like Breakfast Clubs Canada aim to provide these children with a nutritious start to the day. In 2010/11, Breakfast Clubs Canada served 16 million meals to more than 106,000 students in need across Canada. (www.breakfastclubscanada.org)

social marginalization have persisted with only incremental improvements. Despite promises, such as the campaign to end child poverty by the year 2000, very little has actually been achieved. Currently, about one in ten children lives below the Low Income Cut-off. With unemployment rates continuing to hover around 7 per cent, with the global economy still vulnerable to economic depression and experiencing negligible employment growth, and with many politicians focusing on deficit-fighting rather than social agendas, the situation is unlikely to improve, and we may indeed see an erosion of past gains. In this context, the usual groups will continue to suffer as a result of inequalities.

Groups of Canadians vulnerable to economic marginalization include women (especially those in lone-parent families), unattached individuals, Aboriginal people, persons with disabilities, recent immigrants and visible minorities, and the working poor (Collin and Jensen 2009; Hay 2009).

Women

Around the globe, as well as in Canada, women figure prominently among the poorest of the poor, especially those raising children as lone parents and those living as unattached seniors. Canada's 2006 census reported that there were 1.4 million lone-parent families residing in Canada, 80 per cent headed by lone mothers. By 2008, the number of lone mother–headed families living below the poverty line was 20.9 per cent in contrast to 7 per cent of lone father–headed families (Williams 2010, 21). In 2008, the poverty rate for senior women living alone was 17 per cent—nearly seven times the rate for senior families with two adults or more, which sat at 2.6 per cent (Milan and Vezina 2011, 24; Williams 2010, 21).

Gender wage inequities continue to contribute to women's high poverty rates. Although the Pay Equity Act, enacted in 1987, made it illegal to pay someone less for their work on the basis of gender, Canadian women working full-time, full-year, continue to earn approximately 71 per cent of what their male counterparts earn (Williams 2010, 13). The wage gap in turn is interwoven with continued occupational segregation, undervaluing of women's paid work, the restructuring of women's employment through increased privatization and outsourcing, and a lack of child care limiting women's choices for employment (Fleras 2009; Albanese 2012).

Does the Canadian government do enough to support working parents? See "Affordable and Regulated Child Care," Chapter 9, p. 183, for more information on this topic.

Unattached Individuals

Individuals living on their own are, not surprisingly, particularly vulnerable to low income. According to the latest census data (2006), more than 4 million Canadians (17 per cent of women and 16 per cent of men) live alone or with non-family members (Milan, Keown, and Urquijo 2011, 17). In 2009, approximately 1.3 million of these unattached individuals lived on a low income (27 per cent) (Statistics Canada 2011b, 8). Here, both men and women shoulder the likelihood of impoverishment. According to Statistics Canada, 35.7 per cent of unattached (non-elderly) women had a low income in 2000, compared to 30 per cent of males (Collin and Jensen 2009). However, by

2009, 32.5 per cent of unattached non-elderly females and 30.1 per cent of comparable males were living on low income. Indeed, women and men occupying these two categories were characterized by the first and second highest poverty rates in Canada (National Council of Welfare 2012).

Aboriginal People

Most Canadians are well aware that poverty is significantly higher among Aboriginal people (Collin and Jensen 2009). Statistics Canada reports that in 2007, 18.7 per cent of Aboriginal people living in economic families lived in poverty, while 47.8 per cent of unattached Aboriginal people did (Collin and Jensen 2009). Unemployment and geographic isolation partly explain the high rates of poverty; however, a host of other reasons intersect, making Aboriginal people particularly vulnerable to impoverishment (Noel 2009). Many Aboriginal people lack education (42 per cent of Aboriginal Canadians have completed a post-secondary education, compared to 61 per cent of the non-Aboriginal population), and their living and health conditions, especially on remote northern reserves, remain well below those of other Canadians (Noel 2009; Gionet 2009).

For example, in 2006, 28 per cent of all First Nations people and 44 per cent of First Nations people living on reserves had dwellings in need of major repairs—compared to 7 per cent of the non-Aboriginal population (Gionet 2009, 58). Many blame Aboriginal people for their own situation, citing rampant alcoholism, substance abuse, and domestic violence as the self-inflicted cause of their poverty rates. This view ignores the long-standing history of colonial domination and cultural oppression that Aboriginal peoples have faced (Francis 2012).

Many factors have contributed to the lack of education on the part of many Aboriginal Canadians. See "Educational Opportunities and Inequalities" in Chapter 10, p. 206, for a broader discussion.

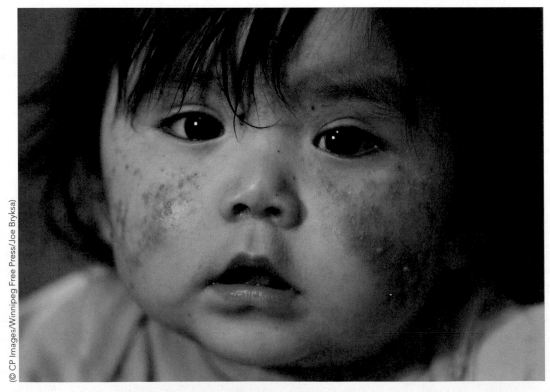

(© CP Images/Winnipeg Free Press/Joe Bryksa)

Many First Nations reserves do not have access to running water. A multitude of health problems can arise from a lack of safe water, including gastrointestinal diseases and skin rashes, as suffered by Lyra Harper, who lives an hour out of Winnipeg at Red Sucker Lake.

New Immigrants and Visible Minorities

According to the 2006 Canadian census, recent immigrants (those who had arrived within the preceding five years) are more vulnerable to living in poverty than other Canadians. They are at greater risk despite having significantly higher education and more potential earners per household. Based on the latest census data (2006), immigrants make up 66 per cent of the **racialized** persons living in poverty in Canada. Within this group, 42 per cent of immigrants who arrived between 2001 and 2006 and 36 per cent of those arriving between 1991 and 2000 were impoverished (National Council of Welfare 2012). There has been a dramatic rise in the educational attainment of new immigrants because of changes to Canada's immigrant selection criteria in 1993; however, this has had little impact on poverty outcomes (Collin and Jensen 2009). Of immigrants who arrived in Canada in 2000 and who experienced chronic poverty (low income for four out of the first five years in Canada), 52 per cent were skilled immigrants, and 41 per cent had a university degree (Picot, Hou, and Coulombe 2007).

These statistics suggest that recent immigrants do not reap the same rewards from their educational qualifications and work experience as those who are Canadian-born. Foreign education and experience is less valued, resulting in immigrant populations needing to update their education in Canada and often taking dead-end survival jobs in an effort to gain some type of Canadian experience. Racism, language difficulties, cultural differences, and poor access to job networks are also used to explain their disproportionate representation among those living with a low income.

People Living with a Disability

Statistics Canada has stated that in 2006, 4.4 million Canadians reported living with a disability. In 2005, disabled Canadians who were of working age (18 to 64 years of age) had an average income 10 per cent lower than those without disabilities, and 17.1 per cent of people with disabilities had earnings below $5000 annually (Collin and Jensen 2009). Human Resources and Skills Development Canada (HRSDC) (2007) reported that people with disabilities are more likely than people without to rely on government supports. They found that in 2005, 59 per cent of people with disabilities relied on a source of income other than wages. The experience of those living with disabilities also varied by gender, with women reporting higher rates of disability as well as lower incomes and employment rates than their male counterparts with disabilities (Collin and Jensen 2009).

Besides physical limitations that may prevent some people with disabilities from carrying out certain types of employment, they are often alienated from the workforce through varying types of discrimination. For example, they are often excluded via institutional discrimination (organizations work or deliver services in a way that prejudices minority groups), environmental discrimination (for example, inaccessible buildings and lack of accessible transportation), and attitudinal discrimination (prevailing attitudes exclude and alienate disabled people). These types of discrimination are forms of ableism—that is, discrimination against people based on preconceived notions about their limitations.

The Working Poor

Although there a number of definitions, the working poor are generally defined as individuals who are not full-time students and who have an income below the low-income threshold (LICO, LIM, or MBM) despite working a minimum of 910 hours in a given year (Collin and Jensen 2009; Fleury and Fortin 2006). Contrary to the impression given by media reports that poor Canadians are unemployed and rely on government transfers, 37 per cent of low-income individuals in 2008 belonged to a family in which someone was employed at least half of the year. In 2009, more than 1.6 million Canadians aged 25 to 64 were living in "employed" low-income families (Luong 2011, 4, 5). Not only are they employed, but they work on average as many hours as other workers (although fewer have full-time, year-round employment) (Fleury and Fortin 2006). Despite similar work efforts, the working poor earn on average 65 per cent of the wages of other salaried workers (Collin and Jensen 2009). They also tend to hold jobs offering fewer benefits, including limited or no access to health insurance, dental care plans, life and disability insurance, and pension plans (Fleury and Fortin 2006).

UNDER the WIRE

Technological Inequality

Poverty has wide-ranging consequences, not the least of which is exclusion from many of the goods and services Canadian society can provide. For example, in 2007 one in five Canadian households was too poor to afford eyeglasses, dental care, or meaningful involvement in community recreational activities (NUPGE 2009). For many poor Canadians, this pattern also extends to access to modern technologies. According to a recent report by the Canadian Centre for Policy Alternatives, *The Affordability Gap*, only one-third of low-income households have high-speed Internet access, only 40 per cent have cellphones, and only 26 per cent have computers. In contrast, 80 per cent or more of wealthy homes have access to these technologies (Kerstetter 2009). These results confirm earlier research indicating that information and communication technologies are slower to "penetrate" low-income households (Sciadas 2002). In a society where education and employment are increasingly linked to information technology, the negative potential of this pattern is clear.

Understanding Poverty

Many people believe that we all start out with the same chances of obtaining the "American Dream"—democracy promises prosperity. This belief system is grounded in **classism**—bias, prejudice, and discrimination on the basis of social class—and often results in **blaming the victim** rather than the system. Coined by William Ryan (1971), blaming the victim is a view that holds individuals entirely responsible for any negative situations that may arise in their lives. Because there is an implicit understanding in Canada that individuals who work hard should be able to prosper, those who do not succeed are seen as at fault and are criticized as lacking motivation or being too weak to help themselves.

In a poverty "classic," anthropologist Oscar Lewis (1996 [1966]) investigated the lives of the poor and argued that people who live in poverty are a subculture with different value systems from the rest of society. He maintained that those who live in this culture of poverty feel inferior and helpless and have a defeatist attitude, which then limits their ability to improve their situation. In this analysis, the responsibility for changing impoverished circumstances is placed squarely on the individual. Contemporary analysts argue that the classism and blaming the victim stance embedded in Lewis's analysis have contributed to "poor-bashing." Facts about poverty and the poor are ignored, and instead stereotypes are repeated. These stereotypes, in turn, may lead to both verbal and physical assaults on the poor.

This approach to the poor and poverty, of course, completely overlooks facts indicating that poverty results from institutional arrangements and even legislation. For example, a great deal of Canadian poverty would immediately disappear if legislation on welfare rates and minimum wage were improved. According to the National Council of Welfare, in 2007 it would have taken $12.6 billion to provide the 3.5 million Canadians living in poverty with enough income to rise above the poverty line. Yet Canadians spend about twice that much each year to deal with the consequences of poverty, such as health problems and crime that derive directly from poverty (Monsebraaten 2011, A12).

As Michael Katz, a well-known poverty researcher in the United States, argues, poverty and inequality are not about specific people and their personal qualities; rather, they are about wealth distribution—some people receive a great deal more than others. He writes, "descriptions of the demography, behavior or beliefs [of people who are poor] can't explain inequality" (Katz 1989, 7). Jean Swanson (2001) furthers this assertion and urges society to stop blaming individuals for their impoverished circumstances so that "we can expose the policies, laws, and economic system that force millions of people in Canada and around the world to compete against each other, driving down wages and creating more poverty" (2001, 8).

Katz and Swanson are employing a perspective often referred to as **blaming the system**. This is more consistent with a sociological view, since it recognizes the systemic discrimination that exists within society. People are poor for many reasons that are beyond their control. There are many structural variables that influence poverty levels, such as deindustrialization (the replacement of well-paid manufacturing jobs with lower-paid service-based jobs), rising costs of living, barriers to opportunities (such as increased tuition for education and training programs), limited access to affordable housing, inability to obtain credit, and so on.

Policies to Address Poverty

There is a very long tradition of efforts to "help" the poor. Initially driven by Christian and Jewish religious ethics, early charities in Canada provided food, clothing, and occasionally shelter for those who had fallen on "hard times." Then, as now, single mothers (often widows), orphaned children, seniors, and the disabled were routinely marginalized. In the absence of government-funded welfare programs, they were often forced to turn to private and religious agencies to beg for whatever support they could find.

SOCIOLOGY in ACTION

Challenging Poverty and Economic Inequality

Sociologists have played a leading role in exposing economic inequalities in Canada, in exploring the sources of such inequalities, and in gauging the societal impact of growing gaps between the haves and the have-nots. While it is very important that this sociological research helps to inform all Canadians about economic inequality in Canada, it is particularly important that government policy—at the municipal, provincial, and federal levels—is informed by rigorous research information. In this regard, sociologists have played a pivotal role in creating and maintaining a variety of organizations that support research, the dissemination of this research, and lobbying government to incorporate accurate research information into legislation. Through the creation and maintenance of groups such as the Canadian Centre for Policy Alternatives, the Canadian Centre for Social Development, and the Caledon Institute of Social Policy, sociologists and other social scientists have been instrumental in developing social policy to address poverty and economic inequalities.

The recent (2005) creation of the Centre d'étude sur la pauvreté et l'exclusion (CEPE) (Centre for the Study of Poverty and Social Exclusion) by the Quebec government is another example of the role that sociologists, along with other social scientists and government officials, play in creating the agencies whose mandate is to provide "reliable and rigorous information" that then can be used to fashion appropriate

social policies. CEPE proposes research topics and, in some instances, funds proposals and makes the resultant reports available to the public through its website (www.cepe.gouv.qc.ca). This information—examining both local and international efforts to combat poverty—is then available to inform future initiatives.

One outstanding initiative to understand and reduce inequalities is the Vibrant Communities program (www.vibrantcommunities.ca). Supported (in part) by the Caledon Institute of Social Policy, Vibrant Communities encourages collaboration between social science researchers, government representatives, businesspeople, and community workers to explore local initiatives to combat poverty. Specific groups involved in the program include, for example, Opportunities Niagara, the Winnipeg Poverty Reduction Council, and the Hamilton Roundtable for Poverty Reduction. The resultant community-level evaluations are now playing a very important role in suggesting specific ways that economically depressed areas can create and introduce new strategies to reduce inequalities and improve community strengths. For example, some communities have effectively mobilized involvement in arts and crafts to both strengthen community ties and create avenues for income generation. Significantly, Vibrant Communities identifies "high use of research to inform the work" as one of the key ingredients in program success.

Throughout the early twentieth century, very little changed for the overwhelming majority of the Canadian population who were not property-owners. Industrial work was harsh, injury and work-related illness were commonplace, and wages were far from reliable. Not surprisingly, increasing numbers of workers and their families rebelled against a system that provided them with so little in the way of personal security. In particular, the Winnipeg General Strike in 1919—a strike that resulted in the deployment of the army to maintain order in Winnipeg—suggested to many that Marx's predictions of class conflict were not far off the mark.

To better understand why Marx felt that conflict between wage-labourers and the owners of the means of production was inevitable, see "Material Processes" in Chapter 14, p. 276.

Then the Great Depression of the 1930s—when unemployment rates soared to 30 per cent—underscored the vulnerability of most workers to impoverishment (Duffy 2011). Predictably, this constellation of events pushed social activists and politicians to formulate legislation that softened the harshest edges of the capitalist economy.

In 1927, the Old Age Pensions Act was introduced, followed by the Unemployment Insurance Act in 1940, the Family Allowance Act in 1944, and in 1947 the first Hospital Insurance Plan. Throughout the postwar period, particularly in the economically buoyant 1960s, a series of policies were implemented—Canada and Quebec Pension Plans (1965), Medicare (1966), Federal Education Grants (1976), and an improved Unemployment Insurance Act (1971). Many of these initiatives were funded by progressive income tax programs that taxed the well-to-do at a significantly higher rate than less well-off citizens. As a net result,

(© CP Images/National Archives of Canada)

Men clear the road to the railway station in Valcartier, Quebec, in January 1934. Thanks to the Relief Act of 1932, single, homeless men were provided with food, clothing, accommodation, and medical assistance in exchange for work on roads, on railways, and in forests.

government bodies and agencies were in place to provide at least some assistance to the elderly, ill, disabled, and out-of-work.

This levelling of the economic playing field was then generally reversed throughout the 1980s and 1990s. Largely in response to the popularization of neo-liberalism as espoused by Ronald Reagan, Margaret Thatcher, and Brian Mulroney, legislators opted to reduce the size of government and place greater burden directly on individuals and their families. Effectively, there has been a steady dismantling of much of the "welfare state." For example, unemployment benefits were increasingly restricted both in terms of eligibility for benefits and the length of the benefit period. Similarly, the cash value of welfare benefits across the country was reduced, and workfare provisions (requiring many welfare recipients to accept any paid work or training in exchange for their benefits) were introduced. In this context, it is not surprising that poverty and economic marginalization remain at the centre of political struggles.

TIME to REFLECT

Who or what is to blame for social inequality? Should individuals be blamed for their lack of motivation and effort, or should society take some responsibility for ensuring an equitable standard of living for all citizens?

Conclusion: Social and Economic Inequalities—Future Trends

Various indicators suggest that economic polarization is increasing rather than decreasing (Goar 2011, A19). This trend is reflected in the fact that business CEOs in Canada are now paid compensation 325 times greater than that of shop-floor and cubicle workers, up from a ratio of 25 to 1 in the 1960s. Not surprisingly, this pattern is reflected in a growing gap between the wealthy and the average Canadian. In Canada, the top 1 per cent of income earners

receive almost 40 per cent of the total national income, up from a mere 8 per cent in the 1950s and 1960s and 33 per cent between 1998 and 2007 (Olive 2011, B1, B4).

Class polarization appears to be particularly alarming for the middle and working classes. Deindustrialization has meant the loss of numerous well-paid and secure manufacturing jobs. The manufacturing jobs that remain are primarily the purview of middle-aged males with long seniority rights, and even these jobs are in jeopardy because of plant closures. In their place are a variety of poorly paid, often precarious (part-time, contract, seasonal, temporary) jobs that do not afford job-holders, even in a dual-income family, the prospect of a secure middle-class existence. At the same time, employment in the public sector (for example, jobs in the federal, provincial, or municipal governments) has also eroded. Neo-liberalism and a penchant for deficit reduction have meant not only that much of this work has disappeared but also that what work remains has become increasingly part-time, contract, or covered through employment agencies.

At the same time that well-paying, secure, full-time employment has become increasingly scarce, the economic pressures on middle-class and working-class families have grown dramatically. For example, undergraduate university tuition increased by 165 per cent between 1991/92 and 2007/8, while graduate and professional students face even greater increases (CAUT 2009, 38; Statistics Canada 2010e). Predictably, more students are shouldering more debt. This is not surprising, since the past few summers have recorded some of the highest rates of student unemployment since records were first collected in 1977 (Statistics Canada 2010c). When these students graduate, they enter a labour force in which statistics in early 2012, for example, revealed an unemployment rate of 7.6 per cent for the general population and a startling 14.5 per cent for those aged 15 to 24 years of age (Statistics Canada 2012c).

Significantly, in 2010, according to Statistics Canada, the non-elite 99 per cent of Canadian tax filers were earning even less of the economic pie than they did in 1982, while the wealthiest families continued to prosper (Statistics Canada 2013). This trend toward increased social inequality is often associated with concerns about the declining middle class. Roger Sauvé recently commented on the growing income inequality in Canada and the United States (2012). Similarly, *The Guardian* published an article entitled "Is the British middle class an endangered species?" If, as seems likely, these concerns are well founded, then we may face the same unsettling conclusion: "the crisis is just beginning" (Beckett 2010).

questions for critical thought

1. What kinds of social class messages are embedded in your day-to-day experiences at university?

2. How do Marx and Durkheim differ in their approach to social stratification, and which theoretical orientation appears most applicable to contemporary Canadian society?

3. What is the basis of the feminist critique of stratification theory?

4. Why would private schools and exclusive clubs be important to the Canadian economic elite?

5. What policies should be put in place to lessen the gap between the haves and the have-nots?

6. Do Canadians appear to be heading toward more or less economic and social inequality in the coming decades?

recommended readings

Rosemary Crompton. 1993. *Class and Stratification*. Cambridge: Polity.
Crompton argues that class processes are not the only factors contributing to the maintenance and reproduction of inequality; rather, cultural practices are deeply involved in both its reproduction and its maintenance.

Ralf Dahrendorf. 1959. *Class and Class Conflict in Industrial Society*. Stanford, CA: Stanford University Press.
Dahrendorf believes that in an age in which property and control have become separated in the industrial world, it is not property but the exercise of or exclusion from authoritative control that establishes class position.

Edward G. Grabb. 2007. *Theories of Social Inequality: Classical and Contemporary Perspectives*. 5th edn. Toronto: Harcourt.
Grabb provides an overview and analysis of theories of social inequality, including theorists such as Marx, Weber, Durkheim, Lenski, Poulantzas, Wright, and Giddens.

Gerhard Lenski. 1966. *Power and Privilege: A Theory of Stratification*. New York: McGraw-Hill.
Lenski contends that classes are aggregations of persons in society who stand in a similar position with respect to some form of power, privilege, or prestige. He shifts from a focus on class structure to processes that generate structure.

Peter S. Li. 1992. "Race and gender as bases of class fractions and their effects on earnings." *Canadian Review of Sociology and Anthropology* 29 (4): 488–510.
Li examines the joint effect of race and gender on income and argues that gender fractionalizes class in two important senses: as the occupational structure changes, gender provides the ground for segregating occupations into men's and women's jobs, and women have become more proletarianized than men in the labour force.

J.A. McMullin. 2004. *Understanding Inequality: Intersections of Class, Age, Gender, Ethnicity, and Race in Canada*. Toronto: Oxford University Press.
McMullin outlines the ways in which opportunities are distributed differentially in society on the basis of things such as class, age, gender, ethnicity, and race and argues for a relational understanding of inequality.

John Porter. 1965. *The Vertical Mosaic: An Analysis of Social Class and Power in Canada*. Toronto: University of Toronto Press.
Porter argues that there is a hierarchical structure of material rewards that acts as a barrier to equal opportunity. He argues that in Canada there is an establishment of a vertical mosaic of class and power, with the Anglo-Saxon charter group at the top of the class and power structures, recruiting their offspring and social equals as future elites.

recommended websites

Canada Without Poverty

www.cwp-csp.ca

Canada Without Poverty is a not-for-profit charitable organization dedicated to the elimination of poverty in Canada.

Human Resources and Skills Development Canada (HRSDC)

www.rhdcc-hrsdc.gc.ca

The HRSDC site offers information on Aboriginal peoples, children, homelessness, and indicators of well-being as well as many links to information on particular policies.

Make Poverty History

www.makepovertyhistory.ca

This site provides information about poverty around the world and includes information and resources for anti-poverty activism.

Organisation for Economic Co-operation and Development (OECD)

www.oecd.org

The OECD brings together governments from around the world to support sustainable economic growth, boost employment, raise living standards, maintain financial stability, assist other countries' economic development, and contribute to growth in world trade.

SocioSite

www.sociosite.net/topics/inequality.php

The section "Social Inequality and Class" offers a comprehensive list of sociological resources on social inequality, class, stratification, and poverty.

chapter 7

Gender and Sexuality

Janet Siltanen, Andrea Doucet, and Patrizia Albanese

In this chapter you will:

▶ Learn some conceptual anchors in sociological thinking about gender and sexuality.

▶ Come to understand the connections and disconnections between gender and sexuality.

▶ See how the sociology of gender and sexuality is grounded in sites such as school, paid work, and family, as well as in increasing globalized representations of identity.

▶ Begin to think sociologically about how gender and sexuality matter in your everyday life and how they intersect with other dimensions of experience such as race/ethnicity, class, and age.

Introduction: Gender, Sexuality, and You

If you were asked to describe yourself, what would first come to mind? Male or female? Straight or gay? Whatever descriptors you use, we nevertheless hope that you will discover in this chapter that we live in a society deeply structured by both gender and **sexuality** as well as implicit values about appropriate gender and sexual behaviour. Put differently, the places where you live, the families who raise you, the television shows you watch, the schools you go to, the computer games you play, and the friends you have are all shaped by gendered and **heteronormative** expectations. Thinking sociologically about gender and sexuality means thinking about how to uncover and assess the social assumptions underlying particular configurations of gender and sexuality structures and experiences.

This chapter is also guided by a fundamental pedagogical principle that you will learn more deeply and meaningfully if you are able to link the material to your own life. We hope that you will be able to connect some of what you read in this chapter with your own life. At the same time, we encourage you to look beyond your own experience to see patterns of social life that are both similar to and different from yours.

Part 1 of the chapter presents some core sociological ideas about gender and sexuality. They are that gender and sexuality are vantage points of critique, are social constructions, and involve relations of power and inequality.

Part 2 encourages you to begin looking at familiar aspects of your experience sociologically by taking you through three social sites where gender and sexuality are in play—school, work, and family. We also discuss how young people navigate their gender and sexual identities through the constant negotiations of complex identities in a global world.

Gender and Sexuality as Critical Vantage Points

The study of gender and sexuality is certainly a central part of sociological study in Canada. Yet not so long ago, sociology was a **heterocentric**, male-centred discipline. This led to two serious consequences. First, those who were *not* male and *not* heterosexual were invisible within the content of sociology. Second, they were also invisible within the profession of sociology.

There were very few female faculty members, reinforcing the impression that sociology was a man's business. In her seminal book *The Everyday World as Problematic* (1987), one of Canada's best-known sociologists, Dorothy Smith, used telling subtitles that captured well the sense of exclusion, isolation, and invisibility of women's perspectives within the discipline of sociology; these subtitles included "Text, talk and power: Women's exclusion" and "Men's standpoint is represented as universal."

Smith and other pioneering sociologists began to develop ways of including women's experiences within sociological research and theory. They imagined, as Smith put it, "how a sociology might look if it began from the view of women's traditional place in it and what happens to a sociology that attempts to deal seriously with that" (1974, 7). Gender has since become a key vantage point of sociological thinking. A vantage point enables us to "see" ourselves, the social institutions around us, and our social worlds in ways that include more experiences and provides an angle to critique the status quo. This process of expanding our vision by adopting new vantage points was repeated within sociology for other dimensions of socially structured experience, including sexuality.

As sociologists turned their attention to widening and deepening the idea of gender as a vantage point of critique, studies of sexuality started to come to the fore. Feminist sociologists who struggled in earlier decades for the acknowledgement of gender were joined by new scholars taking up related but different issues that are particularly salient to contemporary social and cultural agendas.

It is not surprising that sexuality studies have almost always involved challenging fixed and often inaccurate ideas about human sexuality—which makes sexuality studies a vantage point. Much of the early scientific research on sexuality focused on the biomedical aspects of sex and procreation. The development of sexology involved a shift in focus from reproductive processes to the study of sexual practices, but even then, studying sex and sexuality focused on heterosexual sex for procreation in marriage as normal and all other sexual activity and identities as deviant.

A pioneer in the scientific study of sexuality was Henry Havelock Ellis (1859–1939). Unlike others at the time, he tried to demystify sex and challenge many sexual norms of Victorian England, famous for its sexually repressive norms and abundance of clandestine erotic literature (see Kearney 1982). For example, he assured his readers that masturbation did not lead to illness and that homosexuality was not a disease, vice, or amoral choice. Since then, the study of sexuality has continued to challenge accepted norms and has itself shifted its focus to address more complex understandings of sexual identities. More recently, within sociology sexuality is typically studied and understood as being intricately connected to cultural, economic, political, legal, moral, and ethical phenomena. Janice Irvine (2003, 431), for example, notes that from a sociological perspective, "sexuality is a broad social domain involving multiple fields of power, diverse systems of knowledge, and sets of institutional and political discourses."

Many feminist sociologists have questioned and challenged, among other things, the social construction of sex and sexuality, the control of women's bodies and reproduction, the objectification of women, sexual double standards, the link between sex and power, and sexual abuse and oppression (Millett 1969; Greer 1984; Butler 2006 [1990]; Weitz 2002; Benkert 2002). Sexuality has been understood as both "an arena for women's liberation" and "a crucial vector of women's oppression" (Marcus 2005, 193). Queer theory is yet another shift in this area, leading to a new vantage point.

The use of the term *queer* within the gay community began as a ploy to reclaim a slur and highlight the multiple ways that sexual practices, sexual fantasy, and sexual identity "fail to line up consistently" and "expresses an important insight about the complexity of sexuality" (Marcus 2005, 196). Queer theory derives part of its philosophy from the ideas of Michel Foucault (1990), who saw homosexuality as a strategically situated marginal position from which it may be possible to see new and diverse ways of relating to oneself and others. Queer politics rejects forms of gender and sexual oppression, but it intentionally does so from the margins in order to maintain a critical outsider perspective (Baird 2001; Plummer 2003).

Michel Foucault had a wide influence in many disciplines, and his work continues to shape sociological thought. See the Sociology in Action box in Chapter 1, p. 13, to learn more about his remarkable life.

Men's experiences have been part of these developments. Indeed, increasing attention to gender and sexuality on the part of men is evident in popular writing as well as within sociology, where there has been a growing recognition that men's views on and struggles with masculinity need to be a component of studies in gender and sexuality. One impulse in this direction came from male sociologists who began to theorize and research multiple forms of masculinity, including male sexuality.

A male pro-feminist theoretical and activist perspective began to take shape in sociology through the 1980s and 1990s. Male scholars such as Canadian Blye Frank, three American scholars who all share the first name Michael (Messner, Kimmel, Kaufman), R.W. Connell, and many others have pioneered studies of men and masculinities. (R.W. Connell, an Australian sociologist who has made many significant contributions to the study of gender, was male until the 1990s. She is now a woman.) In doing so, these scholars have significantly enriched the content and new directions of sociological scholarship.

TIME to REFLECT

Do you think that young women and young men today are equally affected by the explosion in "sexting"? How might the sociological vantage points of gender and sexuality help to answer this question?

GENDER AND SEXUALITY ARE SOCIAL CONSTRUCTIONS

One of the earliest developments in thinking about gender in sociology was to challenge the notion that gender identities (e.g., masculinity and femininity) could be easily mapped onto biological identities (e.g., male and female). It was argued that ideas about masculinity and femininity, and about appropriate behaviour for women and men, boys and girls, have a social foundation independent of biological necessity. *Gender* was introduced as a term distinct from *sex*: the latter referred to biologically based differences, primarily related to differences in chromosomes and reproductive functions, while gender referred to socially produced differences, primarily of character, ambition, and achievement. Sociology challenged ideas about sex and gender being dichotomous—two-part (male/female; masculine/feminine)—variables and thus being "natural" polar opposites. (Note that in the term "opposite sex," we are assumed to be sexually "drawn" to one another like magnets.) In inaccurately dichotomizing sex and gender, we often also tended to dichotomize sexuality, sexual identity, and sexual orientation into heterosexual or **homosexual** when in fact sexuality, like gender, is considerably more complex.

British sociologist Ann Oakley's classic book *Sex, Gender and Society* (1972) was one of the first to make the case that distinctions of sex are not as clear-cut or as straightforward as people typically think. She and others argued that the cultural and psychological features of gender are so variable historically and cross-culturally that it is impossible to map these features onto biological sex difference. By the end of the 1980s, the distinction between sex and gender commonly appeared in first-year sociology textbooks. This principle of gender studies within sociology—that of gender as a social construction—has meant that taking a gender perspective means we regard being masculine or feminine not as a natural phenomenon but as a very *social* achievement requiring intense effort and scrutiny on the part of individuals and societies.

Further, attributes and inequalities associated with being male and female came to be seen as socially created consequences of the way society is organized around gendered identities.

In the case of sexuality, Jeffrey Weeks (1993, 16) similarly notes that the meanings we give to sexuality are "socially organized, sustained by a variety of languages, which seek to tell us what sex is, what it ought to be—and what it could be." These languages of sex are then "embedded in moral treatises, laws, educational practices, psychological theories, medical definitions, social rituals, pornographic or romantic fictions, popular music and common sense assumptions."

The problem is that once people are packaged into boxes—male or female, masculine or feminine, heterosexual or homosexual—**sexism** (the subordination of one sex, usually female, and the perceived superiority of the other) and **homophobia** (an irrational fear and/or hatred of homosexuals and homosexuality) help to reinforce rigid boundaries and keep people "in their place." A young person who challenges traditional gender ideology or practices is likely to be teased and taunted. Boys and girls who cross the gender divide are often harassed back into stereotypical behaviour. Children and youth learn to avoid ridicule by conforming to prescribed gender and sexual norms. As a result, we come to see certain types of behaviour as normal, natural, and inevitable—the core or **essence** of femininity or masculinity, heterosexuality or homosexuality—when in fact we may have been

(© Thinkstock/iStockphoto collection)

Blue is for boys, pink is for girls, right? You may find it hard to believe, but this gender stereotype is a relatively new one. Prior to the 1940s, it was acceptable and even encouraged to dress boys in the colour pink. So engrained are these colour associations today that a baby boy dressed in pink would undoubtedly be mistaken for a female. This is one of many examples of how gender is socially constructed.

forced to suppress parts of our identities that cross the socially constructed gender and sexual divide. Many have come to treat as natural, inevitable, or **essential** things that are cultural, learned, and open to change. The decoupling of the sex–gender distinction from a division between the social and the natural also loosened the association of gender and sexuality and ushered in a torrent of research activity on sexuality as a socially constructed phenomenon that may or may not have a gendered form.

While much of the sexual revolution of the 1960s and 1970s was very conventional in terms of understandings of women's and men's sexuality, the 1980s saw a stronger development of woman-defined female sexuality and other explorations of sexuality that were not gender-defined. The trend now is to see a more dynamic relationship between identified features of sexed bodies and what these features come to mean in social situations and in personal identities. Thus, with the social construction of gender released from more limited notions of heterosexuality and reproduction, a greater range of behaviours emerged, which expressed a more varied relationship between sexual orientation and the gendered/sexed body.

This tendency has been increasingly taken up by a new generation of scholars, especially individuals who bring together complex and intriguing intersections between sexuality, embodiment, gender, and ethnicity. Emerich Daroya, who completed his MA at Carleton University, provides provocative reflections that typify this move within sociology toward nuanced discussions of how some of these sociological concepts are lodged in people's everyday lives.

HUMAN DIVERSITY

Potatoes and Rice: How Desirability Is Racialized in the Gay Community

Emerich Daroya

Desirability in the gay community is intrinsically linked with race, gender expression, and body types. Whiteness, muscularity, and masculinity intersect in perceptions of desirability, putting gay white, masculine, and muscular men at the top of the gay desirability totem pole. Gay men of colour are considerably lower. Gay Asian men are particularly de-eroticized and inferiorized because they are stereotyped as being feminine and having smaller bodies. In a community that considers them "unsexy," interracial relationships between white men and Asian men are delegitimized by the usage of racialized discourses that reflect these stereotypes.

Within gay communities, a white man who is exclusively attracted to Asian men is called a "rice queen." A rice queen is stereotypically an older white male who is considered unattractive and goes after younger Asian guys because he is not able to get younger white men. A "potato queen" is an Asian man who is exclusively attracted to white men, but because the stereotypes attributed to them render them undesirable, they are seen to be "settling" for older rice queens because they are the closest "desirable" men they can get. The effeminized Asian is also considered passive, which the rice queen fetishizes so that Asian men become objects for white men's fantasies of domination (Han 2007, 57).

These discourses are often used to delegitimize white–Asian relationships in the gay community. This is because when (even younger) Asian–white gay couples are seen, people often see the white man as a rice queen and the Asian man as a potato queen. However, there is no popular discourse to describe a white man who is exclusively attracted to other white men (snow queen?), which tells us that whiteness in the gay community remains unmarked. In my own experience, I have been called a "potato queen" and my partner a "rice queen," which demonstrates that race is (still) a category of exclusion in the gay community. As Chuang (1999) argues, when a gorgeous white man is seen with an Asian man, people wonder why he would choose to be with an Asian man, since he should be able to attract many desirable white men. It is not yet cool for a white guy to have an Asian boyfriend (Chuang 1999, 38). This indicates that desirability is racialized and that the intra-racial relationship between two white men (after all, they are the "desirable" ones) in the gay community is seen as the only legitimate relationship, to the exclusion of all others.

A second issue that troubled earlier ideas about the need to separate the social and embodied experiences of gender and sexuality came when sociologists began to think that perhaps the body *is* important in particular contexts and moments in the life course. As early as 1980, Canadian feminist sociologist Margrit Eichler voiced some of the analytical problems that emerge out of a systematic separation of biological sex and social gender. Other feminists, including feminist theorist Linda Nicholson, agreed that the body "becomes a historically specific variable whose meaning and importance are recognized as potentially different in different historical contexts" (1994, 101).

As the appreciation of the complexity of gender and sexual identities developed, sociologists started to pay attention to how everyday practices work to reproduce and/or challenge existing understandings of what is "normal" or appropriate. There was a particular interest in youth culture and experience. For example, was it possible to observe change in how young people negotiated their gender and sexuality?

A fascinating study by Jade Boyd (2010) reveals the pushes against and pulls toward conventional enactments of heterosexual masculinity and femininity. Examining Vancouver's entertainment district, Boyd argues that the "mainstream" produces, maintains, and reiterates the moral contours of heterosexuality within the city. Boyd shows that nightclubs, as spaces of hypermasculinity and hyperfemininity, offer a prime example of how **governmentality**, surveillance, and private enterprise work together in the maintenance and regulation of social/sexual conformity. Boyd's ethnographic study of Vancouver's entertainment district— the Granville Strip—highlights young adults' perceptions of how hegemonic sexuality and nightlife collide. Boyd explains that through heterosexual hegemony and heteronormativity, heterosexuality has been normalized and is understood as unproblematic and natural rather than revealed as constrained and produced by power relations. Like Adrienne Rich (2003 [1980]), Boyd argues that heterosexuality is a compulsory fiction and political institution, maintained and enforced through state practices. Like Judith Butler (2006 [1990]) and

Foucault (1990), she also theorizes gender as performative in that it re-enacts meaning systems through the constant reiteration of heterosexual norms. All of this, Boyd (2010) argues, ultimately works to conceal the instability and production of sex and gender, thus enabling gender inequality to remain unchallenged.

Young people in Boyd's study commented on the differences in gender dynamics between indie events in the East Side of Vancouver and mainstream events in "glossy bars" on the Granville Strip. One young woman explained as follows:

> Visually there's more hyper-females in mainstream clubs . . . more Barbie doll style. Not to say that they all look like Barbies. But they often have very long hair, they'll be wearing quite a lot of makeup, they'll be wearing very feminine clothes that show off their physical attributes like their boobs and their bum, their waist and hips and stuff. (Boyd 2010, 182)

Boyd showed that (hyper-)(hetero-)sexualized performance in Granville clubs reinforced hegemonic femininity and masculinity and heterosexual hegemony. In contrast, study participants noted that the indie dance scene was more open to diverse sexualities compared to the Granville scene. A male interviewee said that compared to other scenes, the indie scene was fairly diverse in terms of sexuality:

> [Alternative dance spaces are] less homophobic. I'm shocked when I encounter homophobia. But I will encounter it

Do your experiences at nightclubs and bars align with those expressed in Boyd's study? Why or why not?

usually at those shitty nightclubs I try to avoid.

Such as?

Like Stone Temple, anything on Granville, anything on the downtown. All those places are pretty homophobic. I get it at my bar where I work at The Dodson. I've noticed some of those guys are totally homophobic. (Boyd 2010, 183)

How does your own experience of gender and sexuality norms in public spaces compare to what Boyd discovered in her study? Have you encountered "alternative" spaces that reproduce heteronormative identities? How were they different from "alternative" spaces that challenge heteronormative identities? Considering these sorts of questions will help you to identify the social processes and interactions involved in the construction of gender and sexuality identities.

GENDER AND SEXUAL RELATIONS ARE RELATIONS OF POWER AND INEQUALITY

In the 1970s and 1980s, sociologists of gender argued that a systemic feature of society was that gender and sexual relations were marked by persistent inequalities. Feminist sociologists also made this point as they sought to counter prominent sociological approaches, such as structural functionalism, that insisted on the complementarity of male instrumental and female expressive gender roles. Indeed, feminist sociologists were very active in documenting extensive inequalities associated with gender and sexuality. Sociologists of gender argued that "sex differences" have often been exaggerated. Discussions of "sex differences" in temperament, in attitudes, and in capabilities overstated the extent of difference between men and women as social groups. These overstatements hindered women's abilities and achievements and contributed to men's claims of power and authority. Sociologists came to argue that the overstatement of sex difference was becoming itself a form of discrimination and oppression, which largely worked to the advantage of men.

Another claim by sociologists of gender was that inequality in women's and men's life chances is a consequence of how society is organized and of the particular ways in which gender is created and sustained as a significant feature of social and personal life. In Canada, there were several streams of work developing this idea. One was focused on the organizational aspects of inequality, with an emphasis on inequalities in education, employment, incomes, and in the amount and types of work that women and men do. Monica Boyd's early work on occupations is a good example of this (Boyd 1982, 1985; Boyd et al. 1985). The second stream of research in Canada was concerned with larger systemic foundations of gender inequality, captured by analyses of capitalism, **patriarchy**, and what came to be called the sex/gender system. The work of sociologist Roberta Hamilton captures this trend, both in her early studies of relations of patriarchy and capitalism (1978) and in her well-known revision of Canadian sociologist John Porter's (1965) classic work on the Canadian vertical mosaic structured along class lines; Hamilton titled her book the "gendering" of the vertical mosaic (Hamilton 2005 [1996]).

John Porter's seminal work *The Vertical Mosaic* (1965) is discussed in more detail under "From the Vertical to the Colour-Coded Mosaic" in Chapter 8, p. 163.

While these efforts are still regarded as foundational, scholars of gender and sexuality increasingly began to attend to diversity, complexity, nuance, and fragmentation within earlier concepts and arguments. It was clear that context and circumstances mattered. There was thus a move toward regarding the relevance and substance of gender as questions for, and not assumptions of, research.

In Canada, for example, women of colour drew on earlier work by pioneering scholars in the United States and pointed to how the seemingly harmonious Canadian multicultural mosaic was marred by exclusion, discrimination, and, at times, brutality. The work of feminist sociologists Himani Bannerji and Sherene Razak stands out in this regard. Both authors employ the evocative metaphor of the *gaze* to capture relations of oppression and resistance. Bannerji's

Returning the Gaze (1993) and Razak's *Looking White People in the Eye* (1998) depict the active agency, response, and resistance of racialized women who stare back at and challenge injustices in Canadian society. Work with and by Aboriginal women represents important efforts to recognize and address the gender struggles of the most marginalized individuals in our society. These efforts have helped to put the many forms of **racialization** in Canada, and the way they intertwine with gendered and sexual hierarchies, on the sociological agenda.

Growing recognition of the significance of race and ethnicity in identifying different experiences of inequality *among* women has ultimately led analysts to realize that they could not be content with a simple, dichotomous presentation of gender. For example, Sedef Arat-Koc (1989) examined the lives of immigrant women working as live-in domestic workers in Canada, a situation in which housework "becomes the responsibility of *some* [women] with subordinate class, racial and **citizenship** status, who are employed and supervised by those who are liberated from the direct physical burdens" (1989, 53). She concluded that the domestic service relationship adds class and race complexities to gender inequalities (see also Stasiulis and Bakan 2005).

More recently, the words **interlocking** or **intersectional analysis** came to dominate understandings of women's multiple identities as well as their location in multiple structures not only of gender and sexuality but also of dis/ability, class, and race. According to American sociologist Patricia Hill Collins, intersectionality "refers to particular forms of intersecting oppressions, for example, intersections of race and gender, or of sexuality and nation. Intersectional paradigms remind us that oppression cannot be reduced to one fundamental type, and that oppressions work together in producing injustice" (2000, 18).

While the terms seem to be shifting to capture increasing levels of diversity in our society, an important point to emphasize is that issues of difference and disadvantage need to be viewed as multifaceted and as both relational and structural phenomena. They operate at the level of identity or agency (i.e., "I feel discriminated against as an Aboriginal woman, not just as a *woman* and not just as an Aboriginal person but as an Aboriginal woman"), and at the same time they are rooted in the ways in which social institutions such as families, workplaces, and schools are set up and function.

Living Gendered Lives

GENDER AND SEXUALITY IN SCHOOL

Gender differences in the experience of schooling, and in school attainment, have been matters of sociological attention for many decades. Throughout the 1960s and 1970s, the concern was that girls were losing out in education. Sociological research demonstrated that starting as early as elementary school and becoming more pronounced over time, classroom experiences, curriculum design, and measurements of student success highly favoured boys. After successful campaigns and educational changes, the tables seem to have turned. From the early 1980s onwards, the enrolment of women in Canadian universities has exceeded that of men. Statistics Canada has reported that by 2009, women made up close to 60 per cent of undergraduate and MA enrolment. Men still predominate (53 per cent) at the doctoral level, but even here the gender gap appears to be narrowing. Research (Abada and Tenkorang 2009, 201) shows that the gender gap in attending and graduating from university also applies to children of immigrants to Canada, with young immigrant women "60 per cent more likely to have a university education" than their male counterparts. For Aboriginal youths, there is a slight gender gap in favour of women completing a university education, but this is the case in an overall situation of extreme educational disadvantage. In 2001, only 2 per cent of Aboriginal youths (aged 20 to 24) had a university degree (Mendelson 2006).

What does this shift mean? Some have noted (e.g., Davies and Guppy 2006) that degree-level qualifications have become important for careers that girls typically pursue more than boys do (for example, teaching, nursing, and social work). Thus, enrolment equalization reflects changes in the kinds of programs universities are offering and the inflation in degree qualifications required in certain professions. This may help to explain the increased proportion of women in master's-level programs. Supporting this idea is the fact that most students continue to be gender-segregated in terms of the programs and courses they take as undergraduates. Women have made significant inroads into professions such as law and medicine (now both roughly 50 per cent female) and now dominate some degree programs in which they were previously a minority (for example, pharmacology, education, and veterinary medicine). However, overwhelming imbalances continue to exist in traditionally female programs (nursing, social work, and fine arts) where roughly 66 per cent (or more) of the degrees are granted to women. Some male-dominated programs also seem more resistant to change. Programs like architecture, engineering, mathematics, physics, and forestry show an increase in female participation but remain strongly male-dominated. As Davies and Guppy suggest (2006, 114), these are programs (and areas of employment) where a long-standing male-focused culture presents a chilly climate to women daring enough to cross the gender divide; it also persists in the school system for diverse individuals and groups that find themselves at the intersection of race, class, gender, and sexuality. Grassroots organizations and women's and feminist groups continue to work to overcome disadvantage and system prejudice (see Egale's safe schools campaign for some statistics and details on homophobia, biphobia, and transphobia in schools: www.egale.ca).

To get a clearer idea of the gender imbalances in Canadian university programs, see Table 10.3 on p. 207 in Chapter 10 and the surrounding discussion under "Educational Opportunities and Inequalities" on p. 206.

SEXUAL VIOLENCE

There is considerable ambivalence on the part of women's groups and feminists regarding the role of men in cases of sexual violence. Some women's groups and feminists have argued that "Take Back the Night" (www.takebackthenight.org) events should involve women only; others have argued that men also need to be somewhat involved in these events, since sexual violence is not only a "women's issue." At the same time, some men's groups have come up with their own male-centred approaches to ending

sexual violence. Perhaps the best-known is the White Ribbon Campaign, which was started by Canadian sociologist Michael Kaufman. Men are encouraged to wear a white ribbon as a symbolic pledge never to commit, condone, or remain silent about violence against women. The White Ribbon Campaign is bookended by two days that women have designated as important times to reflect on gender and sexual violence: it starts on 25 November, the International Day for the Eradication of Violence against Women, and it ends on 6 December, Canada's National Day of Remembrance and Action on Violence against Women (and the anniversary of the Montreal Massacre. The Montreal Massacre is the name given to a tragic period of 45 minutes on 6 December 1989 when a 25-year-old gunman named Marc Lépine killed 14 women at Montreal's École Polytechnique).

Violence against women can take many forms, but for more information on domestic violence, see "Wife Abuse," Chapter 9, p. 186.

The MA research of Elana Finestone typifies how a younger generation of women is seeking to include men in discussions of rape on campus. Elana argues that since men play a strong role in perpetuating sexual violence, they should also be involved in helping to solve the issue of sexual violence on university campuses and elsewhere. The term **hegemonic masculinity** is introduced here to refer to a dominant form of masculinity in society—one espousing that men be strong, assertive, aggressive, self-reliant, and free of traditional feminine characteristics such as a willingness to display emotion.

TIME to REFLECT

Despite dramatic legal changes—allowing same-sex marriage, for example—in the spring of 2002 the Durham Catholic school board unanimously voted to deny a gay Oshawa high school student, Marc Hall, the right to attend his high school prom with his same-sex partner. Do you support the school board decision? Why? Why not?

OPEN for DISCUSSION

Sexual Assault on Campus

Elana Finestone

During my six years as a student at Queen's and Carleton, sexual assault posters captured my attention in women's bathroom stalls, the University Centre atrium, and the tunnel system on campus. I eyed posters for women's self-defence courses, offering to teach me how to protect myself from sexual assault. Another poster informed me that I should watch my drink at parties to lessen the risk of date rape.

These posters, like most of the sexual assault posters around campus, exclusively target women. They imply that if women fail to protect themselves, they invite it. This message is not only victim-blaming for sexual assault survivors, but it completely ignores the role men can play in ending sexual assault.

Recently, Carleton University administration tried to target men in their sexual assault posters. Through focus groups with first-year Carleton University students, I learned that men did not feel targeted by these posters.

Most of the men *and* women I spoke with felt that men did not feel actively engaged because the posters portrayed all men as exhibiting central traits of hegemonic masculinity: aggressive, emotionless, and slaves to their sex drive. For example, many men and women felt the poster with the catchphrase "Ask First: Any form of sexual activity without consent is sexual assault" talked down to all men as potential rapists.

While posters depicting hegemonic masculinity were unsuccessful, so too were posters depicting characteristics associated with femininity. For example, posters for events encouraging men to share their feelings were unsuccessful. Students' desire to differentiate masculine from feminine traits suggests they view gender as a dichotomy rather than a continuum.

My discussions with first-year students revealed the importance of sexual assault campaigns that target men in ways that recognize the multiplicities of masculinities and femininities. For example, a poster with the slogan "Being a friend means stopping him before he does something stupid: . . . Rape is a man's issue too" was most effective for men. It redefined masculinity in positive ways by constructing men as part of the solution to sexual violence. Universities would do well to involve both genders in university-wide sexual assault prevention efforts.

GENDER AND SEXUALITY IN WORK

Although women have surpassed men in terms of obtaining education credentials, they are less able to turn this educational advantage into dollars when they enter the labour market after university or college. This is partly because the gender segregation in university programs carries students into gender-segregated jobs in the labour market. However, evidence shows that even within the same occupation, young men begin their employment careers with a higher starting salary (MacAlpine 2005).

> Are you shocked that Canadian women continue to earn less than their male counterparts? See "Gendered Work," Chapter 11, p. 222 for a broader discussion on work participation, labour segregation, and the different experiences of racialized women.

But gendered experiences don't end there. A number of scholars of sex and gender have argued that many different workplace and organizational cultures play key roles in creating, maintaining, and undermining sexual identity and promoting gender inequality at work (Hearn and Parkin 1987; Woods and Lucas 1993; Welsh 1999; Dellinger 2002). Dellinger suggests that instead of simply looking at sexuality as something individuals bring to work, we should examine how customs and practices in a workplace constitute a type of **organizational sexuality** or social practice that determines explicit and culturally elaborated rules of behaviour to regulate sexual identities and personal relationships. In other words, different occupational cultures hold different and specific social rules about what constitutes "appropriate" or acceptable sexuality. Workplace norms about sexuality regulate who we say we are, who we "date," how we dress, and how we understand and experience sexual harassment in the workplace.

Woods and Lucas (1993) write about the "corporate closet," which strongly encourages gay men in some professions to keep their sexual identities and relationships hidden. In such work contexts, gays and lesbians intentionally pass as heterosexuals because of the pervasiveness of heteronormative discourses and **heterosexism** in the workplace (Johnson 2002).

Some researchers have noted (Welsh 1999) that some organizations actually mandate the sexualization of their workers, and as a result, in some sexually charged work cultures, degrading or sexualized behaviours become an institutionalized component of work. Take for example a waitress at Hooters Bar, who is required to wear short shorts and a top that shows cleavage—this is not, for the most part, considered sexual harassment. Given these highly sexualized workplace cultures, it is perhaps not surprising that research by Lynn (2009) found that waitresses' tips varied with age, increased with breast size, increased with having blonde hair, and decreased with body size.

Researchers such as Dellinger (2002) have noted that most workplaces, either formally or informally, convey rules of dress and that dress is a well-recognized site of gender construction and sexual identity. She argues that dress and workplace norms "influence people's definition of pleasurable, acceptable, and unacceptable sexuality at work" (2002, 23). As a result, workplace norms and organizational culture affect how sexuality is negotiated at work and, in part, determine what counts as sexual harassment.

It is important to also note that heterosexual norms in the workplace not only exclude or sexualize women but also silence or closet gay men and lesbians and work to constrain the behaviour of heterosexual men, who are at times labelled "unmasculine" when they choose not to participate in "hyper-masculine" stereotypical behaviour (Welsh 1999).

TIME to REFLECT

If an employer required you to dress in a sexually provocative manner, would you consider this a form of sexual harassment? Why or why not?

GENDER AND SEXUALITY IN FAMILY

Whatever your current living situations, most of you will have had some experience of family life that influences the way you think about gender and sexuality both in the family and outside of its boundaries. Sociologists have known for some time that family experience and relations have a profound impact on our sense of self—including our sense of ourselves as gendered and sexual beings. While in earlier decades sociologists were inclined to study the family as a "haven in a heartless world," recent attention has focused on inequalities running through families and their connection to gender and sexual hierarchies.

Inequality within the family and the study of **gender divisions of domestic labour** are now burgeoning areas of research. While this is a large and diverse field of study, four features are worthy of note here.

First, it is important to see domestic labour and the care of children not as a small issue of concern only to women. How societies care, or do not care, for dependent others—both old and young—tells us a great deal about the social fabric, social institutions, and political priorities of that nation, province, territory, or city. For more than three decades, feminist social scientists have highlighted the economic, social, political, and personal costs to women of the gender imbalance in family-based care work. There has also been increasing attention on how *not* caring for others has affected men—including lower lifespans and loneliness or isolation when they live without wives or partners.

A second point relates to something you may have seen in your own household: men doing more domestic work. While there are different interpretations of how much housework Canadian men are actually doing, there is a fairly strong consensus that *more* men are doing *more* housework than they did in previous generations and much of this increase is in child care–related activities (Marshall 2006).

Third, there have been dramatic increases over the past 30 years in the number of men in Canada who are stay-at-home dads; the proportion of single-earner families in which the father is the stay-at-home parent increased from 2 per cent (in 1976) to 10 per cent in

Gender relations in the family are shifting as more men take on household responsibilities, such as doing laundry.

(Florian Franke/Alamy)

2002 (Statistics Canada 2002) to 12.5 per cent in 2007 (Statistics Canada 2008c). With women's full-time employment growing over the past few decades, dual-earner households have also increased. Perhaps the most dramatic social shift in gender relations that straddle family and work is the fact that women are primary breadwinners in nearly one-third of Canadian **two-earner families** (Sussman and Bonnell 2006). These shifts raise intriguing questions about movements in the gender balance of paid and unpaid work.

Families have always existed in diverse forms, but only recently have some families been allowed to legally "count" as families in the Canadian context. In 2000, the passing of Bill C-23 granted same-sex couples the same rights and obligations as common-law heterosexual couples. Following that, in 2005, "equal marriage" legislation came into force with the passage of Bill C-315, the Civil Marriage Act,

which recognized the right of same-sex couples to have access to civil marriage without legal discrimination. The 2011 census results reveal that there is a growing number of same-sex families in Canada, which may also lead us to redefine and rethink the gender division of domestic labour debate.

TIME to REFLECT

Would you expect the division of household labour in same-sex couples to be similar to or different from that in heterosexual couples? Why?

While, as discussed above, young people are constantly negotiating gender relations and sexuality at school, at work, and within their families, they are also negotiating a wide range of gender and sexual identities in an increasingly globalized world.

NEGOTIATING IDENTITIES IN A GLOBAL AGE

A distinguishing aspect of the generational experience of gender negotiation for youth today is that it is being done in a relational context that is *globalized*. Globalizing processes bring a double-sided dimension to gendered and sexual identities. On one side, there is greater exposure to multiple images and practices of masculinity, femininity, and sexuality. On the other, there is a tendency toward a homogenized portrayal, and worse, these portrayals can tend toward conservative, stereotyped, and, at the extreme, exploitative images. As mentioned previously in this chapter, sociologists have used the word *hegemonic* to identify this sort of dominant form of gender identity. Young people negotiate their own gender identity within the pushes, pulls, and pulses of the tensions between multiplicity, homogeneity, and the hegemonic. Adding further complexity are relationships between gender, sexuality, class, race, and other intersecting dimensions of identity and social structures, which set parameters and possibilities for experience.

Through immigration, increased intercultural relationships, and the influence of global media, Canadian youth find themselves confronted with multiple ways of enacting femininity or masculinity. As Bill Osgerby, a British researcher on youth culture and gender, writes (2004, 181), "young people's subject positions have come to operate across, and within, multiple cultural sites—their identities are constituted by the intersection of crisscrossing discourses of age, ethnicity, gender, class, sexuality and so on." If family, friends, and social connections are diverse in cultural traditions, there may be different understandings of appropriate gendered behaviour, and these understandings may very well clash with each other.

Research in Canada has highlighted how young people negotiate gender and sexual identities within relational contexts that can include clashes between dominant and subordinated cultures as well as clashes within cultures. For example, Amita Handa (2003) tells of the "tightrope" that young South Asian girls walk in negotiating the expectations of femininity that vary *within* Asian culture as well as *between* it and the dominant "white" Canadian culture. She highlights bhangra, popular music that takes inspiration from traditional Punjabi culture, as a flashpoint for such clashes. "Bhangra music and dances stand in opposition to dominant white culture in the struggle for cultural space. . . . They also assert girls' resistance to parental attempts to control their sexuality" (Handa 2003, 116).

Becoming oneself involves confronting the contours and power of hegemonic gender and sexual identities. Although the specific characteristics of hegemonic masculinity can vary according to context, it is usually identified with the traditional masculine qualities of "being strong, successful, capable, reliable, in control" (Connell 2000, 10). Hegemonic masculinity is distinguished from other expressions of masculinity that are subordinated and/or marginalized, and it is *especially* distinguished from femininity, or what Connell calls **emphasized femininity**. Both hegemonic masculinity and emphasized femininity have taken on different shapes and forms within a globalized context that includes the ubiquitous presence of Internet pornography, the stunning scale of sex tourism, and the increase in human trafficking for the sex trade. All of these are serious examples of where gender, race, class, and historic processes of colonization and contemporary globalization collide to produce extreme, exploitative versions of hegemonic masculinity and emphasized femininity.

TIME to REFLECT

Advertising is full of assumptions and messages about gender. What criteria could you use to determine whether advertising images are depicting hegemonic masculinity or emphasized femininity? What about criteria that would identify a homophobic attitude?

One does not have to travel the globe to be affected by globalizing trends in the presentation and enactment of gender identities. Stereotyped presentations of gendered bodies are very familiar on television, in

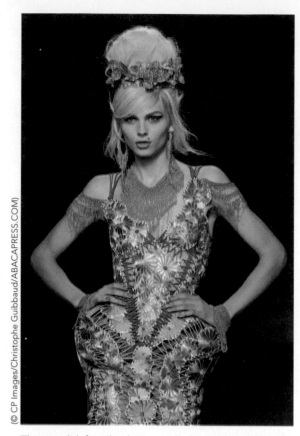

(© CP Images/Christophe Guibbaud/ABACAPRESS.COM)

This model fits the beauty ideals espoused by the fashion industry, right? Would you still agree if you found out this model was a man? Androgynous model Andrej Pejic has caused a sensation in the fashion world, successfully modelling for top fashion designers like Jean Paul Gaultier as both a man and a woman.

magazines, and on celebrity websites; there are many versions of the thin, tall, perfect-complexioned, blonde young woman and the six-packed, clean-shaven young man with the dazzling white smile. Billions of dollars are spent every day on temporary and permanent body products and procedures, and this industry caters increasingly to men as well as to women.

Surgical modification to enhance and produce gendered standards of beauty is an expensive option, but as Zainab Amery explains, it is becoming a normalized practice in many places around the globe.

Conclusion: On to the Future . . . Gender Relations and Social Change

Uncovering strategies and possibilities for change is an important focus of sociological investigations. This brings us to ask the question: how do we identify progress in the ways in which gender and sexuality are structured in society and negotiated in everyday lives? Is progress the eradication of differences or the neutralization of the social, material, and political consequences of differences? Ideas about gender equality and sexuality change with the times, and we need to keep a constant watch on whether our understanding of and platforms for equality are keeping pace with social, economic, and political changes.

Youth are a key source of this energy for change. Many young people in Canada today are involved in campaigns and other activist work to address gender and sexuality issues—from Femmetoxic (the campaign to remove toxic chemicals from women's beauty products) to the involvement of male youth in the White Ribbon Campaign to grassroots organizations like Egale Canada (which advocates for equality and justice for Canadian lesbian, gay, bisexual, and trans-identified people).

Equally ubiquitous are the efforts by many people in their homes, workplaces, schools, neighbourhoods, and city streets to address gender inequality and homophobia in everyday relationships. The feminist insight that the personal is political continues to reverberate in contemporary gender and sexual relations.

While we have tried to write a sociology of gender and sexuality that speaks to you, at the end of the day, it is *you* who knows best how these ideas resonate with your everyday life. Where do these ideas fit your experience—where do they not? We urge you to bring your experiences and perspectives into a conversation with sociology. We believe that both you and the discipline of sociology will benefit from such an engagement.

GLOBAL ISSUES

Body Beautiful: Perfection under Construction

Zainab Amery

Who knew boob jobs and liposuction would be the top two surgical procedures in China and India, according to the 2010 survey of the International Society of Aesthetic Plastic Surgery? With the United States and Brazil taking first and second place as cosmetic surgery nations, China runs a close third, with India not too far behind. There are also reports that customers everywhere are getting younger, with cosmetic surgery becoming one way young women get ready for university.

But it's not about beauty alone: it's about the rewards that being beautiful can bring. Studies show that attractive people achieve a higher degree of success than their less attractive competitors on the labour market. In Brazil, where the body is worshipped and beauty means access to employment, government-run hospitals offer subsidized procedures for low-income people. In Asian countries, business is booming but is racialized, with many young people opting for double-eyelid surgeries to become "Caucasian-looking" in order to get the best jobs.

However, it is Lebanon that takes the prize for the first cosmetic loan program. Billboards advertising the First National Bank's Plastic Surgery program read, "Beauty is no longer a luxury" beside an image of a Caucasian, blonde, blue-eyed, Western-looking woman. Astonishingly, the only stipulations are that the borrower be at least 17 years of age and make a minimum of $600 a month. In a country where beauty is paramount for the purpose of getting (and staying) married, the perfect body can have high significance—especially since there is only one eligible male for every five women in the population. The situation is so serious that mothers escort their daughters to surgeons to raise their odds of finding a husband. But the search for perfection is no longer solely a women's quest. Of the 1.5 million surgeries performed yearly in Lebanon, 30 per cent are on young men (Ajami 2005), with a similar trend occurring globally.

questions for critical thought

1. Gender differences are a systemic feature of our everyday lives. But do these gender differences always have consequences for our choices and opportunities? Thinking about your own life right now, where would you say gender *matters* the most? Can you think of areas of your life where gender does not seem to matter at all?

2. According to Kenneth Plummer (2003, 516), "There is no essential 'sexuality' with a strictly biological base that is cut off from the social." What does this mean? Can you think of ways it is manifested in your life?

3. For decades, feminists have been deeply divided about the roles of pornographic media in promoting heterosexist institutions and relations. What role do you think pornography plays in our understanding of men's and women's sexuality? Has the Internet changed this? If yes, how?

4. What evidence is there to support the idea that gender equality has been achieved? What evidence would suggest that this is not the case?

recommended readings

Mary Louise Adams. 1999. *The Trouble with Normal: Post-War Youth and the Making of Heterosexuality*. Toronto: University of Toronto Press.
Adams writes about the social construction of heterosexuality and the discourses surrounding the notions of "normal" and "heterosexuality" that were imposed on youth in postwar Canada.

Judith Butler. 2006 [1990]. *Gender Troubles: Feminism and the Subversion of Identity*. New York: Routledge Classics.
Butler's work challenges traditional assumptions about the "naturalness" and essentialism of sex and gender and maintains that "masculine" and "feminine" are not biologically fixed categories but rather are culturally determined.

Roberta Hamilton. 2005. *Gendering the Vertical Mosaic: Feminist Perspectives on Canadian Society*. 2nd edn. Toronto: Pearson.
Hamilton provides a discussion of the relationship between sociology, women's studies, and the women's movement. The "vertical mosaic" in the title is a reference to one of the most famous books on social inequality in Canada, written by John Porter.

Barbara Marshall. 2000. *Configuring Gender: Explorations in Theory and Politics*. Peterborough, ON: Broadview.
This book discusses detailed developments in the sociological analysis of gender. It also introduces you to how gender is understood in recent approaches to sociology influenced by post-modernism and post-structuralism.

Janet Siltanen and Andrea Doucet. 2008. *Gender Relations in Canada—Intersectionality and Beyond*. Toronto: Oxford University Press.
This book sets out the value of sociological analysis for understanding gender at different moments of the life course (childhood, adolescence, and adulthood) while also exploring how the concept of *intersectionality* enhances our understandings of gender.

recommended websites

Canadian Feminist Alliance for International Action (FAFIA)
www.fafia-afai.org
FAFIA is a dynamic coalition of more than 75 Canadian women's equality-seeking and related organizations. Its mandate is to further women's equality in Canada through domestic implementation of its international human rights commitments.

Canadian Research Institute for the Advancement of Women (CRIAW)
www.criaw-icref.ca
For more than 30 years, CRIAW has documented the economic and social situation of Canadian women through ground-breaking research that is accessible for public advocacy and education.

Egale Canada
www.egale.ca
Egale Canada is an organization that advances equality and justice for lesbian, gay, bisexual, and trans-identified people and their families across Canada. The site includes summaries of key court cases, press releases, and information on local, national, and international campaigns and events.

Father Involvement Research Alliance (FIRA)
www.fira.ca
FIRA is a Canadian alliance of individuals, organizations, and institutions dedicated to the development and sharing of knowledge focusing on supporting father involvement.

Femmes et Villes International
www.femmesetvilles.org
Femmes et Villes International (Women in Cities International) is a network of city-based initiatives to promote the development of inclusive cities for women and girls. From its headquarters in Montreal, it acts as a knowledge and skills exchange network for those concerned with global gender equality.

Sex Information and Education Council of Canada (SIECCAN)
www.sieccan.org
SIECCAN is dedicated to informing the public and professionals about diverse aspects of human sexuality. It also publishes the *Canadian Journal of Human Sexuality*.

Native Women's Association of Canada: Sisters in Spirit

www.nwac.ca/programs/sisters-spirit

Sisters in Spirit is a research, education, and policy initiative driven and led by Aboriginal women. Their primary goal is to conduct research on and raise awareness of the alarmingly high rates of violence against Aboriginal women and girls in Canada.

Status of Women Canada

www.swc-cfc.gc.ca/index-eng.html

Status of Women Canada is a federal government organization that promotes the full participation of Canadian women in economic, social, and political life. It places particular emphasis on increasing women's economic security and eliminating violence against women.

World Health Organization (WHO): Sexual Health

www.who.int/topics/sexual_health/en

The World Health Organization, a UN agency, provides information on a wide range of health topics, including sexual health and sexual violence. Included here are publications on such subjects as adolescent sexual and reproductive health, sexually transmitted diseases, and female genital mutilation.

XY

www.xyonline.net

XY is a website focused on men, masculinities, and gender politics; it is a space for the exploration of men's and women's everyday lives, issues of gender and sexuality, and personal and social change.

chapter 8

Ethnic and Race Relations

Nikolaos I. Liodakis

In this chapter, you will:

▶ Learn that the meaning of the terms *ethnicity* and *race* are historically specific and are important bases for the formation of social groups.

▶ Understand how Canada has been shaped by the colonization of Aboriginal peoples, the requirements of "nation-building," capitalist economic development, and discriminatory immigration policies.

▶ Find out that multiculturalism and interculturalism are ideological frameworks within which government policies and programs attempt to manage ethnic and race relations and provide social cohesion.

▶ Come to appreciate how, despite improvements in immigration policy and government integration efforts, discrimination and racism continue to permeate many aspects of Canadian social, political, and economic life.

▶ Learn about different theoretical approaches that attempt to explain the economic inequalities among and within ethnic and racial groups.

Introduction

The examination of ethnic and race relations is crucial in our understanding of Canadian society. Canada is, demographically, one of the most multicultural countries in the world. With the exception of Aboriginal peoples, everyone else is either an immigrant to this country or the descendant of one. As sociologists, we are interested in analyzing social relations—that is, relations of power (domination and subordination) among individuals and social groups. Our existing demographic makeup is a product of our history; it is a reflection of Canada's immigration policies and practices, many of which were discriminatory and racist at least until the mid-1960s. Current problems in the economic, social, and political integration of visible minorities and recent immigrants may be partially attributed to racism. The field of ethnic and race relations has been central and continues to grow and assume importance within Canadian sociology. Let us begin by briefly examining how sociologists define the concepts of ethnicity and race and how we can approach the study of ethnic and race relations theoretically.

Defining *Ethnicity* and *Race*

Sociologists argue that the terms *ethnicity* and *race* have historically specific significations—i.e., they mean different things to different people at different times and in different places. Ethnicity and race are not constant or monolithic concepts but represent dynamic social relations in flux. Popular uses of the terms tend to differ from social scientific definitions (Miles and Torres 1996). The term *ethnicity* comes from the Greek word *ethnos*, and it refers to a large group of people. **Ethnic groups** share similar cultural characteristics (language, religion, customs, history, and so on). Race refers to people's assumed but socially significant physical or genetic characteristics (Satzewich and Liodakis 2010, 11).

Émile Durkheim (1964 [1893]) used the concept of collective consciousness as a primary source of identity formation. He emphasized the importance of group sentiments over individual ones. Similarities or "sameness" within the social group created social solidarity and led members to differentiate between themselves and others (non-members) and to prefer their "own kind" over others. The collective consciousness of people leads to a feeling of "us" versus "them," important in social group formation, reproduction, and maintenance.

Max Weber argued that social group formation is associated with practices of inclusion/exclusion, important for the production and distribution of scarce valuable resources (social status and status symbols, goods, services, wages, political power, equality, voting rights and citizenship, access to social programs, human rights, self-determination, and so on).

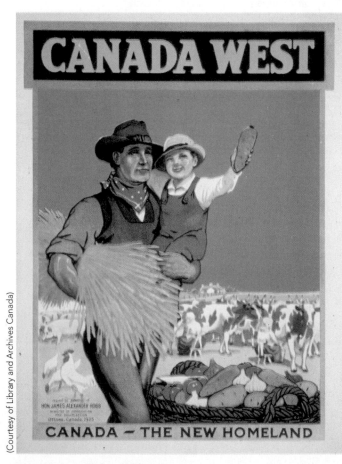

(Courtesy of Library and Archives Canada)

Immigration poster, 1925

According to Weber (1978 [1908]), common descent, tribe, culture (which includes language and other symbolic codes), religion, and nationality are important ethnic markers and determinants of ethnicity. Ethnicity should be seen as a subjective and presumed identity based on a "folk-feeling," not (necessarily) on any blood ties.

Weber used the term *race* to denote the common identity of groups based on biological heredity and endogamous conjugal groups. Visible similarities and differences, however minor, serve as potential sources of affection and appreciation or repulsion and contempt. Cultural and physical differences, produced and reproduced over time, constitute the foundations upon which a "consciousness of kind" is built. The physical characteristics of humans that have been used to classify social groups have included skin colour, eye colour, hair type, nose shape, lip shape, body hair, and cheekbone structure (Driedger 1996, 234–5). Differences can serve as a starting point for the tendency of **monopolistic closure** (Weber 1978 [1908], 386)—i.e., to economic, political, and social processes and practices, often institutionalized, whereby members of the in-group ("we"/"Self") have access to the scarce valuable resources mentioned above, while members of the out-group ("they"/"the Other") are excluded.

Today, sociologists use the term *racialization* to refer to sets of social processes and practices through which social relations among people are structured "by the signification of human biological characteristics in such a way as to define and construct differentiated social collectivities" (Miles and Brown 2003, 99). Social group labelling creates hierarchical social dichotomies by the attribution of negative intellectual, moral, and behavioural characteristics to subordinate populations and the attribution of positive characteristics to the dominant groups. Social positions of superiority and inferiority are thus created, and a social hierarchy is built (Li 1999).

Ethnicity and race are central factors in power relations; they not only set boundaries, but they also designate hierarchical positions of superiority and inferiority among and within social collectivities. The meanings of the categories and the populations they describe or "contain" are not fixed in time and space. When I ask my students how many races there are, they usually answer only one: the human race. But when we begin to discuss colonialism or inequality among social groups, terms such as *white, black, visible minorities, Asians,* and *Aboriginals* cannot be avoided. These terms connote race as real.

Racialization is linked to European colonization, exploitation, and domination of indigenous peoples. During the advent of capitalism, a new social dichotomy slowly emerged, one based on definitions of "Self" and "Other." The "Self" referred to dominant European populations and cultures and was considered superior; the "Other" referred to non-Europeans, who were seen as inferior and subordinate. Prior to the emergence of capitalism, race was used in a legal sense to describe people with common lineage and as a self-identification label for the aristocracy (a category that defined the Self), but with the emergence of the bourgeoisie, the term was used to define "Others," "Others" being "Negroes," "Jews," "Arabs," "Asiatics," and so on. It became an externally imposed label. The classification of certain groups as races was coupled with negative evaluations of their members' biological, social, and behavioural characteristics.

TIME to REFLECT

Do you believe that races exist? If so, how many races are there, and what are their different characteristics? Could all human populations be categorized in terms of inherited physical characteristics? Should they be?

Building a Nation or Two: Canada's Development through Immigration

In the current context of global economic competition, Canada needs a growing population to keep labour costs down, increase the tax base, finance social programs, and maintain its comparative advantage in the oil, gas,

▼ FIGURE 8.1   Immigration in Historical Perspective, 1860–2010

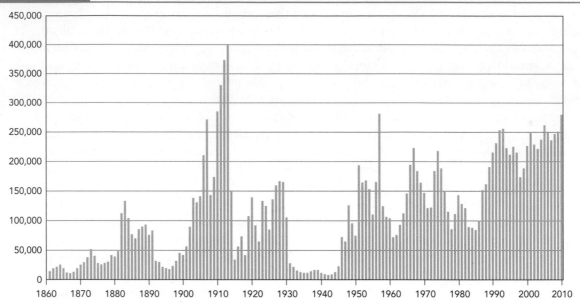

Historical highlights

- 1896 to 1905: The settlement of the West with an offer of free land results in large numbers of immigrants from the United Kingdom, Europe, and the United States.
- 1906: Immigration Act
- 1910: Immigration Act
- 1913: 400,000 immigrants arrive in Canada
- 1914 to 1918: Immigration slump during World War I
- 1928: Opening of Halifax's Pier 21, the Atlantic gateway to Canada
- 1930s: Extremely low levels of immigration during the Depression years
- 1940s: During and after World War II, approximately 48,000 war brides and their 22,000 children arrive in Canada.
- 1950s: Canada receives about one-and-a-half million immigrants from Europe.
- 1952: Immigration Act
- 1956 and 1957: Canada accepts 37,500 Hungarian refugees.
- 1962: New immigration regulations are tabled to eliminate all discrimination based on race, religion, and national origin.
- 1967: The government amends Canada's immigration policy and introduces the point system for the selection of skilled workers and business immigrants.
- 1968 and 1969: Canada takes in 11,000 Czechoslovakian refugees.
- 1972: Canada resettles more than 6175 Ugandan Asians.
- 1973: Canada accepts more than 6000 Chileans.
- 1975 to 1978: Canada resettles almost 9000 Indochinese.
- 1978: Immigration Act (1976) came into effect 10 April 1978.
- 1979 and 1980: 60,000 Vietnamese, Cambodian, and Laotian "boat people" arrive in Canada.
- 1999: Canada accepts more than 7000 Kosovars.
- 2002: Immigration and Refugee Protection Act (IRPA) came into force 28 June 2002.
- 2008: Ministerial instructions change the way the economic immigrant cases are processed under IRPA.
- 2008: Canadian Experience Class (CEC) facilitates access to permanent residence for those who have recent Canadian work experience or have graduated and recently worked in Canada.

SOURCE: Citizenship and Immigration Canada, 2011, *Facts and Figures—Immigration Overview—Permanent and Temporary Residents.* www.cic.gc.ca/english/resources/statistics/facts2010/permanent/01.asp

and other resource extraction industries. It needs immigrants. Until the 1960s, the image of Canada as a nation was based on the idea that the British and French peoples founded this country. These two **charter groups**, by this thinking, built the country; everyone else "joined in" later. The "two founding nations" thesis endures even today, but it is historically inaccurate, in part. The French and the British colonized Canada and sent settlers to this land, but they did this at the expense of the Aboriginals who were already here, and not only did they lose their lands through war and deceitful treaties, but "efforts to assimilate *them*" through Christianity, private property, and competitive individualism left them with long-lasting cultural trauma and without the communal economies that had sustained them. In addition, immigration from other countries began around the time of Confederation. Nation-building required the creation of a national transportation infrastructure (roads, railways, canals), the development of commercial agriculture in western Canada, and capitalist industry in major urban centres. A large influx of mostly northern and central European and American immigrants (except blacks) followed, since what was left of the once-thriving Aboriginal population, it was believed, either did not have the necessary skills or could not adapt to the British/French "ways of doing things." More often than not, Canada's first peoples were seen and treated as "uncivilized savages"—very much "Others." Cultural compatibility was a requirement for immigration to Canada. The offer of free land to European and American settlers (land that was taken away from Aboriginals) resulted in the first wave of immigration to Canada, from 1896 to the beginning of World War I.

Not everyone has always been welcomed in Canada. The Immigration Act of 1910 prohibited the immigration of people who were considered "mentally defective," "idiots, imbeciles, feeble-minded, epileptics, insane, diseased, the physically defective, the dumb, blind, or otherwise handicapped" (McLaren 1990, 56). A 1919 amendment to the Immigration Act decreed that people with "dubious" political loyalties

(e.g., socialists and communists) be excluded outright or, if they were already here, be subject to deportation (Roberts 1988, 19). Immigrants from China and India were of particular "concern" to xenophobic immigration authorities, since they were seen as impossible to assimilate and thus unsuitable for permanent residence. Until the liberalization of immigration in the 1960s, Canadian governments exercised exclusionary policies. Some groups were preferred (mostly northern and central Europeans and Americans). Others were labelled as "non-preferred" and were systematically excluded (the Chinese, black Americans, eastern and southern Europeans, and Indians).

The end of World War II saw some minor improvements in Canadian immigration policy. Gradually, some non-whites were allowed to immigrate. Small numbers of black women were admitted as domestic workers, typists, and nurses. It was not until 1962 that the government eliminated racist criteria in the immigrant selection process and not until 1967 that the points system was introduced, which relied on more objective criteria and assigned more weight to the applicant's age, education

Sikh passengers aboard the *Komagata Maru*.

(Vancouver Public Library, Special Collections, VPL6231)

credentials, job skills, work experience, and English- and/or French-language abilities, not to a person's country of origin. Family reunification provisions led to an increase in the numbers of southern Europeans (Italians, Greeks, Portuguese, and Spanish) in the late 1960s and early 1970s and a moderate rise in non-white immigration to Canada.

> **What would a non-white immigrant face in the job market upon arrival in Canada?** See Chapter 11, "Race and Racialized Work," p. 225, for a broader discussion of the relationship between race, citizenship, and employment.

The New Mosaic: Recent Canadian Immigration Trends

The "colour" of Canadian immigration has changed since the 1980s. Immigration from the traditional European (white) source countries has diminished substantially, since the standard of living in these countries has improved markedly. There has been a remarkable shift in the geographical regions from which Canada admits immigrants. During the 1950s, the United Kingdom and the rest of Europe accounted for almost 90 per cent of all immigration to Canada, but recently the percentage of European immigration dropped to less than 15 per cent. In 2010, immigrants from the UK and France accounted for only 6 per cent of total immigration. On the other hand, immigrants from the Philippines, India, and China accounted for 33 per cent of all immigration to Canada (Citizenship and Immigration Canada 2011; see Table 8.1 below).

In 2010, Canada admitted approximately 280,000 immigrants. Table 8.1 lists the top 10 source countries of immigrants to Canada for that year. Together, they accounted for 52.7 per cent of all immigrants admitted. The top source country was the Philippines (13.03 per cent of all immigrants admitted), and the second-highest percentage belonged to India (10.77 per cent). The third source country was China (10.75 per cent). We have certainly come a long way since the era of the Chinese head tax and the continuous journey policy. The UK, France, and the US were still among the top 10 source countries, but their percentage contributions were small (3.38, 2.47, and 3.29 per cent, respectively).

TABLE 8.1 ▼ Top 10 Source Countries of Immigrants to Canada, 2010

Source Countries	Number	% of Total Immigrants in 2010
Philippines	36,578	13.03
India	30,252	10.77
China, People's Republic of	30,197	10.75
United Kingdom	9,499	03.38
United States	9,243	03.29
France	6,934	02.47
Iran	6,815	02.42
United Arab Emirates	6,796	02.41
Morocco	5,946	02.11
Korea, Republic of	5,539	01.97
All other source countries	127,896	47.30
Total	280,681	100.00

SOURCE: "Immigrants by class according to the 10 main countries of birth, Canada, 2005 to 2007." Based on Citizenship and Immigration Canada, *Annual Report to Parliament on Immigration, 2005 to 2007* and Statistics Canada, *Publication Report on the Demographic Situation in Canada*, Catalogue 91-209-XWE, Issue 2005 and 2006. Released date: 23 July 2008, Table 4.3; www.statcan.gc.ca/bsolc/olc-cel/olc-cel?lang=eng&catno=91-209-X

GLOBAL ISSUES

The Points System for Skilled Workers: Would You Make It?

Do you think you would qualify as an immigrant to your own country? Test whether you qualify as a skilled worker for admission to Canada. The table below outlines the various categories of qualification for which points are rewarded. For example, if at present your education consists of a secondary school diploma but no further diplomas, certificates, or degrees, you will receive five points in this category. In the language category, if you can read, write, speak, and understand English with complete proficiency, you will be granted 16 points, and total proficiency in French will earn you an additional eight points. You will need at least 67 points (out of a possible 100) to be admitted to Canada as a skilled worker. For a complete breakdown of the points system, go to the following website: www.canada-immigration.biz/permanent_skilled.asp.

Selection Criteria	Points Awarded
Education	up to 25
Knowledge of official language(s)	up to 24
Work experience	up to 21
Age: Applicants 21–49 years of age receive maximum points. 2 points are deducted for each year under 21 or over 49, so that someone 16 or younger or 54 or older will receive no points.	up to 10
Arranged employment in Canada	up to 10
Adaptability	up to 10
Spouse's or common-law partner's education	3 to 5
Minimum one year full-time authorized work in Canada	5
Minimum two years post-secondary study in Canada	5
Maximum points awarded	100
Minimum required to pass for skilled worker immigrants	67

Immigrants are divided into four major immigration classes: skilled workers, business immigrants, the family class, and refugees. Data from 2010 show that contrary to public misconceptions, the largest category admitted is that of economic immigrants (skilled workers and business immigrants). They constituted 66.6 per cent of total immigration (186,913 people). Skilled workers are independent applicants who are admitted through the use of the points system (see Global Issues box above).

The family class in 2010 (60,220 people) ranked second, with 21.5 per cent of total immigration. These immigrants are admitted if they have close relatives (spouses or parents) in Canada who are willing to sponsor them and to support them financially for a period of three to ten years after they arrive. Refugees (24,696 people) follow, representing 8.8 per cent (Citizenship and Immigration Canada 2011).

Canada is a signatory to international treaties and is obliged by international law to provide asylum to those who have demonstrably genuine refugee claims.

The distribution of immigrants across Canada is decidedly uneven. Ontario receives 42 per cent of all immigrants; Quebec, 19.2 per cent; British Columbia, 15.7 per cent; Alberta, 11.6 per cent; Manitoba, 5.6 per cent; and Saskatchewan, 2.7 per cent. Immigration to other parts of Canada is negligible (Citizenship and Immigration Canada 2011). There is also a clear urban–rural divide. Immigrants are more attracted to major urban centres, because they usually find more economic opportunities there as well as other immigrants from their own homelands. Today, for example, the majority of Torontonians were born outside Canada, whereas almost all of the residents of Hérouxville, a small farming community in Quebec, are Canadian-born.

TIME to REFLECT

Why does Canada admit immigrants? If you were to (re)design Canada's immigration policy, what criteria would you use for admitting immigrants? Why are these criteria important?

Multiculturalism and Its Critics

Multiculturalism is one of those elusive terms that we use every day, but it means different things to different people. In Canada, we understand the term as having four interrelated dimensions: it is a demographic reality; it is part of pluralist ideology; it is a form of struggle among minority groups for access to economic and political resources; and it is a set of government policies and accompanying programs (Fleras and Elliott 1996, 325). Multiculturalism as policy and ideology gives rise to economic, political, and social practices, which in turn set limits on ethnic and racial group relations in order to maintain social order and manage social change (Satzewich and Liodakis 2010, 175–6).

In Canada, multiculturalism was introduced in 1971 by Prime Minister Pierre Elliott Trudeau. In the 1970s and 1980s, multiculturalism focused primarily on cultural folklore activities (e.g., food, song, and dance). In the 1990s, civic multiculturalism emerged, based on notions of social equality and citizenship, focusing more on society-building (Fleras and Elliott 1996). The policy of multiculturalism has been criticized since its introduction. Some argue that multiculturalism makes Canada a unique and great country; others argue that multiculturalism is useless, unnecessary, and ineffective. In the post-9/11 context, debates about multiculturalism have acquired renewed political importance.

CRITICISMS OF MULTICULTURALISM

There has never been agreement about the necessity, desirability, or effectiveness of this policy and its accompanying programs. Early critics argued that too great an emphasis was placed on depoliticized "song and dance" activities that were non-threatening to British and/or French economic, political, and cultural hegemony. The policy mystified social reality by creating the appearance of change without even addressing inequalities in Canada (Bolaria and Li 1988; Moodley 1983). The identification of only "cultural barriers" to the full participation of immigrants in Canadian society precluded the examination of racism and discrimination as barriers (Bolaria and Li 1988). Economic barriers were not recognized, nor were they examined (Stasiulis 1980, 34). The exclusive focus on cultural and linguistic barriers to equality concealed other, perhaps more fundamental, social inequalities based on property rights, labour market position, education, gender, age, and so on. Canadian society is characterized by ethnic- and gender-based class hierarchies and socio-political struggles not addressed by multiculturalism, because such struggles challenge, if not threaten, these hierarchies. Multiculturalism obfuscates these antagonisms and shifts the struggle to the cultural realm.

In the 1990s, critics claimed that the policy of multiculturalism reproduced stereotypes of ethnic groups, undermined Canadian unity, ghettoized minority issues, and took away from the special claims that francophones and Aboriginal peoples have within Canadian society. A policy that had as one of its underlying intentions the improvement of inter-group relations was seen by many as leading to deteriorating inter-group relations and as a threat to the coherence and stability of Canada. It was argued that "caravans," "folk fests," and other multicultural festivals do not promote serious cultural exchanges but instead are superficial commodity cultures and reproduce cultural, ethnic, and racial stereotypes (Bissoondath 1994, 83). In addition, multiculturalism promotes cultural **relativism** and hence undermines Canadian values and social cohesion (Bibby 1990). We have ended up with a value system that contains nothing exclusively Canadian. Multiculturalism does not offer a vision of unity; it encourages divisions by ghettoizing people into ethnic groups.

These critics seem purposefully vague in describing what constitutes Canadian culture, the definition of what and who is or should be Canadian or what Canadian values are. There is no definition of what constitutes "the Canadian nation, culture, or character," who defines it,

HUMAN DIVERSITY

The "Veil Issue"

Many Muslim women choose to cover parts of their face with veils. It is part of their religious tradition, just as many southern European Christian women in mourning choose to wear long black dresses and cover their heads. In the post 9/11 world, xenophobia and Islamophobia are on the rise worldwide. The "veil issue" has sparked heated debates in the UK, Belgium, France, and elsewhere. Canada is no exception. In September 2007, three federal by-elections took place in Quebec. Marc Mayrand, Canada's chief electoral officer, was under pressure from politicians, the media, and "concerned citizens" to take a stand against allowing veiled Muslim women to vote unless they first showed their faces. Should women wearing veils be allowed to vote? How could their identity be verified? Mayrand argued that veiled Muslim women have the same rights as everyone else. There is nothing in the current electoral law to prevent veiled people from voting. The law allows citizens—for religious reasons—to vote with their face covered provided they show two pieces of valid ID and swear an oath. After all, in the previous federal election, 80,000 people cast votes by mail.

How would you feel if you were a Canadian Muslim woman and were not allowed to vote because you wear a veil? Do you think that veiled women want to hide their identities? Canada is considered a tolerant society and has an official policy of multiculturalism. Freedom of religion is protected by the Charter of Rights and Freedoms. Should we allow veiled citizens to cast ballots? Before you grapple with this last question, you should know that both the Canadian Islamic Congress and the Canadian Council of Muslim Women agreed that veiled women should show their faces before voting.

or whose interests it serves. The implication is that the current system is somehow biased in favour of "non-whites" and "non-Europeans" and that it should not be.

Rhoda Howard-Hassmann (1999) has pointed to a basic fault in the Bibby and Bissoondath critiques: they both assume that multiculturalism calls for individuals to retain their ancestral identities. But the Canadian policy is "liberal," not "illiberal"—that is, it recognizes differences but does not impose the idea of maintaining ethnic differences, nor does it force individuals to identify with ancestral cultures. Far from promoting disloyalty to Canada and things Canadian, multiculturalism has the seemingly ironic consequences of integrating immigrants to the dominant society, promoting national unity, and encouraging "a sense of connection with other Canadians" (1999, 534). The rising number of people who identify their ancestry as Canadian in recent censuses tends to support her argument.

ABORIGINAL PEOPLES, QUÉBÉCOIS, AND MULTICULTURALISM

Another criticism is that multiculturalism undermines the special claims of francophones and Aboriginals. In Quebec, multicultural-ism was seen as an attempt by the federal government to undermine the legitimate Quebec aspirations for "nationhood." By severing culture from language, multiculturalism rejected the "two founding nations" metaphor of Canada's historical development and reduced the status of French Canadians from that of "founding people" to just another ethnic group (Abu-Laban and Stasiulis 1992, 367). Multiculturalism also became a mechanism to "buy" allophone votes. Assimilationist language policies in Quebec, directed toward allophones, can be understood in this context. Successive Quebec governments have pursued a policy of **interculturalism** instead of multiculturalism. According to Kymlicka (1998), interculturalism is based on three important principles: (1) it recognizes French as the language of public life; (2) it respects liberal-democratic values (political rights, equality of opportunity); and (3) it respects pluralism (openness to and tolerance of differences). These principles constitute a "moral contract" between the province of Quebec and immigrant groups. Interculturalism may sound a lot like the federal policy of multiculturalism, but there are some nuanced differences. For example, it promotes linguistic assimilation. The "centre of convergence" for different cultural groups in Quebec is the "collective good" of the French language, which is seen as an indispensable condition for the creation of the *culture publique commune* (common public culture) and the cohesion of Quebec society.

Some researchers have argued that interculturalism is the most advanced form of pluralism today (Karmis 2004, 79), since it combines multiculturalism and multinationalism and is more inclusive than either. It does not apply only to ethnic groups or nations but also to "lifestyle" cultures and world views associated with new social movements, including cultural, gay, punk, environmental, feminist, and other non-ethnic-based identities. In principle, no cultural community is excluded from Québécois identity.

TIME to REFLECT

Would you prefer to live in a country without official multiculturalism and/or interculturalism? Would you rather live in the US, France, or Germany? Why?

Canadian Aboriginals are also critical of and have similar reservations about multiculturalism. Aboriginal leaders argue that multiculturalism reduces them to "just another minority group" and undermines their aspirations for self-government (Abu-Laban and Stasiulis 1992, 376). They claim that they possess a distinct and unique set of rights—now enshrined in the Constitution—that stem from their being the first occupants of Canada. Since Aboriginal peoples do not consider themselves part of the so-called mainstream Canadian pluralist society but as distinct peoples, multiculturalism is seen as a threat to their survival. They prefer to negotiate their future with the federal and provincial governments, which should recognize their collective rights to special status and distinctiveness (Fleras and Elliott 1996, 343).

MULTICULTURALISM IN A CHANGING WORLD

Today, many countries celebrate their multicultural makeup, and some have policies designed to promote the peaceful coexistence of diverse groups. A number of events over the past decade, however, have provided a context for renewed questions about and attacks on multiculturalism, both in Canada and abroad. Certainly, the attacks on the World Trade Center in New York and the Pentagon on 11 September 2001 put many Western governments on alert about the threats that cultural and religious "Others" may pose to the "peace and security" of their countries. In the post-9/11 era of Islamophobia and "big brother" surveillance, two criticisms of multiculturalism are also prevalent: (1) that multiculturalism encourages and tolerates the promotion of cultures and religions that are decidedly intolerant and (2) that multiculturalism is a recipe for home-grown terrorism. Such critiques are often concealed forms of racism. No country has arrived at an ideal management of ethnic and racial diversity. Canada's multicultural approach to diversity issues may not be perfect—indeed, it is rather limited—but many other far more problematic approaches to diversity exist (the US and France spring readily to mind), and we can take pride that we have avoided them so far. Let us now turn, then, to the unresolved issues of racism.

TIME to REFLECT

Are Aboriginal Canadians and the Québécois just ethnic groups? If not, why not?

Prejudice and Racism

Racism is based on "othering" (Simmons 1998). According to Stuart Hall, it is

> not a set of false pleas which swim around in the head . . . not a set of mistaken perceptions. . . . [Racist ideas] have their basis in real material conditions of existence. They arise because of the concrete problems of different classes and groups in society. Racism represents the attempt ideologically to construct those conditions, contradictions, and problems in such a way that they can be dealt with and deflected at the same moment. (in Li 1999, 325)

Many sociologists have suggested (e.g., Bolaria and Li 1988; Li 1999) that race problems often begin as labour problems. Competition for employment among workers from different ethnic/racialized (and gender) groups keeps wages low and profits high. Workers participate in split labour markets in which members of dominant groups may have more secure, full-time, and high-paying jobs, whereas minorities are found in more part-time, low-paying, insecure, and menial occupations. Labour market splits develop over long periods of time and are reproduced by prejudice and discrimination. Often, we have preconceived notions about ethnic/racialized groups. Members of some groups are seen through the prism of stereotypes (Driedger 1996). Some are deemed hard-working, law-abiding, smart, moral, and so on. Others are seen as "lazy," "smelly," "dirty," "stingy," "criminals," "promiscuous," "uncivilized," and the like. Ethnic jokes, which might amuse us uncritically, are based on these stereotypes. Negative stereotypes are often reserved by the majority group for minority groups; positive stereotypes are related to dominant groups, although minority groups use positive self-stereotypes to resist racism. Discrimination refers to behaviours and policies that reproduce ethnic and racial social stereotypes as well as economic and political inequalities. Prejudice refers to the negative views of and attitudes about members of various minority groups. Stereotypes, discrimination, and prejudice maintain and reproduce racism. Expressions of working-class racism may be attributable to labour market conditions of inequality (see Dunk in Satzewich 1998).

Historically, many groups have experienced varying degrees of racism in Canada. First Nations people have been singled out for unequal treatment by Canadian governments. Their lands were taken away through war and through "treaties"; they were forcibly segregated in reserves; and generations of children were sent to residential schools, deprived of their own cultural heritage. During the world wars, members of certain ethnic groups (Germans, Italians, and Japanese) were interned by Canadian authorities. Others (Russians, Ukrainians, and Jews, for example) were seen as communists and were either not allowed to immigrate to Canada or, if they were involved in labour strife, were quickly deported. Canada accepted only a handful of European Jewish refugees in the 1930s. As mentioned previously, early immigration policies excluded the Chinese and Indians.

Today, a more subtle type of discrimination permeates Canadian life. Because it is covert, it is more difficult to identify, resist, and combat. Many face issues of systemic discrimination—impersonal, covert practices that penalize members of minority groups. Also called institutional racism, it is the outcome of the inner workings of institutions (e.g., the economy, education systems, governments) that disadvantage subordinate individuals and groups. For example, in the labour market a minimum educational requirement of a high school diploma may exclude from unskilled jobs some minorities with low educational attainment. Recent immigrants may be excluded from good jobs when governments and employers require long years of "Canadian experience." Members of minority groups may be excluded from police or firefighting forces on the basis of a minimum height requirement (similar regulations have kept many women out of these forces). Non-recognition of educational credentials attained abroad (especially from developing countries) keeps large numbers of visible-minority immigrants out of secure, well-paying jobs.

To learn more about institutions that promote racism, see Chapter 14, "Institutional Processes," p. 281.

Henry and Tator (2005) argue that today, a peculiar form of racism exists in Canada: democratic racism. It is not necessarily based on old racist notions of the biological and social superiority of whites over racialized minorities but rather on contradictions between and conflicts over social values. For example, Canada is supposedly committed to justice, equality, and fairness, but these values coexist with differential treatment of and discrimination against minorities. Democratic racism is an ideology and a mechanism for reducing the conflict inherent in maintaining a commitment to both liberal and non-egalitarian values. It permits and sustains the rationalization, justification, and maintenance of two apparently conflicting sets of values (liberal-democratic versus non-egalitarian).

Racism is reflected in systems of cultural production and representation and in dominant

(© CP Images/Nathan Denette)

Racism continues to be a part of Canadian society. Governor of the Bank of Canada Mark Carney apologized in August 2012 after reports that the new $100 banknote was altered because focus groups responded negatively to the depiction of an Asian woman looking into a microscope. One member of the focus group said, "The person on it appears to be of Asian descent, which doesn't rep(resent) Canada. It is fairly ugly" (Ruparelia 2012).

codes of behaviour. Henry and Tator argue that they are "embedded in the values and meanings, policies and practices of powerful institutions" (2005, 90). Society gives voice to racism through words, images, stories, explanations (or silences), categorizations, justifications, and rationalizations, which in turn produce a shared understanding of the world and of the (inferior) status of people of colour in that world (2005, 91). This discourse is used to extend or defend the traditional interests of the dominant culture.

For example, many people, usually members of dominant groups, claim that they do not "see" colour. "Not seeing colour" masks the reality of the pervasiveness and the historical "baggage" of colour in our everyday lives—policies, programs, and practices that continue to be racist. We speak of equal opportunity, but it is often assumed that we do not have to dismantle dominant (capitalist/white/male) institutions of power in order to achieve it. Just because we exalt tolerance of others through the language and policy of multiculturalism does not mean that multiculturalism necessarily leads to social harmony. The new buzzword—"reasonable accommodation"—is often seen as a hoax (see Open for Discussion box below). We continue to use the dominant values, beliefs, and ideas as measuring sticks for evaluating others. In addition, multiculturalism conceals the structural, economic, and political inequalities in Canada. Multiculturalism has not combated racism or class and gender inequalities.

OPEN for DISCUSSION

Reasonable Accommodation, Xenophobia, and Islamophobia

"Reasonable accommodation" is the new mantra used by proponents of Quebec interculturalism. The term implies that government policies and programs strive not just to tolerate but also to accommodate the cultural differences—the "otherness"—of new immigrants. Not all Quebecers agree with reasonable accommodation. In fact, a clear urban/rural cultural split reflects current socio-demographic realities: urban centres like Montreal have sizable immigrant populations and are more accepting of difference; rural areas are largely homogeneous and culturally conservative, and they would like to keep it that way. For example, in January 2007, Hérouxville, a small (population 1338) Quebec farming community of almost exclusively white, francophone, Catholic residents, gained notoriety when its town council passed a resolution prescribing a code of conduct for immigrants. It set conditions under which new immigrants could be admitted to the town. Immigrants who "cover their face," "carry weapons to school," "stone or burn alive women," or "perform female genital mutilation" were not welcome in Hérouxville. As André Drouin, a town councillor, put it, reasonable accommodation had reached a state of emergency in Quebec. The implication was clear: apparently, interculturalism and reasonable accommodation had gone too far, since, it was presumed, they "allow everything."

You may visit http://herouxville-quebec.blogspot.com and have a look at the town's "character." What do you think are the implications of this issue for the study of race and ethnicity in Canada? Who decides what is "reasonable" in reasonable accommodation? What are the criteria? What should they be?

Culturalism and Political Economy: Explaining Socio-economic Inequalities

Broadly speaking, two major theoretical frameworks attempt to explain ethnicity and race as social phenomena: culturalism and political economy. The central argument of culturalism can be summarized as follows: ethnic and racial groups share common values, religion, beliefs, sentiments, ideas, languages, historical memories and symbols, leaderships, a common past, and so on. If we want to explain their differential socio-economic achievements, we must look into their culture, the key to understanding their differences. Culture is considered the *explanans* (that which explains), not the *explanandum* (that which must be explained). Cultural values affect the psychological composition of group members and produce, it is claimed, "differences in cognitive perception, mental aptitude, and logical reasoning" (Li 1999, 10). In turn, such differences are thought to affect subsequent educational and economic achievements. Thus, some groups, on average, are doing better than others in school and in the labour market. Some cultures foster values conducive to economic achievement (in capitalist conditions); others do not.

The political economy perspective, on the other hand, begins with the tenet that socially constituted individuals belong to social structures that enable but also constrain their social actions. Examples of these structures include those built on social relations of class, gender, race/ethnicity, age, sexual preference, physical ability, mental health/illness, and so on. Societies are characterized by the unequal distribution of property, power, and other resources (both natural and socio-political). Who owns and controls what, when, why, and how are central concerns of political economy (Satzewich 1998, 314). Race and ethnicity are seen as relational concepts. Social class, status, race, and ethnicity constitute an

index of social standing or rank reflected in terms of criteria like wealth, education, style of life, linguistic capacity, residential location, consumptive capacity, or having or lacking respect. Status has to do with one's ranking in a social system *relative to the position of others,* where the ranking involves . . . [positive] self-conception and (de)valuations of others. (Goldberg 1993, 69; emphasis added)

Most immigrant groups have been primarily associated with the lower classes because of the menial jobs they tend to do upon arrival. In contrast, members of the charter groups have been associated with the upper classes and with less labour-intensive, more prestigious occupations. Historically, there appeared to be an overlap between lower-class membership and membership in a minority ethnic/racial group. We shall examine the economic dimensions of ethnic/racial inequalities below.

From the Vertical to the Colour-Coded Mosaic

Over the years, most research on social inequality in Canada has focused on the economic performance of ethnic groups to determine whether Canadian society is hierarchically structured (Agócs and Boyd 1993, 337). John Porter in *The Vertical Mosaic* (1965, 73) argued that immigration and ethnic affiliation were important factors in the process of social class formation in Canada. Canadian society, understood as an ethnic mosaic, is hierarchically structured in terms of the differential distributions of wealth and power among its constituent ethnic groups. The charter groups (British and French) appropriated positions of power and advantage in the social, economic, and political realms and relegated "entrance status" groups to lower, less preferred positions. "Less preferred" groups that arrived in Canada after the charter groups were employed in lower-status occupations and were subject to the assimilation processes laid down by the charter groups (Porter 1965, 63–4). Ethnic affiliation implied blocked social mobility. Upward mobility of ethnic groups depended on the culture of the ethnic group in question and the degree to which it conformed to the rules of assimilation set by the charter groups. The improvement in the position of entrance status groups over time could be determined by their assimilability (1965, 67–73).

Porter found persistent patterns of ethnic inequality. Canadians of Jewish and British origin were at the top, overrepresented in the professional and financial occupations (higher status and income) and under-represented in agricultural and unskilled jobs (lower status and income). The Germans, Scandinavians, and Dutch were closest to the British. Italians, Polish, and Ukrainians were next, with other southern Europeans (Greeks and Portuguese) near the lower end of the spectrum (1965, 90). The French, somewhere between the northern and southern Europeans, were under-represented in professional and financial occupations and overrepresented in agricultural and unskilled jobs. Aboriginal people were at the bottom of the hierarchy (1965, 201–308, 337–416, 520–59).

Even though questions have been raised about the persistence of the **vertical mosaic** for certain European-origin ethnic groups, some suggest that the vertical mosaic persists in a racialized form and that Canada is characterized today by a *colour-coded vertical mosaic* (Galabuzi 2006, 7). In this new mosaic, whites are on top and non-whites on the bottom. In 1984, the Royal Commission on Equality in Employment found substantial income disparities among visible minorities, Aboriginals, and non-visible groups (Royal Commission on Equality in Employment 1984, 84–5). Visible minorities were sometimes denied access to employment because of unfair recruitment procedures and were more likely to be unemployed. Often, education credentials acquired outside Canada were not recognized in the labour market or by governments. Sometimes, Canadian experience was unnecessarily required (1984, 46–51). These disparities were attributed to **systemic discrimination** in the workplace. For Aboriginal peoples, the situation was even worse. Aboriginal men earned 60 per cent of the earnings of non-Aboriginal men; Aboriginal women made 72 per cent of what non-Aboriginal women earned (1984, 33), and this spoke only of those who had jobs—many Aboriginals are isolated in peripheral locations

far from job markets, are unemployed and not seeking employment, and therefore are not counted in unemployment statistics.

Subsequently, several studies found a general trend of convergence of earnings among the European groups, but visible minorities of all educational levels received lower rewards, substantially below the national average (Lian and Matthews 1998, 471, 475). Similar findings were reported by Li (2003) and Galabuzi (2006), who showed that in 2000 the average after-tax income for racialized persons was $20,627, 12.3 per cent less than the average after-tax income of $23,522 for non-racialized persons. Among university degree–holders in 2000, racialized individuals had an average after-tax income of $35,617, while their non-racialized counterparts had an average after-tax income of $38,919, an 8.5 per cent difference. Many researchers argue, then, that race is now *the* fundamental basis of economic inequality in Canada. These researchers tend, however, to treat the categories visible/non-visible as homogeneous, with no internal class, gender, or nativity differences.

Differentials within Ethnic and Racialized Groups: The Roles of Class, Gender, and Place of Birth

Apart from a few notable exceptions (Li 1988, 1992; Nakhaie 1999, 2000; Liodakis 2002), the class dimension of ethnic earnings inequality in Canada has not been adequately examined. Ethnic and racialized groups have internal hierarchies and are themselves stratified. They are not homogeneous. They are differentiated internally by religion, dialect, region of origin, time of arrival in Canada (Porter 1965, 72–3), social class (Li 1988; 1992), gender (Boyd 1992), age, and place of birth (Liodakis 1998; 2002). The vertical and colour-coded mosaic theses should be questioned, not because we have more ethno-racial equality now but arguably because inequality in Canada is still very much based on social class, gender, and place of birth. Ethnicity and race serve as sources of division

(Photo courtesy of TRIEC)

Increasing numbers of immigrants to Canada have impressive credentials and work experience, yet they often are underemployed because their schooling and experience were gained abroad. These posters were part of a public awareness campaign for hireimmigrants.ca, the Toronto Region Immigrant Employment Council (TRIEC).

within the broader class structure (Li 1992). Ethnic inequality cannot be analyzed outside the class context (Li 1988; Nakhaie 1999, 2000; Liodakis 2002; Satzewich and Liodakis 2010).

TIME to REFLECT

Why do some people make more money than others? Do all members of the same ethnic/racialized group have the same income? What do you think are the causes of income inequalities within ethnic and racialized groups?

Statistics Canada defines the following groups as part of the "collectivity" of visible minorities (often called "non-whites"): black, South Asian, Chinese, Korean, Japanese, Southeast Asian, Filipino, Arab/West Asian, Latin American, visible minority not included elsewhere, and multiple visible minority. All other groups are considered non-visible, or "white," groups (Statistics Canada 1996). This dichotomous taxonomy (visible/non-visible, "white/non-white" groups) creates such broad categories that the considerable internal socio-

economic heterogeneity within the two groups we are left with is concealed (Liodakis 2002; Satzewich and Liodakis 2010).

The colour-coded vertical mosaic thesis does not fully explain the patterns of economic inequality in Canada. The racialized vertical mosaic thesis overlooks many anomalous cases that undermine it. For example, "white" southern Europeans (Greeks, Portuguese, and Italians) often have lower educational levels and earn less than many visible-minority groups. Li (1988) and Boyd (1992) have shown that women of Greek, Italian, Portuguese, other European, and Dutch origin make less than the average earnings of all women. Visible-minority native-born women actually make more than their non-visible counterparts (Li 2003).

Table 8.2 shows the social class composition of several groups and provides updated confirmation that ethnic and racialized groups are not homogeneous in class composition. If we examine social inequality from a class perspective, it appears that in the case of workers there is no clear-cut visible/non-visible distinction. The Chinese, for example, are less proletarianized than the Portuguese, the Italians, the Greeks, the British, and the French, and the national

TABLE 8.2 ▼ The Class Composition of Ethnic Groups,[1] 2005 (%)

Ethnic/Racialized Group	Workers	Professionals	Managers and Supervisors	Petite Bourgeoisie	Small Employers
Aboriginal	67.8	18.7	8.0	3.8	1.7
English	53.1	21.6	13.4	6.9	5.0
Caribbean*	64.9	20.4	8.6	4.1	2.0
Chinese	48.4	29.0	9.1	7.1	6.4
Filipino	70.5	20.3	5.6	2.1	1.5
French	51.1	26.8	10.7	7.2	4.2
Greek	48.5	21.5	14.3	7.5	8.2
Italian	50.4	22.3	14.6	5.8	6.9
Jewish	30.0	33.1	13.8	11.9	11.2
Portuguese	65.1	13.2	12.2	5.1	4.5
South Asian**	61.4	19.3	7.6	5.9	5.8
Canada	53.0	23.5	11.7	7.0	4.8

[1] Single origin responses of individual respondents aged 25 to 59 and over who worked at least one week in 2005 in Canada, excluding the territories, Atlantic Canada, and inmates. Percentages may not add up to 100 because of rounding error.
* Excluding Jamaican-origin responses
** Excluding East Indian–origin responses
SOURCE: Calculated from Statistics Canada, 2006 Census, Public Use Microdata File on Individuals.

average. The Portuguese are more proletarianized than all the visible-minority groups except the Filipinos. Aboriginal Canadians are more likely to be found in the working class and less likely to be found in the other classes, although Aboriginal women are, actually, less proletarianized than Aboriginal men (Liodakis 2009). Aboriginal, Caribbean, Filipino, French, and Portuguese individuals are under-represented in the ranks of employers, while British, Chinese, South Asian, Greek, and Jewish individuals are variously overrepresented among the ranks of the petite bourgeoisie. In the professional category, the Chinese are well above the national average, above the charter groups, the Portuguese, the Italians, and the Greeks, and second only to Jewish-origin Canadians. In the small-employer category, the Chinese are the fourth highest group, whereas all other visible groups are under-represented, along with the Portuguese, the French, and Aboriginals.

There is, then, great class variation among and within ethnic and racialized groups. In addition, groups have different gender and nativity compositions. For example, in terms of gender, the Caribbean and Filipino groups have more women than men in the labour market

because of immigration patterns. In all visible groups, the percentage of foreign-born is around 90 per cent, whereas in the non-visible category the percentages are much lower (less than 55 per cent). These differences affect earnings inequalities that exist *within* ethnic groups but are concealed if we only look at them as homogeneous entities (Satzewich and Liodakis 2010). There are considerable differences in the earnings of classes within ethnic groups. Historically, the petite bourgeoisie and the proletarians have mean earnings below the national average, while small employers, semi-autonomous workers, and managers and supervisors have earnings considerably above it (Li 1988, 1992; Liodakis 2002; Satzewich and Liodakis 2010). In addition, women, on average, make less than men in all ethnic groups and in all social classes. In general, internal variations of earnings *within* ethnic/racialized groups are greater than the earnings differentials *among* them (Liodakis 2002; Satzewich and Liodakis 2010).

Moreover, the greater the size of the immigrant component of an ethnic/racialized group, the more likely it is that the group will have lower earnings. Data from the 2006 Canadian census show that earnings differentials exist among the Canadian-born, immigrants, and recent immigrants. Three patterns have emerged over the years: First, immigrants, as a group, make less than Canadian-born individuals. Second, these differences are greater among those with university education. For example, Statistics Canada census data (2006) show that the median 2005 earnings of the Canadian-born with a university degree were $51,656, whereas those of immigrants with a university degree were only $36,451, a difference of $15,205. For those without a university degree, the difference was only $4801 ($32,499 − $27,698). It appears that immigrants with higher education, although they make more than immigrants without a university education, make a lot less than their Canadian-born counterparts. Third, the 2005 median earnings of recent immigrants (i.e., those who had immigrated to Canada during the five years before the census was taken) were much lower than those of immigrants who had been in Canada longer than five years and the Canadian-born. When compared with the Canadian-born with a university degree, recent immigrants with a university degree earned $27,020 less ($51,656 − $24,636). Recent immigrants without a university degree made $13,927 less than their Canadian-born counterparts ($32,499 − $18,572) (Satzewich and Liodakis 2010).

TIME to REFLECT

Do you think that there is a link between a person's ethnic/racial background and his or her moral, intellectual, and behavioural characteristics? If so, can you think of specific examples, without resorting to stereotypes?

A closer look at the general trends of earnings of recent immigrants since the 1980s points to a steady decline in their earnings compared to those of the Canadian-born. Table 8.3 shows median earnings differences among male and female recent immigrants with and without a university degree from 1980 to 2005. Whereas in 1980 recent-immigrant males with a university degree made 77 cents for every dollar their Canadian-born counterparts made, in 1990 they

made 63 cents. In 2000, they made 58 cents; and in 2005, only 48 cents. Female recent immigrants in 1980 with a university degree made 59 cents for every dollar their Canadian-born counterparts made, 63 cents in 1990, 52 cents in 2000, and only 43 cents in 2005. Male recent immigrants without a university degree in 1980 made 84 cents for every dollar their Canadian-born counterparts made. In 1990, they made 67 cents; in 2000, 65 cents; and in 2005, only 61 cents. Female recent immigrants without a university degree in 1980 made 86 cents for every dollar their Canadian-born counterparts made. In 1990, they made 77 cents; in 2000, 66 cents; and in 2005, only 51 cents.

In short, there has been a steady deterioration of recent-immigrant earnings, irrespective of gender and university education. This is a troubling trend, given that today, most recent immigrants have more educational credentials than those who immigrated to Canada in the 1980s. Although there are individual variations (knowledge of official languages and foreign education play important roles in influencing immigrant earnings), in general, immigrant status has a strong, negative impact on earnings. Recent immigrants experience higher levels of earnings inequality. They are more likely to work part-time than full-time, more likely to face unemployment, and less likely to move up the occupational hierarchy. They earn less than Canadian-born workers, and they also face earnings volatility (instability). Those initial earnings differences tend to persist in later years (Ostrovsky 2008, 24–5). The recent recession has had negative effects on the earnings of all Canadian workers but especially on those of recent immigrants.

Conclusion: The Future of Race and Ethnicity

In this chapter, we have argued that ethnicity and race are social relations. As such, they are about power among individuals and social groups. Notions of ethnicity and race are about domination and subordination; they are rooted in the history of colonialism and associated with the development of capitalism. Historical processes that have made some people "minorities" have led to and continue to inform and reproduce the formation of the social,

| TABLE 8.3 ▼ | Median Earnings of Male and Female Recent-Immigrant and Canadian-Born Earners, 1980–2005 | | | | | | | | | | | |

	Recent Immigrant Earners				Canadian-Born Earners				Recent Immigrant to Canadian-Born Earnings Ratio			
	With a university degree		With no university degree		With a university degree		With no university degree		With a university degree		With no university degree	
	Males	Females	Males	Females	Males	Females	Males	Females	Males	Females	Males	Females
Year	2005 constant dollars								Ratio			
1980	48,541	24,317	36,467	18,548	63,040	41,241	43,641	21,463	0.77	0.59	0.84	0.86
1990	38,351	25,959	27,301	17,931	61,332	41,245	40,757	23,267	0.63	0.63	0.67	0.77
2000	35,816	22,511	25,951	16,794	61,505	43,637	39,902	25,622	0.58	0.52	0.65	0.66

Note: The numbers refer to all earners whether or not they worked on a full-time basis for a full year. Individuals with self-employment income are included, while those living in institutions are excluded.
SOURCE: "Median earnings, in 2005 constant dollars, of male and female recent immigrant earners and Canadian-born earners aged 25 to 54, with or without a university degree, Canada, 1980 to 2005," adapted from Statistics Canada, "Income and earnings, 2006 Census," Catalogue 97-563-XWE2006002, Table 8, www.statcan.gc.ca/bsolc/olc-cel/olc-cel?catno=97-563- XWE2006002&lang=end

political, and economic dichotomies of the "Self" and the "Other." Canada's current socio-demographic makeup is linked to the historical (and ongoing) "othering" of Aboriginal peoples, the usurpation of their lands, the destruction of their cultures, and government policies of forced assimilation. It is also intertwined with immigration policies that, for a long time, excluded visible minorities and other "non-preferred" groups from immigrating to Canada.

Race and ethnicity are bases of social inequality. They inform and are part of its class and gender dimensions. In Canada, some groups are doing better than others. If we consider ethnic and racial groups as homogeneous entities, there appears to be a binary social hierarchy based on visibility. When we examine the internal class, gender, and nativity differences among groups, it is clear that the Canadian-born, males, managers and supervisors, professionals, and small employers do better than the foreign-born, females, workers, and the petite bourgeoisie. Canada now has an official policy of multiculturalism that attempts to integrate minorities into the social fabric. But the policy does little to address the economic inequalities in Canadian society and has not been very successful in combating racism or promoting the institutional integration of minorities.

Recent efforts of "reasonable accommodation" have sparked more debates. This is by no means an exclusively Canadian phenomenon.

The wider global context is interesting: in the post-modern, globalized world, the hegemonic economic, political, and cultural powers (e.g., the US, the European Union, Japan) have increasingly pushed for world economic integration through free trade, the free movement of capital across nation-states, the control and surveillance of international labour migration, the weakening of the role of the nation-state, as well as the rise of supranational organizations like the **World Bank**, the **International Monetary Fund**, and the World Trade Organization. A trend toward global cultural homogenization is partly attributable to the export of capitalism and consumer popular culture to developing nations. Today, our world does not seem to be any more peaceful or egalitarian. Nor have ethnic/racial and cultural identities or racism disappeared. On the contrary, we have witnessed the rise of nationalisms; ethnic cleansing; a new racism, xenophobia, and Islamophobia (especially after 9/11); wars in ex-Yugoslavia, Afghanistan, Iraq, and elsewhere; and a general thrust against the protection of individual and group rights and freedoms in all Western, liberal-capitalist democracies—all in the name of fighting "terrorism" and "exporting" what is claimed to be democracy. At the heart of all these matters are race and ethnicity, a major field of study within the social sciences, especially within sociology.

questions for critical thought

1. What criteria would you use to differentiate human populations, and why? What makes you a member (or not) of an ethnic and/or racial group? Should Ontarians be considered an ethnic group? Quebecers? Why? Apply the criteria listed in the first part of this chapter to answer these questions.

2. Can the policy of multiculturalism alone provide solutions to the problems of racism and the attendant issues of immigrant and minority group integration into Canadian political, social, and economic institutions? What should policy-makers do to address the issues of racism and immigrant integration into Canadian society? Explain.

3. What is reasonable accommodation? Who decides what is reasonable? Explain the rise of post-9/11 xenophobia and Islamophobia in the US, Canada, and elsewhere. Choose a particular issue (e.g., the veil), and survey the opinions of your friends and family. What do you conclude?

4. What account better for the economic inequalities among different ethnic/racial groups— cultural or structural differences? Assume that all members of ethnic/racial groups share the same cultural and behavioural characteristics. If culturalist explanations account for the economic inequalities among ethnic/racial groups, what would explain the significant economic inequalities within ethnic/racial groups?

recommended readings

Grace-Edward Galabuzi. 2006. *Canada's Economic Apartheid: The Social Exclusion of Racialized Groups in the New Century.* **Toronto: Canadian Scholars Press.**
In this controversial argument that supports the view of Canada as characterized by a new colour-coded vertical mosaic, Galabuzi presents evidence of persistent income inequalities between racialized and non-racialized Canadians.

Frances Henry and Carol Tator. 2005. *The Colour of Democracy: Racism in Canadian Society.* **3rd edn. Toronto: Thomson Nelson.**
This thorough and caustic critique of racism in Canadian policies and institutions points to the contradictions of multiculturalism and democratic racism in Canadian society.

Peter Li. 2003. *Destination Canada: Immigration Debates and Issues.* **Toronto: Oxford University Press.**
This is an excellent and up-to-date review of the major debates about the social and economic consequences of immigration to Canada.

Vic Satzewich and Nikolaos Liodakis. 2013. *"Race" and Ethnicity in Canada: A Critical Introduction.* **3rd edn. Toronto: Oxford University Press.**
This work summarizes theoretical approaches to the study of race and ethnicity, Canadian immigration policies, Aboriginal–non-Aboriginal relations, economic inequalities among and within ethnic groups, multiculturalism, racism, and transnationalism.

recommended websites

Assembly of First Nations
www.afn.ca
This excellent website of the national organization for status Indians, established in 1982 out of the earlier National Indian Brotherhood, includes press releases, publications, news, policy areas, information on past and future annual assemblies, and links to provincial and territorial organizations. You might also want to check out the fine websites of the other two national Aboriginal organizations in Canada: Inuit Tapiriit

Kanatami, at www.itk.ca, and the Métis National Council, at www.metisnation.ca.

Citizenship and Immigration Canada: Multiculturalism
www.cic.gc.ca/english/multiculturalism/index.asp
This federal department site includes information on multicultural programs, definitions of multiculturalism and diversity, news releases, publications, and links to numerous Canadian and international organizations.

Canadian Race Relations Foundation (CRRF)
www.crr.ca
The CRRF, established by an Act of Parliament in 1991, is the lead government agency that aims to eliminate racism in Canada. Its site outlines programs, includes publications, and has useful links to other sites.

Justicia for Migrant Workers—J4MW
www.justicia4migrantworkers.org
This non-governmental organization, founded in 2001 and based in Toronto with an office in Vancouver, seeks to promote the rights of Mexican and Caribbean migrant workers in Canada. The website, which is bilingual English/Spanish, provides notices on upcoming events, press releases, description of ongoing campaigns, and a "Wall of Shame" of public statements by politicians and other stakeholders showing "the face of racism in Canada."

chapter 9

Families and Personal Life

Maureen Baker

In this chapter, you will:

▶ Learn about patterns and trends in Canadian families.

▶ Gain a clearer knowledge of cross-cultural family variations.

▶ Differentiate among the conceptual frameworks in family sociology.

▶ Learn more about several controversial issues in Canadian families.

Introduction

The media often dwell on the negative side of family life by highlighting violent and broken relationships, yet most Canadians value their families, want to have and raise children, and expect to live within a stable relationship for most of their lives (Baker 2010). Ideally, family life can provide companionship, children, a sense of belonging, love and sexual expression, personal development, and shared resources. However, some families are actually unloving and even abusive.

Governments typically encourage heterosexual marriage and childbearing, because they need future taxpayers, voters, consumers, and workers to maintain the nation. Governments and employers rely on parents to produce children and socialize them to become law-abiding citizens and future employees, and on family members to provide the necessary support so that people can return each day to school or work. This suggests that intimate relationships remain important to the larger society as well as to individuals, but family life and gender relations have changed considerably during the past 30 years (Baker 2010; Siltanen and Doucet 2008).

Since the 1970s, young people have been delaying marriage while they gain an education and prepare for employment. More couples now cohabit without legal marriage, and couples are producing fewer children, who spend more time with non-family caregivers while their parents work. Remarriages form a larger percentage of all marriages as more

relationships now end in separation, and an increasing proportion of children are raised by lone parents or in stepfamilies. People tend to live longer, but more people are also living alone, especially before marriage, after separation, and in widowhood.

This chapter first defines families and outlines some structural variations. It then introduces the different ways that sociologists have explained personal life, followed by a discussion of five controversial issues: sharing domestic work, assisted conception, non-family child care, children and divorce, and wife abuse. Some general conclusions are then drawn from this material.

Family Variations

DEFINING FAMILIES

Many definitions of family have been used in academic research, policy development, and program delivery. Most definitions focus on legal obligations and family structures rather than on love, obligation, or personal services. These definitions always include heterosexual couples and single parents sharing a home with their children, but until recently few definitions encompassed same-sex couples. Most definitions also include parents with dependent children as well as childless couples or those whose children have left home. Others extend the definition of family to grandparents, aunts, uncles, and cousins who share a dwelling.

Sociologists and anthropologists used to talk about "the family" as a monolithic institution with one acceptable structure

Families come in different forms and sizes. What unites families is what they do, not how they look.

and common behavioural patterns (Eichler 2005). Academics used to assume that family members were related by blood, marriage, or adoption and that they shared a dwelling and resources, maintained sexually exclusive relationships, reproduced and raised children together, and cherished and protected each other. Nevertheless, academics always differentiated between nuclear families, which consist of parents and their children sharing a dwelling, and extended families, which include several generations or adult siblings sharing a dwelling and resources with their spouses and children. Both kinds of families continue to be a part of Canadian life, although nuclear families are more prevalent.

The most common definition in policy research is Statistics Canada's **census family**, which includes married couples and cohabitants who have lived together for more than one year, with or without never-married children, as well as single parents living with never-married children. As of 2006, couples can be same-sex or opposite-sex, but this definition excludes the larger kin group. The Canadian government also uses the concept of **household**, which refers to people sharing a dwelling whether or not they are related. For example, a boarder might be part of the household but not part of the family. Table 9.1 shows the percentage of Canadians living in various family types in 2006 compared to 1981, revealing the decline in legal marriage.

In a culturally diverse society like Canada, it is inaccurate to talk about "the family" as though a single family type exists or ever did exist. In fact, cultural groups tend to organize their families differently, depending on their traditions, beliefs, socio-economic situation,

and immigrant or indigenous status (Vanier Institute of the Family 2004). Most Canadians live in nuclear families comprising only parents and their children, but **extended families** remain important as a living arrangement and support group. Even when relatives do not live together, they may reside nearby, visit or telephone regularly, help with child care, provide financial and emotional support, and help to find employment and accommodation for one another. When relatives do not share a household but still rely heavily on one another, they are said to be a **modified extended family**.

In the 1950s, sociologists lamented the isolation of the modern **nuclear family**, suggesting that extended families used to be more prevalent before industrialization (Parsons and Bales 1955). Since then, historians and sociologists have found that nuclear families were always the most prevalent living arrangement in Europe and North America (Goldthorpe 1987; Nett 1981), but extended families were and still are widespread among certain cultural groups, such as some First Nations peoples, southern Europeans, and some South and Western Asians. They are also more prevalent among those with lower incomes, because they provide low-cost accommodation and practical support for young cash-strapped couples, lone mothers, or frail elderly parents in widowhood.

In this chapter, "families" will be used in the plural to indicate the continued existence of different family structures. Qualifying phrases, such as "male-breadwinner families," "lesbian families," and "stepfamilies," will be used for clarification. Although sociological definitions formerly focused on who constitutes a family, more researchers now emphasize what makes a family. This approach downplays sexual preference and the legality of the relationship and focuses instead on patterns of caring and sharing.

MONOGAMY AND POLYGAMY

In all Western countries, it is illegal to marry more than one spouse at a time, but **polygyny**, or having several wives at a time, is practised in some countries in Africa and western Asia, especially those using Islamic law. In sub-Saharan Africa throughout the 1990s, about half of married women were in polygynous unions

TABLE 9.1 ▼	Percentage of Families in Canada by Type, 1981 and 2006	
Type of Family	1981	2006
Legally married couples with children	55	39
Legally married couples without children	28	30
Lone-parent families	11	16
Common-law families without children	4	9
Common-law families with children	2	7

SOURCE: Vanier Institute of the Family (www.vifamily.ca, Virtual Library, 2010).

in Benin, Burkina Faso, and Guinea and more than 40 per cent in Mali, Senegal, and Togo (United Nations 2000, 28). Wealthy men are more likely than those with fewer resources to take on more than one legal wife (Barker 2003).

Polygynous unions, which lead to a proliferation of stepchildren and step-relatives, tend to be associated with patriarchal authority and wide age gaps between husbands and wives. They are more common among rural and less-educated women, as well as among those who do not formally work for pay outside the household (Barker 2003). Multiple wives, who are sometimes sisters, may resent their husband's taking a new partner, but they may also welcome her assistance with household work and horticulture and may value her companionship in a society where spouses are seldom close friends. Furthermore, the husband's second marriage elevates the rank of the first wife, who becomes the supervisor of the younger wife's household work.

Polygamy refers to the practice of having more than one spouse at a time, but polygyny is much more prevalent than **polyandry**, or marriage between one woman and several husbands. When polyandry does occur, the husbands are often brothers attempting to keep family land intact (Ihinger-Tallman and Levinson 2003). Most societies prefer polygyny, because more children can be born with multiple wives, which could be important if children are the main labour source for the family or community. Identifying the father is

particularly important in **patrilineal** societies, because children take their father's surname, belong to his kin group, and inherit from him. Married men are also responsible for supporting their children.

Are polygamous relationships practised anywhere in Canada? If so, how do they circumvent the bigamy laws? See the Open for Discussion box "Polygamy: Do Women Really Choose?" in Chapter 13, p. 270, for more information on this controversial topic.

ARRANGED VERSUS FREE-CHOICE MARRIAGE

Marriages continue to be arranged in parts of the world in order to enhance family resources, reputation, and alliances and because parents feel more qualified to choose their children's partners. The family of either bride or groom may make initial arrangements, but marriage brokers are occasionally used to help families find mates for their offspring.

Middle Eastern and South Asian immigrants living in Canada sometimes have their marriages arranged, which may involve returning to the home country to marry a partner selected by relatives living there or being introduced to a potential partner from the same cultural group in Canada. Young people often expect the opportunity to veto the family's choice, but in the home country they may be pressured to abide by the judgment of elders (Nanda and Warms 2007).

Family solidarity, financial security, and potential heirs are more important in arranged marriages than sexual attraction or love, but new partners are urged to respect each other, and it is hoped that love will develop after marriage. Often, arranged marriages are more stable than free-choice unions, because both families have a stake in marriage stability. Furthermore, divorce may be legally restricted, especially for women, and may involve mothers relinquishing custody of their children and struggling to support themselves outside marriage.

(© CP Images/AP Photo/Khalid Tanveer)

Polygyny is legal in Pakistan and permitted Azhar Haidri to marry both the woman he loves and the woman his family arranged for him to marry when he was a child.

In cultures with arranged marriages, **dowries** have been used to attract partners for daughters, to cement family alliances, and to help establish new households. Dowries may involve payments of money or gifts that accompany brides into marriage and become part of marriage agreements. If women have large dowries, they can find "better" husbands, which usually means wealthier, healthier, better educated, and from more respected families. Dowries could become the property of the groom's family or could be used to establish the new household. Dowries have also been used to provide brides with some measure of insurance in case of divorce or widowhood (Barker 2003).

In other societies practising arranged marriage (such as eastern Indonesia), the groom's family may be expected to pay the bride's parents a **bride price** for permission to marry their daughter. If his family is short of assets, the bride price could be paid through the groom's labour. Although dowries and bride prices are associated with arranged marriages, free-choice marriages have retained symbolic remnants of these practices. For example, trousseaus, wedding receptions, and the honeymoon are remnants of dowries, while the engagement ring and wedding band given to the bride by the groom are remnants of a bride price.

Explaining Family Patterns and Practices

All social studies are based on underlying assumptions about the desired focus of research and what factors are responsible for patterns and changes in social behaviour. These assumptions, often called theoretical frameworks, cannot be proven or disproven but guide our research and help to explain our observations (Klein and White 1996; Cheal 1991). In this section, several theoretical frameworks used to study families will be examined, including their premises, strengths, and weaknesses.

THE POLITICAL ECONOMY APPROACH

Political economists argue that people's relation to wealth, production, and power influences the way they live and view the world. Family formation, personal life, and well-being are all influenced by events in the broader society,

UNDER the WIRE

Internet Dating

In the past, many people met potential dating and marriage partners at community events, through personal introductions, or less often through newspaper advertising. Now, more people are using the Internet. Relationships formed through cyberspace have been called "hyperpersonal," because participants can be less concerned about what they look like and how to initiate a conversation with a potential partner. Instead, they can filter out undesirable candidates, carefully plan their email messages, decide how best to portray themselves, and send their message when they are ready. Once they have contacted a potential partner, they may be better able to articulate their needs and express their emotions online than in face-to-face situations.

One of the differences between initiating a relationship in a face-to-face situation and online may be the depth and breadth of self-disclosure within a short time. People can quickly reveal their life details before they agree to meet, although the accuracy of this information may later prove to be a stumbling block for continuing the relationship (McKenna, Green, and Gleason 2002). Because Internet encounters are initially "disembodied," there is more scope for fantasy and deception, making it possible to explore identities and sexualities (Baker 2010, 46).

Research on Internet dating has demonstrated that people can be strategic and deceptive in the way they present themselves in cyberspace, altering details about their gender and sexuality. They can also pretend to be younger or older, more attractive, wealthier, and more professionally successful. Because of the potential for deception, parents and teachers often worry about Internet safety, since it can be difficult to differentiate between sexual predators and people genuinely searching for lasting relationships. To minimize the risk, the initial face-to-face meeting, if there is one, should normally take place in a safe public place.

such as economic cycles, working conditions, and public policies. This perspective originated in the nineteenth-century work of Karl Marx (1818–83) and Friedrich Engels (1820–95) but has been modified over the years. Political economists continue to argue that social life always involves conflict, especially between the rich and powerful and the poor and marginalized. Conflicting interests remain the major force behind societal change.

With industrialization, men's workplaces were removed from the home, encouraging families to adapt to employers' needs and eroding patriarchal authority. Furthermore, many goods and services formerly produced at home were more cheaply manufactured in factories. This meant that families eventually became units of shared income and consumption rather than units of production and became viewed as private and separate from the public world of business and politics. However, political economists argue that the distinction between public and private is actually misleading, because unpaid household work contributes to corporate profits (Luxton and Corman 2001). The impact of industrialization and employment on family life became the focal point of this approach, as well as the belief that economic changes transform ways of viewing the world.

STRUCTURAL FUNCTIONALISM

Structural functionalists argue that behaviour is governed by social expectations and unspoken rules rather than by economic changes or personal choices. Individuals cannot behave any way they want but must abide by societal or cultural guidelines learned early in life or risk punishment. Within this approach, "the family" is viewed as the major social institution providing emotional support, love, sexual expression, and children. Parents help to maintain social order by socializing and disciplining their children, while families normally cooperate economically and share resources.

Talcott Parsons and Robert F. Bales (1955) theorized that the growth of industrialization and the move to urban areas encouraged parents and children to live separately from their relatives. They assumed that the nuclear family has two basic structures: a hierarchy of generations and a differentiation of adults into instru-

mental and expressive roles. Parsons and Bales assumed that the wife accepts the expressive role, maintaining social relations and caring for others, while the husband takes on the instrumental role of earning household money and dealing with the outside community (Thorne 1982).

Structural functionalists have been criticized for assuming that there is one acceptable family form rather than many variations and for downplaying personal choice. Structural functionalists have also implied that a gendered division of labour has been maintained because it was functional for society, when it may actually benefit heterosexual men more than others (Thorne 1982). **Systems theory** accepts many of the assumptions of structural functionalism but focuses on the interdependence of family members and the way that families often close ranks against outsiders, especially in troubled times. This approach has been particularly useful in family therapy (Braithwaite and Baxter 2005).

Structural functionalists tend to view social change as disruptive rather than normal, while individual opposition to social pressure has been viewed as deviant. Consequently, the structural functionalists have not dealt with conflict and change as well as the political economists, but neither focuses on the dynamic nature of interpersonal relations.

SOCIAL CONSTRUCTIONIST APPROACH

The social constructionist approach assumes that we construct our own social reality based on our personal experiences and choices (Berger and Luckmann 1966). Life does not just happen to us—we make things happen by exerting our will. This approach, also called symbolic interactionism, originated with the work of Americans Charles H. Cooley (1864–1929) and George Herbert Mead (1863–1931), who studied how parents help children develop a sense of self. Within this perspective, the way people define and interpret reality shapes their actions, and this process is aided by non-verbal and verbal cues. Part of socialization is developing the ability to look at the world through the eyes of others and anticipating a particular role before taking it, called anticipatory socialization.

(© ClassicStock/Corbis)

Idealized or romanticized images like this are common in the media, but they do not reflect the reality of family life.

See Chapter 3, "Symbolic Intera-ctionist Frame of Reference," p. 55, for more information on Mead's perspective.

Social constructionists often study family interaction and decision-making in laboratories, sometimes with the assistance of videos. Research is typically centred on communication processes during everyday experiences, but perceptions or "definitions of the situation" are thought to influence behaviour more than objective reality (Holstein and Miller 2006). This perspective could be seen as the precursor of post-structural theory, discussed later in this chapter.

FEMINIST THEORIES

Feminist theorists have focused on women's experiences, on written and visual representations of women, and on "gendered" patterns of behaviour. Some feminist researchers have used a **structural approach** to analyze the ways that gender inequality is perpetuated through social policies and employment practices (Baker 2006; O'Connor, Orloff, and Shaver 1999). Others have concentrated on interpersonal relations, examining non-verbal communication, heterosexual practices, and public discourse about women (Krane 2003; Wall 2009). Still other feminist theorists have studied women's experiences and ways of thinking and knowing (Butler 1992; Smith 1999).

Feminists typically argue that gender differences are socially constructed, are developed through socialization, and are maintained through institutional structures and practices. Most argue that gender differences in priorities and achievements grow out of psychological, physiological, and social experiences, which are shaped through different treatment by parents, teachers, and others (Brook 1999). These scholars continue to argue that whatever is considered "feminine" in our culture is granted lower status than "masculine" achievements or characteristics. Feminists also note that although most adult women are now employed, they continue to accept responsibility for most domestic work (Fox 2009; Ranson 2010). The unequal division of labour within families, including women's "second shift" of unpaid work, is seen as interfering with their employment equity (Hochschild 1989).

Critics of this perspective argue that it glosses over men's experiences, but feminists respond that men's experiences are already well represented in social science. The increasing acceptance of this perspective has been promoted by greater acknowledgement that both perception and reality are socially constructed.

TIME to REFLECT

What empirical or statistical evidence can you identify that shows that female experiences, activities, and accomplishments tend to be undervalued in Canadian society?

POST-STRUCTURAL APPROACHES

These perspectives argue that knowledge and understanding depend on one's social position, that vast differences in family experiences have always existed, and that personal lives continue to change. In Canada and other Western countries, sexuality is increasingly separated from marriage, and marriage is being reconstructed as a contract that can be ended. Child-rearing is no longer necessarily linked with marriage, and the gendered division of labour is continually renegotiated (Beck-Gernsheim 2002). This shows that more people are "writing their own biographies" or making their own decisions about personal life.

Post-structuralists also argue that images of gender and family are shaped by language and public discourse (Giddens 2006). By deconstructing or analyzing the origins and intended meanings of beliefs about gender and family, researchers can understand how these have been socially constructed throughout history. Welfare systems were premised on the male-breadwinner/female-caregiver family, but new lifestyle possibilities have encouraged both men and women to question this gender order as well as **normative heterosexuality**.

This perspective focuses on images of the body, media representations of gender and family, sexual diversity, families of choice, and the "performance" of gender (Smart 2007). However, critics argue that too much emphasis is placed on personal choice and minority living situations rather than on the ways that most people live or the material constraints on their life choices (Baker 2010).

Recent Issues in Canadian Families

In this section, we consider several controversial issues, beginning with the gendered division of labour at home.

SHARING HOUSEHOLD WORK

Over the past 20 years, gendered patterns of employment have changed dramatically. In 1976, 47 per cent of women aged 20 to 64 years who were either married or cohabiting participated in the labour force, but this proportion had increased to 76 per cent by 2009 (Lu and Morissette 2010). However, men are still more likely to work full-time and overtime after parenthood. In particular, mothers with preschool children have lower labour force participation rates than fathers, as Table 9.2 indicates.

Researchers find that most husbands work full-time after parenthood and perform occasional chores around or outside the house. Most wives are employed for fewer hours per week, but they usually take responsibility for routine indoor chores and child care, even when they are employed full-time. Wives are also expected to be "kin keepers" (Rosenthal 1985), which involves maintaining contact

TABLE 9.2 ▼	Canadian Labour Force Participation Rates (%) for Mothers and Fathers with Children under 15 Years of Age, 2006		
Family Type		Mother	Father
Single (never-married) parent with children under 6		61	78
Single (never-married) parent with youngest child age 6–14		80	85
Married parent with children under 6		75	94
Married parent with youngest child age 6–14		82	93
Divorced parents with child under 6		76	90
Divorced parents with youngest child age 6–14		86	90

SOURCE: Vanier Institute of the Family website (www.vifamily.ca), derived from Statistics Canada, 2006 Census.

with relatives and organizing family events. In addition, wives and mothers usually retain responsibility for "emotional work," such as helping children to build their confidence and listening sympathetically to the concerns of family members (Ranson 2009).

Despite this gendered division of labour, wives employed full-time tend to perform less housework than those who work part-time or who are outside the workforce, and employed women did less housework in 2005 than in 1986 (Lindsay 2008b). Yet women retain most of the responsibility for indoor housework and child-rearing tasks, especially those who are older and have less education, which leaves many employed women exhausted (Ranson 2009). Wives employed full-time may lower their housework standards, encourage others to share the work, or hire help. More equitable workloads are apparent among younger, well-educated couples with few or no children. However, Baker (2010, 123) shows that even among university professors with doctorates and full-time jobs, wives tend to do a disproportionate amount of housework. Yet wives' bargaining power may increase slightly when they earn an income comparable to that of their husbands (Statistics Canada 2006b).

Why do employed wives accept so much responsibility for household work? These relations are influenced by gender expectations, opportunities, and experiences, but gender also intersects with culture and social class to influence such relations. Furthermore, partners' working hours and earnings seem less important than marital power relations in determining the allocation of household tasks (Davies and Carrier 1999). Dempsey (1999) concluded

that most Australian husbands use a variety of tactics to avoid doing housework, such as waiting to be asked by their wives, saying they do not know how to do the task, arguing that it does not really need doing yet, and delaying completion.

Considerable research suggests that even when men have time available, most do not choose to spend it on domestic work. Husbands will lend a hand if their wives are pressed for time, but housework and child care are typically viewed as low-status women's work. Cohabiting couples seem to have a less gendered division of labour than married couples (Wu 2000; Baxter, Hewitt, and Haynes 2008), but relative power differences in heterosexual relationships continue to influence patterns of domestic work.

An uneven and gendered division of labour has many implications. More mothers than fathers develop close ties with their children through years of physical and emotional care. In addition, some homemakers are able to pursue hobbies and friendships during the day. At the same time, accepting most of the responsibility for household work reduces the likelihood of working full-time and being promoted to higher-paying positions. Furthermore, women's confidence can be reduced if they are financially dependent, which could translate into reduced decision-making power within marriage and less income in the event of divorce or widowhood. When women accept most of the responsibility for domestic work, they also reinforce traditional role models for their children (Ranson 2009). However, many women feel they have little control over the household division of labour.

Women continue to accept responsibility for the majority of household tasks, but new research shows that there has been a shift, however small, toward a more equitable division of labour. See "Gender and Sexuality in Family" in Chapter 7, p. 143, for more on this topic.

TIME to REFLECT

Do husbands and fathers compensate for their lack of indoor housework through their outdoor work and financial contribution to the household?

MEDICALLY ASSISTED CONCEPTION

Recently, family relationships have been complicated by cohabitation, same-sex partnerships, divorce, and remarriage, but reproductive and genetic technologies may be in the process of fundamentally reshaping families (Eichler 1996). This includes separating biological and social parenthood, changing generational lines, and enabling sex selection. A wide range of procedures have now become routine, such as donor insemination and in vitro fertilization. Freezing sperm, eggs, and embryos makes conception possible after the donors' death, post-menopausal women can bear children, and potential parents can contract with surrogates to bear children for them (Baker 2005). We can now buy eggs, sperm, embryos, and reproductive services—all of which are produced and sold for profit—but these technologies could also raise the potential for eugenic thinking (Eichler 1996). However, little research has been done on the impact of these technologies on family life.

Research suggests that fertility continues to influence social acceptance and gender identity and that conception problems often contribute to feelings of guilt, anger, and depression and to marital disputes (Doyal 1995). Low fertility may be caused by many factors, including exposure to sexually transmitted diseases, long-term use of some contraceptives, environmental pollutants, substance overuse, and prolonged stress (Bryant 1990). The probability of conception also declines as women age. With

the growing availability of fertility clinics, more couples are encouraged to seek assistance with conception problems.

Infertility is usually defined as the inability to conceive a viable pregnancy after one year of unprotected sexual intercourse, but this definition encourages some couples to seek help prematurely. Access to publicly funded treatment varies by jurisdiction but is often limited to young, heterosexual, and childless couples in stable relationships with a diagnosed medical reason for low fertility, although private clinics charging fees may be less selective. Most treatments last for several months and involve drugs that produce side effects such as depression, mood swings, weight gain, and multiple births. Some treatments continue for years (Baker 2005).

Fertility treatments can be expensive, although those who end up with a healthy baby may find these costs acceptable. A few decades ago, the success rates were not as high as many couples anticipated, and the chances of complications were greater than for natural conception. For example, Australian research showed that adverse infant outcomes, such as pre-term delivery, low birth weight, stillbirth, and neonatal death, were more prevalent among assisted-conception births than among all births (Ford et al. 2003). In recent years, however, success rates appear to have improved. Canadian figures from 2009 indicate that the chances of a woman having a single healthy baby through assisted human reproduction still vary by age and were 21 per cent per cycle for women under 35 years old but only 7 per cent for those 40 years old and over (Canadian Fertility and Andrology Society 2011).

Eichler (1996) argues that reproductive technologies and surrogacy arrangements tend to blur the role designations of mother, father, and child. Although sociologists have always been interested in the impact of absent fathers on family life, they are now referring to sperm donors as the new absent fathers (Jamieson 1998, 50). Researchers are also interested in the increasing number of lesbian couples using self-insemination to create families without men. Although assisted conception expands opportunities for parenthood, some technologies are experimental and intrusive, medicalizing the natural act of childbearing. They offer

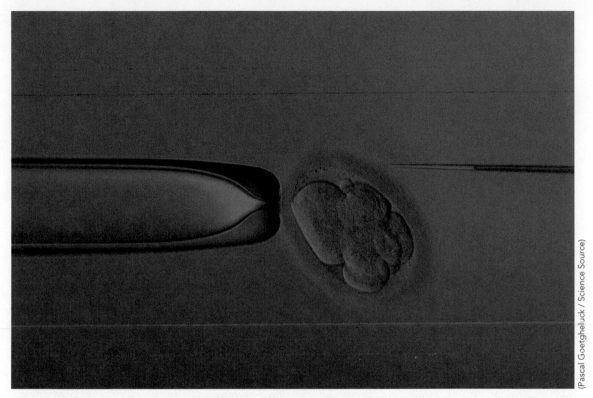

(Pascal Goetgheluck / Science Source)

Before being implanted in the uterus, a cell from the IVF-produced embryo is screened for genetic disorders such as Down syndrome. Although considered a valuable procedure, pre-implantation genetic diagnosis could be used to select a preferred sex and thus raises serious ethical concerns.

costly services that lower-income people often cannot afford and could reinforce the pressure on all women to reproduce. Patriarchal societies could use sex selection to reinforce the cultural preference for males, and working-class women could be exploited through surrogacy arrangements. Sociologists seem to be most supportive of reproductive technologies when they discuss self-insemination within lesbian relationships (Nelson 2001).

AFFORDABLE AND REGULATED CHILD CARE

The dramatic increase in maternal employment has led to higher demands for public child care, although quality assurance remains a problem and costs are still unaffordable for many parents. Since the 1960s, Canadian governments have subsidized child-care spaces for low-income and one-parent households. However, there have never been enough spaces for eligible families (Beach et al. 2008).

Canadian governments offer two forms of child-care support: a federal income tax deduction of up to $7000 per preschool child for employed parents using non-family care (with no family maximum), which is most useful for middle-income parents paying higher taxes. In addition, the provincial governments subsidize spaces for low-income families and lone parents (Baker 2006). Unlike other provinces, Quebec heavily subsidizes care for parents who need it, regardless of their income or work status, at a cost to parents of only $7 per day (Albanese 2006). Not surprisingly, the employment rate of mothers with preschool children is much higher in Quebec than in the rest of the country (Statistics Canada 2006c).

Across Canada, many not-for-profit centres have long waiting lists, but some do not accept children under two. Even if space is available, parents want to ensure that the centre employs adequate staff to keep the infants clean, fed, stimulated, and infection-free. Finding a qualified sitter to come to the child's home or who will welcome an extra child in her home is also difficult, although licensed family homes are available in most jurisdictions (Beach et al. 2008). Sitter care is unregulated by government yet remains the most prevalent type of child care for employed parents. Grandparents (usually grandmothers) sometimes provide care while the parents are working, which can save money, provide culturally sensitive care, and create a solid bond between generations. Yet it might also lead to intergenerational disagreements about child-rearing practices. Child-care concerns have encouraged some mothers to remain at home with their own children, although few can now afford this option.

Centre-based care generally operates during office hours, but some parents need child care in the evening and on weekends. Parents whose children have special needs also experience problems, because with more mothers in the workforce, caregivers may need to be hired.

The quality of child care remains a concern, as provided both in licensed centres and by caregivers in private homes. In some jurisdictions (such as Alberta), child-care employees and sitters are not required to have special training. These jobs pay the minimum wage or less and therefore do not readily attract and retain trained workers. A number of advocacy groups have formed around these concerns, asking governments to tighten regulations, improve training and fringe benefits, and require higher wages for child-care workers. However, this requires more public funding, which calls for making child care a regular election issue in Canada.

DIVORCE AND REPARTNERING: THE IMPACT ON CHILDREN

Since divorce rates began to increase in the 1970s, considerable attention has been devoted to the outcomes for children. Canadian researchers have estimated that about 38 per cent of marriages will end in divorce before their thirtieth anniversary, but only half of these involve children (Vanier Institute of the Family 2004, 33). Children from one-parent families most often live with their mothers and tend to experience higher risks of negative outcomes than children from two-parent families. These outcomes include lower educational attainment, more behavioural problems, leaving home earlier, premarital pregnancy for girls, and higher divorce rates when they marry.

Despite negative media attention given to one-parent families, most children from these families do not experience problems but only higher risks. Furthermore, when studies control for the usual declines in household income after parental separation, the incidence of problems falls, although it does not disappear (Kiernan 1997; Lipman, Offord, and Dooley 1996, 88). Does the high risk of negative outcomes result from parental conflict, the absent father, or some other factor, such as poverty? In Canada and even more in the United States, many children in one-parent families live in poverty, especially if their mother is not employed, as the Global Issues box on the next page indicates. However, one-parent families more often experience economic disadvantage both before and after separation, since lower-income households generally tend to have higher rates of bereavement, separation, and divorce (Pryor and Rodgers 2001). When children are raised in poverty, they are more likely to suffer disadvantages that continue into adulthood.

Distinguishing between the impact of poverty and of parental separation is difficult for researchers. Lower incomes after parental separation seems to be a mediating factor for some negative outcomes but not others. It accounts for a decline in educational attainment but not for rates of delinquency, psychosomatic illnesses, cigarette smoking, or heavy drinking in adulthood (Hope, Power, and Rodgers 1998). However, even children raised in low-income households with two parents are more likely than other children to experience negative behavioural outcomes. These outcomes include delayed school readiness, lower educational attainment, a greater number of serious childhood illnesses, higher childhood accident rates, premature death, high rates of depression, high rates of smoking and alcohol abuse as young adults, and more trouble with school authorities and the law, to name only a few (NLSCY 1996; Canadian Institute of Child Health 2002). Consequently, social researchers must consider household income as an important variable in all discussions of children's outcomes after separation and divorce.

Living in poverty is influenced by living arrangements and parental work status but also by country of residence. Children in Canada and the United States have much higher poverty rates than those in the United Kingdom, Finland, and Sweden, especially when they

GLOBAL ISSUES

Poverty Rates and Children

Poverty Rates of Households with Children in Various Countries, by Working Status of Parents						
Country	1 parent, no worker	1 parent, 1 worker	2 parents, no workers	2 parents, 1 worker	2 parents, 2 workers	Poverty rate, all children
United States	92	36	82	27	6	18
Canada	89	32	81	22	4	13
Australia	68	6	51	8	1	10
New Zealand	48	30	47	21	3	13
United Kingdom	39	7	36	9	1	9
Netherlands	62	27	65	12	2	9
Finland	46	6	23	9	1	4
Sweden	18	6	36	14	1	4
OECD Average	54	21	48	16	4	11

SOURCE: Organisation for Economic Co-operation and Development (OECD), *Society at a Glance 2009: OECD Social Indicators* (Paris: OECD, 2009). Based on Table EQ3.2, p. 93.

reside with one parent outside the workforce (see Global Issues box above). However, if parents can find and keep well-paid jobs and governments provide generous benefits and services, children's poverty rates can be reduced.

Many studies indicate that children who reside with their mothers after divorce tend to experience diminished contact with their fathers and to suffer distress from this loss (Smyth 2004; Qu and Weston 2008). As children grow older, the time spent with the non-resident parent decreases, and about a third lose contact (Amato 2004). However, father–child contact is not the deciding factor in children's adjustment after parental separation, since frequent contact could be detrimental if there is a high degree of conflict surrounding it. If conflict is absent or contained, children benefit from frequent contact with both parents (Amato 2004). In general, a close relationship with both parents is associated with a positive adjustment in children after divorce (Pryor and Rodgers 2001). Whether or not the father continues to pay child support also influences the children's adjustment and household income, and non-resident fathers who regularly see their children are more likely to pay child support.

Parental separation clearly adds stress to children's lives through changes in relationships, living arrangements, and resources, but few studies conclude that problems are severe or prolonged (Baker 2010). Instead, most research finds that the first two years after separation require adjustments by both parents and children. However, adult children of divorced parents are more likely than those from intact marriages to believe in the fragility of marriage, to have poor relationships with their parents, and to end their own marriages with divorce (Cartwright and McDowell 2008; Cunningham and Thornton 2006; Hughes 2005). This may result from poor role models, a history of family conflict, or the acceptance of divorce as a solution to an unhappy marriage.

Never-married mothers who become pregnant before completing their education are particularly vulnerable to low income and children's disciplinary problems. These mothers often repartner within a few years of the child's birth, but the disadvantages of bearing a child at a young age may linger (Edin and Kefalas 2005). Their children are most likely to spend their childhood in one or more stepfamilies, which are often conflictual. This helps to explain the higher rates of behavioural problems among children from never-married mothers (Marcil-Gratton 1998).

Research suggests that stepfamilies require considerable negotiation and that children living in these households are at the same risk of behavioural problems and distress as those growing up in one-parent households. Neither a higher income nor two adults in the home ensures good outcomes for these children (Pryor and Rodgers 2001). One explanation is that parental conflict and separation have a lasting effect on children. Another is that stepparents do not relate to their stepchildren with the same warmth and concern, because they do not see them as their own children and have not lived with them during formative years.

Although researchers usually study separation and divorce as negative life events, parents often experience relief after the initial adjustment, which is reflected in their general outlook and interactions with their children. Consequently, most researchers agree that children living in stable one-parent households are better off than children living in conflict-ridden two-parent households (Cavanagh 2008). Furthermore, children of employed lone mothers tend to accept more egalitarian gender roles, because they see their mothers managing tasks previously defined as masculine. This suggests that separation and divorce could have positive as well as negative outcomes for parents and children.

WIFE ABUSE

Sociologists have studied "family violence" since the 1980s, but the very term is misleading, because men are the perpetrators in the vast majority of cases coming to the attention of authorities (Dobash et al. 1992). The Canadian Urban Victimization Study found that in cases of "spousal violence," physical abuse is not an isolated event. Some women are assaulted on numerous occasions by male partners and have sought help many times from friends, neighbours, social workers, and the police. Furthermore, separated women are more likely to be assaulted than married women (DeKeseredy 2009). Women are also more vulnerable if they view their partner as the household head, if they are or were financially dependent on him, or if they live in a housing development with other single mothers. Violence becomes normalized when it is prevalent within the community or seen as a form of entertainment in the larger society.

Strauss and Gelles (1990) found that marital violence decreased in the United States throughout the 1980s even though reporting increased. They argued that reports to police were influenced by the women's movement, by police campaigns to prosecute perpetrators, and by increasing options for women leaving violent relationships. Yet they also made the controversial claim that women are as likely as men to abuse their partners, although they acknowledged that this behaviour is less reported, less harmful, and often motivated by self-defence. DeKeseredy (2009) criticized the "conflict tactics" scale they used in these studies, which counts the incidences of violence without examining the social context.

The abuse of women may reflect men's rising concern that they are losing authority

SOCIOLOGY in ACTION

The Emotional Scars of Family Violence

"I was raped by my uncle when I was 12 and my husband has beat me for years. For my whole life, when I have gone to the doctor, to my priest, or to a friend to have my wounds patched up, or for a shoulder to cry one, they dwell on my bruises . . . I don't look anything like I did 15 years ago, but it's not my body that I really wish could get fixed. The abuse in my life has taken away my trust in people and in life. It's taken away the laughter in my life . . . It's taken away my faith in God, my faith in goodness winning out in the end, and maybe worse of all, it's taken away my trust in myself. I don't trust myself to be able to take care of the kids, to take care of myself, to do anything to make a difference in my own life or anyone else's. That's the hurt I would like to fix. I can live with my physical scars. It's these emotional scars that drive me near suicide sometimes."

SOURCE: DeKeseredy and Macleod 1997, 5.

in their households, especially those who are experiencing marital separation or unemployment. This kind of violence is also aggravated by alcohol and substance abuse but represents more than an interpersonal problem. The fact that most victims of reported violence are women and that separated women are often the targets indicates important social patterns relating to gender and power.

In the past, the police failed to respond seriously to calls about "domestic violence," because they thought women did not want charges laid or would later withdraw them (DeKeseredy 2009). Policies have now been implemented in most jurisdictions for police to charge abusive men. Yet many women remain with abusive partners because they lack affordable housing, income to support their children, and knowledge about where to turn. Abuse often continues because some women feel that they deserve it, especially those abused as children. In addition, many women fear reprisal from former partners who threaten to kill them if they tell anyone. The number of women killed by their male partners indicates that fear of reprisal is often justified.

Women's groups, social agencies, police, and researchers have developed new ways of dealing with domestic violence against women. Many programs are crisis-oriented, helping women to develop a protection plan that could involve laying charges against the perpetrator, finding transitional housing, engaging a lawyer, gaining a protection order, or acquiring welfare to cover living costs. Through counselling or group therapy, abused women and their abusers can be helped to restructure their thinking about violence and to view it as always unacceptable.

The male abuser is now more often charged with an offence. He is also given opportunities for counselling, including accepting personal responsibility rather than blaming others, learning to manage his anger, developing better communication skills, and learning non-violent behaviour from positive male role models. Action against intimate violence has also included sensitization workshops for professionals to increase their knowledge of program options and the implications of violence. In addition, more support services have been provided for high-risk families.

Governments have voiced concern about violence against women and children, but shortage of funding is a major impediment for new programs. Transition houses are usually funded by donations, staffed by volunteers, and operated with short-term resources. Follow-up counselling also costs money. Despite the

(© Joe Fox / Alamy)

In 2009, less than 22 per cent of spousal violence victims reported the incident to police. (Canadian Centre for Justice Statistics, Statistics Canada, 2011, *Family Violence in Canada: A Statistical Profile,* http://publications.gc.ca/collections/collection_2011/statcan/85-224-X/85-224-x2010000-eng.pdf)

serious nature of this kind of violence, new program funding for the rising number of reported victims and their abusers is often difficult to find (Sev'er 2002).

TIME to REFLECT

What sources of support are available for someone in an abusive relationship? Which of these might people turn to first, and which might be seen as a last resort? Why?

Spousal victimization and perpetration have been associated with childhood exposure to violence and later to dating violence (Gover, Kaukinen, and Fox 2008). Three broad explanations arise from these findings. The intergenerational theory suggests that solving conflicts through physical or verbal violence is learned from early experiences of witnessing parental conflict or being a victim of child abuse or neglect. The solution within this perspective focuses on improving anger management, self-esteem, couple communication, and parenting skills. A second theory sees marital violence as a misguided use of conflict resolution by husbands who feel their authority is threatened. The solution within this systems framework is to offer therapy sessions so that couples can improve their communication skills, manage anger, and learn to become more assertive about feelings without resorting to violence.

In contrast, feminist theories reinforce the fact that marital violence is usually by men against women. This reflects women's lack of interpersonal power, the patriarchal nature of many families, and the social acceptability of violence (Sev'er 2002). The three theories, however, are not incompatible. Not everyone who has witnessed abuse or felt threatened becomes abusive. Furthermore, everyone lives in a society that condones certain kinds of violence, yet only a small minority abuse others. Individually, none of the theories can explain the perpetuation of this form of violence.

Domestic violence clearly cuts across national, cultural, class, and age boundaries and is not confined to cohabitation or marriage. Changing public attitudes require more reporting of such activity, but authorities need to take reports seriously and provide the necessary protection and services.

Conclusion

Intimate relationships remain central to most people, even though families and personal life have changed substantially over recent decades. Cohabitation, separation, and divorce are now more prevalent than they were a generation ago, while marriage and families rates are declining. Cultural variations in personal and family life are also pronounced, with new immigrant people are modifying response.

Social theoretical frameworks personal life and family different aspects and networks presented in theorists differ in their. The chapter also discussed several controversial issues in family life. The first was the sharing of domestic work: despite dramatic increases in women's paid work, female partners still take responsibility for the major portion of housework and child care. The second issue related to the apparent rise in infertility and to concerns about the inherent contradictions in and high costs of medically assisted conception. The third issue related to the cost and quality of child care for employed parents, which makes it difficult, especially for mothers, to combine earning and caring. The fourth involved the impact of separation and repartnering on children, with the suggestion that separation is not always a negative solution and that remarriage is not always the best outcome for children. And the fifth issue related to wife abuse and why it continues despite public efforts to reduce its prevalence.

This chapter has shown that more people now cohabit, separate, repartner, and live with more than one partner over their lifetime. Nevertheless, not all of our living arrangements represent our own choices. Most Canadians still hope to develop loving and stable intimate relationships and to watch their children grow into adults. However, few people anticipate the ways that work requirements, money problems, their partner's actions, and prevalent ideas about marriage will shape their personal lives.

questions for critical thought

1. Why are more young people cohabiting before marriage? What does this indicate about the authority of the church and state?

2. How would you explain the rise in maternal employment with reference to (a) post-structural feminist perspectives, (b) structural functionalism, and (c) political economy theory?

3. Should parents stay together for the sake of the children, or is parental conflict more detrimental to children?

4. Should same-sex couples and women over 40 be permitted to use the services of fertility clinics at the public's expense? Give reasons for your viewpoint.

5. Should parents be required to pay the entire cost of child-care services when they are employed?

recommended readings

Patrizia Albanese. 2009. *Children in Canada Today*. Toronto: Oxford University Press.
This book involves an analysis of the sociology of childhood and youth culture, discussing agents of socialization and Canadian social policies to improve children's lives.

Maureen Baker. 2010. *Choices and Constraints in Family Life*. 2nd edn. Toronto: Oxford University Press.
This book argues that our choices about partners and living arrangements are shaped by economic circumstances, cultural expectations, popular culture, and events in the larger society, including labour market changes and political discourse.

David Cheal, ed. 2010. *Canadian Families Today: New Perspectives*. 2nd edn. Toronto: Oxford University Press.
This edited book contains chapters by 18 experts on various aspects of Canadian families.

Andrea Doucet. 2006. *Do Men Mother? Fathering, Care and Domestic Responsibility*. Toronto: University of Toronto Press.
This book discusses different parenting styles among men and women, based on qualitative interviews with primary-caregiver fathers and some of their partners.

Gillian Ranson. 2009. "Paid and unpaid work: How do families divide their labour?" In Maureen Baker, ed., *Families: Changing Trends in Canada*, 6th edn, 108–29. Toronto: McGraw-Hill Ryerson.
This chapter provides an overview of theories and research on the division of labour in Canadian families.

recommended websites

Child Care Canada: Childcare Resource and Research Unit
www.childcarecanada.org
The Childcare Resource and Research Unit website includes Canadian and cross-national research and other material on child-care issues.

National Association for the Education of Young Children (NAEYC)
www.naeyc.org
This US-based association publishes the journal *Young Children*, which includes reviews of research and practical information.

Statistics Canada
www.statcan.ca
Statistics Canada provides a wide range of census documents and statistics relating to families and households.

Vanier Institute of the Family
www.vifamily.ca
The Vanier Institute of the Family in Ottawa provides educational material, news items, and research on Canadian families.

chapter 10

Education

Terry Wotherspoon

In this chapter, you will:

▶ Come to understand how and why formal education has become a central social institution in Canada and in other nations.

▶ Identify key aspects of the relationship between major social transformations and education systems.

▶ Gain a critical understanding of various forms of lifelong learning beyond formal education.

▶ Learn about the major theoretical perspectives and theories that sociologists employ to explain educational institutions, practices, and outcomes.

▶ Explore the relationship between education and social inequality.

▶ Critically evaluate contemporary debates and controversies over major educational issues.

Introduction

In the context of what is often called the *knowledge* or *learning society*, **education** has been thrust into a central role as individuals, organizations, and nations struggle to keep pace with demands for new knowledge and credentials regarded as essential for jobs, career advancement, and economic and social development. We expect educational institutions to educate and prepare learners by instilling a wide range of technical, social, and personal competencies so that they can cope with changing, often uncertain futures. We also look to schools to respond to the needs of diverse students and communities.

Sociologists are interested in several issues associated with educational processes and outcomes and in the environments within which education operates. This chapter examines several key questions that sociology addresses in its concern to understand education:

- Why is formal education so important in contemporary societies, and how did it get to be that way?

- What are the main dimensions of education and education systems in Canada and in other nations?

- How do sociologists explain the growth of education systems and the outcomes associated with education for different groups?

- What are the main educational experiences and outcomes for different social groups?

- What are the main challenges facing education systems in Canada and other nations?

The Changing Face of Education

Although education is a fundamental characteristic of all human societies, it is generally understood in contemporary contexts as formal learning that takes place in institutions such as schools, colleges, universities, and other sites that provide specific courses, learning activities, or credentials in an organized way. Informal learning also occurs as people undertake specific activities to learn about distinct phenomena or processes. Both formal and informal education are part of the broader process that sociologists typically call socialization, which refers to all direct and indirect learning related to humans' ability to understand and negotiate the rules and expectations of the social world.

For a broader discussion on how school is a socializing agent, see "Schools," Chapter 3, p. 61.

Nearly all Canadians engage in formal education for extended periods of time. Just over a century ago, communities frequently lacked schools or qualified teachers, many children did not go to school, and those who did attend typically left by their early teen years (Guppy and Davies 1998). Today's students and teachers typically exhibit a far greater array of personal, stylistic, and cultural variation than was apparent a century ago, and they have access to extensive learning opportunities and resources. Despite these changes, the casual visitor to classrooms in either time period is not likely to mistake schools for other settings. Education is a unique social institution, but it also reveals characteristics that are integral to the society in which it operates.

TIME to REFLECT

What is the difference between education and socialization? How has the introduction of formal schooling influenced the relationship between these two phenomena?

DIMENSIONS OF EDUCATIONAL GROWTH

Table 10.1 shows that half of the population now hold post-secondary credentials, in stark contrast to the situation in the mid-twentieth century when more than half had less than a Grade 9 education. Growing emphasis on the importance of formal education and credentials has been matched by three interrelated factors: the overall expansion of educational opportunities and requirements, increasing levels of educational attainment among people born in Canada, and recent emphasis on the selection of highly educated immigrants.

In spite of the many and varied changes made to education practices over the past century, the classroom remains a distinctive space that is easily recognized.

In the late nineteenth and early twentieth centuries, relatively few occupations required educational credentials. Early advocates of public **schooling** undertook a mission to convince the public, and especially members of influential groups, of the merits of the education system (for examples, see Lawr and Gidney 1973). They promoted schooling as an efficient enterprise that would serve the public or general interest, unlike narrow, more selective sites such as families, churches, and businesses.

By the mid-twentieth century, more and larger schools were required to accommodate growing educational demands. As credentials became more important for many jobs, people were more likely to extend their schooling into and beyond the high school years. The **baby boom** that occurred after World War II resulted in unprecedented sizes of cohorts of children who were entering and moving through the school system. The figures in Table 10.2 demonstrate that while total enrolment in Canadian

TABLE 10.1 ▼	Educational Attainment in Canada by Percentage of Population Aged 15 and Over, Selected Years, 1951–2011				
	Less than Grade 9	Grades 9–13	Some Post-secondary	Post-secondary Certificate or Diploma	University Degree
1951	51.9	46.1	–	–	1.9
1961	44.1	53.0	–	–	2.9
1971	32.3	45.9	11.2	5.8	4.8
1981	20.1	44.3	16.1	11.5	8.0
1986	17.7	42.5	19.3	12.3	9.6
1991	14.4	43.8	8.8	21.9	11.4
1996	12.3	39.4	8.9	25.9	13.3
2001	9.7	36.9	9.2	28.3	16.0
2006	8.1	35.0	8.1	29.9	18.9
2011	6.3	33.0	8.0	31.2	21.5

Note: Figures are rounded.
SOURCE: Compiled from Statistics Canada, Census data (1951–86), and CANSIM labour force survey, annual averages (1991–2011).

TABLE 10.2 ▼ Full-Time Enrolment in Canada, by Level of Study, Selected Years, 1870–2010 (000s)

	Pre-elementary	Elementary and Secondary	Non-university Post-secondary	University Undergraduate	University Graduate
1870	–	768	–	2	–
1880	–	852	–	3	–
1890	–	943	–	5	<1
1900	–	1055	–	7	<1
1910	–	1318	–	13	<1
1920	–	1834	–	23	<1
1930	–	2099	–	32	1
1940	–	2075	–	35	2
1950	–	2391	–	64	5
1960	146	3997	49	107	7
1970	402	5661	166	276	33
1980	398	4709	261	338	45
1990	468	4669	325	468	64
2000	522	5035	425	505	81
2010*		4965	521	712	139

* Pre-elementary figure for 2010 is included in elementary and secondary total.
SOURCES: Compiled from various editions of Dominion Bureau of Statistics/Statistics Canada, Census data, "Education at a Glance," *Education Quarterly Review*, CANSIM data Tables 477-0013 and 477-0015; and Brockington (2010:21).

public elementary and secondary schools in 1950 was slightly more than twice what it had been in 1900, enrolment more than doubled again over the next two decades (Manzer 1994, 131; CMEC 2008, 8).

Formal education is also expanding throughout the life course, from early childhood and kindergarten programs to post-secondary levels and beyond. The number of graduate students alone is now nearly triple total university enrolments in the early 1950s. There has also been significant growth in other post-secondary options since the introduction and expansion of the community college system in the 1960s and 1970s, offering students several pathways toward certification in specialized trades or vocations or university degrees.

TIME to REFLECT

To what extent has educational enrolment increased in Canada over the past century? What factors account for this growth?

EDUCATION IN THE LEARNING SOCIETY

The growing popularity of terms such as *information society*, *learning society*, and **life-long learning** signifies the central place that education holds within the context of what is commonly designated as the **new economy** or *knowledge-based economy*. The new economy has gained prominence as rapidly changing information technologies and scientific advancements have a growing impact on all major spheres of social life, including work, home, and public life (Wolfe and Gertler 2001). In this climate, what counts is not so much the knowledge that we acquire as our capacities to learn, innovate, and apply knowledge to emergent situations. People are expected not simply to learn more but to develop different ways of learning and transferring knowledge.

As Table 10.2 indicates, more than 6.5 million Canadians (about one-fifth of the entire population) are engaged in full-time schooling, and well over 300,000 more are involved in part-time studies. More than half of Canadians are involved in various forms of adult educa-

OPEN for DISCUSSION

Debating Alternatives to Public Schools

Although strong public support exists for public schooling in Canada, many individuals and groups have advocated in favour of alternative forms of schooling within public school systems or through various types of privately operated schools.

Some critics view education as a marketplace in which parents should "shop" for the kinds of education best suited to their children's needs. Private schools, voucher programs, home schooling, and other measures are advanced as mechanisms for schools to become more responsive and accountable to the varied interests of educational consumers (Maguire 2006).

Other reforms are taking place within public education systems. Most provinces now offer a variety of specialized school alternatives as well as programs to link schools with other public and community agencies. Schools under First Nations control have introduced many innovations or modifications to public models of education, while other groups are seeking more specialized schools in response to particular concerns or interests.

Sociologist George Sefa Dei suggests that black-focused schools can address high dropout and failure rates and related social problems such as violence, unemployment, and drug abuse among inner-city black youth. Observing that present educational practices contribute to youth alienation through disconnection from students' real concerns, Dei (2006, 28) sees these African-centred schools as guided by "a new vision" that stresses

the development of a culture of youth affirmation that fosters a sense of pride by helping to build strong personal, social and cultural identities. For example, such a culture can be achieved when teachers introduce alternative forms of school discipline to replace suspensions, expulsions or the summoning of law enforcement.

Still other researchers indicate that increasing diversity in Canada's public school populations can be beneficial for all students, creating opportunities for critical reflection and broadened understanding of what it means to live and function in a truly global society.

tion, such as in-person, correspondence, or private courses; workshops; apprenticeships; or arts, crafts, and recreation programs. Levels of *informal learning* are even higher as people seek knowledge outside formal schooling, such as learning a new language or computer skills and gaining competencies in conjunction with family, work, or voluntary roles. Nearly all Canadians are involved in learning activities, although the more formal education they have, the more engaged they are likely to be in adult education and informal learning (Livingstone 2004, 36–7; Desjardins et al. 2005, 89).

Canadians are not unique in their growing pursuit of education and training. Emphasis on credentials and lifelong learning is a phenomenon associated with globalization and competitiveness across national settings. Throughout the twentieth century, the degree to which a population was educated came to be recognized as a significant indicator of modernization and development status. The more education one has, the higher the chances of having a job, a better income, good health sta-

tus, and many other factors positively associated with a high standard of living. Conversely, rates of poverty, unemployment, crime, serious illness and injury, and other less desirable characteristics rise when formal education is limited. The Canadian Council on Learning (2010, 10) stresses that "learning and training are more critical now than ever as shifting workforce demographics, rapid advancements in technology and increased global competitive pressures are transforming our society." However, it cautions that "we cannot afford to remain complacent. Lack of progress in lifelong learning threatens to undermine the development of our greatest asset—the potential of our people" (2010, 8).

Despite the expansion of educational opportunities, substantial disparities in educational participation remain across the globe. Figure 10.1 illustrates that those living in the Americas, Europe, and parts of Asia and the Pacific region can expect on average to complete more than 12 years of formal schooling. In other parts of the world, average levels of schooling, particularly

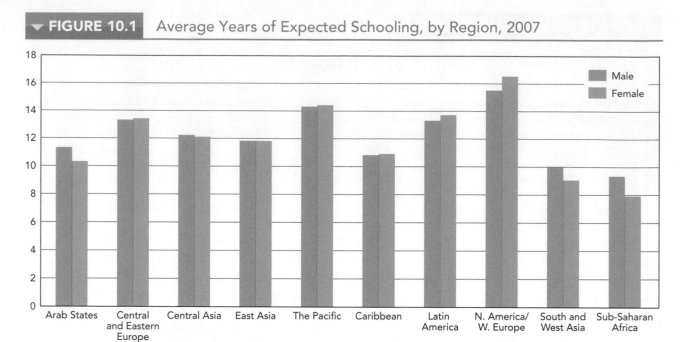

▼ FIGURE 10.1   Average Years of Expected Schooling, by Region, 2007

SOURCE: Based on data in UNESCO, (2010:329)

among female populations, are below high school completion. Educational attainment levels by girls and women in North America and Europe are more than twice those in sub-Saharan Africa.

Alternative Accounts of Educational Growth and Development

There is no uniform way of understanding education. Various educational **ideologies** pose contrasting views about what kinds of education a society should have, who should control and pay for education, and what should be taught in schools. Sociological theories of education, by contrast, are more concerned with describing and explaining education systems, educational processes, and educational change. Two early influential theoretical perspectives (the structural functionalist approach and the symbolic interactionist–interpretive theories)

are contrasted below, followed by examination of two critical challenges (conflict and feminist theories) and more recent integrative orientations to the analysis of education.

STRUCTURAL FUNCTIONALISM

Structural functionalism is concerned primarily with understanding how different parts of the entire social system are interconnected in order to keep the system going. Structural functionalism examines education primarily in terms of its contributions to social order and stability. As society becomes more complex and specialized, educational institutions take on many of the functions previously managed by families, communities, and religious organizations to ensure that successive generations are able to make a seamless **transition** from early childhood and family life through schooling into labour force and adult roles.

Émile Durkheim (1956 [1922], 123) described education as "the means by which society perpetually re-creates the conditions of its very existence." Talcott Parsons (1959) later identified schools' two central functions within contemporary societies as selection (allocating individuals with appropriate skills and talents into necessary jobs and social positions) and socialization (providing people with aptitudes and knowledge required for adult roles and specific jobs).

In the primary grades, schools partially resemble home environments where highly personal, emotional ties prevail, but as students proceed through successive grade levels, the schools are marked by progressively greater degrees of competition, merit, and instrumentality intended to prepare the individual for integration into work and other social settings. Schools also reinforce essential social **norms** (Dreeben 1968), including independence (acting according to expectations without supervision), achievement (actions to meet accepted standards of excellence), universalism (impartial treatment of others based on general categories), and specificity (a focus on selected individual characteristics as opposed to the person as a whole).

Educational expansion is viewed within structural functionalism as a result of the growing complexity of the occupational structure and citizenship requirements in industrialized societies. A related form of analysis, *technical functionalism*, links educational growth to the increasing technical sophistication of jobs and knowledge production (Bell 1973). Functionalist analysis typically assumes a broad social consensus about what should be taught in schools and how educational institutions should be organized. It tends not to question either the legitimacy of educational credentials to determine entry into specified labour market positions or the fairness of the way the education system operates.

Functionalist analysis tends to portray deviation from these ideals as abnormalities or temporary problems that warrant minor reforms rather than as challenges to the education system as a whole. Describing liberal democratic visions of what schools should be like rather than explaining how schooling came about, functionalism presents education as a meritocratic ideal, a means of enabling people to gain opportunities for social or economic success regardless of their social backgrounds. Societies require a careful fit among capability, talent, effort, training, and jobs as social tasks become more complex and specialized. Such claims have led to subsequent research into the definition and measurement of educational inequality, calling into question the degree to which educational realities match the needs of industrial democratic societies.

Human capital theory, an approach with some affinity to structural functionalism, emphasizes education's role as a tool for developing human capacities to advance economic productivity and development. **Human capital** can be enhanced when adequate investment is made in the form of proper training, education, and social support; this approach has been used to justify the massive investment by governments that contributed to the significant growth in post-secondary enrolment observed in Table 10.2. Human capital theories have gained renewed currency as attention turns to the importance of advanced training and educational credentials in knowledge-based societies (Heckman and Krueger 2004).

Employment, income, and other benefits do improve generally with educational attainment. However, structural functionalism, human capital theory, and related orientations are not able to account adequately for the presence of persistent inequalities in educational opportunities, outcomes, and benefits, typically ignoring how initial advantage is likely to contribute to ongoing educational and economic success. The theoretical emphasis on consensus limits consideration of differences in educational values, content, and practices; of how some things get incorporated into schooling while others do not; and of how these differences affect people from different social backgrounds. Alternative theoretical approaches to education attempt to address some of these issues.

TIME to REFLECT

What are the main functions of education identified by structural functionalist approaches to the understanding of schooling?

SYMBOLIC INTERACTIONISM AND MICROSOCIOLOGY

Microsociology or *interpretive theories* are concerned more with interpersonal dynamics and how people make sense of their social interactions than with educational structures. Symbolic interactionism, one of the most influential branches of microsociology, focuses on how meanings and **symbols** are integral to social activity. Symbolic interactionism draws attention directly to the lives and understandings of social participants.

Interpretive analysis of education examines such questions as how schooling contributes to the development of personality and identity, how some forms of knowledge and not others enter the curriculum, and how students and teachers shape learning processes in and outside of the classroom. It focuses on the meanings and possibilities that social actors bring to social settings. Willard Waller depicts schools as "the meeting-point of a large number of intertangled social relationships. These social relationships are the paths pursued by social interaction, the channels in which social influences run. The crisscrossing and interactions of these groups make the school what it is" (1965 [1932], 12). Peter Woods (1979) explores schooling as a series of **negotiations** among teachers, students, and parents, expressed in such phenomena as how pupils select the subjects they take, the role of humour and laughter in the classroom and staffroom, and teacher reports on student progress. Howard Becker (1952) shows how teachers' backgrounds influence their construction of images of the ideal pupil, which in turn affect how they treat and assess students.

For symbolic interactionists, societies and institutions are fluid rather than fixed entities. Institutional patterns are the result of recurrent daily activity and of people's capacities to shape, interpret, reproduce, and modify social arrangements through their social relations. *Ethnomethodology*, a variant of interpretive sociology, examines in detail the methods or approaches that people draw on to construct a sense of reality and continuity in everyday life. Understood this way, classrooms tend to resemble one another not so much because of a given model of schooling but more likely because people act in accordance with images about what is expected of them.

Symbolic interactionism and ethnomethodology offer interesting insights, but their focus on the details of ongoing social activity can restrict their ability to account for social structures and historical processes. Classroom dynamics or how one interprets the curriculum cannot be understood fully without reference to educational policy, power structures, social change, and persistent social inequalities that strongly influence educational processes and outcomes.

Some researchers, such as noted British sociologist Basil Bernstein (1977), have combined interpretive sociology, with its insights into practical social activity, with approaches that pay greater attention to the social contexts in which social action takes place. They are concerned with breaking down barriers between micro- and macrosociology. Educational knowledge and practices are socially constructed, but they are also shaped by wider relations of power and control as they become part of the taken-for-granted assumptions that guide the actions and understandings of teachers and other educational participants, including notions about "what it is to be educated" (Bernstein 1977; Blackledge and Hunt 1985, 290).

TIME to REFLECT

How do symbolic interactionist theories differ from functionalist and conflict approaches to the study of education?

CONFLICT THEORY

Conflict theory highlights inequalities and power relations, emphasizing how institutional structures and social inequalities are maintained or changed through conflict and struggle.

Samuel Bowles and Herbert Gintis, like structural functionalists, emphasize schools' role as mechanisms that select and prepare people for different positions in labour markets and institutional life. However, drawing from Marx, they see the labour market as conditioned more by capitalist interests than by general consensus about social values and needs. Claims that all students have a fair chance to succeed represent democratic ideology that cannot be fulfilled. Bowles and Gintis (1976, 49) posit education, historically, as "a device for allocating individuals to economic positions, where inequality among the positions themselves is inherent in the hierarchical division of labor, differences in the degree of monopoly power of various sectors of the economy, and the power of different occupational groups to limit the supply or increase the monetary returns to their services."

Conflict theorists emphasize the persistent barriers to opportunity and advancement created by deeply rooted relations of domination and subordination. Different social groups are understood to employ education and educational ideologies as tools for pursuing their own interests. Employers rely on formal educational credentials—regardless of the skills demanded by the job—to screen applicants and assess a person's general attributes. Professions control access to education and certification as a way of preserving the status and benefits attached to their occupations. New knowledge and technological advancements in areas such as medicine, nursing, teaching, engineering, and information processing may appear to produce a demand for increasingly more advanced, specialized training. But more often, credential inflation occurs as occupations preserve special privileges by simultaneously claiming the need for superior qualifications and restricting entry into these kinds of jobs (Collins 1979).

Technological developments are not necessarily accompanied by increasing skill requirements for many jobs. Machines and information technology often replace human input for routine technical operations or influence the content of "new jobs" in which people are required to do little but read gauges, respond to signals, or key in information. Harry Braverman (1974, 440) contends that schools serve more as warehouses for delaying people's entrance into the labour force and for dissipating dissatisfaction with the economy's failure to provide a sufficient number of satisfying jobs than as places where effective learning and occupational training take place. Capitalism, in this view, has contributed less to skills upgrading through technological advancement than to processes that erode working skills, degrade workers, and marginalize youth.

In the section "Revolutionary New Technology" in Chapter 11, p. 220, the positive and negative effects of new technologies on employment opportunities and required skills are discussed in more detail.

Students and parents also have different understandings, resources, and time that affect the extent to which they can participate in and benefit from educational opportunities. Government cutbacks and changes to school-funding formulas exacerbate many of these inequalities, posing special difficulties for communities and families unable to provide additional resources to subsidize educational costs. Increases in tuition fees and other costs associated with schooling make it increasingly difficult for students without sufficient resources or unable or unwilling to take on significant debt to attend colleges and universities. Conflict analysis highlights dangers of the growing reliance by educational institutions on corporate donations and sponsorships to make up for shortfalls in government funding. Inequalities are intensified through processes of commercialization and **marketization** in which educational institutions and practices become increasingly organized on the basis of consumer choice, competition, and profitability with the continuing expansion of capitalist relations within a global context (Raduntz 2005).

Conflict theories of education, in short, stress that expectations for schooling to fulfill its promise to offer equal opportunity and social benefits to all are unrealistic or unattainable within current forms of social organization. Barriers that exist at several levels—access to schooling, what is taught and how it is taught, ability to influence educational policy and decision-making, and differential capacity to convert education into labour market and social advantage—deny many individuals or groups the chance to benefit from meaningful forms and levels of education. Conflict theories offer varying assessments of what must be done to ensure that education can be more democratic and equitable. Some analysts stress that educational institutions and organizations themselves must be transformed, while others suggest that any kind of school reform will be limited without more fundamental social and economic changes to ensure that people will be able to use, and be recognized for using, their education and training more effectively.

FEMINIST THEORIES

Feminist analyses of schooling share some of the observations of other conflict theories, though with an explicit emphasis on the existence of and strategies to address social inequalities based on gender. Feminist theory stresses that social equity and justice are not possible as long as males and females have unequal power and status through patriarchy or gendered systems of domination. In the eighteenth century, Mary Wollstonecraft (1986 [1792]) saw access to education as a fundamental right for women; denied such a right historically, women were degraded as "frivolous" or a "backward sex." Later waves of feminism have continued to look to education as a central institution through which to promote women's rights, opportunities, and interests.

Various forms of feminism pose distinct questions for educational research and propose different explanations and strategies for change (Gaskell 1993; Weiner 1994). In general, though, feminist analysis shows that influential mainstream studies of schooling have most often concentrated on the lives of boys and men, with little recognition that girls and women have different experiences and little chance to voice their concerns. Much research in the 1970s and 1980s focused on how such things as classroom activities, language use, images and examples in textbooks and curriculum material (including the absence of women and girls in many instances), treatment of students by teachers, and patterns of subject choice reflected gender-based stereotypes and perpetuated traditional divisions among males and females (Kenway and Modra 1992).

Feminist analysis seeks to do more than simply demonstrate how these social processes contribute to inequalities, focusing as well on strategies to change the conditions that bring these practices about. This focus has shifted as some aspects of the agenda on women's rights and issues have advanced successfully while specific barriers continue to restrict progress on other fronts. For instance, school boards have policies, enforced through human rights legislation, to restrict sexist curricula and to prohibit gender-based **discrimination** in educational programs and institutions. The educational participation rates of and attainment by females have come to exceed those for males. Yet gender parity has not been achieved in several important respects. Female students remain highly under-represented in important fields such as information technologies, engineering, and some natural sciences, while gender-based barriers exist in other areas of schooling. Moreover, educational achievements do not always contribute equitably to successful social and economic outcomes.

Analysis of the feminization of teaching, as female teachers came to outnumber male teachers by the end of the nineteenth century, illustrates the relationship between education and changing gender relations. Teachers often lack the professional recognition that might otherwise accompany the demands and training their work involves. Teachers—and women teachers in particular—have been heavily regulated by governments and by school boards. During the early part of the twentieth century, guidelines often specified such things as what teachers could wear, with whom they could associate, and how they should act in public (Wotherspoon 1995). Until the 1950s, legislation in many provinces required that women resign their teaching positions upon marriage. Although today's teachers have much greater personal and professional autonomy than those of the past, teachers' lives and work remain subject to various forms of scrutiny, guidelines,

(© iStockphoto/asiseeit)

Across Canada, less than 20 per cent of elementary school teachers are male, and these numbers are continuing to fall. However, men still dominate positions of leadership in schools as principals, vice-principals, and directors rather than being based in the classroom.

and informal practices that carry gender-based assumptions or significance. Female teachers predominate in the primary grades, while men tend to be overrepresented in the upper grades and in post-secondary teaching positions, especially in the most senior teaching and educational administrative positions.

Feminist analysis increasingly has come to address interrelationships among gender, sexuality, and other social factors and personal characteristics. Gender-based identities, experiences, and opportunities are affected by race, region, social class, and competing expectations and demands that people face at home, in the workplace, and in other social spheres (Arnot 2011; Dillabough, McLeod, and Mills 2011). Students and teachers from different backgrounds encounter diverse experiences, concerns, and options even within similar educational settings, which in turn affect subsequent educational and personal options.

TIME to REFLECT

What are the main bases of inequality emphasized in conflict theories and feminist theories of education, respectively?

EMERGING ANALYSIS AND RESEARCH IN THE SOCIOLOGY OF EDUCATION

Sociologists commonly employ insights from several models or orientations, acknowledging theory as a tool to help understand and explain phenomena and guide social action.

Critical pedagogy is one approach that draws from different theoretical positions, including conflict theory, feminist theory, and post-modernist challenges, both to explore how domination and power enter into schooling and personal life and to seek to change those aspects that undermine our freedom and humanity (Giroux 1997; Darder, Baltodano, and 2003; McLaren and Kincheloe 2007). Anti-racism education shares similar orientations, further stressing the ways in which domination builds on notions of racial difference to create fundamental inequalities among groups that are defined on the basis of biological differences or cultural variations (Dei 1996).

Pierre Bourdieu (1997; Bourdieu and Passeron 1979) has explored how social structures (the primary focus of structural functionalism and conflict theory) become interrelated with the meanings and actions relevant to social actors (the main concern of symbolic interactionism or interpretative sociology). Bourdieu, as a critical theorist, emphasizes that education contributes to the transmission of power and privilege from one generation to another as it employs assumptions and procedures that advantage some groups and disadvantage others. Educational access, processes, and outcomes are shaped through struggles by different groups to retain or gain advantages relative to one another. However, the mere fact that people hold varying degrees of economic, social, and cultural resources does not guarantee that these resources will be converted automatically into educational advantage. Competition for educational access and credentials increases as different groups look to education to provide a gateway into important occupational and decision-making positions.

Canadian research, influenced by Bourdieu's analysis and other integrative approaches such as life course theory, demonstrates the complex interactions among personal and social structural characteristics that affect the pathways taken by children and youth through education and from schooling into work and other life transitions (Anisef et al. 2000; Taylor 2005; Lehmann 2007). Researchers are also especially interested in the various ways in which education intersects with both local and global dimensions of cultural, economic, and social forces (Apple, Au, and Gandin 2009; Spring 2008). This analysis is drawing attention to the complex relationships that link educational practices and participants and broader socio-economic structures, processes, and transformations.

TIME to REFLECT

What advantages do integrative approaches to the analysis of education offer in comparison to other theories presented earlier in this chapter?

Educational Participants

Educational institutions are highly complex organizations. Sociologists are interested in questions related to the changing nature of who attends and works in these institutions (with respect to gender, race, ethnicity, religion, socio-economics, and other factors), what positions they occupy, and what barriers and opportunities they encounter.

There is increasing diversity in education. The educational participation of girls and women has increased significantly since World War II, especially at the post-secondary level. Immigration has contributed to changing educational profiles, with increasing racial, linguistic, and cultural diversity and variations in educational backgrounds and expectations among groups. Rural-to-urban migration, policy changes, and population growth have increased the concentrations of Aboriginal students in elementary and secondary schools, especially in western and northern Canada. Economic changes have exacerbated many inequalities, especially increasing gaps between high- and low-income families. Poverty and economic marginalization affect up to one-quarter of Canada's children. Classrooms today integrate students who historically have been excluded, such as teen parents or those with physical or learning disabilities. Religious orientation, regional economic variations, distance to essential educational and support services, and many other factors also affect educational participation and outcomes.

Sociological interest extends beyond how formal curricula and structured activities affect students' learning and chances for success. Educational organization, rules, expectations, and practices also contain a **hidden curriculum**, the unwritten purposes or goals of school life. The daily rhythm of school life helps to channel students into selected directions and contributes to taken-for-granted understandings about order, discipline, power relations, and other aspects of social life that favour students from some backgrounds to the detriment of others (Lynch 1989). Schooling can have limited connection with—and produce negative consequences for—the students and communities it is intended to serve (Dei et al. 2000; Stonechild 2006). Practices known as *silencing* inhibit many students from raising concerns that are important to them, often making students or parents uneasy about their own cultural backgrounds in relation to the authority represented by the school. These practices are often reinforced by a *banking model* of **pedagogy** (Freire 1970) in which pre-established curricula are transmitted in a one-way direction from the educator to the student, working especially to the detriment of students from less advantaged backgrounds. Benjamin Levin (2007, 75–6) points to overwhelming comparative evidence "that socioeconomic status remains the most powerful single influence on students' educational and other life outcomes" while cautioning that "[i]n public policy and politics, though, evidence matters only if it affects beliefs, and this does not happen so quickly." Socially selective practices, though often unintended and sometimes resisted by teachers, are difficult to change when they are embedded within highly complex interactions between schooling and other features of social organization.

TIME to REFLECT

What does an understanding of the hidden curriculum tell us about the nature and purposes of schooling?

Educational Policy, Politics, and Ideologies

Educational policy is established and administered in quite different ways in other countries. Many nations, such as Sweden and Japan, have highly centralized systems of education. Canada and the United States, by contrast, do not have uniform or centralized education systems, contributing to what Paul Axelrod (1997, 126) describes as an "educational patchwork." In nearly all nations, however, competing demands for more coordinated educational planning, national standards, and consistency coexist with competing reforms driven by greater responsiveness and **accountability** to local concerns (Manzer 1994; Hoffer 2008).

▼ FIGURE 10.2 Public and Private Spending on Education: Relative Share of Public and Private Expenditure on Education in Canada, Selected Years

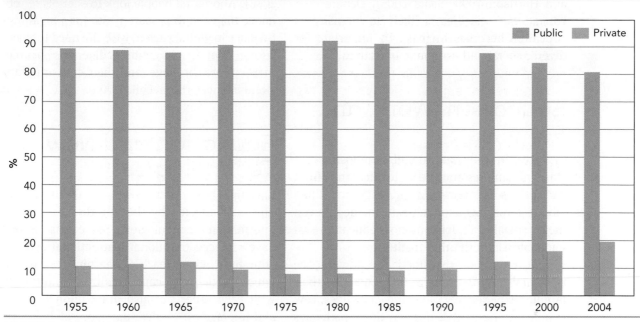

SOURCES: Based on data from Statistics Canada, CANSIM Table 478-0001 and Catalogue number 81-582X Tables B2.2 and B2.4.

Canada's Constitution assigns primary responsibility for education to provincial and territorial governments, although school boards and other local bodies as well as the federal government also play key roles. These relationships are changing as governments seek new ways to organize, administer, and deliver education (CMEC 2008). Figure 10.2 reveals that in Canada, as in most other highly developed nations, education continues to be funded primarily by governments but the share of educational spending from private sources, including tuition fees, is growing.

These trends suggest the risk of increased educational inequalities. Along with tuition fees, other educational costs, and rising living expenses, many students encounter substantial financial burdens. About six out of ten students who graduated from Canadian undergraduate programs in 2009 had some student debt, owing an average of $26,680 (Berger 2009, 185). Elementary and secondary schools also face difficult choices as they weigh the costs and benefits of seeking higher taxes to finance schools, increasing school fees, fundraising, relying on corporate sponsors to cover educational expenses, or cutting school programs and services. Public schools commonly raise funds not only for such activities as school trips, library books, and athletic programs but also for aca-

demic programs, school supplies, and textbooks (Canadian Teachers' Federation 2010). Teachers frequently pay for school materials and activities themselves, while parents or communities "are having to make up for programs that aren't paid for—so then it depends on where you live and who you are. . . . There is a growing concern about equity. There is a growing gap between the 'have' and 'have-not' schools" (Brown 2002).

Educational funding decisions are accompanied by different perceptions about how education systems can best prepare learners for contemporary economic and social conditions. Neo-liberal critics promote the application of business or market-based principles to education and other social services. High-quality education is defined in terms of the excellence of educational "products," measured by such things as standardized test scores, parental choice, and public accountability. Parents and learners become "consumers" who should have the opportunity to select the kinds of education they want. Other observers draw attention to the dangers inherent in treating schooling like a market or reducing it to narrowly defined kinds of outcomes. Some suggest that inequality is likely to increase in the absence of a true commitment to community participation and high-quality education dedicated to the full range of activities and competencies that schools seek to foster (Osborne 1999; Gidney 1999; Kachur and Harrison 1999; Sears 2003). Debate over educational priorities is likely to intensify as education becomes increasingly important for diverse social and economic objectives.

Education, Work, and Families

Changes in the nature and composition of learners' families and the varied demands from workplaces for particular kinds of qualified labour force participants have made it even more crucial to understand how education systems interact with other institutions.

The nature of childhood and adolescence is changing profoundly as students and their families experience various life challenges. Few people experience "traditional" linear pathways from home to school to work. Periods of work and study often overlap, while family, work, and community responsibilities create multiple demands on both children's and parents' time. Tensions sometimes spill over from one site of social life to another, expressed in public concern over phenomena such as bullying, violence, gang warfare, and "risk" among children and youth (although it is also important not to overemphasize the dangers while ignoring the positive experiences and contributions often associated with childhood and youth). Taking their cue from the market model of education, many parents view their children's education as an investment. Uncertainty about job futures heightens expectations on learners (seeking high performance to be competitive) and on teachers and educational administrators (in order to deliver a high-quality product that will yield the best results in the marketplace).

Parental education, along with emphasis on early reading and literacy skills, factors heavily as an influence on children's subsequent educational attainment and success (Statistics Canada 2006a). Parents and community members from diverse backgrounds frequently have differing expectations about the way education should be organized and delivered. Some immigrants, for instance, may feel that the Canadian education system is too unstructured and undemanding in comparison to the systems they were familiar with prior to arriving in Canada, while others take the opposite view (Campey 2002). Aboriginal people look to schools to reconcile the need to prepare youth for a meaningful place in global society with the need to make strong connections with indigenous people, their cultural heritage, and their contemporary circumstances (Stonechild 2006).

Education and New Technologies

Education, like other institutions, has been significantly affected by the introduction of new information technologies. Some institutions have replaced traditional instructional settings with fully wired teaching/learning centres in which participants can not only communicate with each other but also draw upon material and interact with individuals on a global basis (Gergen 2001). Web access and new technologies have also expanded learning resources and opportunities for schools and learners in remote regions. Schools and universities are just beginning to fully explore the opportunities that new technologies are making available to them (even though the World Wide Web originated, in part, in the development of a tool that could be used to produce and share new knowledge among university-based researchers).

New technologies and their use in and impact on education give rise to several important questions. Levin and Riffel raise the still relevant consideration for schools that "it may be that technology is not living up to its promise because it has been seen as an answer to rather than a reason to ask questions about the purposes of schools and the nature of teaching and learning" (1997, 114). Two issues are especially critical in this respect.

First, significant gaps remain between those who have access to computers and reliable electronic connections—and the skills and know-how to use and take advantage of new technologies—and those who do not. This "digital divide" refers mainly to gaps between richer, more technologically developed nations and developing nations. However, even within Canada regular access to up-to-date information technologies, along with the ability to use them productively, depends on such factors as degree of job security, income and education levels, gender, area of residence and work, social class, and racial characteristics (Statistics Canada 2010a; United Nations 2009, 16–20).

Second, it is important to examine how and why new technologies are being adopted as tools and expectations in education. The rapid expansion of new technologies and applications—from text messaging, social networking, blogging, and communities involved in the dissemination of public information resources such as Wikipedia to gaming and electronic surveillance devices—is transforming everyday life for students and their families. However, students and teachers are not always equipped and supported sufficiently to use such technologies to their advantage or to fully understand their implications and limitations.

Issues related to the adoption of information technologies in education reflect more enduring concerns about the relationship of what happens in the classroom with structures and processes outside of schooling. Educational practices are strongly influenced by social, technological, and economic developments and innovations, although they also reveal their own peculiarities and rhythms. Demands for education to prepare people for the changing workplace sit side by side with

(© iStockphoto/MarsBars)

For those on the right side of the "digital divide," new technology allows university and college students to access digitized library resources, re-watch lectures, contribute to class forums, and submit assignments from anywhere.

parallel demands for producing better citizens and persons with multiple competencies to function in a global society.

TIME to REFLECT

What are the main ways in which the introduction of new technologies has influenced formal education?

UNDER the WIRE

One Laptop per Child Project

A global initiative called the One Laptop per Child project seeks to equip students around the world with tools that enable them to become part of the information society. The project aims at providing each child in developing and underdeveloped nations with an inexpensive laptop, giving them access to resources and information that are essential for contemporary education. Widely hailed as a progressive measure, the project nonetheless carries many hidden costs and dangers that illustrate the risk of adopting a one-dimensional orientation to educational problems. Shrestha (2007) cautions that the project appears relatively modest in cost ($100 per computer), but

> for those who really need it . . . there's lots of hidden cost like software cost, maintenance cost,

distribution cost as well. Software should be developed in local languages and the content of the internet and other educational resources should be localized in order to make it accessible to these poor children. Poor countries are not in the condition to buy it on their own. They have to bring in money either as loan or grant through some INGOs (International Non Governmental Organization), international banks like World Bank, International Bank . . . [which will] increase the national debt of these countries.

As information technologies become more pervasive, educators and researchers are being called upon to pose similar questions about the true costs and benefits of new applications within specific educational contexts.

Educational Opportunities and Inequalities

Questions about the relationship of education to social inequality and opportunity structures have long been central to the sociological study of education. As educational participation and attainment rates increase across populations, many traditional forms of inequality diminish or disappear altogether. Nonetheless, significant inequalities persist with respect to many dimensions of educational experience and outcomes.

These trends can be illustrated by examining changes in the composition of the young adult population with post-secondary credentials. In 1981, the proportion of Canadians in the 25- to 34-year-old age cohort with a degree, certificate, or diploma from a university or college was about 32 per cent for both males and females. By 2006, the corresponding figures had risen to 63 per cent for women and 49 per cent for men (Statistics Canada 1984; 2008a). In 2008, 60 per cent of all persons who received university degrees were women, although at the highest end, 56 per cent of doctoral degrees were awarded to men (Statistics Canada 2010d; see also Table 10.3).

Findings from numerous surveys that girls have begun to outperform boys on a number of indicators, especially in areas like reading, have generated controversy over suggestions that gender inequality has reversed to the point that the education system is now "failing" boys (Bussière and Knighton 2004, 38). However, major comparative studies from Canada and several other nations also demonstrate the complex nature of gender inequalities in education. These surveys also draw attention to the interconnections among numerous family, school, and individual characteristics, notably family socio-economic background and immigration status (Alloway 2007; Bussière, Knighton, and Pennock 2007, 37–42).

Women outnumber men in post-secondary enrolment and graduation, but there are strong gender differences in fields of study and types of training programs (see Table 10.3). Programs in areas such as business, management, and commerce, some arts and social sciences, pro-

tection and correction services, and languages are relatively popular among both men and women. Women are much more heavily concentrated in a few fields, such as education, nursing, and social work or social services. Men tend to be more widely dispersed over more fields but outnumber women considerably in areas such as engineering and electrical technologies, computer science, and primary industries.

Differences in fields of study reflect a combination of personal choices and circumstances, institutional practices, and broader socio-economic factors (Arnot 2011; Wotherspoon 2000). Employment options and life pathways are generally associated with the kinds of education and credentials that people attain. Nonetheless, women's rising levels of education do not always translate fully into gains in labour market positions, incomes, or other equitable outcomes (Vosko 2010).

Some educational differences between racial and ethnic groups also appear to have disappeared or diminished significantly in recent decades (Davies and Guppy 2010, 116–20). Immigration policies have simultaneously emphasized the recruitment of immigrants with high educational credentials and made Canada less dependent on immigrants from western Europe and the United States, resulting in growing proportions of highly educated or professionally qualified visible-minority immigrants.

To better understand the requirements skilled workers must meet to be accepted into Canada, see the Global Issues box in Chapter 8, p. 157.

Racial diversity has been accompanied by increasing sensitivity to the impact of racial discrimination and other mechanisms that historically have excluded or discouraged racial-minority students from advancing through the Canadian education system.

As with gender inequalities, analysis of racial and ethnic inequalities in education reveals a complex series of interactions that do not lead to any straightforward conclusions. The short answer to the question of whether some groups are advantaged or dis-

TABLE 10.3 ▼ University Degrees Awarded by Field of Study and Gender, Canada, 2007

Field of Study	Number of Graduates	Rank Order for Female Graduates	Female Graduates in Field as % of All Female Graduates	Females as % of All Graduates in Field	Rank Order for Male Graduates	Male Graduates in Field as % of All Male Graduates	Males as % of All Graduates in Field
Social and behavioural sciences and law	50,529	1	23.3	67.6	2	17.3	32.4
Business, management, and public administration	48,705	2	17.6	52.9	1	24.2	47.1
Education	27,420	3	14.3	76.4	6	6.8	23.6
Humanities	27,222	5	12.0	64.7	4	10.1	35.3
Health, parks, recreation, and fitness	26,226	4	13.9	78.0	8	6.1	22.0
Architecture, engineering, and related technologies	19,434	8	3.2	23.8	3	15.6	76.2
Physical and life sciences and technologies	18,726	6	7.6	59.2	5	8.1	40.8
Visual and performing arts and communications technologies	8,727	7	4.0	67.3	9	3.0	32.7
Mathematics, computer and information sciences	8,547	9	1.7	29.9	7	6.3	70.1
Agriculture, natural resources, and conservation	3,864	10	1.5	57.9	10	1.7	42.4
Other	2,151	11	1.0	64.9	11	0.8	35.3
All fields	241,551		100.1	60.7		100.0	39.3

SOURCE: Compiled with data from Statistics Canada (2009).

advantaged in relation to racial and ethnic criteria is "it depends." Analysis of census data and education indicators over time reveals that Canadians in most categories (based on gender, race, region, age, class, and other factors) have benefited from the expansion of education systems (Davies and Guppy 2010). However, outcomes for specific groups, including Aboriginal people, some immigrant and visible-minority populations, those from working-class backgrounds, and many persons with disabilities, continue to be less favourable relative to other groups. Social class has a strong impact on post-secondary attendance and educational attainment. These general trends are compounded by considerable variation in educational success and attainment within groups.

Research on education for Aboriginal people is instructive in this regard. Many First Nations expressed their desire in the nineteenth-century treaty-making process to have access to formal education in order to keep pace with contemporary social and economic demands. However, the damaging legacy of residential schooling, lack of acceptance or discriminatory treatment in provincial schools, and other social, cultural, and economic factors have left Aboriginal people's overall education levels (especially those of registered Indians who live on reserve) well below national levels (Schissel and Wotherspoon 2003). Despite continuing increases in the levels of educational attainment by Aboriginal people, by 2006 Aboriginal people aged 25 to 44 years were 1.8

© Liam Sharp

The students of the Attawapiskat First Nation school on James Bay, Ontario, have been forced to attend school in rundown, mice-infested portable units since 2000. The issue has helped to shed light on the inequality faced by reserve schools, which receive on average $2000 less funding per student than provincial schools.

times less likely than non-Aboriginal people to have a post-secondary degree or diploma and 3.5 times less likely to have graduated from university but nearly three times as likely not to have completed high school (based on data in Statistics Canada 2008b).

Numerous specific factors, including lack of individual motivation and family or community support and social and educational discrimination, can contribute to educational inequalities. They typically occur through a complex chain of interrelated cause-and-effect mechanisms. Early childhood development and family and social environments in which children are raised are crucial for the development of literacy and language skills, thinking processes, and other capacities that are central to educational success. These conditions, in turn, depend on the socio-economic circumstances of parents, the availability of support networks in the home and community, labour market opportunities for parents and students

coming out of the education system, the extent to which people in particular communities or regions have access to high-quality educational programs and services, and numerous other factors. There are strong associations between social class or socio-economic background and educational attainment. Parents' education levels and household income are strong predictors, both independently and in combination with one another, of the likelihood that a person will continue into post-secondary education (Finnie, McMullen, and Mueller 2010).

Educational institutions also influence these outcomes in many ways, such as how well they are equipped to deal with students from diverse cultural and social backgrounds; the kinds of relationships that prevail between and among teachers, parents, and students; curricular objectives and materials; standards for assessing and evaluating students; and the general social climate within educational institutions. Social class and cultural differences are evident, for instance, in the grouping and **streaming** of students into specific educational programs that contribute, in turn, to diverse educational pathways.

There is general agreement, in the context of global economic developments that place a premium on knowledge and learning, that education is important for all people. The same consensus does not exist, however, with regard to how education should be arranged to fulfill its promise on an equitable basis.

Conclusion

This chapter has examined several dimensions of education and its relevance for sociological inquiry. It has highlighted the phenomenal growth of formal systems of education since the nineteenth century and the accompany-

ing increases in general levels of education throughout the population. It has linked that growth to a strong degree of public faith in the ability of education both to contribute to individual development and to address social needs for knowledge, innovation, and credentials. Educational growth, processes, and outcomes have been understood from diverse theoretical perspectives: structural functionalism (focusing on education's contributions to dominant social and economic requirements); symbolic interactionism and microsociology (highlighting understandings and interactions of various participants within educational processes); conflict theories (emphasizing education's contributions to social inequality and power relations); feminist theories (drawing attention to gender-based educational differences); and integrative approaches (linking insights from

HUMAN DIVERSITY

Education for Canada's Aboriginal People

The educational experiences of Aboriginal people in Canada are instructive for an understanding of how education can both advance and restrict social and economic opportunities. Historical practices and inequities have contributed to a legacy of widespread failure, marginalization, and mistrust, but considerable optimism also accompanies many new initiatives.

Many Aboriginal people in the late nineteenth century looked to schooling as a way of ensuring integration into contemporary societies. Tragically, while some education-related treaty promises were fulfilled, the residential school system and continuing problems with other forms of educational delivery had devastating consequences that many Aboriginal communities and their members are still struggling to cope with. The report of the Royal Commission on Aboriginal Peoples (1996) endorsed the long-standing principle of First Nations control over education along with other measures to ensure that all educational institutions would provide more receptive schooling for Aboriginal people.

Mixed results have ensued so far, as one of the co-chairs of the royal commission has observed:

Considering the primary importance of children in aboriginal cultures, it is not surprising that education was one of the first sectors where aboriginal nations and communities are now administered

locally, and where possible they incorporate aboriginal languages and cultural content in the curriculum. . . . More young people are staying in school to complete a high-school diploma, though a gap still exists between graduation rates of aboriginal and non-aboriginal people. . . . Aboriginal youth are especially vulnerable. They are less likely than mature adults to have attained academic and vocational credentials and they are hardest hit by unemployment. (Erasmus 2002)

Accomplishing educational improvement is difficult in the context of considerable diversity among Aboriginal populations and their educational options, aspirations, and circumstances. A "report card" issued by the Assembly of First Nations (2006, 16–17) on the tenth anniversary of the royal commission report assigned failing grades to all but three of 11 specific recommendations in the section on education. Some Aboriginal communities and educators are reframing success in Aboriginal learning in terms that are not restricted and not oriented to the measurement of learning deficits. Such a model would revitalize holistic notions of education as a lifelong process in which "Aboriginal learning is a fully integrated and potentially all-encompassing process that permeates all aspects of the learner's life and their community" (Canadian Council on Learning 2009, 11).

diverse perspectives). The chapter has also addressed the changing significance of formal schooling to the experiences and social and economic opportunities of different social groups, particularly with respect to gender, race and ethnicity, and social class. All groups have benefited from educational expansion, though in varying degrees. Adequate sociological analysis of education requires an ability to integrate an understanding of what happens in and as a result of formal education with the social context in which education is situated.

questions for critical thought

1. Why is education in most nations organized formally through schools and related institutional structures rather than through some other arrangement, such as families or community-based agencies? To what extent should education be a private as opposed to a public responsibility?

2. Compare and contrast schooling (formal education) with other major social institutions, including businesses, families, prisons, and religious organizations. Describe and explain the major similarities and differences.

3. What is the impact of emerging emphases on lifelong learning and the new economy on education systems? What kinds of alternatives to formal schooling are being developed in response to increasing demands for lifelong learning? Explain and critically discuss the changes (or lack of change) you have identified.

4. Why have education levels increased across populations in Canada and in most other nations? Which theoretical perspectives offer the most adequate explanation of these trends?

5. To what extent and in what ways have educational institutions been influenced by new information technologies? Discuss the relative strengths and limitations of these changes in terms of schooling's ability to meet the needs of learners in contemporary societies.

6. To what extent has education in Canada fulfilled its promise to provide greater opportunities for social and economic advancement to all social groups? Explain your response with reference to at least three different theoretical frameworks.

recommended readings

Scott Davies and Neil Guppy. 2010. *The Schooled Society: An Introduction to the Sociology of Education*. 2nd edn. Toronto: Oxford University Press.
The authors integrate their discussion of core concepts and theories in the sociological analysis of education with material drawn from sociological research and case studies. Both historical and contemporary issues and developments are covered.

Shailaja Fennell and Madeline Arnot, eds. 2009. *Gender Education and Equality in a Global Context*. London: Routledge.
Taking global commitments to achieve equity in basic education by the year 2015 as a starting point, several authors integrate feminist inquiry with empirical research on the ways in which gender inequality is intertwined with poverty, culture, economic systems, and fundamental social conditions in different national contexts.

Hugh Lauder, Phillip Brown, Jo-Anne Dillabough, and A.H. Halsey, eds. 2006. *Education, Globalization, and Social Change*. Oxford: Oxford University Press.
In one of the most comprehensive collections of analyses of education from various perspectives in sociology and other disciplines, influential chapters from different national settings examine the impact of political and economic changes on education, cultural diversity, new conceptions of knowledge and curricula, the reshaping of teaching, and the dynamics of inequality and exclusion in relation to formal education.

Cynthia Levine-Rasky, ed. 2009. *Canadian Perspectives on the Sociology of Education.* Toronto: Oxford University Press.
This volume assembles both theoretical and empirical contributions to the analysis of relationships between school and society, with an explicitly Canadian focus. Chapters include analysis of such issues as educational reform, race, gender and identity in education, socio-economic inequality, and rural schooling.

Terry Wotherspoon. 2014. *The Sociology of Education in Canada: Critical Perspectives.* 4th edn. Toronto: Oxford University Press.
Various dimensions of Canadian education are explored from a critical orientation that emphasizes inequalities based on class, race, gender, region, and other factors. The book addresses contemporary aspects of Canadian education in the context of various theoretical perspectives and historical factors.

recommended websites

Canadian Council on Learning
www.ccl-cca.ca
The Canadian Council on Learning, funded by the federal government, was established to promote lifelong learning in Canada, in part by promoting and co-ordinating evidence-based research about various aspects of education, training, and learning. The website includes useful reports and information related to such key themes as Aboriginal learning, post-secondary education, early childhood and adult learning, and public attitudes toward learning.

Council of Ministers of Education, Canada
www.cmec.ca
The Council of Ministers of Education provides access to major reports and studies conducted through that organization as well as links to each of the provincial and territorial ministries of education and other important Canadian and international education bodies.

Educational Resources Information Center (ERIC)
www.eric.ed.gov
The ERIC database is a comprehensive collection of information (mostly abstracts of journal articles and reports) on various aspects of and fields related to education, including the sociology of education.

Organisation for Economic Co-operation and Development (OECD)
www.oecd.org
The OECD website provides useful and up-to-date information for major international comparisons and developments. It includes report summaries, statistics, and links to major documents on education and related thematic areas that highlight significant trends and issues for 30 member countries and several dozen other nations.

Statistics Canada
www.statcan.gc.ca
Statistics Canada provides a comprehensive body of data and information on education on its website and through its links with other sites.

chapter 11

Work and the Economy

Pamela Sugiman

In this chapter, you will:

▶ Be introduced to some of the main concepts that are used in the sociological analysis of work.

▶ Examine the different ways in which work has been socially organized by employers.

▶ Recognize the impact of flexibility strategies on workers who are located differently in a gendered and racialized capitalist society.

▶ Explore ways in which workers experience work and sometimes resist.

Introduction

Let us begin this chapter on work and the economy by making three key points. These assertions are the premises on which this chapter is based. First, most of us will spend the better part of our lives working, because work is central to our economic well-being. Second, work is a social product and, as such, it is negotiable. Third, people seek meaning in the work that they perform: there is a close relationship between work, life, and identity. Let us look more closely at each of these points.

1. *Work is central to our existence.* What would it be like if you never held a job? Would it be possible? Unless you are incredibly wealthy, unable to work as a result of disability or poor health, or willing (or forced) to live on social assistance or handouts on the street, it is unlikely that you could live without work. If you are like most people, you have no choice but to work in order to secure for yourself the basic necessities (food, clothing, a decent living environment). Most of us will spend a large chunk of our lives working; the majority will work for someone else, on another's terms. This holds true whether you bus tables, drive a truck, stock grocery shelves, trade on Bay Street, or teach in a school. The very wealthy rely heavily on investment income for their economic well-being, and the extremely poor depend on social welfare (transfer payments). But the majority of people in the middle- and highest-income groups in Canada count on wages and salaries for their existence (Jackson and Robinson 2000, 11). In 2008, close to eight in ten persons in Canada aged 15 to 64 participated in the paid labour force (Jackson 2009, 3). It is crucial to think about work, for it has strong implications for how we will live our lives.

2. *Work is a social product.* The second point emerges from the observation that many Canadians view the work they perform as a given. Work is something that we go to every day or night, leave at the end of a career, will do for a good part of our lives. Yet it is important to understand that there is nothing inevitable about the way work is presented and organized. Work is a social product. The way it is structured, the nature of jobs, the rewards of work are all products of **social relationships** between different groups of people. Over time and across cultures, work has taken varied forms. We need to critically examine its current organization with the knowledge that this may be transformed.

3. *People seek meaning in their work.* Although most of us work in order to survive and live comfortably, we also work for more than economic survival or comfort of living. The quality of work matters to workers, young and old.

In order to understand work fully, it is necessary to think about the wider economy in which it is situated. We may define the *economy* as a social institution in which people carry out the production, distribution, and consumption of goods and services. It is critical that we understand how economic systems function, for they have a direct bearing on how we live. The economy and our location in it shape, for instance, the quality of health care, housing, diet and nutrition, consumer spending, and lifestyle. The economic system is, furthermore, linked to a nation's political system, to people's conceptions of democracy and citizenship, and to general measures of success and failure.

TIME to REFLECT

In work that you have done for pay, what, besides the money, did you gain from the work? How do you think work affects a person's self-esteem and feelings of belonging in society? What do you want from your job?

World Economic Systems

In Canada, we currently live in a society that is based on a system of **capitalism**, one in which there are blatant as well as subtle manifestations of inequality. We observe extremes of wealth and poverty every day. On the highway, a shiny new Porsche whirs by a 1998 Chevy Impala. A businessman rushing to pick up a $5000 suit from a Holt Renfrew store walks quickly past a homeless person squatting on the corner. A Filipina nanny on a temporary work permit spends her days taking someone's children to Montessori school and ballet class.

We live in a society in which economic inequalities are complexly wound up with inequalities based on gender, race, and ethnicity.

The power of capitalism is so pervasive that we tend to take for granted many of its central premises. Few of us notice, much less question, the kinds of inequalities that characterize a capitalist society. Concerned about how we can individually climb up the capitalist hierarchy, we seldom stop to question the system itself. But by looking more closely, with a sociological lens, we can see how our present society is the result of historical relationships based on conflict and struggle.

CAPITALISM

Unlike earlier economic systems, capitalism is based on private ownership of the means of production, an exchange relationship between owners and workers, an economy driven by the pursuit of profit, and competitive market relations.

In order to understand capitalism, let us turn to the ideas of the classical social theorist Karl Marx. Marx (1967 [1867]) wrote about the profound changes he observed in nineteenth-century England. He witnessed a gradual but dramatic transition from a feudal agricultural society to an industrialized, capitalist economy. Under capitalism, the capitalist class (or bourgeoisie) owns the means of production, while the majority of people, the working class (or proletariat), does not. Means of production is a concept that refers to wealth-generating property, such as land, factories, machines, and the capital needed to produce and distribute goods and services for exchange in a market. In a capitalist society, capitalists and workers are engaged in a relationship of unequal exchange. Since workers do not own the means of production, they have no choice but to sell their labour to a capitalist employer in exchange for a wage. Working people are forced into this relationship, because in this type of economy, it is almost impossible to survive without money. One can try to feed a family with the produce of a home vegetable garden, wear homemade clothes, and live without electricity, but at some point it is necessary to purchase market goods and services.

The capitalist class organizes production (work) with the specific goal of maximizing profits for personal wealth. For this reason, capitalist employers structure work in the most efficient way imaginable, pay workers the lowest possible wages, and extract the greatest amount of labour from the worker within a working day.

TIME to REFLECT

Would you characterize your family of origin as "capitalist" or "working class"? In what ways, if any, do you believe that your family background has affected your choice of occupation and your attitudes toward work and workplace rights?

CAPITALISM AND INDUSTRIALIZATION

While capitalism is a broad economic system, industrialization refers to a more specific process that has consequences for the nature and organization of work as well as for the division of labour. Industrialization involved the introduction of new forms of energy (steam, electricity) and of transportation (railroads), **urbanization**, and the implementation of new machine technology, all of which contributed to the rise of the factory system of production and the manufacture and mass production of goods. These changes greatly facilitated and heightened capitalist production. As well, and in profound ways, they shaped the ways in which people worked and organized their lives.

The proliferation of factories led to the movement of work from homes and small artisanal workshops to larger, more impersonal sites, to the concentration of larger groups of workers under one roof, and to the introduction of *time discipline* (by the clock), in addition to a more specialized division of labour.

During the period of industrial capitalism, economic inequalities became increasingly visible, and conflict between classes grew. While successful capitalists made huge amounts of money, working-class men toiled in factories or mines for a pittance, women combined long hours of domestic drudgery with sporadic income-generating activities, and children were sent off to factories or domestic work. Many people lived in poverty and misery.

An example of the rise of the factory system is Ganong, Canada's oldest candy company. Founded in 1873 in St Stephen, New Brunswick, Ganong is credited with inventing the chocolate bar. The head office and factory are still located in New Brunswick and employ 400 people.

FAMILY CAPITALISM

In the mid- to late nineteenth century, industrial capitalism was in its early stages. Throughout this period, a small number of individuals and families owned and controlled most of the country's wealth—major companies and financial institutions. Because wealth accrued from business enterprises that were passed on within families, from generation to generation (for example, the Fords and Rockefellers in the United States and the Eatons and Seagrams in Canada), this era is aptly termed that of *family capitalism*.

CORPORATE CAPITALISM

The subsequent phase of economic development, occurring in the late nineteenth to mid-twentieth centuries, is called *corporate* (or *monopoly*) *capitalism*. This phase witnessed the movement of ownership from individuals and families to modern corporations (and their shareholders). A *corporation* is defined as a legal entity distinct from the people who own and control it. As an entity, the corporation itself may enter into contracts and own property. This separation of enterprise from individuals has served to protect owners and chief executives from personal liability and from any debts incurred by the corporation.

Under corporate capitalism, furthermore, there has been a growing concentration of economic power (that is, power in the hands of a few large corporations). One way in which capitalists have increased their economic power is through mergers. By merging, large corporations have been able to create situations of monopoly and oligopoly. We have a monopoly when one corporation has exclusive control over the market. Obviously, this situation is undesirable for consumers, since it restricts their market "choices." The Canadian government has, as a result, implemented various controls to curb the monopolization of an industry.

An *oligopoly* exists when several companies control an industry. The insurance, newspaper, and entertainment industries all are characterized by oligopolistic control. Increased revenues by way of mergers and acquisitions obviously is desirable to corporate owners but may occur at the expense of industrial development, employment, and workers.

The Global Economy

Today, economic activity knows no national borders. Most large companies operate in a global context, setting up businesses in Canada, the United States, parts of Africa, and the new economic "giants" in Asia, such as India. These companies may be called *transnational* or *multinational*. The head offices of transnational corporations are located in one country while production facilities are based in others. We see the products of the global economy everywhere we turn. Look at the clothes you wear, the car you drive, the food you eat. Where are they from? Products of the new global economy typically move through many nations.

Clearly, the goal of transnational corporations is profit. Capitalists are rapidly moving beyond national boundaries in an effort to secure the cheapest available labour, the lowest-cost infrastructure (power, water supply, roads, telephone lines), and production unencumbered by health and safety regulations, minimum-wage and hours-of-work laws, maternity provisions, and the like.

Global capitalism has, furthermore, had an uneven impact on different groups of people around the world. Media exposés of children sewing Nike soccer balls in Pakistani sweatshops for the equivalent of six cents an hour have brought worldwide attention to sweatshop abuses in the garment and sportswear industries. More hidden are the adolescent and teenage girls, often single mothers, who sew clothes in the maquiladora factories of Central America and Mexico for major North American retailers such as Wal-Mart and Gap and the United Kingdom's Marks & Spencer (Maquiladora Solidarity Network 2010).

Garment manufacturers in Central America's free-trade zones, Mexico's maquiladora factories, and Asia's export-processing zones say that they prefer to hire young girls and women because "they have nimble fingers. Workers suspect that children and young people are hired because they are less likely to complain about illegal and unjust conditions. And more important, they are less likely to organize unions" (Maquiladora Solidarity Network 2010). We are seeing the intensification of divisions of labour, globally, along the lines of class, sex, and race.

These developments have direct consequences for the organization of work and for the collective power of working people in the Global North as well. Many Canadians now work under a constant threat of company relocation to lower-cost areas. And this has resulted in a weakening of the political power of workers and their unions. In light of this threat, many people in Canada have agreed to concessions (that is, giving up past gains) such as pay cuts, loss of vacation pay, and unpaid overtime. In the long term, the lingering threat of job loss affects the standard of living and contributes to economic decline in the country as a whole.

For a broader discussion on the globalization of trade and manufacturing that has occurred over the past several decades, see "Capital/Goods/Services" in Chapter 15, p. 308.

(© CP Images/Kevin Van Paassen/The Globe and Mail)

Canada Goose is one Canadian company that has chosen not to move production overseas. The "made in Canada" branding used by the company is one of the reasons CEO Dani Reiss was named Ernst & Young's Entrepreneur of the Year in 2011 (http://theglobeandmail.com/report-on-business/small-business/sb-marketing/sales/manufacturers-wave-maple-leaf-to-marketing-advantage/article2301931/?service=mobile).

The Capitalist Economy: Where People Work

Just as the economy undergoes change throughout history, so does our relationship to work. With the expansion of some economic sectors and the contraction of others, our opportunities for certain kinds of jobs also change. We may identify four major economic sectors in which people in this country find employment: primary and resource industries, manufacturing, the service sector, and social reproduction.

PRIMARY RESOURCE INDUSTRY

Decades ago, most Canadians worked in *primary* (or *resource*) *industry*. Depending on your family origins, your ancestors may have performed primary-sector work. Though not always for pay, Aboriginal peoples have had an important history in the resource industry. Work in the primary sector involves the extraction of natural resources from our environment. Primary-industry jobs may be found, for instance, in agricultural production, ranching, mining, forestry, hunting, and fishing.

Throughout the eighteenth and nineteenth centuries, the primary sector represented the largest growth area in Canada. However, in the twentieth century it began to experience a dramatic decline. Many forces have contributed to its contraction, notably the demise of small family farms and small independent fishing businesses, along with a corresponding rise in corporate farming (or "agribusiness") and large fishing enterprises. These developments have resulted in dwindling opportunities for many people. Moreover, because of the geographic concentration of primary-sector jobs, this decline has devastated some towns (for example, Elliot Lake, Ontario) and entire regions (for example, Atlantic Canada).

MANUFACTURING

Into the twentieth century, growing numbers of Canadians began to work in the *manufacturing* (or *secondary*) *sector*. Manufacturing work involves the processing of raw materials into usable goods and services. If you make your living by assembling vans, knitting socks, packing tuna, or piecing together the parts of Barbie dolls, you are employed in manufacturing.

On the whole, the manufacturing sector in Canada has experienced a slower decline than primary industry. The decline in manufacturing began in the early 1950s. In 1951, manufacturing represented 26.5 per cent of employment in Canada, but by 1995 the employment share of manufacturing had been cut nearly in half, to 15.2 per cent (Jackson and Robinson 2000, 11). By 2002, the manufacturing sector had entered a phase of crisis and restructuring. Between 2002 and 2007, more than 30,000 direct manufacturing jobs were lost, in large part because of plant closures and layoffs resulting from lower production, a corporate drive to intensify productivity, and greater outsourcing (Jackson 2009, 262). Economist Andrew Jackson (2009, 262) notes that the impact of such job loss has been greatest in the unionized manufacturing sector. These losses are significant. On the whole, manufacturing jobs are more likely to be full-time, to offer pensions and benefits, and to be unionized.

THE SERVICE SECTOR

Over the past several decades, numerous new jobs have been created in the rapidly expanding *service* (or *tertiary*) *sector*. Study after study demonstrates that employees who lost jobs in manufacturing have been absorbed by the service industry. Many of you are no doubt currently employed in part-time or temporary service jobs.

The rise of the service industry has been linked to the development of a post-industrial, information-based economy and to the growth of a strong consumer culture. All of this has resulted in a growing need for people to work in information processing and management, marketing, advertising, and servicing. In the course of a day, you will encounter dozens of service-sector employees. Airline reservation agents, taxi drivers, professors, bank employees, computer technicians, librarians, garbage collectors, and Starbucks baristas—all these are service workers.

The service sector embraces a wide range of jobs. So dissimilar are these jobs that some people speak of a polarization of work. In other words, there are some "good," high-skilled, well-paid jobs at one end of the spectrum and many "bad," poorly paid jobs at the other. Jobs in retail trade and food services are at the low end of the hierarchy, while those in finance and business, health, education, and public administration tend to be at the high end.

The experience of service work is also qualitatively different from that of manufacturing. Much service employment involves not only the physical performance of a job but also an emotional component. In the face of an intensely competitive market, how does a company vie for customers? Service. And service rests on a big smile and (artificially) personalized interactions. In *The Managed Heart* (1983), Arlie Hochschild explored the emotional work of flight attendants. According to Hochschild, emotional labour, typically performed by women, is potentially damaging to workers precisely because it involves regulating one's emotional state, sometimes suppressing feelings and often inventing them.

Low-end service work is furthermore characterized by low-trust relationships. With the expectation that their workforce will have only weak loyalties to the company and its goals, managers attempt to control employees largely through close direction and surveillance (Pupo and Noack 2010; Tannock 2001). It is now common practice for employers to use electronic equipment to monitor telephone conversations between employees and clients and to install video security cameras to keep an eye on retail clerks. Another form of surveillance, more common in the United States than in Canada, is drug testing (through urinalysis) of prospective employees. Such testing is standard, for example, at Wal-Mart stores (Ehrenreich 2001; Featherstone 2004).

SOCIAL REPRODUCTION

All the work we have discussed so far is conducted in what social scientists call the *sphere of production*. Production typically occurs in the public world of factory, office, school, and store. Moreover, it involves monetary exchange. The study of work in this country has largely been biased toward production.

However, in Canada as well as elsewhere, many people spend hours and hours each day doing work that is not officially recorded as part of the economy. This type of labour may be called **social reproduction**. Social reproduction involves a range of activities for which there is no direct economic exchange. Often, though not always, this work is performed within family households. Typically, it is done by women. We do not view as economic activity the hours women (and, less typically, men) spend buying groceries, planning and cooking meals, folding laundry, chauffeuring children, buying clothes, cleaning the toilet bowl, managing the household budget, and caring for aging relatives. The instrumental value of such activities has long been hidden. Rather than being viewed as work, they are deemed a labour of love (Luxton 1980).

But what would happen if women and other family members no longer performed this labour? How would it get done? Equally important, who would pay for it? If capitalist employers or the state had to ensure that workforces got fed, clothed, and nurtured, what would the cost be? These kinds of questions perplex economists and social statisticians. Says economist Marilyn Waring, breastfeeding, for example, is "a major reproductive activity carried out only by women, and this thoroughly confuses statisticians' and economists' production models. The reproduction of human life also seems conceptually beyond their rules of imputation. But bodies most certainly have market prices" (1996, 86). According to the Vanier Institute of the Family, family members in Canada spend 20 billion hours annually performing housework. Unpaid labour is valued at no less than $197 billion, or the equivalent of 10 million full-time jobs (cited in Nelson 2010, 253).

The system of capitalism benefits tremendously from the performance of unpaid labour. Yet not only are the unpaid services of housewives and other family members excluded from traditional economic measures, but for many years sociologists did not even consider them "work." This is paradoxical insofar as such work is essential to basic human survival and to the quality of our lives.

Why are women more likely to take on unpaid domestic labour? See "Sharing Household Work" in Chapter 9, p. 180, for more information.

THE INFORMAL ECONOMY

Also hidden from official growth figures—as well as from the public conscience—is a wide range of economic activities that are not officially reported to the government. These activities make up the **informal** (or *underground*) **economy**. Such activities include babysitting, cleaning homes, sewing clothes, peddling watches, playing music on the streets, gambling, and dealing drugs. As you make your way through the downtown core of most major cities, you will see people of all ages trying to eke out a living in the informal sector.

Of course, we do not know the precise size of the underground economy. We have only estimates of its share of officially recognized economies and see much variation across the globe. According to the International Labour Organization (ILO), in developing countries as a whole the informal economy has been estimated to involve one-half to three-quarters of the non-agricultural labour force. In the developing world, informal employment is generally a larger source of employment for women than for men (www.ilo.org/public/english/employment/gems/download/women.pdf).

Informal economies have flourished for a long time in most nations, but this sector has been growing in importance, largely because of economic hardship related to restructuring, globalization, and their effects of dislocation and forced migration. Increasingly, people are turning to "hidden work" in order to survive in the midst of contracting opportunities in the formal economy. It has become a safety net of sorts for the poorest groups in society. Without doubt, workers in this sector have had to be enterprising. Some are highly motivated and possess valuable skills; others lack formally recognized credentials. Unfortunately, most people who rely on the informal economy for a living face precarious, unstable "careers" in unregulated environments.

The Social Organization of Work Today

REVOLUTIONARY NEW TECHNOLOGY

Today, popular writers and scholars alike are talking about the emergence of a new world of work, one that is rooted in a "knowledge

OPEN for DISCUSSION

Hard Work Never Killed Anyone

Hard work never killed anyone! This is an old and familiar phrase. Teenagers are likely to hear it from their parents when they balk at having to cut the grass or shovel snow. But hard work does injure and kill. In 2004, 340,000 Canadian workers were injured on the job severely enough to lose time from work. In the same year, workers' compensation boards across the country accepted 928 fatality claims. Many would regard these numbers as highly conservative estimates. Tens of thousands of workers who have accidents while at work do not report them, while official statistics of workplace fatalities fail to take into account the daily wear and tear of jobs that can take years off one's life—not to mention the problem of occupational disease.

Canadian workers are injured and killed on the job in at least three ways. First, some jobs such as mining, logging, fishing, and farming are dangerous, and accident and fatality rates are unacceptably high. Second, accident rates are related to how fast and how long a person works at a job. The more hours a person works in a day, the greater the likelihood of an accident. Why? Fatigue. If you get tired shovelling snow, you can stop. If you are paid according to the number of laptops or telephone calls you make, you are likely to push yourself beyond safe limits. And if you are manipulating a fast-paced machine with sharp cutting tools, even a brief lapse in attention can result in serious injury. Third, years of working hard can lead to various occupational diseases that are both debilitating and fatal.

The change from an industrial to a "post-industrial" or "information" society has altered patterns of workplace accidents. More than 30 years ago, the dominant form of injury compensated for by provincial compensation boards involved crushed or severed limbs. Now, one-half of all accident/injury claims are related to strains and sprains, especially of the lower back and upper limbs. Musculoskeletal injuries are on the rise because we are being asked to work harder and faster in jobs that are poorly designed and highly repetitive. Under such conditions, our bodies break down. Many experience chronic neck, shoulder, arm, and back pain.

Numerous studies also link long-term exposure to toxic substances and chemicals such as asbestos, lead, benzene, and arsenic to cancer and other deadly diseases. So, too, waiters in bars and casino workers have to deal with unruly customers and sexual harassment, which can lead to high levels of stress and subsequent health problems such as heart disease. Yet these serious workplace health and safety problems rarely find their way into official accident and compensation statistics.

Workers and unions in Canada have long protested these alarming conditions. In the 1970s, such protests resulted in the passage of occupational health and safety laws that gave workers the right to know about the substances they were working with, the right to participate with management in identifying unsafe and unhealthy working conditions, and the right to refuse work they believed to be unsafe.

—Robert Storey, Labour Studies and Sociology, McMaster University

society"—a world that offers opportunity, an increase in leisure time, an experience of work that is far more intrinsically rewarding than in the past. Are these assertions founded? Do people now have better jobs than their parents and grandparents had? Has work been transformed?

Admittedly, most people agree that the new technology may eliminate routine and repetitive tasks, thereby freeing people to perform more challenging work. Think, for example, about preparing a research paper without a word processing system and printer. Moreover, technology has had a positive impact on job creation. Yet some sociologists argue that at the same time, the technology has created new forms of inequality and exacerbated old ones. While it has resulted in new, more challenging jobs for some people, many others have lost their jobs (or skills) as a result of technological change in the workplace.

In the **service economy**, for instance, employers have relied extensively on computers and microelectronics to streamline work processes. In banking, many of the decisions (such as approving a bank loan) that used to be made at the discretion of people are now computer-governed. And the introduction of automated bank machines has made redundant the work of thousands of tellers. As well, in various industries computers have taken over the supervisory function of employee surveillance. With state-of-the-art computer equipment, and without the direct intervention of a supervisor, firms can now effectively enforce productivity quotas and monitor workers, especially those who perform highly routine tasks (Fox and Sugiman 1999; Lewchuk and Robertson 2006).

FLEXIBLE WORK

Alongside information technology, some writers have extolled the benefits of related trends in management methods. Over the past few decades in business circles, one would hear buzzwords such as "workplace restructuring," "downsizing," and "lean production." All of these concepts are part of a managerial approach called flexibility. One popular practice, termed **numerical flexibility**, involves shrinking or eliminating the core workforce (in continuous jobs and full-time positions) and

(© iStockphoto/DaveAlan)

Google is developing technology for driverless cars. If they are successful, what would this new technology mean for industries such as truck driving and taxi driving?

replacing them with workers in *non-standard* (or *contingent*) *employment*. **Non-standard (or precarious) work** is a term used to describe various employment arrangements such as part-time work, temporary (seasonal and other part-year) work, contracting out or outsourcing (work that was previously done in-house), and self-employment. Non-standard work is, in short, based on an employment relationship that is far more tenuous than those of the past (Jackson 2009; Vosko 2003, 2006).

In the current economy, non-standard work arrangements now characterize most spheres of employment. In your own university or college, for example, you may discover that many courses are taught by part-time or sessional instructors, some of whom hold PhDs, others of whom are graduate students. These individuals are paid by the university to teach on a course-by-course or session-by-session basis. Sessional or part-time instructors typically do not work on a full-time basis, and they seldom receive assurances of stable employment.

The proportion of Canadian workers in the most precarious forms of work has remained high over the past two decades. Indeed, non-standard labour represents the fastest-growing type of employment in this country. Not unlike the "reserve army of labour" described by Karl Marx, non-standard employees provide owners and managers with a ready supply of labour to "hire and fire" as the market demands. Employers invest minimally in these workers and offer them only a limited commitment. In order to remain competitive in the global market, corporations must reduce labour costs through downsizing—that is, laying off permanent, full-time workers and replacing them with part-time, temporary, and contract labour (Cranford, Vosko, and Zukewich 2006; Vosko 2006).

Furthermore, non-standard workers as a whole receive relatively low wages and few benefits. Consequently, many people who rely on this type of work must resort to holding multiple jobs in an effort to make ends meet. People carve out a living by stringing together a host of low-paying, part-time, and temporary jobs. Often this involves moonlighting or doing shift work, situations that no doubt put added strain on families.

In light of these trends, for most Canadians the concept of a career is a remnant of the past.

The gold watch for 50 years of continuous service to the same company is not attainable in the new workplace scenario. Says Richard Sennett, "flexibility today brings back this arcane sense of the job, as people do lumps of labor, pieces of work, over the course of a lifetime" (1998, 9). Not surprisingly, living in this era of economic uncertainty, with the attendant worry about layoffs and job loss, is a major source of stress for people in Canada (Jackson 2009, 74–7; Lewchuk and Robertson 2006).

TIME to REFLECT

Have you ever worked or do you now work at what could be termed a "McJob"? Did it or does it fulfill your needs? In what ways, if any, did or does it fall short? What would it be like to work at a "McJob" for the rest of your working life?

The Changing Face of Labour: Diversity among Workers

Just as places of work have changed dramatically over time, so too has the workforce itself. Workplaces today are becoming increasingly diverse. Only a minority of families rely on a single paycheque. Aboriginal Canadians make up a growing proportion of the paid labour force in certain geographic areas. People of colour, some of whom are immigrants to this country, many Canadian-born, currently have a stronger-than-ever presence, particularly in big cities such as Vancouver, Toronto, and Montreal. As well, the workforce has become more highly educated and younger.

GENDERED WORK

The participation of women in the paid labour force has increased steadily over the past four decades. In the mid-1970s, the labour force participation rate of women aged 15 to 64 was slightly over one-half. By 2006, it was close to three-quarters (or 73.5 per cent) (Jackson 2009, 100). Most striking has been a rise in the employment rates of married women and mothers of children under the age of six. The two-breadwinner (also called *dual-earner*) family is now the norm.

HUMAN DIVERSITY

Offshore Migrant Farm Workers: A New Form of Slavery?

Who, if anyone, are the new slaves in Canada? While they are not really slaves in the classical sense of the term, the 16,000 workers who come to Canada every year from the Caribbean and Mexico to work in Canadian agriculture are a form of unfree labour. *Slavery* may be too strong a term to describe who they are, but their condition of unfreedom does bear a strong resemblance to slavery.

What makes these workers different from other Canadians and from immigrants who come here to build better lives for themselves? Migrant workers from the Caribbean and Mexico come to Canada under labour contracts. These contracts specify how long they can remain in the country and the conditions under which they must work. Workers are allowed to stay in Canada for between three and eight months every year. When their contracts expire, or if they breach one of the terms of their contracts, they are expected to leave the country. Workers pay for a portion of their transportation and must pay their employers back to help them cover the costs of accommodation. In some cases, workers bunk five or six to a room and live in hot, overcrowded conditions. However, the main reason that they are considered

unfree labourers stems from their inability to quit or change jobs in Canada without the permission of their employer and a representative of the federal government. If they do quit their jobs with a Canadian employer without permission, they are subject to deportation from the country.

Why does this condition of unfreedom matter? After all, some people think that migrant workers are lucky to be here compared to where they come from. They invariably make more money here than they would back home, so they should be grateful for the opportunity to come here to work, even if only temporarily. Yet even though no one is forcing them to sign a labour contract and come to Canada to work, it does matter that they are a form of unfree labour. Their lack of choice when it comes to whom they work for and their inability to vote with their feet and find better-paying jobs in other sectors of the Canadian economy mean that farm employers have a tremendous degree of power over migrant workers. In many cases, workers are fearful of saying "no" when they are asked to do jobs that are dangerous and might harm their health. And employers who have a captive labour force do not have market incentives to improve wages or working conditions.

—Vic Satzewich, McMaster University

Today, many young women and men entering the labour force are unaware of the blatant sexual inequalities of the past. Whether or not they identify themselves as feminists, women today are building their careers on a feminist foundation. If not for the challenges posed by women's rights activists, university lecture halls would be filled exclusively by men, women would not be permitted entry into the professions or management, and paid employment would simply not be an option after marriage.

But just as women's historical breakthroughs are instructive, so too are the persisting inequalities. In spite of a dramatic increase in female labour force participation, women and men are by no means equal in the labour market. The **social institution** of work is still very much a gendered one. Some women have made inroads in non-traditional fields of manual labour, the professions, and management and administration, but the majority remain concentrated in

female-dominated occupations such as retail salesperson, secretary, cashier, registered nurse, elementary school teacher, babysitter, and receptionist, while men are more commonly truck drivers, janitors, farmers, motor vehicle mechanics, and construction trade helpers, for example (Statistics Canada 2008d).

As well, women (in addition to youth of both sexes) are more likely than men to be employed on a part-time or temporary basis. For years now, women have made up approximately 70 per cent of the part-time workforce in Canada. And while the majority of the self-employed are men, the 1990s witnessed a rapid growth in women's self-employment. In comparing the sexes, we also see that self-employed men are more likely than self-employed women to hire others and that businesses operated by men are more likely to be in the goods sector, whereas female-run businesses are likely to be in the less lucrative service sector (Nelson 2010, 246–7).

(Todd Korol/Aurora Photos/GetStock)

Less than 4 per cent of Fire Services employees are women, demonstrating that female presence in traditionally male professions is still very low (http://www.servicecanada.gc.ca/eng/qc/job_futures/statistics/6262.shtml).

These trends—labour market segregation by sex and the overrepresentation of women in precarious employment—have contributed to gender-based differences in earnings. Currently, among all categories of earners (full-time and part-time), we find that a woman earns 64.5 cents for every dollar earned by a man (Statistics Canada, CANSIM, Table 202-0102). When we compare women employed on a full-time basis with their male counterparts, the gap narrows—although it does not disappear. In fact, the gap persists even when we control for education. While Canadian women posted better academic achievements than men at all levels, women with a post-secondary education still earn on average 63 per cent of the salary of men who possess similar educational qualifications (www.theglobeandmail.com/news/national/women-at-work-still-behind-on-the-bottom-line/article1699176).

The category of "woman," of course, is not a homogenous one. Immigrant women, women of colour (or racialized women), and Aboriginal women bear the brunt of income and occupational polarization by sex. In consequence, their average annual earnings are disproportionately low. Statistics Canada reports that of those employed full-time, full-year in 2000, visible-minority women, for example, had average annual earnings of $32,100, roughly 10 per cent less than their equivalents who are not visible minorities (http://publications.gc.ca/collections/Collection-R/Statcan/89-503-X/0010589-503-XIE.pdf).

Faced with multiple forms of **discrimination**, working-class women of colour and some female immigrants have come to occupy job ghettos. Indeed, many of the jobs that typically are performed by working-class people of colour have a "hidden" quality: the work they do is not noticed; the workers are rendered invisible. All too often, we regard private domestic workers and nannies, hotel and office cleaners, taxi drivers, health-care aides, and dishwashers—all of whom perform indispensable labour—as simply part of the backdrop (Arat-Koc 1990; Das Gupta 1996; Sherman 2007). Not only are they physically out of sight (in basements, in kitchens, working at night when everyone else has gone), they are out of mind.

In documenting sex-based inequalities in employment, social scientists have produced reams of statistics. But there are many other ways in which we may speak of the gendering of work, some not easily quantifiable. Joan Acker (1990) writes about the process by which jobs and organizations come to be gendered regardless of the sex of job-holders. The bureaucratic rules and procedures, hierarchies, and informal organizational culture may rest on a set of gender-biased assumptions, for example. In *Secretaries Talk* (1988), Rosemary Pringle highlights the ways in which gendered family relationships are reproduced in workplace relations between bosses (husbands, fathers) and secretaries (wives, mistresses, daughters). "Male bosses go into their secretaries' offices unannounced, assume the right to pronounce on their clothes and appearance, have them doing housework and personal chores, expect overtime at short notice and assume the right to ring them at home" (Pringle 1988, 51).

Today, many young women plan to both have a professional career and raise a family, but they are not quite sure how they will combine the two. Feminist researchers have demonstrated how the very concept of "career" is gendered, built on a masculine model. Career success depends on the assumption of a wife at home—a helper who will pick up the children from school, arrange dinner parties, and generally free the "breadwinner" to work late at nights or on weekends and for out-of-town business travel.

Furthermore, feminist analysis has called attention to the complex link between paid and unpaid labour, employment and family (Corman and Luxton 2007; Eichler et al. 2010; Fox 2009). With two breadwinners, both of whom spend increasing hours in their paid jobs, families are under enormous pressure. While the demands of paid work have risen over time, so too have pressures on family life. Government restructuring and cutbacks in resources have affected public daycare, after-school programs, special needs programs, and care of the elderly and the disabled. Who picks up the slack? The family. One consequence has been an intensification of (unpaid) family work, more stress, and growing tensions within families as people try to cope.

RACE AND RACIALIZED WORK

Although we now have an abundance of research on the gendering of work, sociologists in Canada have paid far less attention to the relationship between race, citizenship, and employment. Barriers faced by people of colour, Aboriginal Canadians, and some immigrant groups are most often demonstrated in unemployment and earnings disparities. Aboriginal peoples comprise only a tiny percentage of the working-age population, yet this group is growing rapidly and over the next 20 years will constitute a sizable share of new entrants to the labour force in certain parts of Canada (Jackson 2009, 146). Although one should be wary of making broad generalizations about the diverse group of people who identify as Aboriginals, one clear observation is that on the whole they are disadvantaged in the labour market. Disadvantage is linked to systemic discrimination generally, in addition to low levels of education and patterns of geographic residence (Jackson 2009, 146–7).

The **unemployment rate** for Aboriginals is disturbingly high in comparison to that for the Canadian population as a whole (16.1 per cent for Aboriginal men and 13.5 per cent for Aboriginal women). And for Aboriginal youth (aged 20 to 24) specifically, the rate of unemployment is 20.8 per cent (Jackson 2009, 147). In addition, more than half of Aboriginals are in part-time employment—jobs that offer little security—and they are concentrated in marginalized sectors of the economy where they face low pay, seasonal jobs, and high levels of discrimination in hiring (www.canadianlabour.ca/index.php/Aboriginal Workers/464). The economic prospects for those who live on reserves are even more bleak. Close to half of the on-reserve Aboriginal population live in poverty (Jackson and Robinson 2000, 71).

The category "people of colour" is likewise quite diverse, containing notable differences according to class, education, and citizenship status. In Canada, about one in ten workers is defined as being of colour or as a racialized person (the official census term is "visible minority" and excludes Aboriginal Canadians), and currently, one in five Canadians is foreign-born (Jackson 2009, 135). Labour market inequities remain even when we control for age and education. According to the 2006 census, "visible-minority" workers aged 25 to 44 with a university degree earned 74.6 per cent of the median for the group as a whole, while "non-visible"-minority earners made 105 per cent of the median. Even second-generation visible-minority earners in this age and educational category earned less than their non-visible-minority counterparts ($14,675 compared to $46,172) (Jackson 2009, 145–6). Typically, recent immigrants are younger than the labour force as a whole, but they also have more schooling. One problem is that foreign credentials are not always respected in Canada, thus contributing to a high concentration of immigrants of colour in low-wage jobs (Jackson and Robinson 2000, 69–70). Refer to Chapter 8 for more information.

Though telling, statistics reveal only one dimension of the research on disadvantaged groups. It is equally important to recognize that because of racial and cultural differences, people experience the work world in distinct ways. In their classic study *Who Gets the Work*, Frances Henry and Effie Ginzberg (1985) found a striking incidence of discrimination directed at job seekers. For example, when whites and blacks with similar qualifications applied for entry-level positions that had been advertised in a newspaper, jobs were offered three times more often to whites than to black applicants. Similarly, of the job seekers who made inquiries by telephone, those who had accents (especially South Asian and Caribbean) were often quickly screened out by employers.

Furthermore, the role of the Canadian state historically in promoting or facilitating racialized work has been documented extensively (Schecter 1998). Agnes Calliste (1993) notes that between 1950 and 1962, Canadian immigration authorities admitted limited numbers of Caribbean nurses but under rules different from those for white immigrant nurses. Black nurses were expected to have nursing qualifications superior to those demanded of whites. Several scholars (Arat-Koc 1990; Daenzer 1993; Macklin 1992; Stasiulis and Bakan 2005) have also discussed the role of the Canadian state in addressing the need for cheap child-care workers by importing women from the developing world (the Caribbean and the Philippines in particular) to perform domestic labour, without granting them full citizenship rights.

YOUTH AND WORK

In Canada today, youth (persons 15 to 24 years old) constitute a much smaller share of the population than in past years. Nevertheless, the youth labour market is expanding at a significant rate. Study after study suggest that young people are in important ways no different from the majority of Canadian workers. They want high-quality work—work that is interesting and challenging and that provides a sense of accomplishment. And youth have been increasing their human capital to acquire such jobs. Notably, young people are acquiring more education. (While a university degree does not guarantee a job, young people are still better off if they have the formal credentials.) But while Canadian youth are better schooled on the whole, they are also working less and in jobs for which they feel they are overqualified. Young people are most likely to be employed in low-paying service-sector jobs such as in fast-food restaurants, clothing stores, and grocery stores. For most students, contingent work is all that is available.

Some writers argue that the youth labour market makes a perfect accompaniment to the new goals of managerial flexibility. Employers invest in the belief that young people will have a limited commitment to the goals of the firm and that they expect to stay in jobs temporarily as a stop-gap measure discontinuous with their adult careers and identities (Tannock 2001). Stuart Tannock explains that youth themselves partially accept the popular **ideology** that positions them "as a separate class of workers who deserve less than adult workers do. Good jobs are predominantly the privilege of adulthood. Young workers must be content at first to spend their time in a tier of lower-quality service and retail employment. Dreams of meaningful work must be deferred" (2001, 109). Many young people compare themselves not to other workers across the spectrum but exclusively to other youth workers (Sennett 1998). Consequently, youth are more pliable and passive. Also, because their jobs are viewed as transient, youths are not as likely to become unionized. All of these features render them an extremely exploitable source of labour.

But as Tannock points out, youth are not stop-gap workers simply because they are young: they are also stop-gap workers because of the poor conditions under which they have to labour—conditions that have been created by employers in the service sector. Despite the popular view that young people are not especially concerned about their conditions of work, there is now much evidence that points to the contrary: "Teenagers and young adults working in these industries, who expect to have long lives ahead of them, worry that their jobs, which are supposed to be meaningless, stop-gap places of employment, will have lasting and detrimental effects on their bodies and future life activities" (Tannock 2001, 54).

Workers' Coping and Resistance: The Struggle for Dignity and Rights

FINDING MEANING IN WORK

Regardless of the many differences among Canadian workers today, one point remains clear: most Canadians want work that is personally fulfilling (Lowe 2000). People have a powerful desire to maintain dignity at work

(Hodson 2001). Some of us are fortunate enough to hold jobs that offer challenge, jobs in which we can exercise autonomy and from which we can reap fruitful economic rewards. But even the "good jobs" are not always meaningful, and there are many jobs that are rarely rewarding. How do people cope with their work?

Sociologists have found that no matter how meaningless the job, people seek meaning in their work. Sometimes this is done through the culture of the workplace. People who have boring, routine jobs, for example, may make a game out of their work, varying repetitions, altering pace and intensity, imagining the lives of customers. As well, the social component of work (peer relations) is frequently a source of pleasure. In some workplaces, employees regularly exchange gossip, flirt, share personal problems, debate politics, and ridicule management. Relationships with co-workers often make the job itself more bearable if not meaningful. In cases where the organization of work permits such exchanges, the lines between employment and leisure can become blurred.

Job satisfaction studies suggest that work is not all that bad. Most people report that they are generally satisfied with their jobs (Lowe 2000). On close examination, though, discontent broods near the surface. At the same time that they report satisfaction, a majority of workers say that their jobs are somewhat or highly stressful, that they are not sufficiently involved, recognized, and rewarded, and that their talents are underutilized (Lowe 2000). In addition, there are high rates of absenteeism, oppositional attitudes, slacking off, pilfering, and even destruction of company property. Some workers simply quit their jobs. But in the face of a competitive job market, family responsibilities, consumer debt, and, for some, limited marketable skills, this is not always a viable option. Furthermore, it is telling that even though they claim to like their jobs, many people add that they do not want their own children to end up doing the same kind of work (Sennett 1998).

Faced with unfair, unsafe, and sometimes unchallenging work, workers will be discontented. They will find ways to make changes, to resist. The question is, how? Individual acts of coping and resistance may give workers the feeling of agency and control, but insofar as they are individual acts, they rarely result in a fundamental or widespread change in conditions of work. In order to effect large-scale change, people must resort to collective measures.

LABOUR UNIONS AND LABOUR'S AGENDA

When most of us think of unions, strikes come to mind. Some of us may view trade unionists as just a bunch of greedy, overpaid workers demanding higher wages and in the process disrupting our lives, transportation, communication—even our garbage collection. We may owe this perception to dominant media representations of unions, their members, and their leaders.

The labour movement in this country goes far beyond this narrow and unfair characterization. The basic premise of the organized labour movement is to take collective action through the process of bargaining a contract. This *collective agreement* is the outcome of days, weeks, or even months of negotiations between two parties: worker representatives and company representatives. The contract is a legally binding document, an agreement that has been signed by both the employer and the union. Only if the two parties cannot reach an agreement is there potential for strike action. The actual incidence of strikes in Canada is, in fact, low. Recently, throughout the entire country, there have only been 300 to 400 work stoppages per year, and they involved 100,000 to 400,000 workers. While one-third of all employees are members of unions, annual time lost due to strikes has typically been far less than one-tenth of 1 per cent of total working time (Jackson 2009, 202). The strike is usually a measure of last resort. The vast majority of contracts that come up for renewal are settled without the union's resorting to strike action.

Workers in the nineteenth century first struggled to secure union representation in an effort to protect themselves against excessively long workdays, extremely hazardous work environments, low pay, and blatant favouritism on the job. Today, labour–management conflict arises over a host of issues. Not only are wages an item of dispute, but companies and union representatives also negotiate benefits packages, job security, the implementation of technological change, outsourcing, concessions, and anti-harassment policies. Because of the struggles of union members, Canadian workers in offices, stores, and factories now have the

UNDER the WIRE

Privacy in the Workplace

We spend so much of our lives at work: what about our right to privacy as employees? . . . Just as employers are demanding "more work for less pay," they are also demanding or simply taking more and more of our personal information. We are being screened, tested, monitored, and reported like never before. Put simply, organizations have voracious appetites for employee (and lots of other) information, together with the computer communications, surveillance, and other technological means to feed them. Practically all large organizations need to go on personal information diets. . . .

Who knows us better than our employers? Their files and databases include our hiring, pay and benefits information, banking, insurance, family matters, pictures, personal identifiers and contacts, attendance, sick leave, claim and medical information, performance and other career-related records, grievances and other complaint files, "challenges" we're having (at work or otherwise), investigations, discipline . . . the list is a long one. It's just about all there.

In larger organizations, employee information is collected, "shared," used in decision-making, and retained by great numbers of supervisory, personnel, finance, security, and other officials. Increasingly, their operators . . . are computerized. By definition, computers enable far more access to employee information, by far more people, far faster than ever before. The privacy risks of massive breaches are far greater, too, and although violations are usually inadvertent, the damage is sometimes irreparable. . . .

An estimated 75 per cent of companies in the United States electronically monitor their employees. Video surveillance cameras are multiplying like rabbits, and everybody seems to need to wear ID cards these days to enter or move around unthreatened workplaces. Maybe your employer has gone hi-tech with biometric tracking or radio frequency identification (RFID). One would think we all had "top secret" jobs and that none of us could be trusted, regardless of long service.

SOURCE: Sharp 2006.

(© CP Images/Tibor Kolley/The Globe and Mail)

The annual Labour Day parade and celebration in Toronto was inspired by the printers' strike of 1872. The Toronto Typographical Union successfully campaigned for a nine-hour workday (www.thecanadianencyclopedia.com/featured/origins-of-labour-day)

right to refuse unsafe work, the right to participate in company-sponsored pension plans, and, in some cases, access to on-site daycare centres.

The Union Advantage

There is absolutely no doubt that unionization benefits workers (see Table 11.1). Collective bargaining has secured for employees advantages in wages, benefits, job security, and extended health plans. This has been called the *union advantage*. The union wage premium in particular is greatest for (traditionally disadvantaged) workers who would otherwise be low-paid. Unionization tends to compress wage and benefit differentials and thereby promote an equalization of wages and working conditions among unionized workforces. In 2007, for example, average hourly earnings of unionized workers in Canada were $23.48, while for non-unionized workers the average hourly rate was $18.98, thereby representing a union advantage of 24.2 per cent. The difference in wages between unionized and non-unionized women was even greater. In 2007, the union

TABLE 11.1 ▼ The Union Advantage, 2007

	Union in $	Non-Union in $	Union Advantage in $	Union Advantage as % of Non-Union
All	23.58	18.98	4.60	24.2
Men	24.38	21.20	3.18	15.0
Women	22.79	16.71	6.08	36.4
Ages 15–24	14.45	11.63	2.82	24.2
By occupation:				
Professionals in business, finance	30.03	28.94	1.09	3.8
Secretary, administration	22.00	19.05	2.95	15.5
Clerical, supervisors	20.12	15.92	4.20	26.4
Natural sciences	29.61	28.32	1.29	4.6
Heath, nursing	29.96	29.22	0.74	2.5
Assist. health occupation	21.05	18.94	2.11	11.1
Social sciences	26.13	21.64	4.50	20.8
Teacher, professor	30.45	23.44	7.01	29.9
Art, culture, recreation	24.42	19.33	5.09	26.3
Mainly low-wage private services:				
Retail, sales, cashier	13.02	11.40	1.62	14.2
Chefs, cooks	15.22	11.42	3.80	33.2
Protective services	23.68	16.81	6.87	40.9
Child care	17.88	11.56	6.32	54.7
Sales, service, travel	15.18	11.26	3.92	34.8
Blue-collar:				
Construction trades	24.76	18.50	6.26	33.8
Other trades	25.76	19.60	6.16	31.4
Transport equipment	21.62	17.00	4.62	27.2
Trades helpers	21.01	14.41	6.60	45.8
Primary industry	22.29	16.69	5.60	33.5
Machine operators	20.75	17.10	3.65	21.3
Process, manufacturing	17.38	13.07	4.31	32.9

SOURCE: Statistics Canada, *Labour Force Survey* (Ottawa: Statistics Canada, 2007). Taken from Andrew Jackson, *Work and Labour in Canada: Critical Issues*, 2nd edn, p. 207 (Toronto: Canadian Scholars' Press, 2009).

advantage for women was $6.08 as compared to $3.50 for men (Jackson 2009, 208).

TIME to REFLECT

Imagine that you are employed in a non-unionized workplace, and a union organizer is seeking to enlist union members and certify your workplace. Would you support this action? In what ways does union membership shape the experience of work?

Conclusion: Work in the Future, Our Future as Workers

Workers and unions, of course, have limited powers. While newspaper headlines promote the "big" collective bargaining gains of the most strongly organized unions, most unionized workers across the country are still struggling to attain basic rights that others managed to secure years, if not decades, earlier. Every day in small workplaces, employees (unionized and non-unionized) negotiate their rights. More often now than in the past, these employees are women, people of colour, the disabled—not members of the dominant groups in this country.

These struggles have been difficult and continue to be so, particularly in the context of the current assault on unions. Powerful corporations effectively curb workers' rights to organize by simply closing down stores, mounting strong union decertification campaigns, or stalling when it comes time to bargain a first contract. The power of workers and their movements is being even more severely circumscribed by the aggressiveness of global capitalists, many of whom are openly supported by networks of governments in both developing and developed nations. Whether you work part-time at Gap, labour a 60-hour week in a steel factory, freelance as a consultant, or find sporadic office employment through a temporary help agency, you face a challenge.

Regardless of theoretical perspective or political agenda, scholars today are debating the nature of the challenge of the transformation of work. Both young people entering the

labour market for the first time and middle-aged people confronting reconfigured jobs and refashioned workplaces are part of this transformation. Workers, young and old, must work in order to survive, to nurture families, to participate in life. Given this reality, it is crucial to know the debate, engage in it, and perhaps transform the world of work according to your own vision.

questions for critical thought

1. Think about where you are located in the economy. If you are not currently employed, where do you plan to find work? How does this depart from your parents' and grandparents' work histories? What factors have shaped (or constrained) your work-related aspirations?

2. Think about the work that you perform in the course of an average day. What proportion of this is paid and what unpaid? Do you believe that we should define unpaid domestic activities as "work" that is of economic worth? If you were asked to calculate the economic worth of unpaid domestic labour, how would you begin? What factors would you take into account?

3. Most people in Canada today take the new computer technology for granted, but as a sociologist, you must take a closer, critical look. Consider some of the ways in which computer technology has reshaped employment opportunities and the nature of work.

4. A prevailing view is that the youth today are merely "stop-gap" workers. They are young and resilient. As they mature, they will move on to better, more secure and fulfilling employment. Thus, their conditions of work are not problematic. Young people themselves are not concerned about the nature of the jobs that they perform. Why should sociologists bother writing about youth at work?

recommended readings

Meg Luxton and June Corman. 2001. *Getting by in Hard Times: Gendered Labour at Home and on the Job.* Toronto: University of Toronto Press.
In this study, based on a series of interviews with women and men in families having one member employed at Stelco's manufacturing plant in Hamilton, Ontario, the authors demonstrate how working families are coping in the face of the economic restructuring that began in the 1980s.

Norene J. Pupo and Mark P. Thomas, eds. 2010. *Interrogating the Economy: Restructuring Work in the 21st Century.* Toronto: University of Toronto Press.
Pupo and Thomas offer a timely collection of articles based on Canadian research on the many features that define work today in the context of economic and political change.

Richard Sennett. 1998. *The Corrosion of Character: The Personal Consequences of Work in the New Capitalism.* New York: Norton.
This book provides a meaningful, eloquent critique by one of America's finest sociologists of the consequences of the new flexible workplace on individual lives and moral identity.

Rachel Sherman. 2007. *Class Acts: Service and Inequality in Luxury Hotels.* Berkeley: University of California Press.
This is an engaging ethnographic study of the invisible and semi-visible workers in two luxury hotels that makes a sobering comment on class relations and the normalization of inequality in the service industry in the United States.

recommended websites

Canadian Centre for Occupational Health and Safety (CCOHS)
www.ccohs.ca
The CCOHS, based in Hamilton, Ontario, promotes a safe and healthy working environment by providing information and advice about occupational health and safety issues.

Canadian Centre for Policy Alternatives (CCPA)
www.policyalternatives.ca
The CCPA offers an alternative to the message that we have no choice about the policies that affect our lives, undertaking and promoting research on issues of social and economic justice.

International Labour Organization (ILO)
www.ilo.org
The ILO was founded in 1919 and is now an agency of the United Nations. Its mandate is to promote and realize standards, fundamental principles, and rights at work.

LabourStart
www.labourstart.org
LabourStart is a web-based news organization that provides up-to-the-minute information on a wide variety of labour-related issues and developments around the globe. Visitors to this site can find anything from job advertisements in Australia to information on latest strikes in the United Kingdom and reviews of recently published books.

chapter 12

Health Issues

Juanne Clarke

In this chapter, you will:

▶ See how health, illness, and disease need to be differentiated.

▶ Learn that health, illness, disease, and death are integrally related to social inequality globally.

▶ Examine medicare as a system that embodies five principles: portability, universality, comprehensive coverage, public administration, and accessibility.

▶ Consider how privatization is increasing in the Canadian medical system.

▶ Learn that medicalization is a powerful cultural and social force.

Introduction

Canada is a part of a cross-national health research initiative sponsored by the World Health Organization. Every four years since 1990, a survey called the Health Behaviour in School Aged Children (HBSC) has been carried out. It includes answers to questions about the health-related behaviours and attitudes of more than 7000 Canadian students from five grades (6, 7, 8, 9, and 10). Some of you may have been in the survey at one point or another. Taking a **social determinants** approach, the survey explains health in the context of social issues such as socio-economic status, gender, and health or risk-taking behaviours—for instance, cigarette smoking, unprotected sex, and alcohol consumption. You might not be surprised to learn that while most students said that their emotional health was good, between 20 and 30 per cent said they had some form of emotional problem. Girls were more likely to report depression and headaches increasingly as they aged to Grade 10. Boys and girls reported similar levels of irritability and backache. Emotional suffering seemed to be at its highest level in Grade 7, which usually occurs at a time of transition to middle school. Young people who got along better with their parents and had higher socio-economic status withstood this major transition better than those who did not. As this brief illustration demonstrates, health is linked to social, economic, and school policies (among other social variables).

What do you think are some significant health issues facing Canadians today? Do you think immediately of HIV/AIDS, alcoholism, cancer, or heart disease? Or do you think of the medical care system and topics in the news such as long waiting lists for emergency service, the apparent lack of available physicians, or the devastating effects of hospital-acquired infections? This chapter will introduce you to some sociological perspectives on topics such as these that are related to the sociology of health, illness, and medicine.

Health is linked inextricably to the social order. Its very definition, its multitudinous causes, and its consequences all are social. What is considered healthy in one culture or society may not be considered healthy in another. Rates, as well as understandings, of sickness and death vary across time and place. Social classes differ in their definitions of health. What a woman considers health may be different from a man's definition of health. Class and gender differences lead to varying levels of health and sickness and different rates of death.

The first part of this chapter will examine several issues in the sociology of health: the changing health of Canadians over the nineteenth and twentieth centuries; HIV/AIDS; environmental health problems in different parts of Canada; social inequality; social capital and health; the sense of coherence; and obesity and eating disorders. The second part of the chapter will investigate some of the most important sociological concerns in the area of medical sociology, including **medicalization**, the future of the health-care system, and **privatization**.

Theoretical Perspectives

Four theoretical paradigms may be considered the most significant approaches to understanding health and medicine sociologically: structural functionalism, conflict theory, **interpretive theory**, and feminism/anti-racism.

STRUCTURAL FUNCTIONALISM

From the structural functionalist perspective, health is necessary for the smooth running of the social system. In a stable society, all institutional forces work together to create and maintain good health for the population. Your university or college assumes your good health as it organizes its courses and exams—you probably have to get a letter from a doctor for exemption from writing a test or an exam. The smooth functioning of societies depends on the good health of their members. For instance, societies are organized to support a population up to an average **life expectancy** and at a given level of health and ability. This normative standard of health and age at death are reinforced by political, economic, cultural, and educational policy.

A classic statement of the structural functionalist perspective is found in the work of Talcott Parsons (1951), in particular in his concept of the **sick role**. The sick role is to be thought of as a special social role. It exists to prevent sickness from disrupting social life and legitimates what might otherwise be viewed as deviant behaviour. It does this by attributing certain rights and duties to sickness.

There are two rights and two duties for those who want to claim sickness and engage in the sick role. The rights include the right to be exempted from normal social roles and the right to be free of blame or responsibility for the sickness. The duties are to want to get well and to seek and co-operate with technically competent help. However, these theoretically derived ideas do not always have empirical support. For example, it is well known that the right to be exempt from the performance of social roles depends in part on the cause or nature of the sickness. A hangover, for instance, may not be considered a good enough reason to claim the sick role as an excuse for an exam exemption. Many people with HIV/AIDS continue to be stigmatized or blamed for their condition. And with respect to duties, not everyone is expected to want to get well. Indeed, those with a chronic disease such as diabetes are expected to accept their condition and learn to live with it. Parsons assumed the dominance of **allopathic medicine** in his statement that a sick person was to get technically competent help. Today, however, many people believe that the best help may not always come from allopathic medicine even though it is the state-supported type of medical care. Indeed, a substantial minority—about 26 per cent of Canadians—used an alternative approach such as acupuncture, chiropractic, or homeopathic methods to treat a health problem, according to a 2011 international survey (Deloitte Center for Health Solutions 2011, 23).

CONFLICT THEORY

From the perspective of conflict theory, health and ill-health result from inequitable and unjust economic conditions. Questions driving this perspective include: Are the poor more likely to get sick? Is the **mortality rate** (the frequency of death per a specified number of people over a particular period of time) among the poor higher than among the rich? Does racism affect the **morbidity** (sickness) **rate** (the frequency of sickness per a specified number of people over a particular period of time)? In this perspective, health is seen as a good that is inequitably located in society.

More than a quarter of Canadians now seek medical treatment with alternative medicines.

(© iStockphoto/temmuz can arsiray)

A classic statement of this position is found in the work of Friedrich Engels, who often wrote with Karl Marx. In his book *The Condition of the Working Class in England* (1994 [1845]), Engels demonstrated the negative health consequences of early capitalism. He described how the development of capitalism advanced mechanism in agriculture and forced farmworkers off the land and into the cities to survive. Capitalists in the cities sought profit regardless of the cost to the well-being of the workers. Owners maintained low costs through poor wages and long hours of backbreaking labour in filthy and noisy working conditions.

As a consequence, poor labourers and their families lived exceedingly rough lives in shelters that offered little or no privacy, cleanliness, or quiet. They had very little money for food, and the quality of the foodstuffs available in the cities was poor. The slum-like living conditions were perfect breeding grounds for all sorts of diseases, and because of the high density of living quarters, the lack of facilities for toileting and washing, and the frequent lack of clean drinking water, the morbidity and mortality rates in the slums were very high. Infectious diseases spread quickly and with dire results.

Epidemics were almost common in nineteenth-century industrial cities, where overcrowding, overflowing cesspits, garbage piled all around, and unsafe water were the norm. It was only after new discoveries in bacteriology, when it became clear that many of the worst diseases were spread by bacteria and viruses in the water, air, and food, that governments enacted public health measures. These new prevention policies included sewage disposal, garbage removal, cleaned and filtered drinking water, and hygienic handling of food. The death rates began to abate (Crompton 2000).

INTERPRETIVE THEORIES

Interpretation and meaning are the hallmarks of sociology within interpretive theories. What is the meaning, for example, of anorexia and bulimia? Are they medical conditions? Are they the result of a moral choice? Or could they be considered "socio-somatic" conditions—that is, caused by society (Currie 1988)? Various authors have attributed them to women's "hunger strike" against their contradictory positions, against culturally prescribed images, and against lack of opportunities in contemporary society. They have been conceptualized as a means "through which women, both unconsciously and consciously, protest the social conditions of womanhood" (Currie 1988, 208).

Stigma is often attached to the person with HIV/AIDS, lung cancer, or mental illness. Some people think these diseases have connotations of immorality. Good health is even associated with being a good person. A study of the blogs of people who self-identify as having Asperger's (AS) and their parents or caregivers (Clarke and Van Amerom 2008) found that these two groups held not only different but even oppositional interpretations of AS. People who self-identified as having Asperger's rejected the popular but denigrating understanding of AS. They called themselves Aspies. They called others NTs or neurotypicals. They said they were proud of who they were and of the way they thought. They said that they felt the major problems they faced were not due to the "disorder" or the "limitations" they suffered because of AS but resulted from the stigma of AS and the way that others perceived and acted toward them. Parents and caregivers, on the other hand, expressed worry about their children's problems in schooling and in their social lives. Parents tended to accept the dominant and pathologizing view of AS, while the bloggers who self-identified as having AS expressed pride and mutual solidarity.

FEMINISM/ANTI-RACISM

Feminist and anti-racist health sociology recognizes the centrality of gender and racialization to social life. Feminist/anti-racist health sociology investigates whether, how, and why people who are racialized and men and women have different health and illness profiles, as well as different causes and average ages of death. It also often includes a dynamic consideration of the intersection of such things as ethnicity, sexual preference, gender identity, and ability/disability and health. These axes of inequality, therefore, are central issues to be included in designing research, uncovering social injustice, and planning and making social change.

King, in *Pink Ribbons, Inc.*, demonstrates how the focus on consumer activism, especially among white women in the breast cancer movement, "shaped as it is by an ideology of individualism and an imperative for uncomplicated, snappy marketing slogans," has obfuscated prevention efforts and failed to address inequities in incidence and treatment availability (King 2006, 117–18). She argues that the corporations involved in breast cancer awareness and fundraising have benefited from their involvement, possibly to the detriment of women's health.

The Sociology of Health, Illness, Disease, and Sickness

At the broadest level sociologists compare the rates of, causes of, and treatments for health and sickness and causes of death within societies around the world and over time. Here, factors such as wars, famine, drought, epidemics, natural disasters, air and water quality, quantity and quality of foodstuffs, transportation safety, level and type of economic development, technology, available birth control,

GLOBAL ISSUES

Warfare and Human Health

Human health depends on the complex interaction of manifold social determinants that operate across a number of levels, as portrayed in Figure 12.1. An important part of this picture is international and intra-national conflict. The twentieth century was the most violent century in history. Almost three times the number of people who died in conflict during the previous four centuries died in the twentieth century. This is partly due to the huge numbers massacred in World Wars I and II and partly due to the overall frequency of conflict. The Rwandan genocide in 1994, for instance, resulted in the deaths of approximately 1 million people. The civil war in the Democratic Republic of the Congo killed 7 per cent of the population of that country, and the several-decades-old conflict in Sudan has resulted in 2 million deaths and the displacement of 6 million people. Over time, conflict has increasingly occurred in the poorest countries of the world.

The consequences of conflict for health are many. Wars inevitably result in death, disability, and rape. They also result in the destruction of the infrastructure necessary for everyday living for the masses of people affected. This destruction occurs in food production, storage, and distribution systems. It limits or eliminates access to potable water, sewage systems, and electricity, not only for homes but for hospitals. Fundamentals such as roads, houses, schools, and health-care facilities are also affected and frequently destroyed or damaged. Other negative consequences include chronic and acute psychological trauma and distress. The majority of the countries that have experienced war have child death rates that have either stagnated or worsened after the conflicts.

The World Bank has suggested that a civil war reduces the growth of a nation's economy by about 2.2 per cent per year and costs an average of $54 billion for a low-income country. The longer a conflict lasts, the greater the toll on all fronts, from the human to the economic.

immunization, pharmaceuticals, medicalization, culture, and political economy all are considered relevant.

At the next level, sociologists examine morbidity and mortality within societies and cultures and compare people of different social class, educational levels, genders, religiosity, rural/urban locations, occupations, ethnicities, family statuses, and so on. A further level of investigation concerns the way sociopsychological factors, such as level of stress and sense of coherence, are implicated in illness, disease, and sickness.

The next level is an examination of the relationships between various "lifestyle" behaviours, such as smoking, seat-belt use, alcohol consumption, diet, risk-taking behaviours, sexual activity and protection, drug use, and health. Finally, the existential considerations, including the meaning and the experience of morbidity and mortality to individuals, are studied. Figure 12.1 shows these links, beginning from the person.

In this chapter, we will look at specific topics within each of these levels of analysis, beginning with the changing health of Canadians over the nineteenth and twentieth centuries, HIV/AIDS in Canada and around the world, and environmental issues (including the water crisis in Walkerton, Ontario) as examples of first-level concerns. At the second level, we will look at social inequity and social capital. At the third level, the focus will be on sense of coherence. Fourth, we will investigate eating-disordered behaviour and attitudes, including obesity. The fifth and final level is briefly discussed with reference to popular cultural conceptions of illness such as those found in major motion pictures. This separation into levels is artificial and done only for reasons of analytical clarity. In fact, each of the levels influences all the other levels in reciprocal ways.

COMPARATIVE ANALYSES

The Changing Health of Canadians

People generally are living longer and healthier lives today than they did in the past. In the nineteenth century, infectious and communicable diseases such as cholera, typhoid, diphtheria,

▼ **FIGURE 12.1** Components of Health

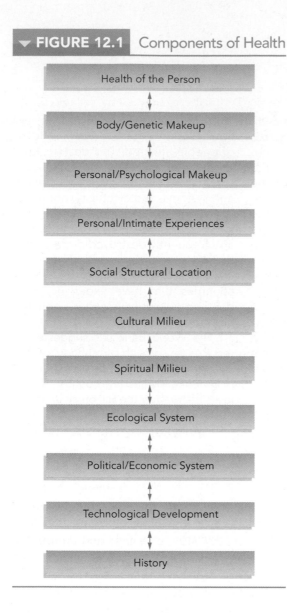

the spread of disease. These measures included improved nutrition, better hygiene through sanitation and water purification practices, and advances in birth control. Interventions such as these brought the average life expectancy to 59 in the 1920s and, largely because of dramatic declines in infant mortality, to 78 in 1990–2 (Crompton 2000, 12).

> Understanding the causes and consequences of population growth informs key health-care policies and practices. See "Demographic Indicators" in Chapter 16, p. 321, for a more detailed discussion.

One other important feature of the declines in mortality or gains in life expectancy is the gap between men and women and how this gap has changed over time. From 1920 to 1922, women lived an average of two years longer than men; from 1990 to 1992, they lived an average of six years longer than men. Now, women live almost five years longer. Part of the explanation for women's greater benefit from the changes of the twentieth century relates

TABLE 12.1 ▼ Health Indicators, Canada, 2009

	Males	Females
Life expectancy at birth (years)*	78.8	83.3
Infant mortality rate (deaths per 1000 live births)**	5.1	4.7
Babies with low birth weight (%)***	5.7	6.5
Health-adjusted life expectancy****	68.3	70.8
Daily smokers (%)*****	22.6	17.7

SOURCES:
* Human Resources and Skills Development Canada, "Health—Life expectancy at birth," www4.hrsdc.gc.ca/.3ndic.1t.4r@-eng.jsp?iid=3
** Human Resources and Skills Development Canada, "Family life—Infant mortality," www4.hrsdc.gc.ca/.3ndic.1t.4r@-eng.jsp?iid=2
*** Human Resources and Skills Development Canada, "Health—Low birth weight," www4.hrsdc.gc.ca/.3ndic.1t.4r@-eng.jsp?iid=4
**** Statistics Canada, "Health-adjusted life expectancy, by sex" www.statcan.gc.ca/tables-tableaux/sum-som/l01/cst01/hlth67-eng.htm
***** Statistics Canada, "Smoking, 2009" www.statcan.gc.ca/pub/82-625-x/2010002/article/11268-eng.htm

and scarlet fever were rampant and often fatal. Wound infections and septicemia were frequent results of dangerous and unhygienic working, living, and medical conditions. Puerperal fever killed many women during and after childbirth.

In 1831, the average life expectancy for Canadian men and women was 39.0 years—38.3 for women and 39.8 for men (Clarke 2008, 50). Today, life expectancies are about double this for Canadian men and women: women can expect to live to 83.3; men, to 78.8 (Statistics Canada 2012a). What has happened to cause this dramatic shift? You might think first of medical interventions such as antibiotics or immunization. However, the most important causes of the increase in life expectancy are related to public health measures that prevented

to the decline in maternal mortality over this period. Another part of the explanation has been the greater tendency for men to engage in risk-taking behaviours such as cigarette smoking and drunk-driving.

TIME to REFLECT

The *HPV* vaccine was first introduced for preteen girls in Canada in 2007. It is now being marketed to young boys. Why was it not introduced for boys at the same time that it was for girls?

TABLE 12.2 ▼ Leading Causes of Death, Canada, 1921–5 and 2008	
1921–5	**Percentage (%)**
Cardiovascular and renal disease	21.5
Influenza, bronchitis, and pneumonia	13.7
Diseases of early infancy	10.8
Tuberculosis	8.3
Cancer	7.4
Gastritis, duodenitis, enteritis, and colitis	7
Accidents	5
Communicable diseases	4.6
2008	**Percentage (%)**
Malignant neoplasms (cancer)	29.6
Heart disease	21.3
Cerebrovascular diseases (stroke)	5.8
Chronic lower respiratory diseases	4.6
Accidents	4.3
Diabetes	3.2
Alzheimer's disease	2.8
Influenza and pneumonia	2.3
Nephritis, nephrotic syndrome and nephrosis (kidney disease)	1.6
Intentional self-harm (suicide)	1.6

Disease categories are not identical over time.
Rates are age-standardized.
SOURCES: Statistics Canada, *Canadian Social Trends*, Catalogue no. 11-008, winter 2000, p.13; Statistics Canada, CANSIM Table 102-0552 and Catalogue no. 840209X, www.statcan.gc.ca/pub/11-008-x/11-008-x2000003-eng.pdf; Statistics Canada, *Leading Causes of Death in Canada, 2008*, www.statcan.gc.ca/pub/84-215-x/2011001/table-tableau/tbl001-eng.htm

HIV/AIDS

HIV/AIDS is a disease of pandemic proportions around the world today (see Figure 12.2). Many people in North America have come to associate the disease with certain categories of other people. For example, they may think of HIV/AIDS as the male "gay disease" (Crossley 2002). In an international context, however, HIV/AIDS is almost as common among heterosexual women as among men: in 1997, 59 per cent of those diagnosed internationally were male, and 41 per cent were female; by the latest count, about 50 per cent were male and 50 per cent female (www.who.int/gender/hiv_aids/en). In sub-Saharan Africa, however, more women than men are HIV-positive (this means that they carry the precursor virus but have not yet developed AIDS). In some of the sub-Saharan African countries where the disease has taken its highest toll, teenage girls are five to six times as likely to be infected as boys. Whether because they themselves are diagnosed with the disease or because they are much more likely to act as caregivers to others who are sick, women are substantially more affected by the AIDS epidemic than men in Africa. Already, too, in Africa, more than 1 million children are living with HIV, and more than 12.1 million children have been orphaned by the disease. Children who are orphaned because of AIDS bear the additional burdens of stigma and decreased access to health and education. In turn, they are more susceptible to becoming infected by HIV/AIDS (UNAIDS 2001, 2). At present, it is estimated that about 34 million people are living with HIV/AIDS globally (range 31.6–35.2) (www.avert.org/worldstats.htm).

Even though the incidence and prevalence of HIV/AIDS is much lower here, Canada is not exempt from the epidemic. By 2009, this country had experienced a cumulative total of 20,746 AIDS cases and 69,844 cases of HIV. Until the mid-1990s, women made up only 7 per cent of the total AIDS cases in Canada. By 2009, they accounted for more than 20 per cent of the new cases each year. Overall, however, the increase in disease incidence reached its peak in 1993, and diagnoses have been gradually declining since then (www.avert.org/canada-aids.htm).

▼ FIGURE 12.2   Estimated Adult and Child Deaths Due to AIDS, 2008

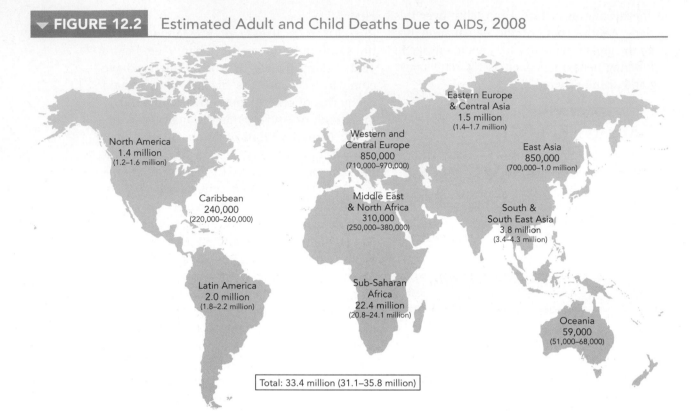

SOURCE: From www.unaids.org/en/KnowledgeCentre/HIVData/EpiUpdate/EpiUpdArchive/2009/default.asp. Reprinted with permission from UNAIDS.

The most common means of transmission in Canada has been among men who have sex with men (MSM). Among women, the majority of cases are attributed to heterosexual contact. HIV/AIDS is overrepresented among Aboriginal people and black Canadians. Aboriginal and black people constituted 3.3 per cent and 2.2 per cent of the population, respectively, but 5.4 per cent and 15.0 per cent of the AIDS cases with known ethnicities in 2007 (www.avert .org/canada-aids.htm). Evidence suggests that the major routes for transmission differ in these two groups. Injecting drugs appears to be the most common cause for Aboriginals, while a large majority of black Canadians appear to have acquired the disease through heterosexual contact (www.avert.org/canada-aids.htm).

ENVIRONMENTAL ISSUES ACROSS THE COUNTRY

Health is dependent on the natural environment and the ways in which we as members of societies maintain the health of the natural environment. Water, air, and soil are among the basic and determining factors. Do you know how safe your drinking water is? Do you know how it is purified or how much is available and for how long? Is there enough water for your generation, for your children and their children, and so on? Good and healthy land and soil are prerequisites to health, because they are the basis for the production of foodstuffs. However, there are threats to the environment all across Canada.

Alberta Oil Sands

In Alberta, the extraction of oil from the oil sands is an ongoing challenge to the health of the people and the environment. While the amount of oil is immense (there are said to be 175 billion barrels of proven oil, second only to the 260 billion barrels in Saudi Arabia), the processes needed to access this oil essentially require the strip mining and consequent removal of the sand to extract the infused oil. This affects soil organisms and water flow in the Athabasca River and water levels in the

A heroin addict in Vancouver's Downtown Eastside, a neighbourhood notorious for its drug addicts and dealers. The area is also home to North America's first safe injection site, set up to counter the spread of HIV and AIDS among the neighbourhood's drug users.

river and, downstream, in Lake Athabasca (huge amounts of water are required to extract the oil, but the water cannot be returned to the river because of its toxicity). In addition, mining of the oil sands displaces animals, increases erosion, and decreases carbon sequestration. Moreover, the energy required to access the oil is already causing public health problems, air pollution, and global warming. Some argue that the damage will be repaired naturally. Many others disagree.

The Walkerton Water Crisis

Water is fundamental to our good health. Walkerton, a small town nestled among rolling hills beside the Saugeen River in southwestern Ontario, was, at least from the outside, a perfect picture-postcard town—until May 2000. That was when the drinking water became polluted with a virulent strain of *E. coli* bacteria that was ingested repeatedly by the townspeople, leading to seven deaths and to illness

in approximately 2300 to 2500 others. The 2002 report of the Walkerton Inquiry, written by Justice Dennis R. O'Connor, detailed the causes of these tragic deaths and sicknesses and suggested that individual behaviours, cultural values, and social structural arrangements all were responsible for the suffering of the people of Walkerton.

Let us examine these causes. First, what were the causes at the level of individuals? Two brothers, Stan and Frank Koebel, were particularly implicated in the tragedy. According to the O'Connor report, Stan Koebel neglected several essential aspects of his job with the Public Utilities Commission (PUC) as the general manager responsible for water chlorination and safety. In addition, he repeatedly lied to officers in the health unit and even after many people had taken sick, reported that the water was "okay." Some of his actions were the result of his lack of understanding of the health consequences of his work. Some were due to the fact that the norms in the PUC culture had been lax for at least 20 years and before Koebel was hired.

As well, there were structural causes for this tragedy. These included the fact that Stan and Frank Koebel were certified on the basis of their experience ("grandfathered") and were not required to take any courses or pass any examinations for continued certification. Another structural deficiency related to the fact that the Ministry of the Environment failed in its responsibility to regulate or to enforce regulations pertaining to the construction and operation of municipal water systems. Budget reductions at the provincial level were also implicated, because they led to the privatization of lab testing and to failure to regulate the reporting responsibilities of private labs whenever unsafe water was detected and to ensure that proactive water quality interventions were made.

Sydney Tar Ponds

On the east side of the country, the "tar ponds" at Sydney, Nova Scotia, contain dangerously contaminated soil and sediment as a result of decades of steel and coke production. The process of heating coal to produce coke for the manufacture of steel produces toxic chemicals such as benzene, kerosene, and napthalene. These chemicals accumulated in the harbour in Sydney. After more than 80 years of this type of coke-oven operation, the ground water and surface water in the area was seriously contaminated with arsenic, lead, and other toxins. In 2004, after years of public lobbying, a $400-million cleanup was announced. According to a press release from the Sydney Tar Ponds Agency on 13 December 2012 at 2 p.m., "In total, 871,650 tonnes of contaminated material have been successfully contained—the equivalent of stacking up 112 football fields, each one a metre deep" to date (http://tarpondscleanup.ca/upload/1355424987Tar%20Ponds%20and%20Coke%20Ovens%20Cleanup%20Marks%20Major%20Milestone.pdf).

To learn more about environmental sociology and issues, see "Cities and Perspectives on the Environment" in Chapter 16, p. 332.

INTRA-SOCIETAL ANALYSES

The Social Determinants of Health

The degree of economic inequality has been increasing in Canada, especially recently, in the last decade of the twentieth century and into the first decade of the twenty-first century. A report for the Organisation for Economic Co-operation and Development (OECD) pointed out that Canada was, in fact, one of the two (out of 30) wealthy nations characterized by the largest growth in income inequality in the 1990s and 2000s (Mikkonen and Raphael 2010). Consider the following statistics. In the years 1984 to 2005, 30 per cent of Canadians had no net worth and over this time became more indebted. By comparison, the average net worth of those in the top 10 per cent increased over this period to $1.2 million (an increase of $659,000 in constant dollars) (Mikkonen and Raphael). Many people are aware of the widening gap between the rich and the poor, the "haves" and the "have-nots" in Canada. What might be less familiar to you is that there is a direct link between income inequality and health. A classic illustration of this relationship can be found in the Whitehall studies, which followed the health of more than 10,000 British civil servants for nearly 20 years and found that both the experience of well-being and a decline in mortality rates were associated with upward mobility in the occupational hierarchy of the British civil service (Marmot et al. 1978; 1991). Positive health benefits were found *in each increase in rank*. Remember, too, that this was a study of the civil service. Thus, all of the jobs under scrutiny were white-collar office jobs with "adequate" incomes. It is interesting that this finding held true even among people who engaged in health-threatening behaviours such as smoking. Thus, for instance, "researchers found that top people who smoked were much less likely to die of smoking-related causes" than those nearer the bottom who did not smoke (National Council of Welfare 2001/2, 5).

Poverty exacerbates health problems from birth onward. In 2007, the child poverty rate in Canada was 15 per cent (*Report Card on Child and Family Poverty in Canada* 2009). Forty-three per cent of children of visible-minority parents and 52 per cent of Aboriginal children live in poverty (www.cich.ca/PDFFiles/

ProfileFactSheets/English/Incomeinequity. pdf). Poor women are more likely to bear low-birth-weight babies. Low birth weight is associated with myriad negative health, disability, learning, and behavioural effects. Children born in the poorest neighbourhoods in Canada (the lowest 20 per cent) live shorter lives, by 2 to 5.5 years. They also tend to spend more of these shorter lives with some degree of disability. Children at the lower end of the social hierarchy have a greater variety of health and developmental deficits than those higher up on the socio-economic status ladder. It is also important to note that these results are situated in the context of a nationally funded medical care system. It is also interesting to note that in a global context, the rate of childhood poverty in Canada is high (www.cich.ca/PDFFiles/ProfileFactSheets/English/Incomeinequity. pdf)—*higher* than in other developed nations such as Sweden, where the incidence of childhood poverty is 3 per cent, the Netherlands (6 per cent), France and Germany (7 per cent), and the United Kingdom (10 per cent) (www. cich.ca). Men and women in neighbourhoods that differ by income have different life expectancies. Men and women in the poorest neighbourhoods can expect to live 74.7 and 80.9 years, respectively. Men and women in the richest neighbourhoods can expect to live 79 and 82.8 years, respectively (Wilkins 2007).

Even though there are significant links between income inequality and both ill-health and death, Canadian health policy continues to involve substantial investments in the health-care system rather than in community-level interventions intended to alleviate inequality, such as a guaranteed annual wage, a national daycare program, or proactive prenatal care for low-income mothers.

The ways in which economic inequality affects health outcomes are complex and contested. Certainly, material needs are part of the explanation. For example, differential ability to pay for ample healthy foodstuffs and for clean, quiet, and temperature-appropriate living quarters is a part of the explanation. What the Whitehall studies suggest, however, is that there is likely something beyond material differences contributing to the explanation. One finding of the Whitehall studies was that while all levels of the civil service had elevated stress levels while at work, blood pressure levels of the senior administrators dropped when they went home; in contrast, the stress levels remained high for those lower in the hierarchy (National Council of Welfare 2001/2). Socio-psychological issues related to perceptions of well-being appear to be implicated in inequities in health outcomes. In other words, people also feel stress and appear to have consequent health difficulties as a result of comparing their socio-economic positions (negatively) to those of others (Marmot et al. 1978; 1991).

Social Capital

Inequality affects a myriad of other aspects of life, all of which have an impact on health. (Wilkinson and Pickett 2009). It is clear from all types of research done today and in the past, in this and in other societies, that social status and health are related. Societies with greater degrees of inequality tend to have poorer overall health outcomes regardless of their overall wealth.

This interesting paradox needs clarification. Explanations for the individual-level correlation have suggested that people with higher incomes, higher occupational prestige scores, and higher educational levels are more able to maintain good health by eating and drinking wisely, avoiding serious threats to health such as cigarette smoking and excessive alcohol consumption, and engaging in prescribed early detection. When those in these higher levels are sick, they can get medical attention immediately and take advantage of the most sophisticated and effective new treatments. They are also able to maintain a sense of well-being through various socio-psychological processes.

Why would the degree of inequality in a society also be important in predicting health and illness outcomes? One explanation is that it is the degree of social cohesion, social capital, or trust that is the link between inequality and health (Mustard 1999; Clarke 2012). A society characterized by inequality is one in which "there is a pronounced status order" (Veenstra 2001, 74). As people compare themselves to one another, it is possible—indeed likely—that those lower in the status hierarchy "will feel this shortcoming quite strongly, given the width of the gap, and consequently will suffer poorer health" (2001, 75). This may result from "damaging emotions such as anxiety and arousal, feelings of inferiority and low self-esteem, shame and embarrassment, and recognition of the need to compete to acquire resources that cannot be gained by any other means" (2001, 75). Social cohesion is thought to be evident in societies to the extent that people are involved in public life and volunteer to work together for the good of the whole. A society with little social cohesion might, for instance, be dominated by market values and characterized by transactions in the interest of profit. Current social policies in Canada that favour market dominance over state intervention exacerbate the degree of inequality in society.

SOCIO-PSYCHOLOGICAL FACTORS: THE SENSE OF COHERENCE

The *sense of coherence* is a socio-psychological concept articulated first by Aaron Antonovsky (1979). Rather than asking what makes people sick, Antonovsky wondered what kept people healthy. Having thought about this and reviewed available research, he defined *sense of coherence* as an orientation to the world and to one's place in it that leads a person to a long-lasting and dynamic feeling of confidence that "things will work out" because (1) life is basically comprehensible, understandable, and predictable; (2) there are sufficient resources for the individual to be able to cope with whatever circumstances arise; and (3) life makes sense or has meaning. These three components of the sense of coherence enable individuals to manage life experience in a positive manner and to establish a basis for resisting disease and handling or coping with suffering.

TIME to REFLECT

What encourages or discourages your involvement in extracurricular activities (which might enhance your social cohesion while at university)?

LIFESTYLE BEHAVIOURS: OBESITY AND EATING DISORDERS

A number of recent articles in the *Canadian Medical Association Journal*, and indeed in the mass media, have reported on seemingly opposite health concerns: obesity, on the one hand, and eating disorders such as anorexia and bulimia, on the other. It seems that both are increasing among children and adults and that both herald other serious medical problems. Why are so many young people facing such problematic and contradictory issues related to food, body image, and control of eating?

Obesity is now pandemic (Katzmarzyk 2002), affecting hundreds of millions of people around the world, especially in rich countries, where between 10 and 20 per cent of the population are obese. *Obesity* is defined as an excess of fatty or adipose tissue; it "results from un-balanced energy budgets. An overweight person consumes food energy in excess of expenditure and stores the surplus in body fat" (Obesity Canada 2001). Excess body fat is associated with higher rates of premature morbidity and death from diseases such as coronary heart disease, stroke, type 2 diabetes mellitus, gallbladder disease, and some cancers. The rate of growth from 1981 to 1996 is estimated at 92 per cent in boys and 57 per cent in girls (Obesity Canada 2001). Our sedentary lifestyle, typified by television viewing and computer games, along with the ubiquitous "fast" food, have played a role in this growing health concern. Children who watch four or more hours of television a day have higher body mass indices and thicker skin folds than those who watch fewer than two hours per day. In addition, caloric intake is positively associated with television viewing (Obesity Canada 2001). By 2010, almost 20 per cent of males and about 17 per cent of females (Statistics Canada 2011c) were considered obese in Canada.

While some children are gaining too much weight, others are losing or trying to lose too much. For example, in a survey of 1739 adolescent females, 23 per cent were dieting to lose weight (Jones et al. 2001, 549). Binge eating was reported by 15 per cent; self-induced vomiting, by 8.2 per cent; and the use of diet pills, by 2.4 per cent. Disordered attitudes toward eating were found in more than 27 per cent of the young women surveyed. Consistent with other studies, disordered eating behaviours and attitudes seemed to increase gradually during adolescence and were more common among girls with higher body mass indices (BMI), an international standard for measuring overweight and obesity (Jones et al. 2001, 549–50).

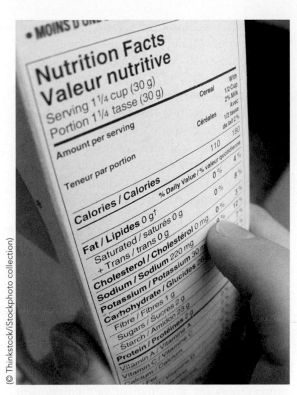

One of the biggest causes of obesity is an unhealthy diet. It is now mandatory for all prepackaged foods to have nutrition labels. These labels make is easier for consumers to compare products and make healthier choices.

TIME to REFLECT

What other social factors are related to disordered eating behaviours and attitudes among adolescents?

THE EXISTENTIAL LEVEL

How do you experience illness? What sorts of illnesses have you had? Have you always gone to the doctor when you felt ill? One compilation of popular notions of illness includes illness as choice, illness as despair, illness as secondary gain, illness as a message of the body, illness as communication, illness as metaphor, illness as tatistical infrequency, and illness as sexual politics (Clarke 2012).

Illness as choice refers to the notion that we choose when to become sick, what type of illness we will have, and so on. In other words, illness episodes are viewed as a reflection of the deep tie between the mind and the body. That illness is a sort of despair is a related notion. Primarily, however, the idea is that ill-ness results from emotional misery. The notion of secondary gain emphasizes the idea that people sometimes benefit from illness—for instance, an ill student might not be able to write an exam for which he or she also hap-pens to be unprepared. Closely related to this notion is the philosophy of illness that suggests that physical symptoms are a means through which the body communicates a message to the consciousness. And related to this, in turn, is the idea that the symptoms are meant to reflect a particular message, a particular set of unmet needs. For example, a cold, with its run-ning nose and eyes, may be said to represent a frustrated desire to cry.

Susan Sontag (1978; 1989) has described some of the metaphors attached to diseases such as tuberculosis, AIDS, and cancer. One illustration of disease metaphor is the idea of a disease as an enemy and the subsequent need for a war against the disease. Illness as statisti-cal infrequency, in contrast, is simply a numeri-cal definition that names as "illness" a bodily functioning or symptom that is infrequent in the population.

Finally, the idea that illness reflects gender politics is related to the patriarchy of the medi-cal profession and its consequent tendency to see women's bodies as basically flawed and women's behaviours as more likely to be pathological (for example, meriting psychiatric diagnosis) than those of men (see Clarke 2012).

The experience of illness has been por-trayed in theatre (in plays such as M. Edson's *Wit*, 1999), movies (such as *Lorenzo's Oil*, 1992), poetry, and other art forms, such as the quilts made to honour those with breast cancer or HIV/AIDS.

Sociology of Medicine

The sociology of medicine examines the socio-logical issues regarding location, definition, diagnosis, and treatments of disease. It includes an examination of the various health-care insti-tutions such as hospitals along with medically related industries and the training, work, and statuses of medical and nursing professionals and other health-care providers today and in historical context.

Because the twentieth century was char-acterized by the increasing dominance of allopathic medicine and its spreading relevance to more and more of life (Zola 1972; Conrad 2005), the term *medicalization* (the tendency for more and more of life to be defined as relevant to medicine) has provided an important conceptual framework for critical analysis.

THE CANADIAN MEDICAL CARE SYSTEM

Our present medical care system was implemented in 1972 after a Royal Commission on Health Care (Hall 1964–5) under Justice Emmett Hall recommended that the federal government work with the provincial governments to establish a program of universal health care. While hospitalization and some medical testing had been covered before that, the new program was designed to cover physicians' fees and other services not already covered under the Hospital Insurance and Diagnostic Services Act (1958).

Four basic principles guided the program. The first was universality. This meant that the plan was to be available to all residents of Canada on equal terms, regardless of prior health record, age, income, non-membership in a group (such as a union or workplace), or other considerations. The second was portability. This meant that individual benefits would travel with the individual across the country, from province to province. The third was comprehensive coverage: the plan was to cover all necessary medical services, including dentistry that required hospitalization. The fourth was public administration. This referred to the fact that the plan was to run on a non-profit basis.

The Canada Health Act of 1984 added a fifth principle, accessibility. The costs of the plan were to be shared by the federal and provincial governments in such a way that the richer provinces paid relatively more than the poorer provinces; thus, the plan would also serve to redistribute wealth across Canada. Doctors, with few exceptions (found mostly in community health clinics), were not salaried by the government. Instead, they were and continue to be private practitioners paid by the government on a fee-for-service basis.

PRIVATIZATION

Despite the presence of the universally available and federally supported national medical care system, there is considerable evidence of privatization within the system. At present, approximately 70 per cent of the Canadian system is public, 30 per cent private (Mikkonen and Raphael 2010, 38). The private aspects of the Canadian system are dominated by multinational corporations involved in providing a variety of health-related goods and services, including additional medical insurance, information technology services, food and laundry for hospitals, long-term and other institutional care, drugs, medical devices, and homecare. The most important impetus for growth in the medical system is in the private sector, particularly in drugs and new (and very expensive) technologies such as MRI, CAT scan, and mammography machines and other increasingly popular diagnostic technologies such as the PSA test for prostate cancer.

Table 12.3 portrays the increase in personal expenditures on medical care from 2003 to 2011. Notice especially the relative rate of growth in expenditures for the often private component of care, pharmaceuticals (both prescribed and over-the-counter) as well as other (unspecified) expenses.

There is considerable debate today about whether or not Canada can continue to afford a publicly funded and universally available medical care system. The mass media are full of stories of overcrowded emergency rooms and long waiting lists for medical services. These sorts of concerns often seem to lead to the argument that the problem is the publicly funded system. However, evidence from a wide variety of sources does not necessarily support this point of view (Canadian Health Services Research Foundation 2002; 2005). For example, Calgary recently moved to a degree of privatization: cataract surgery services are now bought from private companies. This has resulted not only in more costly cataract surgery but also in longer waiting times than in the nearby cities of Lethbridge and Edmonton. According to the Canadian Health Services Research Foundation, not only do parallel private health-care systems not cut waiting lists, but they seem to lengthen lists for those in the public system (2005).

US studies on the effect of governments' buying medical services from for-profit companies demonstrate other problems with privatization. Johns Hopkins University researchers compared more than 3000 patient records and found that

TABLE 12.3 ▼ Health Expenditures, 2003–11 ($ millions)

	2003	2005	2007	2009	2011
Total personal expenditure on consumer goods and services	686,552	758,966	851,603	898,215	980,629
Medical care	15,906	18,386	21,101	23,959	27,255
Hospital care	1,653	1,914	2,199	2,474	2,767
Drugs and pharmaceutical products	13,025	15,092	18,268	20,053	21,119
Other medical care	4,856	5,347	6,085	6,512	6,741
Percentage of all personal expenditure on medical care and health services	5.2	5.4	5.6	5.9	5.9

SOURCE: Statistics Canada, CANSIM, Table 380-0024, www40.statcan.ca/l01/cst01/health48-eng.htm

the for-profit centres had higher death rates, were less likely to refer patients for transplants, and were less likely to treat children with the dialysis method most likely to be of benefit to them (Canadian Health Services Research Foundation 2005). Most US-based research suggests that for-profit (private) care costs more, pays lower salaries to staff, and incurs higher administrative costs but does not provide higher-quality care or greater access. Not-for-profits tend to provide higher rates of immunization, mammography, and other preventive services (Canadian Health Services Research Foundation 2005). On average, people lose two years of life when they are treated in for-profit hospitals (Devereaux et al. 2002, 1402).

MEDICALIZATION

Medicalization is the tendency to see more and more of life as relevant to medicine. Irving Zola (1972) was one of the first social theorists to express criticism of this process. He defined medicalization as including the following four components:

1. An expansion of what in life and in a person is relevant to medicine.
2. The maintenance of absolute control over certain technical procedures by the allopathic medical profession.
3. The maintenance of almost absolute access to certain areas by the medical profession.
4. The spread of medicine's relevance to an increasingly large portion of living.

Ivan Illich (1976) attributes the growth of medicalization to bureaucratization. Vincente

Navarro (1975) claims that medicalization, or medical dominance, is more related to class and class conflict, in particular the upper-class background and position of physicians. He also relates medicalization to the work of physicians who operate as entrepreneurs in the definition of health and illness categories and their relevant treatments.

DISEASE-MONGERING

Capitalism plays a role in medicalization too. Consider the importance of pharmaceutical corporations in **disease-mongering**. Through a series of suggestive anecdotes, Ray Moynihan, Iona Heath, and David Henry (2002) argue for critically examining the ways in which the pharmaceutical industry plays a significant part in creating diseases out of conditions for which they have developed an effective drug. Ostensibly involved in public education about new diseases and treatments and often working alongside doctors, public relations firms, and consumer groups, the pharmaceutical industry has created diseases out of problematic conditions that may well be better seen as part of life. For example, the medicalization of baldness by Merck occurred after the development of their anti-baldness drug, Propecia, in Australia. Around the time of the patenting of the drug, a major Australian newspaper reported on a new study that indicated that about one-third of men experienced hair loss (Hickman 1998). Further, the article emphasized, hair loss sometimes led to panic and other emotional difficulties and had a negative impact on job prospects and well-being. What the newspaper

OPEN for DISCUSSION

The Power of Medicalization

Struggles over the power of medicalization can be illustrated by the case of Tyrell Dueck. He was 13 when, in early October 1999, he was diagnosed with osteogenic sarcoma, or bone cancer. Treatment upon diagnosis usually begins immediately with chemotherapy to shrink the tumour and stop the spread of the disease. Surgery is used next to remove the tumour or sometimes the whole limb if the disease is found to have spread. Chemotherapy may then continue. With immediate treatment and localized disease, the prognosis can be excellent for full recovery.

At the point of diagnosis, Tyrell's father, Tim Dueck, said that the family did not want Tyrell to undergo chemotherapy and surgery but wanted him to try alternative treatments and prayer. The hospital responded by going to court. By 11 December, a couple of months after the diagnosis, the court ordered that the Saskatchewan minister of social services have guardianship over Tyrell. This gave the minister the right to consent to treatment on Tyrell's behalf. After two rounds of chemotherapy, doctors decided Tyrell's leg would have to be amputated and that this surgery would give him a 65 per cent chance of survival but that he would almost certainly die without the amputation of his leg.

Tyrell decided that he did not want to have his leg removed. Nor did he want more chemotherapy. This created a new dilemma. The court order of guardianship had taken the power of consent for treatment away from Tyrell's parents in favour of the hospital. It had not taken it from Tyrell himself. Another hearing began on 13 March. A psychologist and a psychiatrist gave contradictory evidence regarding whether Tyrell was legally mature and thus capable of making the decision against treatment on his own. By 18 March, the court had decided that Tyrell was a "mature minor" and therefore was required to have the prescribed medical treatment. But by this time, further medical investigations had revealed that the time lapse had decreased Tyrell's chances of survival to 10 to 15 per cent. At this point, the minister of social services withdrew the order of treatment, and the Duecks were free to pursue alternative treatment in Mexico. They did so. Tyrell received the treatment. Nonetheless, Tyrell died a few months later (Rogan 1999, 43–52).

Who do you think should have the power to decide in a situation like this: the state, the doctors, the parents, or the young person?

---

failed to report was that the study was funded by Merck and that the "expert" quotations were from the public relations firm hired by Merck. This example is just one illustration of some strategies used by pharmaceutical industries to "establish a need and create a desire" (Cook 2001, cited in Moynihan, Heath, and Henry 2002).

TIME to REFLECT

PlosMedicine (www.plosmedicine.org), a peer-reviewed online journal, has a series of critiques of "pharmaceuticalization," including the development of drugs for male erectile dysfunction, female sexual dysfunction, and ADHD, published in 2006. Take a look at this online journal, and read at least one of the articles on pharmaceuticals. Can you offer a counterargument to the ones put forward in *PlosMedicine*?

MORALE AND BULLYING AMONG DOCTORS

Despite the power of medicine and the relative power and wealth of doctors, medical work is often difficult. Recent research in the United Kingdom has identified workplace bullying as a major source of stress at work for health-care professionals (Quine 2002). One study among doctors who worked for the National Health Service found that one in three reported that they had been bullied in the year previous to the study (Quine 1999). Another study found that bullying, racial harassment, and discrimination were everyday occurrences in the work lives of Asian and black doctors in the United Kingdom (Coker 2001). In the United States too, a few studies have identified mistreatment and bullying experienced by medical students, interns, and residents (Kassebaum and Cutler 1998). Doctors are not immune to discrimination on the job. While studies of bullying have not been done in Canada, there is reason to

UNDER the WIRE

Health Care Online

The Internet has changed health care in the modern world. Nettleton and colleagues argue that this is such a profound alteration that it deserves a new name—e-scaped medicine (2004; 2005). More people go online for medical advice on a daily basis than visit doctors. According to Statistics Canada's Internet Use Survey, 80 per cent of Canadians used the Internet for personal reasons such as email, social networking, and banking in 2009. Almost three-quarters of adult women (74.9 per cent) and about two-thirds of adult men (66 per cent) used the Internet for information about health (www.statcan. gc.ca/daily-quotidien/100510/dq100510a-eng.htm).

This increasing access to and reliance on the Internet has led to changes in doctor–patient relationships as patients have begun to think of themselves as informed. Not all of the information available on the Web is credible, however, and evaluating medical sites is complicated. Websites vary widely as to their validity, timeliness, readability level, sponsorship, and so on. A good proportion of the Canadian population have limitations in literacy (www2 .literacy. bc.ca/facts/inCanada.pdf). Moreover, there are those who argue that the increasing reliance on the Internet for health information may exacerbate health inequalities.

think that the patterns might be generalizable to this country. Such research is particularly important as increasing numbers of Canadian-educated doctors are female and/or from visible-minority backgrounds.

Bullying is one of the causes of increasingly poor morale among doctors around the world

(Edwards, Kornacki, and Silversin 2002). While declining morale is partly the result of doctors' increasing workload, accompanied by a relative decrease in remuneration, according to extensive research it is also, and perhaps more importantly, related to the changing social compact between doctors and the societies in

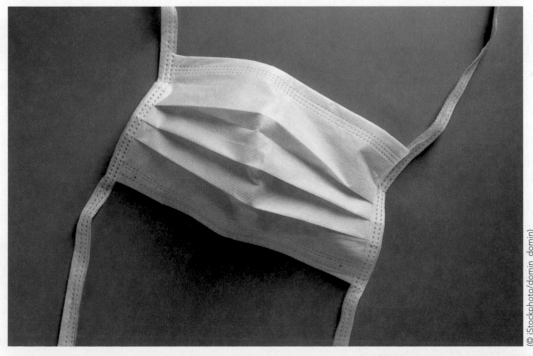

(© iStockphoto/domin_domin)

If you needed medical assistance, who would you expect your doctor to be? Doctors are not drawn in a representative way from across the socio-economic and socio-demographic variation of the whole population of citizens. People from rural areas, black Canadians, and Aboriginals are under-represented among medical students. The Canadian Federation of Medical Students has called for change and for an expansion in the degree to which medical students represent the Canadian population.

which they practise. Doctors who were previously sole practitioners and operated as independent entrepreneurs within a private—even, many suggest, "sacred"—doctor–patient relationship are now under intense surveillance by governments and corporations (such as insurance companies). *Evidence-based medicine* may also contribute to decreasing morale. This new approach to medical practice removes the clinical judgment from the doctor and puts it into the hands of epidemiologists and other scientists who determine best-practice principles that doctors are expected to follow. Moreover, best-practice findings are no longer published only in arcane medical journals but often are easily accessible to insurance company personnel and to individual patients through numerous, disease-specific Internet sites.

TIME to REFLECT

Do you think it is important for the backgrounds of physicians to reflect the cultural, ethnic, and other diverse features of Canada? Explain.

Conclusion

In many ways, health issues are fundamentally social issues. The rates, definitions, and meanings of illness, sickness, disease, and death have varied and continue to vary around the world and over time. Within Canadian society, these differences, particularly in rates, reflect culture and social structure and mirror inequality and marginalization. Medical care is dominated by allopathic medicine today. However, a sizable minority of Canadians are now choosing complementary and alternative care. At the same time, there is increasing evidence of medicalization by the pharmaceutical industry through its entrepreneurial disease-defining work. While there is substantially more privatization in the Canadian medical care system today, it has tended not to reduce costs or to provide better medical service but the reverse. Finally, it appears that doctors in the system are experiencing low levels of job satisfaction and morale today.

questions for critical thought

1. What are the three most important health/social policies that you would recommend the government establish to minimize the rate at which Canadians die from car accidents?

2. Why are more and more people using complementary and alternative health care?

3. Examine three magazines that you commonly read—for their health-related messages, perhaps—focusing on a particular subject such as *depression*. Include both articles and advertisements (for anti-depressants) in your analysis. Consider the portrayal of issues such as gender, ethnicity, and social class in your discussion.

4. One of the most dangerous places to work in Canada today is a hospital. Explain.

recommended readings

Pat Armstrong, Hugh Armstrong, and David Coburn, eds. 2001. *Unhealthy Times: Political Economy Perspectives on Health and Care in Canada.* Toronto: Oxford University Press. This is a fascinating book on the ways that economics and politics influence health in Canada and globally.

Olena Hankivsky, ed. 2011. *Health Inequalities in Canada: Intersectional Frameworks and Practices.* Vancouver: University of British Columbia Press. This is an edited book using an intersectionality approach in analyzing selected health problems and inequities.

Samantha King. 2006. *Pink Ribbons, Inc.: Breast Cancer and the Politics of Philanthropy.* **Minneapolis: University of Minnesota Press.** This book examines the corporate face of fundraising for breast cancer and traces the history of breast cancer from an individually and privately experienced disease to an enormous marketing cause.

Richard G. Wilkinson and Kate Pickett. 2009. *The Spirit Level: Why Greater Equality Makes Societies Stronger.* **London: Bloomsbury Press.** This book empirically documents the links between inequality and all sorts of social problems, including health.

recommended websites

Health Canada
www.hc-sc.gc.ca
Health Canada, a government department, provides health-related information on topics such as healthy living, health care, diseases and conditions, health protection, and media stories.

Public Health Agency of Canada
www.phac.asac.gc.ca
The Public Health Agency of Canada offers access to research and working papers on the social determinants of health, health promotion, and population health perspectives.

Statistics Canada
www.statcan.ca
Statistics Canada publishes myriad studies on Canadian society, including statistics relevant to morbidity, mortality, disease incidence, birth rates, and so on.

World Health Organization
www.who.int
The World Health Organization provides information, fact sheets, reports, and news about health issues around the world. It also covers essential information regarding worldwide epidemics and news about outbreaks of various illnesses in a worldwide context, including epidemic and pandemic alerts and responses.

chapter 13

Religion in Canada

Lori G. Beaman

In this chapter, you will:

▸ Explore definitions of religion and spirituality.

▸ Learn about the changing religious demography of Canada and its potential impact.

▸ Examine the concept of secularization.

▸ Explore the relationship between law and religion.

▸ Think about the gendered dimensions of religious participation.

Introduction

Religion is an important point of identity for many people in Canada. Almost daily, we hear or read about an aspect of someone's religious beliefs that bump up against a regulation, law, or policy. For example, the Supreme Court of British Columbia case *Reference re: Section 293 of the Criminal Code of Canada* (2011), a case on the criminality of polygamy—which is practised by some Fundamentalist Latter-day Saints—has generated considerable discussion and debate, reflected in newspaper and magazine articles, website postings, and letters to the editor (see, for example, Bramham 2010; Stuek and Hunter 2011; Kay 2011; Lewis 2011). The case of Naima Ahmed, a 29-year-old Muslim immigrant to Quebec (from Egypt), made the headlines and stirred the quiet embers of a fire over reasonable accommodation that had only just calmed in Quebec. Naima was ordered to remove her **niqab** when attending her French class. Her complaint to the Quebec Human Rights Commission became public, and heated debate ensued. For Naima, the choice to wear the niqab was an important part of her religious identity. For those opposed to the niqab in the classroom, it was an important reminder of a past that was dominated by what is perceived by some as religious oppression (Peritz 2010; Montpetit 2010; El Akkad 2010). One result of this incident was the tabling of Bill 94 in the Quebec National Assembly on 24 March 2010 that, had it been passed, would have forced women who want to receive public services to remove their niqabs (CBC News 2010). No matter how one may feel personally about religion, it matters to a good many people. For social scientists, religion constitutes an important area of study in our pursuit to better understand social life.

Sociologists of religion do not ask questions about the veracity of particular sets of religious beliefs. In other words, we do not care whether god exists or whether Raelians have really had contact with extraterrestrial beings. Rather, our concern is with how human beings act out their religious beliefs and practices, as well as how religious beliefs and social institutions intersect. How are certain sets of beliefs legitimized? What is constructed as being a "religion"? What are the power relations embedded

in these processes? In other words, who gets to decide whether a religion is really a religion?

MARXIST INFLUENCE

Until relatively recently, sociology—as a discipline—did not take the study of religion particularly seriously. There are a number of reasons for this. First, a good number of scholars accepted the popular wisdom that we live in a secular society. However, religion remains an important part of the Canadian (and global) social fabric and is likely to continue to be so.

Another reason for the lack of attention to religion within sociology can be explained by the strong Marxist tradition, particularly in Canadian sociology. Marx was concerned about the power of religion and in fact stated that "Religion is the sigh of the oppressed creature, the heart of a heartless world" (Marx, as cited in Raines 2002, 167). While he recognized the ability of religion to offer solace in times of trouble, Marx worried that the happiness offered by religion was illusory and that it distracted people from seeking real happiness (which in Marx's view inevitably involved the transformation of economic arrangements and the end of capitalism). Marx concluded that "the abolition of religion as the illusory happiness of the people is the demand for their real happiness" (Marx, as cited in Raines 2002, 167). Some sociologists understood this statement as a licence to minimize the importance of religion in society, to exclude religion as a variable from research, and to ignore its importance in theoretical work. This hardly reflects the spirit in which Marx wrote (one would think something deemed to be so powerful would need to be studied carefully) and has resulted in a paucity of research about religion and social life.

Moreover, on a substantive note, there have been some significant social movements that have been grounded in a combination of religion and Marxism, most specifically liberation theology, which began in South and Central America in the 1960s and was based on the premise that part of the mission of Christianity is to bring "justice to the poor and oppressed, particularly through political activism" (Smith 1991, 12). Its goal was to effect socio-economic change, and indeed it became so threatening that it was condemned by the Vatican. Several Latin American bishops were deposed for their continued fight for social and economic justice based on Marxist principles.

Religion in Profile

What does religion in Canada look like from a demographic perspective? Mainstream Christianity has dominated Canada's historic landscape and, to some extent, continues to do so. Mainstream Christianity includes Roman Catholicism and Protestant groups such as the United Church of Canada and the Anglican Church of Canada. Numbers of affiliates have been approximately equal between Roman Catholics and Protestants. Groups outside of these two broad categories make up a relatively small proportion of the religious picture in Canada, but as we will see below, that picture is rapidly changing. For the most part, Canadians have remained affiliated with the religion of their

TABLE 13.1 ▼	Top 10 Religious Denominations, Canada, 2011	
	Number	%
Roman Catholic	12,728,880	38.7
No religious affiliation	7,850,610	23.9
United Church	2,007,610	6.1
Anglican	1,631,850	5.0
Muslim	1,053,945	3.2
Baptist	635,840	1.9
Protestant	550,965	1.6
Hindu	497,960	1.5
Lutheran	478,185	1.4
Presbyterian	472,385	1.4

SOURCE: Statistics Canada. 2003. 2001 Census: Analysis Series, Religions in Canada, p. 20. Catalogue no. 96F0030XIE2001015. Ottawa: Statistics Canada. Available at www12.statcan.ca/english/census01/products/analytic/companion/rel/pdf/96F0030XIE2001015.pdf

▼ FIGURE 13.1   Religious Affiliation of Population (by Census Division): No Religion

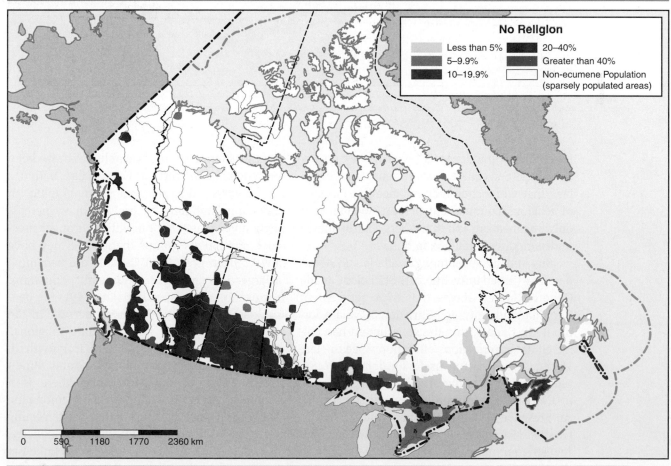

SOURCE: Natural Resources Canada, 2001. *The Atlas of Canada*, http://atlas.nrcan.gc.ca/site/english/maps/peopleandsociety/religion/religion01. Reproduced with the permission of the Minister of Public Works and Government Services Canada, 2013.

▼ **FIGURE 13.2**   Religious Affiliation of Population (by Census Division): Protestant

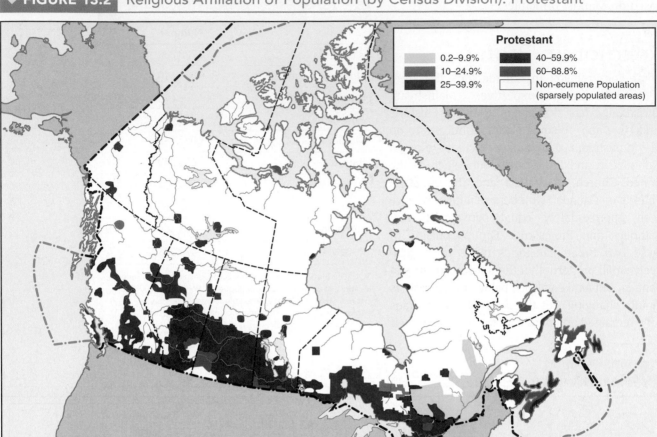

SOURCE: Natural Resources Canada, 2001. *The Atlas of Canada*, http://atlas.nrcan.gc.ca/site/english/maps/peopleandsociety/religion/religion01, Reproduced with the permission of the Minister of Public Works and Government Services Canada, 2013.

parents and grandparents, even if they do not actually attend church. Social scientists have realized that while church attendance is a measure of religious commitment or participation, it is only one measure and thus offers a fairly limited understanding of religion in Canada.

Statistically speaking, Canada is still dominated by Christianity. The 2011 Statistics Canada General Survey shows that 67.3 per cent of Canadians identify as "Christian." We are fortunate in Canada that the government had collected data on religious affiliation since the late 1800s, thus allowing us to formulate a longitudinal understanding of religious participation in Canada. These data also show the historical presence of Sikhs, Muslims, Buddhists, and Hindus. Moreover, we know that the Canadian Jewish community has roots that date back to the 1700s. Thus, while we hear much about the increasing presence of religious groups who are

not Christian, most of these religions have been present since the birth of Canada as a nation.

However, the religious demographic in Canada is changing. We are becoming increasingly diverse as a nation, with a stronger presence of religious groups that, while they have always been present in Canada, are becoming a larger percentage of the overall population. For example, between 1981 and 1991, the census data show a 144 per cent increase in the category of "other non-Christian religions" (Statistics Canada 1993). There is growth in Jewish, Muslim, Sikh, Buddhist, and Hindu communities; at the same time, there is a decline in attendance and belonging among the Canadian Christian communities. Intersecting with these trends are immigration policies, human rights legislation, and policies linked to the Canadian Multiculturalism Act. Religious identity is an important part of what people

▼ FIGURE 13.3 Religious Affiliation of Population (by Census Division): Roman Catholic

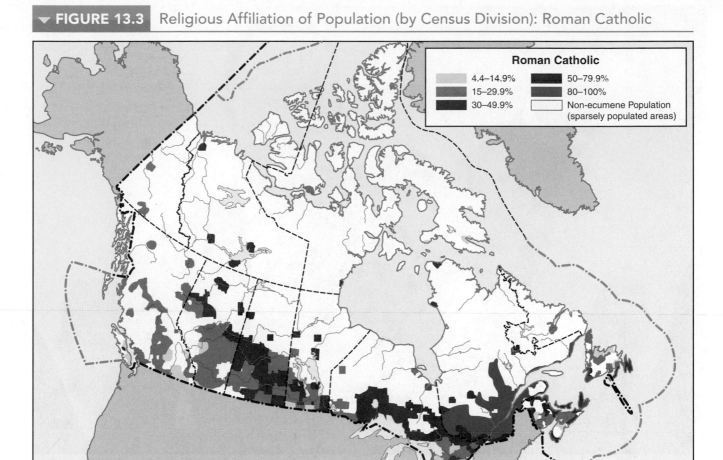

Roman Catholic

- 4.4–14.9%
- 15–29.9%
- 30–49.9%
- 50–79.9%
- 80–100%
- Non-ecumene Population (sparsely populated areas)

0   590   1180   1770   2360 km

SOURCE: Natural Resources Canada, 2001. *The Atlas of Canada*, http://atlas.nrcan.gc.ca/site/english/maps/peopleandsociety/religion/religion01, Reproduced with the permission of the Minister of Public Works and Government Services Canada, 2013.

bring to their roles as employees and employers, their financial choices, their political involvement and decisions, and their conceptualizations of how society should respond to social issues. While religion is, of course, not the only factor in people's decisions, it is nonetheless important to understand the ways in which it informs people in their day-to-day lives.

The data collected by Statistics Canada and researchers like Reginald Bibby (2002) and Michael Adams (2003) provide invaluable information about religious beliefs and behaviours in Canada. However, we need more information about how Canadians are religious and spiritual. In other words, what do religion and spirituality look like in their daily lives? What role do they play in everyday life? What is the nature of religious or spiritual practice at home? How is religion lived? Unfortunately, statistical data can give us little information

about these sorts of questions. Especially lacking is data that give us insight into minority religious communities.

Since the terrorist attacks on various locations in the United States, or "9/11," and subsequent attacks in the UK, Spain, and Bali, discussions about the link between religion and violence have become more frequent. Although this connection might seem recent, it has been present throughout history. We need only to examine Canada's history of violence against and violation of its First Nations peoples to uncover a horrifying picture of the intertwining of religion, political goals, and power relations to understand the intersection of religion and violence.

Does religion cause violence? The answer to this question is not easy. Certainly, religion can provide an ideological justification for violent acts or approaches that do violence to people or their culture in more subtle ways.

In August 2012, Anders Behring Breivik was convicted of murdering 77 and injuring 242 people in Norway. Breivik stated that the motivation for his violent rampage was to prevent Norway from being overrun by Muslims. Is religion to blame for this tragedy? Why or why not?

GLOBAL ISSUES

Securitization and the Link between Religion and Violence

The link between religion and violence has become a central preoccupation of many Western governments as they try to develop a deeper understanding of the ways in which religious ideology can motivate violence. Unfortunately for some groups, the actions of marginal minorities come to represent, in the eyes of many, the face of religion. Some people, like Richard Dawkins, argue that religion is responsible for violence in the world and for the wars we currently witness globally. But the quest to understand the link between religion and violence must go deeper. For example, riots in Paris suburbs in October/November 2005 were superficially linked with Muslim youth (for more information, see CBC News 2007). But some sociological analysis pointed out that the historical disadvantaging of immigrants coupled with racism resulted in a denial of employment opportunities, which in turn led to a lack of social integration. Is the cause of violence then religion or poverty? Recently, governments have begun to focus on the causes of so-called home-grown terrorism. What, they ask, causes young men in particular, who are native-born, to take up causes that inspire them to commit acts of violence, often in the name of religion or a particular religious group? The answer to this question remains open to debate and to illumination through sociological research (Selby 2012; Spalek, El-Awa, and McDonald 2008).

When we think about the power of religious ideology, we can begin to understand why it is important to have a better sense of the role of religion in the lives of Canadians. Religion can provide a source of comfort, direction, and community for people. It can be both prescriptive, in that it offers people direction on important choices, and explanatory, in that it provides a source of explanation for everyday events. It is often an important influence on how people think about issues like same-sex marriage, abortion, and gender roles. It can influence how and why new Canadians feel welcome and a part of Canadian society or feel excluded and marginalized.

Peter Beyer, head of the Religion and Immigrant Young Adult Research Team at the University of Ottawa, situates a sociological understanding of religion in Canada in the context of the global flows of which it is a part. The team has spent six years examining the intersection of religion, youth, and Canadian culture. Participants self-identify as having Islam, Hinduism, Sikhism, Christianity, or Buddhism as part of their religious background, have at least one immigrant parent, were born in Canada or arrived here as an immigrant and had lived in Canada at least eight years, and were between the ages of 18 and 30. More than 300 young adults have participated in the study thus far. Results from this research show that the young adults who participated in the study locate their religious or spiritual quests in a complex web of family and cultural reference points. For these young adults, spiritual definition is their own prerogative, and while they may rely on their parents and extended families to some extent for spiritual or religious information, they take responsibility for their own spiritual and religious journeys. This group of immigrant youth from Toronto, Montreal, Vancouver, Edmonton, Ottawa, and Sydney were generally highly integrated into Canadian society, feeling connected to Canada as their country. Certainly, they had experienced incidents of discrimination, but this was generally explained as a product of individual ignorance rather than a reflection of Canadian society (Beyer 2008; 2012). For these young adults, multiculturalism in Canada is a positive ideal that situates Canada as a progressive nation. Here is how one Muslim participant expressed this idea:

Give it a couple of . . . generations for people to get . . . out of the shell of their own culture, to mix with the world. Because I believe what we have in Canada is an opportunity that a lot of the world doesn't have, I mean, don't get me wrong, there's a lot of blood on the hands of everybody who lives in this country. But we have an opportunity for people to start fresh. We have people from all different backgrounds, all over the world. We are a representation to the world. . . . There are certain points into staying and understanding your own culture and appreciating your own culture. But to be able to evolve and to move on with the times . . . we can show the world here how to live amongst people from all different backgrounds. (Beyer 2008, 36)

TIME to REFLECT

In your opinion, why are many Canadians less committed to religious institutions than they were several decades ago? What are the potential impacts on micro and macro levels of society?

Definitions of *Religion*

What do we mean when we use the word *religion*? Does it include spirituality? And what do we mean by *spirituality*? Sociologists face an ongoing challenge when they attempt to define religion. Meredith McGuire (2005) very simply categorizes definitions of religion into functional definitions and substantive definitions. In short, functional definitions focus on what religion does for the social group and for the individual. The dominant theme running through most functional definitions is social cohesion—in other words, how religion offers a sense of connectedness to others and to a larger picture. Substantive definitions, on the other hand, examine what religion is and what does not count as religion. Substantive definitions attempt to define religion by examining its core elements, most typically a belief in a higher being, a set of prescribed beliefs and rituals, and so on.

TIME to REFLECT

Is hockey a religion?

Émile Durkheim (1965 [1912]) certainly deserves some of the credit for the shape of functional definitions of religion, but his influence can be seen in substantive understandings as well. Durkheim's preoccupation was with social cohesion, and thus he viewed religion through this lens. For Durkheim, religion contributed to social cohesion in that it was fundamentally a reflection of the society in which it existed and it was, at its core, a social or group phenomenon. He argued that society divided the world into the sacred and the profane and that the former was the focus of religion. Durkheim's work had some powerful effects on how sociologists of religion define and think about religion. The **binary** between the sacred and the profane has limited conceptual resonance for some cultures, especially, for example, many Aboriginal groups. Moreover, the emphasis on the social aspects of religion as they are highlighted by Durkheim has resulted in a denigration of sacred practices that are not communally oriented. Wiccans, for example, are often sole practitioners, unconnected to a "faith community" in the traditional Christian sense of the word or in the sense that Durkheim thought was necessary for religious expression.

A contemporary application of Durkheim's functional ideas is reflected in the research of Robert Bellah and his colleagues (1985) in the United States. They spent considerable time exploring the role of religion in social cohesion, or **civil religion**. This elusive and amorphous concept emerged in the American context and was most vocally defended as a "real" phenomenon by Bellah and his colleagues, who argued that it transcended any specific religious tradition and formed an ethical framework that existed apart from any one religion. However, the strong Christian presence in the United States might belie that claim. Perhaps the most important thing to remember about civil religion, its proponents argue, is that it forms an overarching framework that supports a cohesive society. It is equally important to remember that underlying this notion is the idea that society is based on and functions because of shared values and perspectives, something that is highly contested by many scholars. Much of Bellah and his colleagues' work has focused on understanding how society has departed from those common ideals and the consequences of that, which they identify as being largely negative.

In part, narratives of a cohesive society lost, such as that told by Bellah, return us to debates about the definitions of religion and spirituality. Many people neatly divide the two into religion as **organized religion** and spirituality as somehow representing something less institutional and more private. This division is arbitrary at best, and hidden behind the categorization are particular power sedimentations that create a hierarchy in which "religion" is privileged as what counts in terms of spiritual belief and practice. Linda Woodhead (2007) is especially critical of the dominance of functionalist conceptualizations of religion, particularly Durkheimian models that privilege religion over magic despite the fact that both are related to the sacred or transcendent. We see among sociologists a tendency to denigrate or minimize religious or spiritual behaviours that don't fit into organized religion patterns like Christianity. Woodhead also argues that "Religions look remarkably like what Christians think of as religion" (2007, 2). It is important that sociologists think carefully about the work such categories do in the preservation of particular hierarchies of what "counts" as religion.

Substantive definitions focusing on content are equally vulnerable to criticism, primarily on the grounds that they often rely on Christianity to form the basis of the determining criteria. Some important challenges to conventional thinking about definitions of religion have emerged both within sociology and from other disciplines such as anthropology. For example, Talal Asad (1993) calls into question the work that definitions of religion do. He argues that the separating out of religion as something distinct from everyday life is a Christian approach to thinking about spirituality and religion. As Asad states, "It is preeminently the Christian church that has occupied itself with identifying, cultivating and testing beliefs as a verbalizable inner condition of true religion" (1993, 48). By challenging definitions of religion, we also open the possibility of shifting the way religion is measured.

What might an alternative approach be? How would we think about people's involvement with the sacred if we were able to step outside of Christian thinking about religion? Canadian scholar William Closson James (2012) offers a beginning point for the exercise in boundary deconstruction. He argues that "as religion in Canada in the twentieth century becomes more highly personal and individual, we should expect it to continue to be characterized more by an eclectic spirituality cobbled together from various sources rather than a monolithic and unitary superordinating system of beliefs" (2012, 66–7). If we only consider religion that looks a particular way (in the view of the scholars mentioned above, that is religion that looks like Christianity), we will miss a great deal of the richness of Canadians' spiritual lives.

New Religious Movements

There are some very practical implications of decisions about what constitutes a religion. Religious groups in many countries receive privileges simply because they are religious. In Canada, for example, there are certain tax exemptions for religions as charitable organizations. Thus, the determination of a group's status as a religion is not merely an academic discussion. In many countries, religions must register with a central state authority in order to be recognized for some benefits. Moreover, those who are not on official state lists are often persecuted through the harassment of group members, the denial of benefits, and the use of state apparatus such as the criminal justice system to keep groups under close scrutiny. Especially vulnerable are **new religious movements** (NRMs).

The classic study on new religious movements is *The Making of a Moonie*, by Eileen Barker (1984). Barker was intrigued by the increasing frenzy around new religious movements, particularly the talk of **cults**, "brainwashing," and "deprogramming" in the late 1970s and early 1980s. As a social scientist, she decided that she would investigate the workings of the Reverend Sun Myung Moon's Unification Church, also known as the Moonies. As it turned out, the mostly young adults who were joining the Unification Church were not brainwashed, deprived of sleep, or malnourished, as the hysterical discourse around their "conversion" had suggested. Rather, they were simply middle-class young adults who were seeking a spiritual or religious experience and a sense of community. Barker's research (1984; 2005; 2007) had profound implications and triggered a debate that continues to this day.

UNDER the WIRE

Religion on the Internet

As the Internet becomes increasingly integrated into Canadians lives, it should not be surprising that religious activity has also migrated online. Indeed, religious activity has been a part of the online experience for many people since Internet access became possible. Religious activity and debate became so prevalent on the UseNet boards, an early publicly accessible Internet message board, that in 1983 nonreligious users demanded that a new board specifically for religious discussion be created so that other boards did not become overrun with debates and conversations about religion (Helland 2007). Ever since, religious users have matched the pace of technological developments and take full advantage of Web capabilities, developing well-designed, multilingual websites for interested users (Vatican .ca, sgi.org, rael.org, faludafa.org), as well as creating Web 2.0 style websites including social networking sites (wondercafe.ca), video sharing websites (godtube .com), and interactive news sites (onislam.net).

—Morgan Hunter

Susan Palmer is a Canadian researcher who is internationally known for her research on new religious movements. She has studied a number of religious groups, including the Raelians, the Quebec-based UFO cult that claimed several years ago that they had successfully cloned a human being. After 15 years of fieldwork with the Raelians, which involved attending their meetings, countless interviews with members and leaders, and examining video and written materials, Palmer wrote a book about Raelian culture. Her findings described a new religious movement and challenged the stereotypes associated with NRMs. For example, she found that "Raelians with children make no effort to transmit the message to them, true to the Raelian ethic of individual choice" (Palmer 2004, 139). Children cannot be baptized until at least age 15; even when they ask to be baptized as Raelian, they must pass a test "to prove that their choice was not due to parental influence or pressure" (2004, 139). As Palmer discovered, the Raelians have sometimes contradictory beliefs, and as with any social organization, there are power struggles and tensions. In her response to a journalist who wanted to know whether she had observed coercive or manipulative behaviour among the Raelians, Palmer stated, "Well, sure, but no more so than in my women's Bulgarian choir or my PTA meetings. In any human organization you'll find people who try to control other people. Often they have to, just to get the job done" (2004, 6).

Unfortunately, new religious movements still suffer from a great deal of stigma. The language of cults and brainwashing used in the news media and in day-to-day conversation undergoes little critical examination of why it is that we are sometimes quick to marginalize such groups. After all, what is the difference between brainwashing and socialization? This is where questions of agency come into play. What we mean by *agency* is the capacity and ability of a human being to freely make decisions. This sounds simple enough, but ultimately none of us makes decisions "freely" or without constraints. Whether it is the influence of parents, friends, economic constraints, or possibilities, our decisions are shaped by our social world and by social structure. Often, marginal religious groups are conceptualized as exerting "undue influence" on their members, simply because the decisions those members make may be different from the choices we might make.

Theories of Religion and Society

Do we live in a secular society? We frequently hear this question as an affirmative statement with little explanation about what it means. To say a society is secular is to say that it is without religion in its public sphere. **Secularization** is the process by which religion increasingly loses its influence. Whether and how society is secular has occupied a great deal of time and energy among sociologists of religion. The narrative begins like this: Once upon a time, society was very, very religious—everyone participated in religious activity, and religion formed a sacred canopy of meaning over life for the vast majority of people. State and church were one and the same, with no separation between them and no perceived need for a separation. Then along came the Enlightenment, and gradually, science replaced religion (Berger 1967).

To complicate the story, secularization theory developed some very sophisticated versions. In the midst of it all were contested notions of how religion should be defined.

(© Christopher J. Morris/Corbis)

Raelian founder and leader Claude Vorilhon

They are important, because in order to determine whether religion is on the decline, we must first know what religion is. So if people stop attending church but take up yoga and engage in rituals such as meditative walks in **labyrinths**, can we say that we live in a more secular world? If we measure secularization as the decline in people's participation in the rituals and practices of organized religion, such as church attendance, marriage, and baptism, then yes, Canada has definitely secularized. But what happens if the population is increasingly made up of people for whom church attendance is not and has never been a measure of religious participation? How then do we think about secularization? So while one measure of secularization can be the level of individual participation in religious activities, we can see that this presents some interesting measurement challenges.

TIME to REFLECT

Do we live in a secular society?

Another measure of secularization exists at the level of institutions. As religion loses its influence, it has less and less presence in social institutions such as law, education, health care, and so on. And in this process, religion loses its influence as an important social voice. The overt involvement of religion in social institutions, to be sure, is different from what it was in other periods in Canadian history. But the religious voice cannot be discounted entirely. Think, for example, about the religious involvement in the debate over same-sex marriage. The *Reference re: Same-Sex Marriage* (2004) case was decided in 2004; the legislation passed, and the Civil Marriage Act was approved on 20 July 2005. The opinions of a number of religious groups were heard by the Supreme Court of Canada during the Reference process. Some were vehemently opposed to the legislation, but some, such as the Metropolitan Church of Toronto, were instrumental in ensuring that same-sex couples have the right to marry in Canada (see Dickey Young 2012). Religion retains influence over access to public services: for example, in some provinces access to abortion is severely limited because of the influence of religious

lobby groups. In court, witnesses still swear to tell the truth on the bible. Public institutions close on Christian holidays such as Christmas and Easter. In some measure, religious beliefs are so embedded in our social institutions and form part of their histories that it is almost impossible for them to become completely secular or without religious influence.

One important piece of social scientific research on the idea of secularization in recent years is that of José Casanova (1994), whose work employs a multilevel conceptualization of secularization. Casanova argues that secularization theory is actually made up of three interwoven strands of argument: (1) secularization as religious decline; (2) secularization as differentiation; and (3) secularization as privatization. While Casanova says that the idea that religion is differentiated (there is a secular and a sacred sphere) is a possible proposition, it does not follow that religion must be marginalized and privatized. Of course, if we think about world events, Casanova's argument seems plausible. Religion is intertwined with many of the major world events we might think about and in sometimes very public ways.

In Canada, religious participation could be described as **believing without belonging** (Davie 1994), which means that while many Canadians still cite an affiliation with organized religion at census time, many of them do not have much, or any, contact with the churches to which they say they belong. Given current measures of religious life, it is difficult to determine the parameters of belief. The extent to which individuals engage in religious and spiritual activities that are not included in common measures is not known. Home-based religious practices, for example, remain largely invisible, as does participation in yoga classes, labyrinth walking, and meditation. Some scholars argue that such "private" behaviours do not really count when thinking about secularization or when measuring religious behaviour. This is a puzzling argument, because such thinking would exclude many religious groups who engage in religious practice almost exclusively in the realm of the so-called private. Scholars like Robert Orsi (2003), who argues that even prayer is public, have challenged this public–private dichotomy. The essence of Orsi's argument is that we cannot create a meaningful dichotomy between the public and the private. In other words, you take your "private" self with you in the realm of the "public."

Understanding religion in complex ways can give us a rich picture of how people integrate religion and spiritual practices into their daily lives. One of the reasons secularization theory seemed to have so much credibility is the problem of definition. If religion is conceptualized in narrow ways—church attendance, institutional involvement, and so-called other public measures—then without a doubt it has shown a decline of such proportions that it might be reasonable to conclude that it will eventually disappear. But there are alternative practices that are not measured and that form an important part of spiritual identity. Moreover, at an institutional level much of Canada's Christian heritage remains embedded in day-to-day practices, as we will discover in the next section. While some scholars still hold to the validity of secularization theory, many have adopted a more moderate approach that recognizes the continuing importance of religion in our world. The idea of the "post-secular" has gained currency, although this too is problematic for a number of reasons, not least of which is the fact that it assumes that there has existed a secular against which a "post-secular" has now developed. Ultimately, it is probably simply important to recognize that religion, in myriad forms, continues to have relevance at the individual, group, and societal levels.

The Quiet Revolution

The province of Quebec deserves special mention in our consideration of secularization. Its unique cultural position has numerous facets, not least of which is the story of religion in that province. If ever there was a classic story of secularization, Quebec seems to tell it. It had what we might consider an established church; historically, the Roman Catholic church played an enormous role in the lives of Quebec citizens at a personal level as well as institutionally (Simpson 2000, 276). Schools, hospitals, and much of public life were intertwined with the church. Public officials were Roman Catholic, as were most members of Quebec society.

In the late 1960s, it seemed that quite suddenly the church pews were empty. The **Quiet**

(© CP Images/La Presse/MTLP)

Known as the father of the Quiet Revolution, Jean Lesage became premier of Quebec in 1960. With the slogan *C'est le temps que ça change* ("It's time for a change"), Lesage introduced many reforms in areas such as education and health care that saw the Roman Catholic church lose power and favour in Quebec (Canadian Museum of Civilization, "Jean Lesage" in Making Medicare, www.civilization.ca/cmc/exhibitions/hist/medicare/medic-5g06e.shtml).

Revolution had happened. How this seemingly sudden shift came about remains a bit of a mystery, but the perception of the church as anti-modern, oppressive, and representative of an establishment with which the people of Quebec no longer wished to identify combined to create an impetus to abandon what had been a core part of identity in Quebec. David Seljak has argued that the Roman Catholic church did not give up its place in Quebec society; instead, it recreated its public role (2000, 135). The influence of the Roman Catholic church in Quebec institutions has not been completely eliminated, and the relationship between the church and the citizens of Quebec remains a complex one in the process of negotiation.

Recently, a very public debate about the role of religion in society has taken place in Quebec. That debate, in some measure prompted by the *Multani* case (discussed in detail in the next section), has been framed around the notion of "reasonable accommodation" and has focused attention primarily on the religious practices of immigrants, particularly Muslims (although some practices of Orthodox Jews have also been the subject of discussion). The government of Quebec formed the Bouchard–Taylor Commission to examine the nature and extent of the problem that seemed to be emerging around accommodation. The question of how much "accommodation" should be made for religious minorities has resulted in heated debate. For example, Solange Lefebvre has noted that "when it comes to granting religious accommodations to members of minority religions, Québeckers are reacting more strongly and publicly than people in other parts of North America" (Lefebvre 2008, 179). To some extent, the impact of the debate and the report prepared by the commission, *Building the Future: A Time for Reconciliation*, released 22 May 2008, is seen as an issue largely confined to Quebec. But this is not so, because we see similar debates arising all across Canada. The sorts of questions that arise in a religiously diverse society include discussions like the following: Should Sikhs be able to wear their **kirpans** in government legislatures or their turbans (instead of helmets) when riding motorcycles? Should Muslim women be allowed to wear their niqabs to receive government services, to give evidence in court, to attend classes, or to take the oath of citizenship? Should municipal officials be allowed to recite prayers at the beginning of public meetings? These are very real issues that arise in religiously diverse societies. The resolution of such debates was the focus of the Bouchard–Taylor Commission report.

The very language of accommodation leads to another important issue raised by the public discussion around the Bouchard–Taylor report. "Accommodation" is often used interchangeably with the idea of "tolerance." Certainly, liberal principles of diversity management have relied on the notion of tolerance, and it has been a pragmatic strategy used by interfaith and other groups to set the basic ground rules for interacting with those who are different. But as Janet R. Jakobsen and Ann Pellegrini ask, "what does it feel like to be on the receiving end of this tolerance? Does it really feel any different from contempt or exclusion?" (2004, 14). If you think about it, there is a rather large difference between someone tolerating you and someone thinking that you are equal, therefore worthy of respect and your ideas worthy of protection. Understanding religious difference as something that is to be tolerated, dealt with, or managed is therefore problematic. Some people argue that if we eliminate these concepts, then we will be left with nothing and that even these basic positions are better than nothing. We might think, although perhaps optimistically, that it is time to develop an approach to difference that is rooted in a deep understanding of equality rather than a teeth-gritting tolerance of those who are not like us. In summary, the debates that have been most intensely played out in Quebec raise issues that are crucial to all of us as we figure out what it means to live in an increasingly diverse multicultural nation.

The heated debate surrounding reasonable accommodation continues in Quebec, and it is evident from the Open for Discussion box on p. 162 in Chapter 8 that not all Quebecers believe in the concept.

Religion and Law

One important social institution that mediates the ways in which religious beliefs can be expressed through practice is law. For example, if you are a Sikh and you wish to wear your kirpan (ceremonial dagger) to school, you may find yourself, as Gurbaj Multani did, arguing before the courts for your right to do so (*Multani v. Commission scolaire Marguerite-Bourgeoys* 2006). Law sets important boundaries on religious practices. Law provides a forum to which people can come to affirm their right to engage in certain religious practices. It is especially important for minority religious groups, whose practices are more likely to be called into question than those of majority religious groups.

Sections 2(a) and 15 of the Charter of Rights and Freedoms are the core sections dealing with the protection of religious beliefs in Canada:

2. Everyone has the following fundamental freedoms:

a) freedom of conscience and religion;

15. (1) Every individual is equal before and under the law and has the right to the equal protection and equal benefit of the law without discrimination and, in particular, without discrimination based on race, national or ethnic origin, colour, religion, sex, age or mental or physical disability.

Contrary to popular belief, mostly imported from the United States and France, both of which establish the separation of church and state in their founding constitutional documents, there is no legal separation of church and state in Canada. Separation of church and state means that the church has no authority over the state or political decisions. You can see, particularly in the United States, that this is more an ideal than a reality. Keep in mind, though, that while Canada does not have a strict separation of church and state, it also does not have an established church or a church that has authority over the state. So where does religion fit in Canada from a socio-legal perspective?

Since the Charter was enacted in 1982, the Supreme Court of Canada has attempted to find a workable definition of religion that can be applied in its considerations of religious freedom. To this end, the Court has attempted to use a comprehensive definition that employs both functional and substantive elements. For example, in the *Syndicat Northcrest v. Amselem* (2004) decision, the Court stated the following:

In order to define religious freedom, we must first ask ourselves what we mean by "religion." While it is perhaps not possible to define religion precisely, some outer definition is useful since only beliefs, convictions and practices rooted in religion, as opposed to those that are secular, socially based or conscientiously held, are protected by the guarantee of freedom of religion. Defined broadly, religion typically involves a particular and comprehensive system of faith and worship. Religion also tends to involve the belief in a divine, superhuman or controlling power. In essence, religion is about freely and deeply held personal convictions or beliefs connected to an individual's spiritual faith and integrally linked to one's self-definition and spiritual fulfillment, the practices of which allow individuals to foster a connection with the divine or with the subject or object of that spiritual faith.

Trying to define religion is no easy task, as we have already seen. It becomes especially challenging as courts try to distil a very complex concept into a workable definition. Thus, courts are faced with the unenviable task of trying to capture a dynamic idea in a definitional box. Orsi's work on **lived religion** offers important insight into the vast scale of the task of definitions and why it might be especially difficult in law: "The study of lived religion is not about practice rather than ideas, but about ideas, gestures, imaginings, all as media of engagement with the world. Lived religion cannot be separated from other practices of everyday life, from the ways that humans do other necessary and important things, or from other cultural structures and discourses (legal, political, medical, and so on)" (2003, 172). In the definition quoted above, we see the Court using a substantive understanding of religion in its statement that religion is "a particular and comprehensive system of faith and worship." This raises the question of why a religion must be a comprehensive system of faith and worship. We might also question whether that is even a useful way to conceptualize religion, since the religious behaviour of the vast majority of Canadians does not actually seem to fit with this notion of "comprehensiveness." Belief in a divine, superhuman, or controlling power poses some similar problems in that some religions do not have what we might call a central authority figure. How is it possible to determine whether a conviction is "deeply" held? These are the challenges posed by attempts to solidify religious behaviour into manageable definitions for law.

Although the Charter of Rights and Freedoms guarantees religious freedom and equality, the guarantees and rights in the Charter are limited by section 1, which provides a balance of sorts between individual rights and interests and those of society more generally. Section 1 states that the rights and freedoms included in the Charter are subject only to "such reasonable limits prescribed by law as can be demonstrably justified in a free and democratic society." This limitation means a court can find that rights have been violated but the offending legislation or policy can remain because it is a reasonable limit on religious freedom by standards of section 1. Take, for example, a Jehovah's Witness parent who wishes to refuse blood transfusions for her child's cancer treatment. A court may force the child to receive transfusions by assuming temporary custody and overriding the wishes of the parent (and the child). While a court may find that such treatment constitutes a violation of the religious freedom provisions of the Charter, it may also find that such a violation is justifiable under section 1 as representing a societal interest (see Beaman 2008).

To give this discussion a bit more context, let's consider one case in more detail. When we discussed the definition of religion and the matching of definitions and actual religious beliefs and practices as they come before the courts, we questioned whether it is possible to define religion in an inclusive way. The *Multani* case (2006) provides an example of the subtleties of this process. In that case, "G" (the son) and "B" (the father) were fully observant Sikhs, or, as the Court described them, orthodox Sikhs. An arrangement was made to accommodate G's wearing of a kirpan to school; this agreement specified that it be kept under his clothing, sheathed, and sewn shut. The school commission refused to ratify the agreement; however, the superior court set aside that decision. The court of appeal upheld the school commission, and the Supreme Court of Canada allowed the appeal. We might see the carrying of a kirpan as an issue of safety, but given the extent of the provisions the Multanis made to keep the kirpan relatively inaccessible, this is not a viable argument and was not one that the Supreme Court of Canada accepted. Why did the kirpan became an issue to the point that the family was forced to go to the Supreme Court of Canada to be able to exercise their religious beliefs? In part, we can identify the very narrow conceptualization we have of religion and the way it is practised. Fortunately, the Supreme Court was not so limited in its approach.

The naming and construction of the kirpan as a weapon is a discursive practice that relies on a socially constructed set of categories. Manjit Singh comments:

> Rather than go into a detailed explanatory meaning of the kirpan, I would like to talk about another weapon with origins in medieval Europe that has been adopted in Canada and Québec as a symbol of public authority. I am talking about the mace that lies on a table in front of the speaker of the House of Commons in Ottawa as well as in the National Assembly in Québec City. According to Webster's dictionary, a mace is "akin to a staff or club used especially in the Middle Ages for breaking armour" and "an ornamental staff borne as a symbol of authority before a public official or legislative body." It is clear from the above wording that a mace is a weapon. In the context of the two legislative chambers, however, it is a symbol of state authority. No one has ever questioned that some day, some member of one of these chambers, in a fit of rage, could use this weapon to attack a fellow member. The point of this discussion is that through mutual consent and historical tradition, this lethal weapon has come to represent the authority of the state. (Singh 2002)

Singh's insightful commentary points to the constructed nature of religious symbols. James Beckford (2003) employs a moderate social constructionism, which acknowledges the culturally and socially situated position of religion as a concept and as a practice. Beckford notes the definition of religion as shifting throughout time and the link between those shifts and power relations: "what counts as 'really religious' or 'truly Christian' are authorized, challenged and replaced over time" (2003, 17).

Another religious practice that has sparked a heated debate in Canada is the veil worn by some Muslim women. See the Human Diversity box in Chapter 8, p. 159, for a discussion on the veil issue and the law.

Religious groups complicate issues around definition because they may disagree among themselves about who counts as a "real" member of their group. Adherents may challenge others who claim to be members of their group but who don't participate in particular rituals or adhere to specific beliefs fundamental to their religious world view. Thus, some Anglicans, for example, support same-sex marriage while others are opposed to it. Some Muslims support the use of sharia law, others do not, and so on. These tensions can be confusing to those on the outside of the religious group trying to understand the group's religious identity. Some members of a religious group may claim to speak for all members. However, to perceive that all members of a religious group believe and practise in the same way is misleading. Think about the variations of the faith group with which you are most familiar. You will quickly see that religious identity is a complex factor in the consideration of religious belief and practice and its protection.

Religion and Gender

Why is it important to talk about religion and gender? Because there are some decidedly gendered aspects to religious participation. Women tend to make up the bulk of religious congregations, and some argue that it is women's decisions to stop attending that has been the catalyst in the sharp decline in religious participation, at least among Christians. Gender roles are a definite flashpoint in contemporary conversations about the ways in which religion and society intersect.

A number of scholars, most notably Mary Daly (1985) and Naomi Goldenberg (2006), have argued that religion has been a key institutional site of women's oppression. Women have been excluded from positions of power within church structure; they are instead relegated to "domestic" roles within the church. Some of these same debates are emerging in relation to Muslim women. Interpretations over wearing the **hijab** vary; some define it as a cultural rather than a religious symbol, while others see it as a symbol of women's agency or choice and still others perceive it as a sign that a woman is oppressed by her religion. Perhaps most important, but sometimes overlooked in this discussion, are the voices of Muslim women themselves. Research reveals the complexity of this issue but most significantly clearly demonstrates that women's interpretations cannot be excluded from the interpretation of the meaning of a particular practice.

Homa Hoodfar's research (2003) helps us to better understand the complex ways in which women interpret their own choices to wear a hijab. For many of the young women Hoodfar interviewed, the choice to wear the hijab created a newfound sense of freedom from strict parents. All of a sudden, they were free to engage in activities that their parents had previously forbidden: "parents seem to be relieved and assured that you are not going to do stupid things, and your community knows that you are acting like a Muslim woman, you are much freer" (2003, 214). Moreover, for some women it was a strategy to generate respect not only among fellow Muslims but also in the broader society: "I am telling them to see me otherwise. Do not think of my body, but of me as a person, a colleague, and so on" (2003, 221). Many of the women interviewed by Hoodfar were extremely strategic in their choices to wear the hijab, weighing the advantages and disadvantages and often concluding that the advantages outweighed the negatives. For some, it also opened opportunities to discuss their Muslim beliefs and to dispel prejudices and misconceptions.

Ultimately, there are a number of strategic choices involved in women's engagement with religion. Some, like Daly (1985), who is a former Roman Catholic nun, argue that religion is so patriarchal that there is no way that women can freely exercise agency within its confines and that women must therefore abandon traditional religion and create their own spheres for spiritual fulfillment. In part, this has been, if not the goal, the effect of some Wiccan groups. Wendy Griffin's (2000) research on pagan groups has documented the approach of Dianic Wiccan groups, which is largely separationist, and her research on the Circle of the Redwood Moon found that they largely abandoned traditional approaches to religion and spirituality. Naming themselves Dianics after the Roman goddess Diana, they base their holy days largely on seasonal cycles. They conceptualize the divine as female rather than male, and they situate their spirituality in

(Bert Hoferichter / Alamy)

Many Muslim women who choose to wear the hijab find that the head covering allows them greater freedom and opportunity.

feminist analysis that includes political activism. They are largely a women-only group and in this way have separated themselves both from the patriarchy of larger society and from traditional religious practices and beliefs.

Some strategies are less radical and call simply for a reshaping or reframing of religious teachings. For example, while evangelical Christians describe gender roles in rather particular ways (wives, for example, are taught to submit to their husbands), the exact ways in which these roles are interpreted is perhaps not as literal as one might think. Listen to Jane, for example, an evangelical Christian woman who, while she says she is a "submissive" wife, tells the interviewer that all decisions in her marriage are made jointly:

I have had some discussions with women who have a real difficult time with that—wives submit to your husbands. Now, I don't have difficulty with that at all, because in the next breath it says "Husbands love your

wives as Christ loved the church." In my mind, we've got the easy end of the job, they've got the hard one. I mean, they've got to love like Christ. (Beaman 1999, 30–1)

Jane's approach is representative of that of many women who are part of more conservative religious traditions. Women within these groups grow impatient with those who would characterize them as having no choice or agency. While non-members tend to characterize them negatively, they often see themselves as benefiting from the demands of their religious traditions, which create rules for both men and women.

One of the most heated areas of discussion in relation to such teachings is violence against women. The relationship between teachings, such as submission or male headship, and violence against women is rendered even more complex by the valorization of family unity within faith communities (Alkhateeb and Abugideiri 2007; Nason-Clark and Kroeger 2004). This often means that women from conservative faith communities—whether Christian, Muslim, or Jewish—are often especially hesitant to take action if they are abused by their husbands for fear of disrupting the family unit. Thus, such women are "more likely stay in abusive relationships, more likely to return to abusive relationships after counseling, and tend to be more optimistic that abuse will stop if the abuser has some form of counseling" (Nason-Clark and Fisher-Townsend 2007; Nason-Clark 2004).

Violence against women within religious communities is made even more complex by the fact that such communities are reluctant to admit the existence of violence within the family, perpetuating what Nason-Clark and Kroeger (2004) have called a "holy hush" of denial. To further muddy the waters, secular agencies for women are often reluctant to include religious resources in their strategies for helping abused women, thus sometimes excluding a resource that is important to abused women from faith communities.

The intersection of religion and gender often triggers interesting debates. The opposition of some religious groups to same-sex marriage was arguably a reaction to what they perceived to be shifting gender roles. Some groups argued, for example, that marriage

OPEN for DISCUSSION

Polygamy: Do Women Really Choose?

After years of keeping a low profile in BC's lush Creston Valley, the community of Bountiful opened its doors to the public April 21 [2005]—media and protesters alike—to set some records straight.

A group from the community, calling itself the Women of Bountiful, hosted a press conference at a community centre 10 km away in Creston. Their aim was to show Canada that they are fully aware of their lifestyle choice; they enjoy sharing husbands even though they admit polygamy is illegal in Canada, and they will use Canada's Charter of Rights and

Freedoms to argue that plural marriage is covered by their freedom of religion.

"We the women of our community will be silent no more," said Zelpha Chatwin to the 300 people in attendance. "I love the fact that my girls and I only have to cook and clean once a week. [Polygamists are] a team of players who care for each other."

The women also said plural marriages come with various benefits, such as pooling resources and talent and higher household incomes, reported the *National Post*.

—Meghan Wood

was solely the terrain of opposite-sex couples and that it was inherently designed (by god) that way. Heather Shipley (2008, 5) notes that "Defining marriage as an historically religious institution, while inaccurate, is a common argument promoted by religious interest groups who seek to preserve the heterosexual institution of marriage." In the *Reference re: Same-Sex Marriage* (2004), the Supreme Court of Canada rejected the argument that marriage is only possible between a man and a woman, and it is now legally possible for same-sex couples to marry in Canada. However, the legislation has allowed for "the freedom of officials of religious groups who choose not to perform marriages that are not in accordance with their religious beliefs" (para 1.2), preserving a space in which religious voices override basic human rights.

Conclusion

This chapter has considered the contemporary picture of religion in Canada and explored some of the issues that are of key concern to sociologists of religion. We have seen that the religious demographic of Canada is in an interesting period of flux that may have an important impact on Canadian society. Despite their small numbers, religious minorities in Canada play an important role in defining diversity in Canadian society. It is an exciting time to be a sociologist of religion in Canada in this time of rapid change.

We have already discussed to a great extent the limits of existing social scientific research on religion in Canada. Quantitative measures need to be more comprehensive to reflect Canada's shifting demographic. We need to understand how religious beliefs and practices fit into the day-to-day lives of Canadians and, most especially, the religious and spiritual practices of those who have arrived in Canada more recently. We need definitional and measurement standards that are not based on Christian understandings of religion. In other words, our research needs to extend beyond church attendance and bible belief. Our measures of spiritual practices should take an inclusive turn.

Research on religion in Canada is slowly becoming a priority. Sociology has an important role to play in the study of religion in Canada. No matter which theoretical tradition one uses, it brings tools that are invaluable to research. Ethnographic accounts of religious communities will provide insight that is as important as more detailed survey work. Research into important intersections—like youth and religious practice and belief—is central to predicting the role that religion will play in Canada's future. Key, though, to understanding the role of religion in Canada's future are interdisciplinary approaches that seek to draw on the expertise and insights of various traditions of scholarly thought.

questions for critical thought

1. Critically examine your own religious history. Where do you and your family fit in terms of believing and belonging? Are you part of a religious minority or the religious majority?

2. Do we live in a secular Canada? Are there some areas of life that are more or less removed from the influence of religion?

3. How is religion best defined? Explain your decision.

4. Should religion have a say in public policy issues?

5. Why do you think the language of "cults" and "brainwashing" persists?

recommended readings

Lori Beaman, ed. 2012. *Religion and Canadian Society: Contexts, Identities, and Strategies*. 2nd edn. Toronto: Canadian Scholars Press.
Religion and Canadian Society contains chapters by 20 of Canada's most recognized scholars of religion and society from a range of disciplinary perspectives. The topics covered in the book are divided into three themes, offering readers insight into the study of religion in Canada, religious identities in Canada, and strategies for researching religion in Canada.

James Beckford. 2003. *Social Theory and Religion*. Cambridge: Cambridge University Press.
James Beckford presents an important examination of religion by developing clear links between social theory and the social scientific study of religion. Relying on moderate social constructionism, his theory focuses on the ways in which religion is a complex and social phenomenon.

Peter Beyer. 2006. *Religions in Global Society*. London: Routledge.
In this book, Peter Beyer analyzes religion as a dimension of the historical processes of globalization as a means of understanding religion in a contemporary global society. Beyer uses examples ranging from Islam and Hinduism to African traditional religions, resulting in an overview of how religion has developed in a globalized society.

Meredith B. McGuire. 2008. *Lived Religion: Faith and Practice in Everyday Life*. Oxford: Oxford University Press.
McGuire explores how the concept of lived religion can be used to understand the actual religious experiences and practices of people in everyday life.

recommended websites

CBC Archives on Religion and Spirituality
http://archives.cbc.ca/society/religion_spirituality
The CBC archives contain clips from radio and television coverage of religious issues in Canada over the past 60 years.

Centre for Studies in Religion and Society
http://csrs.uvic.ca
The Centre for Studies in Religion and Society, hosted at the University of Victoria, studies the intersection of religion and public life from an interdisciplinary perspective. The website offers information about religious research in Canada.

Religion and Diversity Project
www.religionanddiversity.ca
This University of Ottawa–based project brings together 36 researchers from Canada and other nations to research the contours of religious diversity and possible responses to the opportunities and challenges it presents.

Religion and Violence e-learning (RAVe)
www.theraveproject.com/index.php
Religion and Violence e-learning offers support and provides resources for women, clergy, and other service providers on the issue of violence against women. It is based on sociological research conducted by Nancy Nason-Clark and her Religion and Violence research team.

Statistics Canada: Religions in Canada
www12.statcan.gc.ca/nhs-enm/2011/as-sa/99-010-x/99-010-x2011001-eng.cfm#a6
The Statistics Canada guide to the latest information on religion offers links to tables with data on religion in Canada and links to the most recent Statistics Canada publications on religion.

chapter 14

Politics and Social Movements

Randle Hart, Howard Ramos, Karen Stanbridge, and John Veugelers

In this chapter, you will:

▶ Understand that power is relational and socially determined.

▶ Discover that the state plays a focal role in the sociological analyses of politics, because it shapes the ways that people and groups exercise and negotiate power.

▶ Learn that political sociologists have analyzed politics in terms of control and contests over material, cultural, social, and institutional resources.

▶ See how social movements are studied sociologically.

▶ Review the theoretical approaches to the study of social movements.

▶ Learn how social movements are embedded in national and international politics.

Introduction

Politics is about *power* and its *contestation*—therefore, about political institutions and social and political movements. However, it is not only about the "suits" on Parliament Hill or the activists in the streets—it is also a part of the daily lives of all of us. Sociologists understand politics as endemic to our social existence. It is not only about elections or the "red tape" of government, or protest signs and slogans, but instead it is also about how people negotiate their lives with family, friends, social groups, and institutions of all sorts. These too reflect power relations and challenges to them.

Sociologists use a much broader concept of politics than most of us are used to, one that sees politics playing out in realms of society that we normally consider outside of or unaffected by politics proper (Scott and Marshall 2009). For this reason, the sociological conception of politics is complex and multi-faceted. In this chapter, we will provide you with an overview of some of the key perspectives in political sociology that aim to identify and analyze how power is distributed in society and the sorts of factors on which it is based. We will also provide you with an overview of how sociologists approach power contests—that is, attempts to modify or overthrow existing power relations. We will focus here on **social movements** and their role in political life. When people lend time, energy, and material resources to a cause, their combined efforts create a social movement with a life and force of its own. Examples of present-day social movements include Native, women's, peace, gay and lesbian, anti-nuclear, labour, environmental, ethnic, and regionalist movements.

We will begin by elaborating on the core concept of power and then consider the state and its central, but not exclusive, place in sociological analyses. From there, we will move on to the different ways that political sociologists have conceived of power, looking at who holds it and on what bases it is exercised. We will then look at the characteristics of social movements, consider theoretical approaches to social movements, and then examine examples of social movements in Canada. The chapter ends with a discussion about social movements in today's transnational context.

FIGURE 14.1 Section 15 of the Constitution Act, 1982

Equality before and under law and equal protection and benefit of law

15. (1) Every individual is equal before and under the law and has the right to the equal protection and equal benefit of the law without discrimination and, in particular, without discrimination based on race, national or ethnic origin, colour, religion, sex, age or mental or physical disability.

Affirmative action programs

(2) Subsection (1) does not preclude any law, program or activity that has as its object the amelioration of conditions of disadvantaged individuals or groups including those that are disadvantaged because of race, national or ethnic origin, colour, religion, sex, age or mental or physical disability.(84)

Endnote 84:
(84) Subsection 32(2) provides that section 15 shall not have effect until three years after section 32 comes into force. Section 32 came into force on April 17, 1982; therefore, section 15 had effect on April 17, 1985.

SOURCE: http://laws.justice.gc.ca/en/charter/1.html#anchorbo-ga:l_l-gb:s_15

Power

Max Weber famously defined *power* as the capacity to realize one's will despite the resistance of others. It is the ability to do what you want, when you want, even in the face of opposition. Most people believe that one's condition is determined by one's own decisions, choices, and ambition despite circumstances. But sociologists have found that other factors influence people's capacities to pursue and achieve their goals, such as material wealth, cultural and social recognition, and access to institutions. These factors are defined by social structures that shape power relations and ultimately reward some people who possess or control them more than those who do not.

For example, people who have more money not only can buy more things but usually hold more power than those who have less money. Wealthy people often have more power to influence who owns and controls material resources, such as businesses or factories, and cultural and social resources, such as investing in art and leisure activities or belonging to elite clubs, and because of this, they often have preferred access to institutions of power, such as schools or governments that set standards for others in a society to follow. At first glance, many people think that merely having more money makes one powerful. However, the situation is not so straightforward.

Money is important because people agree that it is so and accept it as a payment for work and goods or services delivered. The power of money, then, is socially negotiated and only has value because people agree that it does. Because of this, it doesn't matter what money *is* but instead that people agree that it is valuable. It is in this sense that sociologists understand power as relational—a phenomenon that only manifests in human relationships—rather than intrinsic to its various representations.

> C. Wright Mills claimed that the elites in society are so powerful that they jeopardize democracy. Do you agree? Turn to "The Wealthy, Elites, and Super Rich" in Chapter 6, p. 118, to read more on this topic.

Because power is relational, it is not fixed. It is a dynamic phenomenon that is under constant negotiation or challenge. Power is continually contested by people who oppose or disagree with its bases and defended by those who benefit from the status quo. For this reason, sociologists tend to treat power as a series of social or **political processes**. Power contests can result in new forms of power and modification of old power relations. Yet challenging and changing the bases of existing power relations is often difficult.

TIME to REFLECT

What reflects political power? Is it fixed and seen, or is it embedded within material, cultural, social, and institutional processes?

Political sociologists would argue that inequalities persist because people and groups who hold and exercise power in a society are generally not ready to give it up or even share it and so muster opposition to those seeking to eliminate old bases of power or gener-

ate new ones. Existing power-holders usually have material, cultural, social, and institutional resources at their disposal that their challengers do not. These resources are the mechanisms that shape the political process that sociologists try to understand. You will be introduced to some of them throughout this chapter.

The State

Perhaps the greatest concentration of power in contemporary Western societies lies in the domain of the state. It is the only institution whose officials have the legal right to tax people, to assault them through the police and military, to permit or force people to commit murder when conscripted into military service, to legally detain people in prison, and, in places where capital punishment exists, even kill them. It is also the only institution that can set policies and laws governing personal behaviour, restrict the ways individuals conduct business and their personal and love relationships, authorize credentials, license professions' activities, and so on. Basically, states set the rules by which other social processes are ordered. And like all rule-makers, the leaders of states hold a lot of power to shape the capacities the rest of us have to realize our wills. But why do states hold so much power?

To answer this question we need to examine Western history. States emerged as one of the many transitions related to the **Industrial Revolution** and the emergence of modernity. As societies became larger and more urbanized and work became more specialized and mechanized, older forms of social order became unworkable. New urban middle classes formed in association with these changes and challenged the traditional authority of aristocracies, and the nature of negotiations around power began to change. Land ownership, for instance, which was once the epitome of material power, was replaced by capital and money as symbolic forms of material power. Divine and heredity rights, which formed the fundamental bases for power in feudal societies, were questioned as new religions emerged and families began to marry outside of ethnic and religious lines. The dominance of churches and other religious institutions was also challenged by science and competing belief systems and their organizations. As the traditional foundations of power, knowledge, trust, and obligation weakened, new social configurations developed. They included new systems of governance, like the modern state, through which leaders managed the social conflicts that accompanied negotiations around the new foundations of power: capital over land, individual over hereditary rights, science and rationality over religion, and so forth.

A key development that accompanied the emergence of the modern state was bureaucracy. It is an organizational form that is ordered by criteria independent of the personal qualities of people holding positions of power. Whereas the authority of organizations of the old order flowed from the personal power of the people who occupied positions in them, bureaucracy enabled power to be exercised through a staff abiding by impersonal practices and procedures less susceptible to individual whims and preferences. This granted modern state leaders a very powerful tool through which they could manage conflicts and set rules around their negotiation.

Bureaucracy is a commonly used term, but what does it mean to sociologists? See Chapter 4, "Bureaucracies," p. 85, for a clear explanation.

TIME to REFLECT

The state is always a central concern in the research of political sociologists, but it is seldom their only concern. Why?

The state thus emerged as a key institution that accompanied the massive changes wrought by shifts in the primary bases of power that came with industrialization. Through its various branches, state leaders today can shape all manner of social processes. Let us now examine three broad groupings of these processes—material, cultural and social, and institutional—and the different ways political sociologists have understood these processes affecting how power is exercised and challenged.

Material Processes

Political sociologists who are concerned with why and how money operates as a source of power are part of a group of scholars who view the possession and control of material resources as central to politics. Material resources include money and other kinds of financial resources but also comprise things like property, technology, natural resources, and different means of communication, transportation, organization, and networking. Materialists generally maintain that the more material resources a person, group, institution, or state has, the greater their capacity to realize their will over others and to exercise and challenge power.

Certainly the most famous scholar to have made the argument that power is determined by possession of material resources is Karl Marx. He said that those who owned and controlled the means of production exercise the most power in human societies. Those who possessed the land to cultivate food, for example, held much power in agrarian societies and the feudal era; they controlled peasants' ability to provide for themselves and their families and dictated much of their daily lives. In the industrial era, those who owned machinery and factories, the bourgeoisie, wielded much power over the workers that kept them running, the proletariat. Again, owners governed, and continue to govern, workers' daily routines, setting their wages and determining the conditions under which they work.

For Marx, individuals' power is contingent on their class position or their relationship to the means of production. If they own the means of production, they hold power and can exercise it by influencing who has access to those means and how and for what purposes they are used. If they do not own the means of production, they are effectively powerless, compelled to submit to the owning class to gain access to the means they need to survive.

But for Marx, the power of the owning class, the dominant minority, went far beyond the manor estate or the factory. Other institutions that comprise a society, like the state, religion, family, and the education and legal systems—what Marx called the superstructure—also reflected and sustained the power of the dominant class.

(Millar, D. / Library and Archives Canada / C-051597)

The Winnipeg General Strike in 1919 is perhaps the most significant instance of organized labour protest in Canadian history. Roughly 94 unions and 30,000 workers participated in the protest, which lasted six weeks.

The system Marx described was one in which the majority subordinate class was deceived by the dominant class into thinking that power inequalities reflected in and sustained by social institutions and the ideologies that sustained them were natural, commonsensical, or at best unchangeable. The subordinate class thus operated under a **false consciousness**, because these phenomena masked the true reasons why elites held power, which was because they controlled or owned the means of production. It was for these reasons, Marx argued, that the bourgeoisie was able to maintain its advantage over the working class.

Later writers critiqued Marx for reducing all politics to class politics. Without denying that significant power could be derived from one's ownership of the means of production and material wealth, Max Weber said that power also flowed from one's control over other sorts of assets, things like social status, professional skills, and institutions. These assets are related to material wealth, because they enhance a person's economic well-being, or "market situation." C. Wright Mills (1956) believed that material assets combine and overlap with other sorts of resources to affect how power is exercised in a society. He argued that the post–World War II US was ruled by a higher circle of corporate, military, and political leaders. They held power because they controlled the massive and interlocking hierarchies of the economy, army, and state that made up the means of power.

TIME to REFLECT

In what ways is Weber's conception of power closer to what most of us understand to be constitutive of class position than Marx's definition?

John Porter (1965), a Canadian sociologist in the tradition of Weber and Mills, witnessed a hierarchical intersection between class, education, political standing, and ethnicity (see Helmes-Hayes 2009, 2002; Helmes-Hayes and Curtis 1998; Satzewich and Liodakis 2010). Porter described Canadian society as a vertical

SOCIOLOGY in ACTION

The Electric Car

By 2012, the first fully electric car, the Nissan Leaf, was available to the global mass market. But did you know that a fully electric car was developed and was on the verge of being made available to the general public in the 1990s?

General Motors introduced a prototype of the EV1 in 1990 and began investigating its commercial viability in California soon after. Despite being wildly popular among the few people the company leased the car to for testing and positive reviews from respected trade magazines, General Motors discontinued production in 1999 and pulled all the existing EV1s off the road in 2003, saying demand for the cars was too low and the costs of its production and maintenance too high. GM executives even had most of the existing EV1s crushed or shredded in an Arizona desert. Why would they do such a thing?

There is considerable controversy around the decision, but the explanation that some people offer for GM's actions suggest the "power elite" that C. Wright Mills said controlled the US in the 1950s was alive and well some 40 years later. According to the critically acclaimed 2006 documentary, *Who Killed the Electric Car?*, GM executives' decision to scrap production of the EV1 had less to do with the real demand for and cost of the car and more to do with the threat the electric car posed for the bottom line of powerful interests in the oil and gas and hydrogen industries.

The documentary suggests that leaders in these industries, along with executives from GM and other major car companies and officials in George W. Bush's government, purposely undermined the viability of the EV1 themselves, lobbying hard against the zero-emission legislation in California that motivated car companies to develop electric prototypes in the first place, understating consumer interest in the vehicle, overstating production costs, and promoting the hydrogen fuel cell as a better alternative to gas than electricity.

Some experts have dismissed the documentary's claims as mere conspiracy theory. And with the major car companies, including GM, now embracing electric and hybrid technology enthusiastically, the suspicions that surrounded the EV1 have faded somewhat. But what *is* known about the episode raises some interesting questions from the perspective of Mills's claims around how the US is run by an "uneasy alliance" (1956, 231) between political, economic, and military elites.

Why would the Bush government join forces with auto and oil executives to lobby hard for repeal of California emission-standards legislation? Is it significant that a key advisor to Bush on this issue, Andrew Card, was a former GM vice-president and president of the American Automobile Manufacturers Association? Was it purely a business decision to kill the electric car or an example of the power elite in action?

mosaic whose own *power elite* was comprised of political, economic, and cultural leaders from the charter groups. These were individuals whose heritage was linked to Canada's English and French "founders." Porter argued that these groups used their material and other advantages to sustain their power and held subsequent migrants to Canada in an *entrance status*. That is, non-charter groups earned lower incomes for their labour, held less prestigious positions, had fewer educational opportunities, and had less access to the state bureaucracy and political system. As a result, there had been little change in the class and ethnic composition of the elites who controlled various power structures.

Porter's influence has been especially prominent in what has become known as the *political*

economy perspective in Canadian scholarship. This tradition focuses on the politics around the acquisition and negotiation of material power within the economic, geographic, and social conditions characterizing the Canadian experience. The importance of Porter's thesis can be seen in its revisiting over the past 20 years (Helmes-Hayes and Curtis 1998). Many of its tenets have been shown to still hold true but on racialized rather than ethnic grounds (cf. Agócs and Boyd 1993; Helmes-Hayes and Curtis 1998; Gosine 2000; Galabuzi 2006; Nakhaie 2007). Visible minorities, rather than all non-charter ethnics, retain their entrance status in a colour-coded vertical mosaic.

We have come some way since Marx and his elaboration of the material bases of power. But while scholars after him have expanded upon and extended his ideas about how material resources configure power relations, his core claim—that control of material fundamentally determines the distribution of power in human societies—remains a key observation in political sociology. Let us now turn to some of the non-material processes of power that sociologists examine.

Cultural and Social Processes

Weber understood power as also stemming from sources other than material. One of these "other" sources was status, the social prestige held by a person. Social prestige is often connected to material advantage but not always, said Weber. He was one among many sociologists who recognized that cultural and social processes affect power relations in ways not captured by purely materialist perspectives.

One of the most notable social thinkers to have pondered how culture affects politics was Antonio Gramsci. He was an Italian Marxist of the early twentieth century who wondered why the working-class masses did not respond to Marxist calls for a class-based revolution. Gramsci reasoned that it was because elites "manufactured" the consent of the masses by communicating ideals supportive of the status quo. He argued that this was accomplished through political and cultural mechanisms like the state, schools, religious institutions, and media. He believed that to mobilize masses to contest power, **counter-hegemonic** positions had to be generated. These positions would lay claim to alternative cultural and social ideals that would reconfigure and challenge the established **hegemonic** order. Gramsci called for "organic intellectuals" to communicate counter-hegemonic ideals through popular culture in ways that would resonate with average people. Max Horkheimer and Theodor Adorno (2006) wrote about similar ideas when they introduced the notion of the **culture industry** and the role cultural production played in the rise of fascism and later American consumer culture. However, they were less optimistic about the potential of organic intellectuals, or anyone for that matter, to challenge the cultural power of elites.

The sociologist who perhaps has gone the furthest in articulating how this works is Pierre Bourdieu. He coined what have become key terms in the field, **cultural capital** and **social capital**. Bourdieu's elaboration of these terms helped scholars to articulate how the different components of culture and other social practices operate in much the same ways as material resources. They act as sources of power and the bases of politics.

Simplifying somewhat, Bourdieu said that cultural capital is anything that reflects and facilitates cultural exchange between people. It includes how people see and understand the social world and the interactions that occur within it, as well as cultural symbols that help them do so, such as language, clothing, custom, and so forth. Social capital is a resource that fosters social relationships and the privileges and obligations that one can draw from them; it is derived from membership in groups. The number and nature of groups to which you belong thus affects the social capital you possess, which in turn can affect the power you are able to exercise over your life and others.

Scholars such as James Coleman and Robert Putnam built upon Bourdieu's concepts. They looked at how social capital and social networks influence political participation. Putnam (2000) observed with some alarm the declining rates of membership in *voluntary associations* (VAs) like social clubs and bowling leagues in the US, arguing that such declines meant that Americans were no longer acquiring the social capital needed to sustain effective political communities. He said that participation in VAs fostered the social interaction that produces reciprocity and trust and confirms social norms, qualities that are essential in well-functioning democracies. Thus, declining VA participation signalled nothing less than the deterioration of civil society.

In his more recent work, Putnam (2007) has continued to warn of the threat to community posed by the dearth of social capital, this time among ethnic communities. It's not that ethnic communities are devoid of social capital, but instead they tend to have too much of the kind that fosters insularity rather than openness. He cautions that the **bonding social capital** that often characterizes these communities could be detrimental to the unity of North American

HUMAN DIVERSITY

Food as a Source of Power

Can food be a source of power? We all need sustenance to do anything, of course, but can the *type* of food we consume allow us to exercise power over other people or challenge existing power arrangements?

A number of political sociologists have begun to explore the political implications of food choice, with some interesting results. Recent years have seen an increase in consumer interest in Canada in organic and **fair trade** products, as well as locally grown and processed produce. A few years ago, the CBC (2009) reported that organic food sales had increased by 20 per cent each year over the past decade. Canadian companies such as Just Us! Coffee Roasters Co-Op in Nova Scotia have seen their profits in fair trade coffee grow over the years, and more restaurateurs are embracing the principles of the "slow food" movement and the "100-mile diet" in response to demands from dining "locavores." Some Canadians are becoming small-scale farmers themselves, growing food and raising livestock in their backyards, even in urban areas.

How can we understand this trend in food consumption and production? Businesses that are part of the movement and their consumers often cite ethical, health, and environmental reasons for adopting these practices. But political sociologists have pondered some of the less obvious reasons that people engage with these trends. These scholars reveal that these "conscientious" businesses and consumers can end up either confirming or confronting the status quo, depending on how they take up the new food trends.

Emily Kennedy and Sara O'Shaughnessy (2010) found that many pursuing these trends understand themselves as activists of sorts by providing "alternative" examples to others in their communities. However, alternative food choices can also serve as a way to consolidate existing power, as Josée Johnston and Shyon Baumann (2009) contend. They observe that most of the people who embrace recent trends in organic/local/fair trade foods are white and affluent. Although they might deny that they are "food snobs," these "foodies" eschew food experiences they deem inauthentic, especially meals from chain restaurants, which the less affluent are more likely to patronize.

The result, say the authors, is that food choice becomes a means by which the privileged distinguish themselves from others, another status marker that signifies their belonging to an economic or cultural elite, and differentiates them from less knowledgeable consumers.

Whether one's food choices represent a challenge to existing power arrangements or further evidence of one's privilege veils what is perhaps the most obvious inequity embedded in this discussion: that having any sort of "relationship" with one's food is in itself a marker of advantage—which is something to think about as we consume our burger or fair trade, organic latte.

society. Putnam recommends that **bridging social capital**, the sort that cultivates many outside and casual interactions, be promoted instead.

Although cultural and social processes can be used to understand how dominant groups sustain their power over subordinate masses, those same resources can be used to challenge existing power arrangements through political movements. Interestingly, some of the earliest and most influential work on how culture and social factors shape political movements was done by a sociologist who completed his doctoral work in the 1940s in Saskatchewan, Seymour Martin Lipset. Like many political sociologists, Lipset was interested in comparative analysis (Schwartz 2007). One of his focuses was on the similarities and differences between Canada and the United States, especially with respect to unionism, values, and institutions. Lipset (1991; 1964; 1963) observed high rates of union membership in Canada as compared to the US and said that the disparity was linked to value differences between the two populations (1990). Canadians tended to be more conservative and supportive of tradition and collective politics than Americans, he said, owing to Canada's history of commitment to loyalist traditions. The US was born of rebellion and revolution, a history that fostered a culture of individualism that discouraged collective responses such as unionism.

A number of prominent Canadian sociologists, however, have challenged Lipset's theory (Bowden 1989, 1990; Grabb and Curtis 2002; Grabb 1994; Baer, Grabb, and Johnston 1987, 1990; Yates 2008). Many found that Canadian attitudes are not significantly different from those of Americans but rather that Canadian institutions have been more supportive of unions than those in the United States. Lipset (1990) himself countered these challenges by asking *why* such institutions were more supportive in the first place, suggesting again that Canadian values have encouraged us to elect politicians who institute collective and union-friendly policies.

In challenging a purely materialist understanding of power relations, Max Weber and other political sociologists after him came up with concepts and identified means that have proven useful for analyzing how cultural and social processes are taken up and how they play into the negotiations that characterize politics in societies. While none of these thinkers would abandon the idea that material resources affect how power is exercised and challenged, they recognize that it alone cannot account for all forms of politics.

Institutional Processes

So far, we have seen how political sociologists have depicted power as shaped by differential ownership of material resources or cultural and social recognition. But there are other sociologists who say these approaches don't consider how institutions configure the circumstances in which people operate. Institutions set the bounds of social interactions, the "rules" and guidelines around how social relations unfold, and they delimit the choices and actions that are available to people to employ under different conditions. In this way, institutions may not determine political outcomes, but they shape them to a significant degree.

Sociologists understand **institutions** as patterns of behaviour that order people's lives in relatively predictable ways. They can be informal and flexible, like a group of friends meeting for happy-hour drinks on a regular basis, or more formal, such as schools, business associations, or the state. Institutions shape social interactions because they exhibit *inertia* and *path dependence*. The first means that they are relatively stable and take concerted effort to modify. Institutions "push back" at attempts to change them by discouraging people from acting, or even thinking of acting, in other ways. The second means that once institutions are established, they affect decision-making down the road, encouraging people to proceed down certain "paths" of action instead of others.

Because of these tendencies, institutions can both help and hinder those engaged in the contestation of power. They help by providing a stable and predictable means through which people can exercise power. They hinder by channelling and delimiting the choices for action available to those who engage with and sustain them. Both can be a boon to power-holders, since it is often difficult, or at least bothersome, for others to change the procedures structuring the distribution of power. But institutions can help challengers too, because once they learn how things operate, challengers can formulate ways of changing the rules, getting around them, or mobilizing them on their own behalf.

The institution that political sociologists are most concerned with is the state. Certainly, many political sociologists analyze how institutions shape formal politics, such as elections, political attitudes, and political parties (see Grabb 1994; Grabb and Curtis 2002), but sociologists also recognize that state institutions influence the politics that happens outside this "official" sphere too. This is because state institutions shape other social processes, such as who is and is not considered a citizen. Your capacity to bring your interests to the fore and exercise power can be limited greatly if you are not recognized by state institutions.

Theda Skocpol is perhaps the best known institutionalist in sociology. In a comparative-historical analysis of the revolutions in China, France, and Russia, she traced the impetus for revolution in each case to the incapacity of existing state structures to meet or resolve crises arising in the international realm, from war, or from economic troubles (Skocpol 1979). Whichever powerful groups ended up exploiting these situations and fostering revolution depended on the relationships that had been conditioned by the state institutions in crisis. Although her subject matter may seem obscure, Skocpol's study was significant, because it reminded sociologists of the important role that state institutions play in configuring class and other antagonisms in different countries.

Michael Mann has elaborated on the capacity of state institutions to shape power relations. In his recent work on genocide, for example, Mann (1999; 2004) challenges popular explanations of genocide as terrible manifestations of rabid "tribal" racisms and points to democracy as spawning these atrocities. Democratic state institutions do not always foster peace by permitting everyone access to the state so that they can resolve group conflicts in an orderly manner, says Mann. In places inhabited by people with many ethnic backgrounds, they can result in the elite power-holding group defining who has legitimate citizenry in ethnic terms. As non-persons, members of subordinate groups and minorities can then be liable to persecution or, at worst, repression or mass murder.

An institutional perspective can inform examinations of less violent events too, of course. In Canadian sociology, Daniel Béland (2005; 2006; 2008; Béland and Hacker 2004) has explored how political "institutional legacies" in the US, Canada, Belgium, and other countries have shaped a range of social phenomena, including nationalism, fiscal policy, health and pension programs, and welfare regimes. Dominique Clément (2008) also offers an overview of how federal policy and funding interacted with and influenced the rise of what he calls Canada's "rights revolution"—that is, the expansion of civil liberty and human rights organizations during the course of the twentieth century. And Jane Jenson and Denis Saint-Martin (2003) draw attention to the important role that state institutions have played in the post–World War II era in helping determine who gets to enjoy rights of citizenship and who does not.

Transnationalism

So far, we have seen how political sociologists depict politics as encompassing contests around material resources, cultural and social factors, and institutions within states or as an attempt to create states. However, with the spread of global capitalism, many have anticipated that we are entering a new era in which old notions of time and social space are collapsing (King 1995; Appadurai 1990) and states are losing their status as the dominant institutions in the world (Jenson and Saint-Martin 2003). In fact, some have surmised that as the world becomes increasingly integrated and political processes become globalized, we are witnessing a massive restructuring of societies rivalling that which accompanied the Industrial Revolution, the emergence of modernity, and the rise of the state. It is a restructuring that these scholars say demands a new form of politics and, perhaps, a new kind of political sociology.

Malcolm Waters (1995) describes globalization as a social process in which the traditional constraints posed by geography, economic activity, culture, and social configurations have receded and have been replaced by processes that extend beyond state boundaries. He and other globalization scholars say that old ways of understanding politics and political movements are of little help today, considering that economies have become increasingly integrated; cultures, homogenized; networks, broadened; and state institutions, challenged. Such developments potentially undermine or at least introduce new and problematic twists to traditional perspectives on political processes.

Take material resources, for example. Globalization scholars note that economies have become increasingly integrated, in part because new technologies have made it easier for people to engage in economic exchanges across national boundaries. This has had repercussions for both elites and labourers within individual countries. Increasing foreign direct investment and trade across states, for example, has generated new international flows of wealth that have altered how national elites respond to and take up these resources. It has also fostered the development of new, sometimes more exploitive labour practices, such as use of **export processing zones (EPZ)**, which circumvent the ability of workers to unionize and challenge power-holders.

If some sociologists say that the circumstances surrounding the distribution and exercise of material power have been altered by globalization, others say that claims to power based on culture have also been undermined. They argue that globalization has been accompanied by cultural homogenization. As Hollywood films gain prominence in international movie theatres (Barber 1995), for instance, and fast-food culture spreads to all corners of the globe (Watson 1997), local cultures are swamped by a hegemonic consumer culture. The result is an overall reduction in the range of unique cultural resources to which people seeking power have access.

These scholars see even institutions as internationalizing. The past 30 years have witnessed a proliferation of international agreements that challenge the sovereignty of existing states. Take, for example, the emergence of the European Union (EU), which integrated most of the economies and governments of western Europe, or the implementation of the **North American Free Trade Agreement (NAFTA)** in Canada, the US, and

Mexico. The prominence of these and other international institutions, such as the United Nations, has led some to declare that a *world society* is arising in which the practices and procedures structuring people's lives and actions are becoming increasingly homogeneous (see Meyer et al. 1997).

Not all political sociologists agree, however, that globalization has changed the world as fundamentally as globalization theorists claim. Peter Urmetzer (2005), for instance, looking at the Canadian case, effectively questions whether or not states have lost control of their economies and the extent to which foreign direct investment is actually globalized. Most trade pacts, and for that matter international agreements, are bilateral, between just two states, rather than multilateral or global. With respect to communication, it is indisputable that we live in an era of unprecedented technological innovation, and for those with material wealth, increased travel and communication is indeed an option. Yet much of the world does not have

(ITAR-TASS Photo Agency/Alamy)

In an increasingly globalized world, institutions of global governance, such as the UN, have become increasingly important.

access to those resources, and in a post-9/11 era, the securitization and monitoring of communication and travel has been unprecedentedly limiting, even for the most privileged populations. When it comes to cultural and social exchange, here too we find that much occurs among wealthy states and the wealthy people within them. Not everyone participates. If culture is becoming so cheerfully homogeneous, then why, as Benjamin Barber (1995) noted, do we at the same time see rising radicalism and nationalist groups seeking independence from, rather than integration into, the international community? Lastly, although there has been a rise of international institutions, few have the force to challenge the will of powerful states. Take for instance the US ignoring UN resolutions when they do not fit that state's agenda, as it did when US leaders decided to launch a war against Iraq in 2003. The United Nations secretary general, Kofi Annan, declared the war illegal and noted that it was not sanctioned by the organizations' security council and was not in accord with the UN's founding charter. For all these reasons, it is likely more accurate to acknowledge the rise of transnational processes or transnationalism between some states and thus pause before calling recent changes truly global.

TIME to REFLECT

Why do some sociologists prefer to characterize the increasing interdependence of the world as transnationalism rather than globalization?

The key difference between globalization and transnationalism is the scale of the processes. The former claims that the entire world is involved, whereas the latter makes a lesser claim, only that more than one state is involved in an interaction with at least one other state. Scholars of transnationalism want us to remember that, as Sidney Tarrow (2005) rightly cautions, it is still states that uphold international norms and implement laws, not international organizations. The ways in which state leaders exercise power, the issues with which they are concerned, and the institutions through which they work have indeed changed over time. But states are by no means withering away.

What Is a Social Movement?

Social movements try to achieve change through the voluntary co-operation of the relatively powerless. Participants may contribute financial or other material resources, recruit new members, or spread a counter-ideology. They may also participate in strikes, sit-ins, boycotts, demonstrations, protest marches, violent action, or civil disobedience. Social movements aim to change attitudes, everyday practices, public opinion, or the policies and procedures of business and government.

Social movements are easier to understand when compared and contrasted with other phenomena studied by sociologists (Diani 1992). A *social trend*, for example, is simply a changing pattern of social behaviour, whereas a social movement is a co-operative effort to achieve social change from below. A *pressure group* is an organization that aims to influence large institutions, particularly the state. A social movement is one kind of pressure group. However, other pressure groups—known as *interest groups*—represent the concerns of specific sets of people. Prominent interest groups include the Canadian Labour Congress, the Canadian Medical Association, Canadian Manufacturers and Exporters, and the Consumers' Association of Canada.

Would you consider the 2011 Occupy Movement a social movement or a pressure group? See the Global Issues box in Chapter 6, p. 122, for an extended discussion of this event.

Since social movements depend on voluntary participation, they are voluntary associations. However, not all VAs seek deeper changes in the distribution of social goods. Some provide social or health services; others organize leisure activities or unite the followers of a spiritual doctrine. VAs that only help people to accept or enjoy the existing social system are not social movements.

Unlike social movements, political parties try to win and keep political power. In principle, a social movement becomes a political party when it fields candidates in elections.

(© CP Images/Graham Hughes)

Pressure groups often mobilize against the state. On 22 May 2012, thousands of people marched in Montreal to mark the 100th day of protests against tuition increases for Quebec university students.

The Green parties in Canada, Germany, France, and Italy, for example, have grown from environmental movements in these countries.

TIME to REFLECT

Do you consider yourself an active participant in any social movement? If not, do you wish you were? What social movement would you become involved in, and what part do you think you could play?

Theoretical Approaches

New approaches have developed in a critical response to earlier approaches, which treated social movements as ailments. This charge arose during the 1960s, a time when social movements supported by mainstream members of society were flourishing in Western democracies. Many sociologists welcomed the new movements against war, racism, sexism, pollution, bureaucracy, and the flaws in the educational system as positive signs of healthy protest against injustice and alienation.

NEW SOCIAL MOVEMENTS

European *new social movement* (NSM) theorists (e.g., Melucci 1989; Touraine 1981) propose that structural changes in Western societies have fundamentally altered people's identities and cultures. This gives rise, they argue, to social movements that are distinct from older class-based movements. NSMs are interested in the politics of cultural recognition; they are concerned less with the redistribution of wealth and status than with securing rights to expressive freedoms, symbolic practices, and/or styles of life. In this sense, the appearance of NSMs may be explained by a value shift (Inglehart 1990).

The NSM perspective focuses largely on the relationship between culture and collective identity. It proposes that social movements are cultural laboratories where people try out new forms of social interaction (Melucci 1989). For NSM activists, important struggles take place in civil society, the areas of social interaction that stand largely outside of the state and the market. In fact, theorists claim that NSMs have come about since the 1960s because state and economic practices have increasingly encroached on people's everyday lives. Slogans such as "the personal is political" are meant to express how everyday life is pervaded by government and corporate activities as well as by dominant cultural ideas that create inequality.

According to this approach, civil society offers greater chances for freedom, equality, and *participatory democracy*, a system of decision-making in which all members of a group exercise control over group decisions. Indeed, NSMs are, in part, characterized by institutional arrangements whereby their members try to organize according to the ideals of equal participation. This is what social movements are good at, and striving for other kinds of success risks perverting these ideals (Cohen 1985).

FRAMING THEORY

Framing theory explains the ways movements create and spread their understandings of the world and how these meanings help to form a sense of collective identity and common purpose.

Drawing on Erving Goffman's ideas, framing theorists define collective action frames as "action-oriented sets of beliefs and meanings that inspire and legitimate the activities and campaigns of a social movement organization" (Benford and Snow 2000, 614). These communal understandings are used to identify and promote grievances.

According to framing theory, a social movement must succeed at three core framing tasks. First, an organization must articulate *diagnostic* frames that define social problems (or injustices) and their guilty agents. Second, *prognostic* frames must propose solutions to these social problems. Prognostic frames give meaning to specific strategies and are used to persuade potential recruits and members that these actions are the best way to solve or address particular social problems. Third, since agreement with diagnostic and prognostic frames does not necessarily translate into

participation, a social movement organization must provide compelling *motivational* frames that persuade people to join.

The process whereby individuals come to adopt the ideology and methods of a particular movement organization is called *frame alignment* (Snow et al. 1986). The alignment of interpretations is a necessary condition for maintaining participation. As Gamson suggests, "any movement that seeks to sustain commitment over a period of time must make the construction of collective identity one of its most central tasks" (Gamson 1991, 27).

THE POLITICAL PROCESS APPROACH

The **political process approach** assumes that the **polity** can be characterized by its opportunities and constraints. Opportunities involve almost anything that provides reasons and resources for people to mobilize—as long as the political climate is not so oppressive that people cannot mobilize without fear or great difficulty. Political opportunities may include economic crises, laws ensuring the right to assemble, a history of previous collective action, even accidents that show the need for social change. Constraints include anything within the polity that may act as a barrier to the mobilization and survival of a social movement, including a repressive police state, inexperience with collective action, even a lack of communication among social movement participants. Opportunities and constraints go hand in hand: no polity is completely open or closed (Tarrow 1998).

Fluctuations in the opportunities and constraints that influence the incidence of collective action create a cycle of contention. For instance, the rise and decline of collective action by Canadian Aboriginal bands from 1981 to 2000 can be seen in Figure 14.2 (Wilkes 2001). Protest events among Native groups in Canada rose dramatically between 1989 and 1991, peaking in the "Indian summer" of 1990. This increase can be attributed to the 78-day armed uprising at Kanesatake (Oka, Quebec) over municipal plans to convert a Mohawk burial ground into a golf course. Indigenous mobilization has continued since the 1990s with incidents such as Ipperwash in 1995, the Mi'kmaq Lobster Crisis in 1999, and the Assembly of First Nations national day of action in 2007. More recently, the Idle No

FIGURE 14.1

Number of Collective Resistance Actions by First Nations, 1981–2000, Canada

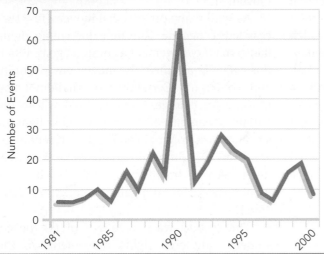

SOURCE: Rima Wilkes, "Competition or colonialism? An analysis of two theories of ethnic collective action" (PhD dissertation, University of Toronto, 2001). Reprinted by permission of the author.

More movement has opposed a government bill affecting waterways, environmental protection, and Native treaties by resorting to traditional forms of protest as well as newer tactics like flash mobs and the use of social media.

The political process model also looks at mobilizing structures, which include levels of informal and formal organization (McCarthy 1996). An example of informal organization is a friendship network. When the cycle of contention is at its lowest point—when there are relatively few (or no) active social movement organizations—the network of friendships among demobilized movement participants keeps the spirit of collective action alive. These latent networks explain why social movements arise when political opportunities appear and when constraints are eased. Although informal communication alone cannot give rise to a social movement, it can become an important resource for mobilization.

The analysis of formal organization looks at the inner dynamics of social movements, which

The well-publicized Oka Crisis resulted in the cancellation of the planned golf course, but more important, it highlighted on an international stage the continuing conflict between First Nations and the Canadian government.

include leadership structures, flows of communication, the entry and exit of members, and the means of identifying, obtaining, and utilizing resources. The study of social movement organizations also includes inter-organization dynamics, such as movement coalitions, which result when two or more social movement organizations share resources. Coalitions can be temporary or enduring, and they can bridge different types of movements. Environmental, feminist, gay and lesbian, labour, peace, and anti-poverty organizations in British Columbia, for example, have formed coalitions based on shared understandings of social injustice (Carroll and Ratner 1996).

TIME to REFLECT

Think about each of the social movement theories. Which one seems the most comprehensive? Can you think of ways to improve or combine these theories?

The Analysis of Social Movements

Why do some movements succeed while others fail? To help answer this question, we will briefly examine two social movements in Canada: the women's movement and the separatist movement in Quebec.

UNITY AND DIVERSITY IN THE CANADIAN WOMEN'S MOVEMENT

The first wave of feminism in Canada began in the late nineteenth century and effectively ended in 1918 when women gained the right to vote in federal elections. During this period, women formed organizations for the protection and education of young single women, such as the Anglican Girls Friendly Society and the Young Women's Christian Association (YWCA). Women's groups also protested against child labour and poor working conditions and pressed for health and welfare reforms.

Feminists of the first wave differed in their religious, class, and ethnic backgrounds. While many were Protestant, others were not. Anglo-Saxon women from the middle and upper classes predominated, especially among the leadership, while language divided anglo-phone and francophone feminists. Moreover, women's organizations had diverse goals. But the battle for women's voting rights unified the movement.

As with many other social movements, success led to decline. The fight for voting rights had given the movement a common goal. When this goal was attained, the movement lost unity and momentum. Certainly, women did not stop pushing for change. Some worked within the labour movement; others continued to fight for social reform or female political representation. Yet after 1918, the Canadian women's movement became fragmented, and four decades would pass before it regained strength (Wilson 1991).

The second wave rose out of the peace, student, and civil rights movements of the 1960s. In some cases, organizations advanced the women's cause by branching out. For example, a Toronto organization called the Voice of Women (VOW) was founded in 1960 as a peace group but gradually adopted other women's issues, and by 1964 it was promoting the legalization of birth control.

As a distinct women's movement emerged in the late 1960s and early 1970s, so did internal diversity. Some members were revolutionary Marxists while others were socialists, liberals, or radical feminists. At times, those who favoured grassroots activism criticized those who worked through high-profile official committees such as the Canadian Advisory Council on the Status of Women. The specific concerns of lesbian, non-white, immigrant, or Native women often were ignored or marginalized by mainstream women's groups. Finally, issues of language and separatism split women's organizations in Quebec from those in the rest of Canada.

Still, the movement found bases for unity. In 1970, a cross-Canada caravan for the repeal of the abortion law attracted publicity. Other coalitions formed around the issues of daycare, violence against women, labour, and poverty. Women's groups also worked together on International Women's Day celebrations.

To better represent their interests, in 1972 Canadian women formed the National Action Committee on the Status of Women (NAC). NAC grew and by the late 1980s had become an umbrella organization for more than 575 women's groups. At the same time, however, debate over the use of assisted reproductive technologies was growing. These technologies include cloning, surrogacy, assisted insemination, in vitro fertilization, embryo research, and prenatal diagnosis techniques. During a first round of consultations about these technologies with the federal government (1989–1993), NAC adopted a position that dissatisfied many of its members. Leaders of the women's organization argued that reproductive technologies were being developed not to meet the needs of ordinary women but to further the interests of the scientific community and the biotechnology industry. These technologies, claimed NAC, "represent the values and priorities of an economically stratified, male-dominated, technocratic science" (NAC 1990, quoted in Montpetit, Scala, and Fortier 2004, 145). Many within NAC disagreed with this position, which was seen as too simple and out of touch with concerns at the grassroots. Those offended included lesbians and infertile women who wished to bear children.

Between 1993 and 1997, therefore, NAC adopted a more open approach to the question. Discussions within the women's organization allowed ample room for the expression of diverse views. NAC now argued that assisted reproductive technologies are acceptable when they reduce inequalities between women.

The Canadian women's movement has organized around many issues. The diversity of its concerns and perspectives not only reflects the many faces of gender inequality but also promotes a diffusion of the movement's ideas and its survival in the face of changing social conditions. Internal arguments may exhaust activists, however. Although factions permit the coexistence of different constituencies, they draw attention and energy away from common interests that unify. When the time for action comes, a movement may lose effectiveness if its factions do not set aside their differences. As with all social movements, the success of the women's movement depends on balancing the trade-offs between diversity and unity (Briskin 1992).

TIME to REFLECT

In what ways, if any, do you believe the women's movement has altered your life and your attitudes about gender? Has the environmental movement had a greater or lesser effect on you than the women's movement?

UNDER the WIRE

G20 Protests in Toronto

In June 2010, world officials met in Toronto to discuss the global economy and to negotiate financial plans. Ever since the 1999 protests in Seattle, security has been strong at these economic summits, and Toronto police and private security firms had planned for months on how to deal with both peaceful and potentially riotous protests. Canadian and worldwide activists came to Toronto for a week of organized activity to help publicize their issues and grievances: worldwide poverty and growing inequality, the expansion of corporate power, colonialism and indigenous rights, women's undervalued global labour, environmental degradation, food security, financial deregulation, and so on. How did so many people get involved in protesting this (and other) financial summits? Why has protest activity now become expected by activists and police forces alike?

The answer is simple: the Internet and the ease of worldwide communication. Now that protest is fully "wired," activists can maintain a strong sense of collective identity and collective efficacy by staying in contact with one another, by reliving their triumphs and/or sorrows on YouTube, by recruiting and staying in touch through Facebook, by organizing and participating in online activist forums, or simply by adding their email address to a listserv, electronic newsletter, blog, or Twitter.

With more than 900 arrests in Toronto, activists have used online communication technologies to help raise money for legal fees and to publicize what some take to be police brutality or government repression. Toronto police are utilizing modern technologies too as they comb through footage of rioters and use advanced face-recognition software to identify those culpable for damages to property and for endangering public safety.

THE SEPARATIST MOVEMENT IN QUEBEC

What came to be known as the Easter Riots began on 28 March 1918 when police in Quebec City arrested a young man for avoiding conscription. As he was escorted to the police station, the suspect was followed by a group of angry sympathizers. Soon the police released him, but by then a crowd of some 2000 people had gathered. Instead of dispersing, they stormed the police station and gave several officers a beating. Next day, about 8000 people attacked the offices of two pro-conscription newspapers before setting fire to the office of the registrar for conscription.

Authorities in Quebec City and Ottawa responded quickly, partly because they feared a repeat of recent revolution and civil war in Mexico, South Africa, Ireland, and Russia. Bolstered by hundreds of English-speaking troops from Ontario and western Canada, over the next few days the army patrolled the streets of Quebec City, guarding key government buildings such as the Legislative Assembly, the Dominion Arsenal, and the Dominion Rifle Factory. This did not prevent a series of violent clashes that left up to 10 civilians dead and dozens of soldiers and civilians wounded (Auger 2008).

Other episodes of collective action for the French-Canadian cause followed, but until the 1960s they were sporadic. What was then known as French-Canadian "nationalism" was conservative. Its goal was to preserve the identity of the French by insulating them from outside influences: not just the English language but the world of politics, business, and the mass media.

Social change accelerated after the Asbestos Strike of 1949, a bitter labour dispute overlaid with ethnic tensions, because the miners who walked off the job for four months were mostly francophone while their managers tended to be English-speaking and the owners of mining companies were American. Through advances in communication—the spread of radio, telephone, and television—the world outside Quebec became ever harder to ignore during the 1950s. This encouraged comparison, self-scrutiny, and awareness that more social change was inevitable. Families relying on agriculture were disappearing, and most of the population was now urban. During the Great Depression, citizens had sought help from the Canadian state, whose reach expanded greatly during the two world wars. French Canadians could not escape modernity. Why not therefore assert control over its direction (Balthazar 1992)?

The 1960s and 1970s witnessed a sharp rise in collective action on behalf of the French in Quebec. In 1962, demonstrators in Montreal protested against the absence of any French speakers on the board of directors of Canadian National Railways. Queen Elizabeth's 1964 visit to Quebec City spurred anti-royalist, anti-British protests. When Prime Minister Trudeau paid a visit to Montreal for the annual Saint-Jean-Baptiste Day parade in 1968, hundreds of hostile and sometimes violent protesters voiced their opposition to the Liberal party and Canadian federalism. That same year, the school board for Saint-Léonard (a Montreal neighbourhood with a significant Italian minority) decided to limit the language of instruction in local schools to French. Immigration to Montreal was increasing, and the school board wanted to halt a trend—the adoption of English by newcomers—that threatened the importance of French. In what came to be known as the Saint-Léonard Crisis, unruly demonstrations continued as backers of Quebec's collective right to protect the French language confronted those who believed parents had a right to choose the language of instruction for their children (Hewitt 1994).

The October Crisis of 1970 is etched in our collective memory. Members of the Front de libération du Québec (FLQ) kidnapped a British diplomat in Montreal, James Cross, and then the provincial Minister of Labour, Pierre Laporte, who was murdered by his captors. This was the peak of contentious politics by nationalists in Quebec. Since its founding in 1963, the FLQ and allied groups had carried out bombings that targeted property and monuments associated with the federal government, big business, and British colonialism. The extremism of the FLQ alienated the majority of Quebecers, however, and indeed can be taken as a sign of its political weakness (Breton 1972; Hewitt 1994). The events of 1970 were the culmination of a wave of contention that subsided quickly thereafter.

Looking back on the period since the October Crisis of 1970, it is difficult to discern a separatist *movement* in Quebec. This raises some provocative questions. If political parties are now its main promoters, has separatism become tamed? As organizations that work within the political system, today the Parti Québécois and the Bloc Québécois push less for the independence of Quebec than for the decentralization of power in Canada. Around the globe, moreover, citizens are turning to social movements as they search for grassroots alternatives to parties. What political options does this leave for those in Quebec who are nationalists yet have no separatist movement to join and believe that the Parti Québécois and the Bloc Québécois are no different from other parties—remote, bureaucratic, and unable to fulfil their promises to voters?

TIME to REFLECT

Given what you have learned about the cyclical nature of social movement activity, what do you think the future holds for the separatist movement in Quebec? Can you justify your ideas with any particular social movement theory?

IS THE FUTURE OF SOCIAL MOVEMENTS GLOBAL?

Will globalization change the potential for social movement formation? Not all sociologists agree that globalization has created a fundamentally new political reality. Leslie Sklair (1994) argues that global politics are very much like national politics, simply on a larger scale. For Sklair, organizations such as Greenpeace International mirror the organizational structures of transnational corporations. He suggests that the global

(© CP Images/Paul Chiasson)

After nine years in opposition, the Parti Québécois won the provincial election in September 2012. However, Pauline Marois and her party will have to govern with a minority and may find it difficult to push their separatist agenda.

environmental movement consists of transnational environmental organizations whose professional members make up a global environmental elite. This elite plays an ideological game with the transnational corporate and governmental elite: each side attempts to have its version of the environmental reality accepted as the truth. For Sklair, this is politics as usual.

Sociologists also question whether the rise of supranational organizations, such as the European Union, will bring about new forms of collective action that link activists across national boundaries. Although the EU does constitute a new political terrain, collective action in Europe remains strongly rooted within the nation-state. While Europeans have many grievances against the EU, most protest against it is domestic rather than transnational. This may simply indicate that activists have yet to develop new transnational strategies and linkages. Nevertheless, domestic politics remains a viable political arena for voicing concerns about the EU (Imig and Tarrow 2001).

Today, the world is more intricately connected than in the past. A variety of new social issues have arisen as a result, and there are now social movements that attack globalization. Each has to identify guilty institutions and actors, however, and states and corporations remain the best choice, because they are largely responsible for the policies and practices that promote globalization.

Generally, three factors are needed for a social movement to be truly global. First, a social movement must frame its grievances as global grievances. By framing environmental risks as global risks, the environmental movement hopes to demonstrate that environmental degradation affects everyone. Second, to be global a social movement needs to have a worldwide membership and organizational structure. On a global scale, membership and frame alignment probably are supported by communication technologies such as email and the World Wide Web. Alternatively, a global movement can arise through a long-term coalition or network of movement organizations. Indigenous peoples across North and South America, Australia, and New Zealand have united against the ongoing effects of colonialism and to ensure that the rights of indigenous populations are recognized. Third, collective identity has to be a globalized identity. Global activists throughout the world would have to see each other as serving the same, common goal. Each would also have to identify cognitively and emotionally with that goal, as well as with other global activists and movement organizations.

TIME to REFLECT

Can you think of any causes that you would be prepared to go to jail or die for? Why are some issues more important to you than other issues?

Conclusion

In this chapter, we have highlighted a number of key perspectives to help you grasp how sociologists understand politics. In doing so, we noted that unlike many other social sciences and vernacular understandings of politics and political movements, sociologists see these processes as being inherently linked to the negotiation of power. Sociologists, moreover, understand power as a relational concept that involves the overt and hidden interactions of individuals and groups, organizations and institutions. We also highlighted that the state plays a prominent role in political sociology, because it remains a key force in structuring political processes and shaping political resources. Throughout the chapter, we illustrated this by looking at material, cultural, social, and institutional resources to understand how they are used to maintain power as well as launch challenges to it through political movements.

Early forms of collective action were poorly organized and relatively sporadic. Often their grievances were tied to local affairs, and usually their targets were local elites. With the rise of nation-states, however, new kinds of social movements appeared. These movements were highly organized and often identified social issues that stemmed from structural conditions such as economic inequality and narrow political representation. They also routinized protest activities: different social movements learned to apply similar methods of protest, such as the mass demonstration. The rise of NSMs in the second half of the twentieth century marks another change. These movements are more concerned with gaining cultural recognition than with the redistribution of social goods. So even though NSMs tend to use traditional forms of protest, they are more concerned with the politics of everyday life (the politics of recognition) than with the traditional politics of governance (the politics of redistribution).

The success of collective action is always linked to the social and political climate. Social and political changes can create opportunities for social movements, or they can impose constraints. According to a theory developed by Herbert Kitschelt (1993), present conditions in Canada have created opportunities that may lead to an increase in social movement activity. Support for social movements usually rises when political parties and interest groups fail to channel citizens' demands. Social movements can then mobilize support, attract resources, and forge alliances among protest groups. According to Kitschelt, however, this surge in social movement activity peaks as resources dwindle, as political parties begin to take up citizens' concerns, and as people's interest in collective mobilization wanes. Social movement activity then falls, only to rise again the next time organizers capitalize on frustration with parties and interest groups. In other words, the short-term pattern of movement activity is cyclical.

The long-term trend, by contrast, is toward an increase in the number of social movements. In the wealthy capitalist democracies, social movement activity has grown steadily since the 1960s. Established parties and politicians have proved increasingly incapable of providing satisfactory solutions to such issues as nuclear power, toxic waste disposal, resource management, and equal rights. Many Canadians now share a distrust of established politicians, political parties, and interest groups. Clearly, the extent of citizen discontent should not be exaggerated: federal elections show that established parties still attract much support. Nevertheless, many burning public questions—around gender; citizen participation; and environmental, ethnic, and Native rights issues—often elude both parties and interest groups. The current climate in Canada, therefore, favours an expansion of social movement activity. Whether organizers will actually exploit this situation remains to be seen. The outcome will depend on social movement leaders and on the political establishment's ability to co-opt them.

questions for critical thought

1. We don't usually think of our capacities to pursue our interests in terms of the *power* we hold relative to others. In what ways is your capacity to "realize your will" or do what you want *enabled* by your access to material, cultural and social, and/or institutional resources?

2. Does the Canadian state influence how you go about your daily life? How does it affect your power, your rights, and your ability to challenge authority?

3. What can account for Quebec nationalism in the 1970s, 1980s, and 1990s? Why have Aboriginal peoples been active in resisting the colonizing efforts of the Canadian government?

4. With regard to the worldwide economic problems that began in 2008, does economic prosperity encourage or hinder the formation of protest movements? Would you expect more protest or less as a result? Which countries do you think will be more likely to experience social movement action? Which would be less likely? Can you draw on social movement theory to justify your answers to these questions?

5. Many people today believe that social movements offer better prospects for democratic participation than political parties or interest groups. However, Roberto Michels's "iron law of oligarchy" says that organization discourages democratic participation because resources, expertise, and status tend to flow to leaders. If you were organizing a social movement, what kind of safeguards would you put in place to prevent social movement leaders from dominating a movement organization? Are there lessons to be learned from the women's movement about decentred decision-making or participatory organizational forms?

6. Why do you think that some social issues provoke social movement campaigning while other issues are hardly addressed by social movement activities? Do you think that these "orphan" issues have something in common that does not resonate with Canadian (or global) society? How might an activist frame an issue to increase the chances that people will pay attention?

recommended readings

Ronald R. Aminzade, Jack A. Goldstone, Doug McAdam, Elizabeth J. Perry, William H. Sewell, Sidney Tarrow, and Charles Tilly., eds. 2001. *Silence and Voice in the Study of Contentious Politics*. New York: Cambridge University Press.
This text is an excellent collection of empirical research testing contentious politics theory.

Douglas Baer, ed. 2002. *Political Sociology: Canadian Perspectives*. Don Mills, ON: Oxford University Press.
This introductory text presents an overview of Canadian scholarship in political sociology and includes many of the area's key luminaries.

Christian Davenport, Hank Johnston, and Carol Mueller, eds. 2005. *Repression and Mobilization*. Minneapolis: University of Minnesota Press.
A collection of essays on state responses to collective action, this is a must-read for students of social movements.

Donatella della Porta, Massimiliano Andretta, Lorenzo Mosca, and Herbert Reiter. 2006. *Globalization from Below: Transnational Activists and Protest Networks*. Minneapolis: University of Minnesota Press.
Challenging the idea that global social movements are merely coalitions of local movements, the authors argue that the global movement against neo-liberalism is a form of collective action that represents important changes in tactics, collective identities, and patterns of organization.

Richard Lachmann. 2010. *States and Power*. Cambridge: Polity Press.
This text offers an overview of how states emerged and how they have come to dominate contemporary

political processes. It introduces students to key perspectives on theories of the state.

Kate Nash and Alan Scott, eds. 2001. *The Blackwell Companion to Political Sociology*. Malden, MA: Blackwell.
An encyclopedia of North American political sociology, this book is a one-stop resource that covers the main debates and innovations in this area of sociology.

David Snow, Sarah A. Soule, and Hanspeter Kriesi, eds. 2004. *The Blackwell Companion to Social Movements*. Oxford: Blackwell.
This is a comprehensive examination of the state of social movement research and what remains to be studied and theorized. Chapters are written by well-known movement scholars.

Suzanne Staggenborg. 2012. *Social Movements*. 2nd edn. Don Mills, ON: Oxford University Press.
Staggenborg provides a thorough introduction to major social movement theories as well as a comprehensive account of the history of important Canadian social movements.

Karen Stanbridge and Howard Ramos. 2012. *Seeing Politics Differently: A Brief Introduction to Political Sociology*. Don Mills, ON: Oxford University Press.
Stanbridge and Ramos provide an introduction to political sociology by challenging the common assumption that people can be "not that into" politics. It looks at much Canadian scholarship and examples to illustrate points.

Sidney Tarrow. 1998. *Power in Movements: Social Movements and Contentious Politics*. 2nd edn. New York: Cambridge University Press.
A scholar versed in theory and empirical work on both sides of the Atlantic, Tarrow presents an up-to-date survey of social movement studies.

recommended websites

AlterNet
www.alternet.org
AlterNet is an award-winning Web magazine dedicated to issues of social justice and the promotion and amplification of alternative voices.

American Sociological Association: Section on Collective Behavior and Social Movements
www.asanet.org/sections/cbsm.cfm
This a good starting place for more information on the sociological study of social movements. Read *Critical Mass*, the section's newsletter, to be informed of new publications, conferences, and the latest research.

Assembly of First Nations
www.afn.ca
This very comprehensive site contains detailed information about social issues pertaining to Canada's First Nations.

Canadian Centre for Policy Alternatives
www.policyalternatives.ca
This is the official website of the Canadian Centre for Policy Alternatives, an independent non-profit organization committed to presenting counter-hegemonic information.

Canadian Lesbian and Gay Archives (CLGA)
www.clga.ca
This site provides information that relates to lesbian, gay, bisexual, and transgender movements. Its focus is mostly Canadian, but the archive also provides plenty of information from around the world.

Canadian Race Relations Foundation
www.crr.ca
The Canadian Race Relations Foundation's primary goal is to end race- and ethnic-based discrimination in Canada. This website provides information about current issues and research.

Centre for Social Justice
www.socialjustice.org
This organization was established in 1997 and is based in Toronto. Its goals are to foster national and international social change through research and advocacy.

Charter of Rights and Freedoms
http://laws-lois.justice.gc.ca/eng/Const/page-15.html#h-39
The Department of Justice hosts this website of the Canadian Charter of Rights and Freedoms, which is the freestanding first 34 sections of the Constitution Act, 1982.

Independent Media
www.independentmedia.ca
This website offers a directory of non-corporate journalism. It lists many news sources that are not widely disseminated or are missed by mainstream audiences.

The Onion
www.theonion.com
The Onion is an alternative spoof newspaper and website. It provides humorous political commentary on current events and news and is both informative and entertaining.

Rabble.ca
www.rabble.ca
Rabble.ca is a prominent alternative Web source of information on Canadian news and politics. It regularly presents articles and essays by politicians, academics, and activists.

PART V

Canadian Society and the Global Context

chapter 15

Globalization and Social Change

Liam Swiss

In this chapter, you will:

▶ Explore different theoretical perspectives on globalization and how they account for social change.

▶ Examine various types of global flows of capital, goods, and people to gain a better understanding of how globalization affects us all.

▶ Learn more about competing global networks of groups actively trying to shape the globalization agenda.

▶ Appreciate the tensions between convergence and divergence associated with globalization and how these processes contribute to social change.

Introduction

How is globalization affecting your daily life? How is it changing the world around you? Do we witness and critically engage with the effects of globalization, or do we take them for granted? These questions underline the contradictory nature of globalization in most lives. It can be at once implicated everywhere and in everything and simultaneously can be overlooked by many in society. Past discussions of globalization have viewed it as primarily an economic process. Indeed, it is often regarded as a homogenizing economic force within global society. Economic policies and development processes lead to a seemingly increasingly similar world where you can just as easily buy an Apple iPhone in suburban Calgary as you can in central New Delhi or Cape Town. Emerging global similarities—like the Apple iPhone—and the effects of neo-liberal economic policies are surely signs of globalization's impact on our world; however, to confine our understanding of globalization to a narrow economic interpretation is to ignore other facets of globalization that have political, cultural, and social implications beyond the scope of economic matters. Furthermore, apart from the homogenizing effects of globalization that hold the potential to promote convergence of different societies toward similar products, policies, and perspectives, we must equally assess the potential of globalization to divide and further differentiate societies and communities at the global and, indeed, national levels. The tension between convergence and divergence has been a central question of the sociology of globalization and will frame this chapter's exploration of globalization(s) and the various sociological views on them.

First, we will engage with the concepts of convergence and divergence to emphasize what we can interpret as evidence of either process of social change occurring at the global level. Next, the chapter outlines a range of ways in which globalization can be conceptualized economically, socio-culturally, and politically. Within the context of this tension between convergence and divergence, these various manifestations of globalization will be interpreted through three prominent sociological approaches to understanding globalization: the world system perspective, the world society perspective, and a range of perspectives on space and time. These theoretical vantage points conceive of globalization in differing yet interrelated ways, allowing sociologists to engage with globalization as a complex and varied set of processes leading to social change. These globalization processes involve a variety of flows and connections that make globalization apparent in everyday life in concrete ways. By examining these flows and the networks of actors involved in enacting and facilitating them through the lens of the various sociological perspectives on globalization, the chapter will close by weighing the evidence for convergence and divergence and arguing that globalization's role in social change is a contradictory one that both levels and divides societies, states, and people on an ongoing basis.

Convergence vs. Divergence

There are many ways in which globalization promotes social change. We cannot address them all in this chapter, but one ongoing debate surrounding globalization and social change that we will examine is the question of convergence versus divergence. These are opposing trends in social change in global society. Convergence can be seen in ways that globalization makes people, societies, and states more similar, uniform, or homogenous. Divergence, on the other hand, can be found in ways that globalization makes the world more unequal, differentiated, or diverse. Are these changes mutually exclusive? If we consider them as absolutes, yes. If we consider the possibility that we might witness convergence and divergence operating simultaneously, then the social change resulting from globalization will be more complex and multidirectional than we might think at first blush. In the remainder of this chapter, as we explore different sociological perspectives on globalization, the global flows associated with the process, and the key actors involved, be mindful of the following questions:

1. Is globalization promoting convergence?
2. Is globalization promoting divergence?
3. Is it leading to convergence and divergence simultaneously?

Sociological Approaches to Globalization

With the wide range of ways that globalization is evident in our daily lives, it is not surprising that sociologists have devised a variety of theoretical perspectives on what globalization is and how it works. These perspectives address different facets of the globalization phenomenon. This chapter will expose you to three perspectives that have influenced the way that sociologists interpret globalization and social change: the *world system perspective*, the *world society perspective*, and a number of perspectives on space and time. Although each perspective offers a unique take on what globalization is and why it happens, sociologists may use all of them to help understand different aspects of globalization.

THE WORLD SYSTEM PERSPECTIVE

When we consider globalization as a process, the first thing that probably comes to mind is its economic dimension. The world system perspective offers one lens through which to view economic globalization, but it does contradict some widespread popular beliefs about the globalization process. In particular, while some see it as a relatively recent phenomenon, supporters of the world system approach argue that economic globalization today is simply a continuation of a series of long economic cycles in the capitalist world system (Arrighi 1994; Chase-Dunn and Grimes 1995; Chase-Dunn 1998; Wallerstein 1976, 1979b).

Emerging initially in the 1970s as a refinement of the dependency theories of economic development and a rejection of the earlier modernization theories, the world system perspective rejects the concept of "national" development and instead emphasizes that the only development that can be observed is within the capitalist world system (Chase-Dunn and Grimes 1995; Wallerstein 1979a, b). The need to view the system as a global whole, acknowledging that states are simply smaller parts of the world system, is one of the main arguments of this perspective.

This focus on the capitalist world system breaks down its component states into three categories: a developed core, the semi-periphery, and an underdeveloped periphery. Capital accumulation flows from periphery to core as a consequence of the overall workings of the world system and the unequal power hierarchy of core and periphery (Chase-Dunn and Grimes 1995). Countries in the periphery can only benefit from the interaction of globalization and economic development through increased integration of the periphery into the world economy in a more competitive fashion (Portes 1997). As the world economy expands, states that are better integrated within it will stand a greater chance of benefitting from global economic expansion (Wallerstein 1979a). Considering each of the three categories in turn will give us a better sense of the roles they play in the globalization process.

Core countries are at the centre of economic and political power on the global stage. Economic production in the core depends on skilled, high-wage labour and requires significant amounts of capital (Chase-Dunn 1998). The core accumulates capital through appropriating the surpluses or profits of the capitalist world system. Through this control of resources, the core is able to evolve more complex modes of production and maintain its global political and military supremacy. Unsurprisingly, the core countries identified in the Figure 15.1 map align very closely to the countries defined as the high-income OECD countries by the World Bank.

In contrast, the **periphery** is that part of the world where we would expect to find labour-intensive economic production, often linked to resource extraction but relying on low-skilled and low-wage labour (Chase-Dunn 1998). The periphery accumulates little of the global capitalist surplus and therefore has few resources on which to develop or expand its share of global wealth and power. Similarly, peripheral countries tend to be on the margins of global political and military power, lacking the power that dominant core countries possess. Figure 15.1 shows that the periphery aligns with the countries in the Global South defined by the World Bank as members of the low-income group.

Not surprisingly, the **semi-periphery** comprises countries that show a mix of both core and peripheral characteristics. This third

FIGURE 15.1   World System Map

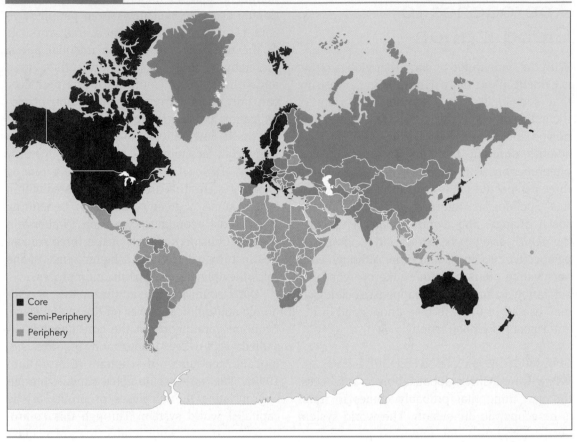

- Core
- Semi-Periphery
- Periphery

SOURCE: Map created by author using data from Jason Beckfield, 2003, "Inequality in the world polity: The structure of international organization." *American Sociological Review* 68 (3): 401–24, and author's own coding.

category is a necessary feature of the world system, preventing overt conflict between core and periphery, with the semi-periphery as "both exploited and exploiter," thus emphasizing the dual nature of such countries (Wallerstein 1979b, 23). It is a buffer between the two extremes of core and periphery, and as the map in Figure 15.1 indicates, it is composed mainly of countries with longer histories of independence as well as a number of the former members of the Soviet bloc.

TIME to REFLECT

Where do you believe Canada fits into the core/semi-periphery/periphery scheme? Can you think of arguments to place it in another category?

This single global division of labour underpins the capitalist world system, but it is not based on any one centre of power. Certain core countries may become dominant or hegemonic in various periods, but this hegemony can shift. In the nineteenth century, Britain held a position of dominance in the world system. After World War II, a period of American hegemony succeeded British dominance (Chase-Dunn 1998). Signs of American decline were becoming apparent to world system researchers in the 1990s, but no new hegemon has emerged within the core. Some speculate about a coming period of Asian hegemony, corresponding to the recent rise of China as an economic superpower, as possibly the next evolution in the world system (Arrighi 1998). Still others suggest that China is unlikely to jump from semi-periphery to core status and instead is more likely to become the site of a proxy battle by other core powers and the interests of multinational corporations (Petras 2006). This underlines one of the main contentions of the world system perspective: it is very difficult for societies/states to move between the three categories of core, semi-periphery, and periphery. Much more likely is movement within categories as countries ebb and flow in terms of economic and political importance. Globalization and social change from the world system perspective thus reflects the evolution of the capitalist world economy as it cycles through periods of expansion and contraction linked to capital accumulation, innovation, political competition, and other power struggles (Arrighi 1994). These systemic cycles of global capitalism, rather than any truly novel form of economic organization, are what we have come to recognize as economic globalization in recent years. The integration of economies into the global capitalist system is not a new phenomenon and indeed simply supports world system arguments that the capitalist world system should be sociologists' chief concern when considering globalization.

If we consider the implications of the world system perspective in the context of our question of convergence and divergence, we can see within the core–periphery divide a very clear argument in favour of globalization as a divergent force. Global capitalist accumulation requires the exploitation of the periphery by the core. While the core benefits and advances economically and politically, the periphery, if not falling further behind, at least experiences relatively persistent levels of deprivation compared to the core and semi-periphery (Chase-Dunn 1998). Globalization from this perspective is primarily an economic manifestation of capitalist exploitation leading to the aggrandisement of the core at the expense of others. With this focus on a narrow interpretation of global capitalism, the world system perspective lens offers a unique view of economic globalization but does little to address some of the other forms of globalization that surround us. To add to our understanding of these other forms, the next two sections explore alternative sociological viewpoints on globalization: the world society and space/time perspectives.

THE WORLD SOCIETY PERSPECTIVE

If you look around the global community, you might take for granted that states appear to share very similar structures and practices. These similarities might include things like central banks, education systems, environmental regulations, and human rights frameworks. Rather than tak-

ing this similarity for granted, sociologists have asked, Why *do* states and other organizations so closely resemble one another despite their widely varying histories? This is the question at the crux of the world society perspective popularized by a group of sociologists associated with John W. Meyer of Stanford University. Meyer and his students argue that the striking similarities we witness in terms of policies, structures, and other institutions of the state arise from a common set of "world cultural" norms, scripts, and models adopted and implemented by states (Meyer 2007; Meyer et al. 1997). Such norms and models spell out what is expected of a legitimate state or other organization in the global community. They arise because of the efforts of international non-state actors like non-governmental organizations, intergovernmental bodies, and networks/communities of experts globally (Boli and Thomas 1997; 1999). These organizations compose what "world society" is and create, spread, and refine these common models and scripts at the global level.

States enact these scripts in order to be deemed legitimate by their peers, citizens, and the others (non-state actors) of world society. This leads to the striking similarities seen globally among states, something sociologists have identified as institutional isomorphism: the similarity of organizational structure emerging from imitation, coercion, or pressures of legitimacy (DiMaggio and Powell 1983). Because states enact similar scripts—the structuring of legal systems to protect human rights, for instance—we begin to see state structures closely resemble one another despite diverse contexts.

What drives states and other actors to enact these scripts? World society researchers have highlighted the influence of two key factors that promote the diffusion of world cultural models among states: (1) embeddedness: the extent to which a state is tied to the rationalized others of world society through global networks of ties, memberships, and treaty adoptions; and (2) model density: the extent to which previous adoption of a model by other states or organizations influences other states to act similarly (Hughes et al. 2009; Swiss 2009, 2012; Yoo 2011). Embeddedness, simply put, involves the influence of NGOs, experts, and global treaties and conferences on states. Model density, on the other hand, represents influence exerted by the actions of other states. Described sometimes as a **contagion** or demonstration effect, we can see density as a form of either peer pressure or as evidence that various models and institutions are worth adopting. The combination of embeddedness and model density have indeed been shown to affect the adoption of world models as varied as women's rights (Paxton, Hughes, and Green 2006; Swiss 2009; Wotipka and Ramirez 2008), environmental protection (Frank, Longhofer, and Schofer 2007; Schofer and Hironaka 2005), and education (Schofer and Meyer 2005).

If these models are so influential, why do we not see institutional isomorphism everywhere and an international community composed of nearly identical states? Evidence suggests that a key feature of the world society perspective is what has been described as either a loose coupling or a complete decoupling of model implementation and intent (Clark 2010; Drori et al. 2003; Swiss 2009). This accounts for the great variation we see in implementation of

world-level models within local contexts and explains the persistent divergence in the global community. One example is states signing on to treaties intended to protect human rights or to reduce greenhouse gas emissions but then failing to protect such rights or cut emissions.

The gap between democracy in intent and democracy in application in many states of the Global South is also evidence of persistent decoupling in the global community. Despite elections held to promote the appearance of free, fair, and accountable government, the actual practices of democracy often fall far short of what we might in Canada deem "free" or "fair." Loose coupling is linked to a number of causes. For instance, Clark (2010) argues that less wealthy, non-Western, and conflict-prone states are more likely to experience loose coupling in the area of human rights. These causes of decoupling suggest that the application of world society models can be very uneven globally, and indeed, other research suggests that world society's reach is unequal and can

(© CP Images/Fred Chartrand)

Canada's failure to follow through with its commitment to cut CO_2 emissions under the Kyoto accord is an example of the decoupling phenomenon. On 12 December 2011, Environment Minister Peter Kent announced that Canada would withdraw from the accord to avoid large fines for not meeting its targets.

exclude parts of the Global South in significant ways (Beckfield 2003; 2008).

TIME to REFLECT

How does Canada's track record on its international commitments to cut greenhouse gas emissions demonstrate decoupling?

A final feature of the world society perspective is the extent to which the models and norms that world society promotes are not static or fixed. Instead, they evolve and are refined as norms become institutionalized by various actors. In this sense, world culture is dynamic and subject to contestation and change. States and other organizations implementing certain models and scripts draw upon their experience of enacting such scripts as they collaborate further with international non-governmental and intergovernmental organizations to tweak and alter the content of world cultural scripts going forward.

In the world society perspective, the focus is placed squarely on institutions and how they appear increasingly similar on the global level. Particular attention is paid to the relationship of states to a world society consisting of international organizations, networks of experts, and other actors that shape world cultural institutional scripts and models. The world society perspective, in this respect, is likely best equipped to explain and characterize questions of political globalization and aspects of global governance. In contrast, it is less equipped to account for economic globalization than the world system perspective. Nor can it explain cultural forms of globalization as readily as we might expect, given its focus on "world cultural models." As we will see in the next section, a group of other perspectives offers a better lens through which to examine the cultural effects of globalization.

SPACE/TIME PERSPECTIVES

In contrast to the relatively unified world system and world society perspectives discussed above, the range of views labelled here as space/time perspectives encompass a number of attempts to describe and understand globali-

zation by examining how the world is becoming increasingly connected through changes in the way that society interacts with space and time. These changes can be seen in societies abandoning conventional relationships with time and space (Giddens 1990), increased global awareness as a result of greater interconnectedness (Robertson 1992; 1995), global networks underpinned by new technologies (Castells 2000), and changing concepts of locality (Sassen 2007). As we will see, this sort of lens on globalization enables us to go beyond the purely economic or institutional globalizations treated by the world system and world society perspectives and provides a means for examining other social and cultural shifts associated with globalization.

Anthony Giddens defined globalization as the "intensification of worldwide social relations which link distant localities in such a way that local happenings are shaped by events occurring many miles away and vice versa " (1990, 64). This intensification of relations leads to greater interconnectedness globally both in the linking of distant places and in the extent to which what happens elsewhere works to shape events in any particular locality. Roland Robertson echoes this notion that what goes on elsewhere in the world matters more to us than it did in the past. He defines globalization as "the compression of the world and the intensification of consciousness of the world as a whole" (1992, 8). Both definitions emphasize the idea that the world is becoming more interconnected and that a process of intensification or compression is at play, connecting localities both in real terms and in terms of awareness in an unprecedented way.

Giddens argues that this process of intensification is linked to increases in the level of time–space distanciation experienced in society. This concept refers to the ways in which "time and space are organised so as to connect presence and absence" (Giddens 1990, 14). With increased levels of time–space distanciation, we see greater global interconnectedness emerge by "fostering relations between 'absent' others, locationally distant from any given situation of face-to-face interaction" (Giddens 1990, 18). This change in the notion of space and place closely parallels a similar concept described as time–space compression, which refers to processes that change the way we view time and space, compressing or accelerating time and shrinking distances through technologies associated with communication or travel (Harvey 1990). These changes in the social functioning of time, facilitated by technologies and emerging networks, have gone so far as to encourage operation of business and social relations globally in "real time" outside of the traditional linear conceptions of time, something Castells refers to as timeless time (2000). These changing social notions of time and space contribute to the shrinking of the world that Robertson identifies and, in turn, help to make individuals more aware of the global.

TIME to REFLECT

How have technological advances and other global networks changed the way people relate to one another in your lifetime?

Building upon notions of space–time compression and the intermixing of global and local, other thinkers in the space/time perspective have emphasized the importance of understanding globalization as building links or networks across borders and societal boundaries, altering traditional notions of place, and breaking down the conventional sense of local (Castells 2000; Sassen 2007). With their emphasis on the networks and spatiality of globalization, both Castells and Sassen echo the notions discussed above of a compressed world, with boundaries between local and foreign blurred. Castells emphasizes, alongside his notion of timeless time, the idea of the space of flows, which refers to the manner in which space has become less connected to actual physical places and is now connected to the flows of ideas, communication, and relations fostered by the network society and underscoring the global economy. Sassen's work on global cities also examines how changing notions of space and the definition of "local" are resulting in new ways of working, communicating, and living in the globalized world. She highlights the important ways in which boundaries and borders that had once separated place and space are now being transformed as a result

of globalization, leading to the emergence of global cities and corresponding transnational communities of financial and economic activity (Sassen 2001). These cities exist at the nexus of global and local and reflect the extent to which local cultures are being reshaped to incorporate global concerns as a result of the changed context of space and place in the global era.

Global cities, like Toronto, Montreal, and Vancouver, are a crucial aspect of the global economic system. For an extended discussion of global cities, turn to the Global Issues box, p. 333 in Chapter 16.

Robertson also draws attention to the overlooked place of culture and identity within the globalization context and argues that the "intensification of consciousness of the world as a whole" led to emerging similarities in social structure and identity, because these things were more often being defined relative to others globally (1992). This process of relativization is an important feature of this view of globalization, since it implies that all features of the global community (states, humankind, individuals, and so on) are constantly being shaped relative to all others. This relativization is a significant indicator of the global awareness Robertson identifies.

Even though states, societies, and individuals might be shaping their identities relative to others globally, this does not mean that we should expect to see a uniform world emerging. Indeed, Robertson suggests that we should instead see the interpenetration of both the universal and the particular as a result of this relativization. This contradiction of convergence and divergence (universal versus particular) is evident in the ways that globalized identities, commodities, and structures are adapted or modified in local practice. Robertson labels this mixing of global and local as **glocalization**, reflecting the mixing of global and local whether strategically or organically (Robertson 1995). Others have referred to this mixing of convergence and divergence as a form of cultural hybridization in which we see emerging out of the globalization process cultures that reflect mixtures of global and local traits and have a relationship to place very different from

Glocalization and the Maharaja Mac

What is glocalization, and how does it function? We might think that seeing the effects of the mixing of global and local might be a difficult thing to do, but we do not have to look much further than the McDonald's restaurants that have so often been a major referent of the **Americanization** of the world associated with globalization.

In India, for instance, the Big Mac has been replaced on the McDonald's menu by the "Maharaja Mac." Originally based on goat or lamb meat, all McDonald's "burgers" in India are now chicken-based. Why would we see a change to such an American staple? Not surprisingly, the double beef patties of the original Big Mac would not go over too well in a country where the majority of the population follows the Hindu faith, revere the cow as sacred, and do not eat

beef. Moreover, some customers might mistake mutton for beef. Thus, the Maharaja Mac was born out of a process of glocalization that still enables Indian customers to partake of the McDonald's experience but in a way that caters to local tastes. Other glocalized items on the McDonald's menu in India include items such as the "McSpicy Paneer" (a battered, deep-fried patty composed of the Indian curdled milk cheese, paneer) or the "McAloo Tikki" (a potato- and pea-based patty in a burger bun with typical burger trimmings, representing a McDonald's version of the traditional "Aloo Tikki" snack common throughout north India). These examples demonstrate the concept of glocalization but provide clear evidence of the mixing of cultures at work in the globalization of fast food.

the way that relationship is conventionally interpreted as fixed and static (Pieterse 1994). This notion of globalization as at once converging and diverging is an important counterpoint to views of globalization that would argue for uniformity as a chief outcome of globalization.

Though less cohesive than either the world system or world society perspectives, the space/time perspective grapples with an equally important aspect of how society is changing in the era of globalization. Through examination of how time and space are reshaped by technological advances and increasing global awareness, this perspective offers a number of convincing models of why we see altogether different forms of social relations emerging in the realms of economics, politics, and culture. This move away from conventional relationships to time and space can be seen in the increased flows of ideas, communication, capital, and people throughout the increasingly compressed global community. At once connecting peoples and societies, removing national boundaries and barriers, and at the same time encouraging hybrid forms of glocal cultural interpretation to emerge, this perspective can simultaneously support arguments for both convergence and divergence—a contradiction we will examine in the following sections.

(© Tim Whitby / Alamy)

Ronald McDonald welcomes visitors with a traditional greeting at a McDonald's restaurant in Bangkok, Thailand. The success of McDonald's in foreign markets like Thailand relies on the food chain's adaptability to local customs and environment.

TABLE 15.1 ▼ Summary of Sociological Perspectives on Globalization

Perspective	Key Thinkers	Key Features	Strengths	Convergence vs. Divergence
World System	– Wallerstein – Chase-Dunn – Arrighi	– Core – Periphery – Semi-periphery – Capitalist world system	– Explains persistent global inequality and exploitation	– Convergence in encompassing all societies globally – Divergence between core and periphery
World Society	– Meyer	– World cultural models – World society composed of international organizations and actors	– Explains institutional isomorphism and common policy models	– Convergence around world cultural norms – Divergence in decoupling of policy from practice
Space/Time	– Giddens – Robertson – Harvey – Castells – Sassen	– Changing social roles for space and time – Effect of global networks and recent technological changes	– Explains increasing global interconnectedness – Explains mixing of global and local: hybridity	– Convergence in shifting relationships to time and place – Divergence in ways that glocalization promotes local adaptation

GLOBALIZATION IN PERSPECTIVE

What do these three perspectives tell us about globalization as a whole? Each perspective has strengths and highlights key features of the globalization process. These highlights are captured in Table 15.1.

What do these perspectives tell us about convergence and divergence? Table 15.1 suggests support for both trends. The capitalist world system suggests convergence in the way that it encompasses all societies globally, but the sharp cleavages within that system between core and periphery reflect divergence. Likewise, the world society perspective explains convergence emerging around world cultural models and the way they are enacted by states. Simultaneously, however, divergence from these models appears in the form of decoupling between intent and implementation—often with the weakest states being most likely to fall short of these models in practice. Finally, the space/time perspective suggests we are seeing a converging world with instant, real-time communication and the building of communities or places over great distance; however, if we consider the exclusion of people in the Global South from these technological and social changes, these changes can be considered a form of divergence. This mixed evidence of convergence and divergence in all three perspectives suggests that we need to look instead at how globalization manifests itself in various global flows—economic, social, cultural, and political.

Global Flows

If we consider each of the perspectives on globalization explored above, we can see that a common feature is the centrality of global interconnectedness manifested through the flow of various things, ideas, and people throughout the global community. By examining global flows, we can learn how globalization does matter in our daily lives and how it is related to processes of convergence and divergence associated with social change. This section looks at three types of flows: (1) capital, goods, and services; (2) transportation and information/communication technologies; and (3) people. Looking at each of these flows, we will ask what patterns have developed in recent decades and what they indicate about globalization and its effects on social change.

CAPITAL/GOODS/SERVICES

Given that globalization is frequently conflated with economics, it is worth considering its economic manifestations through various economic flows. We can identify such flows concretely by simply looking at the manufacturer's tag in your clothing or considering where the banana you ate for breakfast came from. If you are reading this in Canada, it is highly unlikely that those jeans or that banana originated there. This reflects the globalization of trade and manufacturing that has occurred over the past several decades. Figure 15.2, which shows what proportion of global gross domestic product (GDP) is linked to trade, illustrates the growth in trade over the past four decades. In 1970, trade amounted to just over 27 per cent of global GDP. Twenty years later, trade's share of GDP had jumped to almost 39 per cent. Another 20 years later, in 2010, trade accounted for almost 56 per cent of global income. With the share of global income linked to trade doubling in just 40 years, we can see direct evidence of the increased flows of goods and services globally. Bear in mind, though, that these figures represent the global average. To take Canada alone

during this period, the share of trade as percentage of GDP jumped from about 42 per cent in 1970 to an unprecedented level of more than 85 per cent in 2000, then fell back to hover around 60 per cent in 2009 and 2010 (World Bank 2011).

These sharp increases in trade are paralleled by similar increases in global flows of capital investment, both in stock markets (portfolio investment) and directly in capital in foreign countries (foreign direct investment). Figure 15.3 shows both measures, using World Bank data for investment at the global level for the period 1990 to 2010.

These figures tell us a story of accelerated flows of goods, services, and capital in recent years, something that has been influenced by neo-liberalism as a dominant economic model.

▼ **FIGURE 15.2**   Trade as Percentage of Global GDP, 1970–2010

SOURCE: Graph created by author using data from World Bank, *World Development Indicators,* http://databank.worldbank.org/ddp/home.do?Step=12&id=4&CNO=2 (Washington: World Bank 2011).

▼ **FIGURE 15.3**   Global Investment Trends, 1990–2010

SOURCE: Graph created by author using data from World Bank, *World Development Indicators*, http://databank.worldbank.org/ddp/home.do?Step=12&id=4&CNO=2 (Washington: World Bank 2011).

The neo-liberal economic model is based on concepts of free-market libertarianism, rational choice, and the belief that the state should interfere as little as possible in the market economy. To foster economic growth, advocates of neo-liberalism support free trade, privatization of state enterprise, widespread deregulation, the free flow of capital, and austerity measures to curtail government spending (Portes 1997). Neo-liberalism was adopted by both the World Bank and the International Monetary Fund in the 1980s, which led to the implementation of austerity measures called structural adjustment programs in many countries of the developing world (Bradshaw et al. 1993; Portes 1997; Sen 1999; Stiglitz 2002).

These programs and the neo-liberal agenda have been sharply criticized by many social scientists, particularly for the disproportionate negative impact they have on disadvan-taged groups in many countries where they have been applied, leading to criticism even from the former chief economist of the World Bank (Stiglitz 2002). For neo-liberal theorists, economic growth is governed by the market and the free access to trade and investment by firms both nationally and internationally. Only by adopting competitive economic and fiscal policies can states hope to gain from their participation in the global market economy, and thus states compete in offering lucrative incentives to attract foreign capital and investment. Neo-liberal economic growth as a function of globalization is thus primarily an economic process, with an overriding belief that the social benefits of economic growth and development will "trickle down" from economic processes. Sadly, many examples suggest that this trickle-down process tends not to happen (Bradshaw et al. 1993; Stiglitz 2002).

OPEN for DISCUSSION

Neo-liberal Globalizers vs. Democratic Globalizers

What role do key actors play on the global stage to promote globalization? Jackie Smith's book, *Social Movements for Global Democracy* (2008), offers a succinct argument about two competing global networks of individuals, states, and organizations that actively try to promote competing visions of globalization. Smith identifies two loosely structured networks that are contesting how globalization should look: (1) the neo-liberal globalizers and (2) the democratic globalizers.

The transnational neo-liberal globalizers, according to Smith, are a network composed of states, international organizations (World Bank, International Monetary Fund [IMF], and World Trade Organization [WTO]), multinational corporations, and commercial media. This network promotes a form of globalization that holds neo-liberal interests at its core: protection of corporate interest, promotion of **free trade**, reduction in state sovereignty, and the centrality of free-market ideology. By all accounts, members of this network have been rather successful at promoting their vision of globalization, and the dominance of neo-liberalism in our everyday lives is evidence of this efficacy.

The democratic globalization network, on the other hand, is composed of social movement organizations, individual activists, independent media, and other civil society actors. This network has a very loose structure and fluctuating composition but has a shared core belief in promoting a form of globalization that combats neo-liberalism and instead promotes democracy, openness, transparency, state sovereignty over economic development and regulations, and a stronger role for global governance institutions like the United Nations. At times, these groups have been depicted in mainstream accounts as the **anti-globalization** movement linked to key flashpoints of protest that emerged around international meetings and summits of organizations like the IMF and the WTO—1999's "Battle in Seattle," for example. Smith argues that this network is not "anti" globalization so much as promoting an alternate vision of globalization. In recent years, the key gathering for the network has been the **World Social Forum**, a global focal point for anti-neo-liberal activism (Smith 2004). This annual event has been viewed as a counterpoint to the World Economic Forum, which functions as a global gathering of the corporate and political leaders most closely associated with the neo-liberal globalizers.

The competition between these two networks highlights the fact that there is no single vision of globalization and that the process is a contested one. This contestation underscores the extent to which many groups feel that the convergence associated with the neo-liberal practices of globalization have more detrimental than positive effects globally.

With neo-liberalism influencing most global economies and encouraging increased flows of goods and investment, we have seen the emergence of globalized patterns of production in recent decades. This is evident in the significant shift of manufacturing from the high-income economies of North America and western Europe to regions with lower costs of manufacturing, lower wages, and lower labour standards. The result is a pattern of global production and consumption whereby goods are produced at the lowest possible cost by multinational corporations to be sold in high-income countries for maximum profit. Tied to the neo-liberal principles of free trade and foreign investment, this globalized pattern of production and consumption feeds the Western appetite for clothing, electronics, and other goods, while at the same time taking advantage of low-cost labour in the Global South. Recalling the world system perspective and exploitation of the periphery, we can see how such a pattern can reinforce global inequality. It also raises a set of ethical concerns, including questions about the treatment of workers, the exploitation of natural resources, and the environmental hazards of labour-intensive export-oriented manufacturing in the Global South.

TIME to REFLECT

Consider a product you are wearing or using today that was produced in the Global South. What are the ethical implications of your purchase of this product?

(© Alex Segre / Alamy)

Thanks to technological advances over the past century, fashion retailer Zara can design, manufacture, and distribute its products to 82 countries within two weeks.

Along with the spread of neo-liberal ideology, technological changes in transportation and communication over the past century underpin many of these economic flows. The next section examines the impact of these changes on how globalization affects our daily lives.

TRANSPORTATION AND INFORMATION TECHNOLOGIES

Technological change has created a greater sense of interconnectedness around the world. Advances in transportation, for example, have made it easier than ever to move people and objects from point A to point B in a fraction of the time it would have once taken.

If we think back to the mid-nineteenth century, a transatlantic crossing via ship would have taken approximately two weeks. With improving maritime technology, that same trip was reduced to about five days by the end of the century (Hugill 1995). Today, we can board an airplane in any major Canadian city and arrive in Europe in less than 10 hours.

How have these technological advances in transportation shaped global flows? If we consider the two line graphs in the left-hand column of Figure 15.4, we can see how the expansion of air transportation has shaped the growth in the flow of both people and freight in the period from 1970 through 2010. Broken down by major world regions, the graphs show significant increases across the board in both total numbers of passengers carried and total freight carried. Not all of this carriage was trans-national in scope, but the numbers do indicate the extent to which transportation advances have facilitated a changing relationship of societies to space and time, even in some of the more

▼ FIGURE 15.4   Assorted Global Flows by Region, 1970–2010

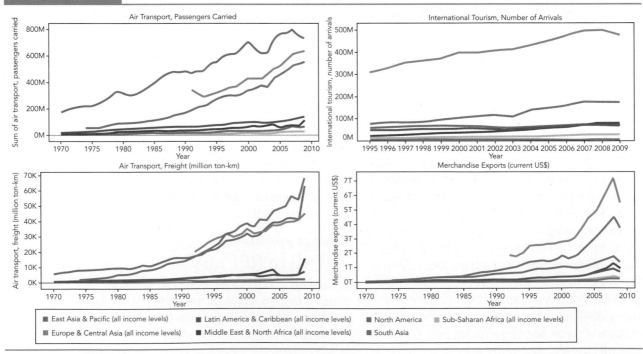

SOURCE: Graphs created by author using data from World Bank, *World Development Indicators*, http://databank.worldbank.org/ddp/home.do?Step=12&id=4&CNO=2 (Washington: World Bank, 2011)

marginalized regions of the world. For instance, while the number of passengers carried in North America rose from about 173.7 million in 1970 to more than 730 million in 2010—a more than four-fold increase—there was an even larger increase in air passenger traffic in regions like East Asia/the Pacific (more than 10 times more traffic in 2010 than in 1974) and in Latin America (more than eight times more traffic in 2010 than in 1970). Similarly, sub-Saharan Africa experienced a six-fold increase in air passenger travel during this period. These patterns suggest that the changes associated with technological advances in transportation are widespread globally, even though the sheer numbers of air passenger traffic are concentrated in the high-income and upper-middle-income regions of the world (North America, Europe, and East Asia). The graph showing trends in air freight traffic also indicates a sharp increase over the same period, illustrating the extent to which advances in transportation have facilitated significant flows of goods within and between countries. This increasing flow of goods is also evident in the bottom right-hand quadrant of Figure 15.4, which shows the growth in merchandise exports over the same 40-year period. The pattern evident in the graphs on air passenger and air freight traffic is repeated here, showing an increase in merchandise exports, with the bulk of the exports from Europe, East Asia, and, to a lesser extent, North America.

More recently, we have witnessed significant innovation in information and communication technologies. The changes brought about by these innovations have been studied by sociologists from the space/time perspective (Castells 2000; Sassen 2007), and a critical factor is the comparative access to these technologies around the world and over time. Figure 15.5 traces trends in the use of telephone (landline) service, mobile phones, and the Internet per 100 people in the seven regions and at the global level from 1990 to 2010. In each regional chart, we can see two corresponding patterns: (1) sharp increases in mobile phone subscription and, to a lesser degree, Internet use; and (2) relative stagnation or even decline in use of conventional fixed telephone lines. In 2010, for instance, the global average of mobile phone subscriptions per 100 people was 78.6, with regional averages ranging from 44.7 in

sub-Saharan Africa to 122.7 per 100 people in Europe and Central Asia. These figures far outstrip the level of mobile phone subscription even 10 years earlier when the global average was only 12.2 per 100 people, and a region like sub-Saharan Africa had an average of less than two subscriptions per 100 people. This massive jump in the number of mobile phone subscriptions is fundamentally altering communication in many developing countries, since the availability of mobile telephones has enabled many countries to significantly expand their telecommunication networks in ways that were not possible with a landline telephone infrastructure.

With the wider availability of new computing technologies and network infrastructure, Internet use has also grown in the period reflected in Figure 15.5. The global average of Internet users per 100 people grew from less than 1 in 1995 to more than 30 in 2010. Regional averages also show significant increases during this period. For instance, North American Internet use grew from fewer than 9 users per 100 persons in 1995 to nearly 80 per 100 in 2010. In contrast to the expansion of mobile telephone use, however, Internet use has not proceeded at the same pace in many of the regions of the Global South. For example, in sub-Saharan Africa, Internet users are estimated at just under 11 per 100 people in contrast to the 44 mobile phone subscriptions per 100 people estimated in 2010. In South Asia, with the massive combined populations of India, Pakistan, and Bangladesh and some of the largest pockets of absolute poverty in the world, Internet use rose from less than 0.5 users per 100 persons in 2000 to just over 8 per 100 in 2010. However, the increase does represent a significant technological change in society, and, more important, along with the other changes in information technology, the Internet directly facilitates the changing social meanings of space and time discussed earlier in this chapter. Further, these advances, not unlike the earlier advances in transportation technology, mediate increased flow of information and communication in revolutionary ways. Email communication, SMS text messaging, video conferencing, the availability of massive amounts of information on the Web: all of these innovations in the way societies communicate lead to increased flows of knowledge and information among people.

▼ FIGURE 15.5   Information and Communication Technology Use/Availability, 1990–2010

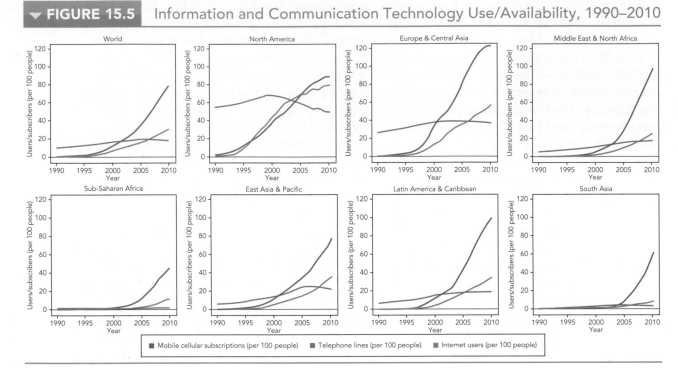

SOURCE: Graphs created by author using data from World Bank, *World Development Indicators,* http://databank.worldbank.org/ddp/home.do?Step=12&id=4&CNO=2 (Washington: World Bank, 2011).

SOCIOLOGY in ACTION

Is Your Phone Contributing to Rape in the Congo?

One of the deadliest wars in recent history, which has received relatively little attention in the West, has been the prolonged conflict in the Democratic Republic of the Congo (DRC). International estimates suggest that upwards of 5 million people died as a result of the conflict between 1997 and 2007. At the same time, the DRC has experienced one of the highest rates of conflict-related rape ever reported, with estimates suggesting that on any given day during the 2006–7 period, more than 1150 women aged 15 to 49 were raped (Peterman, Palermo, and Bredenkamp 2011). Conflict in the DRC has a direct connection to these rapes, with combatants on both sides using rape as a means of dominating and destroying local communities (Baaz and Stern 2009).

How is the phone in your pocket contributing to this use of rape as a weapon of war? The ongoing conflict in the eastern DRC has in large part been perpetuated by various armed groups and the Congolese national armed forces competing over who can control the significant resource wealth in this area. One mineral in particular has garnered interest from these groups: an ore called coltan. This mineral is mined and processed to produce the element tantalum, which is highly sought because of its ability to store electrical charges. Tantalum capacitors are a key component in mobile phones and other electronics. Although the DRC's global share of tantalum production is not overly large, coltan mining is still a significant part of the local economy. Control of the export and sale of this mineral have had a direct effect on the conflict in the DRC and, consequently, on the use of rape in that conflict (Whitman 2012).

The United Nations and other organizations have drawn attention to the role played by coltan and other minerals in the conflict, and this has spurred other actors globally to campaign against the use of "blood coltan" in the manufacture of electronics. Groups like The Enough Project (www.enoughproject .org) have launched awareness and fundraising initiatives to combat sexual violence in the conflict in the Congo. They have also set their sights on educating consumers in the West about the role played by coltan and other minerals in fostering the conflict. Online campaign videos encourage consumers to commit to buying conflict-free electronics and to pressure major electronics manufacturers to eliminate conflict coltan from their products. Still, these conflict-free options have yet to materialize in your neighbourhood electronics store, which suggests that few of us are asking whether our phone is contributing to rape in the Congo.

One corollary of the increased flow of information and communication is the spread and diffusion of shared ideas, norms, and institutions—and these flows are related to the world society perspective. For example, researchers have demonstrated that international telecommunication networks can act as a means through which support for human rights discourse can diffuse through the global community (Clark and Hall 2011). Other research argues that communication using key Internet and mobile phone technologies and platforms (Twitter, Facebook, YouTube) played a critical role in fostering the pro-democracy movements associated with 2011's "Arab Spring" in countries like Tunisia and Egypt (Howard et al. 2011). The same technologies also played a part in the spread of similar protest movements in other countries in the Middle East and North Africa, including Libya, Syria, and Yemen.

This diffusion of a common protest model points to the density or contagion effects often referred to in the world society perspective. It

also highlights how new, rapid flows of information over transnational networks can play an important part in the spread of political ideology across diverse societies.

Increasing interconnection via information and communication technologies reflects a convergence process whereby an increasing amount of commonly accessible information and the means to communicate it rapidly are fundamentally altering social relations among those plugged in. But these technologies might also contribute to divergence, given what has often been labelled the "digital divide"—the gap between individuals and groups who can neither afford nor are sufficiently educated to access the new means of bridging time and space and those who can. The former are thus excluded from the direct flows of globalization that the new technologies facilitate. In this respect, many of the flows we have discussed in this section are beyond the reach of many of the poorest members of most societies, whether in the West or in the Global South.

Some organizations are dedicated to bridging the "digital divide." See the Under the Wire box in Chapter 10, p. 205, which discusses the One Laptop per Child project and the obstacles the organization faces.

(© CP Images/AP Photo/Amine Landoulsi)

Tunisians celebrate the one-year anniversary of the revolution that ended the dictatorship of Zine El Abidine Ben Ali and triggered a spate of uprisings now known as the "Arab Spring."

PEOPLE

Along with that of goods, services, information, and ideas, the movement of people transnationally is another key flow linked to globalization. As we noted in the discussion of air passenger traffic, more people than ever before are crossing national boundaries for either temporary or permanent stays in foreign countries.

In terms of temporary stays, the upper right-hand chart in Figure 15.4 indicates that international tourist travel increased significantly from 1995 to 2010. During that period, international tourist arrivals globally grew from approximately 538 million annually to more than 897 million, a 66 per cent increase. Figure 15.4 also shows that the global growth in tourist flows was not necessarily concentrated in the wealthiest countries or regions but that more countries are welcoming international visitors, no doubt as a result of more available travel options in recent years.

▼ **FIGURE 15.6**   Global Migration Trends, 1960–2010

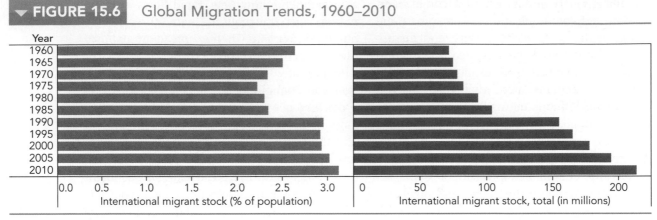

SOURCE: Graphs created by author using data from World Bank, *World Development Indicators*, http://databank.worldbank.org/ddp/home.do?Step=12&id=4&CNO=2 (Washington: World Bank, 2011)

More permanent flows of people involve migrants settling in a country other than that of their birth. Figure 15.6 gives a global estimate of the total stock of international migrants (all the individuals permanently residing in a country other than that of their birth, as estimated by national census data). It shows that international migration has been increasing since 1960, although as a percentage of worldwide population, the growth has not been extreme. Still, with some 213 million migrants in 2010 compared to approximately 72 million in 1960, the sheer number of migrants nearly tripled during in this period. When we consider that more than 3 per cent of the world's population reside in countries other than that of their birth, it is clear that the role of migrant and diaspora groups in shaping other global flows is significant. For example, the International Organization for Migration (IOM) estimates that the more than 213 million migrants worldwide in 2010 sent more than US$440 billion in remittances to communities and family members in their home countries, with more than $325 billion of that total sent to developing countries (International Organization for Migration 2012). The role of these remittances cannot be discounted in terms of promoting development and economic well-being in the countries of origin, and the IOM cautions that the amount of global remittance is probably much larger than these official estimates, because a larger proportion of remittances go unreported. In this way, the flow of people globally is closely linked to the economic and other flows we have already discussed. Furthermore, research suggests that

migrants play a key role in helping to promote support for international norms such as human rights (Clark and Hall 2011).

Conclusion: Convergence, Divergence, and Social Change

This chapter has demonstrated how globalization is a critical transnational process of social change. Theorists have highlighted the ways in which globalization has reshaped economic, social, and political relations worldwide in various ways. A complex set of processes linked to capitalism, institutional isomorphism, and changes in our relationships to time and space, globalization has the potential to promote both convergence and divergence in a variety of ways. We see a greater number of global flows than ever before that are linking societies and states in more uniform ways. The availability of common sets of goods, services, information, and technologies is working to level some of the social, political, and cultural differences that earlier differentiated the world. At the same time, parts of the world are excluded or exploited by the same processes of globalization that are promoting convergence. In this respect, divergence is an unavoidable outcome for many in the globalization era. Impoverished, marginalized, and otherwise excluded from the potential benefits of the globalization, they are outside of the mainstream of globalization. In this respect, the similarities and connections we see emerging around us in an ever-increasing fashion are linked inextricably to aspects of divergence in other locations. The aspects of globalization that at once bring the world together can simultaneously be involved in further differentiating and promoting global inequalities. Social change stemming from globalization, in this way, can be seen to have a dual nature: convergence for some, divergence for others. With contestation over how globalization *should* look, it still remains to be seen whether the current form of globalization will maintain its ability to simultaneously unite and divide in the future or be replaced by another form less rife with contradictions.

questions for critical thought

1. Which of the sociological perspectives on globalization discussed in this chapter appeals most to you? Why?

2. Examine how different global flows affect your life on a daily basis.

3. What evidence do you see of convergence promoted by globalization?

4. What evidence do you see of divergence?

5. How could globalization processes be changed to promote greater equality globally?

recommended readings

John W. Meyer, John Boli, George M. Thomas, and Francisco O. Ramirez. 1997. "World society and the nation-state." *American Journal of Sociology* **103: 144–81.**
This article succinctly summarizes the world society perspective and highlights the key features of how states relate to world society and how this relationship promotes the adoption of common norms, policies, and structures in states and other organizations.

Jackie Smith. 2008. *Social Movements for Global Democracy.* **Baltimore, MD: Johns Hopkins University Press.**

This book highlights the composition, aims, and efficacy of two networks promoting competing visions of globalization on the world stage.

Joseph E. Stiglitz. 2002. *Globalization and Its Discontents.* **New York: W.W. Norton.**
This book, by a former chief economist of the World Bank, is a condemning account of the policies of neo-liberalism promoted by the bank and its counterpart, the IMF.

recommended websites

Gapminder World
www.gapminder.org/world
This website offers an online tool for examining data about global social, economic, and political trends.

World Bank
http://data.worldbank.org
The World Bank website is the source for much of the data on various global flows and development indicators used in this chapter.

World Economic Forum
www.weforum.org
This site outlines the aims, programs, and structures of the World Economic Forum.

chapter 16

Population, Urbanization, and the Environment

Cheryl Teelucksingh

In this chapter, you will:

▶ See how social forces influence human population growth.

▶ Consider the impact of industrialization/ deindustrialization and social inequality on urban sociology perspectives of cities.

▶ Examine the dynamics of population trends in Canadian cities.

▶ Learn about cities' relationships to the environment, including concerns for sustainable development.

▶ Think critically about some solutions to urban sprawl, including attempts to address contemporary concerns about the urban environment.

Introduction

Every two years since 1988, the Population Division of the Department of Economic and Social Affairs of the United Nations updates its projections of urban and rural populations for all countries, globally. According to the 2011 revision of the *World Urbanization Prospects*, between 2011 and 2050 the world's population is expected to increase by 2.3 billion, which is an increase from 7.0 billion to 9.3 billion. During this same period, urban areas, globally, are expected to carry the burden of this population increase as urban populations are projected to go from 3.6 billion in 2011 to 6.3 billion in 2050 (United Nations 2012). As the report argues, higher levels of urbanization, which centralize populations particularly in the developing countries, will improve the effectiveness of the delivery of services such as health care and education as well as provide a wide range of economic opportunities for residents. However, these benefits of urbanization must also be considered in light of the costs associated with mounting urban problems, including deteriorating urban infrastructure, stress on limited energy and water reserves, and urban poverty.

This chapter examines the interrelated issues of population, cities, and the environment from the perspective of Canada and Canadian cities. Examining demography, or human population characteristics, and historical changes is essential to examining how cities evolve over time and to considering cities' dynamic relationships to the natural environment. Cities have become a principal form of settlement as an alternative to living in rural areas. The majority of Canada's population now live in urban areas, a reality that has a major impact on the Canadian way of life, economy, and environment. This is a significant transformation when one considers that in 1851, only 13 per cent of what was then Canada was urbanized (Statistics Canada 2009).

(Mariana Bazo/Reuters)

This shanty town outside of the commercial district in Buenos Aires is an example of the negative effects of urbanization.

We begin this discussion by reviewing the demographic indicators and theories of demographic change, including Thomas Malthus's controversial theory of population and **demographic transition** theory. An overview of the development of Canadian cities and urbanism provides a framework for considering the theories of urbanism presented by the early European urban sociologists, the Chicago School, and the new urban sociology. Particular attention is paid to contemporary urban issues related to deindustrialization and globalization. Since many urban issues in the twenty-first century are increasingly about assessing the limits of urbanism in the context of potential environmental problems, we also examine the dominant perspectives on urban environmental sociology. We look at the challenges posed by urban sprawl in many metropolitan Canadian cities in order to return to critical questions about unregulated urban development.

Demographic Indicators

Demography is the study of the causes and consequences of population growth. To examine the social consequences of population, demographers consider factors such as the size, composition, and geographical variations of population over time. They also study changes in birth rate, infant mortality rate, death rate, **growth rate**, and migration. Demographic trends can inform policies related to health care, immigration, the labour market, and **urban planning**, in addition to providing comparable quantitative measures to assess Canada's well-being relative to other nations. In Canada, the **census**, or the counting of the population every five years, provides a wealth of demographic statistics at different geographic scales. **Birth rates** are an indicator of the reproductive patterns of women of childbearing age. Demographers usually measure the **crude birth rate**, which represents the number of live births in a given year for every 1000 people in a population. In 2011, the crude birth rate in Canada was 10.28 (CIA 2012). As indicated in Table 16.1, Canada's crude birth rate has been stable and is consistent with the crude birth rate in the United States but much lower in comparison to many developing countries (CIA 2012). In 2007, the total fertility rate in Canada was 1.7 children per woman. This is low relative to the **replacement fertility rate**, the average number of children per woman of one generation needed to maintain the population size, which is estimated at 2.1 children per woman (Statistics Canada 2010b). Differences in crude birth rates and fertility rates globally highlight differences in the status of women around the world. Women's freedom to choose at what age they will have their first pregnancy, the number of children they will have, and the frequency of childbirth are tied to a number of factors, including access to education and birth control and female labour market participation, as well as religious and cultural values.

TIME to REFLECT

In July 2010, in response to some Canadians' concerns about personal privacy, the Canadian federal government decided to make completion of the long census form voluntary rather than mandatory. What issues might arise for demographers because of this decision?

TABLE 16.1 ▼ Comparative Crude Birth Rates for Selected Countries, 2011

	Births/1000 population
Japan	7.31
Germany	8.3
Canada	10.28
Norway	10.84
France	12.29
United Kingdom	12.29
China	12.29
United States	13.83
India	20.97
Pakistan	24.81
Philippines	25.34
Afghanistan	37.83
Mali	45.62
Uganda	47.49
Niger	50.54

SOURCE: CIA (Central Intelligence Agency), 2012, *The CIA World Factbook*, New York: Skyhorse Publishing (www.skyhorsepublishing.com/contacts).

The death rate is normally measured in terms of the **crude death rate**, which represents the number of deaths in a given year per 1000 people. According to Statistics Canada (2011a), the crude death rate in Canada in 2008 was 7.2 per 1000 people for all ages and sexes. The crude death rate, as an indicator, is affected by the age distribution. An aging population, as in the case of Canada, will translate into a slow increase in the crude death rate. Statistics Canada defines the **infant mortality rate** as the number of deaths of children less than one year of age per 1000 live births in the same year. In 2008, the infant mortality rate at the national level for both sexes was 5.1 per 1000 live births (Statistics Canada 2011a). The death rate and infant mortality rates are indicators of health-care quality and access as well as living conditions. Life expectancy is the median number of years that a person can expect to live. In 2008, **life expectancy at birth** in Canada reached 80.9 years: 78.5 years for males and 83.1 years for females (Statistics Canada 2011a). Death rates, infant mortality rates, and life expectancies in Canada are similar to those in the United States (National Vital Statistics Report 2011).

Net migration is the difference between the number of immigrants and the number of emigrants between two dates. Immigrants are those entering Canada from international locations, while emigrants are those leaving Canada. Since Confederation, immigration has contributed to the growth in Canada's population. Between 1996 and 2006, Canada's net migration accounted for 7.1 per cent of the 11.4 per cent overall growth rate in comparison to the United States, where net migration only accounted for 4.9 per cent of its 11.5 per cent overall growth rate (Human Resources and Skills Development Canada 2012; Organisation for Economic Co-operation and Development 2009).

The **natural growth rate** is the difference between the crude birth rate and the crude death rate, not taking into account migration or the movement of people into and out of a specific geographical area. At the national level, Canada's population grew by 5.9 per cent during the period 2006 to 2011, including migration. This is a slight increase from the previous census period (2001 to 2006) when population grew by 5.4 per cent. As indicated in Figure 16.1, Canada's population growth between 2006 and 2011 was the highest among G8 countries. In addition, with the exception of Ontario, the Northwest Territories, and Nunavut, every province and Yukon experienced a population increase during this period. Saskatchewan had a strong increase, going from −1.1 per cent

▼ FIGURE 16.1   Population Growth Rate (in Percentages) of the G8 Countries, 2001–6 and 2006–11

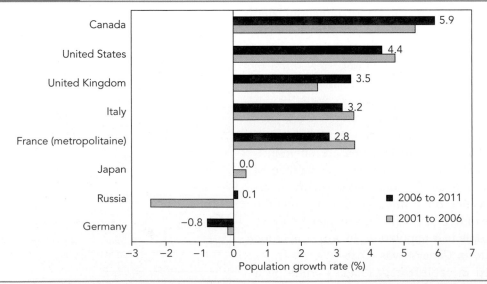

Sources: Statistics Canada, 2011 Census of Population, and calculation from the data of the US Census Bureau—Population Estimates Program, Instituto Nazionale di Statistica (Italy), National Institute of Statistics and Economic Studies (France), United Kingdom Office for National Statistics, Statistics Bureau of Japan, Federal Statistical Office of Germany, and Russian Federation Federal State Statistics Service. Reprinted in Statistics Canada, Catalogue no. 98-310-XWE2011001.

between 2001 and 2006 to 6.7 per cent between 2006 and 2011. The rate of population growth has doubled in Yukon and Manitoba since 2006 (Statistics Canada 2012b).

These demographic statistics are aggregates, applicable to the whole of Canadian society, and therefore do not highlight the variations within the population—for example, from the perspective of lower-income people, racial minorities, or Aboriginal people. Beyond the statistics, demography asks questions about the effects and consequences of population change.

HUMAN DIVERSITY

Youth Boom in India

In contrast to Canada and most Western nations, which are experiencing the consequences of an aging population, in India almost 30 per cent of the population is between the ages of 0 and 14 (CIA 2012). It is estimated that India's population is growing at a rate of 1.4 per cent per year, exceeding China's rate of 0.7 per cent (Bloom 2011). At this pace, India's population will surpass China's by 2030.

India's baby boom is an outcome of a rapid population growth coupled with declines in mortality rates and increased household incomes. The baby boom can also be seen as the beginning of a demographic transition, because India also experiences declining fertility, since fewer births are needed to maintain family needs. India's population pyramid or age structure diagram, below, shows the distribution of its population by age and sex. India and other developing countries have a pyramid-shaped age structure, and in future decades as the population ages, the base of the pyramid will become smaller with an increase in the number of working-age individuals (Bloom 2011).

AGE STRUCTURE in India (2011 Estimate)	
0–14 years	29.7 per cent (male 187,450,635/female 165,415,758)
15–64 years	64.9 per cent (male 398,757,331/female 372,719,379)
65 years and over	5.5 per cent (male 30,831,190/female 33,998,613)

SOURCE: CIA 2012.

India's Population Pyramid, 2010

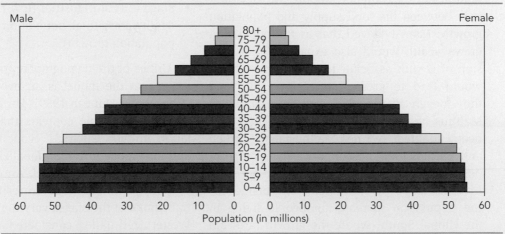

SOURCE: www.nationmaster.com/country/in/Age_distribution

Initially, a young population increases the amount of economic expenditures, because a greater proportion of children and youth in a population means that more resources are needed in terms of food, shelter, and education. However, what is widely anticipated in India is an increased economic growth capacity as the young population moves into working age within the next couple of decades (Bloom 2011). The younger cohort is expected to be more urbanized, healthier, and better educated than previous generations.

MALTHUS'S POPULATION EXPLOSION AND MARX'S RESPONSE

Concerns about possible limits to population growth have existed for some time. In 1798, Reverend Thomas Robert Malthus, an economist, in his book, *Essay on the Principle of Population* (1970 [1798]), outlined an influential theory of human population growth. Malthus's theory starts with the recognition of two constants: people eat, and they reproduce. Based on his analysis, Malthus concluded that while the food supply increases arithmetically over time, population increases exponentially. For Malthus, this scenario would result in an eventual catastrophe, with insufficient resources to enable people to survive. To prevent this crisis, Malthus recommended population control. Because of his own religious convictions, Malthus did not support the idea of birth control but instead suggested that men postpone marriage until later in life when they would be better able to provide for their families. From his perspective, Malthus could not anticipate the gains in food production, the drop in the European birth rate because of the introduction of various forms of birth control, and longer life expectancy because of improvements in health care.

Karl Marx (1967 [1867]) was a critic of Malthusian arguments about the relationship between the food supply and population growth. Marx believed that as the population grew, wealth would also expand. The expansion of wealth associated with overpopulation would lead to greater social inequality and the uneven distribution of resources. Since Malthus first proposed his theories, they have been adopted by neo-Malthusians (Ehrlich and Ehrlich 1990) to support a wide range of population control arguments. Some neo-Malthusians have attributed the blame for the population increase on people living in the Global South, where the growth rates are higher than in the Global North. Based on this claim, many neo-Malthusians have advocated birth control and other efforts to curtail further population growth. Neo-Malthusian sentiments have also been re-ignited by fears about global limits to oil and access to clean water. Those on the other side of the debate, drawing on neo-Marxian perspectives, question the legitimacy of blaming the Global South when those in the Global North consume far more food, fuel, and other resources per capita and create greater amounts of pollution and waste.

DEMOGRAPHIC TRANSITION THEORY

Warren Thompson's demographic transition model, originally conceived in 1929, provides a more complex explanation for demographic change than Malthus's argument. The demographic transition theory distinguishes Western nations, such as Europe, the United States, and Canada, from less industrialized nations. Thompson's (1929) original model of the transitions from high birth rates and high death rates to low birth rates and low death rates, starting in the eighteenth century in Western nations, included three periods of transition: pre-industrial, early industrial, and modern industrial. Recent revisions to this model of population growth in Western societies have been revised to include a further, fourth stage:

- Stage 1: Pre-industrial (high birth rates; high death rates; slow population growth)

- Stage 2: Early industrial and urbanization (fall in death rates; high birth rates continue; rapid population growth)

- Stage 3: Mature industrial (low birth rates; low death rates; slow population growth)

- Stage 4: Post-industrial (low birth rates; low death rates; total population is high; slow population growth)

Critics of the demographic transition model argue that the model is an oversimplification (Hauser and Duncan 1959). For example, political and economic contexts that affect population growth, such as economic recessions and the move toward globalization, are not accounted for in the model. Another limitation is that the time periods corresponding to the transitions in the stages vary depending on the Westernized nation considered. The impact of immigration is also not incorporated into the model. As explained above, in Canada, while the natural population growth rate has slowed as a characteristic of stage 4, immigration from outside of Canada has led to significant population growth.

The demographic transition theory, when considered critically, suggests one monolithic path to development, with a strong emphasis

▼ FIGURE 16.2 Demographic Transition Model

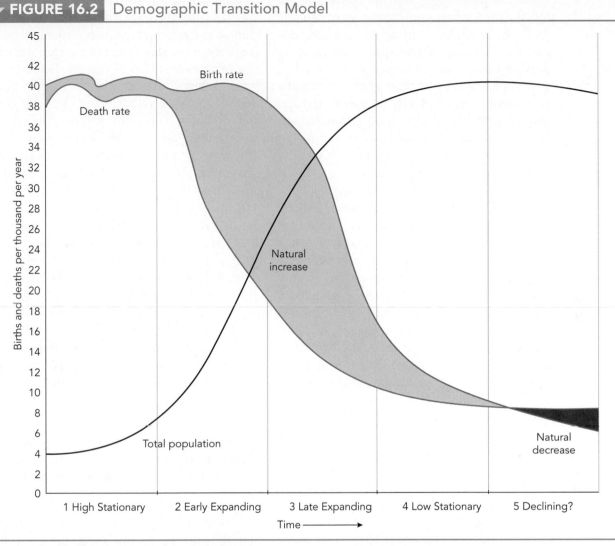

SOURCE: Association of American Geographers, http://globalgeography.aag.org/PopulationandNaturalResources1e/CF_PopNatRes_Jan10/CF_PopNatRes_Jan105. html. Used by permission from Anthony Bennett, www.internetgeography.net

on technology as the instrument to control the natural population growth. Across the model, technology takes various forms, including birth control, medical science, industrialization, and modern infrastructure. The model assumes that technology is universally adopted in the same way by all Westernized nations.

TIME to REFLECT

The demographic transition theory has been heavily criticized because of its perceived Western biases. But what are some of the potential benefits associated with the theory from the perspective of demographers?

Development of Canadian Cities

Urban development is influenced by demographic, economic, ideological, and technological changes at the national and international levels (Bunting and Filion 2006; Stelter and Artibise 1984). Bunting, Filion, and Walker (2010, 19–34) identify five distinct epochs of urban development in Canada. In summarizing these five stages, we have placed an emphasis on uncovering how urbanism evolved in Canada. Urbanism is the process by which a society is transformed from one organized around rural activities to one organized around urban activities, such as transportation, housing, and economic activity.

The earliest stage was the *mercantile era* (1600–1800) when populations were limited. Small settlements, starting in Quebec, originated as colonial outposts for the **staple economy** and the export of natural resources back to France and, later, Britain. Early mercantile settlements in Quebec City, Montreal, Halifax, and St John's were also administratively oriented or military centres (Artibise and Stelter 2012). During this stage, Quebec City and Montreal were the largest cities.

The second period, *urban development* (1800–50), was associated with weaker colonial ties to Britain and an increase in commercial production and consumption. Rural settlements experienced increased population growth as a result of immigration from Europe and accelerated natural growth. In response to agricultural production in rural settlements, cities grew in economic importance as markets and as distribution points (Bunting and Filion 2006). Most urban settlements were still located near accessible waterways, because transportation systems were limited. Toronto, founded in 1793 by John Graves Simcoe, grew in size and importance relative to early Kingston, in part because of Toronto's location close to the agricultural regions of southern Ontario and its military location in relationship to the United States.

At the time of Canada's Confederation in 1867, Canada's population was approximately 3 million people, with about 18 per cent of the population urbanized (Macionis 1997, 575). The building of railways and increased *industrialization* propelled urban growth during the third stage from 1850 to 1945. The Canadian Pacific Railway, completed in 1885, propelled settlement westward to Calgary and Vancouver and other locations along the railway line. Industrialization accelerated in Canada in the latter part of the nineteenth century with the opening of many American branch plants (Foster 1986). Many of the industries were concentrated within the Quebec City to Windsor corridor. Corresponding to the locations of economic activity, urbanization grew more rapidly in southern Ontario and parts of Quebec than in western Canada and the Maritimes (Bunting and Filion 2006).

The *redistribution-oriented government interventions*, such as family allowance, public health care, and subsidized housing, that characterized the fourth epoch following World War II up to 1975 helped to stimulate demographic and economic growth. Urbanization, in the postwar context, involved the spatial expansion of cities to suburban regions, facilitated by the widespread accessibility of cars and home ownership to the middle class. The city cores and outlining suburban regions formed the metropolitan areas as we know them today. The growth of corporations across all sectors of the economy allowed for a concentrated economic base in cities (Artibise and Stelter 2012).

In response to a range of factors, including the oil crisis in the early 1970s and the post-1970 recessions, **deindustrialization** from 1975 to the present signalled the unravelling of the assembly line approach to industrialization and an end to many good-paying blue-collar jobs associated with the previous period of transition. The fifth epoch was also marked by a political shift toward neo-liberalism, with a reduction in government spending on interventions and a shift toward deregulation (Bunting and Filion 2006).

Turn to the Sociology in Action box, p.45 in Chapter 2, for a better understanding of neo-liberal principles.

Urban growth is now predominately concentrated in the metropolitan areas like Vancouver, Calgary, Edmonton, Toronto, Ottawa, and Montreal that are able to draw and employ immigrants (Bunting and Filion 2006). More recently, Calgary and Saskatoon are increasingly able to draw international migrants and migrants within Canada because of the boom in Western economies and declines in the manufacturing sector in other central cities, such as Windsor and Sudbury. Calgary and Edmonton have grown in response to economic opportunities in the oil and gas sector and its spin-off industries. As Table 16.2 reveals, Calgary and Edmonton have experienced population increases of 12.6 per cent and 12.1 per cent, respectively, since 2006 (Statistics Canada, Population and Dwelling Counts Table, www12.statcan.gc.ca/census-recensement/2011/dp-pd/hlt-fst/pd-pl/Table-Tableau.cfm?LANG = Eng&TABID = 1&T = 201&SR = 1&RPP = 150&S = 3&O = D&CMA = 0&PR = 0#C2).

TABLE 16.2 ▼ Top 10 Census Metropolitan Areas, Canada

Geographic Name	Population, 2011	Population 2006	Population, % change	Population Density per Square Kilometre, 2011	National Population Rank, 2011	National Population Rank, 2006
Toronto	5,583,064	5,113,149	9.2	945.3677	1	1
Montreal	3,824,221	3,635,556	5.2	898.06	2	2
Vancouver	2,313,328	2,116,581	9.3	802.5292	3	3
Ottawa – Gatineau	1,236,324	1,133,633	9.1	196.6466	4	4
Calgary	1,214,839	1,079,310	12.6	237.8516	5	5
Edmonton	1,159,869	1,034,945	12.1	123.0405	6	6
Quebec	765,706	719,153	6.5	228.6289	7	7
Winnipeg	730,018	694,668	5.1	137.659	8	8
Hamilton	721,053	692,911	4.1	525.606	9	9
Kitchener-Cambridge-Waterloo	477,160	451,235	5.7	576.6796	10	11

SOURCE: Statistics Canada, 2012, "Population and dwelling counts, for census metropolitan areas and census agglomerations, 2011 and 2006 censuses," www12.statcan.gc.ca/census-recensement/2011/d

Other metropolitan areas are attempting to restructure economically to attract globally oriented "new economy" industries that require highly skilled and educated employees. Much of the settlement during this period has been in the suburban areas of cities. As shown in Figure 16.3, smaller urban centres are now in decline, except for those within commuting distance to metropolitan areas (Artibise and Stelter 2012).

TIME to REFLECT

Population growth in the Montreal census metropolitan area has been only 5.2 per cent since the 2006 census. What do you think accounts for this relatively low population growth in Montreal?

Sociological Perspectives on Cities

FUNCTIONALISM: URBANISM AND THE INDUSTRIAL CITY

Early European urban sociology emerged in response to conditions during the late nineteenth and early twentieth century created by the Industrial Revolution. Sociologists were concerned about the movement of people from rural settings into cities and the potential impact of the demographic shift on social life. The transformation toward urban life and industrialization signalled the disappearance of one kind of human association and its replacement by another (Gusfield 1975).

Many of the early urban sociologists adopted a structural functionalist approach with its concern for social order and stability, which they applied to the move toward city life. German sociologist Ferdinand Tönnies (1957 [1887]) developed the rural/urban typology, or classification, to contrast the two types of social life. The term *Gemeinschaft* referred to a rural or pre-industrial community based on agriculture or a primitive mode of production. Social bonds and relationships existed for their own sake and focused around kinship and neighbourhood. Human motivation for action was natural, and community was assumed to have greater stability. The *Gesellschaft*, in contrast, was the industrial urban community, which involved superficial associations based on contract or exchange. There was less emphasis on the family, and the human motivation for action was rational rather than natural. Lack of social cohesion resulted in social problems.

▼ FIGURE 16.3   Population Growth Rates by Census Metropolitan Area, Canada

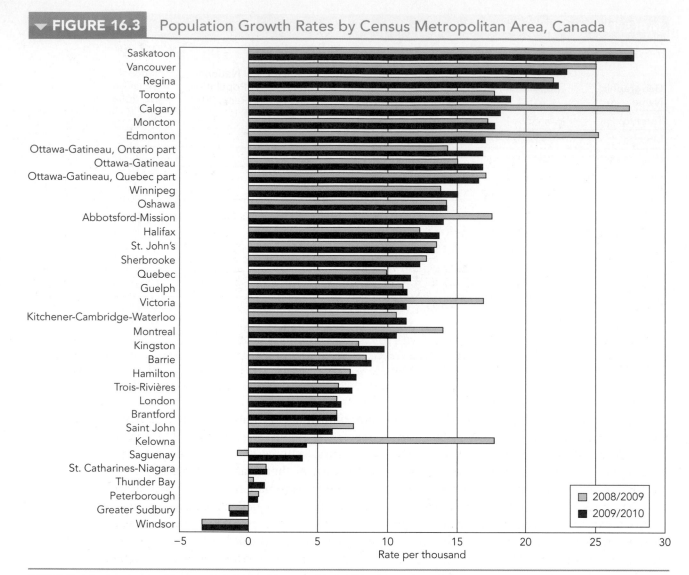

SOURCE: Statistics Canada, Annual Demographic Estimates: Subprovincial Areas 2005 to 2010, p.15, Catalogue no. 91-214-X (Ottawa: Statistics Canada, 2011).

From today's perspective, Tönnies's distinction is useful for explaining, at the structural level, why people might feel isolated in cities, but the *Gemeinschaft* is a crude categorization and the past is over-idealized.

Émile Durkheim (1964 [1893]) provided a rural/urban typology that was much more optimistic about cities. Durkheim classified communities as either "mechanical solidarity" (rural) or "organic solidarity" (urban). The mechanical solidarity of rural life derived from social relationships based on common bonds. Individuals in a rural community were bound to each other without having any choice in the matter. In the city, relationships were based on specialization. The greater division of labour in cities gave the individual freedom and new forms of cohesion. Consistent with structural functionalism and its views on social integration, everyone had a function but was still independent. In cities, people did not have to engage in all forms of labour. For example, if you want to, you can hire someone to clean your house. The division of labour in cities can make individuals dependent on strangers; however, they can also have more free time. But when people or organizations do not do their expected function, chaos may occur.

Georg Simmel explored the meaning of urban life from a micro-level, or social psychological, perspective in his work "The Metropolis and Mental Life" (2002 [1903]). For Simmel, the early industrial city created conditions that predisposed individuals to repress their emotional involvement and to focus on formal interactions with others. In the city, there was an intensification of stimuli and an emphasis on market relations. Simmel suggested that in the urban context, individuals were forced to protect themselves and to become detached and reserved (McGahan 1995). Simmel's work provides a valuable perspective on the urban way of life. However, his writings do not offer a systematic theoretical model. Simmel's regard for urban culture and how people act and behave in cities influenced the Chicago School theorists in North America in the 1920s and 1930s.

Toronto is Canada's largest and most densely populated city. But it doesn't come close to Mumbai, India, which has 29,650 people per square kilometre as opposed to only 2650 per square kilometre in Toronto. (www.citymayors.com/statistics/largest-cities-density-125.html).

THE CHICAGO SCHOOL OF SOCIOLOGY

The beginning of urban sociology in North America took root at the University of Chicago early in the twentieth century. As a collective, the Chicago School of Sociology tended to be more systematic about its insights. In addition to industrialization and its impact on cities, the Chicago School theorists responded to the expansion of Chicago as a result of the influx of immigrants. Therefore, the impact of diversity on the social order was a central question for them.

Louis Wirth's (1938) essay "Urbanism as a Way of Life" presented a formal theory of urbanism that is still relevant to how we understand cities and urbanism today. Wirth's definition of the city as "a relatively large, dense and permanent settlement of heterogeneous individuals" (1938, 1) highlighted social processes in the city and city living. Deriving from this definition, size, density, and heterogeneity were the three criteria that determined the degree of urbanism. A city is larger than a rural settlement, which facilitates segregation. However, a city is much more than its mere size. The higher the density in a city, or the higher the proportion of people per square kilometre, the greater the division of labour.

Heterogeneity in cities provides people with the opportunity to pursue a variety of interests and have regular contact with a wide range of people. For Wirth, population size, density, and diversity presented opportunity for urbanites. A weakness of Wirth's definition of a city is that it does not take into account the need for an administrative centre responsible for governance to deal with the impact of differences associated with heterogeneity on people living in close proximity.

The Chicago School of Sociology, led by Robert Park, developed two approaches to empirically studying the city based on the view that the city represented a sociological laboratory (Lindner 1996). First, drawing on Simmel's earlier work, ethnography was adopted to examine detailed descriptive accounts of lived experience in the city. Field research was used to construct detailed case studies based on participant observation and life histories to identify patterns of social bonding and everyday experiences of people in their natural settings. Many ethnographies profiled the lives of the marginalized, underprivileged, and criminals. One controversial element was that researchers often gained access to the people they were studying by "breaching"—attempting to pass as members of the communities they were studying. Ethnographic narratives such as *The Gang* (Thrasher 1927) and *The Hobo* (Anderson 1923) had popular mass market appeal (McGahan 1995).

The *human ecology approach* (often called the ecological perspective) was the second empirical approach, developed by Robert Park, Ernest Burgess, and Roderick McKenzie (1967[1925]) to examine the social organization of the city in order understand city processes at the macro level. Drawing on components of biology and ecology, **human ecology** conceives of cities as social organisms. People, like species, exist with a division of labour that allows for a balance within society. The city has its own spatial division of labour, but all of the parts fit together (McGahan 1995). In this sense, cities do not grow randomly but rather in an orderly fashion in response to features of the environment. Competition in the city determines the optimal distribution of land and people (Park, Burgess, and McKenzie 1967 [1925]; McKenzie 1967 [1925]). From the perspective of heterogeneity, each social group (i.e., each income group or each immigrant group) has its place in the city, which allows for stable social relations. Competition leads to expansion of the city outward. Invasion and ecological succession is the process whereby one segment of the population takes possession of the urban territory from another population.

The *concentric zone model*, envisioned by Park and Burgess in 1925, provides a visual model for the human ecology perspective. The model places emphasis on function and balance, indicating that every social group and land use has its place. Figure 16.4 shows the

▼ **FIGURE 16.4** | Concentric Zone Model

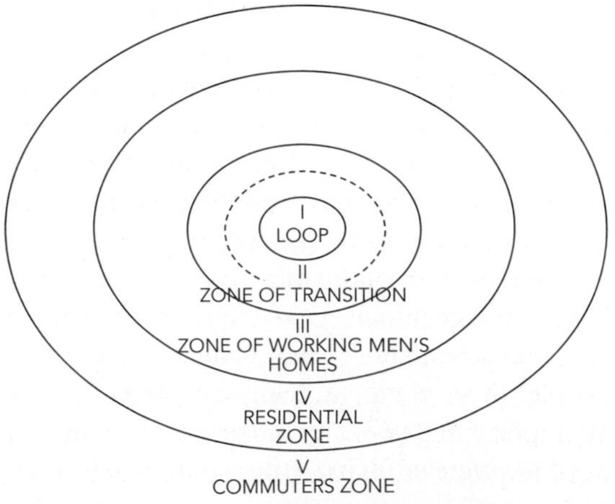

SOURCE: Nina Brown, 2001. "Robert Park and Ernest Burgess: Urban Ecology Studies, 1925." In: *CSISS Classics*, Center for Spatially Integrated Social Science, www.csiss.org/classics/content/26.

five major zones radiating out from the core of the city. These zones are described in terms of housing and social characteristics.

Burgess (1967 [1925]) characterized the zones as follows:

- Zone I was the central business district or commercial heart and centre of the city, consisting of department stores and office buildings. The outer portion of zone 1 was occupied by industrial enterprises that need a centralized location. This was the most valuable zone in the city.

- Zone II was the "zone in transition." It included old residential areas surrounding the commercial core, rundown housing, and rental housing for the poorest populations, including recent immigrants, minorities, and other urban undesirables. This area was characterized by competition between commercial and lower-end residential uses along with high levels of crime. Access to better jobs and money would enable the residents of zone II to move to the better housing in outer zones.

- Zone III was the "zone of working class homes," which were inexpensive semi-detached homes.

- Zone IV consisted of better residential single-family detached homes.

- Zone V, labelled the "commuter zone," included the more expensive detached homes for upper-middle-class and upper-class households. Zones IV and V were associated with economic and social uniformity. Those living in zone V could afford cars to commute to work in the inner zones.

The concentric zone theory was one of the earliest theories to explain the spatial organization of industrial cities. It had great influence on Canadian urban research (e.g., Balakrishnan and Kralt 1987; Anderson 1991). However, the model has a number of weaknesses that limit its applicability, as a general predictive tool, outside of Chicago in the 1930s. For example, in contemporary Canadian cities affected by globalization and deindustrialization, developments such as competition, invasion, and succession are also occurring in the parts of the city, like zone II, that the model conceptualized as undesirable. Many inner zones are experiencing **gentrification** as more affluent people move into previously low-income neighbourhoods. Further, the model assumes that the shape of the city is radial, whereas grid patterns exist in many North American cities. Suburbanization has led to more than one zone I, or central business district area, in many metropolitan cities as companies locate in the suburbs. Lower-income areas are often no longer concentrated but dispersed throughout cities. The model, oriented to explaining structural processes, also gives little attention to the role of individual choice, government regulation, and cultural preferences in settlement (McGahan 1995).

The limitations of the concentric zone theory have been taken up by other theorists, including Homer Hoyt (1939) in his sector theory, which conceived of the city as sectors with different economic activities. Harris and Ullman's (1945) multiple nuclei theory conceived more advanced stages of urbanization in which there could be multiple centres within a larger city. More contemporary approaches to examining the organization of cities attempt to explore the importance of ethnic bonds and lifestyle and the overall significance of the political and economic context. Modelling today often uses geographical information systems to map demographic and land-use variables of interest in terms of the spatial organization of cities.

TIME to REFLECT

Consider some of the reasons that your own city conforms to or deviates from the Chicago School's concentric zone theory.

CONFLICT APPROACH: URBANIZATION AND GLOBALIZATION

Starting in the late 1960s, many urban sociologists, influenced by conflict theory, responded to the lack of consideration of power relations in human ecology and in urban sociology grounded in a functionalist orientation. For the new urban sociology theorists, the political and economic context is the driving force for urban activity (Feagin 1998; Gottdiener and Hutchison 2000; Harvey 1985; Zukin 1980). Much of the sociological work in this approach converges with the work of urban theorists in

urban planning, political science, and geography. The political economy orientation raises questions about inequalities in urban power rooted in capitalist relations. Urban space itself is a commodity that embodies political interests and conflicts. The large urban cities are seen as instrumental sites for the **global economy**.

Joe Feagin (1998), one of the major contributors to defining the new urban sociology, has summarized the central assumptions of the approach. Cities are part of a global system that is oriented around profit, or capitalist accumulation. The new urban sociology is concerned with power inequalities in urban politics and how cities are defined by decision-making processes that are locally defined in each city. This critical perspective on urban processes attempts to highlight the links between capitalism and the workings of racism and patriarchy.

The different political and economic interests of powerful players in cities are central to John Logan and Harvey Molotch's (1987) portrayal of cities as machines fuelled by a drive to grow. Real estate investors, bankers, developers, and corporate officials are examples of the powerful elite in cities who push a pro-growth and pro–urban development mentality. Urban growth leads to competing tensions between community groups and more powerful stakeholders. Those with the most economic and political power are able to position urban development as being good for the whole city. Logan and Molotch (1987) argue that the growth machine influences the workings of municipal governments, which become focused on creating the kind of city that can attract industry and investors, with less attention to community needs.

Critical urban sociological perspectives have also been applied to the role of the city in the transformation from industrialization (or deindustrialization) toward globalization (Harvey 1985; Kipfer and Keil 2002; Sassen 1991). Broadly defined, globalization is the internationalization of the market economy, leading to global exchange of capital. Under industrialization, large-scale manufacturing, such as clothing factories, was predominantly located in one particular city. Starting in the 1980s, with the global expansion of multinational corporations, the production of goods and services can take place in any or several locations where profit can be maximized. With deindustrialization,

there has been a restructuring of the economy and creation of a "new economy," which relies on information- and technology-driven jobs. In the same way that industrialization had a significant impact on the growth and expansion of cities, deindustrialization and globalization also affect cities. According to Global Cities Theory, cities provide the infrastructure that is necessary for global control (Kipfer and Keil 2002). Global cities, including Vancouver, New York, London, and Tokyo, act as command points for centralizing finance, telecommunications, and access to labour markets. Increasingly, global cities are centres for culture as well (Sassen 1991).

As a global city, Toronto has become central in coordinating the international division of labour, which, on one level, involves multinational corporations with various locations of production and distribution and the global movement of financial capital. The head offices of many top Canadian corporations and foreign-owned corporations are now located in Toronto. On another level, the division of labour on both local and global scales results in the uneven development of marginalized communities and people. Since the liberalization of Canadian federal immigration policy in the late 1960s, high levels of new immigrants were drawn to Toronto from developing nations. These new waves of immigrants facilitated the division of labour between the highly skilled and highly paid professional classes and the low-skilled and poorly paid service-sector classes (Sassen 1991). For Sassen (1991), global political economic restructuring has an impact on the spatial organization of the city with the gentrification of inner-city neighbourhoods to accommodate professional classes and groups with capital. Meanwhile, the less-skilled classes are relegated to less desirable areas. The notion of the global city, as conceived by Sassen (1991), links global economics, social divisions of labour, and urban spatial changes. A critical urban sociological perspective draws attention to the fact that culture in the global city is commodified and consumed. The marketing and branding of global cities is seen to be more important than valuing culture, including artists and diverse communities, for their own value. Culture is valued to meet larger political and economic objectives rather than to address the specific needs of local communities.

Cities and Perspectives on the Environment

Environmental sociology, as a distinct area of sociology, emerged in response to growing concern over environmental problems. Environmental sociology recognizes the close relationship between humans and their biophysical environments. As Dunlap and Rosa (2010, 1–2) state, the biophysical environment and human populations are linked in three essential ways: (1) the environment provides resources that maintain human life; (2) in the process of consuming resources, humans generate waste that the environment must absorb; and (3) the environment provides a habitat or home for humans and all living species. In light of this close relationship, environmental problems such as pollution, resource scarcity, and overcrowding or overpopulation can result.

In the twenty-first century, cities have become a focal point for concerns about the environment because of their unrestricted economic growth and the fact that they are sites for the large-scale consumption of goods and services, resulting in high levels of waste and pollution. There is a wide range of environmental problems in Canadian cities. Air pollutants from automobile exhaust and other toxic emissions have increased the levels of ambient air particles. Frequent "smog days" are now a reality of city living. The resulting health problems cause many deaths every year, in spite of the impact of deindustrialization and government controls to reduce urban airborne pollutants. In part because of the lessons learned from the *E. coli* bacteria contamination of the municipal water supply in Walkerton, Ontario, in 2002, maintaining water quality in urban areas has become a priority. But even so, it was estimated that 18 per cent of Canadian cities still did not have adequate sewage treatment for wastewater in 2005 (Canadian Environmental Grantmakers' Network 2005, 11), and Canadians were second only to the United States in the production of solid waste per capita (2005, 12). In Toronto and Montreal, landfill space is limited, and the concern about the potential for land contamination makes it difficult for municipalities to locate new landfill sites. Rising concern about climate change has led to calls for

GLOBAL ISSUES

The Global City and the Knowledge-Based Economy

A global city, also known as a world city, is a "command and control centre" in the global economy (Sassen 1991; 2001). In Canada, Vancouver, Toronto, and Montreal play a complex networking role at the global level by connecting global processes of production, consumption, and distribution. With globalization, business activity is no longer tied to one particular location or city. Rather, in many cases raw materials are extracted at one location; fabrication takes place in another location; and distribution, financing, and marketing, in yet another location. However, human activity is needed to link and coordinate what is occurring in spatially dispersed locations (Shin and Timberlake 2000). Global cities, as conceived by Saskia Sassen (1991), are the few cities at the top of a hierarchy of cities that centralize banking and other specialized services, including finance, culture, and ideology serving a transnational marketplace (Shin and Timberlake 2000). Increasingly, these specialized services are associated with the knowledge-based economy. The knowledge-based economy can be defined as the union of globalization and the trend toward greater reliance on knowledge and high skill levels in response to businesses' needs for quick information. Global cities fuel the knowledge-based economy by providing educated, skilled workers and information infrastructure that foster innovation, such as advances in telecommunication and international transfers of knowledge and capital.

Global cities, as transnational focal points, are sites of innovation, growth, and trade in part because of their ability to draw well-educated migrants who drive the knowledge-based economy (Courchene 2007). Richard Florida (2008) argues that knowledge-based economy workers, whom he calls the "creative class," are drawn to cities with a dynamic culture as an indicator of a city's commitment to risk-taking, diversity, and innovation. For Florida, the culture in global cities is reflected in museums, art galleries, and street festivals as well as multicultural populations and grassroots movements that challenge the status quo. Thus, many of the policies in place in Canadian global cities are intended to entice professional workers and businesses that are globally oriented. Critical urban sociology perspectives raise important questions about what happens to local communities and locally defined needs if global cities favour the dictates of the knowledge-based economy, including international players and international agendas.

residents of Canadian cities to reduce their use of energy, particularly fossil fuels. But energy conservation and energy production are topics of contentious debate in Canada. In cities like Calgary and Edmonton, with economies largely driven by the oil and natural gas industries, energy efficiency is not as much of an urgent priority as it is in most other Canadian urban centres, which are consumers rather than producers of energy and feel the pinch of rising energy prices.

The concept of *ecological footprints*, developed by Canadian William Rees (1992), is a numerical indicator of our lifestyles' impact on the planet in terms of the scarcity of land, fuel, and natural resources. A population's ecological footprint entails how much land and water is used to produce the resources that the population consumes and to absorb the subsequent waste produced (Rees 2001; Wilson and Anielski 2005). The footprint takes into account the population size, the standard of living, "the productivity of the land/water base (whether local or 'imported' in trade goods), and the efficiency of resource harvesting, processing, and use" (Rees 2010, 74). Ecological footprint analysis calculates a population's biocapacity, or natural capital, which is the amount of natural resources for food, energy, and other materials that a population requires relative to the supply of natural resources available.

TIME to REFLECT

Using Figure 16.5, which outlines the ecological footprints of selected Canadian cities, consider the ecological footprint of the city where you live or that is close to where you live. What are some of the reasons for this city's ecological footprint?

▼ **FIGURE 16.5**   Canadian Ecological Footprints

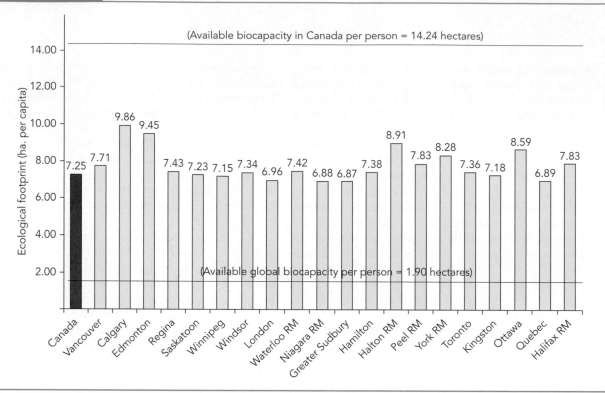

SOURCE: Jeffrey Wilson and Mark Anielski, *Ecological Footprints of Canadian Municipalities and Regions*, p. 6. Prepared for the Canadian Federation of Canadian Municipalities. (Edmonton: Anielski Management Inc., 2005). www.anielski.com/Documents/EFA%20Report%20FINAL%20Feb%202.pdf

It is estimated that 7.25 hectares of land and water resources from throughout the world is needed to sustain Canada's level of consumption per capita (Wilson and Anielski 2005). As shown in Figure 16.5, across Canadian cities footprints vary between 6.87 in Greater Sudbury to 9.86 in the Calgary metropolitan area, reflecting different levels of energy used to sustain consumption needs. Canada has higher levels of natural capital because of its abundance of natural resources; however, some Canadian cities are consuming beyond the world's ecological means. In comparison to other nations, Canada has the seventh largest ecological footprint among 130 nations, with nearly half of this footprint resulting from carbon emissions from fossil fuels (World Wild Life Fund 2010).

The ecological footprint is also a tool for measuring a population's progress toward sustainability. **Sustainable development** has been defined as "development which meets the needs of the present without compromising the ability of future generations to meet their own needs" (Bruntland 1987, 43) and involves an attempt to balance concerns for the three E's: environment, economy, and equity. On one level, sustainable development, as a mandate, means seeking to reconcile the objectives of economic growth and development with the world's resource limits. While this approach to environmentalism has been widely endorsed by various actors, including municipal governments, businesses, and non-governmental organizations, there has been a broad interpretation of the environmental sustainability definition to suit specific actors' own economic and political interests. For some, sustainable development involves recycling programs or new "green" product lines or initiatives. Other actors have pursued a complete restructuring of their objectives, with an even focus on all components of environment, economy, and equity.

Urban sustainability, when adopted, has involved a commitment to using the natural resources of a city within its capacity to sustain its social, economic, and natural significance. Goals associated with urban sustainability are related to improving the quality of life in the city without stealing resources from future generations. Under urban sustainability mandates, some municipal governments, such as Toronto, have installed solar and wind turbines. In other contexts, city planning and development staff have become sensitive to the importance of green space, increasing the density of urban developments, and improving public transportation and facilitating cycling in the city.

FUNCTIONALIST PERSPECTIVES ON THE ENVIRONMENT

Cities are often seen as inconsistent with notions of nature. Discussions of urbanization can mistakenly relegate the natural environment to the rural context where agriculture-based subsistence is seen as closer to nature (Rees 2010). Technological innovations associated with industrialization and globalization tend to blind urbanites to the connection between nature and their own dependence on food, fuel, and other natural resource. Thus, the challenge for sociologists and others has been to conceive of cities as biophysical forms and to consider the impact that urban environments have on shaping social structure and processes.

William Catton and Riley Dunlap (1978) were among the first to criticize sociologists for their lack of consideration of the biological and environmental. They labelled this dominant sociological world view as the human exemptionalist paradigm (HEP). The HEP assumed that humans, because of their use of culture, were distinct from other biological beings; thus, it was possible to reject the significance of biology and the physical in social processes (Harper and Fletcher 2011). Catton and Dunlap (1978) encouraged sociologists to adopt the new ecological paradigm (NEP) that situated humans within an interdependent ecosystem. NEP's world view recognized that while humans' use of culture and technology had allowed for some control over the environment, the carrying capacity of the environment was a reality that could not be avoided (Catton and Dunlap 1978). With the new paradigm, Dunlap and Catton were able to merge an understanding of ecological processes with the structural functionalist perspective's regard for stability and order.

Arguments that recognize the city's biophysical orientation is, in part, reminiscent of components of the Chicago School's human

The Bixi Bikes in Montreal were the first rental bicycles in Canada, and the network now boasts 5120 bikes at 411 stations. The bikes offer a sustainable and affordable alternative to other modes of transport.

(© iStockphoto/carterdayne)

ecology perspective, which conceived of the city as a living organism that grows in a natural and orderly manner. However, the new ecological paradigm (Catton and Dunlap 1978; Dunlap and Catton 1983) situates cities and populations in cities as part of an ecosystem or as ecosystems. "An ecosystem is an interacting set of living organisms (animals and plants) and their nonliving environment (air, land, water) that are bound together by a flow of energy and nutrients (e.g., food chains)" (Dunlap and Rosa 2010, 2). Humans, as only one component of ecosystems, should not disrupt the inherent balance by overusing aspects of an ecosystem.

As an awareness of environmental problems, Canadians' ecological footprints, and the need for urban sustainability have gained greater prominence, some scientists, policymakers, and environmentalists have continued to turn to technocratic solutions to manage urban environments. For example, scientific and technological innovations have made it possible to produce more energy-efficient "smart cars" and hybrid cars. Science is also coming up with ways of addressing the limits of natural resources by developing alternatives to fossil fuels and finding ways of reducing ozone depletion. Counting on the possibility that technology can resolve environmental problems, some policy-makers continue to pursue policies aimed at urban growth rather than encouraging reduced consumption and slower growth.

Energy-efficient cars seem to be a relatively new development, but did you know that an electric car was already in existence in the 1990s? See the Sociology in Action box on p. 278 in Chapter 14 for more information.

THE CONFLICT/POLITICAL ECONOMY APPROACH TO THE ENVIRONMENT

The conflict approach to environmental sociology, conceived by British theorists such as James O'Connor, highlighted the role of power inequalities in struggles over resources. These theorists reworked Marxist analysis to examine the intersection between the oppression of labour and the oppression of the environment within the capitalist production process (Gould, Schnaiberg, and Weinberg 1996; O'Connor 1996). In this sense, the environmental degradation—both in terms of resource depletion as a result of production processes and in terms of pollution as a result of the output of these processes—leads to social consequences that are differentially experienced (Schnaiberg and Gould 1994). By connecting marginalized environments and marginalized communities through capitalism and, by extension, processes of globalization, it was possible to identify why threats to the ecosystem required changes to status quo social relations, not just temporary technological solutions.

In the current context of rising neo-liberalism and the demands of the global economy on cities, many new theorists, under the interdisciplinary label of urban political ecology, have focused on cities as sites where new forms of social and environmental inequalities are emerging from interrelated social, ecological, and political conflicts (Keil and Bourdeau 2006; Heynen et al. 2007). Some of the urban environmental issues that these urban political ecologists have engaged include debates around the privatization of water and utilities (Young and Keil 2007) and deregulation of environmental protection (Overton 2009).

Environmental justice is a sub-theme of urban political ecology. It emerged initially in sociology in the 1980s in the United States in response to the popular environmental justice movement and the recognition that distributive injustices were resulting from the disproportionate burden of environmental degradation and polluting industries borne by poor communities and communities of colour (Bullard 1990; Cole and Foster 2001). In Canada, the undesirable land uses in the former black community of Africville in Halifax and the environmental health problems on many Aboriginal peoples' reserves across Canada point to the link between the oppression of marginalized people and their environment (Gosine and Teelucksingh 2008; Agyeman et al. 2009). Environmental justice research and activism in Canada has emerged more slowly and without the same grassroots and political commitment that characterized the US movement (Agyeman et al. 2009; Haluza-DeLay 2007). However, many experiences of environmental injustice, while not specifically named and labelled as such, have had an enormous impact on the lives of Aboriginal and racialized communities in Canada and have contributed to these communities' marginalized status vis-à-vis the Canadian state (Haluza-DeLay et al. 2009). And environmental justice research is being applied in Canadian cities to better understand uneven development, environmental health risks, and racialization of minorities and new Canadians.

URBAN SPRAWL

Urban sprawl is one of the most significant environmental and social problems affecting many larger cities in Canada. It involves decentralization or the shifting of economic activity and residential patterns away from the central city toward peripheral areas. Urban sprawl is often associated with uncontrolled growth in urban centres as previous suburban regions become extended over time. For example, steady population growth, and the correspond-

SOCIOLOGY in ACTION

Brownfields Redevelopment

Trendy lifestyle-oriented advertising beckons young professionals to come work, live, and play in the modern **metropolis**. Normally, gentrification is associated with upscaling existing lower-income, inner-city neighbourhoods. However, urban renewal in Toronto has currently been targeting underutilized and virtually abandoned industrial brownfields sites. In downtown Toronto, brownfields sites have become hot properties, especially if they are close to the downtown commercial and financial centre and the coveted Lake Ontario waterfront. This instant form of gentrification (Rose 2004, 7) involves the claiming of previously undesirable industrial spaces by the middle-class and upwardly mobile. Tension over scarce resources in downtown Toronto is positioning those on the side of capital (developers, real estate agents, and potential middle-class residents) against the subsistence needs of marginalized groups and marginalized land uses.

Cheryl Teelucksingh, an environmental sociologist in Toronto, used the issue of brownfields redevelopment to examine important environmental justice and citizenship questions, such as who has claims to space in the city and who belongs in the city. Teelucksingh's research considered how universal and egalitarian rights to the city are threatened when stakeholders with fewer resources become vulnerable to environmental inequalities.

The study involved an analysis of various stakeholders' perspectives (e.g., people living near brownfields, affluent residents, and public- and private-sector interests) on brownfields redevelopment in light of competing needs emerging from post-industrialization and shifts toward neo-liberal agendas in Toronto. Based on this analysis, the study found that brownfields gentrification is a unique form of gentrification that has the potential to isolate lower-income and ethno-racial groups into limited neighbourhoods in downtown Toronto, to minimize the focus on creating affordable housing for Toronto's growing population, and, ultimately, to tarnish Toronto's image as the ideal Canadian multicultural urban centre that includes mixed-income neighbourhoods in the downtown core. The development of brownfields in downtown Toronto is resulting in social and environmental inequalities as well as new forms of resistance, such as demonstrations in support of the rights of the homeless and those living in poor-quality housing.

Excerpts taken from C. Teelucksingh, 2009, "Social inequality and brownfields redevelopment in downtown Toronto," in Laurie Adkin, ed., *Environmental Conflict and Democracy in Canada*, 262–78 (Vancouver: University of British Columbia Press). Reprinted with permission of the publisher.

ing growth in residential housing and business expansion, account for Calgary's urban sprawl (Carter and Whitney 2008). It can be seen in large-scale, low-density development that poses serious threats to the natural environment, agricultural land, energy resources, and human health and quality of life. There is now greater awareness of the social and environmental costs associated with urban sprawl, which seems all the more ominous given that the demographic trend is toward smaller families and larger, predominately suburban houses.

Larger housing lots and ease of commuting to the central city often draw residents to suburban communities. However, not only are suburbanites less likely to know and interact with their neighbours, but many suburban communities are class-segregated because of the way new housing developments are designed. Social segregation in low-density communities means less diverse neighbourhoods, which does not foster racial tolerance. As part of urban sprawl, decentralization of economic activity results in the dispersal of workplaces and makes it difficult for those living in the central city to get to work. As people spend more time commuting, their social isolation increases.

One of the most significant environmental consequences of urban sprawl is its threat to farmland. To lessen the threat, some cities, like Portland, Oregon, in 1979, have established a **greenbelt** to contain the sprawl (Carter-Whitney 2008). Suburbanization and urban sprawl also requires construction of more highways. Greater reliance on cars translates into increased fuel consumption and pollution. In many suburban neighbourhoods, public transit options are few, because extensive sprawl makes it difficult to establish and maintain cost-effective transit systems. This disadvantages lower-income people who either live or work in suburban areas.

In an effort to address urban growth in a manner that does not further contribute to urban sprawl, municipalities and developers have been increasingly adopting "smart growth" as a development strategy (Eidelman 2010). Smart growth is an approach to urban development that seeks to make more efficient use of existing inner-city infrastructure by creating higher-density communities. Making better and more efficient use of existing urban space and infrastructure is the alternative to new greenfield development. Some smart growth initiatives in Toronto and Vancouver (Girling 2010) involve the creation of urban villages where people do not need to use their cars to meet their everyday needs. Stores, entertainment, daycare centres, and, ideally, workplaces are all within walking or short public-transit distance. However, many smart growth developments in the form of high-density condominiums, lofts, and townhouses are economically and socially oriented toward young urban dwellers and

older "empty nesters," which limits the ability of people with lower incomes or larger families to benefit from such options.

Vancouver, Calgary, Hamilton, and Toronto have all been experiencing urban renewal in the form of gentrification (Ley and Dobson 2008; Behan, Maoh, and Kanaroglou 2008; Eidelman 2010; Skaburskis and Meligrana 2005). As discussed earlier in the chapter, gentrification involves the upscaling of formerly lower-income or working-class neighbourhoods. Like smart growth developments, gentrification is breathing new life into many inner-city neighbourhoods that have desirable features in terms of access to employment, public transit, and various amenities and offer an alternative to urban sprawl development. However, drawing from conflict approaches to both urbanization and the environment, critics of gentrification point to the displacement of lower-income residents as inner-city neighbourhoods become unaffordable and the fact that the racial and class diversity that once characterized mixed-income neighbourhoods can be lost (Meligrana and Skaburskis 2005).

Do you think Calgary has an urban sprawl issue greater than that of other Canadian cities? Why or why not?

TIME to REFLECT

Based on the arguments presented, is some level of gentrification desirable in lower-income communities? If so, how can gentrification occur without displacing lower-income residents?

Conclusion

Social forces related to changes in the labour market, the family, health care, immigration, and urban planning have all contributed to Canada's current demographic trend toward low fertility rates, an aging population, and a continued reliance on immigration. In this chapter, we have considered demography as the starting point for examining how cities evolve in Canada and the relationship of Canadian cities to their natural environment.

Similarly, we have seen how theoretical perspectives on urbanism and the environment have developed and responded to social transformations. Late nineteenth-century and twentieth-century industrialization led early European and later Chicago School of Sociology theorists to consider the impact of cities on social relations and social order. The Chicago School of Sociology was instrumental in providing urban sociology with a definition of urbanism and systematic methods for studying the city. Subsequent conflict perspectives on urbanism applied the political economy approach to understanding urban inequalities stemming from capitalism and globalization.

As sites for large-scale consumption and high levels of waste and pollution, cities are now central to the drive toward sustainability and a more nuanced regard for humans' place in interdependent ecosystems. It is impossible to predict how today's social and environmental actions will influence future demographic trends and patterns of urbanism. As explained in this chapter, functionalist approaches to urbanism and the environment are focused on maintaining urban growth and development by using science and technology to come up with sustainable solutions. But in the context of heightened inequalities caused by globalization and neo-liberalism, conflict perspectives on urbanism and the environment emphasize the uneven distribution of benefits and costs in current urban development strategies such as suburbanization and gentrification.

questions for critical thought

1. Demography helps us to predict population change. From the perspective of Canada and Canadian cities, what are some of the demographic trends that Canadians will be responding to in the future?

2. What are some of the social benefits and challenges associated with the shift from rural settlements to urban settlements?

3. Are current environmental problems more or less critical than they were before?

4. Sustainable development attempts to balance concerns for environment, economy, and equity. Can these three components exist together, or is sustainable development an unattainable goal?

recommended readings

T.E. Bunting, P. Filion, and R. Walker. 2010. *Canadian Cities in Transition: New Directions in the Twenty-First Century.* **4th edn. Don Mills, ON: Oxford University Press.**
This book examines the major transformation taking place in urban Canada.

P.R. Ehrlich and A.H. Ehrlich. 1990. *The Population Explosion.* **New York: Simon and Schuster.**
The authors examine recent Malthusian perspectives and concerns about population growth.

C.L. Harper and T.H. Fletcher. 2011. *Environment and Society: Human Perspectives on Environmental Issues.* **Canadian edn. Toronto: Pearson Canada.**
This book offers a comprehensive introduction to environmental problems and issues from a Canadian perspective.

R. LeGates and F. Stout, eds. 2003. *The City Reader.* **3rd edn. London, New York: Routledge.**
This anthology includes the best publications on the city, with chapters on globalization, information technology, and urban theory.

recommended websites

Canada Year Book 2011
www.statcan.gc.ca/pub/11-402-x/11-402-x2011000-eng.htm
For more than 140 years, the *Canada Year Book* has been the ultimate source for the latest facts and analyses related to current events, important issues, and trends in Canada.

Centre for Urban & Community Studies, University of Toronto, Urban Affairs e-library
www.urbancentre.utoronto.ca/elibrary.html
This site provides links to scholarly publications on urban issues, including globalization, Aboriginal housing, and urban diversity.

Ecological Footprint: Centre for Sustainable Economy
www.myfootprint.org
The Ecological Footprint Quiz estimates the amount of land and ocean area required to sustain your consumption patterns and absorb your wastes on an annual basis.

United Nations, Department of Economic and Social Affairs
http://esa.un.org/unpd/wup/index.htm
Revised every two years, this site gives estimates and projections of the urban and rural populations of all countries in the world and their major urban agglomerations.

chapter 17

Mass Media and Communication

David Young

In this chapter, you will:

▶ Identify various forms of media ownership and understand concerns about deepening ownership concentration.

▶ Study the role of the state and globalization in relation to the mass media.

▶ Grasp how media content represents the working class, women, and ethno-racial minorities.

▶ Examine how the Internet reflects long-standing issues in the sociology of mass media.

Introduction

You are probably exposed to various mass media every day. You might browse through a newspaper over breakfast, listen to rock songs on your iPod as you head to class that morning, access the Internet to do research for a paper in the afternoon, and relax in the evening by going out to see a movie. The media may play an important role in your life, but you will discover in this chapter that they also play an important role in society.

Sociological Theories of the Media

Four sociological theories—symbolic interactionism, structural functionalism, conflict theory, and feminism—have been described in this book. The focus here will be on considering how useful these theories are for understanding the mass media.

Symbolic interactionism focuses on the microsociological issue of interaction among individuals through shared understanding of verbal and non-verbal symbols such as language or body language. This theory has been used in studies of communication since the 1970s. Faules and Alexander (1978) identified how symbolic interactionism could be employed to examine different forms of communication. They indicated that this theoretical approach can be applied to *interpersonal communication* (face-to-face interaction between two individuals that involves exchange of verbal and non-verbal cues), *group communication* (face-to-face interaction among several individuals in a small context, such as a seminar, that still permits exchange of verbal and non-verbal symbols), and *public communication* (sending messages to various individuals in a large face-to-face setting, as in a lecture, where participants have limited opportunity for exchange of verbal and non-verbal cues). While symbolic interactionism can be useful to scholars who study face-to-face communication, it has more limited applicability with regard to *mass communication* (sending messages to many individuals through media such as newspapers, motion pictures, radio, or television). The theory does not allow sociologists to address macrosociological concerns like the role of media institutions in society.

Structural functionalism is a macrosociological framework that focuses on how order and stability are facilitated by the interconnected parts of society as well as consensus regarding norms and values. This theory was used in studies of the mass media during the 1950s. Wright (1959) argued that media institutions contribute to the maintenance of society by performing four functions. First, news media engage in *surveillance of the environment* by collecting and distributing information so that people know what is happening in the world and can be warned of imminent danger (such as a hurricane). Second, commentaries through media (such as televised speeches by political leaders) enable *correlation of the parts of society* by interpreting information about the environment while prescribing appropriate responses and building consensus about a course of action. Third, various mass media facilitate *transmission of the social heritage* by socializing individuals and helping to ensure that the culture of a society continues across time. Finally, *entertainment* provided by mass media permits the release of emotional tensions that may generate conflict and threaten social order. Although structural functionalism offered some important insights, sociologists had abandoned the theory by the 1970s. In part, this was due to its conservative orientation. The conservative nature of structural functionalism is evident in its emphasis on order and stability. Structural functionalism stresses the role of media institutions (and other social institutions) in maintaining society as it is.

Conflict theory is a macrosociological approach that addresses how social change occurs through conflict between unequal groups such as the capitalist class and the working class. It has been used frequently in studies of the mass media since the 1960s. Rather than justifying the role of media institutions, as structural functionalism does, conflict theory makes it possible to question the role of these institutions. The theory enables sociologists to see how media institutions in capitalist society involve power and reinforce inequality. Through this theoretical approach, sociologists can also see how media institutions are associated with conflict between powerful and less powerful groups in society. Early research based on conflict theory examined linkages between media institutions and power in American society (Schiller 1969) and news coverage of conflict between social institutions and the student movement during the 1960s (Gitlin 1980).

Feminism can be used to understand microsociological issues associated with the lives of women and their experience with inequality, but it also has a strong focus on addressing macrosociological conditions that account for the oppression of women. Feminist theory gave rise to the concept of patriarchy (a society or form of social organization based on male domination), and the theory has had an impact on studies of the mass media since the 1970s. Recent feminist theory has emphasized three themes connected to analysis of media and communication. Wackwitz and Rakow (2004) identify these themes as difference, voice, and representation. *Difference* includes the notion of supposedly biological differences—men being "naturally" more aggressive than women, for example—which feminists see as products of culture that are perpetuated by the media. *Voice* concerns the degree to which women are denied an opportunity to speak in various forms of communication (including interpersonal or group communication) or given a voice only to have their ideas ignored. *Representation* draws attention to the way women are depicted in media content and the way this negatively affects them.

TIME to REFLECT

Consider how a functionalist or a feminist would analyze your favourite television show.

CRITICAL PERSPECTIVES ON THE MEDIA

Conflict theory and feminism have contributed to critical perspectives on the media. Critical perspectives challenge the type of society we have while analyzing the mass media in relation to power, inequality, conflict, and change.

Critical perspectives on the media are often divided into two categories: political economy and cultural studies. Political economy focuses on ownership and control of the media. It examines private corporations and the state in relation to the media as well as the opposition of subordinate groups to the role of powerful media organizations. In contrast, work within cultural studies addresses the ideological aspects of the media. This approach analyzes the ideology embedded in media content, the interpretation of media content by audience members, and efforts to change media representations or disseminate alternative media messages. Adapting the themes that Mosco (1989) associated with political economy and cultural studies, we will now turn to these two critical perspectives.

Political Economy of the Media

While placing a strong emphasis on historical analysis, researchers who specialize in the political economy of media devote particular attention to several issues. The main issues are forms of media ownership, the state and media policy, globalization and the media, and conflict over ownership, policy, and globalization.

FORMS OF MEDIA OWNERSHIP

We can distinguish between public and private media ownership as well as various types of ownership that are private.

Public ownership—ownership of media by the government—has a long history in Canada. Examples of public media ownership in this country include the National Film Board (NFB), the Canadian Broadcasting Corporation (CBC), and the educational television broadcasters operated by some provincial governments. The goal of these organizations is to provide a public service by utilizing the media to satisfy social objectives. Such objectives include providing media that are freely available to citizens, using the media for educational purposes, and ensuring a Canadian voice in the media. Media organizations under public ownership are often supported by government funding, but additional funding may come from advertising or memberships (Lorimer and Gasher 2001).

Private ownership refers to ownership of the media by commercial firms, and it too has long existed in Canada. Most of the media in Canada are under private ownership. The prevalence of private ownership is illustrated in Table 17.1, which presents a list of the leading media organizations in Canada. Only one of these organizations, the CBC, is a public corporation. The goal of private media organizations is "survival and growth in a marketplace driven by profit" (Lorimer and Gasher 2001, 223).

Critical researchers argue that the pursuit of profit through private ownership has significant implications for media content. The interests of private media companies mean that media content "is regarded by their management not as a public service, but as a business cost to be met as inexpensively as possible" (Hackett, Pinet, and Ruggles 1996, 260). For example, the private television network CTV can purchase the rights to broadcast American shows for approximately one-tenth the cost of producing a Canadian series. As Taras (2001, 189) has indicated, this explains why private television broadcasters in Canada "put as little as possible into Canadian content and squeeze the most out of imported Hollywood productions." While noting that private media have done little to reflect Canadian culture in their programming, critical scholars have also been concerned about several specific types of private ownership.

Independent ownership is the most basic and least problematic of these types. It exists when the owners of a media company confine themselves to that one company and are not involved in the ownership of other firms. Their media company usually operates on a small scale. It is often closely associated with a local community and aims to serve that community. This form of ownership means that the newspaper, radio station, or television station in a small town or city might be owned by an entrepreneur who lives in the area. Independent ownership was once quite common in the Canadian media, but it has diminished as large companies have bought small media firms (Lorimer and Gasher 2001).

Horizontal integration (chain ownership) exists when one company owns a number of media organizations in different locations that are doing the same type of business. One company may own several newspapers, for example. Critical scholars contend that this form of ownership has negative implications. For instance, if a company owns a chain of newspapers, it could cut costs by using syndicated news stories across the chain and reducing the number of journalists and local stories at each of the newspapers (Hackett and Gruneau 2000). When an independently owned newspaper becomes part of a chain, a number of jobs disappear along with some of the newspaper's local flavour.

Vertical integration exists when one firm owns media enterprises that link processes such as production, distribution, and exhibition. For instance, Quebecor Media owns the French-language broadcaster TVA as well as Videotron, a cable company in Quebec that carries TVA on its systems. Vertical integration enables a firm to have a guaranteed outlet for its products. However, critical researchers suggest that this form of ownership can result in content from other sources being shut out (Croteau and Hoynes 2000).

Cross-ownership exists when one company owns organizations that are associated with different types of media. Bell Media owns the television network CTV, specialty television channels (such as CTV News Channel and TSN), radio stations, and the sympatico.ca portal. Cross-ownership has certain advantages for a company, including the opportunity to share resources or personnel among media holdings, but critical researchers argue that it can limit the diversity of journalistic opinions or media messages (Hackett, Pinet, and Ruggles 1996).

TABLE 17.1 ▼	The Leading Media Organizations in Canada, 2010
Organization	**Revenues (2010)**
Rogers Communications Inc.	$12,186,000,000
Quebecor Inc.	$4,000,100,000
Shaw Communications Inc.	$3,717,580,000
Lions Gate Entertainment Corp.	$1,727,836,000
Torstar Corp.	$1,479,588,000
Cogeco Inc.	$1,321,694,000
Cineplex Inc.	$1,010,782,000
Astral Media Inc.	$1,010,782,000
Corus Entertainment Inc.	$836,221,000
CBC/Radio-Canada	$567,681,000

SOURCE: Adapted from *Financial Post*, FP500 Database, www.financialpost.com/news/fp500/2011

When one company owns the number of media outlets that Bell Media has, the same news stories and programming will appear across the range of its holdings.

Finally, it is necessary to consider **conglomerate ownership**. A conglomerate is a company containing many firms engaged in a variety of (usually) unrelated business activities. This form of ownership may combine horizontal or vertical integration and cross-ownership. There are also different types of conglomerates. A media conglomerate does most of its business in the media. A non-media conglomerate focuses on other types of business, but it might also own media organizations (Lorimer and Gasher 2001). Critical researchers are concerned about the content of news media held by both types of conglomerates. In this regard, Hackett and Gruneau (2000, 60–1) identify "two worrying implications." First, news media owned by a conglomerate may be required to carry promotional material for other parts of the company. Second, news stories could be suppressed if they contain negative or damaging information about other aspects of the corporate empire.

TIME to REFLECT

How much time do you spend with public media such as the CBC? In your view, how important is it to have public ownership of the media?

THE STATE AND MEDIA POLICY

The concept of the state is sometimes confused with that of the government. However, for sociologists, the state is a much broader term. Cuneo (1990) defines the state in Canada as encompassing various institutions. The latter include all levels of government, regulatory agencies, the legal system, and institutions associated with public education, public health care, and public media that are under different levels of government.

While the state includes public media, other parts of the state have implications for both public and private media. The legal system sets out certain requirements for media organizations. For example, the Broadcasting Act (Canada 1991) indicates what is expected of organizations that provide public and private radio or television in Canada. The legislation makes it clear that these organizations must present Canadian programming. Regulatory agencies are also components of the state that have consequences for the media. Canada has had two independent broadcasting regulators. The Board of Broadcast Governors (BBG) was established in 1958 and replaced in 1968 by what is now referred to as the Canadian Radio-television and Telecommunications Commission (CRTC).

These regulatory agencies were created to help ensure that media organizations comply with media legislation by setting specific rules for the organizations to follow. For example, in relation to the Broadcasting Act, the requirement that broadcasters must present Canadian programming has been reflected in Canadian content regulations. These regulations were established by the BBG in 1960, and they initially required that at least 45 per cent of television programming be Canadian. The CRTC maintained the regulations for television and established similar regulations for radio in 1970. At first, a minimum of 30 per cent of the music on popular music stations had to be Canadian. Over the years, the CRTC has set various percentages of required Canadian content for different types of radio and television programming, but Canadian content regulations remain a key aspect of the agency's policy.

Analysis of media policy is often based on a key point in Marxist theories of the state. As Gold, Lo, and Wright (1975, 31) noted, "Marxist treatments of the state begin with the

(Ei Scan/GetStock.com)

Opponents of Canadian content regulations, especially private broadcasters, claim that CRTC regulations are an attack on the freedom of broadcasters. (Reprinted with permission. Torstar Syndication Services)

fundamental observation that the state in capitalist society broadly serves the interests of the capitalist class." The state in Canada has served the interests of private media companies in a number of ways. For example, the federal government responded to the cable industry's desire for vertical integration by placing a clause in the Broadcasting Act that paved the way for cable companies to own television stations (Raboy 1995). This is now the case, as ownership of the OMNI stations by Rogers Communications illustrates. The CRTC's regulatory process has also done much to assist private media companies. According to Mosco (1989, 57), "this formal regulatory process generally serves the interests of communications companies and large corporate users of communications systems." For instance, since the CRTC has taken "a permissive attitude to industry mergers" (Mosco 1989, 212), the agency has given regulatory approval to the deepening ownership concentration that worries critical scholars.

Some critical scholars suggest that the role of the state has been decreasing as a result of neo-liberalism. Neo-liberalism is an economic doctrine favoured by private companies, and it has been adopted by many governments around the world since the late 1970s. The doctrine of neo-liberalism supports free trade between countries, cuts in social spending, and measures such as deregulation and privatization. Deregulation means that regulatory agencies reduce or eliminate rules they had previously imposed on organizations. For instance, under its 1998 Commercial Radio Policy, the CRTC reduced restrictions on how many radio stations private companies could own in a single market (Canadian Radio-television and Telecommunications Commission 1998). Privatization, which means that organizations under public ownership are transferred to private ownership, has also been apparent in the Canadian media; during the 1990s, the government of Alberta sold The Access Network, its educational television broadcaster, to CHUM.

GLOBALIZATION AND THE MEDIA

In recent decades, the issue of globalization has been the focus of much analysis by sociologists. Globalization involves the flow of goods, services, media, information, and labour between countries around the world. Researchers often examine different but interrelated aspects of globalization. Economic globalization concerns worldwide production and financial transactions, while cultural globalization refers to "the transmission or diffusion across national borders of various forms of media and the arts" (Crane 2002, 1).

Globalization is being driven by a complex mixture of technological, economic, and political factors. Technological factors include the use of computers and satellites to facilitate communication or transmit news between different parts of the world (Nash 2000; Winseck and Pike 2009). Economic factors entail deepening ownership concentration within countries and across national borders as well the international impact of neo-liberalism and free trade between countries. These economic factors are tied to political factors. The latter include the role of the state in assisting private capital, partly through negotiation of the North American Free Trade Agreement (NAFTA) and similar international treaties. Political factors also include the emergence of the World Trade Organization (WTO), an international institution that enforces trade rules on member countries and has thereby reduced the control of governments over their own economies (Karim 2002). These developments have generated a number of issues that concern critical researchers.

Cultural Globalization

In relation to cultural globalization, critical researchers are concerned about the historically deepening and worldwide impact of media industries.

We can illustrate this by looking at the American motion picture industry. The dominance of the American film industry was established soon after the earliest Hollywood productions at the beginning of the twentieth century. By 1939, Hollywood was already supplying 65 per cent of the films shown in theatres worldwide. This export flow expanded dramatically after World War II, and in the 1990s the United States was producing more than 80 per cent of the world's films (Miller et al. 2001). American films generate at least half of the total box-office receipts in all their major markets and sometimes more than two-thirds of total receipts (Scott 2004). In Canada, Hollywood films accounted for 92.7 per cent of box-office receipts during 2010 (Canadian Media Production Association 2011).

Several factors help to explain the dominance of the American film industry. One factor is the ownership structure of the industry, which has played a crucial role. The vertical integration of production, distribution, and exhibition during the early history of the Hollywood studios ensured that the films these studios made were seen in the United States and in many international markets. In Canada and elsewhere, this made it more difficult for domestic films to secure theatrical exhibition (Miller et al. 2001; Pendakur 1990). Hollywood production companies usually do not own movie theatres any more, but they still have substantial distribution operations around the world. Furthermore, as the Hollywood studios have increasingly come under conglomerate ownership since the 1980s, massive and often non-American multinational firms such as the Sony Corporation (which owns Columbia Pictures) have developed strategies to pursue global audiences (Miller et al. 2001).

The state has also contributed to the global dominance of Hollywood. The film industry in the United States has prospered internationally in part because it has "a willing servant in the state" (Miller et al. 2001, 24). Under pressure from the Motion Picture Association of America (MPAA), which represents the major film studios, American federal bureaucracies have pushed governments in other countries to satisfy Hollywood's interests (Scott 2004). In Canada, this has historically resulted in several successful efforts to discourage the federal government from establishing measures to protect the Canadian film industry, including quotas that would have placed limits on the importation of American films (Magder 1993).

Economic Globalization

With regard to economic globalization, critical researchers are concerned about the emergence of an *international division of labour*. Sociologists have analyzed how multinational corporations, including those with holdings in the media and information industries, have spread their production operations around the world. The standard view of this process suggests that it involves shifting jobs from developed, rich countries (such as the United States)

to developing, poor countries (like India). Although the trend is certainly in the direction of moving jobs to the developing world, Mosco (2005, 52) has pointed to "an increasingly complex international division of labour involving far more than simply the transfer of service jobs from high- to low-wage nations."

This is illustrated by the fact that several **developed countries**, especially Canada and Ireland, have been the recipients of much outsourcing and offshoring of jobs in the media and information industries. *Outsourcing* occurs when a company shifts a portion of its production to another entity, typically independent local companies in a foreign country. *Offshoring* exists when a company has one of its own foreign affiliates handle the production. Although **developing countries** offer cheaper labour and other advantages, multinational corporations maintain some outsourcing or offshoring in developed countries, because they need certain jobs to be filled by workers with higher levels of skill or education (Mosco 2005). Because of the value of the dollar and wage rates in these developed countries, multinationals can still enjoy considerable savings on production costs compared to keeping production in the United States. These factors explain the existence of so-called "runaway" productions. Hollywood studios have moved a number of film and television productions from Los Angeles to Canadian cities—everything from the *X-Men* movie trilogy to *The X Files* television series—in order to cut costs while utilizing the expertise of Canadian companies and production crews (Elmer and Gasher 2005).

CONFLICT OVER OWNERSHIP, POLICY, AND GLOBALIZATION

Capitalist interests in ownership, policy, and globalization have generated conflict between private companies and subordinate groups. Although the state serves the interests of the capitalist class, Marxist theory suggests that the state makes some concessions to the working class and its allies. Consequently, despite the power of corporate capital and its influence on the state, subordinate groups have occasionally won victories through their resistance.

This can be illustrated through historical conflict over media ownership and policy. In Canada, subordinate groups won successful battles to establish public ownership of

(© Gregory Holmgren / Alamy)

Colloquially known as Hollywood North, Canada has long been offering Hollywood a cost-effective alternative to shooting in the US. Here, Yonge Street, Toronto, has been made to look like the New York City neighbourhood of Harlem.

broadcasting as well as the policy of Canadian content regulations. Smythe (1981, 165) noted that the period from 1930 to 1936 was marked by "a struggle between the popular forces in Canada fighting for public service broadcasting and those seeking private profit." Trade unions, educational leaders, and other groups that were organized around the Canadian Radio League (CRL) pushed for public radio stations, while the Canadian Association of Broadcasters (CAB), an organization that represented existing private radio stations, wanted broadcasting to be used only for making money. Pressure from the CRL contributed to the decision of the federal government to establish the Canadian Radio Broadcasting Commission (CRBC) as Canada's first public broadcaster in 1932, and the CRBC paved the way for the emergence of the CBC in 1936 (Smythe 1981; Raboy 1990). Similarly, Canadian nationalists and trade unions advocated Canadian content regulations for television and radio to protect Canadian culture and ensure jobs for Canadians working in associated media industries. Despite the views of private broadcasters, who wanted to maximize audiences and advertising revenues by offering popular American television shows and music,

CanCon regulations were established for both television and radio (Raboy 1990).

More recently, much conflict associated with the media has been connected to globalization. This is most obvious in the protests against economic and cultural globalization that social movements have held at WTO meetings and meetings of other international bodies, but conflict over globalization also takes other forms. For instance, in developed countries like the United States, trade unions have resisted outsourcing in the media and information industries. While these unions have resisted the loss of jobs to the **Third World**, they have also challenged the shifting of work to other developed countries (Mosco 2005). For example, there has been opposition from labour in the United States to the movement of film and television production to Canada (Magder and Burston 2001).

Why is it important that television and radio programming reflect Canadian culture? Turn to "Mass Media," in Chapter 3, p. 63, to understand how influential the mass media is on our culture.

OPEN for DISCUSSION

Do We Need CanCon Regulations for Radio?

Canadian content regulations for radio stations in Canada were established in 1970. The regulations are administered by the Canadian Radio-television and Telecommunications Commission (CRTC). Currently, CanCon regulations (as they are often known) stipulate that at least 35 per cent of the music on radio stations featuring popular music must be Canadian. The amount of Canadian content required by the CRTC has varied over time and in accordance with the type of music played by a station. To qualify as Canadian, a piece of music must meet at least two of the following four criteria: the music is composed entirely by a Canadian; the lyrics are written entirely by a Canadian; the music or lyrics are performed principally by a Canadian; or the musical selection consists of a performance that was either recorded wholly in Canada or performed wholly in Canada and broadcast live in Canada.

There has been considerable debate about whether or not we need Canadian content regulations. Opponents of CanCon include private radio broadcasters and some Canadian musicians. Supporters of the regulations include other Canadian musicians, labour unions that represent Canadian musicians, Canadian nationalists, and the owners of Canadian independent record companies. The debate between the opponents and supporters of CanCon has focused on several issues, two of which are outlined below.

The first issue concerns whether or not radio stations should be forced to play Canadian music.

Opponents of CanCon, especially owners of private radio stations, contend that CanCon regulations are an attack on the freedom of broadcasters. They maintain that radio broadcasters should have the right to play whatever music they want and whatever music their listeners want to hear. Supporters of CanCon argue that owners of private radio stations are making money off Canadian airwaves, which are public property and subject to legal requirements under the Broadcasting Act. They believe that private radio broadcasters should meet public service obligations by playing Canadian music in exchange for being given the opportunity to use the public airwaves for profit.

The second issue concerns whether or not Canadian artists need CanCon regulations. Opponents of CanCon argue that Canadian artists who have talent will make it on their own without assistance from the CRTC. In their view, radio stations will play music by Canadian artists as long as their music is good. Supporters of CanCon maintain that Canadian artists will not get on the radio unless they are already well known or unless they are signed to or distributed by one of the multinational conglomerates that dominate the music industry. They contend that developing artists (those who are unsigned or signed to small, independently owned Canadian record companies) will not be heard without regulations that force radio stations to give them airplay.

Now that you have learned about some of the points made on each side of the debate, which side do you agree with?

SOURCE: Adapted from Young 2008.

Cultural Studies of the Media

As noted earlier, while political economy focuses on ownership and control of the media, cultural studies addresses the ideological aspects of the media. Three key issues in cultural studies need to be discussed. They are representation in mainstream media, interpreting and resisting mainstream media, and opposition through alternative media.

REPRESENTATION IN MAINSTREAM MEDIA

The mainstream media include the newspapers, magazines, radio stations, and television channels that most people are exposed to every day. These means of communication are owned by private companies or the government. The mainstream media present *texts* (such as newspaper and magazine articles or television shows) that convey certain messages about society and groups in society. Critical media sociologists argue that these messages reflect the dominant ideology. In other words, the messages express the viewpoints of powerful groups. Capitalist, patriarchal, or racist ideologies illustrate specific forms of the dominant ideology that are embedded in media texts.

We can investigate aspects of the dominant ideology by considering the representation of the working class, women, and racial or ethnic minorities in the mainstream media. Such groups have little power and receive poor representation in media content. They experience under-representation (since members of less powerful groups are usually not seen in the media as frequently as they actually exist in society) and misrepresentation (because members of these groups often are portrayed in ways that are stereotypical and negative).

Representation of the Working Class

Some research has been done on the problematic representation of the working class, and this work is strikingly illustrated in a series of studies conducted on American domestic situation comedies.

After researching all domestic situation comedies that appeared on American television between 1946 and 1990, Butsch (1992) identified the class position of the family in each show through the occupation of the lead male character. The family was considered to be working-class if the lead character was a blue-collar worker, clerical worker, retail worker, or service worker. The criteria for indicating that the family was middle-class included the presence of a professional or manager. Some comedies fell outside these categories, because they featured a lead character who was self-employed or independently wealthy or it was not possible to identify the occupation of the lead character. Once he had categorized the comedies, Butsch examined the data.

He discovered significant differences in the extent to which social classes were represented in domestic situation comedies. Butsch could not specify the occupation of the household head in 11.6 per cent of the comedies, but he found that 5.7 per cent featured a family that was independently wealthy and 1.1 per cent portrayed a family led by a farmer. However, his key findings indicated that 70.5 per cent of domestic situation comedies were about a middle-class family and only 11.0 per cent centred on a working-class family. In earlier research, Butsch and Glennon (1983) noted that similar findings were out of line with the existence of both classes in American society; based on census data, 28.7 per cent of actual household heads in the United States were middle-class while 65.0 per cent were working-class. Thus, based on research conducted up to

1990, the middle class was overrepresented in domestic situation comedies, and the working class was under-represented. Unfortunately, no studies have been done to further update these findings.

In his research on domestic situation comedies, Butsch found that working-class men generally received negative representation. Emphasis was placed on their "ineptitude, immaturity, stupidity, lack of good sense, or emotional outburst" (Butsch 1992, 391). The women in working-class comedies (and sometimes even the children) were portrayed as being much more intelligent and level-headed. In these comedies, the humorous situation typically involved the husband/father. The situation was often one of his own making, and he was usually helped out of it by his wife (Butsch 1992). As Butsch (1995) pointed out, this scenario applied to various working-class domestic situation comedies and their lead male characters in decades from the 1950s through to the 1980s. Consider *The Honeymooners* (Ralph Kramden), *The Flintstones* (Fred Flintstone), *All in the Family* (Archie Bunker), and *The Simpsons* (Homer Simpson).

In contrast, Butsch found that middle-class men often received positive representation. They were portrayed as being "intelligent, rational, mature, and responsible" (Butsch 1992, 391). The women in middle-class families were shown as also having these characteristics in their roles as wives and mothers. In middle-class comedies, the humorous situation typically involved one of the children. The parents guided the child through the situation, and frequently they provided a moral lesson in the process. Examples of these comedies from the 1950s to the 1980s include *Father Knows Best, My Three Sons, The Brady Bunch*, and *The Cosby Show* (Butsch 1992).

In research that extended analysis of domestic situation comedies to the decade of the 1990s, Scharrer (2001, 33) confirmed Butsch's findings. She noted that "the lower the social class of the sitcom father the more foolish the portrayal will be." Such findings are significant. Butsch (1995, 404) argued that the stark differences between the representation of working-class and middle-class men ideologically justify inequality in our class-divided society: "Blue-collar workers are portrayed as requiring supervision, and managers and professionals as intelligent and mature enough to provide it."

Representation of Women

A great deal of research has been done on the problematic representation of women. We can illustrate aspects of this work by looking at a few American and Canadian studies.

Dole (2000; 2001) examined the representation of women as law enforcers in American motion pictures released during the 1980s and 1990s. She argued that the women in these films had "types of power culturally coded as masculine" (2000, 11). The women had power because they occupied the position of law enforcer and because they carried a gun (two characteristics socially defined as "masculine" within our culture). Dole saw the genre of female cop films as emerging in two phases. The earlier films (1987–91), such as *Blue Steel* and *Impulse*, often imitated the physicality and violence of male action films by showing the women using their guns. Because many of these films were commercially unsuccessful, the later films (1991–5) took a softer approach. These films, including *The Silence of the Lambs* and *Copycat*, were more inclined "to privilege intellectual over physical power" (2000, 12). Rather than using their guns, the female law enforcers in the later films relied on their sleuthing skills.

Several other techniques were employed to play down "the threatening image of Woman with a Gun" (Dole 2000, 16). These techniques included *domestication* (portraying the female cops as single mothers or women who have "maternal instincts"), *infantilization* (representing the women as being dependent, vulnerable, helpless, or in need of rescue), and *sexualization* (emphasizing the attractive bodies of the women). Finally, the films that focused on intellectual power utilized what Dole called *splitting strategies*. Splitting strategies distributed among multiple characters the power that would otherwise be concentrated in one character. Through splitting strategies, the power of the female law enforcer was reduced. This can be illustrated by *The Silence of the Lambs*. In that film, intellectual power was split between Clarice Starling (Jodie Foster) and Hannibal Lecter (Anthony Hopkins). Although Starling was intelligent, she needed male assistance in the form of Lecter (Dole 2000, 16). The

ideological message was that a woman is incapable of solving the case and catching the killer on her own. Although female cop films gave women more representation than most movies (because they occupied central roles rather than peripheral roles), the stereotypical and patriarchal misrepresentation of women was still quite evident in these films.

It is also important to consider how the news media are connected to the representation of women or issues associated with women, and some Canadian research in this area has focused on news coverage of what is referred to as the Montreal Massacre. In December 1989, Marc Lépine went to l'École Polytechnique with a semi-automatic rifle. He walked into a classroom, ordered the men to leave, and accused the women of being "a bunch of feminists" before shooting six of them to death. Lépine then entered other classrooms and murdered eight more women. He also injured nine women and four men. At the end of his shooting rampage, he killed himself. In a suicide note found on his body, Lépine cited "political reasons" for the murders: he blamed "the feminists, who have always ruined my life" (cited in Eglin and Hester 1999, 256). There was much coverage of the Montreal Massacre in the news media, and some studies have been done of this coverage.

In one study, Hayford compared newspaper coverage of the Montreal Massacre at the time of the murders to coverage of a similar incident in Chicago during 1966 when eight women were killed by a man named Richard Speck. She found that the killings in Chicago were often interpreted by journalists in individualistic terms as the act of a madman. However, by the time the murders in Montreal occurred 23 years later, the women's movement had experienced some success in raising public awareness about the prevalence of wife-beating, rape, and other acts of violence against women in a patriarchal society. Since this had an impact on at least some journalists, there was media debate about individual versus societal explanations for the murders. Hayford (1992, 209) indicated that "the question of whether Lépine was no more than a demented individual or a reflection of broader social patterns of male violence against women, a question never raised about Speck, became a central issue in coverage of the Montreal killings."

(MGM/Universal/De Laurentiis/The Kobal Collection/Bray, Phil)

FBI agent Clarice Starling, played here by Julianne Moore, wields her firearm in the movie *Hannibal* (2001). Dole, citing films including *Hannibal*'s prequel, *The Silence of the Lambs*, argues that Hollywood has preferred to show women cops using their wits and dependent on males; this scene of a "woman with a gun" is an exception to the rule.

Representation of Racial and Ethnic Minorities

We also need to consider the under-representation and misrepresentation of racial and ethnic minorities in the mainstream media.

Many Canadian studies have documented the under-representation of racial and ethnic minorities. Researchers have found that although Canadian society features growing cultural diversity, this diversity usually is not reflected in media content. For example, my own research shows that ethno-racial minorities have rarely been seen at the annual and nationally televised Juno Awards ceremony for the Canadian music industry. Francophones, blacks, and Aboriginal peoples were almost never among the musical artists who appeared in the ceremony or won Junos during the 1970s and 1980s. There has been some improvement since then, but the Juno Awards ceremony still does not adequately reflect the cultural diversity of artists in Canada's music scene (Young 2006). Other scholars have arrived at similar findings. The general absence of racial and ethnic minorities (relative to their existence in the actual population) is apparent in advertisements, magazines, news, television series, and other forms of media content (Fleras and Kunz 2001; Mahtani 2001). The under-representation of these minorities is significant, because it means that their contributions to Canadian society are trivialized and their roles as Canadian citizens are devalued (Mahtani 2001).

Canadian studies have also shown that racial and ethnic minorities experience misrepresentation. To the extent that they are seen, ethno-racial minorities are frequently portrayed in stereotypical and negative ways. In the news media, this often takes the form of identifying them as social problems; racial and ethnic minorities are depicted as "having problems or creating problems in need of political attention or costly solutions" (Fleras and Kunz 2001, 145). Members of these minorities are presented as social problems in a variety of ways. They are seen to be participating in illegal activities, clashing with police, cheating on welfare, creating difficulties for immigration authorities, and having other undesirable effects (2001, 145). Specific groups—including Aboriginal peoples, Asians, blacks, and Muslims—are often singled out. For instance, Karim (2008) demonstrated that editorials and columns opposing multiculturalism have appeared in Canadian English-language newspapers after news reports about the arrests of Muslim men on terrorism-related charges.

EXPLAINING THE REPRESENTATION

How can we explain the under-representation or misrepresentation of the working class, women, and racial or ethnic minorities? First, we must reject the notion that there is a plot or "conspiracy" by powerful groups against less powerful groups. The circumstances are far more complex than that, and we must return to the concept of the dominant ideology to understand why. According to Hall, the dominant ideology is woven into media texts through **encoding**. Messages are constructed within the economic and technical frameworks of media institutions through a complicated production process that involves (among other things) organizational relations or practices and "meanings and ideas" drawn from the production structure (the media institutions) and "the wider socio-cultural and political structure" (Hall 1980, 129). Therefore, in order to grasp the representation of subordinate groups, we need to consider some of these factors in more depth.

Economic factors associated with media institutions help to partially account for the representation of subordinate groups in the entertainment media. For instance, Butsch (1995) noted that the under-representation of the working class in domestic situation comedies has much to do with the need for broadcasters to develop programs that will attract advertisers by providing a good atmosphere for products. There is a tendency, then, to create shows that feature middle-class characters and occupational groups who can afford to buy the products appearing in the ads. Furthermore, to the limited extent that working-class domestic situation comedies have been made, their persistently negative representation of working-class men exists in part because produc-

ers avoid financial risk by relying on formulas that have proved to be successful. Thus, the popularity of *The Honeymooners* in the 1950s spawned *The Flintstones* in the 1960s.

Factors associated with production and ideology also help to explain the problematic representation of subordinate groups in the entertainment media. Members of less powerful groups often do not hold important positions associated with media production. For example, women have little control over production in the film industry; women comprised only 16 per cent of all executive producers, producers, directors, writers, cinematographers, and editors who worked on the top-grossing American films for the year 2010 (Lauzen 2011). Such exclusion from the process of media production can have a substantial impact on media content.

Butsch (1995) made this clear when he noted that the under-representation of the working class in domestic situation comedies, along with the negative representation of working-class men, can be partly explained by the middle-class background of most producers and writers. Middle-class people develop shows based on what is familiar to them, and when they occasionally focus on working-class characters, they rely on the negative stereotypes of the working class that circulate in our culture as part of the dominant system of meanings and ideas. Such factors also help to account for the representation of subordinate groups in the news media. The need to attract advertising revenues by capturing large

(© iStockphoto/Anthony Brown)

Women and racial minorities are noticeably absent from film and television industries. Their exclusion from roles in front of and behind the camera has a substantial effect on the content of what is being produced and broadcast.

numbers of readers or viewers has contributed to the under-representation of the working class and ethno-racial minorities in news stories. For instance, since advertisers want to reach affluent middle-class audiences, the content of the news is designed to attract these audiences by reflecting their interests or concerns (Hackett and Uzelman 2003). The middle-class, male, white backgrounds of many news personnel also have at least some effect on how less powerful groups are covered (Mahtani 2001). Like that of producers and writers in the entertainment media, the work of journalists is partly shaped by their socio-demographic backgrounds and the dominant meanings and ideas they are exposed to. As Mahtani (2001, 115) has indicated, "journalists are largely bound by the dominant cultures within which they operate, including embedded societal prejudices, stereotypes, and populist frames of thinking."

INTERPRETING AND RESISTING MAINSTREAM MEDIA

In cultural studies, research has gone beyond studying representation in mainstream media to considering interpretation of this representation and resistance to it. We have seen that the dominant ideology is embedded in media texts through the process of encoding, but it is also important to consider the **decoding** of media content by audience members. As part of his encoding/decoding model, Hall argued that the dominant ideology is inscribed as the *dominant or preferred meaning* within media content.

Hall recognized that audience members may not always adopt the dominant meaning when they interpret media messages and identified three possible ways of decoding media texts. A *dominant-hegemonic* reading involves taking the preferred meaning, while an *oppositional* reading involves resisting a message by interpreting it through an alternative ideological framework. A *negotiated* reading contains a mixture of the dominant-hegemonic and oppositional readings. According to Hall (1980, 137), it reflects "the dominant definition of events" while refusing to accept every aspect of the definition. Consequently, "this negotiated version of the dominant ideology is shot through with contradictions" (1980, 137). For example, a worker may accept the argument of

government officials (as presented by the news media) that the "national interest" requires citizens to make economic sacrifices while opposing the related argument that such sacrifices must be made through legislation imposing wage freezes (1980, 137).

Research has been done on the decoding of media content by relatively powerless groups. In order to examine the approaches to decoding that Hall identified, Morley (1980) investigated how groups interpreted the British current affairs television series "Nationwide." Morley's seminal study demonstrated that decoding is affected by one's class position. For instance, in relation to a "Nationwide" program about the effects of budget policy on families, Morley found that no middle-class groups adopted an oppositional reading, while working-class groups produced more oppositional and negotiated readings. Although the research on "Nationwide" is often remembered for analysis of how class position affects interpretation of media texts, Morley (2006) has stressed that his aim was to examine how decoding is also influenced by other types of social position (such as gender, race/ethnicity, and age). These elements of Morley's study have come through more clearly in a statistical re-analysis of his data conducted by Kim. For example, in relation to age, Kim (2004, 88, 91) found that "the *younger* working-class viewers are, the more probability they have of producing *dominant* readings. . . . The more youthful viewers' consent to the preferred meanings can be explained by their relatively low-level of political consciousness, which is commonly found among youths in general."

TIME to REFLECT

How might your class position, gender, race/ethnicity, and age affect your decoding of media messages?

OPPOSITION THROUGH ALTERNATIVE MEDIA

While relatively powerless groups have engaged in resistance to problematic representation and messages in mainstream media, some of these groups have turned to opposition through alternative media. Alternative media are forms of

SOCIOLOGY in ACTION

Watching Homeless Men Watch *Die Hard*

Fiske and Dawson (1996, 297) investigated "the process in which audiences selectively produce meanings and pleasures from texts" by examining how homeless men interpreted television.

The researchers approached authorities who ran a homeless shelter in an American city and received permission to conduct their study. Fiske and Dawson then spent time at the shelter until the homeless men felt comfortable with them. Eventually, they started collecting data on how the men used a television set and video-cassette recorder in the shelter's lounge.

Fiske and Dawson gathered data unobtrusively. They just watched television with the homeless men. The researchers carefully observed reactions of the men to what was being watched and made notes afterwards.

During the study, the homeless men borrowed the film *Die Hard* from a library. Fiske and Dawson analyzed reactions of the men to this movie. The movie's main character is John McClane (Bruce Willis), an off-duty police detective who happens to be in the office tower of the Nakatomi Corporation at the time thieves take company executives hostage. The thieves want the millions of dollars in the company's vaults. The plot of the film involves McClane's efforts to stop the thieves as the police try to contend with the situation from outside the building.

Fiske and Dawson made interesting observations about reactions of the homeless men to *Die Hard*. They found the men paid attention to "violence that was directed against the social order" (1996, 301). For instance, the homeless men cheered when the thieves killed the head of the corporation after he refused to give them a computer code to access the company's vaults. They also cheered after the thieves fired a rocket at an armoured police vehicle, destroying the vehicle and killing the policemen in it. In contrast to the way people are intended to interpret the film, the homeless men were enthusiastic about attacks on corporate capital and the police.

What explains the reactions of homeless men to *Die Hard*? Their reactions must be understood in terms of their position in society and the reasons for their position. Although the dominant view of the homeless assumes they are to blame for their situation, Fiske and Dawson stress that homelessness stems from "the contemporary conditions of US capitalism" rather than individual failings (1996, 301). In the years prior to their study, neo-liberal policies had "minimized the role of the state in social life and maximized that of capital and the market" (1996, 302). Millions of jobs had disappeared, and government assistance to the poor was reduced. This generated increased homelessness. Fiske and Dawson also note that riot police had cleared the homeless from parks in American cities and confronted activist homeless groups.

The experiences of the homeless with capitalism and the police make it possible to understand their reactions to violence in *Die Hard*. Fiske and Dawson conclude that "certain representations of violence enable subordinated people to articulate symbolically their sense of opposition and hostility to the particular forms of domination that oppress them" (1996, 304).

communication used by subordinate groups and social movements to present their own messages, which often involve challenging existing conditions in society.

Many types of alternative media have been used by oppositional movements in Canada. Carroll and Ratner (1999; 2001) examined the use of alternative media when investigating the political strategies of different social movement organizations. They noted that The Centre, an organization for gays and lesbians in Vancouver, was heavily involved in alternative media. The Centre had established the monthly newspaper *Angles* and the "Coming Out Show" on Vancouver Co-operative Radio. End Legislated Poverty (ELP) was another organization studied by Carroll and Ratner. Committed to mobilizing the poor and fighting various state policies that perpetuate poverty, ELP had engaged in popular education through alternative media directed at the poor and the general public. ELP's alternative media included "Fighting Poverty Kits" and a newspaper, *The Long Haul*. Carroll and Ratner found that activists in these movement organizations could talk strategically about how they were using alternative media to struggle for social change. In an interview conducted by Coburn (2010), Carroll suggested that they would have similar findings if these studies were done now.

There is continuing need for alternative media. As Hackett, Pinet, and Ruggles (1996, 271) indicated, "establishment of alternative media is essential to building popular democratic movements, without which the hope of progressive social transformation is in vain."

TIME to REFLECT

Have you ever been exposed to alternative media? What types of media might be effective in helping movements get their messages to you?

The Internet: Extending Political Economy and Cultural Studies

The critical perspectives of political economy and cultural studies have been utilized by sociologists to study so-called "old media" like newspapers, motion pictures, and television. However, these perspectives can also help us to grasp the "new media" of digital communication such as the Internet.

The Internet can be understood through long-standing issues in political economy. Analysis of the Internet must consider the state as well as globalization and private ownership. The state was crucial to the origin of the Internet. The Internet had its beginning in the late 1950s when the US Department of Defense established the Advanced Research Projects Agency (ARPA) to ensure that the Soviet Union would not develop military superiority over the United States in relation to computers and communication. ARPA developed a means of interconnecting computers in such a way that an attack on one server and one part of the network would not knock out other servers or the rest of the network (Cuneo 2002). While the Internet began with the state, its growth has had implications for globalization. The global impact of the Internet is closely tied to private ownership. Like the "old media," the "new media" have become associated with deepening ownership concentration. For instance, in 2000 America Online (AOL) took over the global media conglomerate Time Warner to form AOL/ Time Warner (Taras 2001).

The growing importance of the Internet has led some scholars in political economy to address the **digital divide**. The digital divide refers to inequalities in access to computers and/or the Internet. Most sociologists view the digital divide in terms of access by socioeconomic status and social class (Cuneo 2002). The data presented in Table 17.2 support the view of sociologists that there is an economic and class dimension to the digital divide. The table indicates access to the Internet in relation to the personal income of individuals in Canada for the years 2005, 2007, and 2009. The highest quartile (the top 25 per cent of individuals in terms of income) had consistently more access to the Internet than the lowest quartile. While 83.2 per cent of the highest-income group had access in 2005, only 58.7 per cent of the lowest-income group did. However, the gap between these groups has diminished. In 2009, 92.1 per cent of the highest-income group and 76.2 per cent of the lowest-income group had access to the Internet (Statistics Canada 2010a).

Key issues associated with cultural studies also provide a basis for thinking about the Internet. In many ways, the Internet represents an extension of mainstream media and the content provided by powerful groups.

TABLE 17.2 ▼ Personal Income of Individuals in Canada Using the Internet

Personal Income Quartile	2005	2007	2009
	Percentage of Individuals		
Lowest quartile	58.7	68.8	76.2
Second quartile	56.9	60.7	69.9
Third quartile	71.3	75.5	83.1
Fourth quartile	83.2	87.9	92.1

SOURCE: Adapted from Statistics Canada, "Characteristics of individuals using the Internet," *The Daily* 10 May 2010, www40.statcan .gc.ca/l01/cst01/comm35a-eng.htm. 2010a (Ottawa: Statistics Canada).

UNDER the WIRE

The Internet as Alternative Media

Activists associated with the global justice movement have made use of the Internet to challenge neo-liberalism and other aspects of the agenda that multinational corporations have adopted in relation to globalization. For instance, the Independent Media Centre established a website just before the Ministerial Conference of the World Trade Organization in Seattle in 1999. The aim was to provide coverage and analysis that would counter news of the conference offered by the corporate-dominated mainstream media (Downey and Fenton 2003). Through the website (known as Indymedia), journalists broke stories about the brutality of the police toward the demonstrators. The website had received more than 1 million hits from individual users by the end of the conference. The success of the website spawned other Indymedia websites around the world (Pickard 2006), and these websites continue to exist. Consequently, as Carroll has indicated, it is useful to see the Internet as "a tremendously subversive communications medium" (cited in Coburn 2010, 85).

Mainstream media content and the dominant ideology within this content have spread onto the Internet. Recorded music, motion pictures, and television shows are available for download. The advertising that is crucial for supporting many of the mainstream media is appearing with increasing frequency on websites. Newspapers and television news channels have websites where they can reproduce news stories. Fortunately, as the Under the Wire box makes clear, the Internet can also be seen as a new form of alternative media, which subordinate groups use to challenge the dominant ideology through their own content and messages.

Conclusion

As this chapter has shown, the mass media you are exposed to every day play an important role in society. Sociologists have seen that role in different ways: some have identified the functions of the media for society, while others have shown how the media are connected to conflict and patriarchy. The latter sociologists are critical of the type of society we have and point to how the media are tied to political, economic, and ideological power. This is true of both the old media and the new media, but it is also clear that media can be used by groups committed to change in society.

questions for critical thought

1. Research the background and current status of a media organization identified in Table 17.1 by visiting its website. What types of media have been associated with the organization? Can you connect the organization to one or more forms of ownership and the concerns raised about these ownership forms?

2. Find a newspaper article that reports on a regulatory decision the CRTC has made about radio or television. Does the CRTC's decision favour powerful groups or less powerful groups? What do sociological ideas about the state suggest about the reasons for the CRTC's decision?

3. Review Butsch's findings on the representation of the working class and the middle class in domestic situation comedies. Can you apply his analysis to more recent shows?

4. Examine the content in some form of alternative media (such as Vancouver Co-operative Radio or an Indymedia website). Identify specific ways in which the content is different from that of the mainstream media.

recommended readings

Robert A. Hackett and William K. Carroll. 2006. *Remaking Media: The Struggle to Democratize Public Communication.* **New York: Routledge.**
Hackett and Carroll use interviews with media activists and case studies of social movement organizations in the United States, Britain, and Canada to identify key issues involving the use of media by social movements and the struggles of movements to challenge the mainstream media.

John D. Jackson, Greg M. Nielsen, and Yon Hsu. 2011. *Mediated Society: A Critical Sociology of Media.* **Don Mills, ON: Oxford University Press.**
The authors analyze a variety of media issues (including audiences, advertising, media events, and journalism). They pay particular attention to issues involving Canadian media.

David Taras. 2001. *Power and Betrayal in the Canadian Media.* **updated edn. Peterborough, ON: Broadview.**
Taras examines what he sees as a crisis facing the Canadian media system. His fascinating analysis considers the problems confronting public broadcasting, the detrimental impact of private broadcasting, and the implications of developments such as ownership concentration.

Serra Tinic. 2005. *On Location: Canada's Television Industry in a Global Market.* **Toronto: University of Toronto Press.**
Tinic examines television production in Vancouver with reference to tensions between Hollywood's needs and the need to reflect Canadian culture. Since her analysis draws on political economy and cultural studies, the book is useful for students who want to learn more about these approaches.

recommended websites

Canadian Broadcasting Corporation (CBC)
www.cbc.ca
The CBC's website will enable you to find out more about Canada's national public broadcaster. The website supplies annual reports, corporate documents, and other information.

Canadian Radio-television and Telecommunications Commission (CRTC)
www.crtc.gc.ca
The CRTC's site will help you to learn more about this federal regulatory agency and its various policies.

Department of Canadian Heritage
www.pch.gc.ca
The Department of Canadian Heritage is the federal government agency responsible for broadcasting, film, and other aspects of culture. Its website will give you access to relevant policies and legislation as well as various reports.

Vancouver Co-operative Radio
www.coopradio.org
The website for Vancouver Co-operative Radio will enable you to learn about community radio as a form of alternative media. You can also listen to the station through the website.

glossary

Accountability The expectation that public education, like other state-provided services, has clearly defined objectives that members of the public can identify and use to assess how well and how cost-effectively they are being met.

Aesthetics A system of rules for the appreciation of the beautiful or for the judgment of and reflection on the value of art and other matters of taste.

Agency The human capacity to interpret, evaluate, choose, and act accordingly.

Agents of socialization Organizations and institutions through which culture (norms, values) is transmitted

Aging The multilevel and dynamic process of getting older in the context of the life course.

Allopathic medicine Conventional medicine that treats by opposing something, whether viruses, bacteria, cells, organs, or other pathology.

Americanization The idea that the United States, because of its huge economic superiority, can impose or promote itself as a "model" that other nations should follow and become in a way "Americanized."

Anomie The condition of modern society in which there are too few moral rules and regulations to guide people's conduct.

Anticipatory socialization Explicit or implicit learning in preparation for a future role; in Merton's definition, the acquisition of values and orientations found in statuses and groups in which one is not yet engaged but that one is likely to enter; socialization directed toward the preparation of future roles.

Anti-globalization Associated with many social movements around the world that protest against policies that in their mind are undermining people's rights and the environment by promoting the agenda of free trade and economic liberalization.

Baby boom The dramatic rise in the birth rate in Canada following World War II, lasting until well into the 1960s.

Believing without belonging The idea that today many people may hold religious beliefs without actually belonging to or participating in any religious institution.

Binary The use of either/or concepts (e.g., good/evil, body/mind) in social theory.

Birth rate The number of live births per a given number of persons in a given year.

Blaming the system Analyses that emphasize the structural and institutional sources of inequality. Unequal access to education would, for example, contribute to poverty patterns.

Blaming the victim The tendency to hold individuals entirely responsible for any negative situation that may arise in their lives. As applied to poverty, the poor are poor because of their lack of ambition.

Bonding social capital Social networks, mutual trust, and reciprocal obligations that create attachments between people who are *similar* in important respects (e.g., race, ethnicity, age, gender, class). A term associated with Robert Putnam's work on social capital and civil society.

Bourgeoisie The term used by Marx to refer to the capitalist class—that is, the individuals who own the means of production (factory owners), the merchant (economically dominant) or ruling class.

Bride price Money, property, or labour provided by the groom or his family to a bride's family for permission to marry her.

Bridging social capital Social networks, mutual trust, and reciprocal obligations that create attachments between people who are *different* in important respects (e.g., race, ethnicity, age, gender, class). A term associated with Robert Putnam's work on social capital and civil society.

Bureaucracy The most developed, most efficient formal organization, with formal properties that include written rules, protected careers, and a clear chain of reporting relationships. It is

ordered by criteria independent of the personal qualities of the people who hold positions of power and is a system that is rationalized and associated with states and the post–Industrial Revolution period.

Capitalism An economic system characterized by a relationship of unequal economic exchange between capitalists (employers) and workers. Because they do not own the means of production, workers must sell their labour to employers in exchange for a wage or salary. Capitalism is a market-based system driven by the pursuit of profit for personal gain.

Census A complete count of the population at one point in time, usually taken by a country every five or ten years. The census is distinguished from the vital statistics system, a continuous registration system of births, deaths, marriages, and divorces.

Census family The Statistics Canada definition of the family used in the census, which usually includes married or long-term cohabiting couples, with or without never-married children, as well as single parents living with never-married children.

Charter groups Canadians of British and French origin, who are known as charter groups because they have a special status entrenched in the Canadian Constitution and have effectively determined the dominant cultural characteristics of Canada. Each of these groups has special rights and privileges, especially in terms of the language of the legislature, of the courts, and of education.

Citizenship Rights and privileges granted to people by a recognized state in exchange for their support and loyalty.

Civil religion The idea that society is based on and functions because of shared values and perspectives that serve as the foundation of a cohesive society.

Claims-making The social constructionist process by which groups assert grievances about the troublesome character of people or their behaviour.

Class Inequality among groups of people based on the distribution of material resources and social capital.

Class and status Class, also termed socio-economic class, refers to one's position within a society's economic hierarchy. Typical designations include upper, middle, and lower class. Finer distinctions, such as upper middle class, also appear in the literature. In contrast, status refers to one's social position in terms of privilege and esteem. While often based in economic considerations, status suggests a broader lifestyle dimension. Status may be *achieved* (becoming a CEO) or *ascribed* (born an "untouchable").

Class consciousness The sense of membership in a social class. For Marx, members of the working class would eventually (as a result of their concentration in factories and oppressive working conditions) recognize their common interests and act in concert to overthrow capitalism.

Classism The tendency to discriminate based on social class position.

Community As a broad sociological notion, a group of people living together and sharing common values, a common territory, and a daily life. Often, communities are self-contained, with community members working and living within the same limited geographic area. Community has been opposed to *society* in a radical way, community being the locales for mechanistic solidarity (as defined by Durkheim) while society involves organic solidarity. But this duality can be considered too simplistic, since communities are always being created or recreated within societies.

Concept An abstract idea that cannot be tested directly. Concepts can refer to anything, but in social research they usually refer to characteristics of individuals, groups, or artifacts or to social processes. Some common sociological concepts include religiosity (strength of religious conviction), social class, and alienation.

Conflict theory A theoretical paradigm linked to the work of Marx and Weber that emphasizes conflict and change

as the regular and permanent features of society, because society is made up of various groups that wield varying amounts of power. Conflict theorists often stress the importance of status, economic inequality, and political power.

Conglomerate ownership A form of ownership in which one company owns many firms that engage in a variety of often unrelated business activities. It may combine *Horizontal integration*, *Vertical integration*, and *Cross-ownership*.

Conspicuous consumption A term, popularized by Veblen, describing the many ways in which the well-to-do (the leisure class) display their social status by an ostentatious display of their possessions.

Contagion The rapid spread of something like a fashion, mob mentality, or riot. It is associated with classic collective behaviour accounts of social movement action.

Control theory A category of explanation that maintains that people engage in deviant behaviour when the various controls that might be expected to prohibit them from doing so are weak or absent.

Core Countries at the centre of global economic and political power where wealth becomes increasingly concentrated through the exploitation of the periphery.

Corporate crime Crime committed on behalf of a corporation that victimizes consumers, competing businesses, or governments. It can lead to major social, financial, or physical harm, although often no criminal law has been violated.

Counter-hegemony The ability to launch oppositional views that challenge existing power-holders. See also *Hegemony*.

Cross-ownership A form of ownership in which one company owns organizations associated with different types of media (e.g., a company might own a newspaper and a television network).

Crude birth rate The number of live births in a given year for every 1000 people in a population.

Crude death rate The number of deaths in a given year for every 1000 people in a population.

Cult A popular name for new religious movements. The word *cult* tends to have a negative connotation, and thus scholars of religion prefer to use "new religious movement."

Cultural capital A term coined by Pierre Bourdieu for cultural and linguistic competence, such as prestigious knowledge, tastes, preferences, and educational expertise and credentials, that individuals possess and that influences the likelihood of their educational and occupational success.

Cultural support theory An explanation of deviance that emphasizes an understanding of how deviant values lead to deviant behaviour.

Culture At its broadest, the sum total of the human-produced environment (the objects, artifacts, ideas, beliefs, and values that make up the symbolic and learned aspects of human society), as separate from the natural environment; more often refers to norms, values, beliefs, ideas, and meanings; an assumption that different societies are distinguished by their shared beliefs and customary behaviours; the products and services delivered by a number of industries—theatre, music, film, publishing, and so on.

Culture industry The political economy involved in the production of norms, meanings, values, mores, knowledge, and customs of a society through media, art, literature, and entertainment. A term associated with the work of Max Horkheimer and Theodor Adorno, who argued that the modern culture industry was homogenizing culture, lowering artistic and intellectual standards, and undermining the political consciousness of the working class.

Decoding The process of interpreting or "reading" media content. It may involve a dominant-hegemonic reading, an oppositional reading, or a negotiated reading. See also *Encoding*.

Deindustrialization Withdrawal of investment in factories.

Demographic transition The process by which a country moves from high birth and death rates to low birth and death rates. The shift in fertility rates is often referred to as the fertility transition, while the complementary change in death rates is referred to as the mortality transition. The epidemiological transition theory is a complementary theory to demographic transition theory.

Demography The study of population. Demographers examine changes in birth rate, infant mortality rate, death rate, growth rate, and migration, considering factors such as the size, composition, and geographical variations of population over time.

Developed countries The most industrialized countries of the world. According to the United Nations, these are the countries in Europe and in North America, as well as Australia, New Zealand, and Japan.

Developing countries All the countries not in the developed world. A subdivision of developing countries is the least developed countries, defined by the United Nations as countries with average annual incomes of less than $9000 US. See also *Third World*.

Deviance People, behaviours, and conditions subject to social control.

Digital divide Inequalities in access to computers and/or the Internet. Sociologists usually see socio-economic status and social class as the basis for the digital divide, but gender and national origin are among other characteristics associated with these inequalities.

Discourse A way of talking about and conceptualizing an issue, presented through ideas, concepts, and vocabulary that recur in texts.

Discrimination An action whereby a person is treated differently (usually unfairly) because of his or her membership in a particular group or category.

Disease-mongering Expanding the boundaries of what is considered to be disease, often through the efforts of profit-making pharmaceutical companies.

Dominant ideology The ideas and viewpoints held by the capitalist class or other powerful groups in society. Specific forms of the dominant ideology include capitalist, patriarchal, and racist ideology.

Dowry Money or property provided by a bride's family upon her marriage to help obtain a suitable husband and to be used by her new household (or sometimes to support her in case of divorce or widowhood).

Economic elite Men and women who hold economic power in a society. Contemporary researchers often operationalize this concept in terms of reported financial assets (wealth) and/or leadership positions on the boards of key (largest 100) corporations.

Education The process by which human beings learn and develop capacities through understanding their social and natural environments, which takes place in both formal and informal settings.

Emphasized femininity A form of femininity matched to (and defined by) hegemonic masculinity.

Encoding The process of embedding ideology in media content. Encoding emerges through the complex interplay of economic and technical conditions associated with a media institution, the organizational relations and practices of the institution, and the ideology existing within the institution and the wider society. See also *Decoding*.

Enlightenment An era in the 1700s when theorists believed that human reason could be the instrument of perfecting social life; emotions had to be controlled, and the role of religion, custom, and authority was criticized.

Environmental justice The branch of environmentalism that focuses on the inequitable distribution of environmental risks affecting the poor and racial minorities.

Essence; essentialism; essential nature The idea that a "true" or core reality lies behind appearances, which makes something what it is and which, once identified, can establish its "truth." In the study of sexual and gender identities, for example, many challenge the idea that there is an essence of "femaleness" (something all women share/are) or "maleness" that sets females and males apart from each other.

Ethnic group People sharing a common ethnic identity who are potentially capable of organizing and acting on their ethnic interests.

Ethnicity Sets of social distinctions by which groups differentiate themselves from one another on the basis of presumed biological ties. Members of such groups have a sense of themselves as a common "people" separate and distinct from others.

Export processing zone (EPZ) Special area within a state where its tariff restrictions, laws, and labour practices are not fully enforced and goods are produced for export to other countries. Such zones usually house foreign companies that exploit local workers. The *maquiladoras* along the northern Mexican border with the US are an example of an EPZ.

Extended family Several generations and/or married siblings and their children sharing a residence and co-operating economically.

Fair trade Set of ideas, proposals, and programs to establish direct relations between farmers in the Third World and consumers in the rich countries so that more income is redirected toward the farmers.

False consciousness Misunderstanding by a person of his or her lot in life and the wider social structure and relationships that shape power and politics. A term coined by Karl Marx as a label for ignorance or delusion about one's objective class position.

Feminism A theoretical paradigm, as well as a social movement, that focuses on causes and consequences of inequality between men and women, especially patriarchy and sexism.

Feminization of poverty The fact that globally, most women (as girls, adults, and seniors) are at greater risk of impoverishment than their male counterparts.

First Nations "Indians" in Canadian law; together with Métis and Inuit, they constitute Canada's Aboriginal peoples.

Formal organization An organization with clearly specified goals and a high degree of task differentiation among members.

Framing theory Since any issue can be viewed from a variety of perspectives and be construed as having implications for multiple values or considerations, the process by which people develop a particular conceptualization of an issue or change their thinking about an issue. Goffman defines frames as definitions of a situation that is built up in accordance with social principles of organization that govern them and our subjective involvement in them. Frame analysis is concerned with the organization of experience.

Free trade Policy of trade liberalization promoted by richer states and international institutions like the World Bank and the International Monetary Fund to open economies to external inputs.

G20 Newly designed consultative process involving members of the G8 and some of the "emerging" countries such as China, Brazil, and India.

Gender Socially recognized distinctions of masculinity and femininity.

Gender divisions of domestic labour The identification of specific household tasks as appropriate for men (for example, painting, cutting the grass, putting out the garbage) and for women (for example, cooking, cleaning, child care).

Gender role A set of behaviour patterns, attitudes, and personality characteristics stereotypically perceived as masculine or feminine within a culture.

Gender-role socialization Begins at birth and refers to a set of cultural norms and behaviours considered appropriate for males and females.

Generalized other Mead's final developmental stage of the self whereby we learn cultural rules and values.

Gentrification The process whereby more affluent households purchase and upgrade housing that was previously occupied by lower-income residents.

Global economy A connection of the world's businesses and markets worldwide.

Globalization A social process in which the constraints of geographic, economic, cultural, and social arrangements have receded and have been replaced by processes that extend beyond state boundaries. The flow of goods, services, media, information, and labour between countries around the world; different but interrelated aspects include economic globalization and cultural globalization; worldwide control and co-ordination by large private-sector interests not constrained by local or national boundaries.

Glocalization The process through which universal ideas of globalization are interpreted differently in local contexts.

Governmentality A term coined by Michel Foucault that links the terms "governing" (*gouverner*) and "modes of thought" (*mentalité*). It implies that it is not possible to study power without an analysis of the political rationality underpinning it. The notion itself is complex and has morphed even as Foucault himself used and developed it, but it has included critical reflections on the rationalities and deliberate practices that governments have used to produce citizens that they deem to be best suited to fulfill their needs.

Greenbelt An area around a city where no development is permitted.

Growth rate The difference between births and deaths, taking into account the difference between immigrants and emigrants.

Hegemonic masculinity A dominant form of masculinity. What is identified as hegemonic masculinity may vary depending on the social context. However, hegemonic masculinity typically is the valorization of physical strength, economic power, and heterosexuality and the domination of women and subordinate men.

Hegemony The dominance of ideology and culture by an elite group to the point that few alternatives exist or can be imagined.

Heterocentric Assessing social relations and structures by the norms of heterosexuality.

Heteronormativity The assumption that heterosexuality is a universal norm, therefore making homosexuality invisible or "abnormal."

Heterosexism A set of overt and covert social practices in both the public and private spheres that privileges heterosexuality over other sexual orientations.

Hidden curriculum The understandings that students develop as a result of the institutional requirements and day-to-day realities they encounter in their schooling; typically refers to norms, such as competition, individualism, and obedience, as well as to a sense of one's place in school and social hierarchies.

Hijab A headscarf worn by some Muslim women that covers the hair but leaves the face visible.

Homophobia A term coined by George Weinberg in 1972 to refer to the psychological fear of homosexuality; tends to neglect the wider structural sources of the homosexual taboo essence.

Homosexual Someone who has sex with and/or is attracted to a person of the same sex.

Horizontal integration A form of ownership in which one company owns a number of media organizations in different locations that are doing the same type of business; also known as "chain ownership" (e.g., a company might own several radio stations across Canada).

Household People who share a dwelling whether or not they are related by blood, adoption, or marriage.

Human capital The notion that education, skills development, and other learning processes are investments that enhance our capacities. Human capital theory builds on this notion.

Human ecology The science of ecology as applied to sociological analyses.

Hypotheses Testable statements composed of at least two variables and how they are related.

Identity How we see ourselves and how others see us. How we view ourselves is a product of our history and of our interpretation of others' reactions to us. How others view us is termed "placement" and is other people's reactions to our projections of ourselves, which is termed "announcement."

Ideology A system of beliefs, ideas, and norms, reflecting the interests and experiences of a group, class, or subculture, that legitimizes or justifies the existing unequal distribution of power and privilege; ways of seeing and of understanding the world and its actors. Ideologies function by making the social appear natural or functional rather than constructed for partisan interests and advantage.

Impression management The term used by Erving Goffman to describe how individuals try to shape the impression others have of them.

Industrial Revolution A period of rapid social and political transition from feudal to modern forms of governance beginning in the eighteenth century in western Europe.

Infant mortality rate The number of deaths of children less than one year of age per 1000 live births in the same year.

Informal economy A wide range of legal and illegal economic activities that are not officially reported to the government.

Informal organization An organization with loosely specified goals and little task differentiation between their members.

Institutions Patterns of behaviour that order people's lives in relatively predictable ways. Institutions are comprised of norms and social practices that have calcified to the extent that they create a predictable pattern or map of behaviours that people will usually follow.

Interculturalism Quebec's version of multiculturalism, which discourages the formation of ethno-racial enclaves but promotes linguistic assimilation of minorities in Quebec.

Interlocking/intersectional analysis A way of understanding inequality that takes into account multiple, connecting dimensions. Which dimensions are

significant, and how their interconnections shape inequality, are matters for research. Used in the analysis of gender to draw attention to the importance of looking at gender inequalities as they are connected with and specified by race, class, dis/ability, and so on.

International Monetary Fund (IMF) One of the institutions created in 1944 in Bretton Woods, originally designed to lend money to western European countries for their postwar reconstruction. In the last while, the IMF has been involved mainly in "redressing" Third World states in economic decline by imposing stiff austerity programs.

Interpretive theory An approach that pays close attention to the cultural meanings held by actors, derived from socialization in the group, which is seen as the key to understanding human behaviour and patterns of action.

Intersectionalities The ways in which social inequalities are interwoven in a complex fashion. Gender inequalities, for example, are influenced by social class, disability, sexual orientation, race, ethnicity, age, and immigrant status. Class analysis increasingly pays attention to these intersections.

Intersubjectivity The notion that we adjust our behaviour according to the back-and-forth interpretation of what we think is on others' minds; for example, what I think *you* think of me.

Kirpan Ceremonial dagger worn by some Sikhs as one of the five practices of being an observant Sikh.

Labyrinth A path, as distinct from a maze, that serves as a walking meditation. It has only one winding path, which leads to a centre.

Life expectancy The number of years that an average person in a given population can expect to live.

Life expectancy at birth The average number of years left to live for a newborn in a given period. Life expectancy is distinct from life span, which is the oldest age humans can attain.

Lifelong learning The ongoing expectations for people to acquire new knowledge and capacities through

learning that occurs in various levels and kinds of formal education as well as in other learning contexts; associated with increasing emphasis on the new economy and the continuing transitions that individuals undergo throughout their lives.

Lived religion An understanding of religion that focuses on the actual everyday spiritual practices of people rather than on religious authorities or religious texts.

Low Income Cut-off (LICO) A relative measurement of income used by Statistics Canada. The LICO considers that if a family spends 20 per cent or more of its income on food, shelter, and clothing than the average family, it is in precarious financial circumstances.

Macrosociology The study of social institutions and large social groups; the study of the processes that depict societies as a whole and of the social-structural aspects of a given society.

Marketization The progressive exposure of the public sector to market forces, such as, for example, increased privatization of schooling or health care.

Mass media The technologies, practices, and institutions through which information and entertainment are produced and disseminated on a mass scale.

Master status A status characteristic that overrides other status characteristics in terms of how others see an individual. When a person is assigned a label of "deviant" (for example, "murderer," "drug addict," "cheater"), that label is usually read by others as signifying the most essential aspects of the individual's character.

Means of production A term used by Marxists to refer to wealth-generating property such as land, factories, and machinery; the ways goods are produced for sale on the market, including all the workers, machinery, and capital such production needs.

Medicalization The tendency for more and more of life to be defined as relevant to medical diagnosis and treatment.

Meritocracy A form of social stratification that relies on differences in effort and ability rather than on ascribed statuses such as gender, age, or race.

Metropolis For the early sociologists like Simmel and Tönnies, as well as for Wirth, the great city of their time. In contrast to villages, the metropolis could become an "inhuman" environment because it could destroy traditional social life. But the metropolis can also offer new opportunities for modern individuals. They are exposed to different ways of life and can express their creativity more freely.

Microsociology The analysis of small groups and of the face-to-face interactions that occur within these groups in the everyday.

Modified extended family Several generations who live near each other and maintain close social and economic contact.

Monopolistic closure Weber's concept referring to practices of exclusion of "others" from the distribution of valuable and often scarce economic, social, and political resources, such as property, income and wealth, high social status, power, and high levels of educational attainment.

Morbidity rate The sickness rate per a specified number of people over a specified period of time.

Mortality rate The death rate per a specified number of people over a specified period of time.

Multiculturalism In Canada, a government policy to promote tolerance among cultural groups and to assist ethnic groups in preserving the values and traditions that are important to them; multiculturalism became official policy in 1971 following the report of the Royal Commission on Bilingualism and Biculturalism.

Natural growth rate The difference between the crude birth rate and the crude death rate, not taking into account migration, or the movement of people into and out of a specific geographical area.

Negotiation A discussion intended to produce an agreement.

Neo-liberalism Political philosophy that flourished in the 1980s onwards and that promotes privatization, deregulation, and trade liberalization, as well as fiscal reforms to reduce social expenses and lower taxation of the wealthiest.

Net migration The difference between the number of immigrants and the number of emigrants over a specified period.

New economy A term used to highlight the shift in emphasis from industrial production within specific industries, firms, and nations to economic activities driven by information and high-level technologies, global competition, international networks, and knowledge-based advancement.

New religious movements Religious groups whose development is recent and who often have a less established position in society than more mainstream religious groups.

Niqab A garment worn by Muslim women that covers most of the face but leaves the eyes exposed.

Non-standard (or precarious) work Jobs that are characterized by an increasingly tenuous or precarious relationship between employer and employee, including part-time employment, temporary employment, contract work, multiple job-holding, and self-employment; also termed "contingent work" and "casual work."

Normative heterosexuality The assumption that sexual relations between different-sex couples is the only normal and socially acceptable form of intimacy.

Norms The rules and expectations of appropriate behaviour under various social circumstances. Norms create social consequences that have the effect of regulating appearance and behaviour.

North American Free Trade Agreement (NAFTA) Signed in 1992 by the US, Canada, and Mexico, the "model" of trade liberalization that the most powerful in the world were hoping to extend to the rest of the world. Under NAFTA, capital flows and investments as well as trade have been liberalized. Under chapter 11 of the accord, private entities (companies) are entitled to sue governments if their interests are jeopardized by legislation on issues like labour rights or the environment.

Nuclear family A husband, wife, and their children, sharing a common residence and co-operating economically.

Numerical flexibility Part of a general managerial approach that rests on flexibility in employment; involves shrinking or eliminating the core workforce (in continuous, full-time positions) and replacing them with workers in non-standard employment.

Objective Something completely unaffected by the characteristics of the person or instrument observing it. "Objective" observations were used in the past to establish the truth of scientific theories until it became clear that completely objective observations are impossible.

Operationalization The translation of abstract theories and concepts into observable hypotheses and variables. Once abstract ideas are operationalized, they can be tested in a study.

Organization A set of people connected by regular relationships that conform to shared norms and values.

Organizational sexuality Social practices that determine explicit and culturally elaborated rules of behaviour to regulate sexual identities and personal relationships in the workplace.

Organized religion Institutionalized and public expressions of religion, as opposed to spirituality.

Patriarchy A society or family system in which men have more authority than women.

Patrilineal descent The tracing of relationships and inheritance through the male line.

Pedagogy Processes associated with the organization and practice of teaching; more generally, various kinds of interactions (and how they are understood and organized) in teaching/learning situations.

Periphery Countries exploited by the core for their raw materials and that face poor living conditions and bleak hope for development.

Political process(es) The dynamic contestation of power among dominant elites and subordinate challengers. It is also associated with a branch of social movement theory.

Political process approach An approach that assumes that political constraints and opportunities influence the rise and fall of social movements as well as their institutional organization.

Polity A sovereign political unit.

Polyandry The practice of being legally married to more than one husband at a time.

Polygamy The practice of being legally married to more than one spouse at a time.

Polygyny The practice of being legally married to more than one wife at a time.

Power In the classic formulation, refers to the ability to exercise one's will, even in the face of opposition from others. In Marxist sociology, a social relationship that has a material base. Those who own the means of production have the power to exploit workers through the appropriation of their labour efforts. In Weberian sociology, power is more broadly defined and can reflect the capacity of individuals or groups to exert their will over others. Contemporary analysts point out that power may also involve a wide variety of indirect and subtle manifestations, including the ability to mobilize bias or define a situation in one's own interests.

Prejudice An attitude by which individuals are prejudged on the basis of stereotyped characteristics assumed to be common to all members of the individual's group.

Primary socialization Socialization that takes place during the formative period of life.

Privatization The movement away from universally available and state-funded programs to ones that include profit-making components.

Proletariat Term used by Marx for individuals who provided the labour power to capitalism. Lacking property, the proletariat was forced to survive by selling its labour to the bourgeoisie, who in turn exploited workers' efforts in the pursuit of profit.

Quiet Revolution Decline in church attendance and the power of the Roman Catholic church in Quebec; an example of secularization.

Race A group that is defined on the basis of perceived physical differences such as skin colour.

Racialization Sets of social processes and practices whereby social relations among people are structured according to visible physical difference among them to the advantage of those in the visible majority and the disadvantage of those in visible minorities.

Racialized A term that recognizes the social construction of race, refers to a process whereby race comes to have social significance as well as political and material consequences.

Reciprocal socialization The process of bi-directional socialization whereby we learn from others (e.g., parents, teachers) just as others learn from us.

Relativism The idea that there is no single, unchangeable truth about anything; all things are either true or false only relative to particular standards. Many sociologists who do not view sociology as a science take their stance persuaded by relativism.

Replacement fertility rate The average number of children per woman of one generation needed to maintain the population size.

Resocialization The learning of new roles, norms, and values that are different from those of the past.

Role conflict The conflict experienced when the expectations attached to one role interfere with those attached to another role an individual is playing.

Role-making The process by which individuals creatively adapt and modify the roles they play to fit the situations they encounter.

Role strain The strain an individual experiences as a result of the competing demands built into a single role.

Role-taking The process by which we put ourselves in the position of others and align our actions with theirs.

Roles The specific behaviours, privileges, duties, and obligations expected of a person who occupies a specific status.

Sample The group of people or objects drawn from the whole population that will be studied. In quantitative research, a great deal of time and effort is devoted to the selection of truly random samples, while in qualitative research, samples are often selected on the basis of the theoretical importance of the people or objects.

Schooling Processes that take place within formal educational institutions.

Secondary socialization Socialization that takes place in wider society, such as in the educational system, in peer groups, and from the mass media/technological spheres.

Secularization The process by which religion increasingly loses its influence.

Self In Mead's theory, an emergent entity with a capacity to be both a subject and an object and to assign meaning to itself, as reflected upon in one's own mind. In Goffman's dramaturgical theory, the self is a more shifting "dramatic effect," a staged product of the scenes one performs in.

Semi-periphery Countries that reflect a mix of core and peripheral characteristics and display some hope for development.

Service economy The economic sector in which most Canadians currently are employed. In comparison to primary industry (the extraction of natural resources) and manufacturing (processing raw materials into usable goods and services), the service economy is based on the provision of services rather than on a tangible product, ranging widely from advertising and retailing to entertaining to generating and distributing information. Also called the "tertiary sector."

Sexism Unfair discrimination on the basis of sex. It ranges from the obvious to the (nearly) hidden.

Sexual orientation An individual's sexual preference(s), which could include partners of the opposite sex, same sex, both sexes, or neither.

Sexuality Defined by the World Health Organization (WHO) as a central aspect of being human and encompasses sex, gender identities and roles, sexual orientation, eroticism, pleasure, intimacy, and reproduction. WHO explains that sexuality is experienced in thoughts, fantasies, desires, beliefs, attitudes, values, behaviours, roles, and relationships. It adds that sexuality is influenced by the interaction of biological, psychological, social, economic, political, cultural, ethical, legal, historical, religious, and spiritual factors.

Sick role A conception of illness as comprising a set of rights and responsibilities, with four main aspects: (1) exemption from social responsibilities, which must be authorized by a proper authority such as a doctor; (2) exemption from blame for the illness; (3) a responsibility to get better; and (4) an expectation that the sick person will seek and follow outside medical help.

Significant others Individuals with whom a person interacts and who are important in that person's life, such as a parent or teacher.

Situated transaction A process of social interaction that lasts as long as the individuals find themselves in each other's company. As applied to the study of deviance, the concept of the situated transaction helps us to understand how deviant acts are social and not just individual products.

Social capital A concept widely thought to have been developed by American sociologist James Coleman in 1988 but discussed by Pierre Bourdieu in a similar way in the early 1980s; reflects the power that is derived from ties to social networks.

Social construction A process in which people's experience of reality is determined by the meaning they attach to that reality.

Social constructionism (constructionist) The sociological theory that argues that social problems and issues are less objective conditions than they are collective social definitions based on how they are framed and interpreted.

Social control The various and myriad ways in which members of social groups express their disapproval of people and behaviours. They include name-calling, ridicule, ostracism, incarceration, and even killing.

Social determinants (of health) The factors that contribute to maintaining and improving health and well-being. They include individual lifestyle factors such as diet and smoking, social and community networks, and general socioeconomic, cultural, and environmental conditions. According to the World Health Organization, they are the conditions in which people are born, grow, live, work, and age that are shaped by the distribution of money, power, resources, and policy choices. These conditions are considered responsible for health inequities between individuals and within and between countries.

Social group A number of individuals, defined by formal or informal criteria of membership, who share a feeling of unity or are bound together in stable patterns of interaction; two or more individuals who have a specific common identity and who interact in a reciprocal social relationship. Primary groups are small and involve direct, personal contact, whereas in a secondary group, a member may not interact with every other member.

Social institution A stable, well-acknowledged pattern of social relationships that endures over time, including the family, the economy, education, politics, religion, the mass media, medicine, and science and technology. Social institutions are the result of an enduring set of ideas about how to accomplish various goals generally recognized as important in a society.

Social interaction The process by which people act and react in relationships with others.

Social movement The social form taken by collective actors engaged in struggles against dominance relations; the coordinated, voluntary action of non-elites (people with no control over major resources) for the manifest purpose of changing the distribution of social goods. The outcomes of these struggles are often difficult to grasp. To what extent social actors contribute to social change or toward participating in system regulation remains an open question.

Social network The set of direct and indirect connections among a group of people. Direct connections include links of kinship, friendship, and acquaintance. Information, social support, and other valuable resources flow through incompletely connected, or weakly tied, networks.

Social relationships Interactions of people in a society. Because people share culture and a sense of collective existence, these interactions will to some extent be recurrent and predictable.

Social reproduction A range of unpaid activities that help to reproduce workforces daily and over generations; typically, though not exclusively, performed by women in the family household.

Social stratification The structured patterns of inequality that often appear in societal arrangements. From a macrosociological perspective, it is possible to discern the hierarchical strata of social classes that characterize most contemporary societies.

Social structure Patterns of behaviour or social relationships developed and accepted through time in a given group, organization, or society.

Socialization A lifelong interactive learning process through which individuals acquire a self-identity and the social skills needed to become members of society. See also *Primary socialization*, *Secondary socialization*.

Spontaneous organization An organization that arises quickly to meet a single goal and disbands when the goal is achieved.

Staple economy A reliance on natural resources, such as fish, fur, lumber, agricultural products, and minerals, that are exported to support the economy.

State An institution associated with governing over a specific territory as well as establishing and enforcing rules within that territory. The state in a number of countries (including Canada) is involved in providing various public services. It is a formal bureaucracy that largely shapes material, cultural and social, and institutional political processes.

Status A socially defined position that a person holds in a given social group or organization to which are attached certain rights, duties, and obligations; a relational term, since each status exists only through its relation to one or more other statuses filled by other people.

Status degradation ceremony The rituals by which formal transition is made from non-deviant to deviant status. Examples include the criminal trial and the psychiatric hearing.

Status groups Organized groups comprising people who have similar social status. These groups organize to maintain or expand their social privileges by excluding outsiders from their ranks and by trying to gain status recognition from other groups.

Strain theory Robert Merton's theory that deviance results when people experience a gap between their aspirations and their opportunities.

Stratified Hierarchically ordered; in relation to power, stratification occurs when some groups control more material, cultural and social, and institutional resources than others and block others from challenging their control or gaining access to them.

Streaming Also known as tracking, a practice in elementary and secondary school systems aimed at homogenizing classrooms by placing similar students in the same classroom according to criteria that may include performance on standardized aptitude tests, perceived personal qualities and aspirations, or even social class and ethnic origin.

Structural analysis or approach An approach within organizational theory in the Weberian tradition; focuses on the structural characteristics of organizations and their effect on the people within them. In the context of urban studies, the analysis of the functions cities perform, the size and shape of their governments, and who has what bearing on decisions and outcomes involving cities.

Structural functionalism A theoretical paradigm that emphasizes the way each part of a society functions to fulfill the needs of society as a whole.

Subculture A subset of cultural traits of the larger society that also includes distinctive values, beliefs, norms, style of dress, and behaviour.

Subjective The opposite of objective; refers to the observer's mind, to perceptions, intentions, interpretations, and so on that affect how we act in the world.

Superstructure The overarching cultural, legal, political and social institutions of society, which according to Karl Marx are determined ultimately by class relations.

Surplus That part of the value of goods produced by working people that is taken by the dominant class and used to maintain social inequalities; a measure of the exploitation of the working class.

Sustainable development Refers mainly to the capacity for creating wealth without destroying the environment and preserving the environment for future uses. In the words of the World Commission on Environment and Development report (Bruntland 1987), it means to meet "the needs of the present without compromising the ability of future generations to meet their own needs." The principle is that economic growth and environmental conservation are compatible goals.

Symbolic interactionism An intellectual tradition in sociology akin to interpretive theory, founded in the early twentieth-century work of Charles Horton Cooley and George Herbert Mead, although the term itself was not coined until years later by Herbert Blumer. Symbolic interactionism emphasizes the importance of understanding the meanings of social action and uses ethnographic methods to discover these meanings for individuals in an effort to explain human conduct.

Symbols The heart of cultural systems, for with them we construct thought, ideas, and other ways of representing reality to others and to ourselves; gestures, artifacts, or uses of language that represent something else.

Systemic discrimination Discrimination that is built into the fabric of Canadian life, as in the case of institutional self-segregation.

Systems theory An approach within organizational theory that sees organizations as open systems and that views organizations and their goals as shaped by the interests of their participants and their environments.

Third World Poor countries; an element of a classification in which the First World was made up of western Europe, North America, Australia, and New Zealand; the Second World, of the various communist countries (the Soviet Union, the numerous Soviet satellites, and China); and the Third World, of poorer countries in Asia, Africa, and Latin America. See also *Developing countries*.

Total institution A group or organization that has complete control over an individual and that usually engages in a process of resocialization.

Totalitarian An all-powerful form of government that exerts extreme control over the private lives of its citizens and is often associated with fascist policies of racism and aggressive nationalism.

Transitions The pathways that people follow from family life, into and out of education, and into various jobs or other social situations throughout their life course.

Two-earner family A family in which both adults are employed while raising their children. Now the most common form of family financing in Canada and other post-industrial countries.

Unemployment rate The number of people who do not have a job but are actively looking for a job divided by the labour force (which includes both the employed and unemployed), expressed as a percentage. Those who do not have a job and are not looking for one are considered not in the labour force.

Urban planning The processes leading to the production of urban spaces that professionals, like planners, follow. Urban planning is always historically and culturally characterized. Urban planning decisions can be more or less open to public participation.

Urban sprawl Decentralization or the shifting of economic activity and residential pattern away from the central city toward peripheral areas of the city.

Urban sustainability Involves a commitment to using the natural resources of a city within its capacity to sustain its social, economic, and natural significance. Goals associated with urban sustainability are related to improving the quality of life in the city without stealing resources from future generations.

Urbanism The specific form taken by urban design within a historical moment. But it also includes the processes involved in the production of that form. Urbanism always includes a certain urbanity, defined as the culture of living within a city.

Urbanization The nature, extent, and distribution of cities in the larger society or nation.

Validity The accuracy of a measure, indicator, or study; many different dimensions to validity can be established through formal tests, logic, or depth of understanding.

Variable The operational or observable equivalent of concepts. Many concepts require more than one variable for proper operationalization. The key characteristic of variables is that there must be a range of different values that can be observed.

Vertical integration A form of ownership in which one company owns firms or divisions that link processes such as production, distribution, and exhibition (e.g., a company that owns a movie studio, a movie distributor, and movie theatres).

Vertical mosaic A view of Canadian society as constituting a materially,

educationally, socially, politically, and ethnically divided stratification system, with the charter groups at the top, Native people at the bottom, and other ethnic immigrant groups fitting in depending on their entrance status; from John Porter's *The Vertical Mosaic* (1965).

World Bank Along with the IMF, an important organization promoting neo-liberal policies through conditional lending to developing countries.

World Social Forum Annual consultative process managed by more than 500,000 NGOs worldwide working to develop alternative development proposals focused on rights.

World Trade Organization (WTO) Created in 1995 to facilitate trade liberalization worldwide. WTO has been stalemated in recent times by a growing conflict between the G8 countries and the "emerging" countries over a wide range of economic issues.

references

Aapola, Sinikka, Marnina Gonick, and Anita Harris. 2005. *Young Femininity: Girlhood, Power, and Social Change*. London: Palgrave McMillan.

Abada, Teresa, and Eric Tenkorang. 2009. "Pursuit of university education among immigrant youth in Canada: The roles of parental human capital and social capital." *Journal of Youth Studies* 12 (2): 185–207.

Abbott, P., and R. Sapsford. 1987. *Women and Social Class*. London: Tavistock.

Abu-Laban, Baha, and Daiva Stasiulis. 1992. "Ethnic pluralism under siege: Popular and partisan opposition to multiculturalism." *Canadian Public Policy* 27 (4): 365–86.

Acker, Joan. 1990. "Hierarchics, jobs, and bodies: A theory of gendered organizations." *Gender and Society* 4: 139–58.

Adamic, L., and Eytan Adar. 2005. "How to search a social network." *Social Networks* 27: 187–203.

Adams, Michael. 2003. *Fire and Ice: The United States, Canada and the Myth of Converging Values*. Toronto: Penguin Canada.

Agnew, Robert. 1985. "A revised strain theory of delinquency." *Social Forces* 64 (1): 151–67.

———. 2006. "General strain theory: Current status and directions." In F.T. Cullen, J.P. Wright, and K.R. Blevins, eds, *Taking Stock: The Status of Criminological Theory*. New Brunswick, NJ: Transaction.

Agócs, Carol, and Monica Boyd. 1993. "The Canadian ethnic mosaic recast for the 90s." In James Curtis, Edward Grabb, and Neil Guppy, eds, *Social Inequality in Canada: Patterns, Problems, Policies*, 2nd edn, 330–52. Scarborough, ON: Prentice-Hall Canada.

Agyeman, J., P. Cole, R. Haluza-DeLay, and P. O'Riley. 2009. *Speaking for Ourselves: Environmental Justice in Canada*. Vancouver: University of British Columbia Press.

Ajami, Louisa. 2008. "Nose job nation—In Lebanon, surgical bandages are something to flaunt." *NOW* 2 May. www.nowlebanon.com/NewsArchiveDetails.aspx?ID=40594#ixzz0y6RszOKO.

Akers, R.L., and G.F. Jensen. 2003. *Social Learning Theory and the Explanation of Crime: A Guide for the New Century*, vol. 11, *Advances in Criminological Theory*. New Brunswick, NJ: Transaction.

Alalehto, Tage. 2002. "Eastern prostitution from Russia to Sweden and Finland." *Journal of Scandinavian Studies in Criminology and Crime Prevention* 3 (1): 96–111.

Albanese, Patrizia. 2006. "Small town, big benefits: The ripple effect of $7/day child care." *Canadian Review of Sociology and Anthropology* 43 (2): 125–40.

———. 2009. *Children in Canada Today*. Toronto: Oxford University Press.

———. 2012. "The more things change . . . the more we need child care: On the fortieth anniversary of the report of the Royal Commission on the Status of Women." In Lorne Tepperman and Angela Kalyta, eds., *Reading Sociology: Canadian Perspectives*, 2nd edn., 95–8. Toronto: Oxford University Press.

Albas, Dan, and Cheryl Albas. 1993. "Avoiding the label of cheater during exams." In Lorne Tepperman and James Curtis, eds, *Sociology of Everyday Life: A Reader*, 2nd edn, 217–23. Toronto: McGraw-Hill.

———. 2003. "Aces and bombers: The post-exam impression management strategies of students." In Ramón S. Guerra and Robert Lee Maril, eds, *A Social World: Classic and Contemporary Sociological Readings*, 3rd edn, 27–36. Boston: Pearson Custom Publishing.

Alden, H.L., and K.F. Parker. 2005. "Gender role ideology, homophobia and hate crime: Linking attitudes to macro-level anti-gay and lesbian hate crimes." *Deviant Behavior* 26 (4): 321–43.

Alhabib, D., U. Nur, and R. Jones. 2010. "Domestic violence against women: Systematic review of prevalence studies." *Journal of Family Violence* 25: 369–83.

Alkhateeb, Maha B., and Salma Elkadi Abugideiri. 2007. *Change from Within: Diverse Perspectives on Domestic Violence in Muslim Communities*. Great Falls, VA: Peaceful Families Project.

Alloway, Nola. 2007. "Swimming against the tide: Boys, literacies, and schooling: An Australian story."

Canadian Journal of Education 3 (2): 582–605.

Amato, Paul. 2004. "Parenting through family transitions." *Social Policy Journal of New Zealand* 23 (Dec.): 31–44.

Anderson, K. 1991. *Vancouver's Chinatown: Racial Discourse in Canada (opens in new window), 1875–1980*. Montreal and Kingston: McGill-Queen's University Press.

Anderson, N. 1923. *The Hobo: The Sociology of the Homeless Man*. Chicago: University of Chicago Press.

Anisef, Paul, Paul Axelrod, Etta Baichman-Anisef, Carl James, and Anton Turritin. 2000. *Opportunity and Uncertainty: Life Course Experiences of the Class of '73*. Toronto: University of Toronto Press.

Antonovsky, Aaron. 1979. *Health, Stress and Coping*. San Francisco: Jossey-Bass.

Appadurai, Arjun. 1990. *Disjuncture and Difference in the Global Cultural Economy*. Durham, NC: Duke University Press.

Apple, Michael W., Wayne Au, and Luis Amando Gandin, eds. 2009. *The Routledge International Handbook of Critical Education*. New York: Routledge.

Arat-Koc, Sedef. 1989. "In the privacy of our own home: Foreign domestic workers as solution to the crisis of the domestic sphere in Canada." *Studies in Political Economy* 28: 33–58.

———. 1990. "Importing housewives: Non-citizen domestic workers and the crisis of the domestic sphere in Canada." In Meg Luxton, Harriet Rosenberg, and Sedef Arat-Koc, eds, *Through the Kitchen Window: The Politics of Home and Family*, 2nd edn, 81–103. Toronto: Garamond.

Armstrong, Pat, and Hugh Armstrong. 1994. *The Double Ghetto: Canadian Women and Their Segregated Work*. Toronto: McClelland and Stewart.

Arnot, Madeleine. 2011. *Gender and Education*. New York: Routledge.

Arrighi, Giovanni. 1994. *The Long Twentieth Century: Money, Power, and the Origins of Our Times*. London: Verso Books.

———. 1998. "Globalization and the rise of East Asia." *International Sociology* 13 (1): 59–77.

Arrigo, B.A. 1999. "Can students benefit from an intensive engagement with postmodern criminology?" In J.R. Fuller and E.W. Hickey, eds, *Controversial Issues in Criminology*, 149–56. Boston: Allyn and Bacon.

———. 2004. "Theorizing non-linear communities: On social deviance and housing the homeless." *Deviant Behavior* 25: 193–213.

Artibise, A.F., and G.A. Stelter. 2012. "Urbanization." In *The Canadian Encyclopedia Historia-Dominion*. http://thecanadianencyclopedia.com/articles/urbanization.

Asad, Talal. 1993. *Genealogies of Religion: Discipline and Reasons of Power in Christianity and Islam*. Baltimore, MD: John Hopkins University Press.

Asbridge, M., R.E. Mann, and R. Flam-Zalcman. 2004. "The criminalization of impaired driving in Canada: Assessing the deterrent impact of Canada's first per se law." *Journal of Studies in Alcohol* 65 (4): 450–9.

Assembly of First Nations. 2006. *Royal Commission on Aboriginal People at 10 Years: A Report Card*. Ottawa: Assembly of First Nations.

Atkinson, Michael. 2006. "Masks of masculinity: (Sur)passing narratives and cosmetic surgery." In Dennis Waskul and Phillip Vannini, eds, *Body/Embodiment: Symbolic Interaction and the Sociology of the Body*, 246–62. Hampshire, UK: Ashgate.

———. 2008. "Exploring male femininity in the 'crisis': Men and cosmetic surgery." *Body and Society* 14 (1): 67–87.

Auger, Martin F. 2008. "On the brink of civil war: The Canadian government and the suppression of the 1918 Quebec Easter riots." *Canadian Historical Review* 89 (4): 503–40.

Axelrod, Paul. 1997. *The Promise of Schooling: Education in Canada, 1800–1914*. Toronto: University of Toronto Press.

Baaz, Maria Eriksson, and Maria Stern. 2009. "Why do soldiers rape? Masculinity, violence, and sexuality in the armed forces in the Congo (DRC)." *International Studies Quarterly* 53 (2): 495–518.

Babbie, Earl R. 1988. *The Sociological Spirit: Critical Essays in a Critical Science*. Belmont, CA: Wadsworth.

Baer, Douglas, Edward Grabb, and William A. Johnston. 1987. "Class, crisis, and political ideology in Canada: Recent trends." *Canadian Review of Sociology* 24 (1): 1–22.

———. 1990. "The values of Canadians and Americans: A critical analysis and reassessment." *Social Forces* 68 (3): 693–713.

Baird, Vanessa. 2001. *The No-Nonsense Guide to Sexual Diversity*. Toronto: Between the Lines.

Baker, Maureen. 2005. "Medically assisted conception: Revolutionizing family or perpetuating a nuclear and gendered model?" *Journal of Comparative Family Studies* 36 (4): 521–43.

———. 2006. *Restructuring Family Policies: Divergences and Convergences*. Toronto: University of Toronto Press.

———. 2010. *Choices and Constraints in Family Life*. 2nd edn. Toronto: Oxford University Press.

Balakrishnan, T.R., and J. Kralt. 1987. "Segregation of visible minorities in Montreal, Toronto and Vancouver." In L. Driedger, ed., *Ethnic Canada: Identities and Inequalities*. Toronto: Copp Clark Pitman.

Balthazar, Louis. 1992. "L'évolution du nationalisme québécois." In Gérard Daigle and Guy Rocher, eds, *Le Québec en jeu: comprendre les grands défis*, 647–67. Montreal: Presses de l'Université de Montréal.

Bannerji, H. 1993. *Returning the Gaze: Essays on Feminism, Racism and Politics*. Toronto: Sister Vision Press.

Barber, Benjamin. 1995. *Jihad vs. McWorld*. New York: Ballentine Books.

Barker, Eileen. 1984. *The Making of a Moonie: Choice or Brainwashing?* Oxford: Blackwell.

———. 2005. "New religions and cults in Europe." In L. Jones, ed., *The Encyclopedia of Religion*. New York: The Free Press.

———. 2007. "How do modern European societies deal with new religious movements?" In P. Meusburger, M. Welker, and E. Wunders, eds, *Knowledge and Space: Clashes of Knowledge*, 154–71. Heidelberg: Springer.

Barker, John. 2003. "Dowry." In James J. Ponzetti, ed., *International Encyclopedia of Marriage and Family*, 2nd edn, 495–6. New York: Thomson Gale.

Barry, Doug. 2012. "Binge drinking is especially awesome for wealthy, white college guys." *Jezebel* 20 August. http://jezebel.com/5936126/binge-drinking-is-especially-awesome-for-wealthy-white-college-guys. Copyrighted 2013. Gawker. 97030:113FO.

Baudrillard, Jean. 1998 [1970]. *The Consumer Society: Myths and Structures*. Thousand Oaks, CA: Sage.

Baxter, Janine, Belinda Hewitt, and Michele Haynes. 2008. "Life course transitions and housework: Marriage, parenthood and time spent on housework." *Journal of Marriage and Family* 70 (2): 259–72.

Beach, Jane, Martha Friendly, Carolyn Ferns, Nina Prabhu, and Barry Forer. 2008. *Early Childhood Education and Care in Canada*. Toronto: Childcare Resource and Research Unit.

Beaman, Lori G. 1999. *Shared Beliefs, Different Lives: Women's Identities in Evangelical Context*. St Louis: Chalice Press.

———. 2008. *Defining Harm: Religious Freedom and the Limits of Law*. Vancouver: University of British Columbia Press.

Beck-Gernsheim, Elisabeth. 2002. *Reinventing the Family: In Search of New Lifestyles*. Cambridge: Polity.

Becker, Howard. 1952. "Social class variations in the teacher–student relationship." *Journal of Educational Sociology* 25: 451–65.

———. 1963. *Outsiders: Studies in the Sociology of Deviance*. New York: Free Press.

———. 1982. *Art Worlds*. Berkeley: University of California Press.

Beckett, Andy. 2010. "Is the British middle class an endangered species?" *The Guardian* 14 July. www.guardian.co.uk.

Beckfield, Jason. 2003. "Inequality in the world polity: The structure of international organization." *American Sociological Review* 68 (3): 401–24.

———. 2008. "The dual world polity: Fragmentation and integration in the network of intergovernmental organizations." *Social Problems* 55 (3): 419–42.

Beckford, James A. 2003. *Social Theory and Religion*. Cambridge: Cambridge University Press.

Behan, K., H. Maoh, and P. Kanaroglou. 2008. "Smart growth strategies, transportation and urban sprawl: Simulated futures for Hamilton, Ontario. *Canadian Geographer/Le Géographe Canadien* 52 (3): 291–308.

Béland, Daniel. 2005. "Ideas and social policy: An institutionalist perspective." *Social Policy and Administration* 39 (1): 1–18.

———. 2006. "The politics of social learning: Finance, institutions, and pension reform in the United States and Canada." *Governance* 19 (4): 559–83.

———. 2008. *Nationalism and Social Policy: The Politics of Territorial Solidarity*. Oxford: Oxford University Press.

——— and Jacob S. Hacker. 2004. "Ideas, private institutions, and American welfare state 'exceptionalism': The case of health and old-age insurance, 1915–1965." *International Journal of Social Welfare* 13: 42–54.

Bell, Daniel. 1973. *The Coming of Post-industrial Society*. New York: Basic Books.

Bellah, Robert, Richard Madsen, William M. Sullivan, Ann Swidler, and Steven M. Tipton. 1985. *Habits of the Heart: Individualism and Commitment in American Life*. Berkeley: University of California Press.

Bemiller, Michelle. 2005. "Men who cheer." *Sociological Focus* 38 (3): 205–22.

Benford, Robert D., and David A. Snow. 2000. "Framing processes and social movements: An overview and assessment." *Annual Review of Sociology* 26: 611–39.

Benkert, Holly. 2002. "Liberating insights from a cross-cultural sexuality study about women." *American Behavioral Scientist* 45 (8): 1197–207.

Berger, Joseph. 2009. "Student debt in Canada." In Joseph Berger, Anne Motte, and Andrew Parkin, eds, *The Price of Knowledge: Access and Student Finance in Canada*, 4th edn, 182–205. Montreal: The Canada Millennium Scholarship Foundation.

Berger, Peter L. 1963. *Invitation to Sociology*. New York: Anchor Books.

———. 1967. *The Sacred Canopy: Elements of a Sociological Theory of Religion*. Garden City, NY: Doubleday.

——— and Thomas Luckmann. 1966. *The Social Construction of Reality: Treatise in the Sociology of Knowledge*. Garden City, NY: Anchor.

Berlin, Isaiah. 1963. *Karl Marx: His Life and Environment*. New York: Oxford University Press.

Berman, Jacqueline. 2010. "Biopolitical management, economic calculation and 'trafficked women.'" *International Migration* 48: (4) 84–113.

Bernard, T.J., J.B. Snipes, and A.L. Gerould. 2009. *Vold's Theoretical Criminology*. 6th edn. Oxford: Oxford University Press.

Bernburg, J.G., M.D. Krohn, and C.J. Rivera. 2006. "Official labeling, criminal embeddedness, and subsequent delinquency: A longitudinal test of labeling theory." *Journal of Research in Crime and Delinquency* 43 (1): 67–88.

Bernstein, Basil. 1977. "Class and pedagogies: Visible and invisible." In Jerome Karabel and A.H. Halsey, eds, *Power and Ideology in Education*, 511–34. New York: Oxford University Press.

Bertone, Andrea Marie. 2000. "Sexual trafficking in women: International political economy and the politics of sex." *Gender Issues* 18 (1): 4–22.

Best, Joel. 2004. *More Damned Lies and Statistics*. Berkeley: University of California Press.

———. 2013. *Social Problems*. 2nd edn. New York: W.W. Norton.

Beyer, Peter. 2008. "From far and wide: Canadian religious and cultural diversity in global/local context." In L.G. Beaman and P. Beyer, eds, *Religion and Diversity in Canada*, 9–40. Leiden: Brill Academic Press.

———. 2012. "Religion and immigration in changing Canada: The reasonable accommodation of 'reasonable accommodation'?" In Lori G. Beaman, ed., *Reasonable Accommodation: Managing Religious Diversity*. Vancouver: University of British Columbia Press.

Bibby, Reginald. 1990. *Mosaic Madness*. Toronto: Stoddart.

Bibby, Reginald. 2002. *Restless Gods: The Renaissance of Religion in Canada*. Toronto: Stoddart.

——— with Sarah Russell and Ron Rolheiser. 2009. *The Emerging Millennials: How Canada's Newest Generation Is Responding to Change and Choice*. University of Lethbridge: Project Canada Books.

Bies, Robert J., and Thomas M. Tripp. 1996. "Beyond distrust: 'Getting even' and the 'need for revenge.'" In Roderick M. Kramer and Tom R. Tyler, eds, *Trust in Organizations: Frontiers of Theory and Research*, 246–60. Thousand Oaks, CA: Sage.

Bissoondath, Neil. 1994. *Selling Illusions: The Cult of Multiculturalism*. Toronto: Penguin.

Blackledge, David, and Barry Hunt. 1985. *Sociological Interpretations of Education*. London: Routledge.

Bloom, D.E. 2011. "Population dynamics in India and implications for economic growth." In Chetan Ghate, ed., *The Handbook of the Indian Economy*. Oxford: Oxford University Press.

Bolaria, B. Singh, and Peter Li. 1988. *Racial Oppression in Canada*. 2nd edn. Toronto: Garamond.

Boli, John, and George M. Thomas. 1997. "World culture in the world polity: A century of international non-governmental organization." *American Sociological Review* 62 (2): 171–90.

———. 1999. *Constructing World Culture: International Nongovernmental Organizations since 1875*. Stanford, CA: Stanford University Press.

Bostock, L. 2002. "'God, she's gonna report me': The ethics of child protection in poverty research." *Children and Society* 16 (4): 273–83.

Bourdieu, Pierre. 1984 [1979]. *Distinction: A Social Critique of the Judgement of Taste*. trans. Richard Nice. London: Routledge.

———. 1997. "The forms of capital." trans. Richard Nice. In A.H. Halsey, Hugh Lauder, Phillip Brown, and Amy Stuart Wells, eds, *Education: Culture, Economy, and Society*, 46–58. Oxford: Oxford University Press.

——— and Jean-Claude Passeron. 1979. *The Inheritors: French Students and Their Relations to Culture*. trans.

Richard Nice. Chicago: University of Chicago Press.

Bowden, Gary. 1989. "Labour unions in the public mind: The Canadian case." *Canadian Review of Sociology* 26 (5): 123–42.

———. 1990. "From sociology to theology: A reply to Lipset." *Canadian Review of Sociology* 27 (4): 536–9.

Bowles, Samuel, and Herbert Gintis. 1976. *Schooling in Capitalist America: Education Reform and the Contradictions of Economic Life.* New York: Basic Books.

Boyd, Jade. 2010. "Producing Vancouver's (hetero)normative nightscape." *Gender, Place and Culture: A Journal of Feminist Geography* 17 (2): 169–89.

Boyd, Monica. 1982. "Sex differences in the Canadian occupational attainment process." *Canadian Review of Sociology and Anthropology* 19 (1): 1–28.

———. 1985. "Education and occupational attainments of native-born Canadian men and women." In Monica Boyd et al., eds, *Ascription and Achievement: Studies in Mobility and Status Attainment in Canada,* 229–95. Ottawa: Carleton University Press.

———. 1992. "Gender, visible minority, and immigrant earnings inequality: Reassessing an employment equity premise." In Vic Satzewich, ed., *Deconstructing a Nation: Immigration, Multiculturalism and Racism in '90s Canada,* 279–321. Halifax: Fernwood.

——— et al., eds. 1985. *Ascription and Achievement: Studies in Mobility and Status Attainment in Canada,* Ottawa: Carleton University Press.

Bradshaw, York W., Rita Noonan, Laura Gash, and Claudia Buchmann Sershen. 1993. "Borrowing against the future: Children and Third World indebtedness." *Social Forces* 71 (3): 629–56.

Braithwaite, Dawn O., and Leslie A. Baxter. 2005. *Engaging Theories in Family Communication: Multiple Perspectives.* Thousand Oaks, CA: Sage.

Braithewaite, John. 1979. *Inequality, Crime and Public Policy.* London: Routledge and Kegan Paul.

Bramham, Daphne. 2010. "Polygamy is harmful to society, scholar finds." *Vancouver Sun.* www.vancouversun .com/news/Polygamy + harmful + society + scholar + finds/3290757/ story.html#ixzz0u9ayfizY.

Braverman, Harry. 1974. *Labor and Monopoly Capital: The Degradation of Work in the Twentieth Century.* New York: Monthly Review Press.

Breton, Raymond. 1972. "The socio-political dynamics of the October events." *Canadian Review of Sociology and Anthropology* 9 (1): 33–56.

Briskin, Linda. 1992. "Socialist feminism: From the standpoint of practice." In M. Patricia Connelly and Pat Armstrong, eds, *Feminism in Action: Studies in Political Economy,* 267–93. Toronto: Canadian Scholars Press.

Bromley, David G., and Anson D. Shupe, Jr. 1981. *Strange Gods: The Great American Cult Scare.* Boston: Beacon.

Brook, Barbara. 1999. *Feminist Perspectives on the Body.* London: Longman.

Brown, Louise. 2002. "Two-tier grade schooling feared." *Toronto Star* 31 May: A1, A26.

———. 2010. "Focus on struggling minority students, report recommends." 14 July. www.parentacentral.ca.

Brownlee, Jamie. 2005. *Ruling Canada: Corporate Cohesion and Democracy.* Halifax: Fernwood.

Bruntland, Gro Harlem. 1987. *Our Common Future.* Oxford: Oxford University Press.

Bryant, Heather. 1990. *The Infertility Dilemma: Reproductive Technologies and Prevention.* Ottawa: Canadian Advisory Council on the Status of Women.

Bryman, Alan, Jane J. Teevan, and Edward Bell. 2009. *Social Research Methods.* 2nd Canadian edn. Toronto: Oxford University Press.

Brzozowski, J.A., A. Taylor-Butts, and S. Johnson. 2006. "Victimization and offending among the Aboriginal population in Canada." *Juristat* 26 (3). Ottawa: Statistics Canada.

Bullard, Robert. 1990. *Dumping in Dixie: Race, Class and Environmental Quality.* Boulder, CO: Westview.

Bunting, Trudi, and Pierre Filion, eds. 2006. *Canadian Cities in Transition: Local through Global Perspectives.* 3rd edn. Don Mills, ON: Oxford University Press.

——— and R. Walker, eds. 2010. *Canadian Cities in Transition: New Directions in the Twenty-First Century.* 4th edn. Don Mills, ON: Oxford University Press.

Burgess, Ernest. W. 1967 [1925]. "The growth of the city: An introduction to a research project." In Robert E. Park, Ernest W. Burgess, and Roderick D. McKenzie, *The City,* 47–62. Chicago: University of Chicago Press.

Bussière, Patrick, and Tamara Knighton. 2004. *Measuring Up: Canadian Results of the OECD PISA Study: The Performance of Canada's Youth in Mathematics, Reading, Science and Problem Solving, 2003. First Findings for Canadians Aged 15.* Ottawa: Minister of Industry.

——— and Dianna Pennock. 2007. *Measuring Up: Canadian Results of the OECD PISA Study: The Performance of Canada's Youth in Science, Reading and Mathematics, 2006. First Results for Canadians Aged 15.* Catalogue no. 81-590-XPE, no. 3. Ottawa: Minister of Industry.

Butler, Judith. 1992. "Contingent foundations: Feminism and the question of 'postmodernism.'" In Judith Butler and Joan W. Scott, eds, *Feminists Theorize the Political,* 3–21. New York: Routledge.

———. 2006 [1990]. *Gender Troubles: Feminism and the Subversion of Identity.* New York: Routledge Classics.

Butsch, Richard. 1992. "Class and gender in four decades of television situation comedy: Plus ça change . . . ." *Critical Studies in Mass Communication* 9: 387–99.

———. 1995. "Ralph, Fred, Archie and Homer: Why television keeps recreating the white male working-class buffoon." In Gail Dines and Jean M. Humez, eds, *Gender, Race and Class in Media: A Text-Reader,* 403–12. Thousand Oaks, CA: Sage.

——— and Lynda M. Glennon. 1983. "Social class: Frequency trends in domestic situation comedy,

1946–1978." *Journal of Broadcasting* 27 (1): 77–81.

Butters, Jennifer, and Patricia Erickson. 1999. "Addictions as deviant behaviour: Normalizing the pleasures of intoxication." In Lori G. Beaman, ed., *New Perspectives on Deviance: The Construction of Deviance in Everyday Life*, 67–84. Toronto: Prentice-Hall Allyn and Bacon.

Calavita, K., and H.N. Pontell. 1991. "'Other people's money' revisited: Collective embezzlement in the savings and loan insurance industries." *Social Problems* 38 (1): 94–112.

Calliste, Agnes. 1993. "Sleeping car porters in Canada: An ethnically submerged split labour market." In Graham S. Lowe and Harvey Krahn, eds, *Work in Canada: Readings in the Sociology of Work and Industry*, 139–53. Scarborough, ON: Nelson.

Campey, John. 2002. "Immigrant children in our classrooms: Beyond ESL." *Education Canada* 42 (3): 44–7.

Canada. 1991. *Broadcasting Act*. Statutes of Canada 1991, c. 11.

Canadian Council on Learning. 2009. *The State of Aboriginal Learning in Canada: A Holistic Approach to Measuring Success*. Ottawa: Canadian Council on Learning.

———. 2010. *State of Learning in Canada 2009–2010: A Year in Review*. Ottawa: Canadian Council on Learning.

Canadian Environmental Grantmakers' Network (CEGN). 2005. *Urban Environmental Issues: A Summary of Issues and Approaches*. Toronto: CEGN.

Canadian Fertility and Andrology Society. 2011. "Assisted reproduction and live birth rates for Canada." Press release. www.cfas.ca.

Canadian Health Services Research Foundation. 2002. *Myth: For-Profit Ownership of Facilities Would Lead to Better Health Care*. Ottawa: Canadian Health Services Research Foundation.

———. 2005. *Myth: A Parallel Private System Would Reduce Waiting Times in the Public System*. Ottawa: Canadian Health Services Research Foundation. www.chsrf .ca/publicationsandresources/ Mythbusters/

ArticlcView/05-03-01/5bda3483-f97b-4616-bfe7-d55d0d66b9a0.aspx.

Canadian Institute of Child Health. 2002. *The Health of Canada's Children*. 3rd edn. Ottawa: Canadian Institute of Child Health.

Canadian Media Production Association (CMPA). 2011. *Profile 2011: An Economic Report on the Screen-Based Production Industry in Canada*. Ottawa: CMPA.

Canadian Press. 2011. "Richest Canadians list shows fortunes decreasing." www.cbc.ca/news/ business/story/2011/10/06/rich-canad-ians-list.html.

Canadian Radio-television and Telecommunications Commission (CRTC). 1998. *Commercial Radio Policy*. Broadcasting Public Notice 1998-41, 30 Apr. Ottawa: CRTC.

Canadian Teachers' Federation. 2010. "Fundraising." *Commercialism in Canadian Schools: Who's Calling the Shots?* CTF Fact Sheet. www .ctf-fce.ca/documents/Resources/ en/commercialism_in_school/en/ CISCKitFundraising%28R6%29.pdf.

Carroll, William K. 2010. *Corporate Power in a Globalizing World*. Toronto: Oxford University Press.

——— and R.S. Ratner. 1996. "Master framing and cross-movement networking in contemporary social movements." *Sociological Quarterly* 37: 601–25.

———. 1999. "Media strategies and political projects: A comparative study of social movements." *Canadian Journal of Sociology* 24 (1): 1–34.

———. 2001. "Sustaining oppositional cultures in 'post-socialist' times: A comparative study of three social movement organizations." *Sociology* 35 (3): 605–29.

Carter-Whitney, Maureen. 2008. "Cinching sprawl." *Alternatives Journal* 34 (3): 17.

Cartwright, Claire, and Heather McDowell. 2008. "Young women's life stories and accounts of parental divorce." *Journal of Divorce and Remarriage* 49 (1/2): 56–77.

Casanova, José. 1994. *Public Religion in the Modern World*. Chicago: University of Chicago Press.

Castells, Manuel. 2000. *The Rise of the Network Society*. Oxford: Blackwell.

Catton, William, Jr, and Riley Dunlap. 1978. "Environmental sociology: A new paradigm." *American Sociologist* 13: 41–9.

CAUT (Canadian Association of University Teachers). 2009. *CAUT Almanac of Post-Secondary Education in Canada 2008–09*. Ottawa: CAUT.

Cavanagh, Shannon E. 2008. "Family structure history and adolescent adjustment." *Journal of Family Issues* 29 (7): 944–80.

CBC News. 2007. "Understanding the violence." www.cbc.ca/news/background/paris_riots/timeline.html.

———. 2009. "Going organic: Growing demand, tougher regulations." www.cbc.ca/consumer/ story/2008/05/07/f-food-organic .html.

———. 2010. "Québec will require bare face for service." www.cbc.ca/news/ canada/montreal/story/2010/03/24/ Québec-reasonable-accommodation-law.html.

Chappell, Allison T., and Lonn Lanza-Kaduce. 2010. "Police academy socialization: Understanding the lessons learned in a paramilitary-bureaucratic organization." *Journal of Contemporary Ethnography* 39 (2): 187–214.

Charon, Joel M. 1979. *Symbolic Interactionism: An Introduction, an Interpretation, an Integration*. Englewood Cliffs, NJ: Prentice-Hall.

Chase-Dunn, Christopher K. 1998. *Global Formation: Structures of the World-Economy*. Lanham, MD: Rowman and Littlefield.

——— and Peter Grimes. 1995. "World-systems analysis." *Annual Review of Sociology* 21: 387–417.

Chasteen, Amy L. 2001. "Constructing rape: Feminism, change, and women's everyday understandings of sexual assault." *Sociological Spectrum* 21: 101–39.

Cheal, David. 1991. *Family and the State of Theory*. Toronto: University of Toronto Press.

Chilton, R. 2004. "Regional variations in lethal and non lethal assaults." *Homicide Studies* 8 (1): 40–56.

Chuang, Kent. 1999. "Using chop sticks to eat steak." *Journal of Homosexuality* 36 (3–4): 29–41.

Chung, Donghum, Brahm Daniel DeBuys, and Chang S. Nam. 2007. "Influence of avatar creation on attitude, empathy, presence, and para-social interaction." Lecture Notes in Computer Science, Proceedings of the 12th International Conference on Human–Computer Interaction: Interaction Design and Usability, Beijing, China. Berlin: Springer-Verlag.

Church II, W.T., T. Wharton, and J.K. Taylor. 2009. "An examination of differential association and social theory: Family systems and delinquency." *Youth Violence and Juvenile Justice* 7 (1): 3–15.

CIA (Central Intelligence Agency). 2012. *The World Factbook*. ISSN 1553-8133. https://www.cia.gov/library/publications/the-world-factbook/fields/2054.html.

Citizenship and Immigration Canada. 2011. *Facts and Figures, 2010—Immigration Overview—Permanent and Temporary Residents*. www.cic.gc.ca/english/pdf/research-stats/facts2010.pdf.

Clark, Rob. 2010. "Technical and institutional states: Loose coupling in the human rights sector of the world polity." *Sociological Quarterly* 51 (1): 65–95.

——— and Jason Hall. 2011. "Migration, international telecommunications, and human rights." *Sociological Forum* 26 (4): 870–96.

Clarke, Juanne N. 2008. *Health, Illness and Medicine in Canada*. Toronto: Oxford University Press.

——— and G. Van Amerom. 2008. "The differences between parents and people with Asperger's." *Social Work in Health Care* 46 (3): 85–106.

Clément, Dominique. 2008. *Canada's Rights Revolution: Social Movements and Social Change, 1937–82*. Vancouver: University of British Columbia Press.

Clement, Wallace. 1975. *The Canadian Corporate Elite*. Toronto: McClelland and Stewart.

CMEC (Council of Ministers of Education Canada). 2008. *The Development of Education: Reports for Canada*. Ottawa: CMEC.

Coburn, Elaine. 2010. "'Pulling the monster down': Interview with William K. Carroll." *Socialist Studies* 6 (1): 65–92.

Cohen, Jean L. 1985. "Strategy or identity: New theoretical paradigms and contemporary social movements." *Social Research* 53: 663–716.

Cole, L.W., and S.R. Foster. 2001. *From the Ground Up: Environmental Racism and the Rise of the Environmental Justice Movement*. New York: New York University Press.

Collier, R. 2010. "Medical school admission targets urged for rural and low-income Canadians." *Canadian Medical Association Journal* 182 (8): E327–8.

Collin, C., and H. Jensen. 2009. *A Statistical Profile of Poverty in Canada*. Library of Parliament/Parliamentary Information and Research Services. PRB 09-17E.

Collins, Patricia Hill. 2000. *Black Feminist Thought: Knowledge, Consciousness, and the Politics of Empowerment*. 2nd edn. New York: Routledge.

Collins, R. 2008. *Violence: A Macro-Sociological Theory*. Princeton, NJ: Princeton University Press.

Collins, Randall. 1979. *The Credential Society: An Historical Sociology of Education and Stratification*. New York: Academic Press.

Comack, E. 2008. *Out There/In Here*. Halifax: Fernwood.

Comte, Auguste. 1974. "Positivist philosophy." In Stanislav Andreski, ed., *The Essential Comte*. London: Croom Helm.

Connell, R.W. 1996. "Teaching the boys: New research on masculinity and gender strategies for schools." *Teachers College Record* 98: 206–35.

———. 2000. *Masculinities*. Crows Nest, NSW: Allen & Unwin.

Conrad, Peter. 2005 "The shifting engines of medicalization." *Journal of Health and Social Behaviour* 46 (March): 3–14.

Cook, J. 2001. "Practical guide to medical education." *Pharmaceutical Marketing* 6: 14–22.

Cooley, Charles Horton. 1902. *Human Nature and Social Order*. New York: Scribner.

———. 1962 [1909]. *Social Organization: A Study of the Larger Mind*. Glencoe, IL: Free Press.

Corman, June, and Meg Luxton. 2007. *Getting by in Hard Times: Gendered Labour at Home and on the Job*. Toronto: University of Toronto Press.

Courchene, T.J. 2007. "Global futures for Canada's global cities." *IRPP Policy Matters* 8 (2).

Crane, Diana. 2002. "Culture and globalization: Theoretical models and emerging trends." In Diana Crane, Nobuko Kawashima, and Kenichi Kawasaki, eds, *Global Culture: Media, Arts, Policy, and Globalization*, 1–25. New York: Routledge.

Cranford, Cynthia J., Leah F. Vosko, and Nancy Zukewich. 2006. "The gender of precarious employment in Canada." In Vivian Shalla, ed., *Working in a Global Era: Canadian Perspectives*, 99–119. Toronto: Canadian Scholars Press.

Crockett, Lisa, Mike Losoff, and Anne C. Petersen. 1984. "Perceptions of the peer group and friendship in early adolescence." *Journal of Early Adolescence* 4 (2): 155–81.

Crompton, Susan. 2000. "Health." *Canadian Social Trends* 59: 12–17.

Cromwell, P.F., J.N. Olson, and D.W. Avery. 1991. *Breaking and Entering: An Ethnographic Analysis of Burglary*. Newbury Park, CA: Sage.

Crossley, Michelle L. 2002. "The perils of health promotion and the 'barebacking' backlash." *Health* 6 (1): 47–68.

Croteau, David, and William Hoynes. 2000. *Media/Society: Industries, Images, and Audiences*. 2nd edn. Thousand Oaks, CA: Pine Forge.

Crozier, Michel. 1964. *The Bureaucratic Phenomenon*. Chicago: University of Chicago Press.

Cullen, F.T., J.P. Wright, and K.R. Blevins, eds. 2007. *Taking Stock: The Status of Criminological Theory*. Edison, NJ: Transaction.

Cuneo, Carl. 1990. *Pay Equity: The Labour-Feminist Challenge*. Toronto: Oxford University Press.

———. 2002. "Globalized and localized digital divides along the information highway: A fragile synthesis across bridges, ramps, cloverleaves, and ladders." 33rd Annual Sorokin Lecture, University of Saskatchewan, 31 Jan.

Cunningham, Mick, and Arland Thornton. 2006. "The influence of parents' marital quality on adult children's attitudes toward marriage and its alternatives: Main and moderating effects." *Demography* 43 (4): 659–72.

Curra, John. 2011. *The Relativity of Deviance*. 2nd edn. Thousand Oaks, CA: Sage.

Currie, Dawn. 1988. "Starvation amidst abundance: Female adolescents and anorexia." In B. Singh Bolaria and Harley D. Dickinson, eds, *Sociology of Health Care in Canada*, 198–215. Toronto: Harcourt Brace Jovanovich.

Curtiss, Susan. 1977. *Genie: A Psycholinguistic Study of a Modern Day Wild Child*. New York: Academic Press.

Curwood, S. 2009. "What is poverty?" *Journal of Hunger and Poverty* 1 (December): 9–17.

Daenzer, Patricia. 1993. *Regulating Class Privilege: Immigrant Servants in Canada, 1940s–1990*. Toronto: Canadian Scholars Press.

Daly, Kerry. 2004. *The Changing Culture of Parenting*. Ottawa: Vanier Institute of the Family.

Daly, Mary. 1985. *Beyond God the Father: Towards a Philosophy of Women's Liberation*. Boston: Beacon Books.

Darder, Antonia, Marta Baltodano, and Rodolfo D. Torres, eds. 2003. *The Critical Pedagogy Reader*. New York: Routledge Falmer.

Das Gupta, Tania. 1996. *Racism and Paid Work*. Toronto: Garamond.

Davie, Grace. 1994. *Religion in Britain since 1945: Believing without Belonging*. Oxford: Blackwell.

Davies, Lorraine, and Patricia Jane Carrier. 1999. "The importance of power relations for the division of household labour." *Canadian Journal of Sociology* 24 (1): 35–51.

Davies, Scott, and Neil Guppy. 2006. *The Schooled Society: An Introduction to the Sociology of Education*. Don Mills, ON: Oxford University Press.

——— 2010. *The Schooled Society: An Introduction to the Sociology of Education*. 2nd edn. Toronto: Oxford University Press.

deGroot-Maggetti. 2002. *A Measure of Poverty in Canada: A Guide to the Debate about Poverty Lines*. Ottawa: Citizens for Public Justice.

Dei, George J. Sefa. 1996. *Anti-racism Education: Theory and Practice*. Halifax: Fernwood.

———. 2006. "Black-focused schools: A call for re-visioning." *Education Canada* 46 (3): 27–31.

——— Irma Marcia James, Leeno Luke Karumanchery, Sonia James-Wilson, and Jasmin Zine. 2000. *Removing the Margins: The Challenges and Possibilities of Inclusive Schooling*. Toronto: Canadian Scholars Press.

DeKeseredy, Walter. 2009. "Patterns of family violence." In M. Baker, ed., *Families: Changing Trends in Canada*, 6th edn, 179–205. Toronto: McGraw-Hill Ryerson.

——— and Linda MacLeod. 1997. *Woman Abuse: A Sociological Story*. Toronto: Harcourt Brace. Permission granted by Walter Dekeseredy.

Dellinger, Kirsten. 2002. "Wearing gender and sexuality 'on your sleeve': Dress norms and the importance of occupational and organizational culture at work." *Gender Issues* 20 (1): 3–25.

Deloitte Center for Health Solutions. 2011. *2011 Survey of Health Care Consumers Global Report: Key Findings, Strategic Implications*. Washington: Deloitte Center for Health Solutions. www.deloitte.com/assets/Dcom-UnitedStates/Local%20Assets/Documents/US_CHS_2011ConsumerSurveyGlobal_062111.pdf.

Dempsey, Ken. 1999. *Resistance and Change: Trying to Get Husbands to Do More Housework*. Paper presented at the Australian Sociologists Association annual meeting, Monash University.

Desjardins, Richard, Scott Murray, Yvan Clermont, and Patrick Werquin. 2005. *Learning a Living: First Results of the Adult Literacy and Life Skills Survey*. Ottawa and Paris: Statistics Canada and OECD.

Devereaux, P.J., et al. 2002. "A systematic review and meta-analysis of studies comparing mortality rates of private for-profit and private not-for-profit hospitals." *Canadian Medical Association Journal* 166: 1399–406.

Diani, Mario. 1992. "The concept of social movement." *Sociological Review* 40: 1–25.

Dickey Young, Pamela. 2012. "It's all about sex: The roots of opposition in some Christian churches to gay and lesbian marriages." In Lori G. Beaman, ed., *Religion and Canadian Society: Contexts, Identities, and Strategies*, 2nd edn, 145–56. Canadian Scholars Press.

Dill, Karen E., and Kathryn P. Thill. 2007. "Video game characters and the socialization of gender roles: Young people's perceptions mirror sexist media depictions." *Sex Roles* 57: 851–64.

Dillabough, Jo-Anne, Julie McLeod, and Martin Mills, eds. 2011. *Troubling Gender in Education*. New York: Routledge.

Dimaggio, Paul, and Walter Powell. 1983. "The iron cage revisited: Institutional isomorphism and collective rationality in organizational fields." *American Sociological Review* 48 (2): 147–60.

Dobash, R. Emerson, Russell P. Dobash, Margo Wilson, and Martin Daly. 1992. "The myth of sexual symmetry in marital violence." *Social Problems* 39: 71–91.

Dolan, Kerry A., and Keren Blankfeld. 2011. "Canada's billionaires richer on stock gains." *Forbes*. www.forbes.com/2011/03/14/canada-richest-biolionaires-print.html.

Dole, Carol M. 2000. "Woman with a gun: Cinematic law enforcers on the gender frontier." In Murray Pomerance and John Sakeris, eds, *Bang Bang, Shoot Shoot! Essays on Guns and Popular Culture*, 2nd edn, 11–21. Needham Heights, MA: Pearson Education.

———. 2001. "The gun and the badge: Hollywood and the female lawman." In Martha McCaughey and Neal King, eds, *Reel Knockouts: Violent Women in the Movies*. Austin: University of Texas Press.

Domhoff, G. William. 2009. *Who Rules America: Challenges to Corporate and Class Dominance*. New York: McGraw-Hill.

Downes, D., and P. Rock. 2003. *Understanding Deviance*. 4th edn. Toronto: Oxford University Press.

Downey, John, and Natalie Fenton. 2003. "New media, counter publicity and the public sphere." *New Media and Society* 5 (2): 185–202.

Doyal, Lesley. 1995. *What Makes Women Sick: Gender and the Political Economy of Health*. New Brunswick, NJ: Rutgers University Press.

Dreeben, Robert. 1968. *On What Is Learned in School*. Reading, MA: Addison-Wesley.

Driedger, Leo. 1996. *Multi-ethnic Canada: Identities and Inequalities.* Toronto: Oxford University Press.

Drori, Gili S., John W. Meyer, Francisco O. Ramirez, and Evan Schofer. 2003. "Loose coupling in national science: Policy versus practice." In Gili S. Drori, John W. Meyer, Francisco O. Ramirez, and Evan Schofer, eds, *Science in the Modern World Polity: Institutionalization and Globalization*, 155–73. Stanford, CA: Stanford University Press.

Duffy, Ann D. 1986. "Reconceptualizing power for women." *Canadian Review of Anthropology and Sociology* 23 (1): 21–46.

———. 2011. "Families in tough times: The impact of economic crises on Canadian families." In N. Mandell and A. Duffy, eds, *Canadian Families*, 4th edn, 164–210. Toronto: Nelson.

Dunlap, Riley, and William Catton, Jr. 1983. "What environmental sociologists have in common (whether concerned with 'built' or 'natural' environments)." Sociological Inquiry 53 (2/3): 113–15.

Dunlap , Riley, and E.A. Rosa. 2010. "Environmental sociology." In Edgar F. Borgatta and Rhoda J.V. Montgomery, eds., *Encyclopedia of Sociology*, 2nd edn, 1–7. New York: Macmillan Reference USA (The Gale Group).

Durkheim, Émile. 1964 [1893]. *The Division of Labor in Society.* trans. George Simpson. New York: Free Press.

———. 1951 [1897]. *Suicide: A Study in Sociology.* trans. John A. Spaulding and George Simpson. New York: Free Press.

———. 1965 [1912]. *The Elementary Forms of the Religious Life.* London: Allen and Unwin.

———. 1956 [1922]. *Education and Society.* trans. Sherwood W. Fox. Glencoe, IL: Free Press.

Durkin, K.F. 2009. "There must be some kind of misunderstanding, there must be some kind of mistake: The deviance disavowal strategies of men arrested in Internet sex stings (2008 presidential address)." *Sociological Spectrum* 29 (6): 661–76.

Ebaugh, Helen. 1988. *Becoming an Ex: The Process of Role Exit.* Chicago: University of Chicago Press.

Edin, Kathryn, and Maria J. Kefalas. 2005. *Promises I Can Keep: Why Poor Women Put Motherhood before Marriage.* Berkeley: University of California Press.

Edwards, Nigel, Mary Jane Kornacki, and Jack Silversin. 2002. "Unhappy doctors: What are the causes and what can be done?" *British Medical Journal* 324: 835–8.

Eglin, Peter, and Stephen Hester. 1999. "'You're all a bunch of feminists': Categorization and the politics of terror in the Montreal Massacre." *Human Studies* 22: 253–72.

Ehrenreich, Barbara. 2001. *Nickel and Dimed: On (Not) Getting by in America.* New York: Henry Holt.

Ehrlich, Paul R., and Anne H. Ehrlich. 1990. *The Population Explosion.* London: Hutchinson.

Eichler, Margrit. 1996. "The impact of new reproductive and genetic technologies on families." In Maureen Baker, ed., *Families: Changing Trends in Canada*, 3rd edn, 104–18. Toronto: McGraw-Hill Ryerson.

———. 2005. "Biases in family literature." In Maureen Baker, ed., *Families: Changing Trends in Canada*, 5th edn, 121–42. Toronto: McGraw-Hill Ryerson.

———, Patrizia Albanese, Susan Ferguson, Nicky Hyndman, Lichun Willa Liu, and Ann Matthews. 2010. *More Than It Seems: Household Work and Lifelong Learning.* Toronto: Women's Press.

Eidelman, Gabriel. 2010. "Managing urban sprawl in Ontario: Good policy or good politics?" *Politics and Policy* 38 (6): 1211–36.

El Akkad, Omar. 2010. "Woman shocked by portrayal as hard-lined Islamist." *Globe and Mail.* www .theglobeandmail.com/news/ national/woman-shocked-by- portrayal-as-hard-line-islamist/ article1490612.

Elliott-Buckley, Stephen. 2011. "Seeds of the Occupy Movement." *Our Times* 30 (5): 44.

Elmer, Greg, and Mike Gasher, eds. 2005. *Contracting out Hollywood: Runaway Productions and Foreign Location Shooting.* Lanham, MD: Rowman and Littlefield.

Engels, Friedrich. 1994 [1845]. *The Condition of the Working Class in England.* trans. W.O. Henderson and W.H. Chaloner. Stanford, CA: Stanford University Press.

Erasmus, Georges. 2002. "Why can't we talk." From the 2002 Lafontaine-Baldwin Lecture. *Globe and Mail* 9 March: F6–7.

Eribon, Didier. 1991 [1989]. *Michel Foucault.* trans. Betsy Wing. Cambridge, MA: Harvard University Press.

Erikson, Erik. 1963. *Childhood and Society.* New York: W.W. Norton.

———. 1982. *The Life Cycle Completed: A Review.* New York: W.W. Norton.

Erikson, Kai T. 1966. *Wayward Puritans: A Study in the Sociology of Deviance.* New York: Wiley.

Faules, Don F., and Dennis C. Alexander. 1978. *Communication and Social Behaviour: A Symbolic Interaction Perspective.* Reading, MA: Addison-Wesley.

Feagin, J.R. 1998. *The New Urban Paradigm: Critical Perspectives on the City.* Lanham, MD, and Boulder, CO: Rowman and Littlefield.

Featherstone, Liza. 2004. *Selling Women Short: The Landmark Battle for Workers' Rights at Wal-Mart.* New York: Basic Books.

Ferrao, Vincent. 2010. "Paid work." In Vincent Ferrao and Cara Williams, *Women in Canada: A Gender-Based Statistical Report.* Catalogue no. 89-503-X. Ottawa: Statistics Canada.

Finnie, Ross, Kathryn McMullen, and Richard Mueller. 2010. "New perspectives on access to postsecondary education." *Education Matters: New Insights on Education, Learning and Training in Canada* 7 (1). www.statcan.gc.ca/bsolc/ olc-cel/olc-cel?catno = 81-004- X&chropg = 1&lang = eng.

Firestone, Shulamith. 1970. *The Dialectic of Sex: The Case for Feminist Revolution.* New York: Bantam Books.

Fiske, John, and Robert Dawson. 1996. "Audiencing violence: Watching homeless men watch *Die Hard*." In James Hay, Lawrence Grossberg, and Ellen Wartella, eds,

The Audience and Its Landscape, 297–316. Boulder, CO: Westview.

Fleras, Augie. 2009. *Unequal Relations: An Introduction to Race, Ethnic and Aboriginal Dynamics in Canada*. 6th edn. Scarborough, ON: Prentice-Hall.

——— and Jean Leonard Elliott. 1996. *Unequal Relations: An Introduction to Race, Ethnic and Aboriginal Dynamics in Canada*. Toronto: Prentice-Hall.

——— and Jean Lock Kunz. 2001. *Media and Minorities: Representing Diversity in a Multicultural Canada*. Toronto: Thompson Education.

Fleury, D., and M. Fortin. 2006. *When Working Is Not Enough to Escape Poverty: An Analysis of Canada's Working Poor*. Ottawa: Human Resources and Skills Development Canada.

Florida, R. 2008. *Who's Your City: How the Creative Economy Is Making Where to Live the Most Important Decision of Your Life*. New York: Basic Books.

Force, William Ryan. 2009. "Consumption styles and the fluid complexity of punk authenticity." *Symbolic Interaction* 32 (4): 289–309.

Ford, J., N. Nassar, E. Sullivan, G. Chambers, and P. Lancaster. 2003. *Reproductive Health Indicators, Australia, 2002*. Sydney: Australian Institute of Health and Welfare.

Ford, J.A. 2009. "Nonmedical prescription drug use among adolescents: The influence of bonds to family and school." *Youth and Society* 40: 336–52.

Foster, J.B. 1986. *The Theory of Monopoly Capitalism: An Elaboration of Marxian Political Economy*. New York: Monthly Review Press.

Foucault, Michel. 1990. *The History of Sexuality: An Introduction*. New York: Vintage Books.

Fox, Bonnie. 2009. *When Couples Become Parents: The Creation of Gender in the Transition to Parenthood*. Toronto: University of Toronto Press.

——— and Pamela Sugiman. 1999. "Flexible work, flexible workers: The restructuring of clerical work in a large telecommunications company." *Studies in Political Economy* 60: 59–84.

Fox, James Alan, and Jack Levin. 2001. *The Will to Kill: Making Sense of Senseless Murder*. Boston: Allyn and Bacon.

Francis, Diane. 1986. *Controlling Interest: Who Owns Canada*. Toronto: Macmillan.

———. 2008. *Who Owns Canada Now: Old Money, New Money and the Future of Canadian Business*. Toronto: HarperCollins.

Francis, Margot. 2012. "The imaginary Indian: Unpacking the romance of domination." In D. Brock, R. Raby, and M. Thomas, eds, *Power and Everyday Practices*, 252–76. Toronto: Nelson.

Frank, David John, Wesley Longhofer, and Evan Schofer. 2007. "World society, NGOs and environmental policy reform in Asia." *International Journal of Comparative Sociology* 48 (4): 275–95.

Freire, Paulo. 1970. *Pedagogy of the Oppressed*. trans. Myra Bergman Ramos. New York: Herder and Herder.

Freud, Sigmund. 1938. *The Basic Writings of Sigmund Freud*. trans., ed. Abraham Brill. New York: Modern Library Press.

Friedan, Betty. 1963. *The Feminine Mystique*. New York: W.W. Norton.

Fritsche, I. 2005. "Predicting deviant behavior by neutralization: Myths and findings." *Deviant Behavior* 9 (2): 199–218.

Galabuzi, Grace-Edward. 2006. *Canada's Economic Apartheid: The Social Exclusion of Racialized Groups in the New Century*. Toronto: Canadian Scholars Press.

Gamson, William. 1991. "Commitment and agency in social movements." *Sociological Forum* 6: 27–50.

Gannon, M., K. Mihorean, K. Beatie, A. Taylor-Butts, and R. Kong. 2005. *Criminal Justice Indicators, 2005*. Ottawa: Canadian Centre for Justice Statistics, Statistics Canada.

Garfinkel, Harold. 1956. "Conditions of successful status degradation ceremonies." *American Journal of Sociology* 61: 420–4.

Gaskell, Jane. 1993. "Feminism and its impact on educational scholarship in Canada." In Leonard L. Stewin and Stewart J.H. McCann, eds, *Contemporary Educational Issues: The Canadian Mosaic*, 2nd edn, 145–60. Toronto: Copp Clark Pitman.

Geiger, B. 2006. "Crime, prostitution, drugs, and malingered insanity: Female offenders' resistant strategies to abuse and domination." *International Journal of Offender Therapy and Comparative Criminology* 50 (5): 582–94.

Gergen, Kenneth. 2001. "From mind to relationship: The emerging challenge." *Education Canada* 41 (1): 8–11.

Giddens, Anthony. 1990. *The Consequences of Modernity*. Stanford, CA: Stanford University Press.

———. 2006. *Sociology*. 5th edn. Cambridge: Polity Press.

Gidney, R.D. 1999. *From Hope to Harris: The Reshaping of Ontario's Schools*. Toronto: University of Toronto Press.

Gimlin, D. 2008. "NAAFA: Attempting to neutralize the stigma of the hugely obese body." In E. Goode and D.A. Vail, eds, *Extreme Deviance*, 72–80. Los Angeles and London: Pine Forge Press.

Gionet, Linda. 2009. "First Nations people: Selected findings of the 2006 Census." *Canadian Social Trends* summer, no. 87. Ottawa: Statistics Canada.

Girling, J.L. 2010. *Capital and Power: Political Economy and Social Transformation*. Abingdon, UK: Routledge.

Giroux, Henri. 1997. *Pedagogy and the Politics of Hope: Theory, Culture, and Schooling: A Critical Reader*. Boulder, CO: Westview.

Gitlin, Todd. 1980. *The Whole World Is Watching: Mass Media in the Making and Unmaking of the New Left*. Berkeley: University of California Press.

Goar, Carol. 2011. "Why you should care about inequality." *Toronto Star* 2 January: A19.

Goffman, Erving. 1959. *The Presentation of Self in Everyday Life*. Garden City, NJ: Doubleday-Anchor.

———. 1961. *Asylums: Essays on the Social Situation of Mental Patients and Other Inmates*. New York: Doubleday.

———. 1963. *Stigma: Notes on the Management of Spoiled Identity*. Englewood Cliffs, NJ: Prentice-Hall.

Gold, David A., Clarence Y.H. Lo, and Erik Olin Wright. 1975. "Recent developments in Marxist theories of the capitalist state." *Monthly Review* 27: 29–43.

Goldberg, David Theo. 1993. *Racist Culture: Philosophy and the Politics of Meaning*. Oxford: Blackwell.

Goldenberg, Naomi. 2006. "What's God got to do with it? A call for problematizing basic terms in the feminist analysis of religion." Paper presented at the biannual meeting of the Britain and Ireland School of Feminist Theology, Edinburgh, July.

Goldthorpe, J.E. 1987. *Family Life in Western Societies: A Historical Sociology of Family Relationships in Britain and North America*. Cambridge: Cambridge University Press.

Gosine, A., and C. Teelucksingh. 2008. *Environmental Justice and Racism in Canada: An Introduction*. Toronto: Emond Montgomery.

Gosine, Kevin. 2000. "Revisiting the notion of a 'recast' vertical mosaic in Canada: Does a post secondary education make a difference?" *Canadian Ethnic Studies* 32 (3): 89–104.

Gottdiener, M., and R. Hutchison. 2000. *The New Urban Sociology*. 2nd edn. Boston: McGraw-Hill.

Gottfredson, M., and Travis Hirschi. 1990. *A General Theory of Crime*. Stanford, CA: Stanford University Press.

Gould, K., A. Schnaiberg, and A.S. Weinberg. 1996. *Local Environmental Struggles: Citizen Activism in the Treadmill of Production*. New York: Cambridge University Press.

Gover, Angela R., Catherine Kaukinen, and Kathleen A. Fox. 2008. "The relationship between violence in the family of origin and dating violence among college students." *Journal of Interpersonal Violence* 23 (12): 1667–93.

Grabb, Edward. 1994. "Democratic values in Canada and the United States: Some observations and evidence from the past and present." In J. Dermer, ed., *The Canadian Profile: People, Institutions, and Infrastructure*, 113–39. Toronto: Captus Press.

———. 2007. *Theories of Social Inequality*. 5th edn. Toronto: Thomson Nelson.

——— and James Curtis. 2002. "Comparing central political values in the Canadian and American democracies." In D. Baer, ed., *Political Sociology: Canadian Perspectives*, 37–54. Don Mills, ON: Oxford University Press.

Granovetter, Mark S. 1974. *Getting a Job: A Study of Contacts and Careers*. Cambridge, MA: Harvard University Press.

Grant, Nina, Mark Hamer, and Andrew Steptoe. 2009. "Social isolation and stress-related cardiovascular, lipid, and cortisol responses." *Annals of Behavioural Medicine* 37: 29–37.

Gray, Gary, and Neil Guppy. 2008. *Successful Surveys: Research Methods and Practice*. 4th edn. Toronto: Nelson Thomson.

Grazian, David. 2010. "Neoliberalism and the realities of reality television." *Contexts* 9 (2): 68–71.

Greer, Germaine. 1984. *Sex and Destiny: The Politics of Human Fertility*. London: Martin Secker and Warburg.

Griffin, Wendy. 2000. "The embodied goddess: Feminist witchcraft and female divinity." In S.C. Monahan, W.A. Mirola, and M.O. Emerson, eds., *Sociology of Religion: A Reader*. New York: Prentice-Hall/Penguin Putman.

Griffiths, M. 2001. "Sex on the Internet: Observations and implications for Internet sex addiction." *Journal of Sex Research* 38 (4): 333–42.

Grossman, D. 2009. *On Killing: The Psychological Cost of Learning to Kill in War and Society*. New York: Back Bay Books.

Guppy, Neil, and Scott Davies. 1998. *Education in Canada: Recent Trends and Future Challenges*. Ottawa: Statistics Canada.

Gusfield, J.R. 1975. *Community: A Critical Response*. New York: Harper and Row.

Hackett, Robert A., and Richard Gruneau. 2000. *The Missing News: Filters and Blind Spots in Canada's Press*. Aurora, ON: Garamond.

Hackett, Robert A., Richard Pinet, and Myles Ruggles. 1996. "News for whom: Hegemony and monopoly versus democracy in Canadian media." In Helen Holmes and David Taras, eds, *Seeing Ourselves: Media Power and Policy in Canada*, 2nd edn, 257–72. Toronto: Harcourt Brace Canada.

Hackett, Robert A., and Scott Uzelman. 2003. "Tracing corporate influences on press content: A summary of recent NewsWatch Canada research." *Journalism Studies* 4 (3): 331–46.

Hall, Emmett. 1964–5. *Report of the Royal Commission on Health Services*. Ottawa: Queen's Printer.

Hall, Stuart. 1980. "Encoding/decoding." In Stuart Hall, Dorothy Hobson, Andrew Lowe, and Paul Willis, eds, *Culture, Media, Language: Working Papers in Cultural Studies, 1972–79*, 128–38. London: Hutchinson.

Haluza-Delay, R. 2007. "Environmental justice in Canada." *Local Environment* 12 (6): 557–64.

——— P. O'Riley, P. Cole, and J. Agyeman. 2009. "Introduction." In J. Agyeman, P. Cole, R. Haluza-DeLay, and R. O'Riley, eds., *Speaking for Ourselves: Environmental Justice in Canada*, 1–26. Vancouver: University of British Columbia Press.

Hamilton, Roberta. 1978. *The Liberation of Women*. London: Allen and Unwin.

——— 2005 [1996]. *Gendering the Vertical Mosaic: Feminist Perspectives on Canadian Society*. 2nd edn. Toronto: Pearson.

Han, Chong-suk. 2007. "They don't want to cruise your type: Gay men of colour and the racial politics of exclusion." *Social Identities* 13 (1): 51–67.

Handa, A. 2003. *Of Silk Saris and Mini-Skirts South Asian*. Toronto: Women's Press.

Harper, C.L., and T.H. Fletcher. 2011. *Environment and Society: Human Perspectives on Environmental Issues*. Canadian edn. Toronto: Pearson Canada.

Harris, C.D., and E.L. Ullman. 1945. "The nature of cities." *Annals of the American Academy of Political and Social Science* 242 (1): 7–17.

Harvey, David. 1985. *The Urbanization of Capital: Studies in the History and Theory of Capitalist Urbanization.* Baltimore, MD: Johns Hopkins University Press.

———. 1990. *The Condition of Postmodernity: An Enquiry into the Origins of Cultural Change.* Oxford: Blackwell.

Hathaway, A.D. 2004. "Cannabis users' informal rules for managing stigma and risk." *Deviant Behavior* 25 (6): 559–77.

Hauser, P.M., and O.D. Duncan. 1959. *The Study of Population: An Inventory and Appraisal.* Chicago: University of Chicago Press.

Hay, D.I. 2009. *Poverty Reduction Policies and Programs.* Social Development Report Series. Ottawa: Canadian Council on Social Development.

Hayford, Alison. 1992. "From Chicago 1966 to Montreal 1989: Notes on new(s) paradigms of women as victims." In Marc Grenier, ed., *Critical Studies of Canadian Mass Media,* 201–12. Markham, ON: Butterworths.

Health Canada. 2002. *A Report on Mental Illness in Canada.* Ottawa: Health Canada.

———. 2009. "Canadian alcohol and drug use monitoring survey." www.hc-sc.gc.ca/hc-ps/drugs-drogues/cadums-esccad-eng.php.

Hearn, Jeff, and Wendy Parkin. 1987. *"Sex" and "Work": The Power and Paradox of Organizational Sexuality.* New York: St Martin's.

Heckman, James J., and Alan B. Krueger. 2004. *Inequality in America: What Role for Human Capital Policies?* Cambridge, MA: MIT Press.

Helland, Christopher. 2007. "Diaspora on the electronic frontier: Developing virtual connections with sacred homelands." *Journal of Computer-Mediated Communication* 12 (3). http://jcmc.indiana.edu/vol12/issue3/helland.html.

Helmes-Hayes, Rick. 2002. "John Porter: Canada's most famous sociologist (and his links to American sociology)." *American Sociologist* 33 (1): 79–104.

———. 2009. *Measuring the Mosaic: An Intellectual Biography of John Porter.* Toronto: University of Toronto Press.

——— and James Curtis, eds. 1998. *The Vertical Mosaic Revisited: Social Inequality and Social Justice in Canada, 1965–1995.* Toronto: University of Toronto Press.

Henry, Frances, and Effie Ginzberg. 1985. *Who Gets the Work: A Test of Racial Discrimination in Employment.* Toronto: Urban Alliance on Race Relations and Social Planning Directorate.

Henry, Frances, and Carol Tator. 2005. *The Colour of Democracy: Racism in Canadian Society.* 3rd edn. Toronto: Thomson Nelson.

Hewitt, Christopher. 1994. "The dog that didn't bark: The political consequences of separatist violence in Quebec, 1963–70." *Conflict Quarterly* 14 (1): 9–29.

Hey, Shereen. 1997. *The Company She Keeps: An Ethnography of Girls' Friendships.* Buckingham, UK: Open University Press.

Heynen, N., J. McCarthy, S. Prudham, and P. Robbins. 2007. "Introduction: False promises." In N. Heynen, S. Prudham, and Paul Robbins, eds., *Neoliberal Environments: False Promises and Unnatural Consequences,* 1–21. New York: Routledge.

Hickman, B. 1998. "Men wise up to bald truth." *Australian* 21 (May): 4.

Hilgartner, Stephen, and Charles Bosk. 1988. "The rise and fall of social problems: A public arenas model." *American Journal of Sociology* 94: 53–78.

Hirschi, Travis. 1969. *Causes of Delinquency.* Berkeley: University of California Press.

Hochschild, Arlie. 1983. *The Managed Heart: Commercialization of Human Feeling.* Berkeley: University of California Press.

———. 1989. *The Second Shift: Working Parents and the Revolution at Home.* New York: Viking Penguin.

———. 1997. *The Time Bind: When Work Becomes Home and Home Becomes Work.* New York: Metropolitan Books.

Hodson, Randy. 2001. *Dignity at Work.* Cambridge: Cambridge University Press.

Hoffer, Thomas B. 2008. "Accountability in education." In Maureen T. Hallinan, ed., *Handbook of the Sociology of Education,* 529–44. New York: Springer.

Holmes, Malcolm D., and Judith A. Antell. 2001. "The social construction of American Indian drinking: Perceptions of American Indian and white officials." *Sociological Quarterly* 42: 151–73.

Holstein, James A., and Gale Miller. 2006. *Reconsidering Social Constructionism: Debates in Social Problems Theory.* New York: Aldine de Gruyter.

Hoodfar, Homa. 2003. "More than clothing: Veiling as an adaptive strategy." In S.S. Alvi, H. Hoodfar, and S. McDonough, eds., *The Muslim Veil in North America: Issues and Debates.* Toronto: Women's Press.

Hope, Steven, Chris Power, and Bryan Rodgers. 1998. "The relationship between parental separation in childhood and problem drinking in adulthood." *Addiction* 93 (4): 505–14.

Horkheimer, Max, and Theodor Adorno. 2006. "The culture industry: Enlightenment as mass deception." In Meenakshi Gigi Durham and Douglas M. Kellner, eds, *Media and Cultural Studies: Key Works,* rev. edn. Malden, MA: Blackwell.

Horton, A. 2013. "Flesh hook pulling: Motivations and meaning-making from the 'body side' of life." *Deviant Behavior* 34: 115–34.

Howard, P.N., A. Duffy, D. Freelon, M. Hussain, W. Mari, and M. Mazaid. 2011. "Opening closed regimes: What was the role of social media during the Arab Spring?" In *Project on Information Technology and Political Islam Working Paper,* University of Washington, Dept of Communication.

Howard-Hassmann, Rhoda. 1999. "'Canadian' as an ethnic category: Implications for multiculturalism and national unity." *Canadian Public Policy* 25 (4).

Hoyt, H. 1939. *The Structure and Growth of Residential Neighborhoods in American Cities.* Washington: Federal Housing Administration.

Hughes, Everett. 1945. "Dilemmas and contradictions of status." *American Journal of Sociology* 50: 353–9.

Hughes, Karen. 2005. "The adult children of divorce: Pure relationships and family values?" *Journal of Sociology* 41 (1): 69–86.

Hughes, Melanie M., Lindsey Peterson, Jill A. Harrison, and Pamela Paxton. 2009. "Power and relation in the world polity: The INGO network country score, 1978–1998." *Social Forces* 87 (4): 32.

Hugill, Peter J. 1995. *World Trade since 1431: Geography, Technology, and Capitalism*. Baltimore, MD: Johns Hopkins University Press.

Human Resources and Skills Development Canada (HRSDC). 2007. *Advancing the Inclusion of People with Disabilities—Chapter 3: Income Support, Benefits and Service Delivery*. www.hrsdc.gc.ca/eng/disability_issues/reports/fdr/20007/page05.shtml.

———. 2012. *Indicators of Well-being in Canada*. www4.hrsdc.gc.ca/.3ndic.1t.4r@-eng.jsp?iid = 35.

Humphreys, Laud. 1970. *Tearoom Trade: Impersonal Sex in Public Places*. Chicago: Aldine.

Ihinger-Tallman, Marilyn, and David Levinson. 2003. Definition of marriage, rev. by J.M. White. In J. Ponzetti, Jr, ed., *International Encyclopedia of Marriage and Family*, 2nd edn. New York: Macmillan Reference and Thomson Gale.

Illich, Ivan. 1976. *Limits to Medicine*. Toronto: McClelland and Stewart.

Imershein, Allen W., and Carroll L. Estes. 1996. "From health services to medical markets: The commodity transformation of medical production and the non-profit sector." *International Journal of Health Services* 26: 221–38.

Imig, Doug, and Sidney Tarrow. 2001. "Mapping the Europeanization of contention: Evidence from a quantitative data analysis." In Doug Imig and Sidney Tarrow, eds, *Contentious Europeans: Protest and Politics in an Emerging Polity*, 27–49. New York: Rowman and Littlefield.

Inglehart, Ronald. 1990. "Values, ideology, and cognitive mobilization in new social movements." In R.J. Dalton and M. Kuechler, eds, *Challenging the Political Order*, 23–42. New York: Oxford University Press.

Ingram, R.J., and S. Hinduja. 2008. "Neutralizing music piracy: An empirical examination." *Deviant Behavior* 29 (4): 334–66.

International Organization for Migration. 2012. *Facts and Figures*. Geneva: International Organization for Migration.

Ipsos Reid. 2010. "Weekly Internet usage overtakes television watching." www.ipsos-na.com/news-polls/pressrelease.

Irvine, Janice. 2003. "'The sociologist as voyeur': Social theory and sexual research, 1910–1978." *Qualitative Sociology* 26 (4): 429–56.

Jackson, Andrew. 2009. *Work and Labour in Canada: Critical Issues*. 2nd edn. Toronto: Canadian Scholars Press.

——— and David Robinson. 2000. *Falling Behind: The State of Working Canada, 2000*. Ottawa: Canadian Centre for Policy Alternatives.

Jakobsen, Janet R., and Ann Pellegrini. 2004. *Love the Sin: Sexual Regulation and the Limits of Religious Tolerance*. New York: Beacon Press.

James, Daniel Lee, and Elizabeth A. Craft. 2002. "Protecting one's self from a stigmatized disease . . . once one has it." *Deviant Behavior* 23: 267–99.

James, William Closson. 2012. "Dimorphs and cobbles: Ways of being religious in Canada." In L.G. Beaman, ed., *Religion and Canadian Society: Traditions, Transitions and Innovations*, 2nd edn, 55–68. Toronto: Canadian Scholars Press.

Jamieson, Lynn. 1998. *Intimacy: Personal Relationships in Modern Societies*. Cambridge: Polity Press.

Janis, Irving Lester. 1982. *Groupthink: Psychological Studies of Policy Decisions and Fiascos*. 2nd edn. Boston: Houghton Mifflin.

Jenson, Jane, and Denis Saint-Martin. 2003. "New routes to social cohesion? Citizenship and the social investment state." *Canadian Journal of Sociology* 28 (1): 77–99.

Joanisse, Leanne. 2005. "'This is who I really am': Obese women's conceptions of self following weight loss surgery." In Dorothy Pawluch, William Shaffir, and Charlene Miall, eds, *Doing Ethnography: Studying Everyday Life*, 248–59. Toronto: Canadian Scholars Press.

Johnson, Carol. 2002. "Heteronormative citizenship and the politics of passing." *Sexualities* 5 (3): 317–36.

Johnson, Holly. 1996. *Dangerous Domains: Violence against Women in Canada*. Toronto: Nelson.

Johnston, Josée, and Shyon Bauman. 2009. *Foodies: Democracy and Distinction in the Gourmet Foodscape*. New York: Routledge.

Jones, Jennifer M., Susan Bennett, Marion P. Olmsted, Margaret L. Lawson, and Gary Rodin. 2001. "Disordered eating attitudes and behaviours in teenaged girls: A school-based study." *Canadian Medical Association Journal* 165: 547–52.

Joyce, James. 1968 [1922]. *Ulysses*. Harmondsworth, UK: Penguin.

Kachur, Jerrold L., and Trevor W. Harrison. 1999. "Introduction: Public education, globalization, and democracy: Whither Alberta?" In Trevor W. Harrison and Jerrold L. Kachur, eds, *Contested Classrooms: Education, Globalization, and Democracy in Alberta*, XIII–XXXV. Edmonton: University of Alberta Press and Parkland Institute.

Karakayali, Nedim. 2005. "Duality and diversity in the lives of immigrant children: Rethinking the 'problem of the second generation' in light of immigrant autobiographies." *Canadian Review of Sociology and Anthropology* 42 (2): 325–43.

Karim, Karim H. 2002. "Globalization, communication, and diaspora." In Paul Attallah and Leslie Regan Shade, eds, *Mediascapes: New Patterns in Canadian Communication*, 272–94. Scarborough, ON: Thomson Nelson.

———. 2008. "Press, public sphere, and pluralism: Multiculturalism debates in Canadian English-language newspapers." *Canadian Ethnic Studies* 40 (1): 57–78.

Karmis, Demetrios. 2004. "Pluralism and national identity(ies) in contemporary Quebec: Conceptual clarifications, typology, and discourse analysis." In Alain-G. Gagnon, ed., *Quebec: State and Society*, 69–96. Peterborough, ON: Broadview.

Käsler, Dirk. 1988. *Max Weber: An Introduction to His Life and Work*. Chicago: University of Chicago Press.

Kassebaum, Donald G., and Ellen R. Cutler. 1998. "On the culture of student abuse in medical school." *Academic Medicine* 73: 1149–58.

Katz, M. 1989. *The Undeserving Poor*. New York: Pantheon.

Katzmarzyk, Peter T. 2002. "The Canadian obesity epidemic: 1995–1998." *Canadian Medical Association Journal* 166: 1039–40.

Kay, Jonathan. 2011. "Jonathan Kay on Canada's anti-polygamy law: The B.C. Supreme Court gets it right." *National Post*. November 23. http://fullcomment.nationalpost .com/2011/11/23/jonathan-kay-on-canadas-anti-polygamy-law-the-bc-supreme-court-gets-it-right.

Kearney, Patrick. 1982. *A History of Erotic Literature*. Hong Kong: Parragin Books.

Keil, Roger, and Julie-Anne Boudreau. 2006. "Metropolitics and metabolics: Rolling out environmentalism in Toronto." In Nik Heynen, Maria Kaika, and Erik Swyngedouw, eds, *In the Nature of Cities: Urban Political Ecology and the Politics of Urban Metabolism*, 41–62. London and New York: Routledge.

Kempadoo, Kamala, and Jo Doezema, eds. 1998. *Global Sex Workers: Rights, Resistance, and Redefinition*. New York: Routledge.

Kennedy, Emily H., and Sara O'Shaughnessy. 2010. *Relational Activism: Gender and Environment Reconsidered*. Presentation to the Canadian Sociological Association, 31 May.

Kenway, Jane, and Helen Modra. 1992. "Feminist pedagogy and emancipatory possibilities." In Carmen Luke and Jennifer Gore, eds, *Feminisms and Critical Pedagogy*, 138–66. London: Routledge.

Kerstetter, Steve. 2009. *The Affordability Gap: Spending Differences between Canada's Rich and Poor*. Ottawa: Canadian Centre for Policy Alternatives.

Kessler, R.C., P. Berglund, O. Demler, R. Jin, K.R. Merikangas, and E.E. Walters. 2005. "Lifetime prevalence and age-of-onset distributions of DSM-IV disorders in the National Comorbidity Survey replication." *Archive of General Psychiatry* 62: 593–602.

Kielburger, Craig, and Marc Kielburger. 2011. "Global voices: First Nations education is a national crisis." *Toronto Star* 18 April. www .thestar.com/news/globalvoices/ article/975437--global-voices-first-nations-education-is-a-national-crisis.

Kiernan, Kathleen. 1997. *The Legacy of Parental Divorce: Social, Economic, and Demographic Experiences in Adulthood*. London: Centre for Analysis of Social Exclusion.

Killingsworth, B. 2006. "'Drinking stories' from a playgroup: Alcohol in the lives of middle-class mothers in Australia." *Ethnography* 7 (3): 357–84.

Kim, Sujeong. 2004. "Rereading David Morley's *The 'Nationwide' Audience*." *Cultural Studies* 18 (1): 84–108.

King, Anthony. 1995. "Globalization, modernity and the spatialization of social theory: An introduction." In M. Featherstone, S. Lash, R. Robertson, eds, *Global Modernities*. Thousand Oaks, CA: Sage.

King, Samantha. 2006. *Pink Ribbons, Inc*. Minneapolis: University of Minnesota Press.

Kipfer, Stefan, and Roger Keil. 2002. "Toronto Inc? Planning the competitive city in the new Toronto." *Antipode* 34 (2): 227–64.

Kitschelt, Herbert. 1993. "Social movements, political parties, and democratic theory." *Annals of the American Academy of Political and Social Science* 528 (July): 13–29.

Klein, David M., and James M. White. 1996. *Family Theories: An Introduction*. Thousand Oaks, CA: Sage.

Kohlberg, Lawrence. 1969. "Stage and sequence: The cognitive-development approach to socialization." In David A. Goslin, ed., *Handbook of Socialization: Theory and Research*, 347–80. Chicago: Rand McNally.

———. 1975. "Moral education for a society in moral transition." *Educational Leadership* 33: 46–54.

Krane, Julia. 2003. *What's Mother Got to Do with It? Protecting Children from Sexual Abuse*. Toronto: University of Toronto Press.

Kymlicka, Will. 1998. "The theory and practice of Canadian multiculturalism." *Canadian Federation of the Social Sciences and Humanities* 23 (Nov.): 1–10. www.fedcan.ca/ english/fromold/breakfast-kymlicka1198.cfm.

Lancet. 2003. "Slavery today." 361: 2093.

Langlois, S., and P. Morrison. 2002. "Suicide deaths and suicide attempts." *Health Reports* 13 (2): 9–22.

Laufer, William S., and Freda Adler. 1994. *The Legacy of Anomie Theory: Advances in Criminological Theory*. New Brunswick, NJ: Transaction.

Lauzen, Martha M. 2011. *The Celluloid Ceiling: Behind-the-Scenes Employment of Women on the Top 250 Films of 2010*. San Diego: Center for the Study of Women in Television and Film, School of Theatre, Television and Film, San Diego State University.

Lawr, Douglas, and Robert Gidney, eds. 1973. *Educating Canadians: A Documentary History of Public Education*. Toronto: Van Nostrand Reinhold.

Leavitt, L., and N. Fox, eds. 1993. *The Psychological Effects of War and Violence on Children*. Mahwah, NJ: Lawrence Erlbaum Associates.

Lefebvre, Solange. 2008. "Between law and public opinion: The case of Québec." In Lori G. Beaman and Peter Beyer, eds, *Religion and Diversity in Canada*. Leiden: Brill.

Lehmann, Wolfgang. 2007. "'I just didn't feel like I fit in': The role of habitus in university drop-out decisions." *Canadian Journal of Higher Education* 37 (2).

Lemert, Edwin. 1951. *Social Pathology: A Systematic Approach to the Theory of Sociopathic Behavior*. New York: McGraw-Hill.

Lemish, Dafna, and May Götz, eds. 2007. *Children and Media in Times of Conflict*. Cresskill, NJ: Hampton Press.

Levin, Benjamin. 2007. "Schools, poverty, and the achievement gap." *Phi Delta Kappan* 89 (1): 75–6.

——— and J. Anthony Riffel. 1997. *Schools and the Changing World: Struggling Toward the Future.* London: Falmer.

Levin, J., and E. Madfis. 2009. "Mass murder at school and cumulative strain: A sequential model." *American Behavioral Scientist* 52 (9): 1227–45.

Levitas, Ruth. 1998. *The Inclusive Society? Social Exclusion and New Labour.* Basingstoke, UK: Macmillan.

Lewchuk, Wayne, and David Robertson. 2006. "Listening to workers: The reorganization of work in the Canadian motor vehicle industry." In Vivian Shalla, ed., *Working in a Global Era: Canadian Perspectives*, 53–73. Toronto: Canadian Scholars Press.

Lewicki, Roy J., and Barbara Benedict Bunker. 1996. "Developing and maintaining trust in work relationships." In Roderick M. Kramer and Tom R. Tyler, eds, *Trust in Organizations: Frontiers of Theory and Research*, 114–39. Thousand Oaks, CA: Sage.

Lewis, Charles. 2011. "B.C. polygamy ruling offers 'road map' to avoid prosecution: Lawyer." *National Post* 23 November. http://news.nationalpost.com/2011/11/23/b-c-polygamy-ruling-offers-road-map-to-avoid-prosecution-lawyer.

Lewis, Oscar. 1996 [1966]. "The culture of poverty." In G. Gmelch and W. Zenner, eds, *Urban Life.* Long Grove, IL: Waveland Press.

Ley, D., and C. Dobson. 2008. "Are there limits to gentrification? The contexts of impeded gentrification in Vancouver. *Urban Studies* 45 (12): 2471–98.

Li, Peter. 1988. *Ethnic Inequality in a Class Society.* Toronto: Thompson Educational Publishing.

———. 1992. "Race and gender as bases of class fractions and the effects on earnings." *Canadian Review of Sociology and Anthropology* 29 (4): 488–510.

———, ed. 1999. *Race and Ethnic Relations in Canada.* 2nd edn. Toronto: Oxford University Press.

———. 2003. *Destination Canada: Immigration Debates and Issues.* Toronto: Oxford University Press.

Lian, Jason Z., and Ralph Matthews. 1998. "Does the vertical mosaic still exist? Ethnicity and income in Canada, 1991." *Canadian Review of Sociology and Anthropology* 35 (4): 461–81.

Limoncelli, Stephanie. 2009. "The trouble with trafficking: Conceptualizing women's sexual labor and economic human rights." *Women's Studies International Forum* 32 (4): 261–9.

Lindner, R. 1996. *The Reportage of Urban Culture: Robert Park and the Chicago School.* Cambridge: Cambridge University Press.

Lindsay, Colin. 2008a. "Canadians attend weekly religious services less than 20 years ago." Catalogue no. 89-630-X. *The General Social Survey*, Matter of Fact no. 3. Ottawa: Statistics Canada.

———. 2008b. "Are women spending more time on unpaid domestic work than men in Canada?" Catalogue 89-630-X. *The General Social Survey*, Matter of Fact. Ottawa: Statistics Canada.

Lindsey, L., and S. Beach. 2003. *Essentials of Sociology.* Upper Saddle River, NJ: Prentice-Hall.

Liodakis, Nikolaos. 1998. "The activities of Hellenic-Canadian secular organizations in the context of Canadian multiculturalism." *Études helléniques/Hellenic Studies* 6 (1): 37–58.

———. 2002. "The vertical mosaic within: Class, gender and nativity within ethnicity." (PhD dissertation, McMaster University, Hamilton, ON).

———. 2009. "The social class and gender differences within Aboriginal groups in Canada: 1995–2000." In Dan Beavon and Daniel Jetté, eds., "Journeys of a generation: Broadening the Aboriginal well-being policy research agenda." *Canadian Issues Journal* (winter): 93–7. Montreal: Association for Canadian Studies.

——— and Victor Satzewich. 2003. "From solution to problem: Multiculturalism and 'race relations' as new social problems." In Wayne Antony and Les Samuelson, eds, *Power and Resistance: Critical Thinking about Canadian Social Issues*, 3rd edn, 145–68. Halifax: Fernwood.

Lipman, Ellen L., David R. Offord, and Martin D. Dooley. 1996. "What do we know about children from single-parent families? Questions and answers from the National Longitudinal Survey on Children." In *Growing Up in Canada*, 83–91. Ottawa: Human Resources Development Canada.

Lipset, Seymour Martin. 1963. "The value patterns of democracy: A case study in comparative analysis." *American Sociological Review* 28 (4): 515–31.

———. 1964. "Canada and the United States: A comparative view." *Canadian Review of Sociology* 1 (4): 173–85.

———. 1990. *Continental Divide: The Values and Institutions of the United States and Canada.* New York: Routledge.

———. 1991. "Canada and the United States: The great divide." *Current History* 90 (560): 432–7.

Livingstone, D.W. 2004. *The Education–Jobs Gap: Underemployment or Economic Democracy.* Aurora, ON: Garamond.

Logan, John, and Harvey Molotch. 1987. *Urban Fortunes: The Political Economy of Place.* Berkeley: University of California Press.

Lopez, S.H., R. Hodson, and V.J. Roscigno. 2009. "Power, status, and abuse at work: General and sexual harassment compared." *Sociological Quarterly* 50 (1): 3–27.

Lorimer, Rowland, and Mike Gasher. 2001. *Mass Communication in Canada.* 4th edn. Toronto: Oxford University Press.

Loseke, Donileen R. 2003. *Thinking about Social Problems: An Introduction to Constructionist Perspectives.* New York: Aldine de Gruyter.

Lowe, Graham S. 2000. *The Quality of Work: A People-Centred Agenda.* Toronto: Oxford University Press.

Lu, Yuqian, and René Morissette. 2010. "Women's participation and economic downturns." Catalogue 75-001-X. *Perspectives* (May): 18–22. Ottawa: Statistics Canada.

Luckenbill, David F. 1977. "Criminal homicide as a situational transaction." *Social Problems* 25: 176–86.

Lukes, Steven. 1972. *Émile Durkheim: His Life and Work*. New York: Harper and Row.

———. 1974. *Power: A Radical View*. London: Macmillan.

Luong, May. 2011. "The wealth and finances of employed low-income families." *Perspectives on Labour and Income* 22 July: 3–13.

Luxton, Meg. 1980. *More Than a Labour of Love*. Toronto: Women's Press.

——— and June Corman. 2001. *Getting by in Hard Times: Gendered Labour at Home and on the Job*. Toronto: University of Toronto Press.

Lynch, Kathleen. 1989. *The Hidden Curriculum· Reproduction in Education: A Reappraisal*. London: Falmer.

Lynn, Michael. 2009. "Determinants and consequences of female attractiveness and sexiness: Realistic tests with restaurant waitresses." *Archives of Sexual Behavior* 38: (5) 737–45.

MacAlpine, Karen. 2005. "Ask and you shall receive: An exploration of salary expectations and the gendered earnings gap in Canada." (Unpublished MA thesis, Dalhousie University, Halifax).

McCarthy, John D. 1996. "Constraints and opportunities in adopting, adapting, and inventing." In Doug McAdam, John McCarthy, and Mayer Zald, eds, *Comparative Perspectives on Social Movements*, 141–51. New York: Cambridge University Press.

Macek, S. 2006. *Urban Nightmares*. Minneapolis: University of Minnesota Press.

McGahan, P. 1995. *Urban Sociology in Canada*. 3rd edn. Toronto: Harcourt Brace.

McGuire, Meredith. 2005. *Rethinking Sociology's Sacred/Profane Dichotomy: Historically Contested Boundaries in Western Christianity*. Paper presented at SISR/ISSR, Zagreb.

Macionis, J.J. 1997. *Society: The Basics*. 4th edn. Upper Saddle River, NJ: Prentice Hall.

McKenna, K., A. Green, and M. Gleason. 2002. "Relationship formation on the Internet: What's the big attraction?" *Journal of Social Issues* 58 (1): 9–31.

Mackenzie, Hugh. 2007. *Timing Is Everything: Comparing the Earnings of Canada's Highest-Paid CEOs and the Rest of Us*. Toronto: Canadian Centre for Policy Alternatives.

McKenzie, Roderick D. 1967 [1925]. "The ecological approach to the study of human community." In Robert Park, Ernest W. Burgess, and Roderick D. McKenzie, eds, *The City*. Chicago: University of Chicago Press.

Macklin, Audrey. 1992. "Foreign domestic worker: Surrogate housewife or mail order bride?" *McGill Law Journal* 37: 681–760.

McLaren, Angus. 1990. *Our Own Master Race: Eugenics in Canada, 1885–1945*. Toronto: McClelland and Stewart.

McLaren, Peter, and Joe L. Kincheloe, eds. 2007. *Critical Pedagogy: Where Are We Now?* New York: Peter Lang.

McQuaig, Linda, and Neil Brooks. 2010. *The Trouble with Billionaires*. Toronto: Viking Canada.

Magder, Ted. 1993. *Canada's Hollywood: The Canadian State and Feature Films*. Toronto: University of Toronto Press.

——— and Jonathan Burston. 2001. "Whose Hollywood? Changing forms and relations inside the North American entertainment economy." In Vincent Mosco and Dan Schiller, eds, *Continental Order? Integrating North America for Cybercapitalism*, 207–34. Lanham, MD: Rowman and Littlefield.

Maguire, Patrick. 2006. *Choice in Urban School Districts: The Edmonton Experience*. Kelowna, BC: Society for the Advancement of Excellence in Education.

Mahtani, Minelle. 2001. "Representing minorities: Canadian media and minority identities." *Canadian Ethnic Studies* 33 (3): 99–133.

Malthus, Thomas R. 1970 [1798]. *An Essay on the Principle of Population*. Harmondsworth, UK: Penguin.

Mann, Michael. 1999. *The Dark Side of Democracy*. Cambridge: Cambridge University Press.

———. 2004. *Fascists*. Cambridge: Cambridge University Press.

Manzer, Ronald. 1994. *Public Schools and Political Ideas: Canadian Educational Policy in Historical Perspective*. Toronto: University of Toronto Press.

Maquiladora Solidarity Network. 2010. http://en.maquilasolidarity.org.

Maratea, R.J. 2011. "Screwing the pooch: Legitimizing accounts in a zoophilia on-line community." *Deviant Behavior* 32 (10): 918–43.

Marcil-Gratton, Nicole. 1998. *Growing up with Mom and Dad? The Intricate Family Life Courses of Canadian Children*. Ottawa: Statistics Canada.

Marcus, Sheron. 2005. "Queer theory for everyone: A review essay." *Signs* 31 (1): 191–218.

Markin, K.M. 2005. "Still crazy after all these years: The enduring defamatory power of mental disorder." *Law and Psychology Review* 29: 155–85.

Marmot, Michael G., Geffrey Rose, Martin Shipley, and P.J. Hamilton. 1978. "Employment grade and coronary heart disease in British civil servants." *Journal of Epidemiological Community Health* 32: 244–9.

Marmot, Michael G., George Davey Smith, Stephen Stansfeld, Chandra Patel, Fiona North, Jenny Head, Ian White, Eric Brunner, and Amanda Feeney. 1991. "Health inequalities among British civil servants: The Whitehall II Study." *Lancet* 337: 1387–93.

Marshall, K. 2006. "Converging gender roles." *Perspectives on Labour and Income* 7 (7): 5–17. Ottawa: Statistics Canada.

Marx, Karl. 1967 [1867]. *Capital: A Critical Analysis of Capitalist Production*. ed. Friedrich Engels. London: Lowry.

——— and Friedrich Engels. 1985 [1848]. *The Communist Manifesto*. New York: Penguin Books.

Maslovski, Mikhail. 1996. "Max Weber's concept of patrimonialism and the Soviet system." *Sociological Review* 44: 294–308.

Mead, George Herbert. 1934. *Mind, Self, and Society from the Standpoint of a Social Behaviorist*. Chicago: University of Chicago Press.

Melucci, Alerbero. 1989. *Nomads of the Present: Social Movements and Individual Needs in Contemporary Society*. Philadelphia: Temple University Press.

Mendelson, M. 2006. *Aboriginal Peoples and Postsecondary Education in Canada*. Ottawa: Caledon Institute of Social Policy.

Merton, Robert K. 1938. "Social structure and anomie." *American Sociological Review* 3: 672–82.

————. 1957. *Social Theory and Social Structure*. Glencoe, IL, New York: Free Press.

Meyer, John W. 2007. "Globalization: Theory and trends." *International Journal of Comparative Sociology* 48 (4): 261–73.

————, John Boli, George M. Thomas, and Francisco Ramirez. 1997. "World society and the nation state." *American Journal of Sociology* 103 (1): 144–81.

Mikkonen, J., and D. Raphael. 2010. *Social Determinants of Health: The Canadian Facts*. Toronto: York University, Health Policy and Management. www.thecanadianfacts.org.

Milan, Anne, Leslie-Anne Keown, and Covadonga Robles Urquijo. 2011. "Families, living arrangements and unpaid work." In *Women in Canada: A Gender-Based Statistical Report*. Catalogue no. 89-503-X. Ottawa: Statistics Canada.

Milan, Anne, and Mireille Vezina. 2011. "Senior women." In *Women in Canada: A Gender-Based Statistical Report*. Catalogue # 89-503-X. Ottawa: Statistics Canada.

Miles, Robert, and Malcolm Brown. 2003. *Racism*. 2nd edn. London: Routledge.

Miles, Robert, and Rudy Torres. 1996. "Does 'race' matter? Transatlantic perspectives on racism after 'race relations.'" In V. Amit-Talai and C. Knowles, eds, *Re-situating Identities: The Politics of Race, Ethnicity and Culture*, 24–46. Peterborough, ON: Broadview.

Miller, Gale, and James A. Holstein. 1993. *Constructionist Controversies: Issues in Social Problems Theory*. New York: Aldine de Gruyter.

Miller, Toby, Nitin Govil, John McMurria, and Richard Maxwell. 2001. *Global Hollywood*. London: British Film Institute.

Millett, Kate. 1969. *Sexual Politics*. New York: Doubleday; Avon.

Mills, C. Wright. 1940. "Situated actions and vocabularies of motive." *American Sociological Review* 5 (6): 904–13.

————. 1956. *The Power Elite*. New York: Oxford University Press.

————. 1959. *The Sociological Imagination*. New York: Oxford University Press.

Mitchell, Andrew, and Richard Shillington. 2002. "Poverty, inequality and social inclusion." In Working Paper Series, VII–18. Toronto: Laidlaw Foundation.

Mitchell, Barbara A. 2006. *The Boomerang Age: Transitions to Adulthood in Families*. New Brunswick, NJ: Aldine Transaction.

Monsebraaten, Laurie. 2011. "Canada urged to invest in poor." *Toronto Star* 28 September: A12.

Montpetit, Eric, Francesca Scala, and Isabelle Fortier. 2004. "The paradox of deliberative democracy: The National Action Committee on the Status of Women and Canada's policy on reproductive technology." *Policy Sciences* 37: 137–57.

Montpetit, Jonathan. 2010. "Quebec woman barred from course for second time over refusal to remove niqab." *Winnipeg Free Press*. www.winnipegfreepress.com/canada/breakingnews/quebec-government-kicks-niqab-wearing-woman-out-of-class-for-second-time-87125232.html.

Moodley, Kogila. 1983. "Canadian multiculturalism as ideology." *Ethnic and Racial Studies* 6 (3): 320–31.

Morley, David. 1980. *The "Nationwide" Audience*. London: British Film Institute.

————. 2006. "Unanswered questions in audience research." *Communication Review* 9: 101–21.

Morris, R.G., and G.E. Higgins. 2009. "Neutralizing potential and self-reported digital piracy: A multitheoretical exploration among college undergraduates." *Criminal Justice Review* 34 (2): 173–95.

Mosco, Vincent. 1989. *The Pay-per Society: Computers and Communication in the Information Age*. Toronto: Garamond.

————. 2005. "Here today, outsourced tomorrow: Knowledge workers in the global economy." *Javnost—The Public* 12 (2): 39–55.

Moynihan, Ray, Iona Heath, and David Henry. 2002. "Selling sickness: The pharmaceutical industry and disease mongering." *British Medical Journal* 324: 886–91.

Multani v. Commission scolaire Marguerite-Bourgeoys. 2006. 1 S.C.R. 256, 2006 SCC 6.

Mustard, Fraser. 1999. "Health care and social cohesion." In Daniel Drache and Terry Sullivan, eds, *Market Limits in Health Reform: Public Success, Private Failure*, 329–50. London: Routledge.

Nakhaie, M. Reza, ed. 1999. *Debates on Social Inequality: Class, Gender and Ethnicity in Canada*. Toronto: Harcourt Canada.

————. 2000. "Ownership and management position of Canadian ethnic groups in 1973 and 1989." In Madeline A. Kalbach and Warren Kalbach, eds, *Perspectives on Ethnicity in Canada*. Toronto: Harcourt Canada.

————. 2002. "Class, breadwinner ideology and housework among Canadian husbands." *Review of Radical Political Economics* 34 (2): 137–57.

————. 2007. "Universalism, ascription, and academic rank: Canadian professors 1987–2000." *Canadian Review of Sociology* 44 (3): 361–86.

Nanda, Serena, and Richard Warms. 2007. *Cultural Anthropology*. 9th edn. Belmont, CA: Wadsworth.

Nash, Kate. 2000. *Contemporary Political Sociology: Globalization, Politics, and Power*. Oxford: Blackwell.

Nason-Clark, Nancy. 2004. "When terror strikes at home: The interface between religion and domestic violence." *Journal for the Scientific Study of Religion* 43 (3): 303–10.

———— and Barbara Fisher-Townsend. 2007. "Women, gender and feminism in the sociology of religion: Theory, research and social action." In T. Balsi, ed., *American Sociology of Religion Histories*, 203–21. Leiden: Brill.

Nason-Clark, Nancy, and Catherine Clark Kroeger. 2004. *Refuge from Abuse: Hope and Healing for Abused Christian Women*. Downers Grove, IL: InterVarsity Press.

National Council of Welfare. 2001/2. *The Cost of Poverty*. Ottawa: National Council of Welfare.

————. 2012. *Poverty Profile Special Edition: A Snapshot of Racialized Poverty in Canada*. www.ncw.gc.ca/h.4m.2@-eng.jsp.

National Vital Statistics Reports. 2011. *Death: Preliminary Data for 2009*, vol. 59, issue 4, 16 March.

Navarro, Véase Vicente. 1975. "The industrialization of fetishism or the fetishism of industrialization: A critique of Ivan Illich." *Social Science and Medicine* 9: 351–63.

Nelson, Addie. 2010. *Gender in Canada*. 4th edn. Toronto: Pearson.

Nelson, Fiona. 2001. "Lesbian families." In B.J. Fox, ed., *Family Patterns, Gender Relations*, 441–57. Toronto: Oxford University Press.

Nett, Emily. 1981. "Canadian families in social-historical perspective." *Canadian Journal of Sociology* 6 (3): 239–60.

Nettleton, S., R. Burrows, and L. O'Malley. 2005. "The mundane realities of the everyday lay use of the Internet for health and their consequences for media convergence." *Sociology of Health and Illness* 27 (7): 972–92.

Nettleton, S., L. O'Malley, and I. Watt. 2004. "The emergence of e-scaped medicine." *Sociology* 38 (4): 661–79.

Newman, David M. 2006. *Sociology: Exploring the Architecture of Everyday Life*. Thousand Oaks, CA: Pine Forge Press.

Newton, Michael. 2002. *Savage Girls and Wild Beasts: A History of Feral Children*. New York: St Martin's.

Nicholson, Linda. 1994. "Interpreting gender." *Signs* 20 (1): 79–105.

NLSCY (National Longitudinal Survey of Children and Youth). 1996. *Growing up in Canada*. Ottawa: Human Resources Development Canada and Statistics Canada.

Noel, Alain. 2009. "Aboriginal peoples and poverty in Canada: Can provincial government make a difference?" Paper prepared for the annual meeting of the International Sociological Association Research Committee, Montreal, 20 August. www.cccg .umontreal.ca/RC19/PDF/Noel-A_ Rc192009.pdf.

NUPGE (National Union of Public and General Employees). 2009. *What Poverty Means for Canada's Poorest Households*. www.nupge.ca.

Nylund, D. 2004. "When in Rome: Heterosexism, homophobia and sports talk radio." *Journal of Sport and Social Issues* 28 (2): 136–68.

Oakley, Ann. 1972. *Sex, Gender and Society*. London: Maurice Temple Smith.

Obesity Canada. 2001. *What Is Obesity?* www.obesitycanada.com.

Occhionero, Marisa Ferrari. 1996. "Rethinking public space and power." *International Review of Sociology* 6: 453–64.

O'Connor, James. 1996. "The second contradiction of capitalism." In T. Benton, ed., *The Greening of Marxism*. New York, London: Guilford Press.

O'Connor, Julia S., Ann Shola Orloff, and Sheila Shaver. 1999. *States, Markets, Families: Gender Liberalism and Social Policy in Australia, Canada, Great Britain and the United States*. Cambridge: Cambridge University Press.

Olive, D. 2009. "Income gap has also widened in Canada." *Toronto Star* 10 September, B1, B4.

Organisation for Economic Co-operation and Development (OECD). 2009. *Society at a Glance 2009: OECD Social Indicators*. Paris: OECD.

Orlova, Alexandra. 2004. "Insiders and outcasts: From social dislocation to human trafficking—The Russian case." *Problems of Post-Communism* 51 (6): 14–22.

Orsi, Robert. 2003. "Is the study of lived religion irrelevant to the world we live in?" *Journal for the Scientific Study of Religion* 42 (3): 169–74.

Osborne, Ken. 1999. *Education: A Guide to the Canadian School Debate: Or, Who Wants What and Why?* Toronto: Penguin.

Osgerby, B. 2004. *Youth Media*. New York: Routledge.

Ostrovsky, Yuri. 2008. *Earnings inequality and earnings instability of immigrants in Canada*. Analytical Studies, Research Paper Series no. 309. Catalogue no. 11F0019M. Ottawa: Statistics Canada.

Overton, J. 2009. "Privatization, deregulation, and environmental protection: The case of provincial parks in Newfoundland and Labrador." In Laurie Adkin, ed., *Environmental Conflict and Democracy in Canada*, 159–73. Vancouver: University of British Columbia Press.

Palmer, Susan. 2004. *Aliens Adored: Rael's UDO Religion*. New Brunswick, NJ: Rutgers University Press.

Park, Kristin. 2002. "Stigma management among the voluntarily childless." *Sociological Perspectives* 45 (1): 21–45.

Park, Robert E., Ernest W. Burgess, and Roderick D. McKenzie, eds. 1967 [1925]. *The City*. Chicago: University of Chicago Press.

Parsons, Talcott. 1951. *The Social System*. Glencoe, IL: Free Press.

———. 1959. "The school class as a social system: Some of its functions in American society." *Harvard Educational Review* 29: 297–318.

——— and Robert F. Bales. 1955. *Family Socialization and Interaction Process*. New York: Free Press.

Pascale, R., J. Sternin, and M. Sternin. 2010. *The Power of Positive Deviance*. Cambridge, MA: Harvard Business Press.

Paul, Annie Murphy. 2010. "How to be brilliant." *New York Times* 21 March.

Paxton, Pamela, Melanie M. Hughes, and Jennifer L. Green. 2006. "The international women's movement and women's political representation, 1893–2003." *American Sociological Review* 71: 898–920.

Pendakur, Manjunath. 1990. *Canadian Dreams and American Control: The Political Economy of the Canadian Film Industry*. Detroit: Wayne State University Press.

Peritz, Ingrid. 2010. "Quebec Muslim woman ordered to unveil or leave French class." *Globe and Mail*. www .theglobeandmail.com/news/ national/quebec-muslim-woman- ordered-to-unveil-or-leave-french- course/article1530874.

Perreault, S. 2009. "The incarceration of Aboriginial people in adult correctional services." *Juristat* 29 (3). Ottawa: Statistics Canada.

Peterman, Amber, Tia Palermo, and Caryn Bredenkamp. 2011. "Estimates and determinants of sexual violence against women in the Democratic Republic of Congo." *American Journal of Public Health* 101 (6):1060–7.

Peterson, Richard A. 1994. "Culture studies through the production perspective: Progress and prospects." In Diana Crane, ed., *The Sociology of Culture: Emerging Theoretical*

Perspectives, 163–89. Oxford: Blackwell.

Petras, James. 2006. "Past, present and future of China: From semi-colony to world power?" *Journal of Contemporary Asia* 36 (4): 423–41.

Petzer, Shane, and Gordon Issacs. 1998. "SWEAT: The development and implementation of a sex-worker advocacy and intervention program in post-apartheid South Africa." In Kamala Kempadoo and Jo Doezema, eds, *Global Sex Workers: Rights, Resistance, and Redefinition*, 192–6. New York: Routledge.

Pfuhl, Erdwin H., and Stuart Henry. 1993. *The Deviance Process*. 3rd edn. New York: Aldine de Gruyter.

Piaget, Jean. 1932. *The Moral Judgement of the Child*. London: Routledge and Kegan Paul.

———. 1950. *The Construction of Reality in the Child*. London: Routledge and Kegan Paul.

Pickard, Victor W. 2006. "Assessing the radical democracy of Indymedia: Discursive, technical, and institutional constructions." *Critical Studies in Media Communication* 23 (1): 19–38.

Picot, Garnett, F. Hou, and S. Coulombe. 2007. *Chronic Low Income and Low Income Dynamics among Recent Immigrants*. Analytical Studies Branch, Research Paper Series no. 294. Catalogue no. 11F0019M1E. Ottawa: Statistics Canada.

Pieterse, Jan Nederveen. 1994. "Globalisation as hybridisation." *International Sociology* 9 (2): 161–84.

Piliavin, Erving, and S. Briar. 1964. "Police encounters with juveniles." *American Journal of Sociology* 70: 206–14.

Pines, Christopher L. 1993. *Ideology and False Consciousness: Marx and His Historical Progenitors*. Albany: State University of New York Press.

Plummer, Ken. 2003. "Queers, bodies and postmodern sexualities: A note on revisiting the 'sexual' in symbolic interactionism." *Qualitative Sociology* 26 (4): 515–30.

Porter, John. 1965. *The Vertical Mosaic: An Analysis of Social Class and Power in Canada*. Toronto: University of Toronto Press.

Portes, Alejandro. 1997. "Neoliberalism and the sociology of development: Emerging trends and unanticipated facts." *Population and Development Review* 23 (2): 229–59.

Pratt, T.C., and T.W. Godsey. 2003. "Social support, inequality, and homicide: A cross-national test of an integrated theoretical model." *Criminology* 44 (3): 611–44.

Pringle, Rosemary. 1988. *Secretaries Talk: Sexuality, Power and Work*. London: Verso.

Proudfoot, Shannon. 2010. "Living life by other people's rules." *Vancouver Sun* 3 June.

Pryor, Jan, and Bryan Rodgers. 2001. *Children in Changing Families: Life after Parental Separation*. Oxford: Blackwell.

Pupo, Norene, and Andrea Noack. 2010. "Dialling for service: Transforming the public-sector workplace in Canada." In Norene J. Pupo and Mark P. Thomas, eds., *Interrogating the New Economy: Restructuring Work in the 21st Century*, 111–28. Toronto: University of Toronto Press.

Putnam, Robert D. 2000. *Bowling Alone: The Collapse and Revival of American Community*. New York: Simon and Schuster.

———. 2007. "*E Pluribus Unum*: Diversity and community in the twenty-first century." The 2006 Johan Skytte Prize Lecture. *Scandinavian Political Studies* 30 (2): 137–74.

Qu, Lixia, and Ruth Weston. 2008. "Snapshot of family relationships." *Family Matters* (May).

Quine, Lyn. 1999. "Workplace bullying in NHS community trust: Staff questionnaire survey." *British Medical Journal* 318: 228–32.

———. 2002. "Workplace bullying in junior doctors: Questionnaire survey." *British Medical Journal* 324: 878–9.

Raboy, Marc. 1990. *Missed Opportunities: The Story of Canada's Broadcasting Policy*. Montreal: McGill-Queen's University Press.

———. 1995. "The role of public consultation in shaping the Canadian broadcasting system." *Canadian Journal of Political Science* 28 (3): 455–77.

Raby, Rebecca. 2009. "School rules, bodily discipline, embodied resistance." In Cynthia Levine-Rasky, ed., *Canadian Perspectives on the Sociology of Education*. Don Mills, ON: Oxford University Press.

Raduntz, Helen. 2005. "The marketization of education within the global capitalist economy." In Michael W. Apple, Jane Kenway, and Michael Singh, eds, *Globalizing Education: Policies, Pedagogies, and Politics*, 231–45. New York: Peter Lang.

Raines, John, ed. 2002. *Marx on Religion*. Philadelphia: Temple University Press.

Ranson, Gillian. 2009. "Paid and unpaid work: How do families divide their labour?" In Maureen Baker, ed., *Families: Changing Trends in Canada*, 6th edn, 108–29. Toronto: McGraw-Hill Ryerson.

———. 2010. *Against the Grain: Couples, Gender, and the Reframing of Parenting*. Toronto: University of Toronto Press.

Razak, S. 1998. *Looking White People in the Eye: Gender, Race and Culture in Courtrooms and Classrooms*. Toronto: University of Toronto Press.

Rees, William E. 1992. "Ecological footprints and appropriated carrying capacity: What urban economics leaves out." *Environment and Urbanization* 4: 120–30.

———. 2010. "Getting serious about urban sustainability: Eco-footprints and the vulnerability of twenty-first century cities." In Trudi Bunting, Pierre Filion, and Ryan Walker, *Canadian Cities in Transition: New Directions in the Twenty-First Century*, 4th edn, 70–86. Don Mills: Oxford University Press.

Reference re: Same-Sex Marriage. 2004. 3 S.C.R. 698, 2004 SCC 79.

Reference re: Section 293 of the Criminal Code of Canada. 2011. BCSC 1588.

Reinarman, Craig. 1996. "The social construction of an alcohol problem." In Gary W. Potter and Victor E. Kappeler, eds, *Constructing Crime: Perspectives on Making News and Social Problems*, 193–220. Prospect Heights, IL: Waveland.

Rengert, G.F., and J. Wasilchick. 1985. *Suburban Burglary: A Time and Place for Everything*. Springfield, IL: C.C. Thomas.

Report Card on Child and Family Poverty in Canada. 2009. http://intraspec.ca/2009EnglishC2000NationalReportCard.pdf.

Rich, Adrienne Cecile. 2003. "Compulsory heterosexuality and lesbian existence (1980)." *Project Muse—Journal of Women's History* 15 (3): 11–48.

Ritzer, George. 2000a. *The McDonaldization of Society.* 3rd edn. Thousand Oaks, CA: Pine Forge.

———. 2000b. *Sociological Theory.* 5th edn. New York: McGraw-Hill.

———. 2010. *Globalization: A Basic Text.* Oxford: Wiley-Blackwell.

Roberts, Barbara. 1988. *Whence They Came: Deportation from Canada, 1900–1935.* Ottawa: University of Ottawa Press.

Robertson, Roland. 1992. *Globalization: Social Theory and Global Change.* London: Sage.

———. 1995. "Glocalization: Time-space and heterogeneity-homogeneity." In M. Featherstone, S. Lash, and R. Robertson, eds, *Global Modernities.* Thousand Oaks, CA: Sage.

Roby, Jini. 2005. "Women and children in the global sex trade: Toward more effective policy." *International Journal of Social Work* 48 (2): 136–47.

Rogan, Mary. 1999. "Acts of faith." *Saturday Night* 114 (5): 42–51.

Rose, D. 2004. "The uneasy cohabitation of gentrification and 'social mix': A case study of infill condominiums in Montreal." Working paper, 1–45. Montreal: Institut National de la Recherche Scientifique (INRS), Urbanisation, Culture et Société.

Rosenthal, Carolyn J. 1985. "Kinkeeping in the familial division of labour." *Journal of Marriage and the Family* 47: 965–74.

Ross, David, and Richard Shillington. 1994. *The Canadian Fact Book on Poverty.* Ottawa: Canadian Council on Social Development.

Rothkopf, David. 2008. *Superclass: The Global Power Elite and the World They Are Making.* Toronto: Penguin Canada.

Royal Commission on Aboriginal Peoples (RCAP). 1996. *Report of the Royal Commission on Aboriginal Peoples,* vol. 3, *Gathering Strength.* Ottawa: RCAP.

Royal Commission on Equality in Employment. 1984. *Report.* Ottawa: Supply and Services Canada.

Ruparelia, Rakhi. 2012. "The currency of racism in Canada." *Toronto Star* 22 August. www.thestar.com/opinion/editorialopinion/article/1245720--the-currency-of-racism-in-canada.

Ryan, W. 1971. *Blaming the Victim.* New York: Pantheon.

Rymer, Russ. 1993. *Genie: Escape from a Silent Childhood.* London: Michael Joseph.

Sacco, Vincent F. 2005. *When Crime Waves.* Thousand Oaks, CA: Sage.

——— and L.W. Kennedy. 2012. *The Criminal Event: An Introduction to Criminology.* 5th edn. Scarborough, ON: Thomson.

Sandstrom, Kent L., Dan Martin, and Gary Alan Fine. 2006. *Symbols, Selves, and Social Reality: A Symbolic Interactionist Approach to Sociology and Social Psychology.* 2nd edn. New York: Oxford University Press.

Sarlo, Christopher. 1996. *Poverty in Canada.* 2nd edn. Vancouver: Fraser Institute.

Sassen, S. 1991. *The Global City: New York, London, Tokyo.* Princeton, NJ: Princeton University Press.

———. 2001. *The Global City Revised: New York, London, Tokyo.* Princeton: Princeton University Press.

———. 2007. *A Sociology of Globalization.* New York: W.W. Norton.

Satzewich, Vic, ed. 1998. *Racism and Social Inequality in Canada.* Toronto: Thompson Educational Publishing.

——— and Nikolaos Liodakis. 2010. *"Race" and Ethnicity in Canada: A Critical Introduction.* 2nd edn. Toronto: Oxford University Press.

Sauvé, Roger. 2012. *The Current State of Canadian Family Finances.* Ottawa: Vanier Institute of the Family.

Scharrer, Erica. 2001. "From wise to foolish: The portrayal of the sitcom father, 1950s–1990s." *Journal of Broadcasting and Electronic Media* 45 (1): 23–40.

Schecter, Tanya. 1998. *Race, Class, Women and the State: The Case of Domestic Labour.* Montreal: Black Rose.

Schiller, Herbert I. 1969. *Mass Communication and American Empire.* Boston: Beacon.

Schissel, Bernard, and Terry Wotherspoon. 2003. *The Legacy of School for Aboriginal People: Education, Oppression, and Emancipation.* Toronto: Oxford University Press.

Schnaiberg, A., and K.A. Gould. 1994. *Environment and Society: The Enduring Conflict.* New York: St Martin's Press.

Schneider, Christopher J. 2009. "The musical ringtone as an impression management device: A research note." *Studies in Symbolic Interaction* 33: 35–46.

Schofer, Evan, and Ann Hironaka. 2005. "The effects of world society on environmental protection outcomes." *Social Forces* 84 (1): 25–47.

Schofer, Evan, and John W. Meyer. 2005. "The worldwide expansion of higher education in the twentieth century." *American Sociological Review* 70 (6): 898–920.

Schwartz, Mildred. 2007. "Remembering Seymour Martin Lipset." *Canadian Journal of Sociology Online.* March/April. www.cjsonline.ca/soceye/lipset.html.

Sciadas, George. 2002. *The Digital Divide in Canada.* Ottawa: Statistics Canada.

Scott, Allen J. 2004. "Hollywood and the world: The geography of motion-picture distribution and marketing." *Review of International Political Economy* 11 (1): 33–61.

Scott, John, and Gordon Marshall. 2009. "Political sociology." In John Scott and Gordon Marshall, *A Dictionary of Sociology.* Oxford: Oxford University Press.

Sears, Alan. 2003. *Retooling the Mind Factory: Education in a Lean State.* Aurora, ON: Garamond.

Selby, Jennifer. 2012. "Suburban Muslims: 2004 debates outside Toronto and Paris." In Lori G. Beaman, ed., *Religion and Canadian Society: Contexts, Identities, and Strategies,* 2nd edn, 115–36. Canadian Scholars Press.

Seljak, David. 2000. "Resisting the 'no man's land' of private religion: The Catholic church and the public politics in Quebec." In D. Lyon and M. Van Die, eds., *Rethinking Church, State and Modernity: Canada between Europe and America*, 131–48. Toronto: University of Toronto Press.

Sen, Amartya K. 1999. *Development as Freedom*. New York: Knopf.

———. 2000. *Social Exclusion: Concept, Application, and Scrutiny*. Social Development Papers no.1. Manila: Asian Development Bank.

Sennett, Richard. 1998. *The Corrosion of Character: The Personal Consequences of Work in the New Capitalism*. New York: W.W. Norton.

Sev'er, Aysan. 2002. *Fleeing the House of Horrors: Women Who Have Left Abusive Partners*. Toronto: University of Toronto Press.

Shaffir, William. 1991. "Conversion experiences: Newcomers to and defectors from Orthodox Judaism (*hozrim betshuvah* and *hozrim beshe'elah*)." In Z. Sobel and B. Beit-Hallahmi, eds, *Tradition, Innovation, Conflict: Jewishness and Judaism in Contemporary Israel*, 173–202. Albany: State University of New York Press.

——— and Steven Kleinknecht. 2005. "Death at the polls: Experiencing and coping with political defeat." *Journal of Contemporary Ethnography* 34 (6): 707–38.

Shallhorn, Steve. 2011/12. "Walking with Occupy Toronto." *Our Times* 30 (6): 18–20.

Sharp, Richard. 2006. "Privacy in the workplace." *The Monitor* July. Canadian Centre for Policy Alternatives. www.policyalternatives.ca/publications/monitor/july-privacy-workplace.

Sherman, Rachel. 2007. *Class Acts: Service and Inequality in Luxury Hotels*. Berkeley: University of California Press.

Shibutani, Tamotsu. 1961. *Society and Personality: An Interactionist Approach to Social Psychology*. Englewood Cliffs, NJ: Prentice-Hall.

Shin, K.-H., and M. Timberlake. 2000. "World cities in Asia: Cliques, centrality, and connectedness." *Urban Studies* 37 (12): 2257–85.

Shipley, Heather. 2008. "Accommodating sexuality? Religion, sexual orientation and law in Canada." Concordia University Graduate Conference, Accommodating Religion? Community, Discourse, Definitions, 7 February.

Shon, P.C.H., and B.A. Arrigo. 2006. "Reality-based television and police–citizen encounters: The inter-textual construction and situated meaning of mental illness as punishment." *Punishment and Society* 8 (1): 59–85.

Shrestha, Alok. 2007. "$100 computer! Is it worth what it seems to be?" *Panorama* 18 November. TakingIT Global. www.tigweb.org/express/panorama/article.html?start = 5268& ContentID = 17063.

Siltanen, Janet, and Andrea Doucet. 2008. *Gender Relations in Canada: Intersectionality and Beyond*. Toronto: Oxford University Press.

Simmel, Georg. 2002 [1903]. "The metropolis and mental life." In Gary Bridge and Sophie Watson, eds, *The Blackwell City Reader*, 11–19. Oxford and Malden, MA: Blackwell.

Simmons, Alan. 1998. "Racism and immigration policy." In Vic Satzewich, *Racism and Social Inequality in Canada*. Toronto: Thompson Educational Publishing.

Simon, D. 2007. *Elite Deviance*. 9th edn. Boston: Pearson.

Simpson, John H. 2000. "The politics of the body in Canada and the United States." In D. Lyon and M. Van Die, eds, *Rethinking Church, State and Modernity: Canada between Europe and America*, 263–82. Toronto: University of Toronto Press.

Singh, Manjit. 2002. "All merit respect: Kirpan case revealed double standard." *Montreal Gazette* 28 April, A17.

Skaburskis, A., and J. Meligrana. 2005. "Extent, location and profiles of continuing gentrification in Canadian metropolitan areas, 1981–2001. *Urban Studies* 42 (9): 1569–92.

"Skin-brightening." 2013. In *Shiseido*, http://group.shiseido.com/rd/heritage/brightening.html.

Skinner, Burrhus F. 1953. *Science and Human Behaviour*. Oxford: Macmillan.

Sklair, Leslie. 1994. "Global sociology and global environmental change." In Michael Redclift and Ted Benton, eds, *Social Theory and the Global Environment*, 205–27. London, Routledge.

Skocpol, Theda. 1979. *States and Social Revolutions: A Comparative Analysis of France, Russia, and China*. Cambridge: Cambridge University Press.

Smart, Carol. 2007. *Personal Life*. Cambridge: Polity Press.

Smith, Christian. 1991. *The Emergence of Liberation Theology: Radical Religion and Social Movement Theory*. Chicago: University of Chicago Press.

Smith, Dorothy. 1974. "Women's perspective as a radical critique of sociology." *Sociological Inquiry* 44 (1): 7–13.

———. 1987. *The Everyday World as Problematic: A Feminist Sociology*. Boston: Northeastern University Press.

———. 1999. *Writing the Social: Critique, Theory, and Investigations*. Toronto: University of Toronto Press.

Smith, Jackie. 2004. "The World Social Forum and the challenges of global democracy." *Global Networks* 4 (4): 413–21.

———. 2008. *Social Movements for Global Democracy*. Baltimore, MD: Johns Hopkins University Press.

Smith, Philip. 2001. *Cultural Theory: An Introduction*. Oxford: Blackwell.

Smyth, Bruce, ed. 2004. *Parent–Child Contact and Post-Separation Parenting Arrangements*. Research Report no. 9. Melbourne: Australian Institute of Family Studies.

Smythe, Dallas W. 1981. *Dependency Road: Communications, Capitalism, Consciousness, and Canada*. Norwood, NJ: Ablex.

Snow, David A., E. Burke Rochford, Jr, Steven K. Worden, and Robert D. Benford. 1986. "Frame alignment processes, micromobilization, and movement participation." *American Sociological Review* 51: 464–81.

Sontag, Susan. 1978. *Illness as Metaphor*. New York: Farrar, Straus and Giroux.

———. 1989. *AIDS and Its Metaphors*. New York: Farrar, Straus and Giroux.

———. 2003. *Regarding the Pain of Others*. New York: Picado.

Spalek, Basia, Salwa El-Awa, and Laura McDonald. 2008.

Police–Muslim Engagement and Partnerships for the Purposes of Counter-Terrorism: An Examination. Birmingham, UK: University of Birmingham.

Spector, Malcolm, and John I. Kitsuse. 1977. *Constructing Social Problems*. Menlo Park, CA: Cummings.

Spitzer, Steven. 1975. "Toward a Marxian theory of deviance." *Social Problems* 22: 638–51.

Spring, Joel. 2008. *Globalization of Education: An Introduction*. New York: Routledge.

Stankiewicz, Julie M., and Francine Rosselli. 2008. "Women as sex objects and victims in print advertisements." *Sex Roles* 58: 579–89.

Stasiulis, Daiva. 1980. "The political structuring of ethnic community action." *Canadian Ethnic Studies* 12 (3): 19–44.

——— and Abigail Bakan. 2005. *Negotiating Citizenship: Migrant Women and the Global System*. London: Palgrave-Macmillan.

Statistics Canada. 1984. *School Attendance and Level of Schooling. 1981 Census of Canada. Population*. Catalogue no. 92-914. Ottawa: Minister of Supply and Services Canada.

———. 1993. "1991 Census of Canada highlights: Religion." *The Daily* 1 June. Ottawa: Minister of Supply and Services Canada.

———. 1996. Public Use Microdata File on Individuals User Documentation. Ottawa: Minister of Supply and Services Canada.

———. 2001. *Population Projections of Visible Minority Groups, Canada, Provinces and Regions, 2001 to 2017*. Catalogue no. 91-541-XIE. Ottawa: Minister of Industry.

———. 2002. *Labour Force Survey*. Unpublished data. Ottawa: Statistics Canada.

———. 2006a. *Education in Canada: School Attendance and Levels of Schooling*. Catalogue no. 97F0017XCB2001001. Ottawa: Statistics Canada.

———. 2006b. "General social survey: Paid and unpaid work." *The Daily* 19 July. Ottawa: Statistics Canada.

———. 2006c. "Study: Changing patterns of women in the Canadian labour force." *The Daily* 15 June. Ottawa: Statistics Canada.

———. 2008a. "Highest certificate, diploma or degree, age groups and sex for the population 15 years and over of Canada, provinces, territories, census divisions and census subdivisions." Catalogue no. 97-560-XCB2006008. Ottawa: Statistics Canada, 2006 Census of Population. www12.statcan.gc.ca/census-recensement/2006/dp-pd/tbt/index-eng.cfm.

———. 2008b. "Labour force activity, Aboriginal identity, highest certificate, diploma or degree, area of residence, age groups and sex for the population 15 years and over of Canada, provinces and territories." Catalogue no. 97-560-XCB2006031. Ottawa: Statistics Canada, 2006 Census of Population. www12.statcan.gc.ca/census-recensement/2006/dp-pd/tbt/Lp-eng.

———. 2008c. *Labour Force Survey*. Unpublished data. Ottawa: Statistics Canada.

———. 2008d. "Women in Canada: Paid work." Ottawa: Statistics Canada. www.statcan.gc.ca/daily-quotidien/1012091/dq101209a_eng.htm.

———. 2009. "Census of population, 1851 to 2006." Ottawa: Statistics Canada. www.statcan.gc.ca/tables-tableaux/sum-som/l01/cst01/demo62a-eng.htm.

———. 2010a. "Characteristics of individuals using the Internet." *The Daily* 10 May. Ottawa: Statistics Canada. www40.statcan.gc.ca/l01/cst01/comm35a-eng.htm.

———. 2010b. *Crude Birth Rate, Age-Specific and Total Fertility Rates (Live Births), Canada, Provinces and Territories*. CANSIM Table 102-4505. Ottawa: Statistics Canada.

———. 2010c. "Labour force survey." *The Daily*. Ottawa: Statistics Canada. www.statcan.gc.ca/dai-quo/index-eng.htm.

———. 2010d. "University degrees, diplomas and certificates granted, by program level, classification of instructional programs, primary grouping (CIP_PG) and sex." CANSIM Table 477-0014. www5.statcan.gc.ca/cansim/a26.

———. 2010e. "University tuition fees." *The Daily*. Ottawa: Statistics Canada. www.statcan.gc.ca/dai-quo/index-eng.htm.

———. 2011a. *Canadian Vital Statistics, Birth and Death Databases, and Appendix 1*. CANSIM Table 102-0512.

———. 2011b. *Income in Canada 2009*. Ottawa: Minister of Industry. Catalogue no. 75-202-X.

———. 2011c. "Overweight and obese adults (self-reported), 2010." Ottawa: Statistics Canada. www.statcan.gc.ca/pub/82-625-x/2011001/article/11464-eng.htm.

———. 2012a. "Deaths 2009." Ottawa: Statistics Canada. www.statcan.gc.ca/pub/84f0211x/2009000/after-toc-aprestdm1-eng.htm.

———. 2012b. *The Canadian Population in 2011: Population Counts and Growth*. Catalogue no. 98-310-XWE2011001. Ottawa: Statistics Canada.

———. 2012c. "Labour force survey." *The Daily* 3 February. Ottawa: Statistics Canada.

———. 2013. "High-income trends among Canadian taxfilers, 1982 to 2010." *The Daily* 28 January. www.statcan.gc.ca/daily-quotidien/130128/tdq130128-eng.htm.

Stelter, G.A., and A.F. Artibise. 1984. *The Canadian City: Essays in Urban and Social History*. rev. and enl. edn. Ottawa: Carleton University Press.

Stiglitz, Joseph E. 2002. *Globalization and Its Discontents*. New York: W.W. Norton.

Stone, Gregory P. 1962. "Appearance and the Self." In Arnold Rose, ed., *Human Behavior and Social Processes: An Interactionist Approach*, 86–116. Boston: Houghton-Mifflin.

Stonechild, Blair. 2006. *The New Buffalo: The Struggle for Aboriginal Post-secondary Education in Canada*. Winnipeg: University of Manitoba Press.

Strasburger, Victor C., Barbara J. Wilson, and Amy B. Jordan. 2009. *Children, Adolescents and the Media*. 2nd edn. Thousand Oaks, CA: Sage.

Strauss, Anselm. 1959. *Mirrors and Masks: The Search for Identity*. Chicago: Free Press of Glencoe.

Strauss, Murray A., and Richard J. Gelles. 1990. *Physical Violence in American Families: Risk Factors and Adaptations to Violence in 8,145 Families*. New Brunswick, NJ: Transaction.

Stubera, J., S. Galea, and B.G. Link. 2008. "Smoking and the emergence of a stigmatized social status." *Social Science and Medicine* 67 (3): 420–30.

Stuek, Wendy, and Justine Hunter. 2011. "B.C. court upholds anti-polygamy law as constitutional." *Globe and Mail* 23 November. www.theglobeandmail.com/news/national/british-columbia/bc-politics/bc-court-upholds-anti-polygamy-law-as-constitutional/article2246238.

Sussman, D., and S. Bonnell. 2006. "Wives as primary breadwinners." *Perspectives on Labour and Income* 7 (8): 10–17.

Swain, Jon. 2004. "The right stuff: Fashioning an identity through clothing in a junior school." In M. Webber and K. Bezanson, eds, *Rethinking Society in the 21st Century: Critical Readings in Sociology*, 81–92. Toronto: Canadian Scholars Press.

Swanson, J. 2001. *Poor Bashing: The Politics of Exclusion*. Toronto: Between the Lines.

Swiss, Liam. 2009. "Decoupling values from action: An event-history analysis of the election of women to parliament in the developing world, 1945–90." *International Journal of Comparative Sociology* 50 (1): 69–95.

———. 2012. "The adoption of women and gender as development assistance priorities: An event-history analysis of world polity effects." *International Sociology* 27 (1): 96–119.

Sykes, Gresham M., and David Matza. 1957. "Techniques of neutralization: A theory of deliquency." *American Sociological Review* 22 (6): 664–70.

Syndicat Northcrest v. Amselem. 2004. 2 S.C.R. 551, 2004 SCC 47.

Tannenbaum, Frank. 1938. *Crime and the Community*. Boston: Ginn.

Tanner, Julian. 2009. *Teenage Troubles*. 3rd edn. Toronto: Oxford University Press.

Tannock, Stuart. 2001. *Youth at Work: The Unionized Fast-Food and Grocery Workplace*. Philadelphia: Temple University Press.

Taras, David. 2001. *Power and Betrayal in the Canadian Media*. updated edn. Peterborough, ON: Broadview.

Tarrow, Sidney. 1998. *Power in Movements: Social Movements and Contentious Politics*. 2nd edn. New York: Cambridge University Press.

———. 2005. *The New Transnational Activism*. New York: Cambridge University Press.

Taylor, Allison. 2005. "Finding the future that fits." *Gender and Education* 17 (2): 165–87.

Ten Bos, René. 1997. "Essai: Business ethics and Bauman ethics." *Organization Studies* 18: 997–1014.

Thiessen, Victor. 2009. "The pursuit of postsecondary education: A comparison of First Nations, African, Asian, and European Canadian youth." *Canadian Review of Sociology* 46 (1): 5–40.

Thomas, D.S., and W.I. Thomas. 1928. *The Child in America: Behavior Problems and Programs*. New York: Knopf.

Thomas, Mark. 2012. "Class, state and power: Unpacking social relations in contemporary capitalism." In D. Brock, R. Raby, and M. Thomas, eds, *Power and Everyday Practices*, 110–32. Toronto: Nelson.

Thomas, William I., and Florian Znaniecki. 1958. *The Polish Peasant in Europe and America*, vol. 1. New York: Dover Publications.

Thompson, Warren S. 1929. "Population." *American Journal of Sociology* 34: 959–75.

Thomson, Anthony. 2010. *The Making of Social Theory: Order, Reason, and Desire*. 2nd edn. Don Mills, ON: Oxford University Press.

Thorne, Barry. 1982. "Feminist rethinking of the family: An overview." In Barry Thorne with Marilyn Yalom, eds, *Rethinking the Family: Some Feminist Questions*, 1–24. New York: Longman.

Thrasher, F.M. 1927. *The Gang: A Study of 1,313 Gangs in Chicago*. Chicago: University of Chicago Press.

Tirone, Susan, and Alison Pendlar. 2005. "Leisure, place, and diversity: The experience of ethnic minority youth." *Canadian Ethnic Studies* 37 (2): 32–48.

Tittle, C.R., W.J. Villemez, and D.A. Smith. 1978. "The myth of social class and criminality: An empirical assessment of the empirical evidence." *American Sociological Review* 43: 643–56.

Tönnies, Ferdinand. 1957 [1887]. *Community and Society (Gemeinschaft und Gesellschaft)*. New York: Harper and Row.

Touraine, Alain. 1981. *The Voice and the Eye: An Analysis of Social Movements*. Cambridge: Cambridge University Press.

Trautner, Mary Nell, and Jessica L. Collett. 2010. "Students who strip: The benefits of alternate identities for managing stigma." *Symbolic Interaction* 33 (2): 257–79.

Turk, Austin T. 1976. "Law as a weapon in social conflict." *Social Problems* 23: 276–92.

Twining, Hillary, Arnold Arluke, and Gary Patronek. 2000. "Managing the stigma of outlaw breeds: A case study of pit bull owners." *Society and Animals* 8 (1): 1–28.

Tyyskä, Vappu. 2009. *Youth and Society: The Long and Winding Road*. 2nd edn. Toronto: Canadian Scholars Press.

UNAIDS. 2001. *Children and Young People in a World of AIDS*. Geneva: Joint United Nations Programme on HIV/AIDS.

United Nations. 2000. *The World's Women: Trends and Statistics*. New York: United Nations.

———. 2009. *Information Technology Report 2009: Trends and Outlook in Turbulent Times*. New York and Geneva: United Nations Conference on Trade and Development.

———. 2012. *World Urbanization Prospects: 2011 Revision Highlights*. New York: United Nations Department of Economic and Social Affairs, Population Division.

Urmetzer, Peter. 2005. *Globalization Unplugged: Sovereignty and the Canadian State in the Twenty-First Century*. Toronto: University of Toronto Press.

Vanier Institute of the Family. 2004. *Profiling Canadian Families III*. Ottawa: Vanier Institute of the Family.

Veblen, T. 1899. *The Theory of the Leisure Class*. New York: Penguin.

Veenstra, Gerry. 2001. "Social capital and health." *Canadian Journal of Policy Research* 2: 1672–81.

Venkatesh, S.A. 2008. *Gang Leader for a Day: A Rogue Sociologist Takes to the Streets*. New York: Penguin.

Vosko, Leah. 2003. "Gender differentiation and the standard/non-standard employment distinction in Canada, 1945 to the present." In Danielle Juteau, ed., *Patterns and Processes of Social Differentiation: The Construction of Gender, Age, "Race/Ethnicity" and Locality*. Toronto: University of Toronto Press.

———. 2006. *Precarious Employment: Understanding Labour Market Insecurity in Canada*. Montreal: McGill-Queen's University Press.

———. 2010. *Managing the Margins: Gender, Citizenship, and the International Regulation of Precarious Employment*. Oxford: Oxford University Press.

Wackwitz, Laura A., and Lana F. Rakow. 2004. "Feminist communication theory: An introduction." In Lana F. Rakow and Laura A. Wackwitz, eds, *Feminist Communication Theory: Selections in Context*, 1–10. Thousand Oaks, CA: Sage.

Wall, Glenda. 2009. "Childhood and childrearing." In Maureen Baker, ed., *Families: Changing Trends in Canada*, 6th edn, 91–107. Toronto: McGraw-Hill Ryerson.

Waller, Willard. 1965 [1932]. *The Sociology of Teaching*. New York: Wiley.

Wallerstein, Immanuel. 1976. *The Modern World-System: Capitalist Agriculture and the Origins of the European World-Economy in the Sixteenth Century*. New York: Academic Press.

———. 1979a. "Dependence in an interdependent world: The limited possibilities of transformations within the capitalist world-economy." In Immanuel Wallerstein, ed., *The Capitalist World-Economy: Essays*, 66–94. New York: Cambridge University Press.

———. 1979b. "The rise and future demise of the world capitalist system: Concepts for comparative analysis." In Immanuel Wallerstein, ed., *The Capitalist World-Economy: Essays*, 1–36. New York: Cambridge University Press.

Waring, Marilyn. 1996. *Three Masquerades: Essays on Equality, Work and Human Rights*. Toronto: University of Toronto Press.

Warren, Carol A.B., and Tracy Xavia Karner. 2009. *Discovering Qualitative Methods*. 2nd edn. New York: Oxford University Press.

Waters, Malcolm. 1995. *Globalization: Key Ideas*. London: Routledge.

Watson, James L., ed. 1997. *Golden Arches East: McDonald's in East Asia*. Stanford, CA: Stanford University Press.

Weber, Max. 1958 [1904]. *The Protestant Ethic and the Spirit of Capitalism*. trans. Talcott Parsons. New York: Scribner.

———. 1978 [1908]. *Economy and Society*. trans. Ephraim Fischoff, eds Guenther Roth and Claus Wittich. Berkeley: University of California Press.

———. 1946 [1915]. "Religious rejections of the world and their directions." In H.H. Gerth and C. Wright Mills, *From Max Weber: Essays in Sociology*, 323–59. New York: Oxford University Press.

———. 1958 [1922]. *Essays in Sociology*. trans. H.H. Gerth and C. Wright Mills. New York: Oxford University Press.

Weeks, Jeffrey. 1993. *Sexuality*. London: Routledge.

Weiner, Gaby. 1994. *Feminisms in Education: An Introduction*. Birmingham, UK: Open University Press.

Weitz, Rose, ed. 2002. *The Politics of Women's Bodies: Sexuality, Appearance and Behaviour*. 2nd edn. Oxford: Oxford University Press.

Welsh, Sandy. 1999. "Gender and sexual harassment." *Annual Review of Sociology* 25 (1): 169–90.

Western, Mark, and Erik Olin Wright. "The permeability of class boundaries to intergenerational mobility among men in the United States, Canada, Norway and Sweden." *American Sociological Review* 59(4): 606–29.

Westhues, Kenneth. 1982. *First Sociology*. New York: McGraw-Hill.

White, R., J. Wyn and P. Albanese. 2011. "Youth in a Digital Age" in *Youth and Society: Exploring the Social Dynamics of Youth Experience, 2nd edn.*, 270–3. Don Mills: Oxford University Press.

White, David Manning. 1950. "The 'gatekeeper': A case study in the selection of news." *Journalism Quarterly* 27: 383–90.

Whitman, Shelly. 2012. "Sexual violence, coltan and the Democratic Republic of Congo." In Matthew A. Schnurr and Larry A. Swatuk, eds, *Natural Resources and Social Conflict: Towards Critical Environmental Security*, 128–51. London: Palgrave Macmillan.

Wilkes, Rima. 2001. "Competition or colonialism? An analysis of two theories of ethnic collective action." (PhD dissertation, University of Toronto).

Wilkins, R. 2007. *Mortality by Neighbourhood Income in Urban Canada from 1971 to 2001*. HAMG Seminar, 16 January. Ottawa: Statistics Canada.

Wilkinson, Richard G., and Kate Pickett. 2009. *The Spirit Level: Why Greater Equality Makes Societies Stronger*. London: Bloomsbury Press.

Williams, Cara. 2010. "Economic well-being." In *Women in Canada: A Gender-Based Statistical Report*. Catalogue no. 89-503-X. Ottawa: Statistics Canada.

Williams, F.P., and M. McShane. 2009. *Criminological Theory*. 5th edn. Englewood Cliffs, NJ: Prentice-Hall.

Wilson, Jeffrey, and Mark Anielski. 2005. *Ecological Footprints of Canadian Municipalities and Regions*. Prepared for the Canadian Federation of Canadian Muncipalities. Edmonton: Anielski Management Inc.

Wilson, Sue. 2008. "Socialization." In L. Tepperman, J. Curtis, and P. Albanese, eds, *Sociology: A Canadian Perspective*, 2nd edn, 98–127. Toronto: Oxford University Press.

Wilson, Susannah J. 1991. *Women, Families, and Work*. 3rd edn. Toronto: McGraw-Hill Ryerson.

Wilson, William Julius. 2010, "Why both social structure and culture matter in a holistic analysis of inner-city poverty." *Annals of the American Academy of Political and Social Science* 629 (1): 200–19.

Winseck, Dwayne, and Robert M. Pike. 2009. "The global media and the empire of liberal internationalism, circa 1910–30." *Media History* 15 (1): 31–54.

Wirth, Louis. 1938. "Urbanism as a way of life." *American Journal of Sociology* 44: 1–24.

Wolfe, David A., and Meric S. Gertler. 2001. *The New Economy: An Overview*. Discussion paper produced for the Social Sciences and Humanities Research Council of Canada.

Wolfgang, Marvin, and Franco Ferracuti. 1967. *The Subculture of Violence: Towards an Integrated Theory in Criminology*. Beverly Hills, CA: Sage.

Wollstonecraft, Mary. 1986 [1792]. *Vindication of the Rights of Women*. Middlesex, UK: Penguin.

Woodhead, Linda. 2007. "*Religion as normative, spirituality as fuzzy: Questioning some deep assumptions in the sociology of religion.*" Paper presented at SISR/ISSR, Zagreb.

Woods, James, with Jay Lucas. 1993. *The Corporate Closet: The Professional Lives of Gay Men in America*. New York: Free Press.

Woods, Peter. 1979. *The Divided School*. London: Routledge and Kegan Paul.

World Bank. 2011. *World Development Indicators*. Washington: World Bank. http://databank.worldbank.org/ddp/home.do?Step = 12&id = 4&CNO = 2.

World Wildlife Fund. 2010. *Living Planet Report 2010*. Gland, Switzerland: World Wildlife Fund.

Wortley, Scott. 1999. "A northern taboo: Research on race, crime and criminal justice in Canada." *Canadian Journal of Criminology* 41: 261–74.

Wotherspoon, Terry. 1995. "The incorporation of public school teachers into the industrial order: British Columbia in the first half of the twentieth century." *Studies in Political Economy* 46: 119–51.

———. 2000. "Transforming Canada's education system: The impact on educational inequalities, opportunities, and benefits." In B. Singh Bolaria, ed., *Social Issues and Contradictions in Canadian Society*, 250–72. Toronto: Harcourt Brace.

Wotipka, Christine M., and Francisco O. Ramirez. 2008. "World society and human rights: An event history analysis of the Convention on the Elimination of All Forms of Discrimination against Women." In B.A. Simmons, F. Dobbin, and G. Garrett, eds, *The Global Diffusion of Markets and Democracy*, 303–43. Cambridge: Cambridge University Press.

Wright, Charles R. 1959. *Mass Communication: A Sociological Perspective*. New York: Random House.

Wrong, Dennis. 1961. "The oversocialized concept of man in modern sociology." *American Sociological Review* 26: 183–93.

Wu, Zheng. 2000. *Cohabitation: A New Form of Family Living*. Toronto: Oxford University Press.

Yates, Charlotte. 2008. "Organized labour in Canadian politics: Hugging the middle or pushing the margins?" In Miriam Smith, ed., *Group Politics and Social Movements in Canada*. Toronto: University of Toronto Press.

Yoo, Eunhye. 2011. "International human rights regime, neoliberalism, and women's social rights, 1984–2004."

International Journal of Comparative Sociology 52 (6): 503–28.

Young, David. 2006. "Ethno-racial minorities and the Juno Awards." *Canadian Journal of Sociology* 31 (2): 183–210.

———. 2008. "Why Canadian content regulations are needed to support Canadian music." In Josh Greenberg and Charlene D. Elliott, eds, *Communication in Question: Competing Perspectives on Controversial Issues in Communication Studies*, 216–21. Toronto: Thomson Nelson.

Young, Douglas, and Roger Keil. 2007. "Re-regulating the urban water regime in neoliberal Toronto." In Nike Heynen, James McCarthy, Scott Prudham, and Paul Robbins, eds, *Neoliberal Environments: False Promises and Unnatural Consequence*, 139–52. New York, London: Routledge.

Zola, Irving Kenneth. 1972. "Medicine as an institution of social control." *Sociological Review* 20: 487–504.

Zucker, Lynne G., Michael R. Darby, Marilynn B. Brewer, and Yusheng Peng. 1996. "Collaboration structure and information dilemmas in biotechnology." In Roderick M. Kramer and Tom R. Tyler, eds, *Trust in Organizations: Frontiers of Theory and Research*, 90–113. Thousand Oaks, CA: Sage.

Zukin, S. 1980. "A decade of the new urban sociology." *Theory and Society* 9 (4): 575–601.

Zweigenhaft, Richard L., and G. William Domhoff. 2011. *The New CEOs: Women, African American, Latino, and Asian American Leaders of Fortune 500 Companies*. New York: Rowman and Littlefield.

index

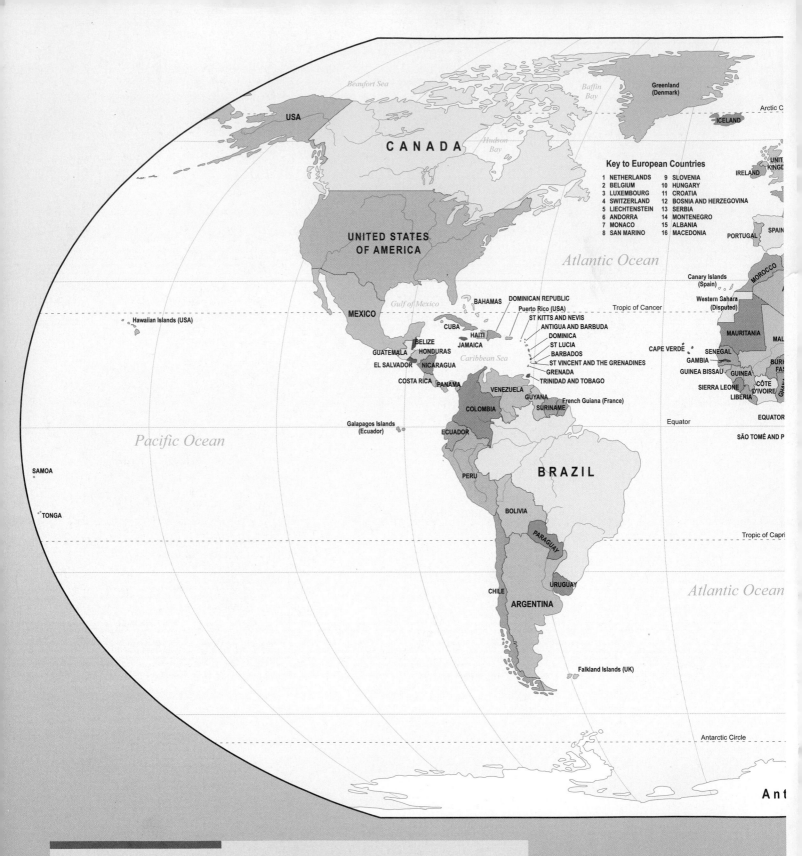

Key to European Countries

1	NETHERLANDS	9	SLOVENIA
2	BELGIUM	10	HUNGARY
3	LUXEMBOURG	11	CROATIA
4	SWITZERLAND	12	BOSNIA AND HERZEGOVINA
5	LIECHTENSTEIN	13	SERBIA
6	ANDORRA	14	MONTENEGRO
7	MONACO	15	ALBANIA
8	SAN MARINO	16	MACEDONIA

SOCIOLOGY: A GLOBAL PERSPECTIVE

Although this is a textbook written for Canadians, by Canadians, the editors and authors never lose sight of the fact that sociology is very much a global discipline. Along with Canadian data, examples, and illustrations, a wealth of information about how humans live and interact around the world is presented in every chapter. This map will help you situate these references in their global context.

Cartography by Douglas Fast